Mr. Rickey's Redbirds

Mr. Rickey's Redbirds

Baseball, Beer, Scandals & Celebrations in St. Louis

Mike Mitchell

ISBN: 978-0-578-69387-3

RickeysRedbirds.com

Table of Contents

Introduction

In the history of the St. Louis Cardinals, one figure towers above all, despite never pitching an inning or taking an at-bat for the team. For decades, the club was defined by his presence – or his absence. From 1876 to 1925, three different National League teams in St. Louis never finished higher than second place. Then everything changed. The St. Louis Cardinals became the league's most dominant team. Over a twenty-one-season period, 1926 to 1946, the Cardinals won nine pennants and six World Series titles. Branch Rickey is the biggest reason why.

Known primarily today outside St. Louis for signing Jackie Robinson and breaking the color barrier in baseball, Rickey spent just eight seasons with the Brooklyn Dodgers. Between the Browns and Cardinals, however, Rickey spent more than thirty years in St. Louis. All six of his children, born between 1913 and 1924, arrived when he was employed by a St. Louis team. St. Louis is where Rickey made his major-league debut as a player, spent his entire managerial career, and first enjoyed the fruits of success as a front office executive. During his early years with the Cardinals, Rickey and baseball survived a World War, the Black Sox Scandal, and Prohibition. The 1920s began with Babe Ruth reshaping baseball strategy and Rickey reshaping baseball development. With Rickey's vision, and owner Sam Breadon's financial backing, the Cardinals took the lead in developing a minor league system that has lasted a century.

Breadon, Gussie Busch (through Anheuser-Busch), and Bill DeWitt Jr. are the most successful owners in the history of the St. Louis Cardinals. Every single World Series title the Cardinals have celebrated has occurred under the stewardship of these three executives. Rickey is the most consequential general manager in the history of the game. Rickey worked for Breadon and Busch. DeWitt's father worked for Rickey.

When Rickey left the Cardinals in the fall of 1942, the club lost more than one man; it lost an entire infrastructure. St. Louis's loss became Brooklyn's gain. The Cardinal Way became the Dodger Way. The Brooklyn farm system, just like the one developed in St. Louis, led to sustained success at the major league level. Rickey developed the blueprint for both.

Rickey spent the final years of his career in the city where it began. The 1964 season, Rickey's last one in baseball, played out in a similar fashion to 1926, the first full season he focused on executive duties and the development of the farm system. In both instances, the Cardinals won a seven-game series against the Yankees, with Rickey playing a role in the front office.

The 1926 and 1964 seasons are just two of many parallels between the Cardinals and Yankees, parallels that began when Rickey joined the Cardinals. Rickey's career, and early professional baseball, were shaped by battles over alcohol. The city of St. Louis has its own unique history tied to the beer industry, and both the city and its teams are linked to a variety of scandals and controversies throughout baseball history. *Mr. Rickey's Redbirds* recounts these various sagas, weaving these tales into the timeline of Rickey's career.

Our story is brought up to date with the final chapter focusing on the modern-day "Branch Rickeys" – the new-age front-office personnel. Prominent in this story are DeWitt, the current chairman of the Cardinals, and Jeff Luhnow, the man he hired to reshape the Cardinals talent evaluation process. Those decisions have helped lead us to where we are in the game today, with an arms race for statistical talent and two new scandals in the past few years.

Rickey's life, career, and impact are an often-told story, but the emphasis is largely on his time with the Brooklyn Dodgers and the story of Jackie Robinson. But even without Robinson, Rickey would still deserve a place in the Hall of Fame. That honor would be deserved because of his pioneering work with the Cardinals. No one casts a longer shadow on St. Louis baseball than Rickey.

Mr. Rickey's Redbirds, though, is not just his story. It's the story of all the incredible players he scouted, signed, or traded and the talented executives he hired, fired, or deeply influenced over the years. It's the story of baseball told through a city and a franchise that proudly claims more World Series titles than any other National League team.

It was in St. Louis where Rickey once read the words of ancient philosophers in the dugout, but claimed he wasn't an educated man. "Why, I've only now gotten to the point where I can translate Caesar from the Latin," he insisted. Rickey had a better vocabulary and a bigger bank account than the men who played for him. The longtime baseball executive was a voracious reader. His players barely read the paper. Rickey enjoyed cigars. His players preferred chewing tobacco. A devout Methodist who refused to go to the ballpark on Sundays, Rickey liked to talk about saintly virtues. His players often thought of him as a demon, especially at contract time. But somehow, the high-minded visionary and his unsophisticated talent clicked.

Over the years, the players, coaches, and staff who embraced Rickey and his methods found an unquestionably loyal partner. Pepper Martin rose to fame playing for the Gashouse Gang Cardinals of the 1930s. After his playing days were over, Martin, like many others, followed Rickey to Brooklyn. Managing in the Dodgers farm system one year, Martin got so upset over a call he began choking an umpire. Following the incident, Commissioner Happy Chandler summoned Martin to his office for an explanation. "What were your intentions?" Chandler asked. "I wanted to kill the buzzard," Martin replied. Chandler suspended him for the rest of the season. The next year, Martin, always one of Rickey's favorites, returned to his duties as manager of the Miami Sun Sox.

*****

Writing a book can be a solitary exercise but the experience is made exponentially better by friends and associates willing to lend a hand or offer advice. Joan Ford, Richard Hamra, and Caroline Pfefferkorn proofread significant portions of the raw manuscript. Jeffrey Kittel proved invaluable in helping me gain a better understanding of baseball's early days in St. Louis. Jacob Pomrenke read the chapter on the St. Louis connections to the Black Sox scandal and graciously provided a roadmap to greater insight. Frank Absher pointed me to resources that helped chronicle the early days of St. Louis radio. Mark Tomasik, who blogs about all things related to Cardinals history at *RetroSimba.com,* read every chapter and provided detailed notes and feedback. Any improvements to the book you are reading are primarily due to their efforts. Any mistakes are mine.

The city and county of St. Louis have wonderful research facilities and incredible venues to research baseball. The staffs at the various branches of the St. Louis Library, the St. Louis County Library, and the Municipal Library Consortium were consistently accommodating and responsive to any questions I had. The Missouri Historical Society and the St. Louis Mercantile Library are great places to delve into the past. Charles Brown at the Mercantile Library was especially helpful.

I am forever grateful to all the historians, researchers and writers who plowed this ground before me. The history of baseball in St. Louis is incredibly rich and diverse. Thanks to people such as Miller Huggins and Branch Rickey, great stories about the Cardinals extend well beyond St. Louis. One can find a lot about the Cardinals by reading the histories of the New York Yankees and Brooklyn Dodgers.

I happened to be reading one such book, *The Lords of Baseball*, a few years ago. The book was written by Harold Parrott, a former sportswriter and one-time traveling secretary for the Dodgers when Rickey was in Brooklyn. The book was republished in 2001 by Parrott's sons and it happened to have an email address inside it. On a whim, I fired off an email, not expecting a response. To my surprise, I got one within minutes.

That sparked an email exchange with Brian Parrott, Harold's son. I was struck how every time he mentioned his father's former boss, he never called him "Branch" or "Rickey," but always, "Mr. Rickey." I was aware, of course, that many of his players and employees had addressed him in that fashion, but Branch Rickey died more than fifty years ago. How many other people do you know get afforded such a title in an informal email exchange? I thought then, and now, that *Mr. Rickey's Redbirds* was the perfect name for what you hold in your hands.

On the February day we traded emails, I heard on the radio that Red Schoendienst had just reported to spring training, an event he'd been a part of for more than seventy years. As we'll see later, Red's early story, like so many others, has a connection to Rickey, a man whose major league career began as a player with the Browns and ended in the front office with the Cardinals. In fact, Rickey's last day with the team in October 1964 occurred on the same day Schoendienst was introduced as the club's new manager. Rickey debuted with the Browns in 1905. Schoendienst passed away in 2018. Thanks to Red and hundreds of others who came before him, Rickey played with, managed, or scouted someone who appeared in a major league uniform for more than 100 straight seasons.

While playing for the Pittsburgh Pirates, shortstop Dick Groat once overheard Rickey tell someone that he should be a .300 hitter. "If Rickey thinks I should hit .300," thought Groat, "I should do it because he knows more about baseball than any man in the world." Rickey "could recognize a great player from the window of a moving train," wrote *Los Angeles Times* columnist Jim Murray. "His legacy was the farm system, the black player, the Gashouse Gang, and, ultimately, the Dodgers Dynasty..."

Infielder Bobby Bragan played for Rickey's Dodgers in the 1940s. Decades later, a reporter asked him about his fondest baseball memory. "My friendship and close association with Branch Rickey is by far the fondest," Bragan said. "I don't know what comes second but there's such a big gap between first and second that it doesn't really matter."

"Such a big gap between first and second" is also a way of describing Rickey's unmatched legacy. And nowhere is that legacy more deeply intertwined than in St. Louis with the Cardinals. When Rickey left the team for Brooklyn in the fall of 1942, a reporter asked his secretary, Mary Murphy, if she would miss him. "Sure, I'll miss him," she replied. "Won't you?" It took years for the Cardinals and their fans to appreciate just how much they did.

Foreword

In October 2019, when Mike Mitchell contacted me and asked if I'd be willing to read a chapter of his manuscript and offer feedback, I agreed, even though we didn't know one another. I accepted the assignment because I like baseball, feel a kinship with those who research and write about it, and respected his resourcefulness.

Mike told me his book was about St. Louis Cardinals baseball history as told through the lens of Branch Rickey and others. I figured I would be a good test audience. I've followed the team since seeing my first game, Cardinals versus New York Mets at the Polo Grounds in New York, in 1963 when I was 7. It was Stan Musial's last appearance in New York as a player and it made a big impression on me. So, I became a Cardinals fan. My lifetime allegiance was assured the following year when the Cardinals beat the mighty New York Yankees for the 1964 World Series championship, earning me bragging rights over all the other kids on my block in Bayonne, N.J.

Baseball and writing have been a prominent part of my life. Before retiring in October 2016, I worked as a newspaper journalist for 40 years, including a stint as a sports reporter, sports editor and member of the Baseball Writers Association of America. I'm also a member of the Society for American Baseball Research, and since 2010 I've produced the most comprehensive blog (RetroSimba.com) about Cardinals history.

I've read dozens of books about baseball and the Cardinals and some of the stories have been retold so often that I skim right over them. Frankly, I wasn't expecting to find much I didn't already know about the Cardinals in Mike's work.

The chapter I received changed my outlook. It began with the story of Miller Huggins, who managed the Cardinals and New York Yankees and got inducted into the Baseball Hall of Fame. I knew about Huggins, or so I thought. As I began reading, the chapter brought to life a Huggins I didn't know, and one I suddenly wanted to know a lot more about. That's one of the best aspects of Mike's book. He writes about familiar figures in unfamiliar ways. Instead of statistics or routine biographical data, the Huggins story connected me to an array of people, from William Howard Taft to George Halas, and captivated my attention as it weaved together topics as varied as false teeth and roller rinks.

As I eagerly read from one paragraph to the next, I found myself caring about Huggins because he was presented as a multi-dimensional person, not a caricature. The same chapter gave the same treatment to the familiar (Branch Rickey, George Sisler, Kenesaw Mountain Landis) as well as the unfamiliar (St. Louis Browns owner Phil Ball and Cardinals manager Jack Hendricks).

When I finished the chapter, Mike invited me to read the rest of the book and, as you'll find, too, it was a treat to get to do so. Mike accepted constructive criticism as enthusiastically as he did praise and he worked with a determination and clarity of purpose that impressed me. I enjoyed our exchanges of ideas about writing, research, baseball and history, and I am certain I gained more from the experience than I gave.

Because Mike is as gifted a researcher as he is a writer, his book is loaded with detail, but it's not dense reading. I appreciated how he did the heavy lifting for the reader, using a discerning eye and a skill for storytelling to select the most interesting anecdotes and information and relay it all in a lively style. His work is factual, credible and accurate. Don't take my word for it. Do yourself a favor and be sure to read the footnotes at the end of each chapter. These footnotes are like mini-stories, carefully crafted, and will inform, entertain and reward you for reading.

Mike's book isn't a complete history of the Cardinals and it wasn't intended to be. He has a talent for collecting stories and themes, tying it all together and providing perspective.

I learned a lot about the Cardinals, and baseball in general, by reading this book, and I also was reminded about a lot that I had forgotten. My biggest takeaway, and what I like best about the book, is it shows how even the best and brightest and most successful people also are deeply flawed and make unwise decisions. Some learn and grow from those decisions; some don't and keep repeating the same mistakes. Mike's book brings out the human element in the characters and does so in a way that helps the reader to understand them better.

Mike's book isn't a fan's gushy tribute to boyhood heroes, or a romanticized recounting of Cardinals glories, nor is it an opinion-filled ranking of bests and worsts. What you get are rich characterizations and authoritative insights into why things happen and the subsequent consequences of those actions.

The central figures in Mike's book, Branch Rickey, Rogers Hornsby, Babe Ruth, Sam Breadon, Gussie Busch, Jacob Ruppert, Leo Durocher, all were incredibly successful and talented, but none were saints. Get ready to have some myths shattered. Gambling, beer, alcohol, gangsters, crime and cheating have been a consistent part of professional baseball, including the Cardinals, and more prevalent than peanuts and Cracker Jack. The revelations of dark, deep connections between prominent baseball figures and unseemly people will open your eyes and stimulate your imagination.

Characters such as Frank Moore, the Kentucky bookmaker who befriended Hornsby, or Carl Zork, a St. Louis garment manufacturer who got entangled in a notorious baseball scandal, aren't names you might associate with St. Louis baseball but they have surprising roles in Cardinals lore.

Reading this book caused me to like some baseball legends more, dislike others more and, above all, appreciate just how thin a line separates success from failure.

Rickey was a smart choice as the character who forms the foundation of the book. Because Rickey's legacy is his successful effort to integrate the major leagues as a Dodgers executive, his innovative work with the Cardinals often gets overlooked by others today. This book makes a compelling case that Rickey is the most important person in Cardinals history and his impact still resonates.

As a history lover, I also appreciated how Mike's book is about more than baseball. I've read sports-themed books that include historic references largely as a timeline. Mike's book uses history to inform, surprise and tell a story.

Figures as well-known and diverse as George Armstrong Custer, Al Capone, Charles Lindbergh, Henry Ford and Ernest Hemingway appear on these pages as naturally as Dizzy Dean and Stan Musial, and their presence enhances the understanding of characters and events, a credit to the imagination and inquisitiveness of the author.

This book changed the way I view the Cardinals and baseball. It challenged me, made me think and inspired me to broaden my perspective. I'd call that a worthy read.

Mark Tomasik, RetroSimba.com

In the Beginning

In the history of St. Louis baseball, scandals came before celebrations. But it was beer and baseball from the beginning. The National League and Budweiser both debuted in 1876. On May 4 of that year, an estimated 500 fans gathered at the Grand Avenue Park to watch the first National League game ever played in the city. With rain falling, the game was cut short in the second inning. Later ensnared in the league's first big scandal, the franchise would be out of business in two years. The discreditable behavior wouldn't be the last in the city.

Exactly two months after the first home opener, St. Louis joined the rest of the nation in celebrating the country's centennial anniversary. The July Fourth revelry would soon be tempered by news of a shocking event that had occurred just days earlier: the slaughter of Lieutenant Colonel George Custer and his 7th Cavalry at the Battle of the Little Bighorn.[1] Two decades later, St. Louis brewer Anheuser-Busch distributed a lithograph of "Custer's Last Fight" to bars across the country, helping spread the mythology surrounding the event.

Custer had risen to the rank of general in the Civil War and now another Civil War general occupied the White House. Because of his marriage to the daughter of a wealthy St. Louis plantation owner, Ulysses S. Grant had a direct connection to the city he once called home. 1876 would mark his last full year as commander-in-chief. In the election that fall, Democrat Samuel J. Tilden won the popular vote but Republican Rutherford B. Hayes won the presidency when a congressional committee awarded him 20 contested electoral votes.

Eleven years after the end of the war, an expanding country was in the midst of rapid technological and industrial progress. The thirty-seven stars on the U.S. flag grew by one when Colorado was admitted to the Union. That same year, Alexander Graham Bell made his first phone call, and the Transcontinental Railroad Express made its first coast-to-coast trip, arriving in San Francisco some 83 hours and 39 minutes after it departed New York.

With the mythology of the American West still evolving – Wyatt Earp started working in Dodge City, Kansas in May and Wild Bill Hickok was killed in a poker game in August – the urbanization of the country had begun. In 1820, just three cities in the United States had populations greater than 10,000. Forty years later, the number of cities boasting those numbers had risen to 101.[2] This concentration of population helped feed the growth of professional sports. Major league teams needed scale to thrive.

St. Louis had only 4,598 residents in 1820. By the 1870s, the Missouri city counted more than three hundred thousand people, making it the fourth largest in the nation, just ahead of Chicago. St. Louis became a center of river commerce and fur trading as well as home to the first grain exchange in the country. Once an importer of flour, St. Louis began to export to Southern markets by the 1840s. "Here in East Tennessee above the Muscle Shoals, and the difficult pass of the Tennessee River through the mountains, we are eating St. Louis flour," a Southern correspondent noted in 1851. "If anyone had a few years ago predicted this feature of our trade, he would have been pronounced demented."[3]

Immigration fueled the rapid rise in population. A city founded by the French and once controlled by the Spanish became increasingly dominated by the Germans and the Irish. By the middle of the nineteenth century, forty-three percent of the St. Louis population were German or Irish natives.[4]

The immigrants instantly embraced the game of "base ball." It would be written as two words until the late nineteenth century. Related to a group of European games that included rounders and cricket, modern baseball developed gradually. In eighteenth-century America, "baseball appears to have sprung up everywhere, like dandelions," wrote baseball historian John Thorn.[5] In his book, *Baseball in the Garden of Eden*, Thorn places a date of *about* 1735 as to when the game took root in America. In 1744, a description of the game appeared in *A Little Pretty Pocket-Book,* a children's book published in England. For the next several decades, the game evolved as a leisure activity, not a spectator sport.[6] The Knickerbocker Base Ball Club of New York organized a formal dues-paying team in 1845. These were professional, white-collar men. "They were more expert with the knife and fork at post-game banquets than with bat and ball on the diamond," wrote Harold Seymour.[7]

From its earliest days, however, the game had widespread appeal. Baseball emerged as a game played by the masses, for the masses, with increasing crowds of spectators adding to the atmosphere. Publishers quickly figured out baseball news sold newspapers. "By the Civil War," noted Seymour, "baseball had taken solid hold on America."

The game needed three elements to vault from a localized affair to a national pastime.[8] Newspaper accounts gave legitimacy to the contests, giving a rooting interest to those who could only read about the events afterward. Published statistics also added credibility. Thirdly, and perhaps most importantly, the element of gambling appealed to more prurient interests. "Adults must care about the outcome, and their willingness to place a wager is a reasonable measure of their interest," Thorn asserted.

Six years after the end of the Civil War, the game had its first professional league. It didn't last long. The National Association played its last season in 1875. It "reeked of corruption," wrote author and baseball historian Lee Allen. Players would jump from team to team. The sobriety of those in uniform was often in question.[9] St. Louis fielded two teams in the league's last year, the Brown Stockings and the Red Stockings. With the start of the National League the following season, St. Louis had one of the eight teams (Brown Stockings). But what fans witnessed at Grand Avenue Park that summer had striking differences from the game we know today.

*****

Transport a twenty-first-century visitor to a nineteenth-century baseball park and she would still see a game with nine players, three bases and a home plate. What she wouldn't see in 1876 was a pitcher's mound. A pitcher delivered the ball from a box 45-feet from home plate. He could not lift his arm above his waist. In early versions of the game, a pitcher didn't have a strategic role in getting the batter out. He merely served as a conduit to get the ball to the waiting hitter. Professional competition began changing the role.

Standing at the plate, the batter could call for a high strike zone or a low strike zone. In its inaugural season, the National League had "fair-foul" hits. Any ball hit that rolled foul before reaching first or third base was considered to be in play. Chicago's Ross Barnes took maximum advantage. Thanks to the fair-foul rule, he led the league in hitting in 1876 with a batting average of .404. When the rule changed the following season, he hit just .276.[10] But foul balls still didn't count as strikes.

There was no screen behind home plate to protect fans from the fouls. The grandstand behind the catcher became known as the "slaughter pens."[11] Almost no thought was given to safety in the game's early days. Catchers didn't wear masks. They would stand a few feet behind home plate and catch the ball on a bounce. "There is about as much sense as putting a lightning rod on a catcher as a mask," declared the *Louisville Courier-Journal*.[12]

A single umpire called the action and was frequently the target of abuse – both verbal and physical – from fans and players. "Mother, may I slug the umpire, May I slug him right away?" was a line in an 1886 poem.[13] Barring illness or injury, an umpire didn't have to track substitutions. They weren't allowed. An exiting pitcher simply swapped positions with his replacement.

The baseball itself was a precious commodity. Teams played as long as possible with just one ball.[14] Bruised and battered by wooden bats and frequently defaced by bare-handed throwers (gloves were almost nonexistent and pitchers were the last to adopt), the white ball grew darker by the inning. Fred Snodgrass played center field in the early twentieth century for the New York Giants. He once described what happened to a baseball on the rare occasion when a new one was put in play. The umpire "would throw the ball out to the pitcher, who would promptly sidestep it. It would go around the infield once or twice and come back to the pitcher as black as the ace of spades. All the infielders were chewing tobacco or licorice, and spitting into their gloves, and they'd give that ball a good going over before it got back to the pitcher. Believe me, that dark ball was hard to see coming out of the shadows of the stands."[15]

In the 1880s, baseball began to allow home team captains the option to bat first. They often accepted because a new and clean baseball was easier to hit. Only with the institution of the rain-out rule in 1892 (a game became official after four-and-a-half innings) did the home team batting last become the norm.[16]

Around this time, many of the rules and practices of the game we know today became common. Brothers George and Alfred Rawlings opened a sporting goods store in St. Louis in 1887. Two years earlier, George Rawlings had been issued a patent for a padded mitt. Fielders began wearing gloves. By this time, catchers had embraced wearing masks, with chest protectors and shin guards soon to follow. Overhand pitching deliveries started by the middle of the 1880s. The pitcher's mound and the current distance of sixty-feet, six-inches became the standard in 1893. Unlimited substitutions began around the same time. In 1896, the league required the home team to provide a dozen baseballs for each game. After multiple iterations, baseball finally settled on four balls for a walk in 1889. Twelve seasons later, the National League started counting foul balls as strikes. In 1911, baseball added a second umpire.

This series of progress by fits and starts neatly encapsulated the experience of St. Louis National League baseball during this period. From 1876 to 1892, the city had three different teams enter the league.

*****

The 1876 St. Louis Brown Stockings (commonly known as the Browns) represented the high-water mark for National League baseball in the city for a half-century. The team tied for second place in the standings, six games behind the league champion Chicago White Stockings. The Browns played 577 innings of baseball that season. George Washington Bradley pitched all but four of them. The 23-year old righthander compiled a record of 45-19, including a win on July 15 that guaranteed him baseball immortality. On that date, he pitched the first no-hitter in National League history, beating Hartford 2-0 at Grand Avenue Park. He took a no-hitter into the ninth inning in his next start. "A man might just as well try to successfully strike his mother-in-law as one of his balls," a Chicago hitter once said of the St. Louis pitcher.[17]

Bradley's success and the team's performance masked underlying issues on the club. Baseball may have had a new league with a new charter, but the men who played were largely the same. The culture of corruption that plagued the National Association followed the game to the National League. Joe Blong started the 1875 season playing for the St. Louis Red Stockings and later played that year for a team in Covington, Kentucky. On both clubs, he was suspected of throwing games.[18] In 1876, he was a starting outfielder for the newly formed Browns.

Dickey Pearce managed and played shortstop for the 1875 National Association Brown Stockings team. His club was widely suspected of conspiring to fix outcomes (called "hippodroming" at the time), including an arrangement with Chicago whereby each team agreed that the home team would win each time they played. In 1876, he served as a backup infielder for the National League team.

Mike McGeary played second base for the National League St. Louis Browns. In a game against New York in the team's inaugural season, he committed two throwing errors. Each one led to three runs scored in a 6-2 Browns loss. McGeary was suspended after the game. "I am authorized to say that the St. Louis club will pay a reward of $250 for any proof that (McGeary) was directly or indirectly interested in any pool, wager, or money consideration on the game alluded to," team vice president C.O. Bishop wrote to a Philadelphia newspaper.[19] With proof lacking, McGeary was later reinstated and continued to play.

The St. Louis second baseman also contributed to Bradley's pitching success. The baseball to be used for the day came to the stadium in a sealed box. McGeary taught the St. Louis pitcher how to steam open the box and then use a vise to crush the ball.[20] The new and now softer baseball was returned to its packaging, with opponents and the umpire apparently none the wiser. When combined with all the other abuses it faced, the mushy and eventually darkened ball proved challenging for hitters to make any significant contact.

While not above gamesmanship, Bradley had no interest in being connected to the more dishonest dealings of his teammates.[21] With no reserve clause in place (it would come a few years later), the pitcher departed to play for Chicago in 1877 ("I had a private misunderstanding with some of the officers of the St. Louis Club," he explained in a letter to the *St. Louis Globe-Democrat*).[22] With Bradley gone, the questionable behavior in St. Louis escalated in the new season. In May, an umpire accused Browns manager George McManus of offering him $250 to help St. Louis beat Louisville. McManus denied the charges and the league took no action.

It wouldn't be the last time St. Louis would be linked to Louisville that season. The game's first big scandal featured the Louisville Grays at the center of it. The St. Louis Browns played a secondary role, but at the end of the season, the impact was identical. Both franchises were out of business.

It began in August when the first-place Louisville team suddenly started losing games under suspicious circumstances, dropping eight in a row at one point. The Louisville slump coincided with a torrid streak by Boston. From August 17 through the end of the season, Boston went 20-1 to win the league. Louisville finished second, seven games back. The late-season struggles caught the attention of a *Courier-Journal* reporter who began pointing fingers and accusing players of dumping the pennant. The club launched an investigation that turned up multiple instances of telegrams between players and gamblers with the code word "sash" used to indicate the fix was on. By the end of October, the franchise moved to expel four players: shortstop Bill Craver, outfielder

George Hall, utility player Al Nichols, and star pitcher Jim Devlin. At a National League meeting in December, the league's board of directors moved to ban all four players from professional baseball.[23]

Hall had a brother-in-law in Brooklyn who had urged him to throw games that season. A New York gambler offered Devlin money to fix contests. The two players began working in concert, first in exhibition games and then in league games.[24]

Hall and Devlin also caught the eye of the St. Louis Browns that summer. In July, manager McManus and second baseman McGeary traveled to Louisville to convince the duo to play for the Browns the following season. St. Louis, which fell to fourth in the standings, was counting heavily on the duo to spark a turnaround in the team's fortunes. Hall was Louisville's best hitter (led the team in batting average, doubles, and triples) and Devlin ranked as one of the game's premier pitchers. He pitched all 559 innings of Louisville baseball in 1877, winning 35 and losing 25 with an ERA of 2.25.

With no Hall, no Devlin, and no money – the franchise had lost thousands of dollars – the St. Louis club folded after just two years in the league.[25] The ownership group accused Louisville of acting out of spite in expelling Hall and Devlin after the Browns had secured their services for the following season.

There was another reason why the St. Louis team never saw 1878. Like the Louisville Grays, members of the Browns had also conspired to fix games. Writing in the *Globe-Democrat,* William Spink presented the evidence under the headline "How St. Louis Was Sold Out." The sports editor of the paper wrote that "it has been evident that several screws have been loose in at least three of the leading clubs of the country – the St. Louis, Louisville, and Chicago," claiming "a small number of strictly first-class ball players have been suspected of co-operating with the gamblers and throwing games..."[26]

Spink contended that St. Louis club officials had evidence to believe that at least two men on the club were playing into the hands of a Chicago gambler named Mike McDonald. On August 24, a day Chicago played St. Louis at Grand Avenue Park, a local man wired McDonald: "Buy wheat. Smith is alright. Jones will assist." Chicago won the game 4-3. Third baseman Joe Battin, and Joe Blong, pitching for the Browns that day and whose reputation for game-fixing preceded his time with the club, were the two players suspected of participating in the conspiracy. Decades later, in the biggest scandal in the game's history, the links between Chicago and St. Louis gamblers and game-fixers would be revisited.

Just days after the Spink article appeared, the *Brooklyn Daily Eagle* reported that Battin and Blong, along with second baseman McGeary and infielder Davy Force had been expelled from the team. "When they do things out West they go the whole hog, whether in enterprise, hospitality, or crookedness," noted the paper.[27] Unlike the Louisville four, however, the St. Louis four were not banished from the game. But at the December league meeting, the franchise officially resigned. The city's first attempt at National League baseball ended in embarrassment, failure, and scandal.

The second attempt didn't fare any better.

*****

"The almost unanimous verdict was, that there had been so much crookedness in the ranks of the various clubs throughout the land, base ball, as a profession, would scarcely recover itself in this city," a pessimistic *St. Louis Post-Dispatch* declared in the fall of 1877. For the next few years, the paper looked prophetic. St. Louis would be absent from the ranks of the National League for the next seven seasons. J.B.C. Lucas II had served as president of the first National League team. Thanks to the efforts of his brother, St. Louis got a second shot.

Henry Lucas was the youngest of twelve children born to James and Marie Lucas. James' father, the original J.B.C. Lucas, had arrived in St. Louis early in the nineteenth century as one of the judges for the Louisiana Territory. He went on to become one of the largest landowners in the area. His portfolio included huge chunks of what eventually developed into downtown St. Louis, real estate holdings that made him one of the city's wealthiest residents. Born in Normandy, France in 1758, the St. Louis County suburb of Normandy sits on land his family once owned. The patriarch passed away in 1842.

Born in 1857, Henry Lucas came into a million-dollar inheritance when his father James died in 1873. In 1880, he married Louise Espenschied, the youngest daughter of Louis Espenschied, a St. Louis businessman and famed wagon maker. An avid baseball enthusiast, Lucas played the game at his five-hundred-acre country estate in Normandy where he invited friends to play ball and enjoy an "elegant spread" afterward.[28] When his brother's team folded, he looked for an angle to bring baseball back to St. Louis. He found his hook in the reserve clause. The clause, which allowed a franchise to control a player's contract in perpetuity, got its start in 1879. At that time, clubs could "reserve" the contracts of five players. It later expanded in the early 1880s to essentially cover an entire roster. Lucas called it "the most arbitrary and unjust rule ever suggested."[29]

The American Association, an upstart league that got its start in the 1882 season, later joined with the National League in enforcing the reserve contract. The two leagues controlled the market for major league talent. Lucas decided to challenge the existing order. He spearheaded the effort to create a new professional league that refused to honor the reserve clause, traveling the country to organize an eight-team circuit known as the Union Association. With local beer money backing him, he rented land in North St. Louis, prepared a field and built a three-story brick clubhouse.[30] The third floor featured a "dressing room, bathroom, reading room, billiard room, card room, and closets for players to store uniforms and personal belongings."[31] The St. Louis Maroons debuted in 1884.

They dominated the league from the very beginning. The Maroons opened the season with a twenty-game winning streak and never looked back.[32] The club finished the year with a record of 94-19, twenty-one games ahead of the Cincinnati Outlaw Reds. Lucas had the money to lure talent to his team. One of his players, infielder Fred "Sure Shot" Dunlap, received a salary of $3,600, a huge sum at the time. A year earlier, playing for Cleveland in the National League, he made $1,300. Sure Shot rewarded Lucas by hitting .412 with 13 home runs, both league-leading numbers.[33]

Even well after the season had started, with a huge lead in the standings, Lucas showed no signs of letting up. In July, after Maroons pitcher Billy Taylor jumped to the American Association, a report surfaced that the St. Louis owner had signed Charles Radbourn, a pitcher for the National League's Providence Grays.[34] "Old Hoss" Radbourn had recently been suspended by the Grays after getting into a dispute with an umpire and appearing to purposefully blow a game. Old Hoss was talented but temperamental. He had a drinking problem. According to his brother, Radbourn would down a quart of whiskey every day. Despite his daily battles with the bottle, Old Hoss sported a record of 24-8 at the time of his suspension. Lucas had reportedly lured him to St. Louis with an offer of $5,000 for the rest of the 1884 season and all of 1885.[35] Radbourn lived in Bloomington, Illinois, only about 160 miles from St. Louis, giving the rumor further credence.

With the fate of Old Hoss still undetermined, another drama began to play out in Providence. The Grays suspended their other starting pitcher, Charlie Sweeney. Accounts vary as to how it came about. It likely involved alcohol or insubordination, or possibly a combination of the two. With Sweeney out, Providence managed to bring back Radbourn by offering to pay him Sweeney's salary on top of his own and void the reserve clause in his contract as long as he made a legitimate push to win the pennant.[36]

Jilted by Old Hoss, Lucas signed Sweeney, a talented pitcher in his own right. In June, he had struck out 19 batters in a game, a major league record that would last for 102 years.[37] For the Maroons, he won 24 games while losing just 7. Combined with his time in Providence, Sweeney won 41 games in 1884. But Radbourn was even better. Rejuvenated by a week-long suspension that gave his arm time to rest, Old Hoss went 35-4 the rest of the way, finishing with 59 wins, a major league single-season record that will never be broken.[38] At one point, he started and completed twenty-two consecutive games. The Providence Grays rode the right arm of Radbourn to a National League pennant. In the first "World Series" that fall between Providence and New York, the champion of the American Association, the Grays swept the Metropolitans in three straight games, with Radbourn the winning pitcher in all three contests.[39] Presented with the opportunity to become a free agent, Old Hoss tore up the agreement and re-signed with Providence for the following season.

From St. Louis, Lucas had indirectly spurred on the National League champions while creating apathy in the league he had created. St. Louis fans responded enthusiastically to his checkbook ownership. "The Maroons, with their silk stockings and lamb's wool sweaters, were a sight to behold when they would march on the Union League field at Jefferson and Cass avenues to the music of a brass band," the *Post-Dispatch* remembered years later.[40] The team drew 116,000 fans to the Union Grounds, the highest attendance in the circuit.[41] It would occasionally be referred to as the "Palace Park of America."[42]

Elsewhere, the uncompetitive league drew a chilly reception. The Washington Nationals attracted 56,000 fans, second-best in the league, but less than half the amount of St. Louis. Most teams drew well under 50,000. In his zeal to create the new league, Lucas helped finance rival teams. By one estimate, he had provided half of the league's capital. Only five of the original eight teams completed the year. The economics were not sustainable. The Union Association folded after just one season.

While Lucas couldn't save the league, he did keep the Maroons' name alive. In January of 1885, Lucas purchased the National League Cleveland Blues and announced plans to move them to St. Louis.[43] With a rumored $2,500 payment to placate the owner of the St. Louis American Association club, the new St. Louis Maroons made their National League debut that spring.[44] When Lucas purchased the Cleveland franchise, he thought he was getting the Blues players. He didn't. Most of them went to Brooklyn.[45] What he wound up with was holdovers from the Union Association team and other players formerly blacklisted by the National League for contract jumping.[46]

Competing in a much tougher National League, the results were diametrically opposite the previous season. The Maroons went from first to worst, finishing 36-72, last place in the eight-team league, forty-nine games behind Chicago. Suddenly, Sure Shot Dunlap didn't look so certain. His batting average fell by 144 points. The volatile Sweeney, just as temperamental and frequently as drunk as his old teammate Radbourn, won just 11 games. Attendance plunged to 62,000.

By the following summer, the financial strain on Lucas had become obvious. Heavily in debt, Lucas sold nearly all his land holdings in July. [47] In August, he resigned from the Maroons organization and walked away from the game. "I'm out of baseball now, and if the citizens of St. Louis came to me with $100,000 and gave it to me to run a baseball club with, I would give it back to them and respectfully decline," he told a reporter.[48] Lucas estimated the final tally on his baseball losses would come to $70,000. A later estimate put the total at more than a quarter-million dollars.[49]

A new ownership group took over the franchise and raised stock but didn't keep it long. By early 1887, the franchise was sold and relocated to Indianapolis.[50] The park was sold at auction later that year and eventually torn down.

Fourteen years after coming into a million-dollar inheritance, Lucas left St. Louis for Minnesota where he worked as a traveling passenger agent for a railroad company. He had started as a ticket-seller.[51] He later moved to Chicago and declared bankruptcy. In 1903, his divorce from his wife drew coverage from *The New York Times*.[52] He spent the last years of his life back in St. Louis working as a city inspector for $75 a month. He died in 1910 at the age of 53.

Backed on two separate occasions by one of the wealthiest families in St. Louis, the city had now twice failed to keep a National League franchise going for longer than two seasons. With back-to-back failures by Lucas-led groups, old money St. Louis shut its collective wallet. For the next several decades, baseball would be kept alive in the city by immigrants and outsiders. Fortunately for St. Louis, a German immigrant had emerged to fill the immediate void. Just blocks from the Union Grounds, the greatest show in nineteenth-century baseball was unfolding.

Reborn in the American Association with new ownership and new players, but a familiar name, the St. Louis Browns were back and better than ever.

---

[1] The news reached St. Louis on July 6. "General Custer And His Command Annihilated," read a headline in the *St. Louis Globe-Democrat*.

[2] Reiss, Steven A. *City Games: The Evolution of American Urban Society and the Rise of Sports*. University of Illinois Press. 1989.

[3] Primm, James Neal. *Lion of the Valley: St. Louis, Missouri 1764 – 1980.* Missouri Historical Society Press. 1981, 1990, 1998.

[4] Ibid.

[5] Thorn, John. *Baseball in the Garden of Eden: The Secret History of the Early Game.* Simon & Schuster Paperbacks. 2011.

[6] Seymour, Harold. *Baseball: The Early Years.* Oxford University Press. 1960, 1989. "Relatively few people watched games."

[7] Ibid.

[8] Thorn, *Baseball in the Garden of Eden.*

[9] Allen, Lee. *The National League Story*. Hill & Wang. 1961.

[10] Ibid.

[11] Hample, Zack. *The Baseball: Stunts, Scandals, and Secrets Beneath the Stitches.* Anchor Books. 2011.

[12] Cook, William A. *The Louisville Grays Scandal of 1877: The Taint of Gambling at the Dawn of the National League.* McFarland & Company, Inc. 2005.

[13] Seymour, *Baseball.*

[14] The last *documented* instance of a major league game played with one ball occurred August 4, 1908 in a game featuring the St. Louis Cardinals and the Brooklyn Superbas (Dodgers) at Brooklyn's Washington Park. Nemec, David. *The Rules of Baseball: An Anecdotal Look at the Rules of Baseball and How They Came To Be.* Lyons & Burford, Publishers. 1994.

[15] Ritter, Lawrence S. *The Glory of Their Times. The Story of the Early Days of Baseball Told by the Men Who Played It.* William Morrow and Company, Inc. 1966/1984.

[16] The home team batting last wasn't written into the rules of the game until 1950. Morris, Peter. *A Game of Inches: The Stories Behind The Innovations That Shaped Baseball: The Game on the Field (Volume 1).* Ivan R. Dee. 2006.

[17] *St. Louis Post-Dispatch*, May 6, 1876.

[18] thisgameofgames.blogspot.com/2007/09/joe-blong.html for more. Blong's brother Andrew was a long-time St. Louis politician.

[19] Ginsburg, Daniel E. *The Fix Is In: A History of Baseball Gambling and Game Fixing Scandals.* McFarland & Company, Inc. 1995.

[20] Engelhardt, Brian. *George Bradley.* SABR.org biography project.

[21]"(T)here were a few guys on the club not a part of this [culture of corruption]and Bradley was one of them. There are statements by Bradley during 1876 that show he was aware of what was happening and he didn't like it. The reason he left the club, I believe, was to get away from the crookedness." Jeffrey Kittel, nineteenth-century baseball historian and blogger in an email exchange with the author. See thisgameofgames.com for more.
[22] *St. Louis Globe-Democrat*, October 18, 1876.
[23] Ginsburg, *The Fix Is In.*
[24] Ibid.
[25] Lee Allen wrote that the team lost $6,000 in 1877. An article in the *New York Clipper* in January of 1878 claimed the team lost $4,000 in its two years of existence. See www.thisgameofgames.com/home/four-thousand-dollars-indebtedness
[26] *St. Louis Globe-Democrat*, November 1, 1877. The article is reproduced in the digital book *Chris Von der Ahe: A Case for Hall of Fame Consideration*. Steve Pona, Editor.
[27] *Brooklyn Daily Eagle*, November 11, 1877.
[28] In the second half of the nineteenth century, wealthy St. Louis residents flocked to the suburbs of Normandy and Ferguson in the summer months. The *Post-Dispatch* described these summer homes as "elegant mansions of brick or stone, richly carpeted and furnished, with pictures from the old masters... In most of these residences they have every modern convenience, including gas and water, and in their stables, scarcely less costly than their houses is found thorough-bred horses, and equipages of every style from the village cart to the elegant family coach." *St. Louis Post-Dispatch*, July 6, 1883. With the completion of a railroad line in 1876, "the country squires had easy access to the city." Primm. *Lion of the Valley.*
[29] Seymour, Harold. "St. Louis and the Union Baseball War," *Missouri Historical Society Review*, Volume 51 Issue 3, April 1957.
[30] One of his investors was Ellis Wainwright, president of the Wainwright Brewing Company, the third-largest brewer in St. Louis at the time, according to Harold Seymour. Contemporaneous reports even refer to the "Lucas-Wainwright organization." See *St. Louis Post-Dispatch* November 6, 1883. At some point, Adolphus Busch became involved. A September 7, 1886 article in the *Post-Dispatch* states the three principal stockholders were Lucas, Fred Espenschied (Henry's brother-in-law), and Adolphus Busch. Joan Thomas later wrote that Anheuser-Busch became an investor when Lucas left the Maroons, "subscribing liberally to the new company." See SABR.org for more.
[31] Thomas, Joan M. *Henry V. Lucas*. SABR.org biography project.
[32] A Wikipedia entry for the Maroons contends the 20-game winning streak was the longest to open a season in American professional sports until the Golden State Warriors opened the 2015-2016 NBA season by reeling off 24 straight victories.
[33] Thomas, *Henry V. Lucas*. *Baseball-Reference.com.*
[34] Taylor had compiled a record of 25-4 for the Maroons with 1.68 ERA.
[35] Achorn, Edward. *Fifty-nine in '84: Old Hoss Radbourn, Barehanded Baseball & The Greatest Season a Pitcher Ever Had.* HarperCollins Publishers. 2010.

[36] Ibid. Also see "Hazard and Tips for Researchers" by James Tackach at the SABR Research Journal Archive. research.sabr.org/journals/hazards-and-tips-for-researchers.
[37] Boston Red Sox pitcher Roger Clemens broke the record with a 20-strikeout performance in 1986. Clemens later equaled the record in a game in 1996. Other pitchers with 20 strikeout performances are Kerry Wood for the Chicago Cubs in 1998 and Max Scherzer for the Washington Nationals in 2016.
[38] Some sources credit Radbourn with 60 victories that season.
[39] The 1884 series was advertised as a "Championship of the United States." Paul E. Doutrich, "Champions, Tantrums and Bad Umps: The 1885 'World Series.' Fall 2017 *Baseball Research Journal*.
[40] *St. Louis Post-Dispatch*, November 16, 1910.
[41] Attendance figures come from baseballchronology.com
[42] Thomas, Joan M. *Union Base Ball Park*. Sabr.org.
[43] *New York Times*, January 7, 1885.
[44] Cash, Jon David. *Before They Were Cardinals: Major League Baseball in Nineteenth-Century St. Louis*. University of Missouri Press. 2002.
[45] Seymour, *Baseball.* Lucas purchased the Cleveland club with $500 down and an agreement to pay an additional $2,000 when the transferred franchise was admitted to the league. When the team didn't include the promised players, Lucas refused to pay and told the group to "play ball with themselves." He counter-sued for $4,500. See *Sporting Life,* February 24, 1886.
[46] The Maroons had so many formerly blacklisted players they became known as the "Black Diamonds."
[47] *St. Louis Post-Dispatch,* July 10, 1886.
[48] Ibid, August 18, 1886.
[49] "In four years he lost more than a quarter-million dollars in an effort to give St. Louis a winning ball team." *St. Louis Post-Dispatch*, November 16, 1910. To a reporter for *The Sporting News*, Lucas admitted to $27,000 in losses. *The Sporting News*, August 23, 1886. Lucas told the publication he sold his interest to brother-in-law Espenschied and L.A. Coquard.
[50] Purchased by John T. Brush, who later owned the Cincinnati Reds and New York Giants, the Indianapolis Hoosiers played for three seasons before folding after the 1889 campaign.
[51] *St. Louis Post-Dispatch,* September 17, 1887.
[52] *New York Times*, June 23, 1903.

From Pennants to a Pauper

By 1860, nearly a third of all St. Louis residents had been born in Germany. Nearly as many kids attended German schools as public schools. Nine German newspapers published in St. Louis at the time. The reign of German papers in the city lasted more than a century with the last one shutting down in 1938.[1] The *Westliche Post* is where Hungarian immigrant Joseph Pulitzer got his start in the newspaper business. He later merged the *St. Louis Post* and the *St. Louis Dispatch*, creating the *St. Louis Post-Dispatch* in 1878.

The Germans brought their skills, habits, and recreational activities with them to the New World. Forty breweries in the city produced nearly 200,000 barrels of beer annually by 1860.[2] Over time, those breweries produced some of the most iconic brands in the industry. Budweiser is the best known but other names such as Stag and Falstaff originated with St. Louis area brewers. The German transplants not only transformed the St. Louis economy but its culture as well. "We found the town inundated with breweries, beer-houses, sausage-shops, Apollo Gardens, Sunday concerts, Swiss cheese, and Holland herrings," the *St. Louis Republican* noted in 1857. "We found it almost necessary to learn the German language before we could ride an omnibus or buy a pair of breeches, and absolutely necessary to drink beer at a Sunday concert."[3]

Gottfried Duden bought land in Warren County, Missouri, west of St. Louis, in the 1820s. He spent the next three years writing about his experiences. He then returned to his homeland and published a book in 1829 – *Report on a Journey to the Western States of North America.* "People in Europe will not and cannot believe how easy and pleasant it is to live in this country," he wrote.[4] Duden's book, and others like it, influenced thousands of Germans to make the trek across the Atlantic Ocean.

One of those who decided to bet on a better life in America arrived in St. Louis by the late 1860s. Chris Von der Ahe landed in New York in 1867 but quickly made his way westward. Born Christian Frederick Wilhelm Von der Ahe in what is now Hille, Germany, he was the oldest of nine children. Often listed with a birth date of October 2, 1851, author Edward Achorn maintains Von der Ahe was born in 1848. Facing compulsory service in the Prussian military at the age of 19, he chose to emigrate, telling authorities he was born three years later. He maintained the fictional birth date for the rest of his life.[5]

Living amongst a thriving German community in St. Louis, Von der Ahe quickly assimilated. By 1870, he was a married man and a partner in a deli and saloon. He married Emma Hoffman, a Missouri-born woman of German ancestry in March of that year. Son Edward soon followed.[6] By the early 1870s, he had bought out his business partner, changed locations and begun expanding the enterprise. He ran a saloon, beer garden and grocery store at the corner of Grand Boulevard and St. Louis Avenue, just down the street from the Grand Avenue Park. His business led to baseball. He became a member of the board of directors of the Grand Avenue Club, a St. Louis amateur team.

After the National League Browns shut down after the 1877 season, the lease on the park lapsed. Von der Ahe and a group that included the future founder of *The Sporting News*, Al Spink, formed the Sportsman's Park and Club Association. Von der Ahe became its largest shareholder and took the title of president. Raising $5,000 in capital, the group tore down the stands of Grand Avenue Park and built a new double-decker grandstand and bleachers. When Sportsman's Park opened in 1881 for the independent St. Louis Browns, it had an 8,000-seat capacity. A $25,000 profit that season whetted the appetite to bring organized professional baseball back to St. Louis.

When the American Association debuted in 1882, it featured teams in six cities, none of which overlapped with the eight-team National League. Three of the teams in the new league, though, included cities once a part of the Senior Circuit. Louisville and St. Louis dropped out after the scandals of 1877. The National League expelled Cincinnati after the 1880 season for refusing to stop selling beer and playing games on Sundays. Beer sales and Sunday games were two of the three pillars of how the American Association would differentiate itself. The new circuit also priced its tickets at twenty-five cents, half the admission price of the National League.

With cheap tickets, abundant beer, and games on Sunday – the only day off for many of the country's recent immigrants – the American Association proved to be a success from the beginning. Attendance at AA games outpaced the National League by thirty percent in its inaugural season. The following year, it became the first league ever to reach one-million in attendance.[7] The National League, seeking to distance itself from the corruption-plagued National Association, desired an affluent audience and wanted to make the game "respectable and honorable."[8] By contrast, the American Association loudly and proudly targeted the immigrant masses. "We Have Brought Baseball to the People," an AA slogan proclaimed.[9]

Critics called the American Association the "Beerball League" and the "Beer and Whiskey Circuit" due to the dominant influence of brewing interests backing the new enterprise. Immigrant saloon-owner Von der Ahe had made money selling beer to the masses, and he viewed baseball as a vehicle to sell more. "The Sunday business was a knockout at Chris' saloon," *Post-Dispatch* columnist J. Roy Stockton wrote years later. "The fans gathered early before the game and drank over the bar."[10] Baseball drew people to his park, but he was happy to use his facility for whatever attracted crowds with money to spend. A hint came early in his ownership. In October of 1881, the mayor granted Von der Ahe permission to apply for a license at the park to use for "athletic games, pyrotechnic displays and lawn parties."[11]

Over the years, Von der Ahe would use his ballparks for fireworks, "Wild West" shows, horse races and political rallies. When Democratic Party presidential candidate William Jennings Bryan arrived at Sportsman's Park to deliver a speech in 1896, he was surprised to learn Von der Ahe had charged admission.[12] With 30,000 people packed inside, the speech was cut short when the platform collapsed.[13]

Ambitious and entrepreneurial, Von der Ahe expanded his grocery and saloon business to include a feed and flour store, a butcher shop, horses, stable, and delivery wagons. He plowed the profits from his saloon and ballpark into more real estate. He owned rooming houses and required his players to live on property he owned. Even before he became a baseball owner, he acquired concession rights to the park. He sold "beer by the mug and whiskey by the shot."[14]

The garish and Gatsbyesque Von der Ahe wore loud clothes and spoke in a thick German accent. With the stadium lacking clubhouse facilities, players would gather before a game at Von der Ahe's saloon. Properly assembled, the players would then parade to the park, with the Browns owner and his two greyhounds, Snoozer and Schnauzer, leading the way.

Married three times and the target of dozens of lawsuits over the years, Von der Ahe could be incredibly cruel or extremely magnanimous, depending on his mood and the size of his bank account. He fined players frequently and fired managers arbitrarily. He watched games with a pair of binoculars and a whistle to better monitor the action and register any disapproval. When flush with cash, he spent lavishly. For a postseason trip to New York in 1888, he paid for the hotel and travel arrangements of some 200 St. Louis fans. The Browns secretary estimated the cost at $20,000. "What of it?" Von der Ahe replied. "An even temperament was not characteristic of Chris," observed George W. Axelson. "It was either sunshine or darkness, with never a trace of twilight in his makeup."[15] Most of the sunshine came early in his baseball career. The darkness came later.

Von der Ahe basked in the success of the Browns teams of the 1880s. Those St. Louis clubs won four consecutive pennants, a feat that wouldn't be repeated until the 1920s when John McGraw's New York Giants pulled it off. The Browns featured colorful players, rowdy fans, and an owner ripe for caricature. Many of the legends that have circulated over the years involve Von der Ahe's supposed lack of knowledge regarding baseball or subtleties of the English language. Once, he supposedly pointed to the infield at Sportsman's Park and proclaimed, "I have the biggest diamond in the world." When informed all diamonds are the same size, he attempted a correction. "What I mean, gentlemen, is that the Browns are playing on the biggest infield in the world." Another time, he was counseled to bury the hatchet with a former Browns player.

When Von der Ahe walked up to Rudy Kemmler with ax in hand, the initially confused catcher accepted his apology. The two men then proceeded, taking turns on a shovel, to bury the ax near home plate.[16]

This portrayal of Von der Ahe as a clueless naïf has received pushback in recent years. "It's ludicrous and beyond belief when you understand who the man really was. He wasn't stupid and he wasn't a clown," contends St. Louis baseball historian Jeffrey Kittel. "He was an outsider who made things work after his 'betters' had failed time and again. While doing so, he earned the eternal enmity of these people and this is reflected in the press he received."[17]

Observing the St. Louis baseball scene of the late nineteenth century, Bill James once contended a very good movie could be made about it. "It's got everything – great teams, unbelievable characters...pennant races, World Series." Chris Von der Ahe made it all possible.

*****

Fans filing into any major league baseball stadium today will see a coach's box on either side of the field. Located in foul territory, the boxes sit outside first and third base. They are there because of the St. Louis Browns. Led by their first baseman and captain Charlie Comiskey, the Browns played a harassing, intimidating style of baseball. Vocal and profane, they practiced psychological warfare on their opponents.

"Comiskey and (shortstop) Bill Gleason used to plant themselves on each side of the visiting catcher and comment on his breeding, personal habits, skill as a receiver, or rather lack of it, until the unlucky backstop was unable to tell whether one or a half dozen balls were coming his way," remembered former Chicago Cubs president James Hart. "Not infrequently the umpire came in for a few remarks."[18] The league put in coach's boxes in 1887 in an attempt to curb the aggressive behavior.

A contemporaneous report of the Browns' antics came from Philadelphia-based *Sporting Life* when the club traveled to the East Coast in June of 1883. "About the toughest and roughest gang that ever struck this city is the nine of the St. Louis club. Vile of speech, insolent of bearing, impatient of restraint, they set at defiance all rules, grossly insulted the umpire and excited the wrath of the spectators." The publication specifically singled out the team's first baseman for criticism. "The captain is an illiterate individual named Comiskey, whose sole claim to distinction rests upon his glib use of profane language."[19] (The Browns captain may have used profanity, but he was not illiterate. He attended St. Mary's College in Kansas.)

Originally a pitcher, Comiskey developed a reputation as perhaps the best defensive first baseman of the nineteenth century. He may not have been the first to play well off the bag as opposed to "hugging the line" as some claim, but he did revolutionize the position.[20] Research by Bill James validates the view that Comiskey was the first to have his pitchers cover first base on ground balls hit to the right side of the infield.[21] James called the Browns teams of this era the best defensive club of the decade.

In addition to playing every day, Comiskey became the team's full-time manager in 1885, following two earlier interim stints. Joining him on the infield of the Browns by the mid-1880s was second baseman Yank Robinson. The ambidextrous Robinson would throw left-handed to catch runners headed to third base. A heavy drinker, he told Von der Ahe he had "hydrophobia," a fear of water.[22] Shortstop Gleason would attempt to trip runners on the base paths and regularly joined Comiskey in haranguing and intimidating opposing hitters while third baseman Arlie Latham was known as "The Freshest Man on Earth." He would entertain fans by faking fainting spells when he disagreed with an umpire's call. Another co-conspirator in heaping abuse on opponents, Latham is thought to be the first to use chatter on the infield ("Hey batter, batter!"). A Chicago paper once complained of his "incessant bellowing." *The Sporting News* credited the Browns with popularizing the sacrifice bunt and called Latham "the most accomplished bunter of his time."[23] This quartet of infielders played together on multiple pennant-winning clubs: the "profane" first baseman, a water-fearing second baseman, a screaming and tripping shortstop, and a loud-mouthed third baseman with acting abilities.

Rounding out the starting lineup for the bulk of the Browns great run were four players known less for their antics and more for their athletic accomplishments. Behind the plate, Doc Bushong pioneered the use of catching the ball with one hand. In the outfield, Curt Welch was considered one of the premier center fielders of his era and a master at intentionally getting hit by a pitch. Left fielder Tip O'Neill won a batting title in 1887 when he hit .492. Walks counted as hits that season but even after adjusting the figures for modern rules, he still hit .435. The Woodstock, Ontario native also hit 14 home runs and generated 123 RBI and is retroactively credited with the Triple Crown. He is remembered today with the Tip O'Neill Award. It is given annually to the best Canadian player in the major leagues. While a great hitter, O'Neill struggled defensively and was considered a poor baserunner. Right fielder Hugh Nicol was his opposite – a fine outfielder and good baserunner who could barely hit. He hit .206 and .207 his last two seasons in St. Louis but had value because of his speed and defensive abilities.

Bob Caruthers and Dave Foutz took top honors on the pitching staff. In his first full season in the league, Caruthers led the American Association in ERA, wins and winning percentage. A year later, in 1886, Foutz led the league in all three categories. Both men frequently played the field when not pitching, often splitting time with Nicol in right field.

These were the St. Louis Browns at their apex – pugilistic, pioneering, and dominating. In winning four consecutive American Association pennants from 1885 to 1888, the Browns won sixty-eight percent of their games. They were even better at home playing in front of their "rowdy, beer-guzzling, insult-belching fans that Comiskey and Von der Ahe had cultivated." Over a seven-season stretch starting in 1883, the Browns won three out of every four ballgames at Sportsman's Park. "Many people felt you just couldn't win in St. Louis," wrote Bill James. "If the fans didn't get to you, they'd get to the umpire."[24]

St. Louis responded immediately and enthusiastically to the Browns, even before the team hit its stride. The 135,000 fans the Browns attracted in their first season led all of baseball, some 10,000 more than the National League White Stockings drew in Chicago. For the entire decade of the 1880s, more than 1.5 million fans watched American Association baseball in St. Louis, the highest figure in the sport. Legend has it the Browns became so famous the Missouri Pacific Railroad named stations after many of them. Bushong, Comiskey, and Latham are towns in Kansas that share the names of St. Louis players.[25]

The year the Browns won their first American Association pennant, 1885, was the same year that Henry Lucas and his Maroons joined the National League. The battle for St. Louis was no contest. The Browns win total of 79 and attendance of 125,000 both represented more than double what the Maroons produced. To compete against Von der Ahe's team, the National League even granted its St. Louis franchise the ability to charge less than the standard fifty-cent admission.[26] But the Browns had a better team, Sunday baseball and beer sales. The trio of factors combined to hasten the demise of Lucas and his Maroons.

Continuing a tradition that had started just a few years earlier, the American Association Browns played the National League Chicago White Stockings in a postseason series. The matchup now had a name. Sportswriter Al Spink is credited with creating the "World Series" moniker.[27] (The modern version played between the champions of the American and National Leagues didn't begin until 1903.) Also referred to as the "World's Championship Series" the 1885 matchup originally called for 12 games in 18 days in seven different cities.[28] Those plans were quickly abandoned. The first game ended in a tie when it became too dark to continue. The second game ended with the Browns arguing with the umpire and Comiskey pulling his team off the field in the sixth inning. "Many specimens of poor umpiring have been seen here this season, but that of Sullivan yesterday takes precedence for out-and-out robbery," an outraged *Post-Dispatch* declared.[29] Umpire Sullivan declared the game a forfeit in favor of Chicago.

The teams then split the next four games. The umpire announced before the seventh game that Chicago no longer claimed the disputed second contest. That meant the series was now tied at two games each (with one tie). With the clubs agreeing to cut the series short, the seventh game represented a winner-take-all matchup. "We each have two victories now and the winner of today's game will be the winner of the series," said Chicago first baseman and manager Cap Anson. The Browns won the game 13-4, but White Stockings president Albert Spalding disagreed with his captain. He claimed afterward his team never agreed to renounce the second game and that Anson lacked "any authority to take such a step." Officially a draw, the teams split the prize money, but the Browns viewed themselves as champions. "All available evidence points to the inescapable conclusion that Al Spalding was a sore loser," a St. Louis author later wrote.[30]

The same two teams, St. Louis and Chicago, met again for a postseason series in 1886. The matchup represented two clubs at the peak of their power. Playing an expanded schedule, the Browns went 93-46, the first of four consecutive 90-win seasons. In compiling a record of 90-34, the White Stockings won their fifth pennant in seven years.

Like the Browns, the White Stockings were led by their captain and first baseman. But Cap Anson was a much better hitter than Charlie Comiskey. The first player in history to generate more than 3,000 hits, Anson had already played five seasons of professional baseball before the National League debuted in 1876. He became so popular in Chicago the team was called the Orphans after he retired in 1897. Baseball historian Lee Allen called Anson the most widely-known player in the game until the arrival of Babe Ruth.[31] Anson's White Stockings and Comiskey's Browns defined major league baseball in the 1880s. They were also influential in driving African-American players out of the professional ranks.

Chicago played a Toledo minor league team in an exhibition game in 1883. Anson refused to take the field because of Toledo's black catcher, Moses Fleetwood Walker. Facing a loss of gate receipts, Anson eventually relented. A similar incident played out four years later when Chicago played an exhibition game against Newark, a club that featured an African-American battery – catcher Walker and pitcher George Stovey.[32]

That same season, the Browns were scheduled to play an exhibition game against the Cuban Giants, a New Jersey team of black players. The night before the game, eight members of the Browns signed a letter addressed to Von der Ahe stating they didn't agree "to play negroes" but added they would "cheerfully play against white people at any time."[33] The game was canceled. The signers of the letter included Latham, O'Neill and Welch. "We didn't want to go over there on Sunday, especially to play a nigger club, and we didn't go," said Latham, reflecting a not uncommon attitude among white players at the time.[34] The actions of the White Stockings and the Browns helped establish an unwritten rule of baseball. Other than some light-skinned Hispanics, players of color disappeared from the established professional ranks for sixty years.

While racial tension was absent in the 1886 series between the clubs, it did feature plenty of drama and some suspicious behavior. Setting the template for the modern version, the matchup was designed as a seven-game series from the beginning. The teams played the first three games in Chicago with the next three scheduled for St. Louis. If necessary, a seventh game would take place in Cincinnati, a neutral site.

Still more informal exhibition than formal postseason series, it took a bet to get the two teams to play. Chicago captain Anson accepted the St. Louis challenge for a rematch with one additional caveat. "We will play you under only one condition," Anson told Von der Ahe, "and that is the winner take all, and by all, I mean every penny that is taken at the gate." The Browns owner agreed to the terms.

After three games, Chicago headed south with a 2-1 lead. The only Browns win, a 12-0 blowout in the second game, fed rumors the game was thrown to extend the series. The absence of Jim McCormick in St. Louis, the White Stocking's number-two pitcher and winner of 31 games in the regular season, also fueled suspicion. "He's got the rheumatism and stayed at home," Anson explained.[35] At Sportsman's Park, the Browns won the fourth game 8-5 to tie the series. "At the Lindell Hotel that evening, the White Stockings, with the exception of Cap Anson, seemed strangely undisturbed by their loss," wrote *Glory Fades Away* author Jerry Lansche. The Chicago players drank champagne, smoked cigars and joked with reporters. "Not surprisingly," Lansche wrote, "the team's unusual behavior caused a resurrection of the charges of hippodroming."[36]

For the fifth game, the White Stockings wanted to start pitcher Mark Baldwin. The righthander hadn't appeared in a single regular-season game for Chicago. He spent the year pitching for Duluth in the Northwestern League and had just recently signed with Anson's club. All year long, Chicago had thrived with three starters and now two of them were sidelined; McCormick with rheumatism while third starter Jocko Flynn "was suffering from the twin curses of booze and a bad arm."[37] With only ace John Clarkson healthy, Chicago had turned to Baldwin. Von der Ahe objected to the ploy, arguing that he had signed up to play the Chicago team that won the National League. The decision went to the three umpires calling the series.[38] They decided to flip a coin. Baldwin was ruled ineligible when St. Louis won the coin toss.[39] The pitcher would resurface in the following decade to become a part of Browns' history.

Denied the chance to use Baldwin and out of arms, Anson decided to give the ball to shortstop Ned Williamson. He gave up two runs in the first inning and was replaced by right fielder Jimmy Ryan who went the rest of the way for Chicago. St. Louis won the game 10-3. Heading to the sixth game with the Browns now leading three games to two, the *Post-Dispatch* noted that the cry of hippodrome "has become universal." The high profile bet of gate receipts had become a source of public fascination and media attention. "A Big Stake," read the headline of the story which estimated the total pot after five games stood at more than $11,000. With the spoils rising with each game played, people had concluded that the teams had incentive to stretch out the series, a charge hotly denied. Chicago president Spalding offered a reward of $10,000 to anyone "who would bring him conclusive evidence of hippodroming."[40]

With accusations flying and the pile of prize money growing, a hobbled Chicago pitching staff counted on their ace to get them to a seventh game. Clarkson made his fourth start of the series. The Browns countered with Caruthers, a thirty-game winner in the regular season, making his third postseason start. The thousands of fans who jammed into Sportsman's Park on that October Saturday afternoon became witnesses to perhaps the most famous game in nineteenth-century baseball.

Chaos broke out in the fifth inning with Chicago leading 2-0. With a light rain falling, fans stormed the field and demanded the umpire call off the game. Police had to intervene. "It required a platoon of blue-coats to keep order."[41] The resumption of play only sharpened the foul mood of St. Louis fans. By the eighth inning, Chicago led 3-0. Both the mood and the scoreboard would soon change.

Comiskey led off in the bottom of the eighth with a base hit, only the second hit of the game for the Browns. A bunt by Welch and a wild throw to first base allowed Comiskey to score and Welch to advance to second. He later stole third base and when Bushong walked, the Browns had two on with two outs with Latham coming to the plate. "Stay there Bush," the Browns' third baseman yelled to Bushong, "and I'll bring you both in." Latham then slapped a ball to left field that made it all the way to the fence. By the time the ball was retrieved and returned to the infield, both runners had scored and Latham stood at third base. Ruled as a triple, *The Sporting News* later called the play an error, claiming Chicago left fielder Abner Dalrymple had misjudged the ball.[42] Either way, the Browns had tied the game and energized the crowd. "The air was full of hats, handkerchiefs and umbrellas."[43] Dalrymple didn't help his cause when he struck out in the ninth inning with a runner on third and the score still tied. The left fielder, who joined the White Stockings in 1879, had one more inning left in his Chicago career.

In the bottom of the tenth inning with the score still tied at three, Welch lined a ball past second base for a single. Foutz, the team's best pitcher (41-16) and part-time outfielder, hit a ground ball that Chicago shortstop Ned Williamson couldn't handle. Both runners moved up when Robinson bunted them over. With runners at second and third and one out, Bushong came to the plate. He never swung the bat. On Chicago pitcher Clarkson's second delivery, the ball eluded catcher Mike "King" Kelly and rolled toward the grandstand. When Welch touched home plate, the Browns had won the game and the series.

St. Louis erupted. Thousands stormed the field to congratulate the Browns. Fans carried players off the field on their backs. "Fifteen minutes after the game," according to one account, "the cheering and excitement had not subsided." For the first and only time, an American Association team could claim an undisputed championship over a National League squad. Chicago had a different reaction. "Anson's Men Defeated By Von Der Ahe's Pets," read a headline from the *Tribune*.[44]

Welch's winning run became known as the "$15,000 slide," referring to the amount of money at stake and how the Browns player crossed home plate. The first part was a slight exaggeration. The second part simply didn't happen. The outfielder didn't have to slide after what was either a passed ball or a wild pitch. "Welch trotted home with the World's Championship run," read an account from *The Sporting News*.[45] As for the money, total gate receipts totaled slightly under $14,000. Once travel and umpire expenses were deducted and Von der Ahe took his half, the dozen Browns players received a little more than $500 each.[46] The Browns owner wanted to proceed with a seventh game in Cincinnati a few days later, but Chicago declined. "We must decline with our compliments," wrote president Spalding. "We know when we've had enough."

The hard-fought extra-inning battle also produced another impact, at least concerning the final game. "Yesterday's play dispelled all suspicion" regarding hippodroming, touted the *St. Louis Globe-Democrat.*[47] "The battle has been for blood – not for fun," noted one Chicago paper.[48]

Dalrymple, the Chicago outfielder fingered by some as the goat of the series, finished his major league career with two years in Pittsburgh and one in Milwaukee. In November of 1896, he boarded a streetcar in St. Louis and paid his fare only to be told by the conductor that his dime was counterfeit. An argument and fistfight ensued. He ended up in a local hospital with a scalp wound and bruises. He claimed the pugilistic conductor was assisted by his passengers.[49] He had better luck with railroads than streetcars. After baseball, he became a conductor for the Northern Pacific.

Dalrymple's teammate in 1886, Kelly, emerged as one of the classiest players in a series better remembered for its bets, taunts, and unruly crowd behavior. The Chicago catcher took responsibility for the pitch that allowed Welch to score the deciding run. "I would say it was a passed ball," he told reporters after the final game. "You can give it to me if you want to. Clarkson told me that it slipped from his hands."[50] He also defended Dalrymple, whose list of critics included the president of his team. "Dal ought to have caught the ball," said Spalding, who looked at Kelly as he spoke. The Chicago player refused to pile on. "I don't know about his catching it," said Kelly.[51]

On Sunday, one day after celebrating victory over Chicago, the Browns began battling the Maroons for the championship of St. Louis, a series that would end in another success for Von der Ahe's team.[52] At the game, Kelly presented the Browns with a "floral tribute" and publicly praised the champions. "They have beaten our club – the Chicago club – fairly (Great applause), and they have beat us on the rattle. (More applause.) I can say that you have treated us well here, and we hope to meet you again in the future." (Cheers.)[53]

On Monday, the Browns were honored at another ceremony at the Mercantile Exchange in downtown St. Louis. Once again, "the irrepressible Mike" addressed the crowd and thanked the Browns, "who are now champions of the world," becoming perhaps the first and last player on a losing team to fete the winners so publicly on consecutive days. Kelly had reason to be in a good mood. A St. Louis grain broker told the *Post-Dispatch* the Chicago catcher had cleared as much as $100,000 by speculating in wheat.[54]

Like Dalrymple, Kelly had played his last game for Chicago. Spalding sold him to Boston in the offseason for $10,000. The White Stockings great run, five pennants in seven years, had come to end. Anson would later call his 1885 and 1886 clubs the strongest team he ever managed. In 1911, he went as far as to call that group of players "the most capable team ever before the public." Hyperbole aside, the most dominant National League team of the 1880s had been bested by the most dominant American Association club of the era. In twelve undisputed games over two seasons, the Browns record against Chicago stood at seven wins, four losses, and one tie.

Although more gradual in retreat, the St. Louis Browns also peaked in 1886. The club did win two more pennants over the next two seasons but were defeated soundly in postseason competition against the National League. In 1887, St. Louis and Detroit agreed to a fifteen-game series, with winners taking seventy-five percent of the gate and the losers getting twenty-five percent. The Wolverines won the series ten games to five. In a best-of-eleven format in 1888 against New York, the Giants claimed their sixth victory and clinched the championship in the eighth game.

The following season, Von der Ahe had reason to suspect his players of betting on games. It began in May when the team dropped three straight contests in Kansas City. It was widely suspected at the time that the team intentionally lost the games as a protest against Von der Ahe's suspension of second baseman Robinson (he had been fined and refused to pay). Robinson was reinstated but the suspicions about the play of certain players remained. By July, Von der Ahe had hired detectives and spoke openly of the investigation into two specific players, pitcher Silver King and third baseman Latham. "I have had both Latham and King up before me, but they deny the matter," the Browns owner told reporters. King forcefully denied the allegations. "I was surprised when Mr. Von der Ahe charged me with throwing games and felt like hitting him."[55]

While Latham also denied the charges, he had far less conviction than his teammate. "Did you see that Athletic game about which they talk so much? We won that in the last inning." A reporter reminded him he had played poorly that game. "Did I?" Latham responded. On August 11, the Browns took action against their third baseman. Von der Ahe suspended him indefinitely and without pay. At a meeting later with the Browns owner and captain Comiskey, Latham admitted he'd been in the company of a man named Lynch – described as a pool-room gambler from Boston – but denied betting against the Browns.[56] Reinstated near the end of August, Latham lasted about a month before trouble surfaced again. With just a few weeks remaining on the schedule and trailing Brooklyn by three-and-a-half games, Von der Ahe fined Latham $200 and suspended him for the rest of the season. "Latham has been a millstone around the neck of the St. Louis Browns since July 1," asserted the *Post-Dispatch*.[57] Other than a brief return to St. Louis in 1896 (managed three games, played in eight), Latham's career with the Browns was over.

As an everyday player with the team from 1883 to 1889, Latham represented both the rise and fall of the Browns. The St. Louis third baseman started for all four pennant-winning teams of the decade. A showman with a flair for the dramatic, his game-tying triple in the bottom of the eighth inning of the sixth game of the 1886 World Series is one of the greatest St. Louis postseason hits of all-time. Animated and vocal, Latham set the pace at the plate and in the field. An accomplished bunter and base stealer, he led the league in runs scored in 1886, plate appearances in 1887, and stolen bases in 1888.

Balancing out the ledger are his connections to a gambler and the suspicions raised about his behavior. Von der Ahe was likely one of the first baseball owners to hire detectives to track down pool hall rumors but he certainly wasn't the last. Thirty years later, as an owner, Comiskey would employ identical tactics to try to get to the bottom of the Black Sox scandal. Suspended twice in 1889, Latham didn't play in seventeen games that season. The Browns went 90-45, finishing second, two games behind Brooklyn. It would be more than three decades before another St. Louis team got that close to winning a pennant.

With the launch of the Players' League in 1890, the Browns roster experienced mass defections. Latham joined Comiskey and O'Neill in playing for the Chicago team in the new league. When it folded after one season, Comiskey and O'Neill returned to St. Louis. Latham went to Cincinnati, where he spent most of his remaining big-league career.

After his playing days were done, New York Giants manager John McGraw hired him as a coach. Latham is thought to be the first contracted base coach in major league history. In 1909, at the age of 49, he appeared in four games for New York and even stole a base. Latham was evidently a better runner than base teacher. Giants outfielder Fred Snodgrass once described him as "probably the worst third-base coach who ever lived."

Latham became an ambassador for the game, spending time in England during World War I, organizing baseball for the troops. He met King George V and showed him how to throw a baseball. "He had a middling fair arm," Latham said of the King, "but it was hard to break him of the habit of his stiff arm way from playing cricket."[58] One winter, McGraw and his wife traveled to England and threw parties each night at their London hotel. Latham had a job as a coat checker at another hotel in the city. Each night after work, the sixty-four-year-old would ride his bike over to where the McGraws had set up residence. He'd dance and tell stories all night, then hop on his bike and head for home only to repeat the sequence the following evening.

When he returned to the United States, he opened a delicatessen in Manhattan and became a press box attendant for both the New York Giants and Yankees.[59] Before he died at the age of 92, he was the oldest living former player in the history of the game. Born a year before the start of the Civil War, Latham died in the fall of 1952.

Writing in *The Sporting News* shortly after Latham's death, Frank Graham called the former Browns third baseman "the first diamond comedian." He also reminded his readers of one of Latham's eternal gifts to the game. When a hard smash came down the third-base line that Latham didn't think he could handle, he would simply wave his right leg in a sign of resignation. "The gesture became legend in baseball," wrote Graham. "For years thereafter whenever a third baseman let a hot shot go by, ball players who had never seen Latham, would say: 'He gave it the Arlie Latham.'"[60]

*****

By the fall of 1891, the Browns had played ten seasons in the American Association, won four pennants, finished second three times, and with the exit of the Maroons, successfully driven the National League out of St. Louis. Largely through the efforts of the Browns, the only team to beat the NL in a postseason series, the AA demonstrated itself a viable competitor to the older and more established league. In December of 1891, the two leagues announced a merger. Four AA teams – St. Louis, Baltimore, Louisville, and Washington – joined an expanded National League that now included twelve teams and featured a 154-game schedule for the first time. "The new organization is a monopoly of the most grinding kind and under its laws players will be little better than slaves," predicted an unimpressed *Post-Dispatch*.[61]

Despite the unhappiness of the local paper, local fans had reason to celebrate. The expanded league allowed Sunday baseball and liquor sales, two issues that had long been points of contention between the two organizations. The first Sunday game in National League history took place in St. Louis on April 17, 1892. The Cincinnati Reds beat the Browns 5-1.

The 1892 Browns got off to an awful start, 2-10 in April, and never recovered. The club finished the season in eleventh place with a record of 56-94. Other than pitcher/outfielder Caruthers, all the stars of the 1880s teams, including Charlie Comiskey, had departed.

A forgettable year for the Browns featured one final campaign from one of the game's early stars. Pitcher James Frances Galvin was a St. Louis native, born in the Irish section of the city known as the "Kerry Patch." He made his professional debut in 1875 for the National Association St. Louis Brown Stockings. The 1892 season was the only other one of his career where he played for a hometown team. "Pud" Galvin became the first National League pitcher to win 300 games in his career. He's also believed to be the first player to use a performance-enhancing steroid-like substance. While playing for Pittsburgh, he took a testosterone potion before a game in 1889. He then shut out Boston 9-0. The Veterans Committee inducted Galvin into the Baseball Hall of Fame in 1965.[62]

The Browns left Sportsman's Park after the 1892 season. "New Sportsman's Park" opened in 1893 just blocks away at the intersection of Vandeventer and Natural Bridge Road. Providing a template for the modern baseball experience, Von der Ahe's creation eventually expanded to include amusement park rides and horse racing.

The *Post-Dispatch* called the new park a "fan's paradise," "without an equal," and praised Von der Ahe for making it possible. It included private boxes, a sweeping press box view that encompassed the Fair Grounds and the city beyond, as well as a "conveniently arranged set of ladies' toilet-rooms" at the back of the grandstand.[63] Opening day began with a parade that embarked from "old" Sportsman's Park. It included twenty-five carriages and "four of Adolphus Busch's finest black Arabian prancers." More than twelve-thousand fans enjoyed the baseball and the beer as the Browns beat Louisville 4-2.

The optimism of opening day didn't last. The new Sportsman's Park 1893 Browns weren't much better than the 1892 version in the old park. St. Louis finished its second National League season in tenth place with a record of 57-75. The following year, the Browns won one less game but finished one position higher in the standings. Then the bottom fell out.

The club finished next-to-last in the standings in both 1895 and 1896. The club cycled through eight different managers over two seasons with Von der Ahe himself taking the reins briefly in both campaigns. When one of the Browns players, Tommy Dowd, promised to pull the Browns up to seventh place, the owner told him, "Don't go to guessing, Tommy; don't count your chickens until they lay eggs already."[64]

Von der Ahe's involvement escalated as the club worsened. The 1897 season featured a record of 29-102, a winning percentage of .221, the worst mark in franchise history. Von der Ahe managed the club for fourteen games, losing twelve of them. The owner was one of four managers of a team that lost eighteen in a row at one point and never won more than two in a row the entire season. The Browns finished the year 63.5 games behind the league champions, the Boston Beaneaters. Thanks in part to a return to the 154-game schedule, St. Louis won ten more games in 1898 but repeated their last-place performance. Manager Tim Hurst somehow survived the entire season, but like every other skipper of the Browns in the 1890s, he didn't return the following year.

The National League St. Louis Browns of the 1890s had completely flipped the script from the 1880s American Association version. A team that consistently won two out of every three games now struggled to win a third of their contests. In their first seven seasons in the National League, the Browns won 307 games and lost 640, a .324 winning percentage, never finishing higher than ninth place. Sportswriter Fred Lieb once described those seven seasons as the "darkest, dankest and direst in St. Louis baseball history."

An economic crisis had swept the country the same year Von der Ahe opened his new park. The panic of 1893 lasted four years with unemployment, by one estimate, reaching eighteen percent. More than one railroad went bankrupt. The stocks of those that survived collapsed. Farm prices plummeted. With extensive real estate holdings, Von der Ahe certainly felt the pinch. Attendance at Browns games, which peaked at 244,000 in 1887, fell to 136,400 by 1897. The Browns owner, widely admired for years, became the subject of media scorn and ridicule. *The Sporting News* mockingly referred to him as "Von der Ha."

During the 1890s depression, Von der Ahe decided to double down on his investment in the new park. In 1895, he announced plans for a "Shoot-the-Chutes" ride. The amusement park experience (like a modern-day log flume) had made its debut in Chicago in 1894. New York's Coney Island had one a year later, and the ride soon became popular across the country. As part of his attempt to make Sportsman's Park the "Coney Island of the West," Von der Ahe's "Chutes" opened in the summer of 1896. Located behind the right-field fence, a ride cost ten cents. It quickly attracted competition. By 1897, St. Louis residents had three such attractions in the city to choose from.[65] At the bottom of the ride at Sportsman's Park, an artificial lake doubled as an ice-skating rink in the winter.

Von der Ahe also added horse racing to the mix of entertainment options during this period, competing with two other tracks in the city, including one at the nearby Fair Grounds. The Browns owner had lights installed at Sportsman's Park to run night-time races. A century ahead of his time, Von der Ahe had transformed his park into a multipurpose entertainment facility. The experiment, however, lasted just a few years. Von der Ahe abandoned the horse track first. A year later, he sold the Shoot-the-Chutes. By the 1898 season, the Browns had returned Sportsman's Park to a baseball-focused venue. Von der Ahe's critics applauded the moves. "If he had worked half as hard to get together a good baseball team as he has to establish a 'dinky merry-go-round,' St. Louis would now have a permanent winning club," wrote *Sporting Life*.[66]

During this period, an old nemesis returned to haunt the Browns owner. Mark Baldwin, denied the opportunity to pitch against St. Louis in the World Series of 1886, had established himself as a quality pitcher and the target of multiple teams. Over three years, he played for three teams in three different leagues – the National League Chicago White Stockings, the American Association Columbus Solons, and the Players' League Chicago Pirates (managed by Charlie Comiskey).

When Baldwin signed with the Pittsburgh Pirates for the 1891 season, he tried to induce a few members of the AA Browns to jump to the National League. Von der Ahe found out and had Baldwin arrested in St. Louis for tampering with his club. The pitcher then fired back with a lawsuit for false imprisonment. It originally went to trial in 1895 and took years to play out. After the original jury had awarded Baldwin $2,500 in damages, a motion for a new trial was granted the following year on the grounds that an attempt had been made to influence the jury. Baldwin won again – this time the jury upped his award to $2,525. With Von der Ahe refusing to pay and the interest on the amount climbing, Pittsburgh authorities and St. Louis lawyers hatched a plot to bring the Browns owner to the Pennsylvania city.

A detective arrived in St. Louis posing as "Robert Smith," a New York businessman. "I have a little private business to discuss with you," read a note sent to Von der Ahe. When the Browns owner arrived, the two men boarded a carriage. The detective quickly slapped one end of a pair of handcuffs on Von der Ahe's wrist with the other attached to his own. The carriage driver, fully engaged in the conspiracy, quickly hustled the two men across the Mississippi River to Illinois where they boarded a train to Pittsburgh. Von der Ahe, fighting and cursing the entire way, had to be forcibly taken aboard. When he arrived in Pittsburgh, "His hat was battered, his coat and vest torn and his shirt front soiled and ruffled."[67]

By refusing to settle voluntarily, Von der Ahe had left his bondsman on the hook. W.A. Nimick either had to pay $1,000 or produce the Browns owner. He chose the latter course. As the former owner of the Pittsburgh franchise, Nimick was no ordinary bail bondsman. The plot to grab Von der Ahe was his idea. He dispatched his attorneys to St. Louis to meet with lawyers who once represented Mark Baldwin, brothers W.C. and J.C. Jones. The St. Louis attorneys signed off on the plan, calling it "entirely legal and offered any assistance in their power."[68] Two decades later, J.C. Jones would emerge as an instrumental force in the fortunes of the St. Louis Cardinals.

Von der Ahe spent nearly two weeks in a Pittsburgh prison while club officials scraped together the money for his release. The total came to $4,000 and included the Baldwin judgment plus interest along with money owed to Nimick. The abduction and jail time represented one piece in a string of humiliations and setbacks for Von der Ahe.

He divorced his second wife in 1898 and married his former housekeeper. Third wife Anna Kaiser was younger than Von der Ahe's son Eddie. He had originally proposed marriage to her in 1895. But he met Della Wells and married her instead. Kaiser sued for breach of promise and was reportedly awarded $3,000 plus court costs. His marriage to Wells didn't last long. Her mother was a Von der Ahe tenant. He evicted her for failing to pay back rent. Daughter Della filed for divorce in early 1898, claiming he was often drunk and beat her.[69] "He did not appreciate quiet evenings at home," said Wells. "The base ball office, the shoot-the-chutes and the night racing was more to him than a loving home."[70] The 47-year-old Von der Ahe then married the 24-year-old Kaiser in August.

In between the end of his second marriage and the beginning of his third, fire struck at Sportsman's Park. It occurred in the second inning of just the second game of the season when a blaze erupted from the east edge of the grandstand. The fire spread rapidly throughout the wooden structure, forced the evacuation of thousands of fans, and caused dozens of injuries. The blaze touched every area of the park except for the right-field bleachers. Von der Ahe's greyhound, "Fly," last seen asleep in the boss's office at the park, was smothered to death by the smoke. "In the clubhouse building I had everything that belonged to me," Von der Ahe told reporters, "including papers that cannot be replaced besides clothing, furniture and jewelry." Lost in the fire were all the Browns championship trophies from the 1880s. Early estimates of the damages put the loss at $60,000 to $70,000. Von der Ahe had insurance for $34,500.[71]

Dozens of laborers worked through the night to remove debris and erect temporary stands. Amazingly, St. Louis and Chicago played the next day. Chicago won the game 14-1 in a year that saw the Browns lose 111 games. Fans injured in the fire filed personal injury lawsuits, putting additional financial strain on the St. Louis owner.

It should be noted the events of 1898 didn't create Von der Ahe's woes, they only compounded them. In January of that year, the Browns reportedly had liabilities of $108,000. The club filed a chattel deed of trust listing Von der Ahe as both the trustee and the preferred creditor in the amount of $91,000. The Browns owed other parties an additional $17,000 with Anheuser-Busch listed as the largest outside creditor. Team secretary Benjamin Muckenfuss said Von der Ahe was essentially bankrupt. "Mr. Von der Ahe is not at all concerned about what he owes personally, as he is to all intents and purposes insolvent."[72] This declaration by Muckenfuss occurred *before* Von der Ahe's abduction and arrest and three months before the devastating Sportsman's Park fire.

The series of unfortunate events accelerated the inevitable. Assets including the ballpark property were sold on the St. Louis County courthouse steps in the winter of 1899, bringing an end to the Von der Ahe reign. The German immigrant had accomplished what old money St. Louis failed to do – keep National League baseball alive in the city for more than two years. Over the years, Von der Ahe had refurbished one ballpark, built another, established the American Association as a credible rival to the National League, and experimented with unique ballpark amenities a hundred years before other owners dared to try. Even his critics recognized his enormous contributions. "He has done more for base ball than any man, living or dead," wrote *Sporting Life*.[73]

Stripped of his ball club, Von der Ahe returned to his saloon. He filed for bankruptcy in 1908, listing assets of $200 and liabilities of nearly $28,000.[74] A baseball charity game that summer raised nearly $5,000 for him. His old captain, Charlie Comiskey, now the owner of the Chicago White Sox, contributed $500. Von der Ahe died in June of 1913 at the age of 61 from cirrhosis of the liver. Comiskey served as a pallbearer along with several other former Browns players and American League president Ban Johnson. The former Browns first baseman called the former Browns owner "the grandest figure baseball has ever known." Von der Ahe is buried at Bellefontaine Cemetery in St. Louis beneath a life-sized statue of himself. [75]

As for the new owners of the Browns, Frank and Stanley Robison took over operations after a series of transactions. The brothers from Ohio also owned the Cleveland franchise, known as the Spiders. Cleveland president Frank Robison had been linked to St. Louis as early as 1897. Upset about opposition to his team playing Sunday games in Cleveland, he began to issue threats that he would move his team to another city.[76] He was true to his word.

To escape Von der Ahe's legal woes, the National League moved to dissolve the St. Louis franchise after the 1898 season. The Sportsman's Park and Club Association, the corporation that owned the assets of the Browns, was replaced by the American Baseball & Exhibition Company. With the new legal entity in place, Robison then performed a wholesale swap – with Cleveland players coming to St. Louis and the rag-tag Browns bound for Ohio. The 1899 Cleveland squad, featuring many of the same players who had donned a uniform in St. Louis the year before, finished the season 20-134, a winning percentage of .130, the worst mark in major league history. Things got so dire for Cleveland the club stopped playing games at their home park, ending the year with 112 road games. When the National League contracted to eight clubs in 1900, Cleveland was one of the casualties. The downsizing paved the way for the birth of the American League the following year.

Things worked out far better for National League fans in St. Louis. With new players and a new name, the "Perfectos," St. Louis went 84-67, a forty-five-win improvement over the prior season and good enough for fifth place. In addition to the name change, the new owners introduced a new color scheme – going from brown to red – and brought a new attitude to the ballpark. "No beer waiters, peanut vendors or score card boys will annoy patrons during games," announced new club president Frank Robison. It is this franchise, essentially the *fourth* effort at National League baseball in St. Louis, that fans flock to Busch Stadium III by the millions every year to watch. Today's St. Louis Cardinals were yesterday's Cleveland Spiders.

With the dawning of a new century, the team would see more ownership changes and years of struggle. But thanks to the arrival in St. Louis of a ballplayer from Texas and an attorney and former player from Ohio, the fortunes of the franchise would take a dramatic turn.

---

[1] Merkel, Jim. *Beer, Brats and Baseball: St. Louis Germans*. Reedy Press. 2012.
[2] Primm, *Lion of the Valley.*
[3] Ibid.
[4]www.teachushistory.org/nineteenth-century-immigration/resources/duden-recommends-immigrating.
[5] Achorn, Edward. *The Summer of Beer and Whiskey: How Brewers, Barkeeps, Rowdies, Immigrants, and a Wild Pennant Fight Made Baseball America's Game*. Public Affairs, Perseus Books Group. 2013.
[6] Hetrick, J. Thomas. *Chris Von der Ahe and the St. Louis Browns*. Scarecrow Press, Inc. 1999.
[7] Cash, *Before They Were Cardinals.* Columbus and New York joined the American Association in 1883, making it an eight-team league.
[8] Seymour, *Baseball.*
[9] Cash, *Before They Were Cardinals.*
[10] *St. Louis Post-Dispatch*, December 9, 1928.
[11] Ibid, October 12, 1881.
[12] Hetrick, *Chris Von der Ahe and the St. Louis Browns.*
[13] *St. Louis Post-Dispatch*, September 13, 1896.
[14] Achorn, *The Summer* of *Beer and Whiskey.*
[15] *St. Louis Post-Dispatch*, November 16, 1919.
[16] Nemec, David (editor). *Major League Baseball Profiles, 1871-1900 (Volume 1). The Ballplayers Who Built the Game*. University of Nebraska Press. 2001.
[17] Email to the author, March 23, 2017.
[18] *St. Louis Post-Dispatch*, November 13, 1919.
[19] *Sporting Life*, June 10, 1883.
[20] Harold Seymour called it a "tenacious" myth that Comiskey was the first to play back and off the base instead of anchoring to the bag. "But the truth of the matter is that the method of play was familiar and commonly used back in the 1860s, at least twenty years before Comiskey supposed to have introduced it." See Seymour, *Baseball.*

---

[21] "In 1886 St. Louis pitchers recorded 106 putouts, whereas the record for a team before 1886 was 81." James, Bill. *The New Bill James Historical Baseball Abstract.* The Free Press. 2001.
[22] Hetrick, *Chris Von der Ahe and the St. Louis Browns*.
[23] *The Sporting News*, October 30, 1887. Von der Ahe biographer J. Thomas Hetrick wrote that Comiskey would order players to sacrifice in close games. If the player didn't comply, Comiskey would walk to the plate and punch them in the mouth.
[24] James, *The New Bill James Historical Baseball Abstract*.
[25] The town of Bushong was originally named Weeks. A Wikipedia entry credits the Missouri Pacific Railroad for renaming the town (2010 population of 34) in honor of the Browns catcher. Comiskey is now a ghost town. It was located in Lyon County, Kansas. A Wikipedia entry for Latham says the town *may* have been named for a railroad official. It was laid out in 1885 – a timeframe that supports the idea of the Browns third baseman as the inspiration.
[26] Seymour, *Baseball*. Relief for the Maroons may have come too late. "St. Louis, Washington, and Philadelphia were granted a 25-cent tariff and St. Louis the privilege of Sunday exhibition games." *St. Louis Post-Dispatch*, November 19, 1886. The Maroons left for Indianapolis the following year.
[27] Cash, *Before They Were Cardinals.* The NL White Stockings played the AA Cincinnati Reds for two games in 1882 with each team winning one. The 1884 matchup was chronicled in the previous chapter.
[28] Ibid. *The Sporting News*, October 13, 1986. Von der Ahe referred to the "World's Championship Series" in a letter to the White Sox in 1886. St. Louis is also credited with giving Chicago the White Stockings nickname. When a Chicago team took the field in St. Louis in April of 1870, a fan called out, "Oh, look at the white stockings!" *Sporting Life*, October 28, 1885.
[29] *St. Louis Post-Dispatch*, October 16, 1885.
[30] Lansche, Jerry. *Glory Fades Away: The Nineteenth Century World Series Rediscovered.* Taylor Publishing. 1991. Competition between St. Louis and Chicago resumed two weeks later at the Union Grounds, home of the Maroons. Only this time the contest wasn't a baseball game. It was a foot race between Browns third baseman Arlie Latham and Chicago outfielder and future evangelist Billy Sunday. In a 100-yard dash, Sunday unofficially clocked in at ten-and-a-quarter seconds and won by three yards. Four representatives from Chicago, including Anson, bet heavily on Sunday and cleaned up – "the quartet must have lugged away $3,500 between them," the *Post-Dispatch* observed. Browns owner Von der Ahe and pitcher Dave Foutz lost money but many of the St. Louis players refused to back their teammate. Outfielder Curt Welch openly bet against him. Sunday won a purse of $400 and the title of "champion base-ball sprinter of the United States." *St. Louis Post-Dispatch*, November 7, 1885.
[31] Allen, Lee. *The Hot Stove League*. A.S. Barnes and Company. 1955.

---

[32] Walker played his only season of American Association baseball in 1884. One of his teammates was Curt Welch.
[33] *New York Times,* September 12, 1887. The *Times* story is headlined "A Color Line In Baseball" and begins this way: "The Philadelphia Times will say to-morrow that for the first time in the history of baseball the color line has been drawn and that the "world's champions," the St. Louis Browns, are the men who have established the precedent that white players must not play with colored men." There is pushback on the idea that what motivated the Browns was solely racism and that the significance of the event is overstated. Some have pointed out that the Browns team was banged up and wanted an off day. www.thisgameofgames.com/home/the-color-line-has-been-drawn.
[34] Hetrick, *Chris Von der Ahe and the St. Louis Browns.*
[35] *St. Louis Post-Dispatch*, October 21, 1886. Charges of hippodroming were mentioned in the same article.
[36] Lansche, *Glory Fades Away.*
[37] Murphy, Justin. *Jocko Flynn*. SABR.org biography project. "I was all broken up by the sickness of McCormick and by the lameness of Flynn's arm," Chicago president Albert Spalding told the *Post-Dispatch*, October 23, 1886.
[38] "Quest umpired for Chicago, McQuade for St. Louis and Kelly officiated between the pitcher's box and second base as the referee," is how one newspaper described the setup. *The Times (Philadelphia),* October 23, 1886.
[39] *St. Louis Post-Dispatch*, October 23, 1886. Umpire McQuade won the coin toss and ruled Baldwin ineligible.
[40] Ibid.
[41] *Chicago Tribune,* October 24, 1886.
[42]seamheads.com/blog/2009/04/06/baseballs-first-world-series-goat-abner-dalrymple-and-game-six-of-the-1886-world-series/. The story quotes from an article in *The Sporting News* dated December 31, 1898. The publication had a different take in 1886. "Dalrymple made a very bad attempt to judge the ball, but it is doubtful if he could have reached it." *The Sporting News*, October 30, 1886. Also see *Sporting Life*, November 3, 1886.
[43] *St. Louis Globe-Democrat*, October 24, 1886.
[44] Chicago Tribune, October 24, 1886.
[45] *The Sporting News*, October 30, 1886.
[46] *St. Louis Post-Dispatch*, October 25, 1886. An account in the *St. Louis Globe-Democrat* put the payout at $580 per player.
[47] *St. Louis Globe-Democrat*, October 24, 1886.
[48] *The Daily Inter Ocean* (Chicago), October 24, 1886.
[49] *St. Louis Post-Dispatch*, November 15, 1896.
[50] Ibid, October 25, 1886. John Thorn wrote that the play was a result of a pitchout gone awry. Thorn, *Baseball in the Garden of Eden.*
[51] *The Sporting News*, October 30, 1886.

---

[52] The two teams played six games that fall. The Browns won five of them. *St. Louis Globe-Democrat*, November 1, 1886.
[53] www.thisgameofgames.com/home/the-1886-world-series-kellys-tribute. Boston Daily Globe, October 28, 1886.
[54] *St. Louis Post-Dispatch*, October 30, 1886.
[55] Ibid, July 17, 1889.
[56] *Boston Daily Globe*, August 15, 1889. Also see Hetrick, *Chris Von der Ahe and the St. Louis Browns*.
[57] *St. Louis Post-Dispatch*, September 28, 1889.
[58] Nemec, (editor). *Major League Baseball Profiles, 1871-1900 (Volume 2).*
[59] "I wish they [players and writers] knew a little more about Chris Von der Ahe," Latham said in 1944. The Browns owner "would be worth two columns a day," he told Grantland Rice. *Baseball Digest*, March 1944.
[60] *The Sporting News*, December 10, 1952.
[61] *St. Louis Post-Dispatch*, December 19, 1891.
[62] Abrams, Roger I. *The Dark Side of the Diamond: Gambling, Violence, Drugs And Alcoholism In The National Pastime*. Rounder Books. 2007. According to a 2006 NPR story, Galvin took something called the elixir of Brown-Sequard – "essentially testosterone drained from the gonads of an animal."
www.npr.org/templates/story/story.php?storyId=5314753
[63] *St. Louis Post-Dispatch*, April 19 and 23, 1893.
[64] *Sporting Life*, August 15, 1896.
[65] *St. Louis Post-Dispatch*, May 9, 1897.
[66] *Sporting Life*, January 2, 1897.
[67] Ibid, February 12, 1898.
[68] Ibid.
[69] Hetrick, *Chris Von der Ahe and the St. Louis Browns.*
[70] *St. Louis Post-Dispatch,* February 5, 1898.
[71] Ibid, April 17 and 18, 1898.
[72] *The Sporting News*, January 15, 1898.
[73] *Sporting Life*, December 25, 1897.
[74] *St. Louis Post-Dispatch*, February 3, 1908. In 1894, Von der Ahe had mortgaged his saloon for $44,000 and put the money in the Browns.
[75] Some have claimed Von der Ahe's statue stood outside Sportsman's Park when he owned the team. In the summer of 1889, the *Post-Dispatch* carried an article titled "A Day With The Dead" about the statues, tombs and monuments in Bellefontaine Cemetery. It featured this sentence: "Upon Laburnum avenue may be found the heroic statue of Chris Von der Ahe, the noted base ball man, which is posed in the center of a lot which, contrary to all rules of the proprieties, is a square instead of a green diamond." *St. Louis Post-Dispatch*, July 28, 1889.
[76] *St. Louis Post-Dispatch*, February 1, 1897.

The Rajah and the Lovely Shade

There are memories of the past every time a fan enters Busch Stadium III in St. Louis. A mural along the left-field wall features images of Hall of Fame players and managers as well as the names and retired jerseys of the men who have defined the Cardinals franchise. The tribute honors players Ozzie Smith, Red Schoendienst, Stan Musial, Enos Slaughter, Ken Boyer, Dizzy Dean, Lou Brock, Bruce Sutter, and Bob Gibson, managers Whitey Herzog and Tony La Russa, broadcaster Jack Buck, and owner Gussie Busch. It also features the name of Brooklyn Dodgers great Jackie Robinson, whose number 42 is now permanently retired across the game, and a man who owed his start in Major League Baseball to Branch Rickey, the visionary executive who spent the majority of his career in St. Louis.

In all, fifteen men are featured on the mural. It begins with the name and image of a Hall of Fame player with no number because there were no numbers on jerseys when he played for the Cardinals.[1] His name is Hornsby. Rogers Hornsby. One of the greatest players in the history of the game, he may be the least known of the group to the modern-day Cardinals fan. Making his major-league debut in 1915, he defined St. Louis Cardinals baseball in the 1920s.

For the entire decade of the twenties, his batting average was .382. In 1924, he hit .424, the highest single-season batting average of the modern era.[2] It will never be duplicated. Neither will his stretch from 1921 to 1925. Hornsby had 2,679 at-bats during this period. He delivered 1,078 hits. That translates to a five-year batting average of .402. He also averaged 29 home runs and 129 RBI in that same five-year window.

Hornsby hit better than .400 three times in four years, including the 1922 season when he won the first of two Triple Crowns. That season, he batted. 401 (47 points higher than second place), hit 42 home runs (16 more than his nearest rival), and drove in 152 runs (20 RBI better than anyone else in the league). He also led the league in hits (250), doubles (46), extra-base hits (102), total bases (450), runs scored (141), on-base percentage (.459), and slugging percentage (.722).

At the height of his career, he was the highest-paid player in his league. Only Babe Ruth could claim a bigger paycheck. The Ruth mention is apt because the two players were compared and contrasted frequently throughout the decade. Ruth was the best player in the American League. Hornsby was the best player in the National League. Baseball historian and sabermetrics pioneer Bill James once listed the single-best performances for every year in baseball history. For the decade of the 1920s, James listed Ruth seven times and Hornsby three times. No other player made the list.

One of Ruth's many nicknames was the "Sultan of Swat." Hornsby was called the "Rajah of Swat."[3] Over time, the nickname was shortened but stuck to Hornsby throughout his career. The Rajah and the Babe both loved to play the ponies, lost money frequently at the horse track, and would have to borrow money from teammates or club officials. Ruth once had to borrow money to pay his income taxes. Hornsby would borrow money to continue betting.

Both men were married multiple times (two marriages for Ruth, three for Hornsby), had extra-marital affairs and had relationships with women who suffered from depression and died under unusual circumstances. Ruth's first wife died in a house fire long after the couple separated. In between his second and third wives, Hornsby lived with a woman who died by jumping out a third-story window. "In case of accident, notify Rogers Hornsby," read the note left in her purse.[4]

Neither man was intellectually curious. Both expressed an aversion to reading and even avoided watching movies. Both Hornsby and Ruth claimed a flickering screen hurt their eyesight. They were contemporaries. Ruth was born one year earlier and made it to the big leagues a season before Hornsby. The Babe took his last at-bat in 1935. Hornsby last appeared in a game in 1937.

Despite the similarities, the differences were even more profound. On the diamond, the right-handed hitting Hornsby smacked line drives and played the infield. The left-handed-hitting Ruth launched towering home runs and roamed the outfield. Ruth struck out more frequently but also walked more often. From 1917 through 1928, Hornsby never struck out more than fifty times in a season. From 1918 through 1930, Ruth never fanned less than fifty-eight times a year. In 1923, Ruth struck out ninety-three times while also leading the league in walks with 170. In thirteen different seasons, Ruth's walk totals exceeded the century mark. Hornsby only accomplished the feat once, in 1928.

Away from the game, when he wasn't at the horse track, Hornsby would sit in hotel lobbies and watch people pass by. Ruth would venture down to the hotel lobby on the way out the door for a drink or a date and quietly sneak back through it when he stayed out long past the team curfew. Hornsby didn't drink. "I have never touched beer in my life." He didn't smoke. "Lady nicotine and I never mix." Ruth was always shoving something in his mouth, be it food, liquor, or a cigar.

Stark contrasts can be found in their personalities and how they're remembered today. An icon of the game and the subject of multiple movies and documentaries, Ruth is still revered while Hornsby is a footnote to history, an answer to a trivia question. He has the second-highest batting average of all-time, only behind Ty Cobb. Do modern baseball fans really know much more about him? Part of why they do not has to do with the era in which he competed, long before television broadcasts and instant Internet analysis. Hornsby's best years even came before daily radio broadcasts. So did Ruth's, but the Babe's career blossomed under the spotlight of year-round newspaper coverage provided by a frequently worshipful press in America's largest city. In the prime of his career, Hornsby competed in a far smaller Midwestern market. Hornsby only played in two World Series. Ruth appeared in three for the Boston Red Sox and competed in seven for the Yankees. It's also hard for a slashing line-drive hitter to stoke the imagination of fans the way a revolutionary home-run hitter can.

Ruth was fun and frivolous and full of life. Hornsby was serious and sober, and focused on hitting a baseball or winning a bet. Ruth was a partier and a prankster. Hornsby was, in the words of pitcher Les Tietje, "a real P-R-I-C-K."

The Rajah was blunt and stubborn. He offered his unfiltered opinion to anyone, including his many bosses over the years. "Why couldn't I talk back to important baseball people?" he once asked while also conceding, "I call a spade a spade and sometimes I think this got me in more trouble than I would have gotten in if I had been a drinker."[5]

In his autobiography, Hornsby tells the story of being in spring training in California one year when he spotted "two carloads of those little midgets driving up and running out on the field where we were trying to get in shape to play baseball." Hornsby ran all of them off except for one who refused to budge. "So I picked him up by the seat of his pants and collar and threw him over the railing." Problem solved. "We didn't have any more midgets around after that."[6] Hornsby's book was appropriately titled *My War with Baseball.*

Long-time sportswriter Fred Lieb claimed that Hornsby told him he was a member of the KKK.[7] "Hornsby didn't like Catholics and Jews," said Gene Karst, who worked as a sportswriter in St. Louis before becoming the first publicist in baseball when he joined the Cardinals. "He was really prejudiced against blacks and Jews, Catholics and everyone else."[8]

Hornsby could sometimes be barely tolerant of those who appreciated him and wanted to like him. In 1950, Hornsby managed the Beaumont Roughnecks to a first-place finish in the Texas League. On "Rogers Hornsby Day," a crowd of more than 6,000 fans looked on as the mayor presented him with a Stetson hat and the keys to a new Cadillac sedan. Hornsby took the hat and keys and shot the car a glance. "It's nice," he said. "Now get it outta here so we can start the game."[9]

He loved the game of baseball. "Any physically able American boy who doesn't play baseball is *not,* in my opinion, an American." He hated the game of football. "That's a goddamn lousy sport," he told a group of sportswriters. In St. Louis, he clashed with his manager. "That Ohio Wesleyan bastard," he once called Branch Rickey. He made it clear he had no use for "front-office bossing," once demanding Cardinals owner Sam Breadon "get the hell out of my clubhouse!"

That's the essence of Rogers Hornsby. A Hall-of-Fame baseball player. A major-league prick.

*****

He was born in Winters, Texas in April of 1896, the youngest of five children. According to Hornsby biographer Charles C. Alexander, the Hornsby family can trace its American roots to the pre-Revolutionary war era. By the 1830s, Rogers' ancestors were living in what is now Travis County, Texas, the first Anglo family to do so. Hornsby's Bend is just outside Austin, the Texas state capital. Rogers was his mother's maiden name.

His father, Ed, died when Rogers was just two years old. He "fell ill and sank rapidly," according to one account. The cause of death was apparently never recorded.[10] Years later, the family would tell the story of how on his last trip to town before he passed away, Ed Hornsby bought a bat and ball for his youngest son. His mother, Mary Rogers Hornsby, moved the family to Forth Worth in the winter of 1902-03. Biographer Alexander called it "the transforming event in the life of six-year-old Rogers Hornsby."

Young Rogers had a devotion to his mother, who made his first baseball uniform, and a love for the game. "It was nothing for us to play three games on a Saturday. We began early and finished late," he remembered.[11] His brother, Everett, spent time in the minor leagues as a pitcher and later briefly scouted for the Browns. By the time he was 15, Rogers was playing with adults in the Fort Worth city league. In 1914, he was a minor-league player in the Class D Texas-Oklahoma league, first for Hugo, Oklahoma, then Denison, Texas, after the Sooner State team folded. In 1915, he returned to Denison. The Railroaders paid him $90 a month. Fans called him "Sugar" due to his fondness for ice cream and candy.[12]

The St. Louis Cardinals spent their spring training of 1915 in Texas. Charley Reese, a railroad conductor, recommended the team look at Hornsby. "A Texas friend touted Hornsby heavily, wrote me repeatedly about the kid," manager Miller Huggins later recalled.[13] The Cardinals had a split-squad team play a three-game series against the Railroaders. "It was my big break," Hornsby later said. Cardinals scout Bob Connery was in Denison for the series and liked what he saw. "The more I looked at the kid, the better I liked him," Connery remembered. "He was green and awkward but possessed a great pair of hands. He fielded bad hoppers neatly and got the ball away quickly."[14]

Playing shortstop for the Railroaders that year, Hornsby hit .277 and committed 58 errors. Even though he had never played above Class D minor league baseball, the Cardinals purchased Hornsby's contract late in the season for $500.[15] With the entry of the Federal League as a competitor to the National and American Leagues in 1914, St. Louis now had three professional teams in town, the Cardinals, Browns, and the Terriers, also known as the "SlouFeds." Dozens of players jumped to the new league.[16]

The competition sparked an intense search for talent. The Cardinals, a resource-deprived organization, had to get creative in their search for young players. Searching for talent in the upper minor leagues was a waste of time, manager Huggins told Connery late in the 1914 season. "Even if you like a certain player," the manager told the scout, "we can't afford the price tag."[17] Hornsby was young, raw, and the price was right. It may have been the best $500 the organization ever spent. Nineteen-year-old Rogers Hornsby packed his bags and headed out. It marked the first time in his life he had ever been north of Tulsa, Oklahoma.

In forty-six September at-bats for the Cardinals, Hornsby recorded 14 hits, all but two of them were singles. His .246 average showed he wasn't completely overwhelmed by major league pitching, but his game needed work. He stood nearly six feet tall and weighed just 135 pounds. "Kid, you're a little light but you got the makings," manager Huggins told the rookie. "I think I'll farm you out next year."

Huggins and Hornsby had very different definitions for "farm." Huggins meant the inexperienced and thin young infielder would likely be spending the next season in the minor leagues. Hornsby took him literally. "I thought he meant a real farm and go to work," Hornsby later wrote in his autobiography. He spent the winter at his uncle's farm in Lockhart, Texas. He ate steak and chicken and drank "all the milk I could." He reported to spring training in 1916 about 30 pounds heavier. "He has grown from a gangling boy into a well-developed specimen," noted one observer.

Observers also noticed a change in his batting stance. When he had first arrived in the big leagues, the Cardinals tried to get Hornsby to bend over and choke up on the bat. A heavier and stronger Hornsby now returned to his old minor-league stance – more upright, holding the bat near the knob, and standing deep in the batter's box. "I never saw a batter stand farther away from the plate," Ted Williams once said.[18] The transformation was not just physical. Hornsby had more confidence. "I had the power," he said. The player called "Sugar" in Texas now had a new nickname. "Hornsby is called 'Pep' by his teammates because he is always full of life and never shows signs of fatigue on the ball field," explained Harry Pierce in the *St. Louis Star*.[19] (Hornsby's brother Everett had also been called Pep.)

At the age of twenty, in his first full season with the Cardinals, Hornsby hit .313, fourth-best in the league. He hit six home runs, had 65 RBI, and stole 17 bases. He started the season batting seventh and playing shortstop. By the end of the year, he was batting cleanup and playing third base. The Cardinals had a budding star on their hands. They desperately needed one. The club finished the 1916 season 60-83, a seventh-place finish in an eight-team league. But with Hornsby on the ascent and the Federal League shut down (it folded after the 1915 season) there were reasons for optimism. It would soon fade.

Hornsby played the 1916 season for owner Helene Hathaway Robison Britton. She had inherited the team in 1911 when her uncle, Stanley Robison, passed away. She owned the club for six seasons, but in November of 1916, she filed for divorce from her husband. She sold the Cardinals in February of 1917. The next few years would be some of the darkest in franchise history. That's no small statement for a club that had finished last or second-to-last twelve times in the previous twenty-two seasons.

*****

Brothers Frank and Stanley Robison bought the St. Louis franchise in 1899 for $40,000. They quickly went about eliminating the vestiges of Chris von der Ahe's disastrous last few seasons as owner of the Browns. The team's change in uniform colors from brown to red inspired another move. After one season of being called the "Perfectos," the franchise got a new name in 1900. "What a lovely shade of Cardinal!" was the phrase a sportswriter supposedly overheard. The National League franchise in St. Louis has been known as the Cardinals ever since.

The 1900 St. Louis Cardinals featured five future Hall-of-Famers. Two of them, shortstop Bobby Wallace and outfielder Jesse Burkett defected to the Browns in 1902. Another two are honored in Cooperstown, not because of their playing talent, but rather their managing abilities. When the National League condensed from 12 teams to eight after the 1899 season, the Baltimore franchise was one of the casualties. Both Wilbert Robinson and John McGraw became St. Louis Cardinals. Robinson went on to a successful career managing in Brooklyn. During his reign, the Dodgers were known as the Robins. The name came from their manager. Robinson spent 18 years in Brooklyn, winning two National League pennants.

John McGraw hated his time in St. Louis. The weather left a lasting impression. "A St. Louis ball club, because of the city's summer climate wearing down the players, must be twenty-five per cent stronger than any other club to win."[20] He reportedly tried to get thrown out of games so he could spend more time at the nearby racetrack. As a player, he had a reputation as an umpire-baiter. Before he was National League president, John Heydler worked as an umpire in the 1890s. "I've seen umpires bathe their feet by the hour after McGraw and others spiked them through their shoes. The worst of it was they got away with much of their browbeating and hooliganism."[21] As a manager, McGraw had an admirer in Rogers Hornsby, who called him "probably the smartest cheater of all time."

McGraw left St. Louis to manage the new Baltimore team in the American League. He didn't stay long. New York Giants owner Andrew Freedman convinced him to return to his National League roots. McGraw's Giants won ten pennants, including four straight from 1921 to 1924, becoming the first team to accomplish that feat since the St. Louis Browns of the 1880s. He won his first pennant with the Giants in 1904. There was no World Series that year. McGraw refused to play American League champion Boston. His departure from Baltimore in the middle of the 1902 season sparked a long-lasting feud with AL president Ban Johnson.

McGraw's teams perfected "small-ball" – employing bunts, using the hit-and-run, and aggressively running the bases. His 1911 squad set the modern-day record with 347 stolen bases. The only National League team to approach that total in the last hundred years is Whitey Herzog's 1985 Cardinals with 314.[22] McGraw's style of play dominated baseball until Babe Ruth arrived in New York in 1920. The manager's decisions over the years would have big impacts on both the Yankees and the Cardinals.

The fifth Hall of Fame player from the 1900 St. Louis team was Denton True "Cy" Young. The man whose name is synonymous with pitching excellence and an annual award in MLB came to St. Louis from Cleveland with the new owners. Of his 511 career wins, 45 of them came for the Cardinals. When the American League launched in 1901, Young took the opportunity to bolt for Boston. Despite being thirty-four years old when he made his AL debut, Young added 225 more wins to his career totals after he left St. Louis.

With none of those five players around in 1903, the Cardinals finished in last place, fifty-one games below .500. They proceeded to compound their woes with an unforced error. Of the club's 43 wins that year, nine of them were delivered by a rookie righthander. Mordecai Peter Centennial Brown grew up on an Indiana farm. His second middle-name comes from the year he was born, 1876, the one-hundredth anniversary of the country's founding. During his childhood, he lost part of his right index finger in a farm machinery accident. He later broke two other fingers on the same hand. They never healed properly. With a permanently bent middle finger and a stump for an index-finger, he became known as "Three Finger" Brown. The deformed hand proved to be an advantage. "That old paw served me pretty well in its time. It gave me a firmer grip on the ball, so I could spin it over the hump. It gave me a greater dip."[23]

His nine wins in his rookie season tied for the club lead, and his 2.60 ERA was the best on the team. In December, the Cardinals traded him. St. Louis sent him to the Chicago Cubs for pitcher Jack Taylor. While Taylor pitched well for the Cardinals, winning 43 games in two-and-a-half seasons in St. Louis, Brown was spectacular for the Cubs. In nine years in Chicago, Brown won 186 games. In 1906, he led the Cubs to their first pennant since 1886, going 26-6 and leading the league with a 1.04 ERA.

For the first and only time in franchise history, the Cubs won back-to-back World Series titles in 1907 and 1908. Brown won 49 games for Chicago over those two seasons and recorded three more victories in World Series play. The Cubs became the National League's first great team of the twentieth century, winning two world championships and four pennants in the five years from 1906 to 1910. During that same five-year stretch, the Cardinals proceeded to win 270 games and lose 492, a winning percentage of .354. While there would be later lopsided trades that greatly benefitted St. Louis, the first significant deal of the century involving the Cardinals and the Cubs helped turn Chicago into something they've never been called since – a dynasty.

In losing two future Hall of Fame pitchers in such a short time, Cardinal fans can only ponder the possibilities and speculate with "what-if" scenarios. But here's one statistic that provides perspective. In 1908, former St. Louis pitchers Three Finger Brown and Cy Young combined to win 50 games. In that same season, the entire Cardinals' pitching staff won 49.

*****

On Monday, July 10, 1911, the Cardinals lost a game in Philadelphia to the Phillies and their rookie pitcher Grover Cleveland Alexander. Scheduled to be in Boston for a doubleheader on Tuesday, the Cardinals left the stadium for the train station. They departed Philadelphia that night at 7:24 p.m. Originating in Washington D.C., the overnight train trip to Boston was scheduled to last thirteen-and-a-half hours.

One of the reasons the trip lasted so long involved the logistics of train travel through New York City during this era. At Jersey City, New Jersey, the railroad cars were taken to the docks, loaded on steam barges, and chugged across New York Harbor. At the Harlem Yards, the cars were then arranged for the trip north. [24]

Departing Philadelphia, the Cardinals' Pullman cars were directly behind the engine. St. Louis player-manager Roger Bresnahan and members of his team supposedly complained about the location to the train's conductors. How could the team get any sleep directly behind the roar and the racket of a steam locomotive with its constant whistling?

"The protest of Mr. Bresnahan and the players was made between Washington and Jersey City," said brakeman Daniel Kissner. "And when the train reached Harlem Yards it was made up anew."[25]

The Pullman sleeper cars for the St. Louis team were now located at the rear of the train. The Cardinals would later vigorously deny they had anything to do with the order of the railroad cars. In their defense, there is evidence the positioning was random. "The different cars were switched backward and forward a number of times before the train was ready to leave the yards," Kissner told *The New York Times.*[26]

Reassembled and ready to go, the "Federal Express" departed New York. Its crew included a new engineer. Arthur Curtis primarily worked as an engineer on freight trains, not passenger trains filled to capacity. Running almost an hour late, the locomotive had the ability to make up time. The "ten-wheeler" could reach 100 mph.

Trouble came in Bridgeport, Connecticut at 3:32 a.m. The train was supposed to switch tracks to make its next stop. The speed limit for the crossover was 15 mph. The train flew off the rails at an estimated 60 mph. The locomotive, a day coach, two baggage cars, and three sleeper cars all crash-landed at the bottom of a twenty-foot embankment. The coupling broke between the sixth and seventh cars. The last three sleeper cars were upright. The last two of them, carrying members of the St. Louis Cardinals, were still on the rails.

From his sleeper car, Bresnahan looked out a window. "Boys, we are needed up front," he shouted to his players. The manager and his team sprang to action. Dazed and confused, some in bare feet and pajamas, they quickly made their way to the bottom of the embankment. It was the middle of the night. Sparked by the crash, a fire in one of the baggage cars provided the only light.

"We got axes from our cars and the next one," outfielder Steve Evans told reporters in Boston later that day, "and started clearing away the wreckage so we could get at the bodies of the dead and the dying."[27]

Their quick action saved lives. Bresnahan and catcher Ivey Wingo pulled a woman out of the window of one of the capsized cars. Another player found two infants, alive but crying. "He picked them up," said Evans, "and started in search of their mothers. He didn't find them." Other infants were not as fortunate. "Two babies were found," noted the *Post-Dispatch* in its story later that day, "one with its head severed and the other impaled on a splinter."[28]

Engineer Curtis was among the dead. Why he approached the crossover that morning at such a high rate of speed will never be known. The throttle was later discovered wide open. In all, the train crash killed fourteen people and seriously injured dozens more. It could have been much worse. Because it happened in the middle of the night, most of the passengers were in their sleeping berths. "The very fact that they were not in the aisles playing around aimlessly explains why the loss of life is not numbered by scores instead of by tens," pointed out the *Post-Dispatch.*[29]

The survivors included every member of the St. Louis Cardinals. Spared by their move to the back of the train, the team acted as first responders until medical help could arrive. The players praised their manager. "If ever a man lived who possessed a cooler head, I have not heard of him," infielder Lee Magee said of Bresnahan. The press praised the team. "The ballplayers were worth a thousand ordinary helpers in an affair of this sort," reported the *Philadelphia Inquirer*. "When the firemen and police and the first squad of physicians arrived, they found the ballplayers working like Trojans and many lives were undoubtedly saved by them."[30]

The affair also took its toll. "The screams of the injured were bloodcurdling," Bresnahan remembered. His team took another train to Boston that morning where the scheduled doubleheader was postponed until the following day. "Crowd Out to See the Heroes of the Wreck," read a headline from the July 12 *Boston Globe*. The Cardinals did win six of their next eight games but struggled the rest of the way. The team won only 27 of its final 67 games, finishing the season at 75-74, 22 games behind McGraw's New York Giants. "Some of the players will never forget that accident," the *Post-Dispatch* noted in October. "It preyed on their minds for weeks afterwards and affected their playing."[31]

Among those spared that morning in Bridgeport, Connecticut was St. Louis second baseman Miller Huggins. The future manager of both the Cardinals and Yankees, Huggins had graduated from law school at the University of Cincinnati before focusing on pro baseball. He counted William Howard Taft as one of his professors. In 1911, Taft was President of the United States. The President frequently took that same Federal Express train, attaching his private car for trips to his alma mater, Yale, or for spending time at his summer home in Massachusetts. After the Bridgeport train wreck, the White House announced changes. Anytime President Taft was aboard the Federal Express, a "pilot engine" would precede it and test the track.[32]

*****

In the spring of 1911, Chicago businessman Charles Weeghman wanted to buy the St. Louis Cardinals. As the owner of a string of lunchrooms, movie theaters and a pool hall, Weeghman had the money. One of his lunch counters at the corner of Madison and Dearborn reportedly served more than thirty-thousand people a day. At his peak, "Lucky Charlie" had an estimated net worth of at least $8 million.[33]

"Yes, I am after the St. Louis National League team," admitted Weeghman in late March.[34] He was on his way to Cleveland to meet with the new owners of the club. For the second time in three years, a death in the Robison family meant changes for the Cardinals franchise. Stanley Robison passed away on March 24, 1911. He had assumed sole control of the Cardinals after his brother Frank had died just a few years earlier. In his will, Stanley left seventy-five percent of the team to his niece, Helene Britton, and the other twenty-five percent to Helene's mother, Sarah, Frank's widow.

Stanley, who never married, was especially close to his niece. "I was more of a sister than a niece to him," Britton once said. The mother of two, Helene and her husband Schuyler made their home in Cleveland, where the family fortune was launched. Helene's father and maternal grandfather started a streetcar business in 1877. Hathaway and Robison, Street Railway Contractors and Builders, did business throughout the United States and Canada. The Olive Street streetcar line in St. Louis was built by Helene's grandfather.[35]

Helene's mother, Sarah, traced her family to the *Mayflower*. The Robisons appeared in a listing of the Cleveland Blue Book, a social register. Helene attended a private all-girls school.[36] With the death of her uncle, she now found herself in a very public spotlight. A female owner of a major league team? The idea was simply inconceivable to the men who ran baseball.

"If Robison's heirs are his female relatives, it is likely that they, as well as members of the National League, will desire that the club be sold," said Cincinnati Reds owner and National Commission chairman Garry Herrmann. The story making the rounds was that the Cardinals could be purchased for $350,000. Charles Weeghman was on his way to Cleveland to see if a deal could be struck.

But Weeghman never got the chance to meet with Britton. She put him off in Cleveland. He later traveled to St. Louis to meet with her. Over two days, he met with different Britton representatives, but he never got the chance to make his pitch to Helene. On April 5, just six days before the Bridgeport train wreck, Schuyler Britton made it official. His wife was keeping the team. "The Cardinal ball club is not for sale," he announced at the Hotel Jefferson with his wife standing behind him. "Mrs. Britton has decided to retain the ball club."[37]

With that decision, history was made. The St. Louis Cardinals became the first major professional sports team with a female owner. Britton quickly demonstrated she was no figurehead. One of her early decisions was to ban a liquor bar at the Cardinals home park, Robison Field. Alcohol-fueled rowdiness was common at ballparks in the early twentieth century. She instituted Ladies' Day promotions and sought to widen the appeal of the game to a female audience. The *St. Louis Star* assured its readers that Britton and her mother "know a base hit from a foul ball."[38]

Her first year of ownership ended as one of her more successful seasons. Despite the fade after the Connecticut train crash, the Cardinals finished above .500 for the first time in a decade. Nearly 450,000 fans came to Robison Field that season. The team made a profit of $120,000.[39] Bresnahan was signed to a new five-year contract.

Sustained success proved elusive. The 1912 Cardinals finished 27 games below .500. Attendance plunged by 200,000. In the days before media and licensing rights, teams relied almost exclusively on gate attendance and concession stands for revenue. With such roller-coaster economics common throughout Britton's ownership reign, rumors frequently spread that the team was for sale. Millionaire oilman Harry Sinclair was among those supposedly interested. Bresnahan made an offer of a half-million dollars to buy the club. Even Harry Frazee, the man made famous by trading Babe Ruth to the New York Yankees, enquired at one point. Frazee, who owned the Boston Red Sox from 1916 to 1923, grew up in Peoria, Illinois.[40]

Other suitors linked to the Cardinals included various owners of the Browns. Phil Ball, Robert Hedges and Otto Stifel all had interest or were rumored to have made offers at one time or another. When the Federal League folded after the 1915 season, the owners of the Baltimore franchise supposedly wanted to move the Cardinals east.

Charles Weeghman found his future in the Federal League. Rebuffed by Britton and the Cardinals, Weeghman returned to Chicago and became one of the founders of the fledgling league. He built a park for his team on the north side of town. On grounds that once housed a seminary, Weeghman Park opened on April 23, 1914. When the league shut down, Weeghman and a group of investors bought the Cubs and moved the team to the new ballpark. Chicago's entry in the National League has played its home games there ever since. Fans know it today as Wrigley Field.

*****

If 1911 marked the apex of Bresnahan's career in St. Louis, the 1912 season served as its low point. One year after leading his club to a winning season for the first time since 1901 and being treated as a hero for his actions at Bridgeport, Bresnahan clashed with ownership and was accused in a game-fixing scandal. The season was his last in a Cardinals uniform.

Bresnahan came to St. Louis from the New York Giants, where he spent the most productive years of his career. One of the few men in baseball history to play all nine positions at the big-league level, Bresnahan is best known as a catcher, where he is credited with pioneering the use of shin guards. He also experimented with an early version of a batting helmet. The son of Irish parents, his nickname was "The Duke of Tralee."

Like his manager, John McGraw, Bresnahan was known as a tough competitor with a quick temper and foul mouth. "Highly strung and almost abnormally emotional," was the description provided by one reporter.[41] He worked as a hotel detective in his hometown of Toledo, Ohio in the offseason.

Originally an outfielder for the Giants, Bresnahan shifted to catching full-time. In 1905, the Giants won the World Series against the Philadelphia Athletics behind Christy Mathewson's three shutouts. Bresnahan caught all 27 scoreless innings.

Knowing his catcher wanted to manage, McGraw arranged a meeting with the Cardinals following the 1908 season. St. Louis had finished last that season, winning just 49 games while losing 105. Cardinals manager John McCloskey's three-year reign had come to an end. In December of that year, New York and St. Louis worked out a trade.

Bresnahan continued to catch while managing in St. Louis. In 1909, the big improvement wasn't on the field where the Cardinals won just five more games than the previous season, but at the box office. Bresnahan's name carried clout with Cardinal fans. Attendance jumped by nearly fifty percent. Performance and attendance climbed each of the next two seasons. The 1911 attendance of 447,768 wouldn't be topped for another eleven years.

Flush with cash and full of hope, new owner Britton signed Bresnahan to a new five-year contract which paid him $10,000 a year plus ten percent of the profits. One year later, Britton was saying the club couldn't afford such an expensive manager.[42]

In fact, relations between the owner and manager frayed over an issue nearly as old as the game itself. Who has the final say over player trades? Bresnahan wanted it. Britton refused to grant it to him. The rift became public in July of 1912. "Many Cards Trades Fail," read part of a headline in the *Post-Dispatch,* noting the only man authorized to make trades for the Cardinals was newly installed team president J.C. Jones, a man who was "seldom if ever seen at Robison Field."[43] Columnist John Wray sided with Bresnahan, pointing out the team was handicapping a man "paid a bank president's salary to be responsible."[44]

The simmering feud came to a boil over the final few months of the season. Wray noted "the present acrimony" between Britton and Bresnahan in August. In September, Britton had to deny rumors of friction between the two. "Will Bresnahan be retained as manager?" a reporter asked her. "Of course he will," Britton replied with a smile. "I've never considered anyone else for manager and I am at a loss to know why you should be in doubt about the security of Mr. Bresnahan's position."[45]

"Mr. Bresnahan's position" was also coming under fire outside St. Louis. Philadelphia Phillies President Horace Fogel charged that the 1912 National League race was fixed. He specifically criticized Bresnahan, accusing him of having the Cardinals "take it easy" against the eventual champion New York Giants and his old boss, John McGraw. The Cardinals did go 7-15 against the Giants that season. In a three-game series in August in St. Louis, the Cardinals dropped all three games, getting outscored 21-4. But St. Louis also went 7-15 that season against both the Cubs and Pirates while compiling a 60-93 record on the season. The Giants didn't need a lot of help to beat the sixth-place Cardinals. They won the pennant by ten games.

Fellow National League owners were furious with Fogel. They moved to ban him from the game. For different reasons, one National League owner was furious with Bresnahan. Britton fired him. "Success weighed heavily on him," *Post-Dispatch* columnist John Wray explained to his readers years later. Bresnahan "began to lose control...especially of his temper." The relationship between Bresnahan and Britton "was completely ruptured one day when Roger is said to have rudely left her presence, slamming the door with an air that distinctly intimated HE would be boss."[46]

The final showdown between Bresnahan and Britton is eerily similar to another famous fight between a different St. Louis Cardinals owner and the club's player-manager. As we'll see later, that relationship was also ruptured with one final slam of a door.

Bresnahan's departure is full of irony. In 1913, he signed with the Chicago Cubs where he played his final three seasons in the big leagues. In 1915, he also managed the Cubs. But when Weeghman bought the team after the Federal League ended, rosters had to be consolidated. Weeghman also had to pick a manager. The Chicago businessman had to choose between Cubs manager Bresnahan and Whales manager Joe Tinker (of Tinker to Evers to Chance fame). With Tinker's longstanding ties to Chicago, it was obvious who Weeghman preferred. Bresnahan was let go in Chicago by the man he could have worked for in St. Louis had Britton decided to sell in 1911.

When it sued Organized Baseball (as MLB was then called) on anti-trust grounds, the Federal League brought Bresnahan into the argument over the treatment of players. The Feds claimed Bresnahan, the man who never received trade approval from management, once traded a player for a bird dog. Bresnahan first saw the dog on a hunting trip to Tennessee with pitcher Booth Hopper. That spring, Bresnahan was prepared to ship Hopper to the minor leagues when the owner of the Springfield, Illinois club asked the Cardinals manager about pitching prospects. Bresnahan mentioned Hopper and a deal was made. But before departing St. Louis, Hopper needed money and asked Bresnahan if he would buy his dog. A second deal was then struck. Bresnahan had to file an affidavit in the case to clear up the confusion. "The statement that I traded Booth Hopper for a bird dog is an absolute falsehood," he explained.[47]

Bresnahan's legacy also includes a trade that wasn't made. In the summer of 1912, Bresnahan wanted to trade second baseman Miller Huggins to the Cincinnati Reds for outfielder Mike Mitchell (no relation to the author). "I thought I had the better of the swap," Bresnahan explained the day after he was fired by the Cardinals. "Hug is getting along in years and his arm is none too strong." Britton blocked the trade. "I will admit that I blocked deals started by Mr. Bresnahan because I did not think the Cardinals were getting an equal share in what was offered," she conceded the following month.[48]

Britton fired Bresnahan in October of 1912. The man whom Cardinal fans called the "Rabbit" – the player Bresnahan had attempted to trade – agreed to manage the team just a few weeks later. "We have reached an agreement with Mr. Huggins," announced the club's attorney on November 4.[49] Miller Huggins would manage in the big leagues for the rest of his life.

Even as the Cardinals were hiring Huggins, they were still battling Bresnahan over the remainder of his contract. It took a special meeting of National League owners to finally resolve the dispute. Bresnahan agreed to a $20,000 settlement. Seeking to repair the damage from a difficult year, the Cardinals made score cards free and had backs attached to bleacher seats for the 1913 season.

When Bresnahan left the Cubs, he became an owner. He bought a minor-league team in Cleveland and moved it to his hometown of Toledo. He owned the club for eight years. After selling out, he became a coach for McGraw's Giants. Retiring in 1928, he saw much of his life savings wiped out by the stock market crash of 1929 and the Great Depression that followed. In December of 1944, he died of a heart attack at the age of sixty-five. He was elected to the Baseball Hall of Fame the following year, becoming only the second catcher inducted at Cooperstown and the first who played in the twentieth century.[50]

Looking back now, more than a century later, it's hard to imagine Bresnahan as one of the most successful managers in the history of St. Louis baseball. Yet, at the time, that's exactly what his resume represented. Since the franchise had entered the National League in 1892, no manager had served longer or won more games than Bresnahan. One has to go back to the days of Charlie Comiskey and the American Association to find a manager who won more games or stayed on the job longer.

What Bresnahan's stint with the Cardinals demonstrated was a thirst in the city for quality National League baseball. The year before Bresnahan came to St. Louis, the Browns outdrew the Cardinals by more than 400,000 fans. In 1911, Bresnahan's only winning campaign, the Cardinals outdrew the Browns by 240,000. In the annual attendance battle between the two teams, the disparity in favor of the Cardinals wouldn't exceed that amount until 1926. By that time, it would be Hornsby in the role as player-manager of the team.

The man Hornsby replaced as manager had been fired from the job, a move that forever changed St. Louis baseball history. The end of the fired manager's reign marked the beginning of a Hall of Fame front-office career. But before he ever wore the uniform of the Cardinals, Branch Rickey was a St. Louis Brown.

---

[1] The vast majority of Hornsby's career with the Cardinals occurred before the team started wearing numbers on the back of uniforms in 1932. The Cardinals did display numbers on the left sleeve of their uniforms in 1923. Hornsby wore number 6. *St. Louis Star*, April 3, 1923. When he returned to the Cardinals briefly in 1933, Hornsby wore number 4. www.baseball-reference.com/teams/STL/1933-uniform-numbers.shtml

---

[2] Napoleon Lajoie hit .426 for the Philadelphia A's in 1901, but foul balls did not count as strikes in the first two years of the American League. The rule was changed in 1903. The 1901 season was the only .400 year of Lajoie's career. His .338 career batting average is 20 points below that of Hornsby.

[3] An Arabian craze hit the United States in 1921 when Rudolph Valentino starred in the silent film *The Sheik*, according to C. Paul III's SABR.org biography of Hornsby. The author of this book could find no reference to Hornsby as Rajah until 1922. It was not until 1926 that writers in St. Louis began to routinely refer to Hornsby as Rajah.

[4] Bernadette Harris threw herself from the third-floor window of a Chicago hotel on Labor Day, 1953. Hornsby was in St. Louis that day, as manager of the Cincinnati Reds.

[5] Hornsby, Rogers and Surface, Bill. *My War With Baseball*. Coward-McCann, Inc. 1962.

[6] Ibid.

[7] Lieb, Fred. *Baseball As I Have Known It*. University of Nebraska Press. 1977.

[8] Golenbock, Peter. *The Spirit of St. Louis: A History of the St. Louis Cardinals and Browns*. Avon Books, Inc. 2000.

[9] Alexander, Charles C. *Rogers Hornsby: A Biography*. Henry Holt and Company, Inc. 1995.

[10] Ibid. Associated Press, October 14, 1926.

[11] *St. Louis Globe-Democrat*, January 9, 1929.

[12] *St. Louis Star*, April 11, 1917. "At the Denison ball park there is a vendor's booth directly behind the home players' bench. Fans in the Texas city declare Hornsby would often walk up to the booth four or five times during a game to buy an ice cream cone, a bag of candy, or a bottle of pop."

[13] *St. Louis Globe-Democrat,* October 11, 1926.

[14] Alexander, *Rogers Hornsby*.

[15] Reports on what the Cardinals paid for Hornsby range from $500 to $750. "Hornsby was purchased by the Cardinals for $500 – not a dime more," wrote Sid Keener. "The owner of the Denison club, then operating in the Western Association, wanted $750 but Connery, who in those days had to drive a bargain down to the last penny, finally closed the deal at $500." *St. Louis Star*, June 11, 1931.

[16] The Cardinals lost outfielders Rebel Oakes and Steve Evans to the Federal League teams in 1914. Third baseman Lee Magee and catcher Paddy O'Connor followed suit one year later. Other players who wanted out of St. Louis jumped to the Federal League only to be enticed to return when the Cardinals granted them a trade to another organization.

[17] Alexander, *Rogers Hornsby*.

[18] Bradlee, Ben Jr. *The Kid: The Immortal Life of Ted Williams.* Little Brown and Company. 2013.

[19] *St. Louis Star*, March 20, 1916.

[20] Lieb, Frederick G. *The St. Louis Cardinals: The Story of a Great Baseball Club*. Reprinted by Southern Illinois University Press. 2001.

---

[21] Lieb, Frederick G. *The Baltimore Orioles: The History of a Colorful Team in Baltimore and St. Louis.* Southern Illinois University Press. 2005.
[22] Over in the American League, the 1976 Oakland A's stole 341 bases.
[23] Mordecai Brown virtual museum. MordecaiBrown.com.
[24] Amore, Don. "Heroes Off The Field: In 1911, St. Louis Cardinals Became A Team Of Rescuers." *Hartford Courant.* July 10, 2011.
[25] Ibid.
[26] *New York Times*, July 12, 1911.
[27] *Hartford Courant*, July 10, 2011.
[28] *St. Louis Post-Dispatch,* July 11, 1911.
[29] Ibid.
[30] *Philadelphia Inquirer*, July 12, 1911.
[31] *St. Louis Post-Dispatch*, October 7, 1911.
[32] Another famous accident involving the *Federal Express* took place in Washington D.C. in January of 1953 when the train overran its track and crashed into the Union Station concourse. Forty-three people were injured but no one was killed. That accident inspired the closing scene of the 1976 movie*, Silver Streak.*
[33] Oakley, Andy. "Boys In The Hoods." *Chicago Reader.* September 26, 1996. "I was worth between eight and ten million dollars," Weeghman is quoted in a 1936 article. See jackbales.com/from-weeghman-to-wrigley/.
[34] *St. Louis Post-Dispatch*, March 30, 1911.
[35] Thomas, Joan M. *Baseball's First Lady: Helene Hathaway Robison Britton and the St. Louis Cardinals.* Reedy Press. 2010.
[36] Ibid.
[37] Deveney, Sean. *Before Wrigley Became Wrigley: The Inside Story of The First Years Of The Cubs' Home Field.* Sports Publishing. 2014. Also see *Chicago Tribune*, April 6, 1911. A separate denial regarding the selling of the club came a month later. See *St. Louis Post-Dispatch*, May 3, 1911.
[38] Thomas, *Baseball's First Lady.*
[39] *St. Louis Post-Dispatch*, March 16, 1915.
[40] The Bresnahan and Frazee offers were likely related. "I made one bid for the club, that for Mr. Frazee, and that before Mrs. Britton had come to St. Louis to take charge of her property," Bresnahan explained. Most references to Bresnahan's offer omit the link to Frazee. See *Post-Dispatch*, May 21, 1912.
[41] Thomas, Joan M. *Roger Bresnahan*. SABR.org biography project.
[42] *New York Times*, October 31, 1912.
[43] *St. Louis Post-Dispatch*, July 19, 1912.
[44] Ibid.
[45] *St. Louis Post-Dispatch*, September 6, 1912.
[46] Ibid*,* April 6, 1919.

---

[47] "Bresnahan Did Not Trade Hopper For A Bird Dog," *St. Louis Post-Dispatch*, January 18, 1915.
[48] *Sporting Life,* November 16, 1912.
[49] *St. Louis Post-Dispatch*, November 4, 1912.
[50] Fleitz, David L. *Ghosts in the Gallery in Cooperstown: Sixteen Little-Known Members of the Hall of Fame.* McFarland & Company, Inc. 2004.

Branch Takes Root in St. Louis

Where to begin the story of a man who accomplished so much? He was a college football player and coach, a college baseball player and coach, a big-league player, manager, owner, a deal maker and a barrier breaker. Away from sports, he was an educator and an attorney, a devout Methodist and die-hard Prohibitionist. In the culture wars of the first half of the twentieth century, he took strong stands on the issues of his day. Sunday baseball? Refused to play or manage. Alcohol? Refused to drink. The integration of baseball? Refused to go along with the crowd.

He pioneered or popularized batting cages, sliding pits, tryout camps, and the idea of pitchers shagging fly balls in the outfield to stay in shape. As manager of the Cardinals, he once explored the idea of hiring a track coach to increase the speed of his players.[1] The iconic birds on the bat of the Cardinals uniform? His idea. The concept of a vertically integrated minor league system for professional baseball? Not only did he develop the template, he demonstrated proof of concept. What New York Giants manager John McGraw once called "the stupidest idea in baseball" led to nine pennants and six World Series titles in St. Louis in a twenty-one-year period.

"I don't think the greatest man in baseball was Cobb or Ruth or Wagner," said infielder Al Bridwell, who played for McGraw's Giants. "I think it was Branch Rickey. I think he's done more for baseball than any man who ever lived."[2] And what a life it was.

Rickey had an eye and an ear for talent. Sitting in the stands during a spring training workout one morning, he heard the crack of a bat and looked up to see the ball sail over the outfield wall and bounce off the bleachers. "Judas Priest, who hit that ball?" he demanded to know. "Pitcher Chick Hafey," came the reply from a coach. "You mean he *was* a pitcher," Rickey told him. "Tell him he's no longer one. He's an outfielder." Charles James "Chick" Hafey had 4,625 career at-bats in the big leagues and zero innings pitched. Rickey's call led to a Hall of Fame career. "He is considered," J. Roy Stockton informed the readers of the *Saturday Evening Post*, "the greatest judge of ballplayers in the world."

A frenetic workaholic, Rickey had a zest for life, a desire to push boundaries, a refusal to accept the status quo. He wanted his players to think the same way. As the baseball coach at Michigan, he once had his slow-footed catcher attempt a stolen base. The play wasn't close. "I was out by ten feet," remembered Russ Baer. Back in the dugout, his teammates applauded him, and his coach encouraged him. "Adventure, Russell, adventure," a smiling Rickey shouted.[3]

On the ballfield or in the classroom, Rickey had a preferred style. Attack. Just out of high school, he became a primary school teacher. He sized up one of his students as "criminally inclined, strong talking, vile talking, and a roughneck." Rickey challenged him. According to biographer Murray Polner, "Rickey beat him in a bloody fist fight." In another brawl with a different student, he took a beating. "The fellow nearly killed me a couple of times, but I was not whipped," Rickey recalled.[4]

The experience with "vile talking" rowdies may have influenced his baseball career. For the rest of his life, Rickey preferred players who mirrored the traits of students he found in his one-room school. "Although Rickey was a kind of snob who didn't drink, swear, or attend baseball games on Sundays, his teams... were always the hardest-drinking, loudest-swearing, most-raucous in the league," Bill James once wrote. It was this mix of the pious and the practical that drive his critics crazy. Baseball Commissioner Kenesaw Mountain Landis called him "a hypocritical Protestant bastard."[5]

Settling into a front-office position in St. Louis by the mid-1920s, a role that defined his career, Rickey was always on the prowl for the next great talent, always tinkering with his teams, always trading. He once dealt a player in between games of a doubleheader. Outfielder Cliff Heathcote had just driven in the game-winning run against the Cubs and was snoozing in the clubhouse when Rickey rousted him with the news. "Had to have a leadoff man. I've traded you for Max Flack," Rickey told him. "You have on the wrong uniform and you're in the wrong clubhouse." Flack lived in St. Louis near Sportsman's Park and had gone home in between games. He left as a Cub and returned as a Cardinal.[6]

Rickey had incentive to sell players. First in St. Louis and later in Brooklyn, Rickey's compensation included ten percent of every player contract sold. He was making a comfortable six-figure salary by the 1940s. Sportswriter Sid Keener once estimated the Cardinals made $2 million from player sales from 1922 to 1942.[7]

Despite the money he made from baseball, Rickey struggled with his finances for decades. "In my entire life I have never made any money of my own," he once confessed. "For the past fifty years, I have never been out of debt – not one minute."[8] He could also be brutally frugal with his players. "He was always going to the vault," remembered Cardinals outfielder Enos Slaughter, "for a nickel's change."

While he clashed with players over contracts, the teetotaling Rickey spent much of his career working for owners with markedly different attitudes toward alcohol. "So you're the goddamned Prohibitionist!" St. Louis Browns owner Phil Ball reportedly exclaimed upon meeting Rickey. Cardinals owner Sam Breadon liked to belt out a song or two after enjoying a few Irish whiskeys. When Dodgers owner Walter O'Malley built Chavez Ravine in Los Angeles, it opened with no water fountains other than in the dugouts. All the better for beer sales. Or so the rumor went.[9] Rickey worked for all three men and ultimately had a falling out with each. The mixture of beer and baseball played a role in every departure.

It's not the departures that defined Rickey, but rather the successes he had before he moved on. His role in integrating baseball alone makes him one of the sport's historic figures. But Rickey's teams also won championships. And nowhere were championships more elusive than in St. Louis in the early twentieth century. "St. Louis at this time had the most inept baseball players gathered in one place since the invention of the foul lines," was how writer Jimmy Breslin described it. The Browns were bad and "their crosstown rivals, the Cardinals, were even worse."[10] That all began to change in the 1920s. Branch Rickey is the biggest reason why.

*****

Wesley Branch Rickey was born in rural southcentral Ohio in December of 1881. He grew up on a farm just outside Lucasville, in Scioto County. On the family's one-hundred-acre property, his father Frank planted corn and sorghum and raised cows and hogs. He worked the land Monday through Saturday and traveled into town for church on Sunday. The Rickeys were Methodists.

Frank and Emily Rickey named their second son after John Wesley, a founder of the Methodist faith. Branch dropped his first name at a young age. He had cousins known as Wesley. His early life reads like something from an Abraham Lincoln biography. Days spent on the farm or in a one-room schoolhouse. Nights spent reading by kerosene light. A portrait of President Lincoln would later hang in Rickey's office.

Branch had a special bond with his mother, Emily, and a close relationship with his paternal grandfather, Ephraim Wanzer Rickey. Both influenced his baseball career. At a young age, Branch had pledged to his mother he wouldn't play baseball on Sundays. Later in life, he described the commitment as "a deeply personal thing. A man's promise, a promise to his mother. Not involving condemnation of baseball on Sunday, nor of others who might desire to play it or watch it on Sundays," Rickey told *Sports Illustrated*.[11]

Branch's grandfather Ephraim was one of the largest landholders in Scioto County. He also developed into a skilled horse trader. During the Civil War, he supplied the Union Army with horses. The secret to good horse-trading was to "know more about the other fellow's animals than your own," Ephraim told his young grandson. It was a lesson Branch Rickey would remember for the rest of his life.[12]

Branch followed in the footsteps of his older brother Orla and began playing baseball at a young age. He became a catcher. His reputation soon spread. After high school and two years of teaching, where he learned to use his fertile mind as well as his fists, Rickey enrolled at Ohio Wesleyan University.

Rickey played both football and baseball at Ohio Wesleyan. He scored the winning touchdown in a 10-6 victory over Ohio State. Sportswriters voted him the starting halfback on an all-Ohio team for 1901. He was the starting catcher on the baseball team the following spring. He continued playing baseball that summer, joining a semi-professional team in Portsmouth, Ohio that paid him $25 a week.[13] When he returned to campus that fall, a Columbus, Ohio newspaper had gotten wind of the arrangement and published a story that Rickey had violated his amateur status by accepting money.

The president of OWU, Dr. James Bashford, sent for Rickey. When he arrived, Bashford showed him a letter from the owner of the Portsmouth team. "Whoever said I paid Branch Rickey any money was a goddamned liar," the letter began. "I never paid him a cent." Rickey silently read the letter and handed it back. "It's not true," he told Bashford.[14] The college president came away from the meeting impressed with Rickey's honesty. Later, when the school needed a new baseball coach that spring, Bashford offered Rickey the position. His college playing career was over, but his coaching career was just getting started. Rickey was twenty-one years old.

Rickey's 1903 Ohio Wesleyan baseball team featured Charles "Tommy" Thomas, the only black player on the club. In fact, Thomas was thought to be one of the few black students on the Ohio Wesleyan campus. Rickey already knew Thomas. The two had been teammates on the football team. More than four decades before Jackie Robinson broke the color barrier in the big leagues, the new coach was about to get a look at how a black player would be treated by white opponents and fans.

In a game that spring at the University of Kentucky, Thomas heard chants of "get that nigger off the field!" Rickey ran over to the Kentucky bench. "We won't play without him!" he yelled to the opposing coach. They didn't. After an hour delay, the Kentucky team relented. The game continued without incident.[15]

Another incident that spring later became the subject of a frequently told Rickey story. Ohio Wesleyan had traveled to South Bend, Indiana to play Notre Dame. Checking into a hotel, the clerk wouldn't let Thomas register. Only whites were allowed to stay there. Rickey talked the hotel manager into allowing the player to stay in his room. It's what happened next that left such an impression on the young coach. Once inside the room, Thomas began rubbing his skin. "Black skin...black skin. If I could only make'em white," he said. "He kept rubbing and rubbing," remembered Rickey, "as though he could remove the blackness by sheer friction."[16]

Some have wondered over the years whether the story is more tale than true story. Various versions of it circulated widely after Jackie Robinson debuted with the Brooklyn Dodgers in 1947. One of the questions raised is this: Did the Thomas incident provide the spark that drove Rickey to integrate baseball?

"The Charlie Thomas story, though based in fact, is vintage Rickey," wrote Jules Tygiel, author of *The Great Experiment*. "The allegory is almost biblical, and the sermonlike quality of the tale invites skepticism."

The link to Robinson may be tenuous and the story perhaps somewhat exaggerated. But it's also largely true. The Ohio Wesleyan baseball team that season featured Rickey as a coach, Thomas as one of his players, and Notre Dame on the schedule. It also doesn't take a lot of imagination to picture a hotel clerk in 1903 denying admittance to a black guest. While the episode may or may not have been the impetus for the Robinson decision years later, Rickey should be credited with a commitment to racial equality decades before his peers. Raw racism was rampant in the early twentieth century, an era in which *The New Yorker* magazine published a cartoon with the caption, "Niggers all look alike to me."[17]

Thomas always appreciated what Rickey did for him. "From the very first day I entered OWU, Rickey took a special interest in me," he said years later. "During the three years I was at OWU, no man could have treated me better."[18]

Rickey and Thomas became lifelong friends. After college, Thomas became a dentist. He began his practice in St. Louis. Several years later, he moved to Albuquerque, New Mexico, where, by some accounts, he was one of the first black dentists in the state. While living in New Mexico, he returned to St. Louis to meet with his old college coach. Rickey met with him in his office. The grandstand at Sportsman's Park was still segregated. Thomas remembered Rickey telling him, "Tommy, some day we'll have that changed."[19]

*****

Rickey graduated in 1904 and left Ohio Wesleyan. Professional baseball came calling. He played that summer for the Dallas team in the Texas League. He met and became a friend of Charley Barrett, who was playing for Houston. Barrett, like Rickey, had an eye for talent and a real passion for the game of baseball. A St. Louis native, Barrett became a scout after his playing days were over. His relationship with Rickey would last for the rest of his life.

The big leagues were Rickey's next stop. The Cincinnati Reds purchased his contract in August. Although he saw action in an exhibition game, he never played in a major league game with the Reds. The Cincinnati manager wanted no part of a player who refused to play on Sundays. Taking a job that winter at Allegheny College in Pennsylvania, he taught English, Shakespeare, and freshman history, in addition to coaching the baseball and football teams.

The Chicago White Sox claimed Rickey in a Rule 5 draft of minor league players, but he never played for them either. The White Sox owner, former St. Louis first baseman Charlie Comiskey, the man who captained the team to four straight American Association pennants in the 1880s, made perhaps an even larger contribution to the city's baseball history with a decision to trade Rickey to the Browns for catcher Frank Roth.[20] Newspaper accounts identified the new St. Louis receiver as "Warren Rickey." [21] For the majority of the next sixty years, working for either the Browns or Cardinals, Rickey drew a paycheck in St. Louis.

He made his big-league debut on June 16, 1905 in Philadelphia. Facing A's lefthander Rube Waddell, a future Hall-of-Famer and first-class eccentric, Rickey struck out on three pitches. He went 0-3 that night and found out after the game his mother was ill back at home in Ohio. His mother recovered, but when Rickey returned, the Browns decided he would be better off playing every day in the minor leagues. He finished the season back in Dallas.

Rickey coached and taught again in the offseason before he joined the Browns for the 1906 campaign. He also married his hometown sweetheart, Jennie Moulton, in June. Her father owned the general store in Lucasville and was a state senator in Ohio. Branch and Jennie – known as Jane – "will make their home in St. Louis," the *Post-Dispatch* informed its readers.[22]

Local papers took turns touting the Browns new catcher. "Rickey weighs about 175 pounds and is the very model of what a ballplayer should be," enthused the *Post-Dispatch* on April 4, calling him "the ideal of an athlete," and "one of the most promising baseball players that has come into major league company in many years."[23] One day later, a caption above Rickey in the *Globe-Democrat* hailed him as "McAleer's Newest Star." While he had a solid campaign in 1906, the reality didn't match the rhetoric. He appeared in 65 games, batting .284. He admitted the St. Louis summer wore him down. "In all my life I have never had such a summer as this and let us hope I may never have another like it."[24] His refusal to play on Sundays, not for the last time, drew endless questions from the media. "I can't help it, it was bred in me," he said when asked about his weekend habits. "I won't play Sunday ball. I made them put it in my contract that I don't have to. Instead I go to church," said Rickey, who claimed membership in the St. Louis YMCA. [25]

Before the season ended, he clashed with his manager, Jimmy McAleer. Rickey, now back at Ohio Wesleyan in the offseason as its athletic director, wanted to leave the team by the middle of September and return to campus. McAleer insisted he stay until the end of the season. With Rickey already unavailable one of every seven days, the request to leave early may have been the last straw.[26] The Browns traded him that offseason to the New York Highlanders, the team known today as the Yankees.[27]

Rickey's thoughts had already turned to his post-baseball career. He promised his wife and her parents the 1907 season would be his last. He wanted to go to law school. He got his wish. 1907 was indeed his last season as a player in the big leagues. It ended in an inglorious fashion.

Rickey had a bad shoulder that season. He traveled to Hot Springs, Arkansas to see if mineral baths could provide relief. After two weeks in the spas and his shoulder no better, he returned to the Highlanders. On June 28, Rickey was behind the plate in a game against the Washington Senators. The Senators stole 13 consecutive bases against the sore-shouldered catcher. Rickey's days of wearing a chest protector and shin guards were over. He finished the season in New York playing some outfield and first base. In 137 at-bats, he hit just .182. Other than two plates appearances in the 1914 season, those were the final at-bats of his major league career.

Rickey eventually got to law school, but he took a few detours along the way. He completed some additional college courses, campaigned for fellow Ohioan William Howard Taft in the presidential election of 1908 and became active in the Anti-Saloon

League. Rickey, a lifelong Republican, strongly believed in the message of Prohibition forces. He roamed his home state one summer, delivering talks on the evils of alcohol at $10 a speech, plus expenses. He maintained these activities all the while still teaching, coaching, and running the athletic program at Ohio Wesleyan. As a Brooklyn fan later described him, "He is a man of many faucets, all running at once."

He also stayed in touch with St. Louis Browns owner Robert Hedges. If Rickey accomplished one thing in his big-league career, it was the impression he left on Hedges. Typical throughout his life, Rickey's intellect and vocabulary could be intimidating or off-putting to those less educated or uninterested in hearing his message. But starting with the president of Ohio Wesleyan, Rickey's style made powerful men want to give him responsibility. Rickey may have left St. Louis over disagreements with his manager. He eventually returned because of his relationship with its owner.

*****

When the American League debuted in 1901, it didn't include a team in St. Louis. Hedges bought the Milwaukee franchise and moved it south. The American League St. Louis Browns started play with the 1902 season. After the Baltimore franchise moved to New York in 1903, major league baseball didn't have a team relocate for half a century. The long era of stability in the sport featured two leagues with sixteen teams playing in ten cities. New York had three teams; the Giants, and the teams we know today as the Yankees and the Dodgers (Brooklyn became a borough of New York City in 1898). Cities with two teams included Boston, Chicago, Philadelphia and St. Louis. Of those four cities, St. Louis featured the smallest metropolitan population by a wide margin. Boston, Chicago and Philadelphia all had metro populations above one-million people. The St. Louis metro area in 1900 tallied a little more than 600,000 residents.[28] Rounding out the leagues were five teams in five cities: Cleveland, Detroit, and Washington in the American League: Cincinnati and Pittsburgh in the National League.

Browns owner Hedges was born just south of Kansas City in Hickman Mills, Missouri. He made his money in Ohio in the buggy manufacturing business, selling out at close to the top in 1900, just as the automobile began its ascendance. While there, he befriended a Cincinnati sportswriter by the name of Ban Johnson, the future president of the American League. It was Johnson who talked Hedges into buying the Milwaukee franchise and relocating it to St. Louis where it found a home in Sportsman's Park. The price tag was $35,000. [29]

Arriving in town in 1902, the St. Louis Browns did what all teams in upstart leagues do. They pillaged the rosters of other clubs. A formal arrangement between the American and National Leagues didn't come about until the following season. The peace agreement of 1903 ensured that each league would respect existing contracts. With no accord in place for the first two years of the American League, it was open season on National League talent. The hometown rival Cardinals proved to be an easy target. "Never before, and perhaps never since, did one team so deplete another team," noted baseball historian Steve Steinberg.[30]

Pitchers Jack Harper, Jack Powell and Willie Sudhoff, infielders Dick Padden and Bobby Wallace, and outfielders Jesse Burkett and Emmet Heidrick all played for the Cardinals in 1901. They all wore the uniform of the Browns in 1902. The trio of pitchers combined to win 49 games. The four position players combined to generate more than 200 RBI and score more than 300 runs. Both shortstop Wallace and outfielder Burkett would have Hall of Fame careers. Wallace played 14 more seasons for the Browns, becoming the first American League shortstop inducted in Cooperstown. At one point, he was the highest-paid player in the AL. Burkett hit .306 for the Browns in 1902 after a long career in the National League that featured three batting titles, including a .376 mark for the Cardinals the previous season.

The Cardinals, having abandoned Sportsman's Park after the 1892 season and the Browns name after the 1898 season, watched as their American League rivals took the city by storm. In their debut season in St. Louis, the Browns finished in second place in the American League with a record of 78-58, five games behind champion Philadelphia. Attendance of 272,000 was nearly double the previous year in Milwaukee and 45,000 more than the Cardinals. The Browns outdrew their National League counterparts for seven of their first eight seasons. "When I went to St. Louis," said infielder Jimmy Austin in *The Glory of Their Times*, "the Browns were *the* team in that town, you know." The 1908 Browns drew more than 600,000 fans, a high-water mark for attendance in the city that stood until 1922.[31]

It proved easier to beat the Cardinals at the box office than their fellow American League teams on the field. In their entire 52-year run in St. Louis, the Browns only finished as high as second three times. The Cardinals lost more than 100 games in back-to-back seasons of 1907 and 1908. The Browns did them one worse, breaking the century mark in losses for three straight seasons starting in 1910. Baseball in St. Louis was equally dismal in 1913. The Browns lost 96 games that year. The Cardinals lost 99.

Hedges did have some notable achievements. He remodeled and expanded Sportsman's Park. St. Louis had one of the first steel and concrete grandstands. A believer in Prohibition, he curbed alcohol sales and encouraged Ladies' Day promotions. "He realized the game must have a popular appeal," *The Sporting News* once noted. "Other club owners, realizing that such policies paid off in the long run, followed his example."[32] A baseball visionary, he instituted profit-sharing, took out life insurance policies on his players, and experimented with a massive circus-like tent to protect the field during rainstorms. It took three forty-foot wagons to assemble.[33] Hedges also had the idea of linking minor league teams to major league franchises even before he hired Rickey to run his front office. A *Post-Dispatch* article from 1907 carried the headline, "Hedges Will Buy Minor League Club," explaining the team could be "used as sort of a recruiting station for the Browns."[34]

But the owner *Sporting Life* once described as "the man with the perpetual smile" never had a more competitive team than the one he fielded his first year in town. Like other magnates, Hedges came to realize business success didn't necessarily translate into a winning baseball team. "Baseball is a curious business," he once said. "I have been interested in other ventures and always managed to make them a success. A man may work himself to death, yet his personal efforts will count for so little in baseball that he is forced to the end of his rope."[35]

Hedges even conceded the raid on the Cardinals was a mistake. The way to do it, he decided, was the model the American League New York franchise adopted – take National League talent from *other* cities.[36] It must have dawned on Hedges and the Robison brothers, owners of the Cardinals, that being the smallest population two-team market in baseball was always going to be an uphill battle. After the 1903 season, the two sides discussed consolidating franchises.[37] While those talks ultimately went nowhere, it signaled a future in St. Louis where only one team would survive.

The Browns developed a reputation, a stigma that forever clung to the franchise. "First in morals, first in sobriety, first in bed, first in the field, first in the front bench at church, and last in the American League," was how writer John Sheridan described the team in 1915.[38] With a nod to local manufacturers and breweries, fans eventually came to prefer a shorter motto. "First in shoes, first in booze, and last in the American League," went the slogan adopted in later years of the franchise.

One of those "last in the American League" teams is remembered today, not for their 107-loss season, but rather for their role in one of baseball's great scandals. It was, in the words of *The Fix Is In* author, Daniel E. Ginsburg, "one of the most sordid in baseball history."

*****

On the last day of the 1910 baseball season, Napoleon Lajoie prepared to play a doubleheader in St. Louis. The second baseman, better known as "Nap" or "Larry" Lajoie, had joined the American League Cleveland team in 1902. He became such a popular figure with fans that the nickname of the club during his era was the Naps. Only after he left did the franchise feature the name we recognize today, the Cleveland Indians.

Lajoie (lazh-uh-way) was one of the game's greatest hitters. His lifetime batting average of .338 included five batting titles and a 1901 season where he hit .426, the highest single-season batting average in American League history. With two games left in the 1910 season, Lajoie had a batting average of .376. He trailed the leader, Detroit Tigers outfielder Ty Cobb, by seven points. More than a batting title was on the line. The Chalmers Motor Company had announced before the season they would award a new car to the baseball player with the highest batting average.[39]

The Cobb-Lajoie competition provided the only intrigue on the final Sunday. The Browns would end the season 57 games behind the American League champion Philadelphia A's. Cleveland finished in fifth place, ten games below .500. Despite the losing records, more than 10,000 fans turned out to watch baseball on a sunny and cool early autumn day in St. Louis.[40] The Chalmers race had captured the attention of the country. The Browns, like their fans and much of the American League, had a rooting interest in the battle between Cobb and Lajoie. Adored and embraced by fans and players alike, Lajoie was both popular and respected. The surly Cobb had even his teammates rooting against him. Many fans had more than pride on the line. Gamblers took notice of the action and placed odds on the event. "There was a great deal of money wagered on the outcome," L. Jon Wertheim pointed out at *Sports Illustrated* years later, "Already there were abundant signs that baseball was becoming a serious business, with real money to be made, legitimately and illegitimately."[41]

Cobb didn't play his last few scheduled games against the Chicago White Sox. He ended the year with a .383 batting average. It would take a perfect day for Lajoie to surpass him. Thanks to the St. Louis Browns, that's exactly what he delivered.

Lajoie's day began with a stand-up triple after an outfielder lost the ball in the sun. He barely swung the bat again. With Browns rookie shortstop Red Corriden moved over to play a deep third base, Lajoie bunted seven times and hit one ground ball to the shortstop who proceeded to make a wild throw to first base. For the day, the official scorer credited him with eight hits and one sacrifice. The perfect eight-for-eight day pushed Lajoie's batting average to .384, one point ahead of Cobb. Lajoie appeared to have won the 1910 batting title. A congratulatory telegram arrived from the Detroit Tigers, signed by eight of Cobb's teammates.[42] The matter was far from settled.

The stunning performance on the last day of the season naturally raised eyebrows. "After today's disgrace," wrote the *Detroit Free Press*, "a hippodrome (game-fixing) ... should be investigated by the highest authorities."[43] When American League president Ban Johnson heard about what happened, he called for an investigation. He discovered that pitcher-coach Harry Howell, not in uniform that day, made repeated visits to the press box.[44] The official scorer reportedly received a note promising an expensive suit of clothes if Lajoie received the benefit of the doubt on close plays. He declined the offer. The Browns let Howell go at the end of the season. His major league career was over.

Browns shortstop Corriden, who had moved over to play third the final day of the season, was absolved in the scandal. It was common at the time for players to play out of position on the last day and while his positioning was unusually deep, he was only following the orders of his manager. Johnson focused on the man calling the shots.

Browns manager Jack "Peach Pie" O'Connor was a St. Louis native.[45] He had a "long history of sordid dealings." As a player in 1892, he was suspended for "habitual drunkenness, disorderly conduct and insubordination." After his career with the Browns, he managed in the Federal League, where he once broke the jaw of an umpire during a heated argument. Umpire Jack McNulty sued O'Connor, winning a judgment of $1,250.[46]

On the day in question, O'Connor ordered third baseman Corriden to play at the edge of the grass. "On the edge of the grass?" Corriden asked, in one accounting of the story. "On the edge of the grass, I said," repeated an angry O'Connor.[47] Questioned by a reporter after the game about his positioning, Corriden explained, "I wasn't going to get killed playing in on Lajoie." The same reporter raised the question of a possible investigation of the matter to O'Connor. "Investigation be damned," O'Connor said. "It doesn't make a bit of difference to me, because as far as I know, there is nothing to investigate."[48]

Johnson's probe into the matter formally cleared O'Connor or anyone else of wrongdoing. "Manager O'Connor attributed Lajoie's success in making infield hits to his shrewdness in switching from the driving system he usually employs to bunting," the AL president wrote in his decision, "thereby springing the unexpected on Corriden." Browns owner Hedges immediately moved to fire his manager.[49] O'Connor, in the middle of a contract, promptly sued the St. Louis team. He was later awarded $5,000.

The investigation and year-end review of the numbers did spark changes in the AL batting race. Cobb's batting average jumped to .385, one point better than Lajoie. The American League office, mistakenly or intentionally, but certainly suspiciously, double-counted Cobb's 2-3 performance in a game on September 24. Six days after the season ended, Cobb got credit for two extra hits, lifting his batting average by two points. Cobb, not Lajoie, officially won the AL batting title. "I will certify...that Cobb has a clear title to the leadership of the American League batsmen for 1910," read Johnson's statement, "and is therefore entitled to the Chalmers trophy." The Chalmers Automobile Company ultimately decided to give a car to both men, awarding each of them a roadster that retailed for $2,000.

Nearly seventy-one years later, *The Sporting News* published the results of an investigation that revealed the mistakenly awarded Cobb hits. Back at the league office in 1910, duplicate entries for the September 24 game had been crossed out on every Detroit player's sheet – except the one for Cobb. In 1981, Commissioner Bowie Kuhn, citing among other things, "a certain statute of limitations," refused to alter the records.[50] One of the eternal charms of the game of baseball is how certain statistics are burned into the brains of fans. One of those hallowed numbers – 4,191 – is the number of career hits we associate with Cobb, the American League's all-time leader. But the actual figure is 4,189.[51] We may have recalled that lower number all along had it not been for the actions of certain members of the St. Louis Browns at Sportsman's Park on Sunday afternoon, October 9, 1910.

*****

Rickey observed the end of the 1910 big-league season from Ann Arbor, Michigan. In true multi-tasking Rickey style, he was in the middle of completing a three-year law school program in two years while also coaching the Wolverines baseball team. Just as at Ohio Wesleyan, a previous baseball coach at Michigan had quit the job. And just like at OWU, administrators awarded the job to Rickey. The fact that he was so active was somewhat of a miracle. The previous year, he survived a major health scare.

In 1909, Rickey dropped thirty pounds and was coughing up blood. When he finally went to see a doctor, he was diagnosed with tuberculosis. At the time, the infectious disease then known as "consumption" had no known cure. In early twentieth-century America, ten percent of deaths could be blamed on it.[52]

The prescription was rest and preferably in a dry climate. Rickey spent time at a sanitarium in upstate New York. He needed to gain weight. On a doctor's order, he even drank beer. Combined with high-calorie meals – six glasses of milk every day along with six raw eggs and cream soups – Rickey started putting on pounds and gradually began to regain his health. Discharged in May of 1909, he continued sleeping outdoors as much as possible to strengthen his lungs.[53]

He started law school that fall. He added baseball coaching duties a year later. Athletic director Phil Bartelme (who later worked for Rickey in St. Louis) offered him the job under the condition the dean of the law school gave his consent. When the dean agreed, Rickey was back on the diamond doing what he loved, teaching young men the game of baseball. He focused on the fundamentals. "Rick drilled us for hours on cutoff plays, the squeeze – we beat Notre Dame in eighteen innings on a squeeze play," remembered one player.[54] His methods of instruction and his passion for the game caught the attention of others. Detroit Tigers players and coaches would make the trip to Ann Arbor to observe Rickey in action.[55]

Browns owner Robert Hedges was also among those keeping tabs. He arrived on the Michigan campus in the spring of 1912 with a job offer. Hedges had the idea to buy a minor league team in Kansas City and have Rickey run it. The coach of the Wolverines turned him down. The Browns owner then made him another offer. Hedges wanted someone to scout talent in the Pacific Coast League over the summer. Rickey accepted the challenge.

The reason Rickey rejected the first offer while accepting the second had to do with his other career. After graduating from law school in 1911, he began working as an attorney over the summer in Boise, Idaho. Rickey left in the fall to return to Michigan but promised his two partners, fellow Ohio Wesleyan alums, he would return in the summer of 1912. Boise offered proximity to Pacific Coast League talent, and the mountainous, dry air proved to be an ideal setting for someone recovering from tuberculosis.

Rickey's law career in Boise didn't last long. He had all of one client in the two summers he spent there. Acting as a public defender, Rickey met the man in his jail cell. The suspect, charged with multiple offenses, greeted his attorney by spitting at his feet. "I never knew a man could be guilty of so many crimes," Rickey later recalled.[56]

Once again, Hedges emerged with a path out of law and back into a full-time baseball career. Meeting in Salt Lake City in August of 1912, the Browns owner now offered Rickey a management position with his team. Hedges wanted someone to scout and evaluate talent, negotiate contracts and make trades. In November, the news broke that Rickey would become the team's secretary in the new year (the term "general manager" had yet to be coined). Rickey accepted the position with conditions (negotiations with him were never easy). He had an obligation at Michigan to coach the baseball team. He wanted to return for one final season and then report to St. Louis. Hedges agreed. Michigan paid him $1,500 to coach baseball and Hedges offered him $7,500 to run the front office. "Jane, $9,000," Rickey told his wife. "It's more than we ever dreamed."[57]

Rickey's last team at Michigan was his best. The 1913 Wolverines compiled a record of 22-4-1 and featured two players that would soon be playing for the Browns in St. Louis, first baseman George Sisler and shortstop Johnny "Doc" Lavan.[58] Sisler hit .445 that spring, showcasing the talents that later sparked a war for his services. With his final campaign in Ann Arbor concluded, Rickey headed to St. Louis. He arrived in town to find a team in turmoil.

*****

The first and only spring training George Stovall conducted for the St. Louis Browns came in 1913. As the club's first baseman, he had replaced shortstop Bobby Wallace as manager midway through the prior season after the Browns got off to a poor start on the way to a 53-101 record and a seventh-place finish. Only a fifty-win New York Highlanders (Yankees) effort saved the Browns from last place in 1912.

The Browns spent spring training 1913 in Waco, Texas. Greeting each player upon arrival was a list of rules from their manager. The rules laid out by Stovall made such an impression the *Post-Dispatch* referred to him in a headline as the "Iron-Handed Taskmaster of the Club."[59] One of the rules of the "iron-handed taskmaster" was no smoking before breakfast. While conceding he smoked and chewed tobacco himself, Stovall didn't like the idea of his players getting a nicotine fix before getting a bite to eat. "I imagine a drag on a cigarette at that early hour must have a very bad effect on a man's system," he said. He also placed a 50-cent limit on poker games and installed a midnight curfew for players when at home. On the road, he wanted players in bed by 11:30. Whenever they ventured down to the hotel lobby or café, Stovall demanded his players wear a white collar. That last rule was aimed at "bushers" who come up every year and "whose dress often unfits them as residents of first-class hotels."[60]

"Work hard and hustle" was his motto. While he made no promises of a "first-division" finish (top half of the standings), Stovall indicated he thought it was a possibility if the team followed his instructions. Despite a challenging spring in which games were marred by Texas sand storms and wind blowing so hard "it caused the men to blink every time they faced a pitcher," the Browns started the season with a competitive 8-9 record in April.[61] Things quickly unraveled in early May.

On Saturday, May 3, the Browns played the Cleveland Naps at Sportsman's Park. In the sixth inning, Stovall, the Browns first baseman, came to the plate. Umpire Charlie Ferguson called a strike on a pitch Stovall thought was a ball. He vocally registered his complaint to the umpire. After a second called strike, Stovall blew his stack. He grabbed the umpire's hat and threw it to the ground. Ejected from the game, it's what Stovall did next that caused him trouble. After retrieving his glove, the Browns skipper returned to confront the umpire. "George let fly with a big blog of tobacco juice – p-tooey! – that just splattered all over Ferguson's face and coat and everywhere else," recalled teammate Jimmy Austin. "George always did chew an uncommonly large wad, you know."[62]

News of the confrontation quickly made its way to AL president Johnson. He moved to suspend Stovall indefinitely and launched an investigation. He also threatened to strip Stovall of his manager's duties permanently.[63] In the end, though, Johnson's bark proved worse than his bite. On May 22, he reinstated Stovall. The Browns manager had to pay a $100 fine and write a letter of apology to the umpire.

Stovall's troubles mirrored those of his team. The Browns finished the month of May ten games under .500. The team didn't have a winning month all season. Rickey had arrived in St. Louis in June and was soon followed by his Michigan shortstop, Johnny Lavan, nicknamed "Doc" because he attended medical school at Michigan (and later became a physician in St. Louis). Lavan became a source of friction between Rickey and Stovall. The front office executive, with years of experience in a university setting, preferred players with college experience.[64] The field manager was not a fan. In August, the Browns sold Lavan to the Philadelphia A's over Rickey's objections (Rickey re-acquired him in the offseason). Shortly thereafter, the Browns lost nine games in a row. Owner Hedges then made his move. He fired Stovall as manager in early September but retained him as a player. The Browns finished the season in last place.

Stovall jumped to the upstart Federal League the following season, becoming the first player in Organized Baseball to do so. "No player had yet broken his reserve contract to go with the Federal League. But I argued that somebody had to be the first and it might as well be I."[65] He became the player-manager of the Kansas City Packers where he once slugged an umpire. The ejection from the game forced Kansas City management to delay a planned "George Stovall Day" at the ballpark.

With Stovall gone in St. Louis, Hedges wanted to replace him with his secretary. But Rickey, demonstrating the horse-trading skills he learned from his grandfather, always considered any offer and then asked for more. He wanted an ownership stake in the team, something Hedges was not willing to give him. With the two sides at an impasse, third baseman Jimmy Austin managed the club for eight games in September of 1913.

When Hedges and Rickey ultimately reached an agreement, the new field captain didn't get stock in the team, but he did get a raise and a possible bonus. Three months shy of his thirty-second birthday, Rickey was a big-league manager in addition to his front office duties (he was made a vice president at the end of the year). "Baseball men generally agree that Rickey is the keenest baseball man Hedges has had around since he entered the national game," *Sporting Life* told its readers after the deal was announced. "Rickey is a practical baseball man in every sense of the word, having made good as a player, coach, and scout. Naturally, judging from what he has already accomplished, he ought to become one of the really great leaders of the national game."[66]

The Browns had their new manager in place shortly before the end of the 1913 season. Their hometown rivals, the Cardinals, began the 1913 season with their new manager. In just a few years, the two men would be working for the same club, setting in motion a chain of events that would impact baseball both in St. Louis and New York for years to come.

---

[1] Before the 1924 season, Rickey unsuccessfully attempted to hire St. Louis University trainer Paddy Fitzgerald. *St. Louis Post-Dispatch,* March 3, 1924.
[2] Ritter, *The Glory of Their Times.*
[3] Polner, Murray. *Branch Rickey: A Biography.* Atheneum. 1982.
[4] Ibid.
[5] D'Antonio, Michael. *Forever Blue: The True Story of Walter O'Malley, Baseball's Most Controversial Owner, and the Dodgers of Brooklyn and Los Angeles*. Riverhead Books. 2009.
[6] Steinberg, Steve. *Baseball in St. Louis 1900-1925.* Arcadia Publishing. 2004.
[7] Polner, *Branch Rickey.*
[8] Ibid.
[9] *Los Angeles Times*, August 10, 1979. "There was conjecture that this was no oversight [lack of water fountains] but it was designed to spur beer sales," wrote Penelope McMillan. "O'Malley never commented." A later *Times* story stated that O'Malley called the lack of water fountains an oversight. *Los Angeles Times,* April 3, 2011.
[10] Breslin, Jimmy. *Branch Rickey*. Penguin Group. 2011.
[11] *Sports Illustrated*, March 7, 1955.
[12] Lowenfish, Lee. *Branch Rickey: Baseball's Ferocious Gentleman*. University of Nebraska Press. 2007.
[13] Ibid.
[14] Ibid.
[15] Ibid.
[16] Polner, *Branch Rickey.*
[17] Bryson, Bill. *One Summer: America 1927*. Doubleday. 2013.
[18] Lowenfish, *Branch Rickey.*
[19] Lamb, Chris. "Did Branch Rickey Sign Jackie Robinson To Right A 40-Year Wrong?" *Black Ball*. Volume 6. McFarland & Company, Inc. 2013.
[20] Rickey was a Comiskey fan. "I followed him in the early 1890s through a weekly edition of the *Cincinnati Enquirer*. He could do everything – hit and play first and manage. He was a giant in my memory," he wrote in *The American Diamond*.
[21] *Topeka Daily State Journal*, February 14, 1906. Rickey's path to St. Louis is a bit convoluted. Comiskey took Rickey in the Rule 5 draft in September of 1905 and traded him to the Browns in February of 1906. But Rickey debuted for the Browns the prior season, in June of 1905. *Baseball Reference* records no transaction that places Rickey in St. Louis that season.

---

[22] *St. Louis Post-Dispatch*, June 2, 1906.
[23] Ibid, April 4, 1906.
[24] Polner, *Branch Rickey.*
[25] Lowenfish, *Branch Rickey.*
[26] Biographer Murray Polner says Rickey requested the trade. Lee Lowenfish claims manager McAleer grew tired of Rickey's Sunday absences. Perhaps the decision was mutual.
[27] The Browns received infielder Joe Yeager in the deal. He hit .239 for the 1907 Browns and was out of major league baseball after 10 games in 1908.
[28] See www.peakbagger.com/pbgeog/histmetropop.aspx for details.
[29] Estimates range as high as $50,000. See sabr.org/research/st-louis-browns-team-ownership-history. Hedges had partners. Later estimates placed his personal investment at $30,000.
[30] Steinberg, Steve. *Baseball in St. Louis 1900-1925.* Arcadia Publishing. 2004.
[31] "Colonel Hedges' profits that season [1908] amounted to $165,000." *St. Louis Star*, August 18, 1916. The Browns finished fourth in the American League with a record of 83-79 but their attendance was second highest in the league.
[32] *The Sporting News*, April 28, 1932.
[33] *St. Louis Post-Dispatch*, May 7, 1908. "These wagons will be pulled out onto the grounds and set end to end overlapping each other and the cranks turned, rolling down the canvas in a tent shape from each side. This canvas will be spiked down onto the grass at the edge of the diamond."
[34] Ibid, September 4, 1907.
[35] *Sporting Life*, March 11, 1905.
[36] Steinberg, Steve. *Robert Hedges*. SABR.org biography project.
[37] *Sporting Life*, December 5, 1903.
[38] *St. Louis Globe-Democrat,* May 4, 1915.
[39] Many accounts of the Chalmers race state the company awarded an automobile to the highest batting average in each league. There was only one award. In his statement affirming Cobb as the AL batting champion, Ban Johnson wrote that Cobb "is therefore entitled to the Chalmers trophy as none of the National League batters approached his record."
[40] *Sports Illustrated*, September 20, 2010.
[41] Ibid.
[42] *The Sporting News*, April 18, 1981.
[43] Ginsburg, Daniel E. *The Fix Is In: A History of Baseball and Gambling and Game Fixing Scandals*. McFarland & Company, Inc. 1995.
[44] Depending on the account, Howell is identified as a pitcher, a coach, a pitcher-coach or a scout.
[45] Exactly when he was born is a source of confusion. His obituary in *The Sporting News* states he was born March 3, 1867. *Baseball Reference* and a *Wikipedia* entry place his birth

date as June 2, 1866. Author Daniel Ginsburg wrote that he was born in 1869. O'Connor and Rickey were teammates on the 1906 Browns.

[46] Ginsburg, *The Fix Is In.* Also see *The Sporting News*, November 18, 1937.

[47] "Lajoie's Eight-Hit Day," *The New York Times*, September 9, 1948.

[48] *St. Louis Post-Dispatch,* October 11, 1910.

[49] Ibid, October 16, 1910. Many accounts of the incident claim that Johnson banned O'Connor following the investigation. In fact, O'Connor was cleared by Johnson and fired by Hedges. In reality, it may be a distinction without a difference.

[50] *The Sporting News*, April 18, 1981.

[51] *Baseball Reference* has removed the two hits from its ledger and records Cobb's total at 4,189. www.baseball-reference.com/players/c/cobbty01-bat.shtml. The site also credits Lajoie with winning the 1910 batting title.

[52] Lowenfish, *Branch Rickey.*

[53] Ibid.

[54] Polner, *Branch Rickey.*

[55] Lowenfish, *Branch Rickey.*

[56] Ibid.

[57] Ibid.

[58] Ibid. Pitcher Ernie Koob also joined the Browns in 1915. A star at Western Michigan (known as Western State Normal School at the time), Koob first caught Rickey's eye in a game against the Wolverines. Koob and Sisler dueled for 14 scoreless innings. Koob pitched a no-hitter for the Browns against the Chicago White Sox in 1917.

[59] *St. Louis Post-Dispatch*, March 5, 1913.

[60] Ibid.

[61] Ibid, March 25, 1913.

[62] Ritter, *The Glory of Their Times.*

[63] *St. Louis Post-Dispatch*, May 6, 1913.

[64] "Rickey, educated in the old rough and ready baseball school, dreamed of an entire club of college men – athletes who would listen and who would be capable of carrying out his theories," wrote syndicated columnist Harry Grayson. *St. Louis Star-Times,* February 25, 1935.

[65] Seymour, Harold. *Baseball: The Golden Age*. Oxford University Press. 1971.

[66] *Sporting Life*, September 20, 1913.

The Hug and Branch Show

"There may be harder tasks than piloting the Cardinals to victory," wrote J.R. McDermott on the pages of *Baseball Magazine* in 1913, "but if so we do not know them."[1] The man assuming that tall task in St. Louis that season measured five feet five inches high and weighed 140 pounds. Many didn't believe he was that big.[2] One of his many nicknames over the years was "The Midget Manager," and if that sounds harsh or cruel to modern sensibilities, it was one of the many appellations he heard. In New York, Babe Ruth called him "The Little Boy" or "The Flea" and once allegedly dangled him upside down over the side of a train following an argument. "Here comes the mouse!" fans would chant when he left the dugout.[3] An umpire once mistook him for a batboy.

Miller Huggins never let his diminutive size get in the way of success. He managed every single New York Yankees World Series team of the 1920s, including the legendary 1927 squad that went 110-44 in the regular season and swept the Pittsburgh Pirates in the Fall Classic. He is celebrated and remembered today with plaques at both the Hall of Fame in Cooperstown and Monument Park in Yankee Stadium. But before he ever became associated with the Bronx Bombers, Huggins cut his managerial teeth in St. Louis. And if things had worked out differently, if things had worked out as Huggins had wanted, he may have never left.

He arrived in St. Louis in a trade with Cincinnati following the 1909 season. Huggins, a Cincinnati native, had a background similar to Branch Rickey. Both grew up in Methodist families not far from one another in Ohio – Lucasville is less than 100 miles from Cincinnati – at around the same time. Huggins was born in March of 1878, three years and nine months before Rickey.[4] Like Rickey, Huggins faced the dilemma of Sunday baseball. But instead of refusing to play, Huggins did so under an assumed name as a teenager. "I played under the name of Proctor, as my dad didn't relish the idea of Sunday baseball."[5]

Just like Rickey, Huggins had a law degree. He captained the baseball team at the University of Cincinnati while also attending to his studies. Professor William Howard Taft, the future President and Chief Justice of the Supreme Court, gave him the advice that changed his life. "You can become a pleader or a player – not both," Taft told Huggins. "Try baseball; you seem to like it better."[6]

Huggins was a second baseman and a switch-hitter. His first year in the big leagues came in 1904 for his hometown Cincinnati Reds, the team Rickey joined, but never played for, at the end of that same season. Huggins led the National League in walks four times, including his first season in St. Louis, and had at least 30 stolen bases six times in his career. He played and managed his first four years with the Cardinals. After making just 14 plate appearances in 1916, his playing career ended at the age of 38.

His first season as player-manager proved challenging. The Cardinals finished 1913 in last place with a record of 51-99. It was the only team Huggins ever managed that finished last. His style proved quite a contrast to the emotional and high-strung Roger Bresnahan. "Huggins rules by persuasion, common sense, by moderation," noted *Baseball Magazine*. But the disastrous first year in St. Louis soon had skeptics growling. "A little fellow can't manage the big fellows," Sid Keener wrote in the *St. Louis Times*.[7]

His style eventually won converts. "Huggins was sort of a fatherly guy," remembered Yankees pitcher Waite Hoyt. "He was sort of a baseball father and sort of a psychiatrist. He had a couch in his office, and I was on that couch more than I was on the field." That "fatherly guy" never married and never had children of his own. His players became his family. "He loved me like a father and I loved him like a son," said Leo Durocher, who broke in with the Yankees under Huggins and later starred with the Cardinals as a member of the Gashouse Gang in the 1930s.[8] "Huggins was the only friend I had, the only one who thought I might make good some day."

Huggins was the first big-league manager Lou Gehrig ever played for. "He is the best teacher I ever had the privilege of being with," said the Yankees first baseman. The role of teacher made Huggins especially effective with younger players. "If I were a youngster breaking into the game, and especially a pitcher, I would ask nothing better than to have Huggins as my manager," said New York Giants skipper John McGraw in 1915. "There is no smarter man in baseball today than Miller Huggins."[9]

It was the 1914 season that signaled Huggins arrival as a manager. In late August, his team was in a virtual three-way tie for first place with the New York Giants and Boston Braves before fading. The Cardinals finished the year 81-72 and jumped five places in the standings. The win total and the third-place finish marked, at the time, the best Cardinals' performance of the twentieth century. The St. Louis team ERA of 2.38 was the best in the National League.

Huggins had a way of coaching players up and a knack for letting them down easily. Early in his career with the Yankees, Huggins had to release a struggling young outfielder by the name of George Halas. "I am forever grateful for the manner in which Miller Huggins told me my big-league career was over," Halas wrote in his autobiography. "Through the years, whenever I had to cut a player, I have tried to emulate his grace and consideration," remembered the man who left pro baseball for pro football and a Hall of Fame career as coach and owner of the Chicago Bears.[10]

Juggling a roster and managing the various personalities on a team didn't come easily for Huggins. An external calm that bolstered the confidence of younger players disguised an internal churn. "He was nervous and irritable, an insomniac – a neurotic," wrote author Robert Weintraub. "He had false teeth, and they didn't fit properly in his gums. He was forever suffering from sinus headaches, eye strains and indigestion."[11] When he managed the Yankees, the stressed-out bachelor shared an apartment in Manhattan with his sister. His personality couldn't have been more different from his boisterous, brash star player, Babe Ruth. They were forever oil and water. When Ruth was introduced to Claire Hodgson, the woman who became his second wife, she proceeded to tell him he drank too much. "You sound like Miller Huggins," the Babe replied.

Off the field, Huggins had a passion for stocks and real estate and a reputation as a shrewd investor. "I know a prominent business man of St. Louis who congratulated me a while ago on my business sagacity," recalled Huggins in 1913. The man told Huggins he had heard the manager was "worth in the neighborhood of a half a million." The manager's reaction? "I nearly fainted." One of his players told him "that if I was not worth eighty-thousand dollars he would eat my shirt." Huggins denied the claim and added, "I only wish it was as easy to make money as some people think it is."[12]

Huggins got an early start as a business owner. When the minor league St. Paul Saints sold his contract to the Cincinnati Reds for $3,500 in the fall of 1903, the owner of the team gave Huggins $1,000 of the purchase price. He invested the money in a cigar store and the largest roller-skating rink in Cincinnati. He was twenty-five years old. Huggins had a fascination with roller rinks, visiting different ones in his travels. His goal was to own a chain of rinks. He later owned an orange grove and several properties in Florida. "What are you, Miller – a real estate man or a baseball manager?" Yankees owner Jacob Ruppert once asked him.[13] What Huggins truly wanted was ownership of a baseball team. While he had a silent interest in the St. Paul Saints in the 1920s, he aspired to have a piece of a major league franchise.[14] It was a dream to be denied by the St. Louis Cardinals.

Beyond the roller rinks and real estate, Huggins had another habit his biographers never fail to mention. "As a young man, he had a suppressed desire to be a drum major, and he yearned for the glittering baton and the tall hat," wrote baseball historian Lee Allen. "Even after he made the grade in the majors, Huggins used to imitate the strut of a drum major...demonstrating his prowess with an umbrella."[15]

If Huggins marched to the beat of his own drum, so too did the man leading the St. Louis Browns. Like Huggins, Rickey had hobbies, habits, and interests that had long fascinated the writers who covered him. "Certainly for peculiarity, Branch Rickey, the backstop, is in a class by himself," noted the *Post-Dispatch* in 1906.[16] Now managing the team he once played for, the "peculiar" Rickey was preparing to introduce techniques he had learned while coaching at the collegiate level. Even before his first full season as manager got underway, he and Huggins began clashing over different approaches to the game of baseball.

*****

At the beginning of the 1914 season, a sportswriter spotted Rickey doing something most baseball managers simply did not do. He was reading a book. And not just any book. The Browns manager was enjoying *Enchiridion* by the Stoic philosopher Epictetus.[17] "Imagine any manager of the old ilk," observed the reporter who caught Rickey red-handed, "attempting to even pronounce the name."[18]

Rickey, a man who had spent years in college classrooms, brought an academic-like focus to baseball. The Browns conducted spring training that season in St. Petersburg, beginning a long St. Louis baseball connection to the Florida city. Rickey set up a classroom "with blackboards and charts and gave his players a lesson in theoretic baseball every morning. He proposed problems, and the players were called upon in turn to provide instant solutions."

This focus on theory served as a flashpoint of disagreement in the offseason. Rickey laid out his ambitious spring training plans in December. In addition to classroom exercises, the Browns manager wanted sliding pits, handball courts and batting cages for his players in St. Petersburg, and then predicted, "I expect Huggins to do likewise before he is through as manager." The manager of the Cardinals was underwhelmed by the advice. "I believe Manager Rickey has a lot of good ideas, but I'm not strong for this theory stuff," Huggins said. "No ball player can learn how to steal by sliding into sand pits."[19]

Since he was silent on the other ideas, Huggins was presumably less opposed to Rickey's more pragmatic suggestions. "Handball will help my players get in condition, brighten their eyes, and make them alert," he contended. The batting cages demonstrated how Rickey's theories could have practical effects. The Browns manager contrived four cages made of wire netting. Now, instead of one batter standing at home plate waiting on a pitch, four hitters could take cuts simultaneously. The confined space of the cages, which allowed for quicker retrieval of the balls, only increased the exponential impact. Rickey, the former catcher, had conceived the idea of the batting cage while at Michigan to help his backstops. The cages freed his catchers from receiving duties.[20]

Rickey and the Browns had been lured to Florida that spring by local businessman and future St. Pete mayor Al Lang. In classic Rickey fashion, the Browns manager and business manager negotiated a deal whereby the city of St. Petersburg paid for the team's travel expenses and living expenses in Florida and agreed to foot the bill for five reporters covering the team. The Browns saved money. The city got media exposure and potentially more Northern visitors. In the only spring training game in St. Pete that year, the Browns and the Chicago Cubs drew four thousand fans.[21] Later, the Cardinals under general manager Rickey and the Yankees under manager Huggins began spending their springs in St. Pete.[22]

Rickey's years with the Browns sparked other relationships that lasted decades and reaffirmed other connections in his growing network. Just as he did as a player, manager Rickey insisted he would not be at the ballpark on Sundays. In 1914, Burt Shotton became his Sunday manager.[23] Shotton, an outfielder who stole more than 40 bases in four consecutive seasons, spent every year but one as a player with either the Browns or the Cardinals. He got his start as a manager in the Cardinals minor league system in 1926. He would have a role in Rickey's career for years to come.

Bill DeWitt Sr., the father of the current Chairman and CEO of the St. Louis Cardinals, broke into baseball with the Browns. The teenager had been selling concessions at Sportsman's Park when he got his big break. The Browns had another teen, Roscoe Hillenkoetter, who worked as an "office boy" for Rickey. Hillenkoetter had an appointment to the U.S. Naval Academy but he enjoyed working for Rickey so much he planned to decline the opportunity. "We all adored him," Hillenkoetter said of his boss.[24]

Hillenkoetter's boss, though, soon discovered the plan. A huge believer in education, Rickey was horrified. "Roscoe, if you don't go, I'll fire you and you'll never get another job," the Browns manager told him.[25] Roscoe went to Annapolis. He graduated from the Naval Academy in 1919. The St. Louis native rose to the ranks of Admiral. He was on the island of Oahu when the Japanese attacked on December 7, 1941. He was wounded in the attack on Pearl Harbor when the battleship *West Virginia* was sunk. After World War II, when the United States government created the Central Intelligence Agency, Hillenkoetter became its first director.[26]

When Hillenkoetter left the Browns, Rickey asked him to recommend a replacement. He named DeWitt, then a thirteen-year-old soda and peanut vendor at the ballpark. After being subjected to a torrent of questions from Rickey, DeWitt got the job. For most of the next forty years, he worked for either the Cardinals or Browns, rising to the ranks of vice president for the former and later becoming an owner of the latter.[27]

Rickey also rekindled his relationship with scout Charley Barrett when he returned to the Browns. The two had faced each other in the minor leagues. Barrett had speed – he once had more than 50 stolen bases in a season – but he couldn't hit. "I would chase a curve ball to first base."[28] When his minor-league career ended, he returned to his native St. Louis. Retired from the game, he was working at a sporting goods store when he met Robert Hedges in 1909. Barrett tried to convince the Browns owner to open a downtown ticket office. Hedges turned the tables on the former minor leaguer and offered him a job with the team. Barrett worked as a scout for the next thirty years, nearly all of them with Rickey. *The Sporting News* once estimated Barrett traveled nearly a million miles in his career, "by railroad, bus, airplane, automobile, and even tractor," signing dozens of players along the way who eventually made their way to the major leagues.[29] He is the unsung hero of St. Louis baseball.

Like Shotton and DeWitt, Barrett eventually followed Rickey from the Browns to the Cardinals. With the Browns, Barrett represented the entire scouting department. To combat the shortage of resources, Rickey began working from a playbook he would hone to perfection with the Cardinals. In a draft of minor-league players in September 1913, 108 players were selected. The Browns took 30 of them. In addition to stockpiling talent, Hedges and Rickey sought better relations with minor league teams. Before Rickey and the Cardinals altered the structure beginning in the 1920s, minor league baseball teams had no loyalty or affiliation with their major league counterparts. They were locally-owned independent parties. Other than an end-of-season draft, the only way for a major league team to acquire a minor league player was to purchase his contract. The arguments in those days mirrored the ones starting in the 1970s when free-agency took off: Only the wealthy teams could buy the best talent.

Hedges found a group of businessmen in Montgomery, Alabama interested in buying a minor league club. He loaned them the money to buy a team with the understanding the Browns would have first rights to any player ready for the big leagues. Hedges and Rickey became interested in Montgomery as a source of talent after acquiring second baseman Del Pratt before the 1912 season.[30]

The deal with the Montgomery businessmen ultimately fell through. By January of 1914, baseball officials stepped in. The National Commission banned major league teams from owning minor league clubs.[31] Stymied by authority and starved of resources, Rickey had few alternatives. He did, however, have an ace up his sleeve. Little did anyone know at the time the uproar it would cause, and that the decision would start the downfall of baseball's ruling order.

*****

Just like Huggins and Rickey, George Sisler was born and raised in Ohio. He grew up in a hamlet just outside of Akron. The future first baseman attracted early attention, not for his batting talents but his pitching prowess. When Sisler tried out for the baseball team at Michigan in the winter of 1912, Rickey got a first-hand look at his abilities. "His left-handed speed and control made him almost unhittable," remembered the coach of the Wolverines. "He was a major league pitcher right there!"[32] Rickey would have to wait a year to play him. Freshmen couldn't play varsity baseball.

Rickey wasn't the first to appreciate Sisler's abilities on the mound. Pro scouts also took notice. At the age of seventeen, Sisler signed a minor-league contract with the Akron team in the Ohio-Pennsylvania League. He never played in a game and never took any money. "They tried to get me to accept some cash," said Sisler, "but I would not, nor did I ever get any money." The left-hander's talents were so obvious the contract was later transferred to a team in Columbus and then purchased by the Pittsburgh Pirates. Pittsburgh owner Barney Dreyfuss paid $5,000 to secure the rights to Sisler.[33]

One of many early baseball magnates with German roots, Dreyfuss arrived in America in 1881, first settling in Paducah, Kentucky with relatives of his grandfather. When the family distillery business expanded, he moved to Louisville and became a baseball owner. He owned the Louisville Colonels, a team in the American Association which became a part of the National League when the two leagues merged. When the

N.L. contracted after the 1899 season, the Louisville franchise was shuttered. Dreyfuss then bought the Pittsburgh Pirates. He owned them until he died in 1932.[34]

In the summer of 1912, Dreyfuss wanted what he had paid for, the services of left-handed pitcher Sisler. "If he (Sisler) refuses to report to the team which has purchased him he will be blacklisted, and will never be allowed to play in organized ball," threatened the Pittsburgh owner who had Sisler placed on the suspended list.

Sisler, who initially kept the contract signing a secret from his parents, went to his college baseball coach for advice. Attorney Rickey viewed the contract as nonbinding. Sisler was a minor at the time and had signed without the consent of a parent or a guardian. But Rickey wasn't taking any chances. He engaged Detroit judge George Codd to take up Sisler's case. They took the matter before the National Commission, baseball's ruling body.

The National Commission came out of the peace agreement between the American and National Leagues in 1903. The three-man panel included the presidents of both leagues and a third member who acted as the chairman. The one and only chairman the National Commission ever had was Cincinnati Reds owner Garry Herrmann. Originally, he was acceptable to National League owners because he was one of them. American League owners found him palatable because of Herrmann's friendship with AL president Ban Johnson.

Rickey had Sisler and his father write letters to the commission, with the player claiming he did not "in any way understand the nature of the contract." Rickey turned the case into a matter of trust. "For who is going to trust you if you cajole minors into signing contracts and declare them suspended – as you have tried to suspend Sisler – when they change their mind?" asked the lawyer and college baseball coach.[35]

With the presidents of the two leagues expected to remain loyal to their side, the vote came down to a decision from chairman Herrmann. While sympathetic to the minor argument, he also came to the issue from the perspective of an owner and appreciated the merits of Dreyfuss's position. Herrmann wanted to make Sisler a free agent and encourage him to sign with Pittsburgh. But no final decision was forthcoming. In August of 1912, with the baseball season almost over and Sisler preparing to return to Michigan for his sophomore year, the commission decided to postpone a verdict.

Sisler returned to Ann Arbor, where, for the first of three straight years, he received All-American honors. In his sophomore season, his first on the Michigan varsity roster and Rickey's last year as coach, he pitched – once striking out fourteen of fifteen batters he faced in a game – and he played the field – finishing the season with a batting average of .445.

Sisler graduated from Michigan in June of 1915 with a degree in mechanical engineering. By this time, the only question surrounding his abilities was the position he would play. The cloud over his status had been lifted the previous fall. After seeking legal advice, the National Commission ruled that Sisler's minor league contract was invalid. He was free to sign with any team he chose.

Pittsburgh owner Dreyfuss offered Sisler a pro-rated contract and bonus of $5,200. Dreyfuss may have been under the impression that he would be the only bidder for Sisler's services.[36] He was wrong. Rickey and the Browns topped the offer from the Pirates, offering the Michigan grad a pro-rated contract and bonus of $7,400. More money and the chance to play for his old college coach made it an easy decision. Sisler chose the Browns.

Dreyfuss was outraged. He accused Rickey of tampering with the college star. He filed a formal complaint with the National Commission and pushed American League president Johnson to suspend the Browns new player. But Johnson was reluctant to get involved without the full backing of the commission. Once again, it came down to a decision from chairman Herrmann. And once again, Herrmann delayed. The formal ruling didn't come until June of 1916, a full year after Sisler had joined the Browns. In a nineteen-page typewritten decision, Herrmann reaffirmed the earlier findings. Sisler's original minor league contract was null and void. The Browns were within their rights to sign him.

Dreyfuss fired back at baseball's ruling body with a twelve-thousand-word opinion of his own. "An outsider, some person not affiliated with either league, should be placed at the head of the National Commission. The finding in the Sisler case is a freak of baseball legislation."[37] The Pittsburgh owner never forgave Herrmann for the Sisler decision and resented Ban Johnson as well. He began a battle to upend baseball's governing structure.

A series of rulings by the commission over the next few years would spark anger and outrage from other owners. The National League Boston Braves and American League Philadelphia Athletics clashed over a pitcher. A minor league player assigned to the Yankees angered White Sox owner Charles Comiskey, fracturing his relationship with American League president Ban Johnson.

The owners of the Yankees and Red Sox would later join with Comiskey in seeking to end Johnson's control over the league. Boston right-hander Carl Mays had walked off the mound in frustration in a game in 1919 and left the team. League President Johnson declared that no team could trade for Mays until he rejoined the Red Sox. Boston and New York ignored the command. Ban Johnson was having breakfast in St. Louis when he read in the paper the Red Sox had traded Mays to the Yankees. "I thought he would hit the ceiling," recalled the publisher of *The Sporting News*, J.G. Taylor Spink. "I never saw him more riled."[38] Furious with the clubs, Johnson tried to block the deal, but the Yankees went to court and got a temporary restraining order against the league president.

An all-out war then erupted among American League owners with the White Sox, Red Sox, and Yankees wanting to fire Johnson. They were dubbed the insurrectionists. The owners of the other five clubs, known as the loyalists, remained committed to their league president. At one point, the insurrectionists even threatened to move their clubs to the National League. Johnson survived the challenge and remained in charge of the

AL, but in February of 1920, Garry Herrmann resigned as chairman of the National Commission. He was never replaced. When allegations of a 1919 World Series fix became public in the fall of 1920, baseball was rudderless. In November of 1920, owners hired Federal District Court Judge Kenesaw Mountain Landis as the first commissioner. The National Commission was no longer in charge. Baseball had a new ruling structure.

With Commissioner Landis in place, gone were the days of decision by committee. Baseball now had an autocratic regime. The Landis era would last nearly a quarter-century and prove to be enormously influential. His decisions set standards baseball would follow for decades. The reforms instituted by the judge included a much tougher stance toward gambling and fixing of games. One by one, Landis began to ban those tied to various conspiracies. The purge of players, the headlines associated with various scandals, and suspicions about outcomes would last through much of the 1920s. His role in the game's history began with the downfall of the National Commission, a ruling body that broke down largely over player disputes.

Those disputes started with Rickey's Browns signing George Sisler and ended with Huggins' Yankees trading for Carl Mays.[39]

*****

One of the reasons baseball officials selected and felt comfortable with Landis running the game was his involvement in an earlier legal case. In 1915, the Federal League sued the American and National Leagues on antitrust grounds. The new league had declared itself a major league the prior year and had started raiding the rosters of the established clubs.

The upstart eight-team league that included a team in St. Louis thought it had found a sympathetic ear in Judge Landis when it filed its case in the U.S. District Court in Northern Illinois. Landis had a reputation as a trustbuster, once imposing a $29 million fine on Standard Oil, a decision later overturned by the Supreme Court. Landis had a knack for attention-getting cases. During World War I, he wanted to indict Kaiser Wilhelm after the ocean liner *Lusitania* was sunk by a German submarine. Sportswriter Red Smith, who spent years in St. Louis before becoming prominent in New York, described Landis as "a gimlet-eyed tyrant off the federal bench with a white fright wig and the face of a sanctified billy goat."[40]

Landis was the son of a Union Army surgeon. Abraham Landis lost a leg at the Battle of Kennesaw Mountain, Georgia when a Confederate cannonball ricocheted off a tree and into his body. He named his son after the site, dropping one "n" in the process.

Kenesaw Landis started practicing law in Chicago in 1891. He later spent time in Washington D.C., working for Secretary of State Walter Gresham. President Roosevelt appointed him to the bench in 1905. A decade later, he found himself trying a case about the sport he loved dearly. Landis was a huge baseball fan, something attorneys in the Federal League case quickly discovered. "I think you gentlemen here all understand that a blow at this thing called baseball – both sides understand this perfectly – will be regarded by this court as a blow at a national institution," the judge declared during the trial.[41]

Reluctant to rule, Landis sat on the case. By the end of the year, the Federal League was out of business. Twenty-four teams across three leagues simply wasn't economically viable. The boost the competition gave to players' salaries – St. Louis Cardinals catcher Ivey Wingo made $2,600 in 1913 and $6,500 by 1915 – proved to be a bust for owners' bottom lines. Eager to settle, the American and National Leagues paid $600,000 to the Federals to drop the case. Five of the eight Federal League teams agreed to terms with established baseball and simply shut down their franchises. Two of the Federal League magnates, Charles Weeghman in Chicago and Phil Ball in St. Louis, merged their clubs with existing teams. Weeghman bought the Cubs, while Ball, after being one of many rejected by Helene Britton and the Cardinals, bought the Browns from Hedges.

Britton had another potential suitor during this period. The one team that refused to come to terms was the Federal League's Baltimore franchise. The Baltimore owners would have settled if they had been allowed to buy a team in the established leagues. The Cardinals were one of the clubs thought to be in play at the time. At a meeting with Baltimore representatives, Cincinnati Reds owner and National Commission chairman Garry Herrmann acknowledged the Cardinals might be for sale. But at an owners' meeting in December of 1915, it all fell apart for Baltimore. Chicago White Sox owner Comiskey mocked the Maryland city. "Baltimore, a Minor League city and not a hell of a good one at that," said the former St. Louis Browns captain. Brooklyn owner Charles Ebbets piled on. "You have too many colored population to begin with," he told an attorney representing Baltimore. "They are a cheap population when it gets down to paying money at the gate."[42]

Denied the opportunity to secure a franchise, Baltimore owners pursued a legal remedy and filed an antitrust case three months later. The suit eventually made its way to the Supreme Court where justices ruled in 1922 that baseball was not interstate commerce, making it exempt from antitrust laws. Had St. Louis owner Britton decided to sell to the Baltimore Feds, the landmark case would not have been heard and baseball history would have pursued a different path. Today we remember the St. Louis Browns as the team that eventually became the Baltimore Orioles. Had Britton succumbed to the pressure to sell in 1915, it could have been the Cardinals.

*****

The end of the Federal League had enormous consequences for baseball in St. Louis. Phil Ball's purchase of the Browns impacted the career trajectories of both Rickey and Huggins. Rickey was the first to move. For the first of three straight ownership groups he worked for, Rickey clashed with his bosses over alcohol and the business of baseball. Prohibitionist Rickey also never said anything stronger than "Judas Priest." Ball, on the other hand, "could cuss with anybody without asking the odds," *The Sporting News* once noted.[43]

It was Ball's other career that allowed him to become a baseball mogul. The son of a former Union Army captain, Ball grew up in the family business of ice machines and refrigeration plants. As a teenager, he followed his father to construction sites around the country, including Memphis, Tennessee, Sherman, Texas, Shreveport, Louisiana, and Paducah, Kentucky. "Those were happy days in Paducah," Ball recalled years later. "We used to have fun showing the innocents how to kick a nail keg up the wall with our backs turned to the keg."[44]

He did have dreams of playing baseball, but his career was cut short in an altercation with a man who nearly cut off his left hand. The hand healed but he carried scars from the incident for the rest of his life. He thought about becoming a civil engineer but realized he could make more money in the family business. He settled in St. Louis in 1890 and later bought out his father's interest in the Ice & Cold Machine Company for $20,000. He greatly expanded the operation, selling ice machines to meatpackers, railroads and breweries. Ball counted a locally-owned brewery as one of his customers. "St. Louis doesn't know that he built the biggest ice-making machine in the whole world, the one at Anheuser-Busch," claimed Ball's secretary, Ella Jacoby.[45]

Ball may have been the wealthiest baseball owner in St. Louis history until Anheuser-Busch bought the Cardinals in the 1950s. When a doctor diagnosed him in the 1920s with just a short time to live, Ball sold his business for more than $5 million.[46] A few years later and his health revived, Ball decided to return to the industry, becoming a stockholder and director in 156 ice plants in the United States, Canada, and Mexico. He also owned a ten-thousand-acre farm in Texas, oil wells in Oklahoma and California, real estate in St. Louis, and "other interests in various states."[47]

Ball's partner in the Browns was Otto Stifel, one of the many beer brewers in St. Louis with a German heritage.[48] The Union Brewing Company competed with Anheuser-Busch, already considered by 1915 the largest beer maker on the planet. "They make beer for the world," said Stifel. "I try to make beer for a part of the good people of St. Louis."[49] Like Ball, Stifel followed in his father's footsteps. "The German people all drink beer. Children drink it from infancy, and the German people are the greatest nation in the world," a belief shared by many in St. Louis at the time, and an opinion many came to regret just a few years later.

The Browns had one owner who was a brewer and another who regarded Rickey as a "goddamned Prohibitionist." The writing was on the wall. It was also in the local papers. "Pressure May Oust Rickey," read the headline of a John Wray column in the *Post-Dispatch* in January of 1916. "If Branch Rickey is railroaded out of all connection with the St. Louis American League club," Wray began, "he may thank his prohibition speeches and his 'anti-wet' stand for his retirement from the Mound City."[50]

At their first meeting, Ball informed Rickey he would no longer manage the team. Fielder Jones, who had guided Ball's 1915 St. Louis Federal League team to a second-place finish, would now run the Browns from the field. "Rickey, you're out as manager and Jones is in. You'll be my business manager," Ball told him. The impatient and gruff owner then asked Rickey what his plans were for the team that had finished in sixth place the previous season. A flustered Rickey could barely respond before his new boss interrupted. "Well, goddamnit, do it. You're the boss." On that note, Ball got up and walked out the door.[51] The two men took an immediate dislike to one another. Rickey was miserable working for Ball and wanted out. Thanks to the other team in town, he soon got his opportunity.

*****

1916 was a season to forget for the St. Louis Cardinals. The team ended the year with a 14-game losing streak on the way to a seventh-place finish, thirty-three games below .500. The Cardinals finished last in the league in attendance, losing $20,000 in the process. Then in November, its owner filed for divorce.

Helene Britton had filed for divorce once before. But she and her husband Schuyler had reconciled in 1911. Schuyler became president of the Cardinals in 1913. Three years later, it all came to an end.

In the early morning hours of November 6, 1916, a drunk Schuyler Britton returned to the family home to find the front door locked. He started pounding on it so loudly it woke up the neighbors. He eventually kicked down the door, and according to Helene, proceeded to "terrorize her and her household." She had the door repaired and barricaded it with a piano only to have him engage in a repeat performance the next night. Ten days later, she filed for divorce in St. Louis Circuit Court. She claimed he was a habitual drunk (a charge later withdrawn), used "vulgar, profane and obscene" language, treated her "often with great brutality," and that he frequently struck her.[52] Schuyler resigned as president of the team. A divorce was officially granted in February of 1917.

In the interim, renewed rumors filled the sports pages that the Cardinals were up for sale. In December, former Browns owner Hedges, flush with cash after selling his club to a group headed by Phil Ball for at least $425,000, became interested in buying the Cardinals.[53] Hedges decided to back off when other bidders emerged. "Every time I come downtown to lunch I hear of another syndicate being formed to buy the team. Competition is getting too keen to please me."[54]

One of those competing syndicates included the manager of the Cardinals. Huggins had always dreamed of owning a baseball team. He returned to his hometown to line up financing for a bid. Brothers Julius and Max Fleischmann had a yeast empire in Cincinnati.[55] The duo also owned a stake in the Cincinnati Reds. Julius was a former Cincinnati mayor and president of the Fleischmann Yeast Company. With Fleischmann money backing him, Huggins thought he had a legitimate shot at getting Britton to sell him the team. She decided to go in a different direction.[56]

The Cardinals owner, who had rejected overtures and interest over the years from everyone from Charles Weeghman in Chicago to Federal League owners in Baltimore, decided to sell the franchise to the people of St. Louis. Britton attorney and former team president James C. Jones came up with the concept. For $25, anyone could buy a share of stock in the National League club. In effect, the Cardinals would become a "fan-owned" team. "We intend to have a ball club run by St. Louis and for St. Louis," Jones said.[57] Britton sold the franchise to the syndicate for $350,000 or $75,000 less than the Browns fetched a little more than a year earlier. On March 5, 1917, Jones presented Britton with a $25,000 check as earnest money. The ex-wife was now an ex-owner. In less than a month, Helene Britton got divorced and sold her baseball team. The six-year run of the first female-owned major sports franchise had come to an end. The Cardinals had new ownership and needed a new president.

It was already an open secret the Cardinals were pursuing Rickey for that role. "It is understood that Branch Rickey, now business manager of the St. Louis Americans, and formerly manager of that team, has been talked of as head of the new Nationals," the *Post-Dispatch* noted the same day Britton received the down payment.[58] Members of the press could confidently make these claims because they had been a part of the decision-making process. Jones had assembled a group of seven local sportswriters and editors and asked them who should be president of the Cardinals. The vote was unanimous. Every single one recommended Rickey for the role.[59]

The Cardinals formally introduced Rickey as the club president at a luncheon two weeks later. His three-year contract called for a $15,000 annual salary. As he did when he joined the Browns, Rickey would wear multiple hats. "If I am to be president, I will also be scout," he said. The Cardinals already had two scouts in Bob Connery and Eddie Herr.[60] Rickey "will increase the scouting corps by giving the present ivory hunters a substantial lift," the *Post-Dispatch* predicted. Contacted in San Antonio, where the Cardinals were in the middle of spring training, manager Huggins voiced his support. "I have known Rickey for several years and I believe there is not a more astute man in baseball."[61]

Rickey and the Cardinals quickly faced two battles: one financial and one legal. The initial $25,000 payment in early March represented just a fraction of what the syndicate was trying to raise. The group needed an additional $325,000 to complete the purchase of the franchise and $150,000 to run the operations of the team. By mid-April, members had raised $175,000 from 700 different investors, ranging in contribution from $25 to $5,000. To get to the full half-million needed, *Sporting Life* estimated the team might need 5,000 investors. "Think of trying to manage the ball team for 5,000 stockholders," the publication pondered.[62]

Like Huggins, Rickey had designs on ownership from his earliest days in management. Combined with the thought of an unwieldy fan-financed scheme, Rickey now had the opportunity and incentive to make his move. He announced in April he had secured an option to buy the Cardinals. His backer was believed to be former Browns owner Hedges. Hedges was in Honolulu at the time, "but he told his friends before he left this country that he intended to aid Rickey in putting over a certain baseball deal," according to one report.[63] The Hedges-Rickey partnership never came to fruition and the option was never exercised. While Rickey did eventually acquire an ownership stake in the team (his parents mortgaged their farm so he could buy 200 shares for $5,000), the search for additional syndicate investors continued.[64]

The Cardinals other challenge came from Rickey's old boss, Phil Ball, and the American League. AL president Ban Johnson hated the idea of losing anyone to the National League. Long before the days of interleague play, the American and National Leagues acted in parallel universes. Launched twenty-five years apart, the leagues had different histories, different owners, different approaches. With a reserve clause in place that tied a player's baseball life to a team in perpetuity, it was not uncommon for a player to spend his entire career with one team. Even when traded, most players spent their baseball lives in one league. The two leagues competed for fans, talent, and media attention.

The Browns moved to block the Rickey move and wanted the National Commission to settle the issue. But the Cardinals, likely knowing that Johnson was behind the resistance to let Rickey go, declared the American League president "utterly unfit" to decide the case.[65] With Johnson's prodding, Ball and the St. Louis Americans then went to court to block the deal. A judge issued a restraining order preventing Rickey from switching teams. The two sides eventually settled on a compromise. Rickey was allowed to join the Cardinals. In exchange, the new team president and his club couldn't have any contact with three specific college prospects until July 1, a small price to pay.[66] "It was a historic moment," wrote Fred Lieb, "for no man in baseball...with the possible exception of Judge Landis and Babe Ruth, has left so deep an impress on the game as Branch Rickey."[67] For the next twenty-five years. Rickey would work for the St. Louis Cardinals and develop the blueprint for baseball's modern farm system.

"Luck is the residue of design," Rickey liked to say. With a little bit of luck and a track record and resume that impressed many, including members of the St. Louis media, the new St. Louis Cardinals president had escaped Phil Ball and the St. Louis Browns. But in jumping to the National League, Rickey had earned the enmity of American League president Johnson. As he plotted his revenge in the summer of 1917, Johnson zeroed in on one target. Just like Rickey, this man earned his living in St. Louis.

*****

Denied the only legitimate shot he would have at owning a major league baseball team, Huggins demonstrated in 1917 why many considered him one of the best managers in the game. The Cardinals went 82-70, finishing third in the National League for the second time in four years. In winning twenty-two more games than in 1916, the team scored 531 runs for the year, while allowing 567. Based on a popular statistical formula that estimates wins and losses based on runs scored and allowed, the Cardinals projected to win only 71 games that season.[68] Huggins got the credit for the improvement.

In calling him the "Little Miracle Worker of the West," *The Sporting News* framed the unique challenges Huggins faced managing the Cardinals in 1917. "Let us pay tribute," wrote the St. Louis-based publication, "to his loyalty and tact, for the proposition of managing a ball team owned by some 1,500 stockholders and in chief control of a man who himself has been a manager and is bound to have ideas of his own and to reject them is not one every team leader could cope with."[69] Huggins had to navigate a fan-owned franchise whose stockholders had more than doubled by the summer of 1917, while working for Rickey, a man who had very definite and often different ideas about the teachings of the game.

As early as the 1914 season, the two men had clashed over philosophical approaches, or what Huggins had called "this theory stuff." Rickey's salary of $15,000 was double what the team paid Huggins. *Post-Dispatch* columnist Wray wrote that "friction was inevitable." Rickey also began carving out territory more often controlled by the field manager, the scouting and signing of players. Rickey's decisions regarding players "left Huggins nothing to do but direct them." The modern general manager's role was beginning to take shape. Just as Rickey chafed under Browns owner Phil Ball, Huggins now had to wonder what kind of future he had with the Cardinals and their new president. But his resume, enhanced by the third-place finish in 1917, made him an attractive target. "His record, considering that he had little money at his disposal, has been remarkable," Wray told his St. Louis readers.[70]

The impressive performance caught the attention of AL president Johnson. Upset about Rickey's defection to the National League, Johnson viewed Huggins as a means to exact his revenge. The motive to court Huggins came from the New York Yankees, who finished the season at 71-82, sixth place in the American League. 1917 was the last year in New York for manager Bill Donovan. The opportunity presented itself thanks to Johnson's relationship with a St. Louis journalist.

The Sporting News publisher J.G. Taylor Spink was a longtime friend of the AL president. The relationship between Johnson and the Spink family stretched back years. Johnson knew Spink's father, Charles, who had served as publisher of the baseball weekly until he died in 1914. "I grew up with a tremendous admiration for Ban Johnson," Taylor Spink admitted.[71] Through *The Sporting News,* the Spinks were early boosters of the American League, something Johnson always appreciated.

Founded in 1886 by Alfred Spink, Taylor's uncle, *The Sporting News* became known as the Bible of Baseball. "That nickname was neither hyperbole nor overstatement," contends the St. Louis chapter of the Baseball Writers Association of America. "In fact, it could be argued, that the nickname was an UNDERstatement. The publication was read in every owner's suite, every clubhouse, in every barber shop and even the front lines of WWI, WWII, Korea and Vietnam."[72]

In a twenty-first-century age of ubiquitous and instant information provided by a flood of media outlets, it may be difficult to imagine the enormous influence the St. Louis weekly had over the game. It had little competition. *Sports Illustrated* didn't publish its first issue until 1954. "For a great many baseball-loving Americans," *The Saturday Evening Post* writer Stanley Frank informed his readers in the 1940s, "*The Sporting News* is their only extracurricular reading material."[73]

In 1917, New Yankees co-owner Tillinghast L'Hommedieu Huston found himself in France in the middle of World War I. America had entered the conflict earlier that year. An engineer by training, Huston had served as a captain in Cuba in the Spanish-American War. Known as "Til" or "Colonel," Huston then made his fortune working on harbor projects following the war. In 1915, he and Jacob Ruppert purchased the Yankees. Two years later, Huston arrived in France and rose to the rank of lieutenant colonel. Sensing that troops were starved for baseball news, he convinced the American League to purchase 150,000 copies of *The Sporting News* for free distribution. Given the nature of the relationship between publisher Spink and league president Johnson, the request likely met little resistance.

The arrival of *The Sporting News* proved to be a hit with the troops and a savior for its publisher. Other than *The Stars and Stripes*, the St. Louis weekly became the most popular publication among America's servicemen. The timing couldn't have been better for Spink as the periodical was "close to failure," according to one account. Circulation had dwindled to 5,000 copies during the war.[74]

With Huston away in Europe, Johnson began selling Yankees co-owner Ruppert on the talents of the St. Louis manager. When Johnson first broached the idea, Ruppert recoiled. "What! Huggins?" he said. "Why, he couldn't manage a dog house for me." Johnson persisted. "You got the wrong impression," the league president assured him. "He's a man we ought to have in our league somewhere."[75]

Eventually convinced, Ruppert and Johnson now needed a middle man to make it happen. Enter Taylor Spink. With the Cardinals in New York for a late-season series in 1917, Spink arranged for a clandestine meeting between Huggins and Ruppert. It marked the first time the two men had ever met. No decision was made but when the season ended, Huggins left for New York and a second meeting with the Yankees co-owner.

On the train to the city, the pipe-smoking Huggins had walked out to the observation platform where he was surprised to see Rickey. With the World Series underway between the Chicago White Sox and the New York Giants, the Cardinals president was on his way to the Polo Grounds. When Huggins told his boss he was making the trip to watch baseball at his own expense, Rickey began to get suspicious. "Rickey knew it was highly improbably that Huggins, who was canny with a dollar, would spend a dime to see the coronation of the King of England and the eruption of Mount Vesuvius if both were billed on the same program," recalled Spink, who once again had arranged a secret meeting.[76]

The publisher registered Huggins under an assumed name at a New York City hotel. He then led the manager "through devious back alleys to clandestine meetings with Ruppert."[77] Huggins' cover was ultimately blown by Ban Johnson. The AL president had given National League manager Huggins a ticket to the World Series in a section of the Polo Grounds occupied by the American League delegation.

Huggins' deal with the New York Yankees became public in late October. He signed a two-year contract at $12,000 a season.[78] Huggins became the ninth manager in the short history of the Yankees.[79] The *New York Times* called him "one of the smartest managers in the game" and "one of the brainiest second basemen in the game when he played with Cincinnati and St. Louis."

"Huggins must have materially bettered himself in going to the Yankees," said Rickey in St. Louis. "I offered him $10,000 and 10 percent of all profits over $25,000 to remain with us next season." Papers in both New York and St. Louis made note of Ban Johnson's role in securing Huggins' service for the Yankees. "He sighted Huggins as the best timber on the horizon to succeed a manifest failure, Bill Donovan," Wray opined in the *Post-Dispatch.*[80]

While the role of Taylor Spink wouldn't be revealed until years later, the arrival of Huggins in New York in 1918 meant that favors between the Yankees and *The Sporting News* had been reciprocated. A request by one of the owners of the Yankees helped save the publication while the St. Louis weekly's publisher helped deliver a future Hall of Fame manager to the American League team.

Despite the many parallels in their early lives and careers, the 1917 season marked the only full campaign that Ohio natives and law school graduates Rickey and Huggins worked for the same organization. Like Rickey, Huggins started with the Cincinnati Reds and came to St. Louis via a trade. Both men eventually managed the team in St. Louis that traded for them. Both expressed a desire to be a baseball owner. Both ended up in career-defining or legacy-shaping roles thanks, in part, to the St. Louis media. Both had scouts who followed them to their new team. Charley Barrett, who left the Browns in 1916 to go to the Detroit Tigers, rejoined Rickey a few years later with the Cardinals and even took a pay cut to do so. Huggins insisted to the Yankees that scout Bob Connery – the man who discovered Rogers Hornsby – join him in New York.

It is conventional wisdom that Huggins was ready to leave the Cardinals after Britton denied him the chance to buy the team. Conflicts with Rickey only enhanced the belief that Huggins couldn't wait to depart. But did he really want to go to New York? According to Babe Ruth biographer Marshall Smelser, Huggins was reluctant to take the job with the Yankees. Like the Cardinals, the Yankees had experienced little success. Neither team had won a pennant. According to Smelser, it was Taylor Spink who "bullied and coaxed him" into taking it.[81] In New York, Huggins had wealthy owners and, beginning with the arrival of Babe Ruth in 1920, great talent. His Hall of Fame career is due entirely to his time with the Yankees. His managerial record with the Cardinals was under .500. But there was something about St. Louis that he always appreciated and fondly remembered. Scout Bob Connery was a lifelong friend. "We were together in both places, and those five years with the Cardinals were happier than any five years in New York, even when Huggins was winning pennants."[82]

*****

By the spring of 1919, baseball had survived an incredibly difficult five-year period. It began with the challenge of the Federal League in 1914, players jumping contracts, and a lawsuit that went all the way to the Supreme Court. With the rival league eliminated by the 1916 season, attendance jumped nearly thirty-four percent. But just as the game started to restore its financial health, the United States entered World War I. Attendance fell in 1917 and plunged in 1918. The sixteen teams that welcomed nearly six-and-a-half million fans in 1916 saw that number drop by nearly four million in two years.[83] As the First World War ended in the fall, the country found itself fighting a new enemy: a worldwide Spanish Flu pandemic that killed more than 600,000 Americans. Fearful of what the future might hold, baseball officials announced that a reduced schedule implemented in 1918 would continue. Nowhere were the prospects more grim than in St. Louis with the Cardinals.

Team president Rickey became manager of the club in 1919. In part, this was due to the club's poor performance the previous year under Jack Hendricks, the man who replaced Huggins. Playing their only season for Hendricks in 1918, the Cardinals fell to the bottom of the standings. The team lost 15 players to the draft and service enlistments. The first-year manager repeatedly clashed with his talented young player, Rogers Hornsby, to the point that the infielder told Rickey he wouldn't play for the Cardinals as long as Hendricks managed the team.[84]

The move was also done to save money. The franchise had little left. The team lacked the resources to travel for spring training. It set up shop at nearby Washington University. The situation was so dire the club couldn't even afford new uniforms. "This is not to be a money-making venture," syndicate leader Jones had announced to the media back in 1917. He was true to his word. In January of 1919, the syndicate of investors still owed Helene Britton more than $100,000, and notes worth $89,000 on a second mortgage of the team's ballpark were due. Rumors again filled the papers that the team may be sold or go on the auction block. Some of this drama unfolded with Rickey away from the team.

Married with four children and approaching his thirty-seventh birthday, Rickey decided in the summer of 1918 he wanted to contribute to the war effort. "Perhaps it was foolish," he admitted, "but I developed a deep desire to fight, in combat if possible." His wife was shocked by the decision. "I thought about leaving him," Jane Rickey admitted years later.[85]

Commissioned as a major, Rickey went to France as part of the 1st Gas Regiment of the Chemical Warfare Service. He set sail from New York aboard the *USS President Grant*. Dozens of men on the ship never saw Europe. The flu pandemic that killed millions worldwide claimed the lives of more than 100 servicemen aboard.[86] Rickey also got sick but was diagnosed with bronchial pneumonia. He spent three weeks at a hospital in England, then arrived in France for training near the front lines. A Rickey adventure was never complete without some intellectual stimulation. "I am learning

French rapidly," he wrote to Cardinals treasurer H.W. Mason on October 18, "already have picked up enough to make myself understood."[87]

The Chemical Warfare Service attracted the stars of baseball. Rickey's unit eventually included Ty Cobb, Christy Mathewson and George Sisler, all future Hall of Fame players.[88] "Christy Mathewson and Branch Rickey are in Chemical," Cobb once explained as his reasons for joining. "They are guys I like and are friends." In France, the regiment taught doughboys defense techniques against poison gas. "We wound up drilling the damnedest bunch of culls that World War I ever grouped in one outfit," Cobb remembered. "The theory was that they would listen to well-known sports personalities – and to some extent it was effective. Those that gave us trouble and didn't heed orders didn't last long, for we weren't fooling around with simulated death when we entered the gas chambers."[89]

Thanks to the Armistice on November 11, Rickey's time in Europe was brief. He returned to New York from France on Christmas Day. On a ten-day furlough and still wearing his uniform, Major Rickey traveled to St. Louis on December 30. "I wasn't able to get in an actual battle," Rickey told reporters. "I have seen some sights I will remember all my life and later, when I have plenty of time, I want to describe them in detail."[90]

Out of the country and away from the game for months, Rickey was reluctant to talk baseball. "I succeeded in escaping a battery of newspapermen in New York," he said in St. Louis. "I refused to be interviewed after I had landed for the reason that baseball topics were strange to me, hence I feared I might say the wrong thing."[91]

Discharged from the Chemical Warfare Service in early 1919, Ricky resumed his role running the Cardinals. He also reunited with his ever-expanding family that had left for Ohio in his absence. In January, Rickey, his wife, mother-in-law, four children, and a maid, returned to St. Louis. There was much to do. Many of the tough decisions regarding the Cardinals had been postponed during the Rickey hiatus. The community-owned club had failed to meet its stockholder goals. The financial condition of the franchise had deteriorated to the point that a sale at auction was now seen as inevitable.

"Gardner To Bid At Auction Sale," read a *Post-Dispatch* headline on January 16. Russell Gardner was a multi-millionaire businessman whose automobile plant in St. Louis assembled Chevrolets and manufactured the bodies for the car company. He later sold his Chevrolet business to General Motors and launched the Gardner Motor Company, which produced a line of autos from 1920 to 1931. "I believe baseball is coming back better than ever," Gardner confidently and accurately predicted, "and my agents will be at the auction of the club prepared to go to the limit."[92]

The sale at auction, feared because the Cardinals lacked the money to pay off noteholders on a second mortgage of the team's ballpark, never materialized. It likely took a good negotiator to pull it off, and fortunately for the Cardinals, they had one. Twelve days after the auction story appeared, Rickey announced the second mortgage controversy had been settled. The terms were not disclosed.[93] Rickey would only say that the matter had been settled to the mutual satisfaction of all parties and that the club would not be sold.[94] Russell Gardner joined a long list of those who publicly stated a desire to buy the Cardinals only to come up short.

An "immensely pleased" Rickey also announced he had a new focus. Team vice president and major stockholder James C. Jones "has relieved me of all responsibilities connected to the financing of the Cardinals," Rickey said. "It's a well-known fact that I had time for little else last year. This alone has greatly encouraged me for I will now be able to devote my entire time to developing the club."[95]

Just days before, Rickey had officially added the title of Cardinals manager to his resume. The club reached a financial settlement with Jack Hendricks, who agreed to terminate his contract.[96] The news was the worst kept secret in St. Louis. Hendricks had been rumored to be on the way out since the end of the previous season. If there was ever any doubt, Hornsby helped seal his fate with an ultimatum in December. "If he returns as manager, I don't want to come back and I'll say frankly I don't have to." Hornsby told the press. "Mr. Rickey and I are the best of friends and if he manages the club, I'll be out there giving the best that's in me."[97]

Rickey had defended his star player in September. "Hornsby is not a hard boy to handle," he said at the end of the 1918 season, adding that Hendricks "rode him," called him "overrated," and a "$50,000 lemon." He also left no doubt what he considered the most crucial role on a team. "I consider a manager's job 90 percent of a baseball club," he stated not long before departing for Europe.[98]

The new manager found things just as challenging as the old manager did. Playing 137 games of a 140-game schedule, the Cardinals finished in seventh place in 1919, forty-and-a-half games behind the National League champion Cincinnati Reds. Rickey's Cardinals won 54 contests, just three more than the team did under Hendricks the previous season, also a shortened campaign in which the team played just 129 games.

St. Louis did make baseball history in 1919. For the first and only time in the major leagues, the Cardinals now had three straight managers with law degrees. Hendricks had graduated from law school at Northwestern and passed the bar in 1897. Along with Huggins (Cincinnati) and Rickey (Michigan), the trio are part of a group of just seven managers in the history of the game who once aspired to a career in law. (Years later, the Cardinals would add a fourth name to their list when the club hired Tony La Russa, a 1978 law school graduate of Florida State University.)[99]

Despite Rickey's impressive curriculum vitae, baseball wasn't in the business of awarding extra credit for knowledge of torts and contract law. The team was a consistent loser on the field and at the box office. While overall attendance came roaring back in 1919 – more than 6.5 million fans represented a jump of 131 percent from the prior year – the Cardinals finished last in all of baseball. The National League club's attendance of 167,059 amounted to a little more than half of what their hometown rival Browns attracted.[100]

The poor attendance came despite a vast community outreach program started by the new owners of the Cardinals. Any shareholder who spent $50 to buy two shares of stock gave the fan the right to give a season pass to a St. Louis youth. Insurance executive W.E. Billheimer is often credited with coming up with the idea that became known as the "Knothole Gang." But it was Rickey who greatly expanded the concept, essentially making it possible for any boy between the ages of 10 and 16 to attend a game for free. He partnered with organizations such as the Boy Scouts and the YMCA to get the word out and set up an executive committee to approve new members. The boys had to sign a pledge – "I will not at any time skip school to attend a game" – it read in part. A violation of the rules terminated club membership. With the pledge signed, a new member received a pass and a button. The Cardinals even set up a special outfield entrance for the Knothole Gang, whose members ran into the thousands. "The idea is big," wrote St. Louis sportswriter W.J. O'Connor, "and it is going over with a bang."[101]

With this program and other initiatives, team vice president Jones began talking of the "Cardinal Idea." The team introduced "noiseless" vendors and free scorecards. While the muzzle on the vendors "may have lessened the sale of pop and peanuts," wrote the *Post-Dispatch*, "it was a pleasant surprise to those who paid to see the game."[102] But as the 1919 attendance demonstrated, the courting of fans could only go so far without a competitive team. With Rickey, the Cardinals had innovative and experienced management. With Hornsby, the team had a talented player on the verge of stardom. What the franchise needed was a committed owner with the resources to end the chronic cash shortfalls.

Sam Breadon, much like unsuccessful Cardinals' suitor Russell Gardner, had made his money in the automobile industry. Partnering in St. Louis with Marion Lambert, Breadon launched a successful dealership in the early twentieth century. A small investor in the fan-owned syndicate, Breadon later increased his stake in the Cardinals and even loaned the team money. As he took a greater interest in the Cardinals, the team took a greater interest in him. Vice president Jones turned to Breadon after the 1919 season with an offer to become president of the franchise. He accepted with the condition the club reduce the number of people on its board of directors. The community-owned organization had nearly two-dozen directors telling management how to run the team. Breadon wanted the number cut to five. The two sides eventually compromised at seven.[103] With Breadon in charge, Rickey became a vice president while continuing to manage the club. The two men would work together for the next twenty-three seasons.

The hiring of the new team president proved to be one final stitch in the symmetrical knitting in the careers of Huggins and Rickey. In St. Louis, Rickey now had the owner he needed to acquire the necessary resources to compete in the National League against the likes of John McGraw's New York Giants. Right around the same time in Manhattan, Huggins got the player he wanted to steal the spotlight from McGraw's Giants. The new acquisition for the Yankees made front-page news on January 5, 1920. The new president for the Cardinals generated headlines exactly one week later, January 12, 1920.

It was a new year and a new era.

1920. The year Prohibition became law and changed American society.

1920. The year the Black Sox Scandal became public and changed baseball culture.

1920. The year Babe Ruth arrived in New York and changed everything.

---

[1] McDermott, J.R. "Miller Huggins, The Midget Manager." *Baseball Magazine*, October 1913.

[2] Writing at the National Pastime Museum website, Lawrence Richards estimated Huggins to be five feet three inches tall and 120 pounds. See thenationalpastimemuseum.com/article/miller-huggins. At the *Society For American Baseball Research* website, Steve Steinberg estimated Huggins was probably five feet one to five feet two inches tall and 125 pounds. See *Miller Huggins*, SABR.org. biography project.

[3] Other nicknames included "The Mighty Atom," "The Mighty Mite," "Little Everywhere," "Hug," and "Shrimp."

[4] *St. Louis Globe-Democrat*, January 5, 1914. Huggins insisted during his career he was born in 1880, a common move by players of his era who wanted to understate their age. "Huggins says, in telling of his experience on the ball field, that he was born March 27, 1880, reports to the contrary notwithstanding." According to biographers Stenberg and Spatz, his cemetery record lists his birth year as 1880, but "1878" is etched into the headstone.

[5] Ibid.

[6] Weintraub, Robert. *The House That Ruth Built: A New Stadium, The First Yankees Championship, And The Redemption of 1923*. Little, Brown & Company. 2911. Also see *St. Louis Star-Times*, June 9, 1943.

[7] *St. Louis Times,* May 4, 1914.

[8] Durocher, Leo with Ed Linn. *Nice Guys Finish Last*. Simon and Schuster. 1975. In the book, Durocher called Huggins "the best manager in baseball."

[9] *St. Louis Globe-Democrat*, March 7, 1915.

[10] Steinberg, Steve and Spatz, Lyle. *The Colonel and Hug: The Partnership That Transformed The New York Yankees.* University of Nebraska Press. 2015.

[11] Weintraub, *The House That Ruth Built.*

[12] *Baseball Magazine*, October 1913.

[13] Steinberg and Spatz, *The Colonel and Hug*. Ruppert and Huggins joined forces in a Florida real estate development. Huggins was a partner in the Smitz-Freeman Corporation, a real estate firm that owned a fifty-percent interest in Ruppert Beach. Ruppert owned the other fifty percent. Huggins was elected vice-president of the Ruppert Beach Development corporation in the fall of 1925. *Tampa Bay Times*, November 18 and December 31, 1925.

---

[14] Bob Connery, the scout who discovered Hornsby, purchased the St. Paul Saints at the end of 1924. Only after Miller Huggins died was it revealed that he owned a one-third interest in the team. Connery always refused to name his partners. St. Louis banker Leo Daly was thought to be a third investor. After the acquisition, the Yankees spent hundreds of thousands of dollars acquiring players from the St. Paul team. See *The St. Paul-New York Underground Railroad* by Steve Steinberg at SABR.org, originally published in the *2012 The National Pastime.* Scout Eddie Herr joined the Yankees after Connery left.
[15] Allen, Lee. *The Hot Stove League.* A.S. Barnes & Co. 1955.
[16] *St. Louis Post-Dispatch*, June 2, 1906.
[17] Ryan Holiday, author of *The Daily Stoic*, once described Epictetus and the *Enchiridion* this way: "Unlike the other powerful Stoics, Epictetus overcame incredible adversity. A slave who was banished from Rome, he eventually became a philosopher and opened a small school. Notes from his classes survive to us in what is called the *Enchiridion*, which translates as 'a small manual or a handbook' and it is exactly that. It is the perfect introduction to Epictetus as it is packed with short Stoic maxims and principles." See ryanholiday.net/ for more.
[18] *St. Louis Post-Dispatch*, July 5, 1914.
[19] Ibid, December 21, 1913.
[20] Lowenfish, *Branch Rickey.*
[21] Fountain, Charles. *Under The March Sun: The Story Of Spring Training.* Oxford University Press. 2009. The Cubs trained that spring in Tampa.
[22] When Al Lang Stadium opened in 1947, the Cardinals and Yankees were the spring training tenants.
[23] Shotton served as Rickey's Sunday manager starting in 1914 but infielder Jimmy Austin also served in the same role that season. According to a May 16, 1914 article in *Sporting Life*, Rickey was so pleased with Austin's performance, he was considering elevating him to the full-time manager's job.
[24] Polner, *Branch Rickey.*
[25] Ibid.
[26] *New York Times*, June 21, 1982. Hillenkoetter ran the CIA until 1950 and the outbreak of the Korean War. He then asked to return to the military. He died in 1982 at the age of 85. He is buried at Arlington National Cemetery.
[27] Both Bill Sr. and older brother Charley were vendors at Sportsman's Park. According to Charley, when Rickey switched teams in 1917, "the first employee he hired for the Cards" was his brother. Charley later became a scout for the Cardinals. *St. Louis Post-Dispatch*, February 3, 1949.
[28] *The Sporting News*, July 13, 1939.
[29] Ibid.
[30] Steinberg, Steve. *Del Pratt.* SABR.org biography project. Pratt, a University of Alabama graduate, played thirteen seasons in the major leagues, nine of them with either the

---

Browns or the Yankees. He played under both Rickey and Huggins and "was arguably was the best second-baseman of the second decade of the twentieth century."
[31] Steinberg, Steve. *Robert Hedges.* SABR.org biography project.
[32] Rickey, Branch. *The American Diamond: A Documentary of the Game of Baseball.* Simon & Schuster. 1965.
[33] Huhn, Rick. *The Sizzler: George Sisler, Baseball's Forgotten Great*. University of Missouri Press. 2004.
[34] *New York Times*, February 6, 1932.
[35] Huhn, *The Sizzler.*
[36] Ibid.
[37] Allen, Lee. *The American League Story*. Hill & Wang. 1962.
[38] Spink, J.G. Taylor. *Judge Landis and Twenty-Five Years of Baseball*. Thomas Y. Crowell Company. 1947.
[39] According to Steve Steinberg, Huggins had mixed feelings about the Mays acquisition. "Huggins was seen as a protégé of league president Ban Johnson." *Miller Huggins*, SABR.org biography project.
[40] Carney, Gene. *Burying The Black Sox. How Baseball's Cover-Up of the 1919 World Series Almost Succeeded*. Potomac Books, Inc. 2006.
[41] Levitt, Daniel R. *The Battle That Forged Modern Baseball: The Federal League Challenge And Its Legacy*. Ivan R. Dee. 2012.
[42] Ibid.
[43] *The Sporting News*, October 26, 1933.
[44] Ibid, October 20, 1932.
[45] Ibid.
[46] Ibid.
[47] *Baseball Magazine*, October 1915.
[48] Stifel is mentioned prominently during this period as a business partner of Phil Ball. The October 1915 *Baseball Magazine* article discusses the origins of ownership of the St. Louis Federal League team. A group of investors, known as the Thousand Dollar Club, "one by one melted away until there was only Phil Ball and myself remaining," Stifel is quoted as saying. An article from *The Sporting News* in 1917 describes Stifel as "one of the heavy stockholders in the St. Louis American League club." Phil Ball, late in his life, mentioned a different partner. "Harry Sinclair, the oil man, and I owned the franchise for St. Louis in the Federal League..." (*The Sporting News*, October 20, 1932.) Sinclair owned the Newark team in the Federal League. Cross-ownership and silent partners were common in the era. Ball also had interests in the oil industry. In a 1917 article, he is described as an "oil magnate." See *Sporting Life*, March 31, 1917.
[49] *Baseball Magazine*, October 1915.
[50] *St. Louis Post-Dispatch*, January 6, 1916.
[51] Lowenfish, *Branch Rickey.*
[52] Thomas, *Baseball's First Lady.*

---

[53] Ibid. Steinberg, *Baseball In St. Louis 1900-1925*. Steinberg estimated the price tag on the Browns was between $425,00 and $525,000. The St Louis Browns Historical Society has an excerpt from an undated and unnamed newspaper article showing the purchase price at $525,000. See www.thestlbrowns.com/#/history/the-early-years. *The Sporting News* obit on Hedges, April 28, 1932, put the price at $425,000. The difference may be explained by the fact that the new owners purchased the team and the Dodier Realty Company, which owned the ballpark. Counting salary and dividends, Hedges turned $30,000 into an estimated $765,000 in 14 years. *St. Louis Globe-Democrat*, February 1, 1916. Hedges' son, Robert Hedges Jr., married Sam Breadon's daughter, Frances, in 1929.
[54] *St. Louis Post-Dispatch*, December 19, 1916.
[55] When Julius Fleischmann died in 1925, he left an estate valued at more than $20 million. *Dayton Daily News*, May 15, 1925.
[56] *St. Louis Post-Dispatch*, October 26, 1917, Huggins "suffered a bitter disappointment in not being given a chance to buy the club himself – a chance promised him by Mrs. Britton," wrote John Wray.
[57] Ibid, February 28, 1917.
[58] Ibid, March 6, 1917.
[59] This explanation is frequently cited as the reason why the St. Louis Cardinals chose Rickey. There is also an alternative or additional explanation. According to an article in *Sporting Life*, the syndicate hit a wall in their fundraising efforts because none of the members had experience running a baseball team. "As a dying chance, Jones and his colleagues decided to put the popular Rickey at the head of the organization..." See *Sporting Life*, March 31, 1917.
[60] Herr had joined the Cardinals as a scout in 1913 for Miller Huggins. He later scouted for the Tigers where he is credited with discovering pitcher Carl Hubbell. He began scouting for the Yankees in 1926. Herr was a St. Louis native. *St. Louis Globe-Democrat,* December 16, 1928.
[61] *St. Louis Post-Dispatch*, March 6, 1917.
[62] *Sporting Life*, April 14, 1917.
[63] Ibid. Hedges never returned to the game as an owner. While he made money in baseball, he was clearly frustrated by the Browns' losing ways. "I'm sick and tired of having a loser and am determined to produce a winner or get out of baseball." *St. Louis Post-Dispatch*, January 26, 1913.
[64] Lowenfish, *Branch Rickey.*
[65] Sporting Life, April 7, 1917.
[66] Ibid, April 14, 1917. The three prospects are listed as "Legore of Yale, Brandel of Michigan, and Wright of Ohio State University." *Baseball Reference* lists Rasty Wright as a major league pitcher who played his college ball at Ohio State. He performed for the St. Louis Browns from 1917 to 1923, winning 24 and losing 19 games with an ERA of 4.05. See www.baseball-reference.com/players/w/wrighra02.shtml. *Baseball Reference* does not list anyone with the last names of Legore or Brandel playing in the relevant period, although

---

Elmer Brandell played one season of minor league baseball in 1917. The agreement also specified that Rickey and the Cardinals would use their best efforts to turn over to the Browns infielder Clyde "Tony" DeFate. DeFate played 14 games for the Cardinals and three more for the Detroit Tigers in 1917. He never played for the Browns and never appeared in a big-league game again after 1917.

[67] Lieb, *The St. Louis Cardinals.*

[68] Pythagorean winning percentage is an estimate of a team's winning percentage given their runs scored and runs allowed. It was developed by Bill James. See www.sports-reference.com/blog/baseball-reference-faqs/ for more.

[69] *The Sporting News*, July 12, 1917.

[70] *St. Louis Post-Dispatch*, October 26, 1917.

[71] Spink, *Judge Landis and Twenty-Five Years of Baseball.*

[72] See www.stlouisbbwaa.com/history/ for more.

[73] Frank, Stanley, "Bible of Baseball." *The Saturday Evening Post*, June 20, 1942.

[74] Ibid.

[75] Ibid, March 28, 1931.

[76] Spink, *Judge Landis and Twenty-Five Years of Baseball.*

[77] *The Saturday Evening Post*, June 20, 1942.

[78] Several accounts of Huggins' signing with the Yankees mention January of 1918 as to when the contract was signed. Writing in *The Sporting News* on October 21, 1943, Taylor Spink wrote that Jacob Ruppert kept delaying the offer until then. However, other accounts make clear the deal was done in October 1917. See *St. Louis Post-Dispatch* and *New York Times,* October 26, 1917. The headline of the *Times* article reads "Huggins Signed As Manager Of Yanks."

[79] *New York Times,* October 26, 1917.

[80] *St. Louis Post-Dispatch*, October 26, 1917. A sidebar wire service story says Huggins' salary with the Yankees was at least $10,000 and a small percentage of the profits. Other stories put his salary at $12,000. See *New York Times*, October 29, 1920.

[81] Smelser, Marshall. *The Life That Ruth Built.* Quadrangle/New York Times Book Co. 1975.

[82] Lieb, *The St. Louis Cardinals.*

[83] See ballparksofbaseball.com/1910-19attendance.htm for details.

[84] *St. Louis Post-Dispatch*, September 6, 1918.

[85] Polner, *Branch Rickey.* When Rickey left for Europe, his family returned to Ohio and put an ad in the paper. "RENT THE HOME OF Maj. Branch Rickey," it read. Located at 5405 Bartmer Avenue, the home had "11 rooms, 2 baths, hotwater heat, large garage; lot 67x230." *St. Louis Post-Dispatch*, August 25, 1918. A week earlier, a similar ad in the *Globe-Democrat* positioned the property for sale and noted it cost $17,000. "Sell My House At Once I'm Going Over," the ad quotes Rickey as saying. *St. Louis Globe-Democrat*, August 18,1918.

---

[86] Original estimates of the global number of people who died during the pandemic were in the 21 to 22 million range. More recent estimates put the totals at 50 million or more. www.cdc.gov/flu/pandemic-resources/1918-pandemic-h1n1.html.
[87] *St. Louis Post-Dispatch*, November 8, 1918.
[88] Cobb, Mathewson, and Rickey all spent time in France. Sisler was preparing to deploy when the Armistice was signed.
[89] Gurtowski, Richard. "Remembering Baseball Hall of Famers Who Served in the Chemical Corps." *Army Chemical Review*, July-December 2005. Gurtowski cites Cobb's autobiography *My Life In Baseball: The True Record.*
[90] *St. Louis Post-Dispatch*, December 30, 1918.
[91] Ibid.
[92] Ibid, January 16, 1919.
[93] Ibid, May 8, 1922. When Sam Breadon took a controlling interest in the Cardinals in 1922, the prior financial difficulties of the team were chronicled and perhaps gave a clue as to how the mortgage debt was settled. "At one stage, 70 members assessed themselves $90,000 to make a payment." That payment likely went for the mortgage or to pay Helene Britton.
[94] Ibid, January 28, 1919.
[95] Ibid.
[96] *New York Times*, January 26, 1919.
[97] *St. Louis Post-Dispatch*, December 17, 1918.
[98] Ibid, September 6, 1918.
[99] The seven men with law degrees are Jack Hendricks, Miller Huggins, Hughie Jennings, Tony La Russa, Branch Rickey, Muddy Ruel, and Monte Ward. Ruel is a St. Louis native who broke into the big leagues with the St. Louis Browns and attended law school at Washington University, giving the city a connection to five of the seven. When Cleveland's Ray Chapman in 1920 became the only player ever hit and killed by a baseball, Carl Mays was the pitcher. Ruel was the catcher.
[100] The Browns drew 349,350 fans that season. See ballparksofbaseball.com/1910-19attendance.htm.
[101] Rickey biographers and Cardinal historians typically credit Billheimer with the plan but others, such as James C. Jones, played a role. An April 1, 1917 article in the *St. Louis Post-Dispatch* mentions the "boy idea" and says it was "conceived by Jones and executed by W.E. Billheimer." But as W.J. O'Connor's article makes clear, the original idea and Rickey's concept of a Knothole Gang were two entirely different systems. By June of 1917, only 1,415 stockholder passes had been issued. "Approximately 1,000 of these have been reassigned to the club to use under the new system," wrote O'Connor. "Rickey estimates that at least 30,000 different boys will be reached," he added. Neither Billheimer nor Jones is mentioned. See *St. Louis Post-Dispatch*, June 26, 1917.
[102] *St. Louis Post-Dispatch*, April 1, 1917.
[103] The club had 21 directors in 1919. The number dropped to seven by 1922. *St. Louis Star*, January 14, 1919, *St. Louis Post-Dispatch*, January 25, 1922.

Things Happened in St. Louis

As a sportswriter for the New York *Daily News*, Marshall Hunt's job was to cover Babe Ruth. Not the Yankees, the team Ruth joined in 1920. JUST Ruth. The baseball calendar didn't matter. "We covered him twelve months of the year," Hunt recalled.[1] "I don't think he was ever aware of his role as a circulation builder." As a result, the two men, the famous ballplayer and the chronicler of all things Bambino, spent a lot of time together.

The duo was on their way to Hot Springs, Arkansas one winter before the start of spring training. Coming from the East Coast, they had to change trains in St. Louis. "There was one whale of a crowd in St. Louis," remembered Hunt. The travelers had just enough time to get a bite to eat before the nine o'clock train to Hot Springs. They navigated their way through the gathered masses toward the taxi stand with the Babe complying with multiple autograph requests. "Babe was autographing any old thing, ladies' sweaters, anything that would take ink."

When the commotion finally dissipated, the taxi driver asked Ruth where he wanted to go. To the House of Good Shepherd came the reply. "Of course, that was St. Louis' leading hook shop. And everyone in the audience knew it," remembered Hunt. "And they thought Babe deserved a hand on that one, and he got it, too." As the taxi pulled away from the curb, a pack of children followed along. "To the House of Good Shepherd," they cried. Once there, the two men had dinner and the Babe had something else in mind for dessert. He paid for the company of one young woman and then got a bonus. "I think he got one on the house that night. Then we went down and got on the train."

Hunt made no mention of his after-dinner activities, but he was impressed with the cuisine at the St. Louis bordello. "The House of Good Shepherd served the best steaks ever served in this world."

During his twenty-two-year big-league career, the Babe appeared in 360 regular-season games against the Browns and five regular-season contests against the Cardinals at the end of his career, along with 11 World Series games against the Redbirds. From 1914 to 1935, Ruth played at Sportsman's Park 178 times in the regular season. He enjoyed his frequent visits to the city. "I always had a lot of high-living friends [in St. Louis]," Ruth remembered after his playing days were over. "St. Louis might have been Ruth's favorite town on the road," wrote Ruth biographer Leigh Montville. "Things happened in St. Louis." Indeed they did. Some of the stories may even be true.

There was the time Ruth and the Yankees came to town during a brutal heatwave. The Babe went through 22 silk shirts in three days. He left all of them to the hotel maid.

Ruth had a ritual when he left town. "Whenever we left St. Louis, we left out of what they call Brandon Avenue, this suburban station," remembered long-time Ruth teammate Waite Hoyt. "Ruth knew some people, and he always, when we left like that, he'd have a few gallons of home brew delivered to the train plus about 15 or 20 racks of spareribs."[2]

The Yankees had their own car on the train which meant the ladies' room was always unoccupied. "Ruth would take over the ladies' room and set up shop and for 50 cents you could have all the beer and spareribs you wanted."

One sparerib story involving Ruth featured a different form of transportation. After the final game of a series against the Browns, Ruth's attendance was requested at a local event that required him to miss the train. Hunt, Ruth's constant traveling companion, phoned Yankees general manager Ed Barrow and asked if they could miss the train and catch a flight that night instead. "Goddamn you. You're going to kill that bastard yet!" came the reply from Barrow, who reluctantly agreed to the arrangement.

At the airport that night, the plane was delayed until a package arrived for Ruth. In another version of the story, Ruth already had the package in hand because it was given to him by a woman at a party that evening. Either way, when the pilot enquired as to the content, Ruth replied, "Spareribs. I'm gonna open'em up right now 'cause I'm hungry."

The plane – "an old TWA shaker" – had only two passengers, Ruth and Hunt. As the two men chowed down, the smell of the spareribs made its way up to the cockpit. A surprised Hunt looked up to see the pilot walking back toward them. "I think he had it on automatic," Hunt suspected.

The pilot joined in the feast and asked Hunt to go to the cabin and watch the controls. By the time the plane landed, about thirty pounds of ribs were gone. "We ate them all," remembered Hunt. "I've often wondered what the janitor thought when he cleaned up that plane. Piles and piles of sparerib bones. They were delicious."

In 1921, the Southern Presbyterian General Assembly held a banquet in St. Louis. Ruth was invited to be the guest speaker. We are left to guess what the libertine slugger told the assembled. A two-paragraph story in *The New York Times* makes no mention of the specifics of the Babe's speech, but we do know he couldn't stay long. The home-run king left the dinner because of another engagement.[3]

Whenever Ruth couldn't come to the fans, the fans would come to him. One year in the locker room in St. Louis, three cowboys were ushered in to meet him. They had ridden on horseback for three days to a depot in Wyoming where they boarded a train for Missouri. "Baby Ruth," said one of the cowboys, "I've ridden all the way to St. Louis to see you hit home runs."[4]

Over the years, hundreds of thousands of fans in St. Louis saw him do just that. Of Babe Ruth's 714 career home runs, 58 of them were hit at Sportsman's Park, the third-highest total of any visiting stadium. The one hit on July 21, 1915 was called the "longest home run ever witnessed at the American League ball park."[5] Four years later, in 1919, his last year with the Boston Red Sox, he hit an even longer home run in St. Louis. Sportsman's Park was one of four stadiums that season where Ruth was credited with the longest home run in history. A 1921 home run in St. Louis traveled an estimated 550 feet.[6] His most significant home runs in St. Louis didn't come against the Browns in the regular season, but rather against the Cardinals in the World Series. Of the Babe's 15 career World Series home runs, seven of them came against the Cardinals. All but one of those came in St. Louis. Many of Ruth's most famous and infamous World Series moments as a Yankee have a St. Louis connection. As we'll see later, those iconic accomplishments are still a part of baseball lore and mythology.

Perhaps it's no surprise that Ruth, the son of parents with German roots and the product of a Catholic education, identified so strongly with St. Louis, a city whose baseball history was strongly influenced by its German-Catholic heritage. A loosely tethered connection still exists between the Babe, his hometown of Baltimore, and St. Louis. When the Browns left St. Louis after the 1953 season, the team became the Baltimore Orioles. Before the Orioles, Baltimore lost an American League team to New York in 1903. That team eventually became known as the Yankees. The greatest stretch in Orioles history occurred from 1969 to 1971 when the team won three consecutive pennants and one World Series title. Their manager was St. Louis native Earl Weaver. Weaver's father was a dry cleaner who used to clean the uniforms of both the Browns and the Cardinals. Ruth's father operated a saloon on Camden Street in Baltimore. The location of that saloon is now shallow center field in Camden Yards, where the Orioles have played their home games since 1992.

*****

George Herman Ruth Jr. was born in Baltimore in February of 1895. George Sr., his saloon-keeping father, and Kate, his mother, had at least six children, possibly as many as eight.[7] Only two survived infancy, George and a younger sister, Mary Margaret, known as Mamie.

George Sr. and Kate's surviving son was a hell-raiser almost from the start. An often-told story from his youth has young George taking money from the till at his father's saloon and spending it on ice cream for his friends. When his father found out, he beat him with a horsewhip. "Daddy used to beat him something terrible," Mamie once admitted.[8]

The future home-run king was not deterred. He responded by stealing even more money out of the cash register. "I honestly don't remember being aware of the difference between right and wrong," Ruth later confessed. He spent a lot of time on the streets of Baltimore, not uncommon for children of his era. "Most city children of medium-poor parents grew up in the streets, unguided," wrote historian and Ruth biographer Marshall Smelser. "His early childhood was bleak, but not crippling."[9] Speaking of the working-class neighborhood of Baltimore known as Pigtown, the Babe later described it as "a rough, tough neighborhood, but I liked it."

While he enjoyed it, others around him did not appreciate his behavior. "I learned to fear and hate the coppers and to throw apples and eggs at the truck drivers," remembered Ruth.[10] Labeled "incorrigible or vicious" and "beyond the control" of his mother and father, his parents sent their son packing in June of 1902. [11] His father dropped him off at the St. Mary's Industrial School for Orphans, Delinquent, Incorrigible, and Wayward Boys located four miles southwest of downtown Baltimore. Young George was seven years old.

A more modern interpretation may reveal the source of Ruth's issues. "He had ADHD (Attention Deficit Hyperactive Disorder), no doubt about it," said his granddaughter Linda Tosetti. "He was always moving. He couldn't sleep, didn't have to sleep."[12]

Another issue was the relationship between Ruth's parents. They were getting a divorce. "His mother and father separated," said Julia Ruth Stevens. The Babe's adopted daughter, who died in 2019 at the age of 102, once told writer Jane Leavy, "He stayed with his father until he couldn't control him anymore and sent him off to St. Mary's."[13]

Life at St. Mary's must have come as quite a shock to a seven-year-old child accustomed to roaming the streets of Baltimore. Run by the Xaverian Brothers, a Roman Catholic order, the school, described as "part reformatory, part orphanage, part trade school and part foster home," by the *Baltimore Sun*, put a big focus on discipline.[14]

A bell rang every morning at 6:00 a.m. to wake up the approximately eight hundred students, ranging in age from 5 to 21. They made their beds, attended mass and had breakfast (meals eaten in silence) before the start of class at 7:30. Bedtime was 8:00 p.m. The school day was spent divided between classwork and learning an industrial trade. At the age of 12, Ruth went to work in the tailor shop and learned to make shirts. The Babe's second wife, Julia's mother, used to enjoy watching her husband, making $80,000 a year at the height of his fame, "carefully turning the collars of his $30 Sulka shirts by himself, and doing a perfect job."[15]

At St. Mary's, Ruth took communion and adopted the Catholic faith which he practiced for the rest of his life. New York sportswriter Westbrook Pegler recalled running into Ruth one Sunday morning at the St. Louis Cathedral on the city's Central West End. The Babe, whose "mornings began when evenings ended," would frequently drag along his Saturday night companion to an early morning mass.[16]

A couple of things happened during his time at St. Mary's that would have an impact on Ruth for years to come. The Babe's physical features, notably his lips and broad nose, attracted the attention of his fellow students. They nicknamed him "Niggerlips."

Rumors about Ruth's ancestry would follow him to the big leagues. "Some of Babe's teammates on the Boston Red Sox were convinced he had Negro blood," recalled long-time sportswriter Fred Lieb. "There was quite a bit of talk about that. Many of the players, when they wanted to badger him, called him 'nigger.'"[17]

The biggest impact at St. Mary's came from the man who changed Ruth's life, Brother Matthias Boutlier. Brother Matthias stood six feet six inches tall and weighed 250 pounds. At St. Mary's, he was the prefect of discipline. The boys at the school referred to him as the Boss. "He was the greatest man I have ever known," Ruth said about him on more than one occasion. Ruth also paid close attention to the way Brother Matthias swung a baseball bat. "I would just stand there and watch him, bug-eyed," he remembered. "I think I was born as a hitter the first day I ever saw him hit a baseball."[18] With his uppercut swing, the Boss could hit long, impressive fly balls and he ran with a pigeon-toed stride that Ruth imitated.

Brother Matthias was in charge of physical activity. In early twentieth-century America, when the game truly was the national pastime, that primarily meant baseball. St. Mary's had dozens of baseball teams. Ruth played every day from March to October. He probably played 200 games a year, including three contests every Sunday. Ruth played all over the field but mainly at catcher for many seasons. A left-handed thrower playing with a right-handed glove, he would catch the ball, dispose of the mitt while tossing the ball in the air, snag it and fire it back to the pitcher.

Ruth didn't get on the mound until he was 16 years old. "Ruth took to pitching because he was big and left-handed and could throw hard," wrote biographer Robert Creamer.[19] It didn't take long for others to notice his ability. Jack Dunn, owner of the minor league Baltimore Orioles in the International League, came calling in early 1914. On Valentine's Day, he made it official. He signed Ruth to a contract for $600 a year.[20] The new professional soon left for spring training in Fayetteville, North Carolina. At the age of 19, Ruth left the city of Baltimore for the first time in his life. When a player in camp asked who the new lefthander was, someone supposedly replied, "He's one of Jack Dunn's babes."[21] The nickname stuck. He's been Babe Ruth ever since.

He didn't stay in Baltimore long. The Federal League, an upstart challenger to Organized Baseball, had a team in Baltimore. The Baltimore Terriers stadium was directly across the street from the Orioles. The Terriers opener drew 28,000. The Orioles exhibition game that day drew 1,000. The Orioles played one game that year in front of 17 fans. Owner Dunn began considering moving the franchise. Needing cash, he started selling players. Ruth, pitcher Ernie Shore, and catcher Ben Egan were soon sold to the Boston Red Sox. The price tag has been estimated as low as $8,500 and as high as $25,000.

Ruth and his teammates took an overnight train to Boston. Less than five months after leaving St. Mary's, he was in the big leagues. The Babe pitched and won the very next day, the first big league game he ever saw. By the fall, he was a married man. It was in Boston that his personality began to fully emerge, with stories about his behavior and habits that would only be amplified once he had the money and the media spotlight that New York provided.

Of the woman he married in the fall of 1914, Ruth wrote in his autobiography that Helen Woodring, a Boston coffee-shop waitress, hailed from Nova Scotia. Actually, Helen *Woodford* was born in Boston.[22]

At a St. Louis speakeasy one night, Ruth opened up to a New York sportswriter about his memory issues. "You know, it's damn embarrassing. I can't remember names. I can remember every ball pitched to me, what I hit, and what I didn't hit. But names go like that. Like the other day this guy comes in to pitch against us. I've known him for ten years but I couldn't remember his name. So I called over to whatchamacallit in centerfield."

"Whatchamacallit in centerfield" was Ruth's longtime Yankee teammate Earle Combs. As the story continued, Ruth ordered another drink and then told the writer, "But I think I'm getting better, Joe." Ruth's drinking partner that night in St. Louis was *John* Drebinger of *The New York Times*. "I almost slid off the couch," remembered Drebinger years later. "To his dying day, he never called me anything but Joe."[23]

Many of Ruth's drinking stories are told in a light-hearted fashion, full of mirth and merriment, but there is a darker side here. Author Glenn Stout put it bluntly. Ruth was likely an alcoholic. "It's a measure of Ruth's enduring power that so few of his biographers have ever uttered the word alcoholic in the same sentence as the name Babe Ruth, because that's almost certainly what he was."[24]

Ruth himself admitted he had a violent temper much like his father. It occasionally found an outlet on the baseball field. Pitching for the Red Sox in 1917, Ruth walked the first batter of the game. He expressed his disapproval of the ball-strike calls to the home plate umpire. The exchange escalated. Umpire Brick Owens ejected Ruth from the game. Ruth responded by punching Owens. "Manager Barry and several policemen had to drag Ruth off the field," according to an account from the Boston Globe.[25]

Ruth's replacement was Ernie Shore. The baserunner was retired on a steal attempt and Shore proceeded to retire the next twenty-six batters in a row. For years baseball treated it as a perfect game for Shore. In 1991, a committee revised it to a two-man no-hitter – Ruth and Shore. It's the only no-hitter of Ruth's career.

The offseason following the no-hitter, Ruth was involved in a car wreck. The Babe had a role in numerous accidents over the years (again, alcohol a likely role-player), leading to frequent rumors that Ruth was either dead or severely injured. On this night, he tried to drive his car between two trolley cars near Fenway Park. Ruth was not injured, but an unnamed woman with him required hospitalization.[26]

Red Sox historian Stout noted that the area around Fenway Park was known as a red-light district when Ruth played there. His teammates suspected Ruth's young bride, 17 at the time of their marriage, was likely either the first woman he had sex with or the first he didn't have to pay. He didn't stay faithful long, and while he frequently preferred the no-strings-attached method of sex for cash, he wasn't above seeking companionship from a married woman. "Stories of Ruth's nighttime escapades were well known among Boston's working men...and some of their wives," Stout wrote. [27]

Abused by his father, abandoned by his mother, the Babe adopted the Mae West philosophy to life: "Too much of a good thing can be wonderful." He drank too much. He ate too much. Careless in his personal life, he wrecked cars, blew through money, and wasn't picky about his women. "I never saw him on an expedition with anybody who was very attractive and he had some awful horses up in Boston," said one acquaintance. Marshall Hunt agreed. "Some of Babe's paramours for a day would only appeal to a man who was just stepping out of prison after serving a fifteen-year sentence."[28]

He was also one hell of a pitcher. Ruth's Red Sox won three World Series titles during his time in Boston. In 1915, the Sox beat the Philadelphia Phillies. Ruth didn't pitch in that series but did make one pinch-hitting appearance against Grover Cleveland Alexander. He grounded out to first base. Ruth and Alexander wouldn't face each other again until the 1926 World Series.

Ruth pitched brilliantly in both the 1916 and 1918 World Series. He recorded 29 2/3 innings of shutout baseball, a World Series record that would last 43 years. After 1918, Ruth never pitched again in a World Series. He finished his career with a perfect 3-0 record in postseason play.

An accomplished regular-season pitcher as well, Ruth won 47 games over a two-season stretch and led the American League with a 1.75 ERA in 1916. But the longer he pitched, the less he enjoyed it. Ruth, who grew up admiring Brother Matthias and those long fly balls on the playgrounds of St. Mary's, wanted to hit and play every day. Short of players because of World War I, the Red Sox gradually gave Ruth his chances. In 1918, Ruth started his first game in the outfield. It came against the St. Louis Browns. In 317 at-bats, he hit 11 home runs that season – tied for the league lead.

In another game against St. Louis that same year, he pitched and beat the Browns 3-1. On that very night, August 24, 1918, his father lay dying on the streets of Baltimore. George Sr. got into a fight with his brother-in-law outside his bar in Baltimore. He fell on the street and fractured his skull. Taken to a hospital, he died shortly thereafter. Citing self-defense, the coroner dropped all charges. Ruth never spoke publicly about his father's death.

The tipping point in Ruth's career came in the 1919 season. He appeared as a pitcher in just 17 games, starting 15 of them, and compiling just 133 1/3 innings, his lowest marks since his rookie season of 1914. But as a hitter, Ruth made 543 plate appearances. His 29 home runs and 113 RBI led the league. He also hit .322 that year.

After making his case in 1919 to be an everyday player, Ruth wanted more money. Red Sox owner Harry Frazee, though, needed more cash. Frazee owned the Red Sox but not Fenway Park. Frazee, who made his money as a Broadway producer, had financed his purchase of the Boston club. The note was held by the previous owner, John Lannin. A payment on the note was due. Frazee also wanted to buy Fenway Park (not owned by Lannin but a separate group) and was in negotiations to buy the Harris Theatre in New York. The Red Sox owner, along with the owners of the Chicago White Sox and New York Yankees, was also in the middle of a bitter feud with American League president Ban Johnson. They wanted to oust him from the job. But the owners of the other five American League clubs, notably Phil Ball of the St. Louis Browns, remained steadfast Johnson loyalists.

Frazee had just given Ruth a new contract before the 1919 season, a three-year deal at $10,000 a season. Now Ruth was demanding more money. From Frazee's perspective, he had a valuable asset in Ruth but also a temperamental star who had proven to be quite a pain in the ass. The Red Sox owner had adjusted Ruth's contract in the middle of the 1918 season when the pitcher-turned-outfielder clashed with his manager over his role and threatened to play baseball for a shipyard in Chester, Pennsylvania. On the last day of the 1919 season, Ruth left the team to play in an exhibition game in Baltimore. Now he wanted $20,000 a year or else. The Babe was dropping hints that he had options, including a potential career as a professional boxer. Now Frazee had to weigh his options. Maybe it was time to sell high. Could Ruth top that 1919 campaign? The idea then that a hitter could consistently pile up large home run numbers was met with incredible skepticism. This was the Deadball Era, where home runs were thought to be more happy accident than skillful display.

Because of the feud with AL president Johnson, Frazee only had two reliable trading partners, the White Sox and the Yankees. The White Sox offered outfielder Joe Jackson and $60,000. Frazee turned down the offer. The Red Sox owner needed more leverage to swing a better deal. He found it in St. Louis.

Cardinals second baseman Rogers Hornsby was just 23 years old in 1919. He hit .318 that season, the third time in four years he had crossed the .300 mark. The New York Giants wanted him. Giants manager John McGraw was reportedly offering the Cardinals four players and $70,000.[29] St. Louis didn't make the deal, but Frazee had to ask if the Cardinals could get that much for Hornsby, what could he get for Ruth? He was about to find out.[30]

With the business of Broadway his focus, Frazee lived on New York's Upper East Side, the same area of the city Yankees co-owner Jacob Ruppert called home. Frazee was a frequent drinking partner of the other Yankees owner, Til Huston. Ruppert and Huston could give Frazee what he wanted most; the cash to pay off Lannin, finance the purchase of the ballpark and pursue his other real estate interests.

The men who ran the Yankees had their own issues. Huston and Ruppert paid rent to the New York Giants for their team to play at the Polo Grounds. American League president Johnson was trying to gain control of the lease to force new ownership on the Yankees. [31] With an uncertain future at the Polo Grounds and playing in the same ballpark with the far more successful Giants, the Yankees needed star power to compete. "For years, the Yankees had been what the St. Louis Browns would later become, an afterthought in their own town, virtually colorless, the beat nobody wanted," is how one writer described them.[32] Ruppert had asked Yankees manager Miller Huggins what the team needed after the 1919 season. "Get me Ruth," came the reply from Huggins, who joined the Yankees in 1918 after managing the St. Louis Cardinals. Finally, with Prohibition starting in January 1920, the brewery-owning Ruppert needed baseball more than ever.

This confluence of events led to what is viewed in hindsight as the most lopsided trade in baseball history, but at the time, met a variety of needs on both sides of the deal. The Yankees got Ruth for $100,000 (reported then at $125,000) and Ruppert made a personal loan to Frazee for $300,000. The collateral for the loan was Fenway Park, which the Red Sox owner purchased with the proceeds. Frazee got the money he needed. The Yankees got the star they desired.

Ruth didn't hit his first home run for the Yankees until May 1, 1920. He hit eleven more home runs that month. On July 15, against the St. Louis Browns, he hit his 29th home run of the year, tying the record he set the previous year. He still had 61 games left to play. That same month, the *New York Times* proclaimed, "The New York fandom has surrendered to the Yankees..."[33] New York was a Giants town when the 1920s began. That was changing. John McGraw's team won the World Series in 1905 and won four pennants in the 1910s. The Yankees had yet to win a single pennant. That would soon change. The Babe finished the 1920 season with 54 home runs. He also hit .376, had 135 RBI, scored 158 runs and walked 150 times. Freed from pitching duties (he appeared as a pitcher in just one game in 1920), Ruth led the league in home runs, RBI, runs scored, walks, on-base and slugging percentage for a third-place Yankees team. Ruth finished second in the league in total bases behind George Sisler. The St. Louis Browns first baseman also won the batting title with an average of .407. Otherwise, it was an almost clean sweep of the major offensive categories for the Yankee outfielder. Ruth alone hit more home runs than 14 of the other 15 teams in baseball.

Validation for the Yankees owners came at the turnstiles. Nearly 1.3 million fans came to the Polo Grounds that season to watch American League baseball. The Yankees became the first team in baseball history to attract a million fans in a season. They outdrew their landlord, the National League Giants, by more than 300,000. The Yankees pre-tax profit for 1920 was $660,000.[34]

Fans clearly preferred long ball to dead ball. In 1918, when Ruth tied for the American League lead in home runs with 11, the entire league hit 96. In 1920, total American League home runs jumped nearly four-fold to 369. Two years later, the total stood at 525. Many factors played a role: the spitball made illegal, better quality baseballs, and more of them. Clean white balls began to replace soiled ones with increasing frequency after the death of Cleveland's Ray Chapman (hit in the head with a pitch in a game against Ruth's Yankees in 1920).

The influence of Ruth, however, was undeniable. Before the Babe, the emphasis was on small ball, generating offense by making contact, employing the hit-and-run, and stealing bases. Ruth wasn't satisfied to just make contact, he was trying to hit home runs. "I swing as hard as I can," he would tell reporters. Standing deep in the box, he took an uppercut swing and never choked up. The Babe made it acceptable to strikeout. Other players noticed. Other owners did too. "I have yet to hear a fan boo a home run," said St. Louis Cardinals president Sam Breadon.[35]

Ruth's pioneering approach at the plate was a revelation and a revolution. "The change between the baseball of the teens and the baseball of the twenties was the most sudden and dramatic change of the twentieth century," wrote Bill James.

*****

The Babe made at least $35,000 in 1920 – and likely a lot more – from baseball, endorsements, a postseason barnstorming tour, and a movie called *Headin' Home*.[36] Shot during the season in New Jersey, Ruth would act in the morning and play baseball in the afternoon, showing up at the park in makeup and mascara. Paid $15,000 upfront, he received another check for $35,000. When he went to cash the second check, he was told the movie company was bankrupt and out of business. The silent film, based on a mythologized history of Ruth's life, had its debut at Madison Square Garden.

That same year featured perhaps the most famous of all Ruth's car wrecks. The Babe was driving from Washington to New York on the night of July 6 accompanied by wife Helen, two Yankee teammates and a coach. Just outside Wawa, Pennsylvania, the car, with Ruth at the wheel, skidded off the road and flipped over into a ditch. Amazingly, outside of a few bumps and bruises, the Babe and his four passengers were all relatively unscathed. Ruth's crew spent the night at a farmhouse down the road. When a mechanic came out to inspect the damaged car the next day, Ruth told him to sell it. "Take whatever you can get for it. I'm through with it."[37]

Ruth and his traveling companions got a ride into Philadelphia where they discovered to their surprise the news of their accident had made headlines. RUTH REPORTEDLY KILLED IN CAR CRASH.[38] Although he banged up his knee in the wreck, Ruth was still very much alive. The next day at the Polo Grounds, he was back in the lineup and hit a triple, having arrived in New York in a brand-new car.

The Babe went on a barnstorming tour after the season was over and then left for a trip to Cuba in late October. New York Giants manager John McGraw had organized a team to play in a dozen games. While there, Ruth was the victim of a sting at the racetrack. The swindlers offered him a "sure-thing" bet. When the Babe won big, he continued taking their advice. The hook was set. When it was all over, Ruth had lost thousands of dollars. Whatever the amount (estimates range from $25,000 to $130,000), the Babe may have lost more money at the track than he had made in his entire baseball career.[39] Ruth biographer Kal Wagenheim says the slugger twice telegraphed his bank in New York for more money and had to escape a mob of angry bookmakers. When he confessed to wife Helen, "I'm cleaned out," she produced a checking account with $30,000 in it that she had kept secret from her husband.[40] The Ruths were able to leave the island debt free. Returning to the states short of cash,

Ruth played exhibition basketball that winter. He had to borrow money to pay his income taxes.

Ruth was not the only American gambler to discover in the fall of 1920 that he had been the victim of a fix. The Chicago "Black Sox" Scandal became public news in late September of that year. Eight Chicago White Sox players were indicted for their role in allegedly attempting to fix the 1919 World Series won by the Cincinnati Reds.

Viewed in a vacuum, gambling on horses didn't necessarily present a problem for the Babe or any other player. The larger issue was the potential threat it posed. Ruth became quickly indebted to bookmakers in Cuba – "cleaned out" – what if it somehow happened again? How far would he or any other ballplayer be willing to go to pay them back? It's here where the potential goes from betting on an uncertain outcome to the temptation of conspiring to fix a pre-determined fate.

No one has suggested Ruth had anything to do with the Black Sox scandal or any other game-fixing affair, but it's easy to see how the worlds of gamblers and ballplayers intermingled in those days. Ruth played for many years in Boston where gambling in the stands was rampant. One of the suspected ringleaders of the Black Sox scandal was a Boston gambler by the name of Sport Sullivan, estimated to have made $50,000 off the 1919 World Series. "Sullivan was familiar to every Red Sox player of the era," wrote Stout.[41] When Ruth left Boston for New York, he moved into the Ansonia Hotel on Manhattan's Upper West Side. It's alleged that one of the planning meetings of the 1919 World Series fix took place there. Arnold Rothstein, a financier of the plot, lived at the Ansonia for a time. Giants manager McGraw, who organized Ruth's trip to Cuba, was a partner with Rothstein in a New York City pool hall. Rothstein had season tickets to Giants games. Ruth's 1920 movie may have been partially financed by Abe Attell, another prominent name mentioned in connection with the fix.

The Black Sox scandal would lay open just how influential bettors had become and the damage wrought by years of looking the other way when it came to gamblers and their impact on the sport. When the day of reckoning came, baseball would emerge as a very different business. As we've seen, one of those shifts in the game was the meteoric rise of the home run, a charge led by Ruth in the American League. Talent development and the alignment of the minor leagues with major league counterparts would be another dramatic innovation. Rickey and the Cardinals would be at the forefront of that development. Finally, baseball's feuding owners settled on a new ruling structure that put absolute power in the hands of one man, Commissioner Kenesaw Mountain Landis, a man both Ruth and Rickey clashed with over the years.

With Landis in charge, the Black Sox Scandal was ultimately settled. And just as with the life of Ruth, the connections to St. Louis are many. Former Browns first baseman Comiskey now owned the Chicago White Sox. Just days after the 1919 World Series ended, he sent investigators to the city he once called home.

St. Louis gamblers had a story to tell.

---

[1] Holtzman, Jerome. (editor). *No Cheering in the Press Box.* Holt, Rinehart and Winston. 1974.
[2] Montville, Leigh. *The Big Bam. The Life and Times of Babe Ruth.* Doubleday. 2006. Hoyt was likely referring to the train stop at Bremen Avenue.
[3] *New York Times*, May 21, 1921.
[4] Wagenheim, Karl. *Babe Ruth: His Life And Legend*. Praeger Publishers. 1974.
[5] Smelser, *The Life That Ruth Built.*
[6] Ibid.
[7] Leavy, Jane. *The Big Fella: Babe Ruth and The World He Created*. Harper. 2018. "The births of six children and the deaths of four them have been verified," Leavy wrote. Ruth's sister Mamie told biographer Smelser there were eight births and six deaths.
[8] Leavy, Jane. "Being Babe Ruth's Daughter." Grantland.com. January 3, 2012.
[9] Smelser, *The Life That Ruth Built.*
[10] Creamer, Robert W. *Babe: The Legend Comes To Life*. Simon & Schuster Paperbacks. 1974, 2005.
[11] Ibid.
[12] Montville, *The Big Bam.*
[13] Leavy, "Being Babe Ruth's Daughter." Ruth's parents were divorced in 1906. George Sr. was awarded custody of the children.
[14] *Baltimore Sun*, February 3, 1995.
[15] Creamer, *Babe.*
[16] Smelser, *The Life That Ruth Built.*
[17] Holtzman, *No Cheering in the Press Box.*
[18] Considine, Bob and Ruth, Babe. *The Babe Ruth Story.* E.P. Dutton. 1948.
[19] Creamer, *Babe.*
[20] Accounts vary. Montville places the value of the contract at $250 a month. One of the men who joined Dunn in scouting Ruth was Fritz Maisel. Maisel was a Maryland native who played six seasons in the big leagues, his last one for the St. Louis Browns in 1918.
[21] In another version of the story, players began calling him "a babe in the woods."
[22] Wagenheim, *Babe Ruth* and Leavy, *The Big Fella.* Mary Ellen "Helen" Woodford was born on October 20, 1896. She was six days shy of her eighteenth birthday when she married Ruth on October 14, 1914.
[23] Holtzman, *No Cheering in the Press Box.*
[24] Stout, *The Selling of the Babe.*
[25] MLB.com. June 23, 2015. "Ernie Shore once threw a quasi-perfect game...after Babe Ruth punched an umpire."
[26] Smelser, *The Life That Ruth Built.*
[27] Stout, Glenn. *The Selling of the Babe: The Deal That Changed Baseball and Created a Legend*. St. Martin's Press. 2016.
[28] Wagenheim, *Babe Ruth.*

---

[29] *New York Tribune*, December 23, 1919. Even higher offers for Hornsby would come later.
[30] Hornsby and Ruth played briefly for Charles Schwab's Bethlehem Steel League in the fall of 1918. With World War I still ongoing, the government had a "work-or-fight" rule in place. It meant ballplayers either had to join the military or work for a defense-related industry. As in the case of Hornsby and Ruth, many ballplayers "work" consisted of playing baseball for an industrial league team. See Stout, *The Selling of the Babe* and usa.arcelormittal.com/news-and-media/our-stories/2017/aug/08-31-2017 for more. Hornsby started at the plant in Wilmington, Delaware but transferred to Pennsylvania in October of 1918. *Reading Times*, October 10, 1918.
[31] Stout, *The Selling of the Babe.*
[32] Ibid.
[33] *New York Times*, June 7, 1920.
[34] Stout, *The Selling of the Babe.*
[35] Smelser, *The Life That Ruth Built.*
[36] Smelser places the figure at $60,000. Wagenheim says Ruth earned $90,000 just from his fall barnstorming tour. His earnings from the Christy Walsh syndicate, detailed by Jane Leavy, didn't begin until 1921.
[37] Creamer, *Babe.*
[38] Ibid.
[39] Montville, *The Big Bam.* Jane Leavy placed the estimates at between $60,000 and $130,000 – "the amount depended on which magazine exclusive you believed," she wrote. Leavy, *The Big Fella*.
[40] Wagenheim, *Babe Ruth.*
[41] Stout, *The Selling of the Babe.*

Did the Sox Go Black in St. Louis?

Henry "Kid" Becker ran a gambling empire in St. Louis. Out of a secret office in the city, Becker oversaw "bookkeepers, stenographers, an expert cost accountant, adding machines, filing cabinets and card indexes."[1] At its peak, betting volume at his bookmaking business was a million dollars a year.

Becker was a St. Louis native who had learned to shoot dice before he was ten years old. As an adult, legend has it that he once won $100,000 playing poker in Hot Springs, Arkansas. The game started on a Saturday night and ended on a Tuesday morning. [2] He left the city in 1905 when Missouri governor "Holy Joe" Folk began cracking down on gambling. But after twice being convicted of setting up gambling houses in Madison County, Illinois, he returned to Missouri in 1917. He found a more tolerant environment this time around.

Becker set up shop at Campbell's Forest Home, described as a "notorious gambling resort of St. Louis County." In May, a *St. Louis Star* reporter paid a visit to the facility located in the suburb of Richmond Heights that "operated practically under the noses" of the sheriff and prosecuting attorney. He found 52 men spread out among two large craps tables and a corner area where people were placing bets on out-of-state horse races.[3] A wooden partition separated the craps room from a bar. The operation, which violated both state and county laws, would remain open until 1920.

In 1918, Becker had a bold idea to fix the World Series.[4] The matchup that season featured the Chicago Cubs and Babe Ruth's Boston Red Sox. Becker later decided he lacked the resources to pull off the fix, but rumors of an attempt reached Chicago and American League president Ban Johnson. After the Series was over, Johnson took the rumors seriously and decided he wanted to investigate. He asked American League owners to pony up the money to provide the necessary backing. They refused.[5] World War I had inflicted serious economic damage on the business of baseball, and with the war in Europe still raging (it would end two months later), owners preferred to keep their money in their pockets and their heads buried in the sand when it came to the issues of gambling and game-fixing.

The following spring, in April of 1919, Becker was at his home in St. Louis when three men appeared, intent on robbing him. The "highwaymen," in the newspaper parlance of the time, wanted cash and what better man to get the money from than a bookie who dealt in cash transactions? During the robbery, Becker reached for his wallet in his back pocket. One of the robbers, thinking he was reaching for a gun, shot him.[6] Rushed to a hospital, Becker died early the next morning. One week later, the baseball season opened in St. Louis. The Browns hosted the Chicago White Sox.

The 1919 Chicago "Black Sox" scandal is one of baseball's enduring mysteries. Even today, more than a century after the event, the pieces of the puzzle still don't fit quite right. What began as conversations with gamblers ended in banishment from the game for eight members of the team.

Seemingly every detail of the case has multiple versions from multiple people. Almost always, those versions conflict. What did they know and when did they know it? Baseball's Watergate has frustrated and fascinated historians and baseball researchers for decades. One of the sources of confusion is simply the basics behind the scandal. It turns out there were likely multiple fixes involving multiple groups and everyone involved – from the ballplayers to the gamblers to the baseball establishment – had every incentive to hide the truth.

"The Black Sox scandal," wrote Arnold Rothstein biographer David Pietrusza, "is not just a riddle wrapped in an enigma inside a mystery. It is a labyrinth of fixes, double-crossers, cover-ups and a con so big, so audacious, it nearly ruined professional baseball."[7] Or as one of those double-crossers and con men, Abe Attell, so succinctly put it, the Black Sox affair was "cheaters cheating cheaters." A complete accounting of the scandal is beyond the scope of these pages. The reader is encouraged to peruse the many books that have covered the fix in exhaustive detail. However, a basic overview is necessary to complete a bridge to our focus – the role St. Louis played in the affair and its impact on the fortunes of both the Browns and the Cardinals.

Here's what we know. The Chicago White Sox met the Cincinnati Reds in the 1919 World Series. Sometime during the season, a group of White Sox players, led by pitcher Eddie Cicotte and first baseman Arnold "Chick" Gandil, met with, maybe even sought out, multiple gamblers to hatch a plot. In exchange for throwing the Series, the White Sox players wanted cash. The gamblers provided it (although not as much as the players wanted), knowing they could recoup their investment by betting on Cincinnati to win the Series. And that's exactly what happened. The Reds won the 1919 World Series in eight games (it was a best-of-nine format in 1919).

Suspicions were raised even before the Series began. People were talking. Rumors were flying. In fact, Chicago sportswriter Hugh Fullerton arrived in Cincinnati for Game One only to find the hotel lobby full of chatter: The White Sox were going in the tank. Take the Reds. The fix was in. *Sporting News* publisher Taylor Spink, an official scorer for the Series, noticed the same thing. "I saw gamblers going around, hocking their rings, raising anything they could, to bet on the Reds."[8]

Becoming so alarmed about the apparent plot, Fullerton wired this headline to newspapers that printed his syndicated writings the night before the Series began:

ADVISE ALL NOT TO BET ON THIS SERIES. UGLY RUMORS AFLOAT.

Eight games and nine days later, the winning Reds celebrated a World Series championship. The losing White Sox faced a long offseason. The owner of the team, former St. Louis Browns captain Charles Comiskey, hired a detective agency to start an investigation and withheld World Series checks from several members of his club.

Fullerton wrote the day after the World Series ended that "there are seven men on the [White Sox] team who will not be there when the gongs sound next Spring..." He gave no names and did not indicate why they wouldn't return. He would later admit he got the information from White Sox owner Comiskey. During the Series, Fullerton, along with Hall of Fame pitcher Christy Mathewson who covered the games for a New York paper, diagrammed every questionable play. "Comparing notes, [they] marked seven plays by the White Sox as highly suspect."[9]

By December, Fullerton was writing for the *New York Evening World*. He penned a series of articles outlining his suspicions about the World Series. "Professional baseball has reached a crisis," he began a story that appeared on December 15. Describing the chatter he heard in his hotel the night before Game One, Fullerton wrote that he "discovered that two persons were extremely active in the betting and before turning in knew that the 'heavy' work was by St. Louisans."[10]

In a piece two days later, Fullerton gave baseball a blueprint for how to get to the bottom of the scandal. He named names. He recommended Judge Kenesaw Mountain Landis (not yet commissioner) get involved and interrogate several people. "The fans are entitled to know if baseball is on the square or not," he wrote. Fullerton recommended that Landis speak to several gamblers and a few sportswriters. Three of the gamblers Fullerton mentioned were from St. Louis.[11] More on them later. One of the other names mentioned was the biggest speculator of all, Arnold Rothstein. In a case with little consensus, and a bewildering number of questions and dead-end leads, there is near-universal agreement among Black Sox researchers that the man largely responsible for financing this operation was Rothstein. The man known as "The Big Bankroll" had a well-earned reputation.

*****

Born in New York in January of 1882, Rothstein came of age in the city at a time when gambling and speculation on everything from stocks and bonds to boxing and baseball ran rampant. "Is there any gambling in New York?" an observer of the scene asked in 1904. "Why, there is almost nothing else!"[12] Rothstein played cards, became a pool hustler (once winning $4,000 in a 32-hour marathon in 1909), and began lending money to others at a 20 percent rate due on Monday afternoons. Collecting the money was an obsession. "Arnold Rothstein is a man who waits in doorways," his lawyer William J. Fallon once said, "a mouse, waiting in the doorway for his cheese."[13]

He met New York Giants manager John McGraw at his pool hall on Herald Square. Rothstein reportedly became McGraw's silent partner in the venture. He was also friends with Giants owner Charles Stoneham. The two men also had some interesting business partnerships that included a shady stock brokerage business.

It was horse racing where Rothstein likely first learned to fix outcomes. He owned part of a racetrack in Maryland. A common trick at the time was to put sponges in a horse's nostrils. Hard for a horse to finish in the money when it's having trouble breathing.[14] Rothstein had some spectacular payoffs with the ponies, once winning $300,000 on a single race in Laurel, Maryland in 1917. Four years later, he earned $850,000 on a race under suspicious circumstances.[15]

He also ran gambling rooms. He set up two parlors for gambling at his home in 1909. When police began to crack down, Rothstein "would invent floating crap games that would move from hotel to hotel, apartment to apartment and warehouse to warehouse."[16] At one of those floating crap games in Harlem one night, robbers took him for $28,000. At some point, Rothstein started carrying a gun.

In January of 1919, police raided a high stakes dice game in New York City that Rothstein was hosting. Suspecting they were robbers, Rothstein opened fire. Three of the cops had minor wounds, one to the shoulder and two on the arm. Rothstein fled the scene but was found on a second-floor fire escape. He was arrested along with other gamblers.

A grand jury was convened. The judge was Francis Xavier McQuade, a man who had done business with Rothstein in the past and who served as treasurer of the New York Giants. Charges against all but Rothstein were dismissed. But no one testified against Rothstein at the trial. Case dismissed. It was likely a fait accompli before it ever got to that point. While the case was in front of the grand jury, *The New York Times* reported, "rumors that several thousand dollars were spent by a wealthy gambler to keep the facts hidden and prevent prosecution."[17]

Rothstein had money, a well-deserved reputation, and plenty of contacts from baseball to the underworld. He also had a lifetime of learning how to survive the corrupt world of New York City machine politics. Paying New York cops for protection was an estimated $3 million a year business in the city at the turn of the century. As the 1919 shooting case likely demonstrated, bribery was also on his resume. He did business with or had a connection to almost every gambler in the Black Sox case. Nearly all the circumstantial evidence points to Rothstein as the man behind the fix. So why did Rothstein biographer Pietrusza write that "The scheme *began* in St. Louis in early 1919..."?

He isn't the only one who suspected St. Louis had a role. "Chicago, New York, Cincinnati, and St. Louis gamblers are bleeding baseball and corrupting players," grand jury foreman Henry H. Brigham told reporters in September of 1920.[18]

Readers of the *St. Louis Post-Dispatch* opened their papers on March 26, 1921, to see this headline:

ST. LOUIS GAMBLERS ACCUSED OF ARRANGING 1919 BASEBALL PLOT.

Fullerton stated he "knew that the 'heavy' work was by St. Louisans" even before the Series began.

Why were so many suspicious eyes cast toward St. Louis in a World Series plot featuring teams from Cincinnati and Chicago thought to be backed by money coming from New York? Is there a thread that connects Rothstein to gamblers in the Midwest? It turns out there are two links that connect Rothstein to St. Louis. One of them was his business partner in a New York resort. That partner, Nat Evans, grew up in St. Louis.

*****

Born in Russia in 1876, Nathanial Isaac Evensky emigrated with his family to the United States in 1883. Settling in St. Louis, his father and older brother ran a tinware shop.[19] Nat, who eventually Americanized his name to Evans (sometimes spelled "Evens"), worked in the family shop for a brief period in the 1890s. He married and had a child only to abandon his family. He moved to Memphis and then to Florida, where by 1902, he was already a well-known name in Southern "sporting" circles, according to some newspaper reports.[20]

He moved on to Georgia, where he spent some time in Savannah, Augusta, and Atlanta. In Savannah, he was shot through the lungs in a saloon gunfight one night. He recovered but received a $500 fine from a judge because he started the incident. He was acquitted in another shooting incident just a month later.[21]

By 1910, Evans was in New York and doing business with Rothstein. One of their early ventures was the Holly Arms hotel in Hewlett, Long Island. They bought it to set up – what else? – a gambling resort. With more than 300 formally attired people on hand for a dance one evening in 1911, police raided the place. Among the gambling paraphernalia carted away that evening were two roulette tables and equipment for playing craps and faro.[22]

Evans and Rothstein became partners in The Brook in 1919, a home in Saratoga Springs, New York they converted into a premier casino. The partnership seemed a natural fit. The two men had been working together for nearly a decade and had years of experience setting up gambling houses. Both men demonstrated they weren't afraid to fire their weapons and somehow wiggle away from legal consequences. They were comfortable using money to buy influence. A $60,000 bribe from Rothstein to local Republicans made running The Brook a little easier. The political graft was nonpartisan. Rothstein also gave $10,000 to the local Democratic boss. It was money well spent. When police did raid the place, Rothstein and Evans knew it was coming. Perhaps a good night to close early? "A place near Greenfield Center [The Brook] was visited last night but the house was dark and the piazzas covered with fresh paint."[23]

"It may have been the nation's most exclusive nightspot," wrote Pietrusza of The Brook. The dress code was strict. Men couldn't enter without wearing formal attire. The resort attracted the biggest gamblers in the country including "Nick the Greek" Dandolos from Chicago, millionaires like New York Giants owner Stoneham and wealthy oilmen like Harry Sinclair, founder of Sinclair Oil. Sinclair, who later served six months in prison for his role in the Teapot Dome Scandal, dropped $48,000 one night at The Brook. He had a good time doing it. He left a $2,000 tip.[24] Stoneham once had a sprained knee and couldn't make it out to the resort. He called Rothstein to tell him he wanted to bet on the roulette wheel. Over the phone, he would tell Rothstein the color and the amount of the bet. Stoneham eventually lost $70,000.[25]

This is the backdrop to baseball's biggest scandal. It is the summer of 1919. An upstate New York casino resort is being run by two successful and notorious gamblers. One of them, Rothstein, has a reputation for fixing horse races. His partner Evans is known to be a heavy bettor on baseball. They're respected and known by gamblers across the country. They have access to information, to the criminal justice system, to the owners of industry and sport. And now with their ownership of The Brook, they have a legitimacy they've never had. The wealthy and powerful clientele that visit the place are daily affirmations of how far they've come. Money is pouring in. "In 1919, [Rothstein] had done so well that a motor cycle guard accompanied a 'money car' from the Brook to a hotel in Saratoga at the end of play each morning."[26] World War I has ended and Prohibition has yet to start. Alcohol, money, and information flow freely. Gamblers talked of their biggest scores of the past and fantasized or plotted about payoffs yet to come. It is here, The Brook, in the summer of 1919, where former Chicago Cubs owner Charles Weeghman said he first heard of a World Series fix from Chicago gambler Mont Tennes, who "had gambling and underworld sources nationwide."[27] Tennes, Weeghman claimed, got the information directly from Rothstein.[28]

*****

Evans grew up in the same St. Louis neighborhood as Carl Zork, a man long associated with gambling in the city. Zork is mentioned in a July 11, 1913 story in the *Post-Dispatch* with the headline, "Police Fail To Stop Gambling At Ball Parks." (Zork was an associate of Kid Becker, who was also named in the same article).[29] Just two years younger than Evans, Zork was born in 1878. The lifelong St. Louisan spent many years in the garment industry and was identified in the papers at the time of the Black Sox scandal as a "shirtwaist manufacturer." In 1919, his title was president of the Supreme Waist Company in St. Louis. A vice president of the firm was Joseph Evans, who may have been related to Nat.[30]

While the ties between Evans and Zork are circumstantial, Zork did have a direct and long relationship with another Rothstein associate, Abe Attell. Known as the "Little Champ," Attell stood five feet four inches tall and was the champion of the featherweight class (122 pounds) for many years in the early twentieth century. His first fight in St. Louis took place in November of 1901 when he defeated former featherweight champ George Dixon.[31]

Attell only lost ten fights in his career.[32] Several of those losses happened in St. Louis at the city's West End Club. Attell became the featherweight champion in 1904. After knocking out Harry Forbes in the fifth round, a column appeared in the *Post-Dispatch* under Attell's byline with the headline, "How I Won The World's Featherweight Championship." Attell described for readers the action in the ring and the action in the crowd before the match. He was especially proud that gamblers were betting on him. "Some had $20 bills in their hands and most of them were offering odds on me. This made my chest expansion increase about six inches."[33]

Around this time, Attell became familiar with Zork. The St. Louis gambler attended an Attell fight in Indianapolis. Coincidentally or not, Attell's long and colorful history of corruption in the ring began around the same time Zork began showing up.

The West End Club in St. Louis suspended Attell for six months after a fight in December of 1904. Following an investigation, the directors of the club concluded that Attell and his opponent, Johnny Regan, staged a "fake" fight. "Charge Attell With Faking Against Neil," read a headline in 1908. "Sullivan and Abe Fake Again," read another one just a few months later. An Attell fight became a full-blown theatrical production. The featherweight champ was called the "greatest actor in the ring" in 1912 by the *Post-Dispatch*.[34] Attell lost his title that year to Johnny Kilbane. He never wore the championship belt again, but Attell and Zork had one last trick up their sleeves.

Zork promoted an Attell fight in late 1912 against St. Louis boxer Oliver Kirk. Attell quit the fight at the end of the sixth round.[35] He went to the ropes and announced to the crowd, "Gentlemen, I am through as a fighter. I have been bluffing it for more than a year but the time has come when I must quit."[36] His retirement didn't last long. Attell and Kirk scheduled a rematch just a few months later. This fight took place in New York at a club Attell partially owned. Attell won the bout in three rounds. His victory, said the *Post-Dispatch*, proved he "quit" in the first match and that the mock retirement was just "a trick to cover lack of condition." Merely out of shape, or were Attell and Zork out for a big score? *Collyer's Eye* smelled a fix. The gambling publication accused Zork of betting heavily on Kirk in the first fight, then turning around and coordinating a rematch where he bet on Attell. The periodical called it "one of the rawest deals ever pulled in a prize ring."[37]

*****

By the fall of 1919, Zork had a reputation. He may have known Rothstein partner Evans as a child. He definitely knew Rothstein associate Attell as an adult. He'd already been linked to baseball gambling and suspected of fixing fights. Now White Sox owner Comiskey wanted to know what Zork and others in St. Louis knew of a possible World Series fix.

The St. Louis trip had its origins in a proposal Comiskey made right after the Series ended. He offered $10,000 to anyone with information that could prove the World

Series was fixed. Gamblers in St. Louis took notice and spoke up. Just a few days after the final game, White Sox manager Kid Gleason, along with business manager Norris O'Neill, arrived in the area. One of the people they interviewed was theater owner Harry Redmon. The operator of the Majestic Theatre in East St. Louis claimed to have lost $6,500 betting on the Series. According to Black Sox researcher Gene Carney, Redmon gave the names of seven gamblers and eight Chicago White Sox players to the investigators. But he would only go so far. He wouldn't implicate any of the gamblers, only saying the bettors had conversations with the players.[38]

Redmon, along with St. Louis bookmaker Joe Pesch, later traveled to Chicago to meet with White Sox officials. Redmon repeated what he heard in front of Comiskey, his attorney Alfred Austrian, and White Sox secretary Harry Grabiner. (Grabiner's diary, discovered years later, was among the items that revealed White Sox officials, like sportswriters, knew early on that something about the Series was amiss.)[39]

"I only had a hearsay story but Joseph Pesch who came with me had the 'goods' direct," Redmon said in Chicago in the fall of 1920. "While we were in Mr. Austrian's office with Comiskey and Grabiner we all compared notes regarding the players under suspicion. Pesch's list of eight suspected players tallied exactly with the list Austrian and Comiskey had."[40]

Redmon also knew Zork. He "is in the silk business, supposed to be," Redmon later told a Chicago grand jury, "but he does more gambling than anything else..."[41]

Another St. Louis connection to speak with the White Sox was Joe Gedeon, a former New York Yankee and now the starting second baseman for the Browns. When St. Louis Cardinals manager Miller Huggins left town after the 1917 season, the first trade he made after joining the Yankees was to send Gedeon and four other players to the Browns in exchange for second baseman Del Pratt and future Hall of Fame pitcher Eddie Plank.[42] Gedeon led American League second basemen in fielding percentage in both 1918 and 1919. A 1918 spring training profile noted that a "ground ball will never cause 'scrap iron' Joe Gedeon to raise his head or close his eyes."[43] He was singled out for his defense in a game in 1919 but for a different reason. His throwing error, which allowed two runners to score, was the difference in a game lost by the Browns 3-2. The opponent that day was the Chicago White Sox.[44]

Gedeon was a friend of White Sox shortstop Swede Risberg. Gedeon would later admit to the grand jury that he won between $600 and $700 betting on the Reds to win the 1919 World Series. While on the witness stand, he wouldn't name the player he got the information from. It later emerged that Risberg sent Gedeon a telegram before the Series started, letting him in on the fix.[45]

Gedeon took the information provided by Risberg and went straight to Zork. On two separate visits, the Browns second baseman gave him $500, a total of $1,000, to bet on the Reds. Whether the two men had a previous relationship or Gedeon knew Zork by reputation is not clear. Gedeon also advised Zork to make a substantial bet on Cincinnati.

The Gedeon-Zork connection would emerge in grand jury testimony in 1920. In the fall of 1919, Zork was far more circumspect. Hearing rumors of White Sox officials sniffing around St. Louis, a *Post-Dispatch* reporter tracked Zork down and asked him to comment. Zork said he bet on the Reds in the Series, but he told the paper that his books would show that he "wagered no more than I usually do on the world's championship." He added that "I broke about even, owing to bets on individual games." In the paragraph preceding those quotes, the reporter wrote that Zork "bet heavily on the Reds, but hedged out later..." Zork reportedly bet as much as $50,000 on Cincinnati.[46] (Whether or not he hedged his bet, he had money to invest by the end of 1919. In January of 1920, he purchased the Aline apartment building, located in the Central West End of St. Louis, which produced annual rental income of $3,360.)[47]

The White Sox didn't find the Zork claims all that convincing. Comiskey hired Hunter's Secret Service of Illinois to investigate the rumors of a World Series fix. The detectives primarily focused on the off-season activities of suspected White Sox ballplayers. But one of his investigators took a night-time train out of Chicago on the evening of November 7, 1919 and headed south.

Identified by initials in his reports, "E.W.M." arrived in St. Louis the morning of November 8. Over twenty-seven days, he sent eight letters back to his supervisors, played a lot of billiards at Joe Pesch's pool hall and found out almost nothing.

On his sixth day in town, the investigator finally spoke to Zork. "This morning, I interviewed Mr. Zork at his place of business under a misleading pretext, so that I would know him when we should meet at the hotel." He saw Zork at the hotel that evening but "he did not recognize me." The St. Louis gambler was focused on the task at hand. "I noticed him cutting some coupons from Liberty Bonds."[48]

The detective from Hunter's Secret Service never did speak with Zork about the reason for his visit, gambling on the 1919 World Series. Zork was always with his wife and always on the move. The investigator also came to St. Louis to speak with Attell. He didn't locate him either. Since Attell's name wasn't in the city directory (he lived in New York), the detective speculated that "Abe Attell" might be a fake name.

Hitting one dead end after another, the detective left town on the evening of December 4. While the St. Louis trip did not produce any confessions, it may have added to the lexicon of history. It was in St. Louis where the first documented use of the term "Black Sox" may have occurred. The detective overheard a gambler at Pesch's pool hall say, "I want to bet on the Black Sox, as they can't call themselves 'White Sox' any longer. They do not play white baseball. With them a man does not get a good chance for his money." The investigator never got the man's name.[49]

By the summer of 1920, it was back to business as usual in baseball. The story of the Black Sox may have ended here had it not been for a game in Chicago in August of that season. But this game didn't involve the White Sox but the team on the north side of town.

*****

On August 31, 1920, the Chicago Cubs played the Philadelphia Phillies at Cubs Park. Claude Hendrix was scheduled to pitch that day for the home team, but Cubs president Bill Veeck Sr. began receiving phone calls and telegrams that the game was fixed. Gamblers were betting on the Phillies to win. Taking the charges seriously, Chicago decided to switch pitchers. Instead of Hendrix, the Cubs tapped Grover Cleveland Alexander to take the mound. Chicago lost the game anyway, 3-0. But Veeck and the Cubs continued to pursue the matter. They turned the information over to law enforcement. One of the interesting nuggets they were able to uncover concerned the six telegrams that Veeck received. Curiously, they all arrived during a 45-minute period. None of the senders was ever located.[50]

Whatever the motives of the telegram senders, they succeeded in getting baseball to finally take seriously the impact gambling was having on the game. A Cook County grand jury convened in September. Their focus quickly widened. What started as an investigation into a Chicago Cubs game ended with a target on the World Series of 1919 and the behavior of the Chicago White Sox. By the end of the month, four White Sox players had confessed to receiving money. The grand jury moved to indict eight players and five gamblers. Rothstein, who took the stand in Chicago, was not indicted. He claimed he lost $6,000 betting on the White Sox and blamed Attell (who was indicted) for the fix. Like Rothstein, Zork and Evans also escaped indictment. (Evans had communicated with the players using a fake name. "Rachael Brown" was indicted but never located.)

The "heavy work" done by St. Louisans in the scandal had escaped the notice of the grand jury. A few weeks after it adjourned, though, American League president Johnson told *The Sporting News* he had a St. Louis gambler on his list. According to Johnson, this man had worked in the past with at least 20 ballplayers to throw games. "If I could have secured the indictment of a certain St. Louis man," Johnson said, "I am sure we would have brought out evidence we need to convict these men and throw them out of baseball."[51]

Johnson didn't name that "certain St. Louis man," but one who certainly fit the description would have been Zork. In 2012, authors Timothy Newman and Bruce Stuckman outlined why they believed Zork conspired with White Sox players to fix regular-season games during the 1919 season. Chicago's Lefty Williams, an Aurora, Missouri native, pitched poorly against St. Louis that year in his home park. In three starts against the Browns in Chicago, Williams gave up ten runs in just 6 1/3 innings pitched. For the entire season, Williams allowed 87 earned runs in 297 innings, an earned run average of 2.64. Oscar "Happy" Felsch also raised eyebrows with his performance against the Browns, making several poor plays in the outfield.[52]

Williams had played minor league baseball with Gedeon, the Browns second baseman who placed a 1919 World Series bet with Zork. Williams and Gedeon were teammates on the 1915 Salt Lake City team in the Pacific Coast League, a club some suspected of throwing games.[53] "He may be asked," the *New York Times* wrote of

Williams after the pitcher was indicted, "as to his knowledge of a scandal regarding fixed games after Salt Lake entered the league."[54]

Contemporaneous evidence of illicit cooperation between St. Louis and Chicago came from sportswriter Fullerton. A St. Louis gambler boasted "he had three of the Chicago White Sox on his pay roll and one man on another club and could fix a game whenever he wanted to," Fullerton wrote in December of 1919.[55]

AL president Johnson, just like White Sox owner Comiskey, had good reason to suspect St. Louis played a key role. However, it would take an election, a *second* grand jury, and some enterprising efforts by St. Louis detectives to put the city and its gamblers in the spotlight.

*****

Americans went to the polls in the fall of 1920 and elected a new President. In the battle to replace two-term Democrat Woodrow Wilson, Republican Warren Harding defeated Democrat James Cox. He was joined in Washington D.C. by Republican majorities in both the House and Senate. The country's first election since women won the right to vote and Prohibition started brought a GOP landslide. Republicans picked up 63 seats in the House and ten new members in the Senate.

It meant changes in Chicago as well. Robert E. Crowe won the Cook County State's Attorney election. When the former circuit judge looked at the Black Sox case in early 1921, he saw a mess. In his view, improper handling of evidence and potential witness corruption had made a farce of the case. When a judge set a quick trial date, Crowe dismissed the original indictments and took other cases off the court calendar.[56] A new grand jury was convened.

By late March of 1921, the second grand jury to examine the Black Sox evidence returned 18 indictments, adding five new names to the list. One of the freshly indicted was Zork. This grand jury also indicted a second man from St. Louis, a gambler by the name of Benjamin Franklin. The case had a new look and a new focus. State's Attorney Crowe said these two St. Louis men, Franklin and Zork, were the ringleaders. "I told you when we dropped some of the baseball cases a few days ago that the first investigation had been bungled and that the real men behind the conspiracy had not been indicted," Crowe told reporters. "We have handled this investigation carefully and have not overlooked a single legal point."[57]

Zork responded to the indictments the same day they were announced. "I know nothing of the reported crookedness in connection with the series, and cannot understand why the Chicago Grand Jury indicted me." Franklin didn't immediately speak to the press. The man "known as a heavy bettor on baseball and horse racing" was said to be in Tulsa, Oklahoma. Franklin's wife telegraphed him the news of the indictment, and he quickly returned home.

Two days later, Franklin and Zork came out with a joint statement in the presence of their attorney. Denying the charges, the two men said they would go to Chicago and seek a quick trial. Franklin admitted winning $5,000 on the World Series and dismissed it as not that big a deal. "Why, I have bet more than $5,000 on a single horse race." Described as a lifelong St. Louisan, the 42-year old Franklin was in business with his brother at the National Stockyards. During World War I, the men had contracts to supply the Allies with horses.[58]

Zork's story had slightly changed since his initial contact with a reporter nearly two years before. Instead of breaking even on the 1919 World Series, Zork now said he lost between $500 and $1,500. He had also lost something else, the ability to attend local baseball games. The Browns and Cardinals announced they were barring all men whose names were mentioned in connection with the scandal.

Before the proceedings got underway in Chicago, additional evidence emerged. This, too, came from St. Louis, thanks to the efforts of a pair of the city's cops. Elias Hoagland was doing routine checks of downtown St. Louis hotels. The detective-sergeant and his partner Jim Vasey noticed a few guests at the Jefferson Hotel that looked out of place.

"They were wearing loud sport jackets and other clothing that didn't fit into the local scene at all," Hoagland recalled years later. "You could spot'em at once as out-of-towners and they seemed so busy moving up and down on the elevators, going into the dining room, etc., that we decided to keep an eye on them."[59]

The big break in the case came about a week later. "We saw them coming out of a smoke shop that frequently had been raided as a bookmaking establishment." Hoagland and Vasey stepped up their monitoring of the group and "found them associating and meeting with characters the police had been arresting often as 'big-name' gamblers." The cops followed them to their hotel room one night. "We're taking you to headquarters for investigation," Hoagland told the four men.

With the quartet at police headquarters, Hoagland and his partner decided to return to the room at the Jefferson Hotel. "Our search turned up a lot of important telegrams and other communications from well-known gamblers all over the land. One of these telegrams I will never forget. It read: 'Beware of Dickle [sic] Kerr - POISON!'"[60]

Kerr, the White Sox pitcher who won two games for Chicago in the 1919 World Series, was not one of the players under indictment. Kerr's victory in the third game of the World Series wiped out a few of the gamblers betting on the Reds, but certainly not the savvy ones. Rothstein's name comes to mind. One of the men arrested that day in St. Louis was Rothstein's former business partner Evans.[61]

The timing of the arrest of Evans and the evidence discovered by St. Louis police raises several fascinating questions about the case:

- Why did Evans choose to come to St. Louis just days after a Chicago grand jury had indicted St. Louis gamblers Zork and Franklin? The two men were indicted and identified as ringleaders of the scandal by prosecutors on Saturday, March 26. Evans, according to *The New York Times*, arrived in St. Louis from Florida on Wednesday, March 30. Evans and the others were arrested on Friday, April 1.

- Did Evans and the other three men choose to bring evidence of communication with gamblers with them to St. Louis or acquire it after arriving? "Up and down the line these wires named names...," St. Louis cop Hoagland remembered years later. Those names included those indicted in the scandal. The telegram reference to Kerr was potentially more than a year old by this point. Why keep it? Was it sloppy or purposeful on their part? And if purposeful, what was their aim? Judging by Hoagland's comments, their clothing and behavior could not have been more conspicuous. If they were trying to get arrested, they succeeded.
- In its story on April 2, the *Times* identifies Evans as the "missing link" in the scandal. If a newspaper could make that charge, why didn't prosecutors in Chicago? While "Rachael Brown" was indicted in Illinois, Evans never was.
- Finally, what ultimately happened to the evidence in the hotel room? Hoagland said he asked for and received permission to turn over the telegrams and letters to *Sporting News* publisher Spink. Spink then told American League president Johnson he needed to come to St. Louis to review the items. He did, but it's unclear what happened to the information from that point. Did the prosecutors review the telegrams and letters? Were they preserved? If so, where are those items today?

Thanks to his discovery, Hoagland did become a lifelong friend of the American League president. "In fact, every time Mr. Johnson came to St. Louis to visit his old friend Phil Ball, then owner of the Browns, he'd invite me down to his hotel to have dinner with him."

Hoagland served 53 years with the St. Louis police department. He retired as a captain and died at the age of 89 in November of 1976.[62] In his *New York Times* obituary, Hoagland is described as "instrumental in solving the Chicago Black Sox baseball scandal..." Based on the calendar, that's more hyperbole than fact. By the time Hoagland arrested Evans and three other men and discovered the communication with gamblers, two separate grand juries had already returned indictments against the eight players. The trial was just months away. But the case is just one more example of how St. Louis proved to be a central point of interest for both investigators and the men who bet on baseball.

*****

By the time of opening arguments in mid-July, the state had evidence and momentum on its side. A second grand jury had expanded the investigation and indicted gamblers from St. Louis, long suspected to be a source of trouble by both White Sox owner Comiskey and AL president Johnson. It had confessions from three players – pitchers Cicotte and Williams and outfielder "Shoeless Joe" Jackson – that they had accepted money from gamblers while a fourth player, outfielder Felsch, had confessed to a newspaper reporter that he received cash. In addition, Bill Burns, one of the indicted gamblers, had agreed to turn state's evidence.[63] Yet the prosecution's case quickly collapsed.

On July 22, the jury heard from Redmon, the state's main witness against Zork. "Zork told me he started the whole deal and it didn't cost him a cent," the East St. Louis theatre operator testified.[64] "He said he and another man, a little red-headed fellow from St. Louis, had started the whole thing."[65]

Redmon also had a connection to the second indicted St. Louis gambler, Ben Franklin. Franklin's brother-in-law was Redmon's partner in his East St. Louis theater.[66] Redmon claimed to the jury that Franklin told him in Chicago during the Series that eight White Sox players were conspiring to fix outcomes. "Franklin told me that further games could be thrown for $20,000 each and wanted to know if I wanted to put up $5,000." Redmon refused. The same offer was made to St. Louis pool hall operator Joe Pesch. According to Redmon, he also refused.

Redmon also stated on the stand that "Zork said that games had been fixed during the year." The judge ordered that statement stricken from the record.[67] He also wasn't buying the rest of Redmon's testimony. Even before Zork's defense could call witnesses to the stand, Judge Hugo Friend said he would direct the jury to return not guilty verdicts in the case of Zork unless new evidence was introduced against him.[68] As described by the prosecution, Zork was one of the chief plotters. If the case against him was crumbling, did authorities really have a chance of getting any guilty verdicts?

The answer came on August 2, 1921 after jurors deliberated for two hours and 47 minutes. Not guilty. The ballplayers and gamblers were free to go. The courtroom erupted in celebration. "Hooray for the Clean Sox!" yelled a crowd of hundreds while jurors lifted players on their shoulders.[69]

"I am entirely innocent, and the jury has proven that," said White Sox shortstop Risberg, conveniently forgetting his telegram about the fix to St. Louis Browns second baseman Gedeon before the Series even started.

"I am not guilty and never had anything to do with any so-called conspiracy," said outfielder Felsch, a man who had told a reporter less than a year before, "I am as guilty as the rest of them. We were in it alike."

"I don't know why they brought me up here," said Zork, a man linked to Attell and suspicious behavior in sporting events going back a decade or more.

With their consciences clear and their comments to reporters concluded, both the players and the jurors decide to celebrate with a dinner. Coincidentally, players and jurors just happened to pick the same Italian restaurant on Chicago's West Side. As luck would have it, they were in adjoining rooms. When they discovered each other, "doors were thrown open and the party became one."[70]

And so it went until the early morning hours of the next day: conversation, food, drink, and eventually song. Players and jurors left the restaurant together singing "Hail, hail, the gang's all here."

*****

The players' celebration was short-lived. The day after the verdict, Commissioner Kenesaw Mountain Landis announced his decision. "Regardless of the verdict of the juries, no player that throws a ball game, no player that entertains proposals or promises to throw a game, no player that sits in a conference with a bunch of crooked players and gamblers where the ways and means of throwing games are discussed and does not promptly tell the club about it, will ever play professional baseball." Suspended with just days to go in the 1920 season, the White Sox players, *Eight Men Out*, in the words of author Eliot Asinof, never appeared in the big leagues again.

Three months later, Landis added another player to the list. Joe Gedeon was scheduled to take part in a game with some minor league players from the Pacific Coast League. The president of the PCL asked Landis for clarification on Gedeon's status. Landis told him he was ineligible. The "ninth man out" in the Black Sox scandal was the second baseman of the St. Louis Browns. Other players ensnared in the scandal such as New York Giants first baseman Hal Chase, who allegedly won money on the World Series, also never appeared in another major league game.

All the gamblers in the case escaped legal action. Only the cases against Zork and David Zelcer of Des Moines, Iowa, even went to the jury. Some like Attell, "Rachael Brown," and Sport Sullivan were never extradited to Chicago to stand trial. Others had their cases dismissed by the judge. The case of Ben Franklin of St. Louis lapsed and never went to trial. Rothstein was not indicted and moved on to bigger fixes in boxing and horse racing. Biographer Pietrusza estimates Rothstein made $350,000 from the 1919 World Series.

Did the Sox go Black in St. Louis? No, they didn't, but actions in the city contributed to the cloud cover over the team. The rumors of 1918 may have also unduly influenced investigators to believe St. Louis gamblers played an outsized role. Those rumors likely influenced the behavior of the White Sox players who initiated the fix. "Even though the White Sox players probably had no idea who Kid Becker was," contends Black Sox researcher Jacob Pomrenke, "what they had *heard* about the 1918 Series was an important plot point in why the 1919 Series was fixed."[71] Redmon's confession to Comiskey's men shortly after the World Series ended put a bullseye on the city. Fullerton's columns suggest St. Louis gamblers were actively communicating with White Sox players during both the regular season and postseason of 1919. Ban Johnson's mention of a St. Louis gambler that had conspired with 20 players to throw games indicated authorities were well aware of the city's gambling influences. The arrests of Evans and three other gamblers in the city in April of 1921 adds additional speculation that something specific was going on in St. Louis.

There were certainly gamblers in St. Louis with knowledge of the fix and who chose to participate in it. Perhaps they were tipped by Attell or Evans, both men with connections to the city and Rothstein.

Gedeon is another likely source of how the information spread. After getting word from Risberg of the White Sox that the fix was in, the Browns second basemen placed his bets on the Reds through Zork. Did Gedeon tip him off or did Zork already know? In Gedeon's biography at the website of the Society for American Baseball Research (SABR), author Rick Swaine describes the Browns second baseman as redheaded. Is this who Redmon had in mind when he spoke about Zork's connection to "a little red-headed fellow from St. Louis"?[72]

Zork and Franklin were trying to jump-start the effort to throw games after it appeared the fix collapsed when the White Sox won Game Three. The driving forces behind the scandal, though, were the White Sox players and their ties to the men and money of the East Coast. Those roads led to Rothstein. Few men, if any, had his experience, connections and resources.

"Why was this man never indicted?" asked St. Louis attorney A.M. Frumberg in closing arguments before the Chicago jury in August of 1921. "Why were Brown, Sullivan, Attell and Chase allowed to escape? Why were these underpaid ballplayers, these penny-ante gamblers from Des Moines and St. Louis, who bet a few nickels perhaps on the World Series, brought here to be the goats in this case?" While definitive answers may never be forthcoming, the questions are as relevant today as they were almost a century ago.[73]

In 1961, Attell was asked if the World Series could be fixed again. "Not a chance," he replied. "That kind of cheating died when they buried Arnold Rothstein."

*****

A few final questions deserve to be raised about the gamblers of St. Louis. How did Zork go from unindicted observer in the eyes of grand jury number one to chief plotter in the view of grand jury number two? And if baseball officials were so worried about St. Louis gamblers and their influence on players in Chicago, could those same gamblers get to a player in the city they called home? The answers are possibly related through the story of a former St. Louis Cardinal.

Gene Paulette made his first big league appearance for McGraw's New York Giants in 1911 then bounced around the minor leagues for several years until St. Louis Browns manager Rickey acquired him in the fall of 1915. His luck wasn't much better with the Browns where he found himself playing behind George Sisler. When Rickey moved on to the Cardinals, the St. Louis National League team claimed Paulette off waivers in June of 1917.

At some point, he became acquainted with a couple of St. Louis gamblers. One of them was Elmer Farrar, a former city and state champion pool player. The other one was Zork. The men struck a deal in early 1919. Farrar supplied Paulette with cash. In return, Farrar and Zork wanted help in game-fixing. Paulette was ready to cooperate, going so far as to write a letter to Farrar telling him he could get two other St. Louis players to participate in a fix.[74]

In July of 1919, the Cardinals and Phillies made a trade.[75] St. Louis sent Paulette and pitcher Lee Meadows to Philadelphia in exchange for three players. According to Black Sox researcher Bill Lamb, both the Cardinals and Phillies were aware of Paulette's association with St. Louis gamblers. Philadelphia owner Howard Baker had come into possession of the letter that Paulette sent to Farrar.[76] That letter eventually made its way to Commissioner Landis. On March 7, 1921, Landis summoned Paulette to Chicago for a face-to-face meeting. He refused to go but did give the commissioner a statement.[77]

On March 24, Landis revealed his decision regarding Paulette.

"Paulette denies that he had ever thrown a ball game and asserts that during the last playing season he held himself aloof from corrupting associations; but the fact remains that he offered to betray his team and that he put himself in the vicious power of Farrar and Zork," read the statement from the commissioner. "He will go on the ineligible list."[78]

No one should have been surprised when baseball's new man in charge later made his decision regarding the Black Sox players. He had set the precedent months before. The first player ever banned by Landis was former St. Louis Cardinal Gene Paulette.

Two days after the commissioner banned Paulette, the Black Sox grand jury indicted Zork.[79]

*****

There is one final connection between the St. Louis Cardinals and the 1919 Chicago White Sox. It involves Kerr, the lefthander who won two games for Chicago in the World Series against the Reds, including a three-hit shutout in Game Three. That performance caught Black Sox gamblers off-guard and cost them a lot of money. "I heard later that that game cost the gamblers between $125,000 and $150,000," Kerr once said.[80]

Richard Henry "Dickey" Kerr was born in St. Louis in July of 1893. Starting his professional career at the age of sixteen in Paragould, Arkansas, Kerr played ten years of minor-league baseball. He finally made it to the big leagues in 1919. One of the "Clean Sox," he went 13-7 for Chicago in his rookie season.

Kerr later became a minor-league manager. In 1940, the St. Louis Cardinals hired him to manage the Daytona Beach Islanders in the Florida State League. The Islanders had a young left-handed pitcher who was struggling with his control. Under manager Kerr, Stan Musial thrived. He went 18-5 in 1940 with a 2.62 ERA. His walks per nine innings dropped from 8.3 to 5.9. He also played the outfield on days he didn't pitch and showed promise as a hitter with a batting average of .311.

Musial and his pregnant wife Lil moved in with Kerr and his wife Cora during the season. When it came time to deliver the baby, it was Kerr who drove Lil to the hospital "four or five miles away, in five minutes, against red lights," he later recalled.[81] Stan and Lil named their first child Richard in honor of the minor-league manager.

In the same month Richard was born, Stan suffered an injury in the outfield. Attempting to make a shoe-string catch, Musial fell on his left shoulder. He made the catch but battled shoulder soreness the rest of the season. Just nineteen-years-old with a wife and a young son, Musial began having doubts about his career. He thought about quitting. His manager wouldn't let him do it. "You won't make it to the top as a pitcher, but you'll get there some way because you're a damn fine ballplayer and a big-league hitter," Kerr told Musial.[82]

Musial's days as a pitcher were over, but he was just getting started as a full-time hitter. He hit .343 with two minor-league clubs in 1941 and was in the big leagues with the Cardinals by September of that season. Musial hit .426 in 47 at-bats with St. Louis and never played minor league baseball again. By the time he retired, Musial had racked up 3,630 hits, a tally that included 475 home runs. A three-time National League MVP, the first-ballot Hall-of-Famer won seven batting titles and retired with a career average of .331.

In 1958, Kerr was sixty-five-years old and working as a bookkeeper for a construction manager. He and Cora were living in Houston, Texas. They moved into a new home that year, a home purchased by Musial. To express his gratitude to the man who wouldn't let him quit, Musial bought the house and gave the deed to the Kerrs.

Kerr lived there until he died in 1963, the same year Musial retired. At Kerr's funeral, Musial was among those in attendance. Loyal to the end, Musial never forgot what his former manager did for him. "I became discouraged and was afraid Dickey would tell me to forget about baseball. Then Dickey gave me the big pat on the back I needed – and just at the right time," Musial told *The Sporting News* after Kerr's death. "The Kerrs treated Lil and me as they would their own children. They were wonderful."[83]

*****

We end this chapter where we began with the story of Kid Becker, the St. Louis bookmaker shot and killed outside his home in the spring of 1919. Prosecutors in Chicago knew of Becker and brought his name up at the 1921 Black Sox trial. E.P. Melrose was a character witness for Zork. He claimed to have dinner with him the night of the fourth game of the 1919 World Series. "Did Becker's name come up at the dinner with Zork," asked Assistant State's Attorney George Gorman, "or did anyone say anything about Becker previously having fixed regular season games?"

"He was never mentioned and I know nothing about him," Melrose replied.[84]

Becker's estate left some clues about the state of baseball during this period and its relaxed stance toward those who frequently associated with gamblers and bookmakers. Among Becker's more than $264,000 in assets were three notes in excess of $38,000 signed by Otto Stifel ("Stifel was a heavy plunger on horses," noted the *St. Louis Star*).[85] Stifel was president of the Union Brewery in St. Louis. Along with Phil Ball, he was one of the principal stockholders in the St. Louis Browns.

Stifel was among those in St. Louis who heard early rumors of a fix in the 1919 World Series, thanks to his friendship with a local bookmaker. Tom Kearney had concluded the Series was fixed, based on bets he handled for Game One. "Men who would ordinarily bet a small sum were wagering thousands, because it was a sure thing."[86]

He went to Stifel with the information. "Get Ban Johnson on the phone at once," Kearney told him. "Tell him the first game was thrown and the players have sold out the entire Series."[87]

Stifel dismissed the claims with a laugh. "Tom, if I did not know you so well I would think that you were crazy."[88] Stifel chose not to pass along the information. Johnson would later say if he had heard the news after the first game, there was a probability the World Series "would have been halted or perhaps called off, until the atmosphere could be cleared."[89] History can turn on the smallest of decisions.

The information that Stifel owed St. Louis's gambling kingpin Becker nearly $40,000 became public in May of 1919. By the end of the year, Stifel had sold his baseball interest to local businessman Walter Fritsch. By the summer of 1920, he was officially a candidate for Congress, nominated by Republicans on the third of August. Fifteen days later, on the morning of August 18, he was at his farm near Valley Park in St. Louis County. His son would later say that Stifel had become extremely nervous in recent days. An unidentified bookmaker was quoted as saying that the beer magnate and former baseball owner had "lost two or three fortunes in the last few years."

Stifel left a note: "This is for the benefit of the public and my creditors. It is a brief review of how I came to get into a financial jam. Prohibition is the main trouble."[90] In the note, Stifel also admitted he had reached out to the owners of the Browns. "I lost my head and appealed to Walter Fritsch and Phil Ball," he wrote. "I was showered with kindness by these choice Masonic friends in every manner possible."[91]

Stifel's body was found on a bed, a revolver still in his hand. He had shot himself in the head, a suicide sparked by Prohibition and gambling debts.[92]

---

[1] *St. Louis Post-Dispatch*, April 16, 1919.

[2] *St. Louis Star*, April 15, 1919.

[3] Ibid, May 21, 1917.

[4] Pietrusza, David. *Rothstein: The Life, Times and Murder of the Criminal Genius Who Fixed The 1919 World Series*. Carroll & Graf Publishers. 2003.

[5] Carney, Gene. *Burying The Black Sox: How Baseball's Cover-Up of the 1919 World Series Fix Almost Succeeded.* Potomac Books, Inc. 2006. The World Series in 1918 was played in September. The season was cut short by World War I.

[6] Becker was shot by members of a St. Louis group known as the Cuckoo Gang. Waugh, Daniel. *Egan's Rats: The Untold Story of the Prohibition-Era Gang That Ruled St. Louis.* Cumberland House Publishing, Inc. 2007.

[7] Pietrusza, *Rothstein.*

---

[8] Spink, *Judge Landis and Twenty-Five Years of Baseball*. Spink voiced his concerns to Ban Johnson after Game 1. "Do you know," the American League president replied, "Hughie Fullerton told me the same thing."
[9] Carney, *Burying The Black Sox*.
[10] *New York Evening World*, December 15, 1919.
[11] Ibid, December 17, 1919. The three from St. Louis Fullerton mentioned were Carl Zork, Joe Pesch and Harry Redmon (Fullerton calls him Redmond).
[12] Pietrusza, *Rothstein.*
[13] Asinof, Eliot. *1919: America's Loss Of Innocence.* Donald I. Fine, Inc. 1990.
[14] Pietrusza, *Rothstein*.
[15] Ibid.
[16] Ibid.
[17] Ibid.
[18] *St. Louis Post-Dispatch*, September 24, 1920.
[19] Allardice, Bruce. *Nat Evans*. SABR.org biography project.
[20] Ibid.
[21] Ibid.
[22] Ibid.
[23] Pietrusza, *Rothstein.*
[24] Ibid.
[25] Ibid.
[26] *New York Herald*, October 4, 1920.
[27] Pietrusza, *Rothstein.*
[28] Both Weeghman and Tennes testified to the grand jury in 1920. Tennes denied telling Weeghman about the plot.
[29] The article claims Becker's chief assistant "was a man known to the gamblers of the city as 'Sammy the Gook.'" Zork would accompany bookmaker Joe Pesch and his brother Will to whatever park was open that day. The Cardinals and Browns had separate stadiums at the time. *St. Louis Post-Dispatch*, July 11, 1913.
[30] Allardice, Bruce. *SABR Black Scandal Research Committee Newsletter*, December 2014.
[31] Attell is frequently and incorrectly credited with winning the featherweight title with his victory over Dixon, but Dixon had already lost the title to Terry McGovern by the time they fought. See *New York Times*, January 10, 1900. McGovern also prevailed in a rematch in June of the same year. See *New York Times*, June 24, 1900. McGovern lost the title to "Young Corbett" (William Rockwell) the following year. See *New York Times*, November 29, 1901.
[32] *New York Times*, February 7, 1970. The *Times* says his record was 91 wins, 10 losses with 67 other fights that were "draws or no decision, a common practice in boxing's early days."
[33] Attell, Abe. "How I Won The World's Featherweight Championship," *St. Louis Post-Dispatch*, February 7, 1904.
[34] *St. Louis Post-Dispatch*, January 28, 1912.

---

[35] The loss to Kirk in 1912 meant at least five of Attell's ten defeats occurred in St. Louis.
[36] *St. Louis Post-Dispatch*, March 23, 1913.
[37] Allardice, *SABR Newsletter*, December 2014.
[38] Carney, *Burying The Black Sox.*
[39] Veeck, Bill with Ed Linn. *The Hustler's Handbook*. Simon & Schuster Inc. 1965. In addition to the diary, Black Sox researchers also point to other evidence. In 1930, White Sox owner Comiskey gave an interview to Sid Keener of the *St. Louis Star* in which he revealed he heard reports about the fix before Game One was played. "I blame Ban Johnson for allowing the series to be completed," Comiskey told Keener. "Why didn't he stop it?" *St. Louis Star*, December 13, 1930.
[40] *New York Evening World*, October 27, 1920. Redmon also insisted he wasn't looking for the $10,000 reward money Comiskey had offered. He did say Comiskey later sent him a check to cover his expenses to Chicago.
[41] Redmon's grand jury testimony from the Black Sox files at the Chicago History Museum. The author reviewed the files on August 19, 2015.
[42] The trade, described as a "blockbuster deal" by *Baseball Reference* sent Pratt and Plank to the Yankees in exchange for Gedeon, Fritz Maisel (the man who accompanied Jack Dunn on his scouting trip of Babe Ruth), pitcher Nick Cullop, catcher Les Nunamaker, and pitcher Urban Shocker, who became the ace of the Browns staff.
[43] *St. Louis Post-Dispatch*, March 15, 1918.
[44] Ibid, June 29, 1919. The sub-headline to the piece reads, "Gedeon's Error Is Break That Wins For Chicago Sox."
[45] Carney, *Burying The Black Sox*. Carney cites his source as *The Sporting News* obituary on Gedeon. In fact, it's the paper's obituary on Risberg in 1975 that says the Browns second baseman learned of the fix from Risberg via a telegram "couching the details in what amounted to a code."
[46] Newman, Timothy and Stuckman, Bruce. "They Were Black Sox Long Before the 1919 World Series." *Base Ball: A Journal of the Early Game, Vol. 6, No. 1.* McFarland & Company, Inc. 2012. Exactly how much Zork bet on the Reds in the 1919 World Series is a point of disagreement among Black Sox researchers. Researcher Bruce Allardice told the author in an email exchange he thinks the figure was likely $5,000. See Bill Lamb's book, *Black Sox in the Courtroom: The Grand Jury, Criminal Trial and Civil Litigation* and Alllardice's work at *SABR.org* for more.
[47] *St. Louis Globe-Democrat*, January 18, 1920.
[48] Carney, Gene. "Comiskey's Detectives". *SABR Research Journal.* Fall 2009.
[49] Ibid.
[50] Carney, *Burying The Black Sox.*
[51] *Sporting News*, November 11, 1920.
[52] Newman and Stuckman, "They Were Black Sox Long Before the 1919 World Series."
[53] Ibid. "Later, there was some suggestion that the 1915 Salt Lake City club fixed games."

---

[54] *New York Times*, September 29, 1920. Some Black Sox researchers believe the *Times* reference is to the gambling scandal in the Pacific Coast League in 1919, and not about anything related to 1915.
[55] *New York Evening World*, December 15, 1919.
[56] Lamb, William F. "The Black Sox Scandal." *Scandal on the South Side: The 1919 Chicago White Sox.* Jacob Pomrenke, editor. Society for American Baseball Research, Inc. 2015.
[57] *New York Times,* March 27, 1921.
[58] *St. Louis Post-Dispatch*, March 28, 1921.
[59] *Sporting News*, October 9, 1957.
[60] Ibid.
[61] *New York Times*, April 2, 1921. The other men arrested with Evans, identified in the story as "Nate Evens," were Sydny Stajer, Hyman Cohen and Elias Fink.
[62] *New York Times*, November 18, 1976.
[63] Burns' gambling partner was Billy Maharg. While not indicted, Maharg was also a witness for the prosecution. When Maharg spilled details of the scandal to the *Philadelphia North American* newspaper on September 27, 1920, player confessions soon followed. Maharg was a longtime friend of Grover Cleveland Alexander, a player mentioned in Grabiner's diary.
[64] *St. Louis Post-Dispatch*, July 22, 1921.
[65] *Alton Evening Telegraph,* July 22, 1921. There are conflicting reports if Redmon means to describe only Zork or Zork and a partner. On July 28, the *St. Louis Post-Dispatch* quoted Redmon as saying on the stand that Zork told him, "I am the little red head from St. Louis who started the whole thing." One day earlier, the *New York Times* quoted Redmon saying Zork told him that he and "a redheaded fellow from St. Louis" fixed the series. See *New York Times*, July 27, 1921.
[66] Allardice, Bruce. "The St. Louis connection. Carl Zork & Ben Franklin." *SABR Black Sox Scandal Research Committee Newsletter*, Vol. 6, No. 2, December 1914.
[67] *St. Louis Post-Dispatch*, July 22, 1921.
[68] Ibid, July 27, 1921.
[69] *New York Times*, August 3, 1921.
[70] *St. Louis Post-Dispatch,* August 3, 1921.
[71] Email exchange with the author.
[72] Gedeon was redheaded and so was Zork, Redmon describes Zork as a "red-headed Jew" in his grand jury testimony.
[73] One theory is that investigators prosecuted these men in an attempt to get at their higher-ups in the plot. Another possibility is that Rothstein simply bribed his way out of an indictment.
[74] Lamb, Bill. *Gene Paulette.* SABR.org biography project. The two other players were never identified but Landis later said Paulette denied "that he had any basis whatever for using the names of these players and asserted that so far as he knew they were honest men."

---

[75] This was the second trade Rickey made with the Phillies in 1919. The Cardinals had previously sent three players to Philadelphia in January. One of them was pitcher Gene Packard. Harry Grabiner's diary contained an unexplained notation next to Packard's name: "1918 World Series fixer." Veeck, *The Hustler's Handbook*. Veeck published excerpts. The original diary has never been located. chicagobaseballmuseum.org/wp-content/uploads/CBM-Harrys-Diary-20121228.pdf. Two pages of the diary were posted online at BlackBetsy.com. (Black Betsy was the name of Shoeless Joe Jackson's bat.) Calling it "pure speculation," author Gene Carney wrote, "Perhaps it was Gene *Paulette* and not Gene *Packard* beside whose name Harry Grabiner jotted in his famous diary."
[76] Lamb, *Gene Paulette*.
[77] Ginsburg, Daniel E. *The Fix Is In. A History of Baseball Gambling and Game Fixing Scandals.* McFarland & Company, Inc. 1995.
[78] Ibid.
[79] The judge in the criminal trial bløcked testimony about Zork's fixing of earlier games. See Allardice, "The St. Louis connection."
[80] *The Sporting News*, May 18, 1963.
[81] Ibid.
[82] Vecsey, George. *Stan Musial: An American Life.* ESPN Books. 2011.
[83] *The Sporting News*, May 18, 1963.
[84] *St. Louis Post-Dispatch*, July 28, 1921.
[85] *St. Louis Star,* August 19 and October 27, 1920. The details of the three notes totaling $38,742 are covered in the August story. The October story mentions that Stifel also owed Tom Kearney $10,000.
[86] Carney, *Burying The Black Sox.*
[87] *St. Louis Post-Dispatch*, February 16, 1929.
[88] Ibid.
[89] Ibid. Johnson and Comiskey were feuding at the time and not on speaking terms. When Comiskey, through an intermediary, eventually relayed his concerns about his players to Johnson (after Game 2), the AL president dismissed the claims. "Comiskey has lost two games He's crying, he's calling this series a fake simply because he's the loser," Johnson said (according to Comiskey*). St. Louis Star*, December 13, 1930. Other evidence suggests Johnson was aware of something after Game 1 (see endnote 7 of this chapter).
[90] Ibid, August 19, 1920.
[91] *St. Louis Post-Dispatch* and *St. Louis Star*, August 18, 1920.
[92] Suicides by prominent St. Louis German-Americans, which included a number of brewers, became so notorious that their affliction became known as the "Dutch Act." Those brewers included Stifel, August Busch Sr. and four members of the Lemp family. www.beerhistory.com/library/holdings/lemp6.shtml.

Beer and Baseball

Beer was in his blood. His grandfather started in the brewery business after emigrating from Germany in the nineteenth-century. His father continued in the family business. As the third-generation brewer, he started working in the family operation in his twenties. Under his leadership, the company prospered. It brought him fortune. He owned multiple homes, a yacht, and prize-winning animals. He took delight in taking the reins of a horse-drawn beer wagon.

It was baseball that gave him fame. At first, he didn't want the franchise he purchased. He wasn't a fan. The team had an undistinguished early history. It was a second-class citizen in its own city for the first two decades of the century. The hometown club in the other league was more profitable and more successful in that era. The second-class status extended to the ballpark. The team he acquired paid rent to the hometown rival.

Fans of the St. Louis Cardinals may recognize this as the story of Anheuser-Busch and the company's iconic leader, August A. Busch Jr., better known as "Gussie." But fans of the New York Yankees may also claim the description. Like Busch, Jacob Ruppert was a third-generation beer baron. Both joined the family business as young men. Both were fiercely proud of their German heritage. Each spoke the language. Ruppert, despite being a second-generation American, even spoke with a German accent. He always called Babe Ruth "Root." As an anti-German backlash erupted in the country with the entry of the United States into World War I in 1917, both families and their companies were forced to prove their American bona fides.

Neither man grew up as part of the establishment in his hometown. The Protestant natives viewed the German-Catholic brewers with suspicion. Ostentatious displays of wealth by Gussie's family were termed "Buschy" in St. Louis. In New York, Ruppert's family met with similar doubts. "As a nouveau riche family who made their fortune brewing beer and were Catholic rather than Protestant, they were never part of the 'Four Hundred,'" wrote Ruppert biographers Steve Steinberg and Lyle Spatz.[1]

Both men were active in Democratic Party politics. In 1898, Ruppert ran for Congress and won. He served four terms. In 1906, the *Washington Post* named him as one of fourteen millionaires serving in the House of Representatives.[2] Busch worked to elect fellow Missourian Harry Truman as President in 1948 and diligently raised money for John F. Kennedy in the election of 1960. "All you had to do was tell Gussie that money was getting tight and more was needed," recalled Massachusetts congressman and later Speaker of the House Tip O'Neill. "In a few days, a package would drop from heaven. Gussie raised it faster and easier than anybody in that era."[3] Busch found a kindred spirit in Lyndon Baines Johnson. Anheuser-Busch biographers Peter Hernon and Terry Ganey went so far as to describe LBJ as "Gussie's true soul mate."[4] Busch and Johnson shared many traits, including a domineering personality and a propensity to do business anywhere, including the bathroom.[5]

Busch joined the military in World War II and left with the rank of colonel. Ruppert joined the National Guard as a young man and later received an honorary title from the Governor of New York. He was known as Colonel Ruppert. Busch's family frequently spent their summers at their home in Cooperstown, New York, better known today as the home of the Baseball Hall of Fame. Ruppert often spent his winters in the resort town of French Lick, Indiana, better known today as the hometown of NBA legend and lifelong St. Louis Cardinals fan Larry Bird.[6]

When Ruppert, along with Til Huston, bought the Yankees in 1915, he wanted to name the team "Knickerbockers" after one of his beers. When Busch, through the Anheuser-Busch corporation, acquired the Cardinals in 1953, he wanted to rename his home park "Budweiser" in honor of the iconic A-B brand. Both moves backfired. Neither man got his wish.

Both companies, Anheuser-Busch and the Jacob Ruppert Brewery, survived Prohibition. The vast majority of brewers in the country did not. They survived through creativity. Both companies used the spare capacity in their plants to make other products such as malt syrup and non-alcoholic beverages.

The beginning and end of Prohibition generated milestone moments for Ruppert and Busch. The Yankees' acquisition of Babe Ruth made front-page news on January 5, 1920. Prohibition started eleven days later. On the day beer sales became legal again, Busch arranged for a case of his company's product to be delivered to President Franklin Roosevelt. On April 7, 1933, the Budweiser Clydesdales trotted down Pennsylvania Avenue.

What is less known is that a separate team of Clydesdales also paraded up the streets of Manhattan on the same day. Anheuser-Busch wanted to thank New York Governor Al Smith. The first case of beer produced by the Jacob Ruppert Brewery after the ban was lifted also went to Smith, the Democrat who unsuccessfully opposed Herbert Hoover in the presidential election in 1928 and pledged to overturn Prohibition.

While the business lives of the two titans only briefly overlapped – Ruppert was born thirty-two years earlier and died fifty years before Busch – the themes of beer and baseball were central to the careers of both. Ruppert needed Ruth and the Yankees in

1920 because he no longer had beer. With the end of Prohibition in 1933, Busch had beer and eventually figured out baseball would help him sell even more.

*****

"The 1920s was in many ways the most strange and wondrous decade in American history," wrote author Bill Bryson, "and nothing made it more so than Prohibition." Other than race, perhaps no issue has ever divided the country as much as alcohol did in the late nineteenth and early twentieth centuries.

The roots of the battle mirrored those faced by baseball in its early days and the wars between the American Association and the National League. When the leagues merged, the sale of beer at parks became more accepted and Sunday games grew increasingly common. St. Louis Browns owner Chris Von der Ahe and other baseball "wets" declared victory. Outside of the sport, though, the "drys" were undeterred. With anti-alcohol groups such as the Women's Christian Temperance Union and the Anti-Saloon League taking root in the nineteenth century, activists focused their early efforts on states and municipalities. Their message on the evils of alcohol, delivered countless times by women like Carrie Nation and men such as Branch Rickey, found an enthusiastic audience.

By 1917, twenty-seven of the forty-eight states in the country were already dry. In states where alcohol was still legal, many counties placed bans on the product. In Missouri, ninety-six counties were dry by 1917. Only eighteen counties and the city of St. Louis were wet.[7]

The divide in Missouri reflected the disagreement over alcohol nationwide. The battle over Prohibition pitted rural versus urban, Protestant versus Catholic, native-born Americans versus newly arrived immigrants. Another battle cut across class lines. The wealthy in America wanted no part of alcoholic abstinence. Historian Frederick Lewis Allen wrote that "among the prosperous classes which set the standards of national society behavior, alcohol flowed more freely than ever before..."[8] In 1925, a federal grand jury in New York began investigating a nationwide bootleg syndicate. Investigators traced illicit alcohol shipments to seventy cities, including St. Louis. The prospective customer list included every member of the St. Louis Country Club.[9]

War gave a final push toward a national prohibition. Those who wanted to ban alcohol often made no distinction between America's enemies in World War I and brewers in the United States with European heritage. "We are fighting three enemies," proclaimed a patriotic ad for cereal-maker Kellogg's, "Germany, Austria, and drink."[10]

An anti-German backlash that began with the outbreak of war in Europe in 1914 developed into a full-blown hysteria a few years later. Sauerkraut became "Liberty cabbage," the St. Louis symphony stopped performing the works of German composers, and Berlin Avenue in the city was renamed Pershing.[11]

One of the ugliest incidents took place in Collinsville, Illinois, just across the Mississippi River from St. Louis. Robert Paul Prager was a German-born coal miner suspected of trying to convert Illinois miners to socialism. His activism backfired when a group of miners seized him in April of 1918. They made him walk barefoot on the streets of the town with an American flag on his back.

Fearing for his safety, the Collinsville police put him in jail. The move failed to protect him. An angry mob stormed the jail and dragged him away. In front of a crowd of two-hundred people, Prager was hanged on a tree just outside of town. Eleven Collinsville residents were charged in the case. A jury took forty-five minutes to deliberate and then declared them all not guilty. Prager is buried in a South St. Louis cemetery where his tombstone reads, "the victim of a mob."[12]

The backlash and suspicion caused issues for bachelor Ruppert in New York and members of the Busch family in St. Louis. Ruppert donated to many German causes right up to the outbreak of war. He later had to distance himself from his German roots. "Germany must be whipped, and whipped thoroughly," Ruppert said at one point. "The war first, baseball last," he said in May of 1918.[13]

Born in 1899, Busch was a teenager during World War I. His family was at their home in Germany when bullets started flying in the summer of 1914. While the rest of the Busch clan quickly returned to the United States, Gussie's grandmother Lilly remained in Germany with her two married daughters until 1918. When she finally returned home, she was detained by government officials for forty hours in Key West, Florida and was subjected to a strip search, including "a very thorough examination of her vagina and womb."[14]

During the war, Gussie's father, August Busch Sr., gave $100,000 to the Red Cross, publicly announced he was buying $1.5 million worth of Liberty Bonds, and started wearing an American flag button on his lapel. As president of Anheuser-Busch, August Sr. had every incentive to demonstrate his loyalty to America. He had a company and a reputation to protect. Both of his sisters married German men who supported the German war effort. A New York minister accused Anheuser-Busch of sending $400,000 annually to the German Kaiser. Busch blamed the rumors on "gossip mongers," "fanatic zealots," and "jealous competitors."[15]

By December of 1917, eight months after the United States had entered World War I, both the House and Senate passed Prohibition. The measure then went to the states. When Nebraska became the thirty-sixth state to ratify the Eighteenth Amendment in January of 1919 (later that same day, Missouri became the thirty-seventh state to ratify), the clock began ticking toward making alcohol illegal. The country had one year to shut down a $2 billion industry, the fifth-largest in the nation. The move had major economic consequences, almost all of them disastrous.

Most brewers in the country closed their doors and laid off their workers. They did so with no compensation from the government. States such as New York had relied on liquor taxes to generate much of their revenue. The federal government received hundreds of millions of dollars annually from liquor taxes. It was now all gone. In addition, the government now had to spend millions every year on enforcement. It fought a losing battle from the start.

The government hired 1,500 Prohibition agents to police the activities of 100 million people in a country with 3.5 million square miles of territory and 18,700 miles of coastlines and borders.[16] Bribery was common. Corruption was rampant. A thriving and legal industry was transferred into the hands of violent gangs that ruled by bullets and intimidation. In the first two-and-a-half years of Prohibition, thirty federal agents were killed. The national murder rate spiked by more than thirty percent during the decade.[17]

In New York City, restaurants and hotels that relied on alcohol sales shut down while speakeasies blossomed on every corner. In Manhattan, the Knickerbocker Hotel was converted to offices in 1921. The home of the dry martini reportedly generated $4,000 a day from alcohol before Prohibition. The legendary New York restaurant Delmonico's closed its doors in 1923. At the same time, illegal alcohol flowed freely. In one Manhattan block, an estimated 32 speakeasies were open for business.[18] Legend has it that when the mayor of Berlin visited in the fall of 1929, he asked his New York City counterpart, Mayor Jimmy Walker, "When does the Prohibition law go into effect?" It had been the law of the land for nearly a decade.[19] "It cannot be truthfully said that Prohibition enforcement has failed in New York," remarked Assistant U.S. Attorney Mabel Willebrandt. "It has not yet been attempted."

From his brewery on the Upper West Side of Manhattan, Yankees owner Ruppert was perhaps one of the few in the city to comply with the law. Born in 1867, Ruppert became general manager of the family brewing business at the age of twenty-three. He split his time between the family home on Fifth Avenue in Manhattan and a country estate in Garrison, New York, where he raised prize-winning St. Bernard's and had a stable of horses. In a comment that could have just as easily been said by Gussie Busch, Ruppert admitted he enjoyed driving his company's brewery-wagon horses. "Brewery teams were as pretty to see operate as a nicely stepping ball-team." A lifelong bachelor, he was known to be intensely private, impeccably dressed, punctual, and fastidious. "You could eat off the floor," Yankees pitcher Waite Hoyt once said of Ruppert's office. "You could not imagine it was a brewery."[20]

Ruppert grew up a fan of the National League New York Giants, the dominant team in the city at the time. Ironically, it was the Giants manager John McGraw who convinced him and Til Houston to purchase the Yankees in 1915. "To us, the Giants were the only game in town," Ruppert said, "but McGraw convinced us."[21]

Five years later when the Eighteenth Amendment took effect, Ruppert decided to challenge the Volstead Act, the law that gave Prohibition its enforcement teeth. The suit went all the way to the Supreme Court, where the justices ruled 5-4 that the act was legal. Having lost in court, Ruppert fell in line. "From all indications," wrote Ruppert biographers Steinburg and Spatz, "he fully complied with Prohibition for its entire duration." The Yankees owner "was almost fanatical in his adherence to the law. He would not even have real beer in his home."[22]

The same adherence to the law did not extend to his ball club. "Yankees Training On Scotch," read one often cited spring training headline. They were led on the field and off by their slugging outfielder, Babe Ruth, who had just turned 27 years old in February of that year. "Ruth ignored many laws of civilized society, but the one he flouted with most contempt was Prohibition," wrote author Robert Weintraub. "Booze, in staggering amounts – is a key cog in the Ruthian myth."[23]

Later in the decade, when the Yankees would travel to St. Louis to play the Browns, Ruth and Lou Gehrig often played a round of golf at a country club in the suburbs of the city. Two players from the Browns would round out the foursome on an off day during the season. Longtime Kirkwood, Missouri resident Earl Maschmeier worked as a caddie in his youth. "They usually had five caddies," Maschmeier remembered, "four caddies for carrying clubs and the like and usually one caddy to carry a gallon or so of Gin Rickeys. That was par for the course in those days."[24]

St. Louis had its own unique history during the Prohibition Era. A *New York Times* writer arrived in the city during Prohibition surprised to find so few speakeasies in the city. "St. Louis probably has fewer speakeasies than any city of its class," wrote *Times* reporter Louis La Coss. "This may be due, as has been explained, that St. Louisans are beer drinkers and home brew is a staple commodity in many homes."[25]

The city had an estimated 1,000 speakeasies and another 14,000 "beer flats" that served home brew and other drinks during Prohibition, according to St. Louis historian Robbi Courtaway. That's 15,000 establishments in a city with roughly 800,000 residents in the 1920s. Perhaps not as many as other urban areas, but residents still had plenty of options to get their thirst quenched and keep law enforcement busy. Front and center in the Prohibition Era stories in St. Louis were Gussie Busch and other members of his dynastic family.

*****

In late May of 1922, nearly four years after the end of World War I, August Busch Sr. set sail for the family home in Germany. Departing from New York, the luxury liner *George Washington* soon became a floating bar, serving up French wine, Scotch whisky, English and German beers. To an American beer maker living under Prohibition, this came as quite a surprise. To add insult to injury, the ship was owned by the United States Shipping Board, part of the federal government.

Reaching port in Cherbourg, France, Busch fired off a telegram that made its way to President Harding. He included in the note one of the ship's wine lists. "This makes the United States incomparably the biggest bootlegger in the world."[26] The letter quickly went public.

Harding turned the matter over to Albert Lasker, the chairman of the Shipping Board. He also happened to be one of the owners of the Chicago Cubs. Responding to Busch's letter, Lasker cited a technicality, pointing out the sale of alcohol occurred outside the three-mile limit on national jurisdiction over the seas. He also went on the attack. While Busch saw a hypocritical government profiting from liquor sales on open water while denying its citizens the same right on dry land, Lasker saw more than a whiff of hypocrisy in the actions of the brewer. "I believe your letter to be thoroughly selfish and that you are acting in the hope of creating a revolt against prohibition so that you may again revive the sale of your liquors," Lasker wrote in part.

In closing, Lasker dredged up old rumors about Busch family connections to Germany. "It is, of course, notorious that the Adolphus Busch who founded your brewery was possibly the Kaiser's closest friend in America, and that your family for many years has maintained a castle in Germany."[27]

The *St. Louis Post-Dispatch*, Busch's hometown paper, was outraged. Under the headline, "National Hypocrisy," the paper called the Shipping Board "a shining mausoleum of moral corruption" and asked, "Why should the Government destroy the great breweries which made and sold only beer, while it promotes its own shipping business by selling all kinds of highly intoxicating liquor?"[28]

With August Sr. away in Europe, it fell to his oldest son, Adolphus III (Gussie's brother), to give the brewery's response to Lasker's charges. "You have misunderstood, and therefore assailed our motive in writing the President," wrote the Anheuser-Busch vice president. "The temperature in my office is well above 90," he noted in closing, "and the law prohibits me from making here in America a glass of wholesome beer... Yet, as I write...the Shipping Board [is] approving vouchers for the disbursement of American Government money from the treasury in payment for German and British beers and wines to be sold by our Government at a profit. The prospect does not, I assure, tend to lower the temperature."[29]

The battle between the Shipping Board and Anheuser-Busch went on for weeks. Everyone from the Attorney General to the Anti-Saloon League felt compelled to weigh in on the matter. The tide of public opinion began shifting in favor of the Busch position. "Even a brewer," *The New York Times* editorialized, "has the right to report a violation of the Volstead Act." Added the editors of the *New York World*: "What could be a more shameful spectacle than a Government that breaks its own laws?"[30]

The Busch family advocacy paid off. The government moved to ban liquor onboard American ships and extend its range of jurisdiction. Any foreign ship approaching the United States now had to lock up its liquor or toss it overboard once it came within 12 miles of the country's coastline.[31] In a skirmish over alcohol, the future owners of the Cardinals bested the one-time owner of the Cubs.

*****

On the night of December 31, 1922, more than 2,000 revelers gathered at the Chase Hotel in the Central West End of St. Louis to ring in the New Year. They paid $10 a plate to listen to the music of the Paul Whiteman Orchestra. Given the crowd and the occasion, Prohibition agents also thought it a good idea to go to the Chase that night. When they arrived, the party was in full swing. Agents spotted liquor being served at one of the tables. One of the officers attempted to place a guest under arrest. Then all hell broke loose.

"Bullets, Chairs and Tableware Fly in Riot As St. Louisans Run Dry Squad Out of Hotel," read the front-page headline in *The New York Times* a few days later. When the officers attempted to make the arrest, someone threw a chair, according to the *Times* account. "Excitement followed and a shot was fired."[32]

Two men were shot and wounded that night. One of them was hit below the knee as he was dancing with his wife. Another man was shot in the foot. The New Year's Eve celebrants didn't appreciate the rude arrival of the party crashers and decided to fight back.

They hurled "chairs, glassware, plates, knives and forks" at the agents and police officers. "It seemed to me a good-natured affair at first, but it developed into a rough and tumble," said one Sergeant Glasco. "I don't know who fired the shots. We couldn't do anything. One woman had me by the collar as we were leaving."[33]

The shooter was later identified as St. Louis police detective Edward Sullivan, who claimed he was attacked by a mob. "I was attacked by several men, all of whom were striking me from the rear." Sullivan had a lacerated lip, four loose front teeth and bruises on his back and sides. He claimed the crowd, containing "about 250 drunks," was yelling "lynch them" and "throw them out." [34]

The outnumbered authorities fled the building and didn't return. "I know that some of the best people in St. Louis were in the room," said Prohibition agent Gus Nations, "and I decided it was better for us to lose and retreat than to injure any of them."[35]

One of those "best people in St. Louis" attending the party that night was 18-year old Alice Busch, Gussie's younger sister and the reigning queen of the Veiled Prophet Ball, an annual St. Louis society event. After her coronation in October, the *Post-Dispatch* described her as "5 feet and 7 inches tall," with "medium blonde-chestnut" hair, "somewhat slender," with "very dainty" hands and small feet.[36] As for the events of New Year's Eve, the youngest daughter of August Sr. claimed the trouble started when a Prohibition agent lifted a tablecloth on an adjoining table.[37]

No arrests were made at the Chase that evening. With law enforcement out of the way, the party continued until daylight.

*****

Owen Patrick Smith is considered the "Father of Modern Greyhound Racing." He invented the mechanical rabbit, which the greyhounds chase around the track. He opened the first dog track in America in Emeryville, California in 1919. The next year, he introduced electric light to a track in Tulsa, Oklahoma, making night racing possible. From there, he expanded to tracks around the country, including Chicago and East St. Louis, Illinois.[38]

Smith used a St. Louis attorney, Edward Joseph "Eddie" O'Hare, when he decided to patent the mechanical rabbit. When Smith passed away, O'Hare bought the patent from Smith's wife and got in the dog track business. After divorcing his wife in 1927, O'Hare moved to Chicago.

O'Hare wanted to open a dog track in Cicero, a Chicago suburb. He had a competitor who not only owned racetracks but had a multi-million-dollar business empire. The two men decided to merge their racing interests. O'Hare now had a silent partner. His name was Al Capone. The gangster's involvement made life easier for O'Hare. Betting on greyhound racing was illegal in Illinois. Police would occasionally raid the place, shut it down, and force O'Hare to answer questions about the business. His response to an assistant state's attorney illustrates why O'Hare was sometimes referred to as "Fast Eddie."

When asked if gambling took place at the track, O'Hare explained, "Persons coming to the track do not wager. They make contributions for the better development of greyhounds."[39] Authorities never kept the track shut down for long. In a few years, it was generating more than $100,000 in annual profits.[40]

O'Hare's partner, Capone, the Prohibition era's most famous criminal, came to Chicago from New York in 1919. A facial wound from a knife attack gave him a nickname he despised, "Scarface." In 1925, he replaced Johnny Torrio as the crime boss of Chicago. His gangs controlled the bootleg alcohol business in the city, estimated at $60 million a year. Illegal alcohol was just one piece of his vast domain. He controlled gaming establishments, "vice, dancehalls, roadhouses, and other resorts." Capone's men would famously offer "protection" for a business owner in exchange for cash. Or else. "It prospered because the victim soon learned that if he did not pay, his shop would be bombed, or his trucks wrecked, or he himself might be shot in cold blood..."[41] The State Attorney's office estimated there were seventy-five active rackets in operation in the city. The cost to the citizens of Chicago? $136 million annually.[42]

Prohibition proved to be a wonderful boon to Capone's business. In a city with 10,000 speakeasies, alcohol was always in high demand. To satisfy demand, Capone had six breweries in the city, turning out real beer. But he needed material and equipment, including the device used to tap beer kegs. Enter Gussie Busch.

The brewery had heard Capone's gangs were stealing their keg taps. Sensing a business opportunity, August Sr. sent Gussie to meet with the crime boss. According to biographers Hernon and Ganey, the meeting took place in Miami. The two men struck a deal. Busch would deliver taps to Capone. In turn, Capone would provide sales for Anheuser-Busch's yeast and other products the brewery was making to survive the lean years of Prohibition.

Capone's bootleg business kept humming right along throughout the 1920s. So did his dog track business with O'Hare. It later expanded to locations in Florida, Massachusetts and West Memphis, Arkansas. One of O'Hare's partners in the Miami Beach Kennel Club was St. Louis Browns owner Phil Ball.[43] O'Hare's original dog track in Cicero, Illinois was eventually converted to a horse track. O'Hare dubbed it "Sportsman's Park," the same name of the stadium owned by Ball and shared by the Browns and Cardinals in St. Louis.

In 1930, attorney O'Hare returned to St. Louis for a meeting at the Missouri Athletic Club with an Internal Revenue Service agent and a *Post-Dispatch* reporter who had coordinated it. Capone biographer Jonathan Eig described John T. Rogers as "the paper's shining star." Rogers' reporting on an abusive federal judge forced his resignation. For his investigative efforts, Rogers won a Pulitzer Prize.[44] Joining O'Hare and Rogers that day in St. Louis was IRS agent Frank Wilson.

At the meeting, O'Hare turned over to Wilson records related to Capone. The gangster's wealth attracted attention from many interested parties, including the IRS, which had determined Capone had never filed a tax return. Included in the information O'Hare gave were the names of two Capone bookkeepers. O'Hare's information helped lead to Capone being charged with income tax evasion the following year. In November 1931, Capone was convicted and sentenced to eleven years in federal prison. O'Hare's "contributions to the investigation of Al Capone ought to be put in proper perspective," said Ed Burke, the longest-serving alderman in Chicago history, "and without his cooperation, there never would have been a case against Capone."[45]

Suffering from gonorrhea and syphilis, as well as withdrawal symptoms from cocaine addiction, Capone entered the federal prison system in Atlanta in May of 1932. Federal authorities later transferred him to Alcatraz Federal Penitentiary off the coast of San Francisco. He was paroled on November 16, 1939.

Eight days before Capone's release, on Wednesday, November 8, O'Hare departed Sportsman's Park for the day. The fall season at the track ended the previous Saturday. O'Hare was wrapping up business and preparing to head to Florida for the winter. Driving on the southwest side of Chicago, O'Hare's Lincoln Zephyr was crowded to the curb by one or more vehicles. Two shotgun blasts struck his head and neck. His coupe struck a light pole. O'Hare was dead, "assassinated in gangster fashion."[46]

When he divorced his wife and departed for Chicago, O'Hare left behind a family in St. Louis, two daughters and a son, Edward "Butch" O'Hare. Butch grew up with a fascination for flying airplanes. He got it honestly from his father, who once flew with Charles Lindbergh in his mail plane. Butch wanted to become a Navy Pilot. Thanks to his father's St. Louis political connections, the younger O'Hare received an appointment to the U.S. Naval Academy. One of the theories developed over the years is that Eddie O'Hare cooperated with authorities in the Capone investigation in exchange for helping his son secure the appointment. "Does he realize...he is taking his life in his hands?" IRS Wilson asked reporter Rogers about the elder O'Hare and that fateful meeting in St. Louis in 1930. "Hell, Frank, if Eddie had ten lives to live he'd jeopardize every one of them for that boy Butch," Rogers replied.[47]

In February of 1942, Butch O'Hare was a navy pilot aboard the *USS Lexington*. The aircraft carrier was in the Pacific because of the Japanese attack on Pearl Harbor two months earlier. America had entered World War II. Steaming toward Australia, the *Lexington* found itself under attack by Japanese bombers. With a second wave of attacks imminent, O'Hare launched his fighter plane from the deck of the carrier. He found the enemy bombers flying in a V formation just minutes away from the *Lexington*. O'Hare swooped down and opened fire. He shot down five Japanese planes in less than four minutes.[48]

Butch O'Hare's actions became front-page news across the United States. He returned home to a hero's welcome. At a White House ceremony, President Franklin Roosevelt promoted Butch to lieutenant commander and awarded him the Medal of Honor. His wife Rita, a nurse at Deaconess Hospital in St. Louis, hung the medal around his neck. He then returned to his hometown where the crowd for his parade was estimated at 60,000 people and compared to the one St. Louis gave for Charles Lindbergh following his successful trans-Atlantic flight in 1927.[49]

O'Hare returned to action in the Pacific Theater. In August of 1943, the Navy promoted Butch to air-group commander. He oversaw three squadrons. Three months later, he was assigned to the *USS Enterprise*. On the night of November 26, O'Hare's Hellcat fighter plane was shot down. Official word came on December 9. Butch O'Hare was missing in action. A Mass of Requiem was offered for the Navy pilot at the St. Louis Cathedral on December 20, 1943.[50]

In the spring of 1947, Colonel Robert McCormick, the publisher of the *Chicago Tribune,* floated the idea of changing the name of Chicago's Orchard Depot Airport to honor Butch O'Hare. Just days later, Frank Wilson revealed to *Collier's* the role that Butch's father played in prosecuting Capone. "On the inside of the gang I had one of the best undercover-men I have ever known: Eddie O'Hare," the IRS agent told the magazine.[51] In death, as in life, the stories of father and son were intertwined. Momentum began to build for a tribute to Butch. The idea became reality two years later. The fourth-busiest airport in the world is named for a man who never lived in Chicago. O'Hare Airport is named for Butch O'Hare, the St. Louis native and World War II hero.

The business interests of his father add another link to the St. Louis-Chicago chain. After Eddie O'Hare's death, Sportsman's Park, the Illinois race track, was sold to the Bidwill family, the same Bidwill family that owned the Chicago Cardinals of the NFL.[52] The same Bidwill family that moved the Cardinals to St. Louis in 1960, and then following the 1987 season, to Phoenix, where the Arizona Cardinals play today. While in St. Louis, the football Cardinals played their games at the original Sportsman's Park (by then called Busch Stadium) for their first six seasons in town as tenants of the baseball Cardinals, owned at the time by Anheuser-Busch.

The murder of Eddie O'Hare was never solved. Associates and family of his former business partner, Al Capone, were natural suspects.[53] Capone died in Miami in 1947. Both before and after his prison sentence, Capone resided in the winter on Palm Island on Biscayne Bay. The Florida home he purchased in 1926 was built by Clarence M. Busch. The last name is likely just an ironic coincidence. Some writers have claimed that Clarence was an Anheuser-Busch heir, but there doesn't appear to be evidence to back up the allegation.[54]

The Chicago gangster, though, will always be a part of Anheuser-Busch lore. Capone, the Chicago crime boss, struck an unwritten deal during Prohibition with Busch, the St.

Louis beer baron. "Daddy took it," wrote Gussie's daughter Lotsie, "and Capone was true to his word. Daddy made the brewery a fortune."[55]

*****

Prohibition also directly impacted the fortunes of the St. Louis Cardinals for decades to come. In this instance, it had nothing to do with Anheuser-Busch. Rather it concerned the life and career of Frank Wanzer Rickey. In the 1920s, Rickey became a federal marshal. Working in Michigan, he served in the Prohibition enforcement wing of the U.S. Treasury Department. Coming from a family of teetotalers, Rickey was a true believer in the cause.[56]

In 1923, Rickey went undercover in the resort town of Mount Clemens, north of Detroit. Posing as "Colonel Russell, from Louisville, Kentucky," Rickey made the rounds in the town, introducing himself as a Southern gentleman and telling anyone who would listen that he suffered from rheumatism. The cure was "usually nothing less than a quart of whiskey..."[57] He found it in abundance in the city's hotels and cafes.

"I am satisfied that Mount Clemens was one of the wettest towns in the country," Rickey told reporters after a series of raids resulted in fourteen arrests. "The bars had rear rooms in which women and men congregated at all hours and drank beer, whiskey, and even champagne, which is a rare drink in the East now."[58]

Rickey escaped that undercover assignment unscathed. However, an incident in January of 1924 turned deadly. During a moonshine raid near Monroe, Michigan, Rickey was accused of firing his revolver. The bullet struck twenty-two-year-old Philip Kalb, who died within minutes. At an inquest the same month, five people pointed to Rickey as the man who fired the fatal shot.[59] Rickey was charged with murder.

The case went to trial that summer. Before the verdict came down, Rickey and his family got a second scare. Outside the hotel in Detroit where his family stayed during the trial, Rickey's twelve-year-old daughter Julia was nearly kidnapped. She was walking across the street when she heard a voice. "Hey little girl, I'll help you," someone called to her. With a quick look at the stranger, Julia instinctively knew something was wrong. She ran back inside the hotel lobby, foiling a kidnapping attempt by a bootlegger looking for revenge. For the rest of her father's trial, she never ventured outside alone.[60]

At trial, the same five people who accused Rickey at the inquest again pointed to him as the trigger man. The two federal agents who accompanied Rickey in the raid testified for the defense.[61] It soon became obvious which side jurors found more credible.

When the case went to the jury, it didn't take long for the twelve members to make up their minds. Deliberating less than two hours, jurors returned a verdict of not guilty. In addition, jurors prepared a statement exonerating Rickey "and commending him for the manner in which he had been discharging his duties."[62] When the jury foreman read the words "not guilty," Rickey's wife embraced him. "Those were the two finest words I ever heard spoken," she said.

Frank Rickey was a free man, but he soon chose to leave his job. He went to work as a baseball scout. During the time he worked for his brother, Frank Rickey is credited with scouting or signing players such as Marty Marion, Terry Moore, and Johnny Mize, the cousin of Babe Ruth's second wife, who later set a team record of 43 home runs that stood for nearly sixty years.

The dangers of Prohibition drove Frank Rickey, brother of Branch, straight into the arms of the St. Louis Cardinals.

---

[1] Steinberg and Spatz, *The Colonel and Hug.*
[2] Ibid.
[3] Hernon, Peter and Ganey, Terry. *Under The Influence: The Unauthorized Story of the Anheuser-Busch Dynasty.* Simon & Schuster. 1991.
[4] Ibid.
[5] Robert Baskowitz Jr. told authors Hernon and Ganey that Gussie Busch didn't like being alone. "Even in the can, when he went to the can, I'd be in there and he'd be sitting there doing his business."
[6] Bird's biography at NBA.com notes that he "has a passion for country music, auto racing, golf and the St. Louis Cardinals..."
[7] Courtaway, Robbi. *Wetter Than The Mississippi: Prohibition in St. Louis and Beyond.* Reedy Press. 2008.
[8] Lewis, Frederick Allen. *Only Yesterday: An Informal History of the 1920s.* Harper & Row Publishers, Inc. 1931
[9] Courtaway, *Wetter Than The Mississippi.*
[10] Bryson, Bill. *One Summer: America, 1927*. Doubleday. 2013.
[11] Ibid.
[12] Merkel, Jim. *Beer, Brats and Baseball. St. Louis Germans*. Reedy Press. 2012.
[13] Steinberg and Spatz, *The Colonel and Hug.*
[14] Hernon and Ganey, *Under The Influence.*
[15] Ibid.
[16] Bryson, *One Summer.*
[17] Ibid.
[18] Ibid.
[19] Lerner, Michael. *Dry Manhattan. Prohibition in New York City.* First Harvard University Press. 2007.
[20] Steinberg and Spatz, *The Colonel and Hug.*
[21] Ibid.
[22] Ibid.
[23] Weintraub, Robert. *The House That Ruth Built; A New Stadium, The First Yankees Championship, And The Redemption of 1923.* Little, Brown and Company. 2011.
[24] Courtaway, *Wetter Than The Mississippi.*
[25] *New York Times*, March 16, 1930.

---

[26] Hernon and Ganey, *Under The Influence.*
[27] *New York Times,* June 15, 1922.
[28] *St. Louis Post-Dispatch,* June 14, 1922.
[29] Ibid, June 15, 1922.
[30] Ibid.
[31] Hernon and Ganey, *Under The Influence.* Prohibition gave rise to "booze cruises" whereby ships would make an out-and-back trip just beyond U.S. territorial waters. Okrent, Daniel. *Last Call: The Rise and Fall of Prohibition.* Scribner. 2010.
[32] *New York Times,* January 2, 1923.
[33] Ibid.
[34] *St. Louis Globe-Democrat*, January 2, 1923, and *St. Louis Star*, January 5, 1923.
[35] Courtaway, *Wetter Than The Mississippi.* Nations had applied for a search warrant after seeing liquor in the hotel dining room on October 3rd. *St Louis Star*, January 4, 1923.
[36] *St. Louis Post-Dispatch*, October 4, 1922.
[37] Courtaway, *Wetter Than The Mississippi.*
[38] *Saturday Evening Post*, January 6, 1940.
[39] Eig, Jonathan. *Get Capone: The Secret Plot That Captured America's Most Wanted Gangster.* Simon & Schuster. 2010.
[40] Ibid.
[41] Lewis, *Only Yesterday.*
[42] Ibid.
[43] *St. Louis Post-Dispatch*, August 24, 1935. The paper called the Miami Beach Kennel Club "about the handsomest greyhound plant in the country." It was purchased by O'Hare, Ball, and "others from the Tex Rickard estate."
[44] Eig, *Get Capone.*
[45] *Chicago Tribune*, January 13, 2010. O'Hare also tipped off the judge that Capone had bribed several members of the juror pool. Judge James Wilkerson then swapped the panel with another judge who had a case scheduled to start the same day.
[46] *New York Times*, November 9, 1939.
[47] Eig, *Get Capone*.
[48] Offner, Larry. "The Butch O'Hare Story." *St. Louis Magazine*, July 29, 2006.
[49] Ibid.
[50] Ibid.
[51] *Chicago Tribune*, April 21, 1947.
[52] O'Hare also had a stake in the Chicago Cardinals.
[53] In 2010, Chicago police, at the request of Alderman Ed Burke, agreed to take another look at the case. It remains unsolved. One month after O'Hare's death, his former mistress was married to Frank Nitti, Capone's successor. Bair, Deirdre. *Capone: His Life, Legacy, and Legend*. Nan A. Talese. Doubleday. 2016.

---

[54] In an "abridged" family tree that appears in *Under The Influence* no Clarence M. Busch is listed. At *FloridaMemory.com,* a woman claiming to be Clarence's granddaughter says her grandfather was not a part of the beer brewing family.
[55] Hernon and Ganey, *Under The Influence.*
[56] Lowenfish, *Branch Rickey.*
[57] *New York Times*, July 26, 1923.
[58] Ibid.
[59] *The Escanaba Daily Press*, January 31, 1924.
[60] Lowenfish, *Branch Rickey*. Lowenfish says the trial happened in the summer of 1925. In fact, it happened in 1924.
[61] *The Portsmouth Daily Times*, July 17, 1924.
[62] Ibid, July 24, 1924.

A Lot of Baseball and a Little World Series

They poured into Sportsman's Park that summer. The St. Louis Browns and Cardinals combined to draw more than 1.2 million fans in 1922, a figure not eclipsed until after the Second World War.[1] They came by taxi, streetcar, or just walked to the intersection of Grand and Dodier in North St. Louis. Few drove to the game. Parking spots proved sparse in the residential neighborhood.[2]

With Prohibition the law of the land for more than two years, fans arrived at a stadium with no alcohol sales. It also had no public-address system. A man with a megaphone patrolled the park, announcing changes to the crowd along the first-base line, then walking over to the other side and repeating the words to the fans on the third-base side of the field. With no names or numbers on jerseys, a pinch-hitter could be retired before many in attendance ever knew who was standing at the plate.[3] Whatever the message, white fans likely heard it first. Blacks were relegated to the bleachers and the right-field pavilion. Segregation at Sportsman's Park remained in place until 1944.

The Browns and Cardinals shared the same home field from 1920 through 1953. In the days of a 154-game schedule, each team played 77 games at home. As a result, almost every day, from April to September, a St. Louis fan had an opportunity to watch big league baseball. The daily action and the harsh St. Louis summers took its toll on the field. "The infield grass got browner and soggier as the summer progressed," remembered Gene Karst, a St. Louis sportswriter and later publicist for the Cardinals. "The outfield wasn't much better." Groundskeepers of the 1920s would sometimes spread gasoline around the infield and set it on fire to dry it out.[4]

When action got underway, fans watched a game played at a brisk pace. Only the rare contest lasted any longer than two hours. One year in St. Louis, the Browns and Yankees played a doubleheader at Sportsman's Park that lasted a *combined* two hours and seven minutes. The longer first game – lasting one hour and twelve minutes – featured 25 hits. The shorter second one – which took all of fifty-five minutes – had 20 hits.[5]

At the beginning of the decade, complete games by starting pitchers were the rule, not the exception. Also helping to speed up play – no one had to wait on television timeouts or radio commercials in the early 1920s. Almost no one had to retrieve a glove from a dugout, either. That's because players frequently left their mitts on the field when the side was retired and the half-inning complete. As the fielders made their way to the dugout, they passed a row of bats lined up on the ground on the edge of the grass. Bat racks were not common.

With bat in hand, a player walked to the plate with no batting helmet. Despite Cleveland's Ray Chapman getting hit in the head and later dying from a pitched ball delivered by the Yankees' Carl Mays in a game in 1920, helmets were not made mandatory until 1971. Fear of injury (or worse) didn't come just at the plate. Infielders battled runners with raised cleats and outfielders battled walls with no padding.

Foul balls came with expectations in the game's early days. The umpires and club owners wanted them returned to the field of play. Chicago Cubs owner Charles Weeghman is credited with being the first to allow fans to keep baseballs. Other cities didn't give up the fight so easily. The New York Giants ejected a fan in 1921 for failing to turn over a foul ball. Reuben Berman then sued the Giants and won, collecting $100 for mental and physical distress. The Phillies once jailed a fan overnight for declining to return a ball.[6]

When fans weren't battling ushers over foul balls or hectoring players from their seats, they could stroll to the concession stand and choose from a wide variety of items. Peanuts, hot dogs, and Cracker Jack (introduced at the 1893 World's Fair in Chicago) were staple ballpark items by the 1920s. (The song "Take Me Out to the Ball Game" was written in 1908.) Some of the more unique offerings at Sportsman's Park over the years included boiled-egg and tongue sandwiches. With alcohol off the menu, fans could still enjoy an assortment of tobacco products. Vendors sold chewing tobacco as well as cigarettes and cigars. During Prohibition, a ballpark cigar would typically cost fifteen to twenty cents.[7]

When the game ended, visiting players returned to their hotel. In St. Louis, the Chase Hotel in the city's Central West End was a popular destination. In the days before air conditioning, players would haul their mattresses out to a balcony to cool down or even try sleeping across the street in Forest Park. With their mornings and evenings free, visiting players typically stayed up late.

Two teams sharing one stadium meant extended durations in front of home crowds and lengthy trips on the road. For the entire 1922 season, the Browns and Cardinals had just five home stands apiece. Typical was a stretch in July where the Cardinals played twenty-three games in twenty-one days, all at Sportsman's Park. During that same period, the Browns played eighteen games in twenty days, all on the road.

Sunday baseball laws complicated travel. Midwestern cities with large German immigrant populations like St. Louis and Cincinnati were the first to adopt Sunday baseball (and beer sales). The more established cities on the East Coast resisted the change. New York didn't adopt Sunday baseball until 1919. The states of Massachusetts and Pennsylvania, homes of the Puritans and the Quakers, were the last holdouts. The

Boston Braves and Red Sox couldn't host Sunday games until 1929. Pennsylvania held out until 1934, when finally, the Philadelphia Athletics, Philadelphia Phillies, and Pittsburgh Pirates were allowed to play baseball on the Sabbath. During the Browns road trip in July of 1922, the team finished a series in Philadelphia on a Saturday, left for Detroit to play a single game on Sunday, then returned to the East Coast to start a series with the Yankees on Tuesday. All road trips involved trains. Commercial air service didn't exist.

Train travel brought its own set of unique hurdles, not the least of which was simply keeping track of time. "The human relationship with time changed dramatically with the arrival of modernity – trains and telegraphs and wristwatches all around," explained *Time Travel* author James Gleick.[8] Calendars measured time in days and months, not minutes and hours. Until the second half of the nineteenth century, it simply didn't matter whether the minute-hand on clocks in Cincinnati and St. Louis agreed. Technology, and the accelerating pace of life, changed that. Daylight Saving Time in the 1920s was not standardized. Cities such as Chicago, New York and Philadelphia observed it. Other cities like St. Louis did not.

Once aboard the train, players would hang their sweaty and soiled uniforms out the window to dry out. "You should have seen how some of the passengers would lose their appetites when they passed through our car en route to the diner," remembered longtime big-league manager Joe McCarthy.[9]

Players wore heavy wool uniforms in those days, "which weighed eight ounces to the yard, even before it was soaked in sweat." With a blazer, tie, dress shirt and slacks, an umpire's gear was equally cumbersome. Attire of the fans was also frequently unprepared to deal with the elements. Heat waves could wreak havoc on the population. A brutal stretch of boiling temperatures in 1897 killed forty-two people in St. Louis by early July. Two baseball players, St. Louis infielder Mike Grady and Brooklyn catcher Aleck Smith were among the "numerous prostrations," meaning they had collapsed and could no longer stand upright.[10]

In an era with no night games, baking under the summer sun undoubtedly contributed to the irritability of fans, who often needed little provocation to lash out at umpires or opposing teams. Before Prohibition, alcohol-fueled crowds would show their disapproval by flinging anything handy onto the field of play. "These objects were of great variety," remembered longtime New York sportswriter Westbrook Pegler, "being decanters, beer bottles, beer crocks, and the arms of chairs, as well as the occasional walking cane."[11]

Soda bottles tossed at umpires proved to be such an issue for the Cardinals in 1917 that Rickey announced the club had hired plain-clothed detectives to monitor the crowd. "How are you going to stop it – abolish the selling of soda?" said an exasperated Rickey.[12]

Three years later, Prohibition eliminated any beer bottles from the stands, but the soda bottles remained. Umpire Billy Evans had been struck by a thrown bottle at

Sportsman's Park in 1907. It fractured his skull.[13] Fifteen years later, he was in uniform and on the field in St. Louis when a bottle from the stands made its way to the field of play. This one didn't hit an umpire, though. It landed on the forehead of an outfielder in the ninth inning of a one-run game. It knocked him out cold. The incident took place in the first game of a three-game series that the press was calling the "Little World Series." In September of 1922, pennant fever had finally arrived in St. Louis.

*****

The Browns of 1922 are the greatest St. Louis team most fans have never heard of. They were the first twentieth-century St. Louis team to win more than 90 games. The club featured the American League batting title champion as well as the home run and RBI leader. The offense led the league in batting, slugging, runs, triples, stolen bases, and walks. Six regulars hit over .300 and four players had 100 RBI seasons – the first time in American League history. The pitching staff led the league in strikeouts, saves and ERA.[14]

For the first time, in 1922, the American League named a Most Valuable Player. Browns first baseman George Sisler received the honor. He hit a career-high .420 that season, driving in 105 runs and leading the league with 51 stolen bases, 18 triples and 246 hits. Since joining the Browns in 1915, Rickey's star player at Michigan had demonstrated why his services had sparked such a battle. While the Browns had experimented with him as a pitcher when he first arrived, his hitting skills were simply too valuable not to play every day.[15] His batting title in 1922 was the second of his career, following a .407 season in 1920. In the earlier campaign, Sisler delivered 257 hits, a major league record that lasted 84 years.[16] In 1922, Sisler hit in 41 straight games, an American League record that lasted until 1941 when Joe DiMaggio hit in 56 straight.

Sisler's manager in 1922 was Lee Fohl. When the Browns first baseman had signed his first professional contract as a teenager in Akron, the contract that baseball later voided, Fohl was the manager of the Ohio minor league club. The general manager of the Browns in 1922 was Bob Quinn. Fohl and Quinn had a relationship that dated back to their minor league days in Ohio. When Sisler's original contract was transferred to Columbus, Quinn was running that team. It was Quinn who sold Sisler's contract to the Pirates, launching the battle that Pittsburgh owner Barney Dreyfuss ultimately lost.

Browns owner Phil Ball had targeted Quinn after Rickey left to join the Cardinals in 1917. "There's really nothing to the job," Ball had written to him. "All you need is bunk and bluff." Not liking the description, Quinn wrote him back. "I am very sorry, but I don't qualify for your job. I have never practiced bunk or bluff in my life." Impressed with Quinn's honesty, Ball managed to hire him away from the Columbus minor league team.[17]

Fohl had joined the club in 1921, leading the Browns to a third-place finish and an 81-73 record, the team's best performance since an 83-win season back in 1908. The 1921 everyday lineup returned intact for the 1922 season. In addition to Sisler, manager

Fohl received big years from outfielders William Chester "Baby Doll" Jacobson and Ken Williams as well as second baseman Marty McManus.

In a team lost to history, Jacobson is a player largely forgotten. He shouldn't be. The Cable, Illinois native hit .311 for his career and batted higher than .300 seven straight seasons from 1919 to 1925. His best season took place in 1920 when he batted .355 with 122 RBI. "Although he never received more than a passing glance in the Hall of Fame voting," *The Sporting News* noted at the time of his death, "Jacobson's credentials are superior to many of the old-timers who have been enshrined." Stressing that Jacobson was more than just a good hitter, the St. Louis weekly noted that Jacobson "patrolled center field with skill and daring." At one point, he held 13 fielding records including a season where he logged 488 putouts and seven assists. The putout record lasted until 1948 when it was broken by Boston Red Sox outfielder Dom DiMaggio.[18]

At six feet three inches tall and weighing 215 pounds, Jacobson stood about five inches taller and weighed forty to fifty pounds more than the typical player of his era. He was "Bill" Jacobson until a minor league game in Mobile, Alabama in 1912. "It was opening day and a band was playing. Just before the first pitch, they struck up, 'Oh, You Beautiful Doll,' a popular song at the time," he recalled years later. "Well, I led off with a homer on the first pitch and a lady sitting behind the plate jumped up and shouted: 'You must be that beautiful doll they were talking about.' The name stuck with me and that was it."[19] In 1922, the Browns center fielder hit .317 with nine home runs and 102 RBI. Jacobson had career-highs in stolen bases (19) and in triples (16). Three of those triples came in one game against the Detroit Tigers.

Flanking Jacobson in left field was Ken Williams, a right-handed thrower with a left-handed swing perfectly suited for Sportsman's Park. Of his 196 career home runs, Williams blasted 138 of them in St. Louis. He led the league with 39 home runs and 155 RBI in 1922, a year that also saw him reach career highs in runs scored, slugging percentage, and stolen bases. He became the first player in the big leagues ever to hit more than 30 home runs and steal more than 30 bases (37) in a season. Rounding out the quartet of Browns hitters with 100 RBI seasons was second baseman Marty McManus. At the age of 22, in just his second full year in the big leagues, McManus had 11 home runs and 109 RBI, while batting .312. He played 12 more seasons, but his RBI total never again eclipsed the century mark.

The Browns pitching staff featured a veteran spitball pitcher who loved to face the Yankees and two young pitchers with ties to the region. Urban Shocker appeared twelve times against New York in 1922, ten times as a starter. The Browns had acquired him from the Yankees in a trade that sent second baseman Del Pratt to New York after the 1917 season.

Baseball changed the rules of pitching in 1920, banning the spitball and other pitches involving a foreign substance. Before that season, pitchers had free rein to moisten the ball. Fortunately for Shocker, he was one of 17 players to receive a lifetime exemption. "Urban is one of those slobbery spitballers," wrote Damon Runyon. "He almost eats the old apple while he is wetting it up and is very deliberate."[20] No one benefitted more from the rule change and exemption than Shocker. From 1920 to 1924, Shocker won 107 games, the most in baseball. His 27 wins led the league in 1921. He followed up that season by winning 24 in 1922 and leading the league in strikeouts. A superstitious player, Shocker always placed his glove on the dirt when leaving the field, never on the grass part of the diamond.[21]

Browns pitcher Elam Vangilder won a career-high 19 games in 1922, second-best on the staff. The righthander from Cape Girardeau, Missouri possessed great control that season, walking just 48 hitters in 245 innings pitched.[22] The next year, he beat New York in a game at Sportsman's Park that's remembered today for a different reason. A young Yankees first baseman by the name of Lou Gehrig got the first big league hit of his career off Vangilder in a game won by the Browns, 13-3.

The righthander was joined on the Browns staff in 1922 by another Missouri native. Hub Pruett was born in the Bootheel town of Malden in 1900. Plucked from the University of Missouri campus, Pruett made his big-league debut at the age of 21. He never swore, preferring instead to simply say, "Aw, Shucks." A lefthander, "Shucks" Pruett threw a screwball that Babe Ruth found almost impossible to hit.

Like so many other players in the region during this era, Pruett was discovered by legendary scout Charley Barrett. "If you ever want to play pro ball," Barrett had told him after watching him pitch, "come on up to St. Louis and we'll see what we can do for you." Pruett took him up on the offer and made the trip. The Cardinals were out of town and he ended up speaking with Browns general manager Quinn. "Does it make any difference what St. Louis team you would play for?" Quinn asked him. "No, all I want to do is play ball," Pruett replied.[23] The Browns signed him. Pitching mainly out of the bullpen in 1922, Pruett finished 23 games and compiled seven saves, good for second-best in the league.

Led by Shocker, boosted by the career year from Vangilder, and bolstered by the presence of Pruett, the Browns of 1922 finally had a pitching staff to match their prodigious offense. "Lee Fohl has succeeded in injecting a great deal of confidence into his players," noted the *Post-Dispatch* in early April, "and they seriously believe that they have as good a chance as any club in the American League to win the pennant."[24]

By the end of April, the Browns had a record of 11-5 and were tied with the Yankees for first place. A glimpse of things to come took place on April 22. On that day, St. Louis beat the Chicago White Sox 10-7, and Browns outfielder Williams made history. In four trips to the plate, Williams hit three home runs. His first blast left the park and landed on Grand Avenue. "For sheer distance, it is doubtful if Williams' initial drive in the opening inning has ever been excelled," wrote reporter Joseph F. Holland.[25] The other two long balls landed in the bleachers. The three home runs marked the first time the feat had ever happened in an American League game. No one in the league, not even Ruth, had done it before.

The home runs by Williams were the first three of the year for him. He proceeded to go on a week-long tear, capped off by hitting two in a game against Cleveland with the final one tying the game in the ninth inning. The Browns won it in the tenth. By April 29, Williams had nine home runs. His exploits drew media scrutiny and inevitable comparisons to the games' preeminent slugger. Williams "is a funny sort of guy," *The Sporting News* explained. "He actually plays ball as if he likes the game," noting the Browns outfielder "never golfs, or signs up with the movies, or anything like that – and he talks baseball night and day. He's so different from Babe Ruth that it's almost a crime."[26]

His performance had St. Louis sportswriters giddy. In his "Sport Salad" column, *Post-Dispatch* writer L.C. Davis penned a poem that read in part:

Who is our most admired youth?
Ken Williams.
Who makes the fans forget Babe Ruth?
Ken Williams.
Who is the guy so calm and cool?
Who swings his trusty batting tool
And knocks the pellet for a gool?
Ken Williams.[27]

Williams' performance had filled a void in the game and on the pages of the nation's newspapers. In the unlikely event any fans had forgotten Babe Ruth by early May of 1922, the reason had to do with the Yankee outfielder's absence from the game. Suspended in the offseason by Commissioner Landis, the Babe had yet to a play in a single contest in the young season. But that would soon change. When his suspension finally lifted, Ruth made his season debut in New York at the Polo Grounds. By coincidence, the opponent on the schedule that day was the St. Louis Browns.

*****

Ruth followed up a spectacular 1920 season in New York with an even better 1921. For the third consecutive year, he set the single-season record for home runs. He broke his 1920 record of 54 home runs, hitting number 55 against the Browns. It happened in the Polo Grounds on September 15 in the first game of a doubleheader. "His was not the only home run of the afternoon," noted *The New York Times*, but "Ruth's tremendous slash stood forth among all the drives of the dual affray like an antelope among ants." Ruth, referred to as the "Caliph of Crash" by the *Times*, hit four more home runs that season to end the year with 59.

While his legendary 1927 season, with its 60 home-run campaign, is frequently cited, the Babe's 1921 effort was better by nearly every measure. He led the league in home runs, RBI (168), walks (145), on-base percentage (.512), slugging percentage (.846), and total bases (457). His batting average of .378 tied for the second-best of his career.

Except for the one additional home run he hit in 1927, every other mark was better in Ruth's 1921 season.

The Babe's back-to-back 50-home-run seasons forever altered the game. "Babe Ruth changed everything," wrote Bill James.[28] "The number of runs scored per game in the major leagues increased from 3.59 in 1917 to 5.19 in 1929, while the number of home runs quadrupled."[29] While the long ball soared, stolen bases plummeted. In the ten years from 1911 to 1920, major league players compiled more than nearly 27,000 stolen bases. In the decade from 1921 to 1930, the number dropped to less than 14,000.[30] With the stolen base deemphasized and a priority attached to power, teams started to place a premium on the ability to turn a double play. As a result, second base gradually changed from an offensive position in the early 1920s to a defensive position by 1940.[31]

Like all talented showmen, Ruth had great timing, not all of it his own making. His rise to fame "coincided precisely with the birth of tabloid newspapers, newsreel films, fan magazines and radio...and his arrival in New York brought him into the throbbing heart of the media world."[32] More than just a great baseball player, Ruth was now a celebrity, receiving 200 fan letters a day. "Keep the ones with the checks and the ones from the broads," he'd tell his teammates. "It was delightful," recalled Yankees pitcher Waite Hoyt. "The ladies were quite frank in their invitations."[33]

A private phone installed in his apartment proved futile. Within a few weeks, scores of strangers had the number, phoning the Babe at all hours of the night. A pay phone was installed in the Yankees' clubhouse, primarily for Ruth. It, too, rang constantly. The Babe began endorsing all types of products. Whether he liked or ever used the items himself was irrelevant. Over the course of his career, he advertised everything from cigarettes, shaving cream, and underwear to baseball gloves, biscuits and bread. [34]

Seeking to capitalize on Babe Ruth mania, the Curtiss Candy Company renamed its Kandy Kake offering in 1921 as the Baby Ruth candy bar. The company would later claim the confection was named for President Grover Cleveland's daughter – known as "Baby Ruth" Cleveland. Ruth Cleveland died in 1904. Her father hadn't been President since 1897. Ruth and his agent, Christy Walsh, went to court over the name and launched a competing product, Ruth's Home Run candy bar. Both efforts failed.[35]

While the candy bar litigation would take years to play out, the Babe could seemingly do no wrong in 1921. Led by their slugging outfielder, the Yankees won the American League pennant for the first time in the club's history. Not even a loss in the World Series to John McGraw's New York Giants could slow him down. Two days after the final game, Ruth and two teammates – outfielder Bob Meusel and pitcher Bill Piercy – traveled to Buffalo to play in the first of a series of exhibition games.

In the early twentieth century, postseason barnstorming tours proved popular with fans and players alike. Baseball fans outside the major metropolitan areas embraced the chance to see athletes they had only read about in newspapers or magazines. Players enjoyed the extra money the exhibition games provided. By one estimate, Ruth was paid $30,000 for the tour, as much money as he made playing for the Yankees in

1921.[36] There was just one problem. Baseball had a rule that made it illegal for players on World Series teams to participate in such an event, fearing it would dilute the impact of the real Fall Classic.[37]

Disregarding an order from Commissioner Landis, Ruth, Meusel and Piercy played in the game in Buffalo. After the game, an openly defiant Ruth explained why he chose to ignore Landis. "He had no right to bar us from participating in a postseason exhibition game," Ruth told reporters. "We think that our action was for the best interests of baseball."[38]

Six days later, the Babe bowed to pressure and decided to abandon the tour. By cutting the barnstorming tour short, the press began to speculate that Ruth wouldn't be suspended, but rather receive a heavy fine and reprimand from Landis.[39] The commissioner had different ideas.

Landis waited until December 5 to announce his decision. Saying the players had "willfully and defiantly" violated the rules of baseball, the commissioner suspended Ruth and his two teammates until May 20. The trio would miss the first 33 games of the 1922 season. The action also cost the players their World Series money. The fine cost Ruth $3,326.32.[40] By this time, the Babe was already off on another offseason venture. In November, he had started performing in a vaudeville act that paid him $3,000 a week. The contract called for him to perform in "rapid fire comedy repartee" as well as "risk his popularity by singing a baseball song or two."[41]

The money kept rolling in the following spring. The Yankees offered him a $50,000 contract for the 1922 season, a huge jump from the prior year.[42] Ruth demanded $52,000, saying he wanted to make $1,000 a week. In Hot Springs, Arkansas for his annual preseason visit to the bathhouses, Ruth and Til Huston decided to settle the matter. The Yankees star and co-owner agreed to a coin flip. The Babe called tails. When it landed heads down, Ruth had his grand-a-week salary.

The money was going out as fast – or faster – than it was coming in. Ruth bought a 155-acre farmhouse in Sudbury, Massachusetts. He also bought a Cadillac for his old school, St. Mary's Industrial in Baltimore. It cost $5,000. The day before his suspension lifted, Ruth was spotted at a racetrack. "Pretty good day yesterday. I cleaned up a little more than $18,000," he said. In the case of Ruth, any winnings were just temporary advances against future losses. The Babe's first manager, Jack Dunn, was at the track that day. He watched Ruth bet $5,000 on the first race and then $3,000 on the second.[43]

Despite the suspension to start the season, Ruth could participate in spring training games. The Babe and Huston left Hot Springs and went to New Orleans where the Yankees trained. The Cardinals and Yankees played two exhibition games that spring. The focus was on Ruth and the Cardinals young star, Rogers Hornsby. One New Orleans writer wondered the same thing New York Giants manager John McGraw had been pondering for years. "As a New Yorker, Hornsby would be a serious rival of the great Ruth."[44] Baseball fans would have to wait a few years to find out the accuracy of that prediction.

Hornsby had hosted a party for Ruth that offseason at the Congress Hotel in Chicago. Midway through the affair, the Cardinals infielder instructed an entourage of young women to put on their party dresses made of paper. Once dressed, he had them bend down in a large, galvanized tub, "the kind used by farmers to feed their animals," filled with lukewarm water. When they stood back up, the paper disappeared and the party now had a room full of naked women. "It was kind of pointless," said one guest, "but that was Rogers' idea of a joke, and the Babe got a tremendous kick out of it."[45]

The temptations were always present in Ruth's life: women, booze, and endless attempts by others to separate him from his money. Spring training in New Orleans didn't help. It was here in 1922 when the famous "Yankees Training On Scotch" headline supposedly appeared. The Babe and his teammates were, in the words of biographer Robert Creamer, "a rowdy group of drinkers, gamblers, and wenchers ...(who) raised hell every night."

The description certainly fit Ruth, who drank, gambled and consorted with lewd women. With a six-week suspension to start the season, he now had more time for all three pursuits. What Ruth didn't realize at the time was that 1922 would turn out to be one of the most challenging seasons in his career. He fought with teammates, fans, and baseball officials; and had to explain why a baby had suddenly surfaced in the Ruth household.

*****

Ruth and Meusel, two-thirds of the Yankees starting outfield, had combined for 83 home runs and 306 RBI in 1921. Their New York teammates barely noticed their absence at the start of the 1922 season. The Yankees played .667 baseball their first 33 games, winning 22 and losing 11. Opening a series in the Polo Grounds on Saturday, May 20, New York welcomed the return of the powerful outfield duo and the St. Louis Browns. Thirty-eight thousand fans joined them. They watched Ruth get presented with a floral wreath and a silver bat before the game got underway.

The Browns, just two games behind the Yankees at the start of the day, sent Shocker to the mound that afternoon. Already 7-4 on the season when the day began, the spitballer went eight innings, gave up just three hits and two runs, both unearned. New York second baseman Aaron Ward hit a two-run home run in the bottom of the sixth inning following an error by Browns right fielder Jack Tobin.

The Browns went to bat in the ninth inning down 2-1 to Yankees pitcher Sam Jones. With two outs and no one on base, consecutive Browns pinch-hitters delivered back-to-back singles, putting runners at first and third. Leadoff hitter Tobin sent a ball toward the first-base line knocked down by Wally Pipp. The Yankee first baseman threw the ball to Jones who raced over to cover the bag ahead of the Browns outfielder. The umpire signaled a game-ending out. But Jones had dropped the ball. When the umpire reversed his decision, the runner from third scored and the Browns had tied the game. The next four St. Louis hitters proceeded to reach base, capped off by a Baby Doll Jacobson grand slam. Down to their last out, the Browns sent seven men to the plate and all seven scored. Billy Bayne came on in relief of Shocker in the bottom of the ninth and retired the side in order. The Browns had won the game 8-2, stunning the Yankees and silencing the crowd. Making their season debuts, both Ruth and Meusel went 0-4.

The series went on for three more games with the Yankees winning the next two. Ruth delivered his first home run of the year in the third game. In the fourth and final game, Shocker got another start for the Browns. He beat the Yankees again and now had a 9-4 record, thanks, in part, to teammate Williams. The Browns outfielder hit his twelfth home run of the year in an 11-3 victory. St. Louis left New York in the same place as when they arrived. "The Missourians are still two games behind," observed *The New York Times*, "and the prospects are that they will stay there unless Urban Shocker can be persuaded to pitch every other game for the Fohl clan."[46]

Over the next several weeks, the Browns proved the *Times* wrong. St. Louis won twenty-one of its thirty-six games while the Yankees dropped nineteen of thirty-four contests, including eight in a row at one point. The Browns entered July in first place with a three-game lead over their New York rivals. But the month would not be kind to St. Louis baseball. By the end of it, their pennant prospects had changed. One particular move had St. Louis fans howling and baseball authorities pondering a change in the rules.

*****

Ruth was the best and most famous former Boston Red Sox player on the Yankees 1922 roster, but he was far from the only one. In the everyday lineup, catcher Wally Schang and shortstop Everett Scott had arrived in trades from Boston. But the real story of Red Sox owner Harry Frazee's dealings with New York over the years had to do with the Yankees pitching staff. Joe Bush, Sam Jones, Carl Mays and Waite Hoyt – four-fifths of the starting staff – arrived in New York via Boston. The quartet won 71 games for the Yankees in 1922 and started all but 36 of New York's games. Only Bob Shawkey, purchased from the Philadelphia Athletics in 1915, came from somewhere other than Boston. Frazee engaged in so many lopsided deals with Yankee co-owners Til Huston and Jacob Ruppert that it became known as the "Rape of the Red Sox."

The Yankees started the 1922 season with Frank Baker at third base. "Home Run" Baker had gained fame in the Deadball Era while playing for Connie Mack's Philadelphia A's. He led the league in home runs for three straight years from 1911 to 1913, never hitting more than a dozen in any season. He was now thirty-six years old. 1922 was his last season in the big leagues.

The Red Sox started the year with Joe Dugan at third base. Like Baker, he had started his career in Philadelphia. In 1920, Mack's team conducted spring training in Texas and played several exhibition games against Rickey's Cardinals. Rickey developed a friendship with the Philadelphia manager. "I'd known Mack since my American League playing days, but I saw him in a new light," said the Cardinals manager. Another friendship developed that spring between Dugan and Hornsby. Dugan was deeply influenced by the Cardinals infielder. "Nobody will ever know how much help Hornsby has been to me. I listen to him like a father."[47]

It was in Philadelphia where Dugan acquired the nickname "Jumping Joe" because he frequently left the team. "I used to jump the club," he admitted years later. "I didn't like the place or the fans. How many times? I stopped counting."[48] After hitting a career-high ten home runs for Philadelphia in 1921, the A's traded him to the Red Sox.

In early July of 1922, the St. Louis Browns were in Boston to play Dugan's Red Sox. The teams were scheduled to play a doubleheader on July 6. Despite a sunny afternoon "that had the field in a near dusty condition," the games were postponed. That decision meant the Browns and Red Sox would now have to play three consecutive doubleheaders to complete the six-game series. With the Browns scheduled to play the Yankees next, St. Louis accused Boston owner Frazee of trying to exhaust the visitor's pitching staff. "I am certain that Frazee postponed the games today deliberately to aid the Yankees," said Browns vice president Walter Fritsch. "The deals between the two clubs...in the past two years show how closely these two clubs' owners are united."[49]

If Frazee's actions in early July had the Browns upset, what he did later in the month sparked outrage and objections all over St. Louis. On July 23, the Red Sox and Yankees made another trade – the fifth major deal between the two teams since 1919. New York received Dugan and backup outfielder Elmer Smith. In exchange for acquiring their new starting third baseman and an accomplished pinch-hitter, the Yankees gave up three backups and a player to be named later.[50] The move ignited immediate protests. The St. Louis Chamber of Commerce fired off letters to the presidents of both leagues as well as to Commissioner Landis. "No red-blooded American can cheer," proclaimed the Chamber, "while a team that purchases the pennant...romps on to victory over less fortunate, smaller and consequently more moderately financed teams."[51]

The Browns even found an empathetic voice in their hometown rival. "Show me one valid reason why there shouldn't be a rule limiting all trades between big league clubs to the offseason, except by waiver," said Cardinals manager Rickey. "There is none."[52]

What upset many, including Rickey, was not the content of the deal but the timing of it, coming in late July. "Deals of this sort in midseason are regrettable and must be discouraged and legislated against," said American League president Ban Johnson the day after the trade.[53] Johnson and other baseball officials waited until the offseason to make their move. At a joint meeting of the two leagues in December, baseball responded to the backlash over the Dugan deal by imposing a new trade deadline of June 15. That deadline remained in effect until the 1980s and became a part of baseball lore. Some of the biggest deals in the game's history occurred on that date.[54]

*****

Frazee's gamesmanship in early July, and his trade with the Yankees in late July, were just two of the indignities the Browns faced that month. The team also lost a starting pitcher for the season and lost an unusual game in Philadelphia. That one loss would loom larger in the aftermath of the season.

In the middle of July, the first-place St. Louis Browns arrived in Philadelphia to begin a four-game series with the A's. The Browns had their ace, Shocker, on the mound that day. The pitcher taking the ball for Philadelphia requires some explanation. Twenty-eight-year-old Adolph "Otto" Rettig had never appeared in a big-league game before but was considered a semi-pro legend in New Jersey. He had grabbed the attention of John McGraw and the New York Giants back in October 1916. Pitching for the Paterson Silk Sox, he shut out the Giants on three hits and struck out 13 batters in an exhibition game. Reports surfaced that the Giants would sign him.[55] They didn't. From 1917 until the summer of 1922, he continued to pitch for semi-pro teams.[56]

Philadelphia A's backup catcher Frank Bruggy knew Rettig. The two had been college teammates at Seton Hall and had stayed in communication over the years. Rettig would badger Bruggy about another audition. Bruggy, in turn, would pass the word on to A's manager Mack. At some point Mack acquiesced, and Rettig found himself on a train to Philadelphia. When he arrived at the park, Mack asked him to work out. Rettig told the manager he preferred to pitch in a game. Amazingly, Mack agreed. "Of course, that was very strange, but so was my ball club, and I figured we would lose the game anyway," the manager confessed to Westbrook Pegler years later.[57] That is how, on Wednesday, July 19, 1922, the St. Louis Browns came to face Otto Rettig.

With Shocker on the mound, the Browns were certainly heavy favorites. From the beginning of 1919 through his one previous start in 1922 against the A's, Shocker's record against Philadelphia was 12-1. Two months before the matchup with Rettig, Shocker had pitched a complete-game victory in Philadelphia, allowing three runs while striking out eight.

Against Rettig, the Browns got off to a promising start, scoring a run in the first and adding to the lead with a run in the fourth. Shocker took a 2-0 lead into the bottom of the sixth inning when Philadelphia scored twice to tie the game. The A's broke open the game with a four-run eighth inning. The Browns got one back in the ninth, but it was too little, too late. Philadelphia won the game 6-3. Despite giving up nine hits and five walks, Rettig, "a sleek-haired factory league hurler," had defeated Shocker and the first-place Browns.

The defeat marked the Browns seventh loss in their last eleven games, all coming since Frazee's questionable postponement in Boston. On the night of the loss against Rettig, club vice president Fritsch decided to break the slump with a party. "He bought cigarettes and mints and a few other things, took the boys to his suite of rooms and told them to sing, talk and yell about anything but baseball," reported the *Post-Dispatch.* The next morning, "the mints were untouched, but the cigarettes and other things were gone."[58] The Browns proceeded to beat the A's the next three games.

Rettig's victory in the first game of the series against St. Louis earned him additional playing time for Mack's club. A week after his debut, he pitched and lost in Cleveland 2-0, despite giving up just four hits in seven innings. In his next start at Detroit, he gave up six runs, five earned, while lasting just two and one-third innings. He then faced the

Browns in St. Louis. He walked the first two batters of the game, throwing eight balls in nine pitches. With Sisler coming up next, manager Mack pulled his starter from the game before he retired a single batter. On reliever Charlie Eckhart's third pitch to Sisler, the Browns first baseman lined into a triple play.[59]

On the night Rettig beat the Browns in Philadelphia, Sisler told a writer for *The Sporting News*, "I'll make a little bet that this fellow doesn't win another ballgame from us."[60] Little did he know at the time how prophetic he would be. Rettig never pitched again in the big leagues after departing the mound at Sportsman's Park. Philadelphia released him eleven days later. He returned to his job as a theater manager in New Jersey.[61] His one and only victory in his major league career came against the St. Louis Browns.

*****

Dave Danforth has been called the Forest Gump of baseball.[62] In his two-decade career, "Dandy Dave" or "Dauntless Dave" as he was also known, played for or with some of the legends of the game and on some of the most famous or infamous teams in history. He played for Connie Mack in the major leagues, called Babe Ruth a teammate in the minor leagues, and taught Chicago White Sox pitcher Eddie Cicotte the "shine ball."

A controversial figure, Danforth had a reputation for tampering with the baseball and had such an unusual pitching motion, opposing teams were constantly accusing him of a balk. He learned the shine ball in the minor leagues. "I was having control trouble, so I resorted to putting resin on my pants, and rubbing that spot to get a firm grip on the ball," Danforth recalled. "We used old baseballs then, and the combination of the oil slick and the dirty turf discolored the balls and made them look black and shiny. Hence, my shine ball."[63]

Danforth cashed a World Series check with the White Sox in 1917, a year in which he went 11-6. Fohl, managing Cleveland at the time, started collecting suspicious baseballs from games against the White Sox and complained about "unfair tactics." His star player, outfielder Tris Speaker, who was knocked unconscious by a Danforth delivery that season, was more direct in his criticism. "The game will go to the dogs unless a stop is put to doctoring of the ball by Cicotte and Danforth."[64]

Danforth was a member of the infamous Black Sox team in 1919 until Chicago traded him in late August to Columbus of the American Association. He always had tantalizing ability. Early in his career, *Baseball Magazine* wrote that the pitcher had shown the "promise of developing into one of the greatest lefthanders in the game" when he was with Mack's Philadelphia A's, but "the jump was apparently too great for the youngster."[65]

Pitching for Columbus in 1921, Danforth led the American Association in strikeouts and ERA. When hitters did reach first base, the lefthander kept them close to the bag, frequently provoking cries of balk from the opposing dugout. "It is impossible to tell whether Danforth is about to throw to first or to the plate," is how St. Louis sportswriter Roy Stockton later described his delivery.[66]

His 25-win season in 1921, which tied for the league lead, attracted the attention of the Browns. In December, the club traded 11 players – a collection of journeymen and minor leaguers – to Columbus to secure his services. *The Sporting News* called it "probably the most unique deal ever recorded in baseball."[67]

"If Danforth wins 15 games for the St. Louis Browns, I figure it will be a great deal for the St. Louis Browns," said general manager Quinn. His new manager had similar expectations. "If Danforth can win a dozen games, I will be satisfied," said Fohl, switching sides from accuser to supporter of the lefthander. Fohl's backing of his new pitcher proved fleeting.

Danforth had a reputation that preceded his Browns' debut. Rather than bury his past, he embraced his status and tried to exploit any potential advantage. "There's no rule against rubbing a ball with your hands. Often I did it a long time deliberately for psychological effect," he admitted long after his playing days were done.[68] That reputation proved to be a two-edged sword. His behavior meant umpires and opposing players constantly monitored pitches and scrutinized baseballs that didn't look quite right. Trouble first emerged in June of 1922 against the Yankees.

Danforth went the distance that day at Sportsman's Park in a 13-4 Browns victory. After he retired the Yankees in the top of the first inning, a New York player brought a baseball to the attention of the umpire. The ball appeared to have a substance rubbed into the seams.[69] Umpire Billy Evans showed it to Danforth and Browns manager Fohl. The pitcher denied he had doctored the baseball. He got off with a warning. Danforth improved to 4-0 on the season.

Six weeks later under similar circumstances – at Sportsman's Park and again playing the Yankees – Danforth entered a tie-game in the tenth inning with two runners on base and no outs. After he struck out pinch-hitter Fred Hoffman, the Yankees requested umpire Brick Owens examine the ball. A quick look is all Owens needed. He immediately tossed Danforth out of the game. After Hoffman had fouled off a pitch for the second strike, the umpire put a new ball in play. "I knew the ball was new and clean when I delivered it to catcher (Hank) Severeid," Owens explained after the game, "and when I next saw it I was convinced that it was what we term a 'loaded' ball."

One of the ironies of the 1922 Browns was that the team had a pitcher who thrived by throwing an illegal pitch and did it with baseball's blessing. But unlike spitballer Shocker, Danforth didn't receive a lifetime exemption. His crimes also went beyond moistening the ball. Years before the spitball ban, American League president Ban Johnson had banned the "emery ball," done by defacing the baseball with emery paper. Danforth was repeatedly suspected of defacing the ball. "He was said to have a nail on his left thumb that was so sharp that he could slit the seams or so rough that he could make an abrasion on the ball," wrote baseball historian Steve Steinberg, adding that the pitcher was rumored to have slept while soaking his pitching hand in a tray of pickle brine "to make his skin as abrasive as emery paper."[70]

Whatever he did to the ball that day against the Yankees, Danforth faced an automatic ten-day suspension and a skeptical manager. "Dave has been warned often enough," said Fohl after the game.[71] When his suspension expired, the Browns put Danforth on waivers. No team claimed him. He spent the rest of the year pitching for a minor league team in Tulsa.

In less than a week, St. Louis watched the Yankees gain a key player in a trade while the Browns lost a key pitcher for the rest of the year. A St. Louis team that once led New York by 3.5 games in June entered September down by 2.5 games. Thanks to a stretch where the team won nine of 11 contests, the Browns managed to close the gap to just a half game by September 16. On that date, the Yankees arrived for the first of three games at Sportsman's Park.

Baseball in St. Louis hadn't mattered this late in the season since the 1880s.

*****

In the lobby of a St. Louis hotel in the summer of 1922, a man walked up to Wally Schang and introduced himself by telling the Yankee catcher the two men had met before. Ballplayers were always meeting people in hotel lobbies, so Schang accepted the premise, and the two men quickly struck up a conversation. The man, known as Kelly, endeared himself to Schang and a few of his teammates by inviting them up to his room where he had cases of beer on ice. Over drinks, Kelly asked the players if they liked to play the ponies, indicating he had some horse racing connections. He took their bets and returned the next day with the players' winnings. A drinker and a gambler, Kelly became a hit with the Yankees. The players invited him to come along with them to Chicago, the next stop on their western swing of the American League.

At Comiskey Park one afternoon, Kelly extended another invitation to the Yankees. A friend of his was having a party at a brewery in nearby Joliet. The fact that this was during the middle of Prohibition gave no one pause. Besides, the timing was perfect since the Yankees had the following day off before their next game in Cleveland. Multiple players, including Ruth, accepted the offer. The party was a hit; big mugs of beer, even bigger steaks, lots of laughs. Kelly had thought of everything, including arranging for a photographer to take a picture of the group and having the men sign their autographs to a copy. That photograph made its way to Yankee co-owners Til Huston and Jacob Ruppert. They, in turn, passed it along to Commissioner Landis.[72]

Kelly was no mere bon vivant. He was private detective Jimmy Kelly, hired by the Yankee owners to investigate the off-field behavior of their players. After Landis received the Joliet photograph, he showed up in the Yankees clubhouse before a game with the proof. The commissioner had all the details on the drinks in the St. Louis hotel room, the betting on the horses, and the party at the brewery. He rebuked the players for their partying and gambling ways. Just one year after banning the Black Sox, the last thing Landis wanted was another scandal. Ruth's days of publicly bragging about a day at the track were now behind him.

Landis was not the only baseball official Ruth clashed with in 1922. American League president Ban Johnson had Ruth in his crosshairs multiple times that season, the first instance coming in May less than a week after being reinstated. In the third inning of a game at the Polo Grounds against the Washington Senators, Ruth tried to stretch a single into a double. Umpire George Hildebrand called Ruth out as he slid into the bag. The Babe responded by throwing dirt in the umpire's face. Now ejected from the game and walking back to the bench, Ruth became further incensed by heckling fans. Hearing something he didn't like, he jumped on top of the dugout and started climbing over the tops of seats in an attempt to confront his tormentor. Some fans interceded as Ruth began screaming at the agitator while other bystanders yelled, "Hit the big stiff!" With nothing more than verbal volleys exchanged, tensions dissipated. The Babe then returned to the dugout and walked across the field to the clubhouse. He left the park to a mix of boos and cheers.[73]

Ruth missed one game, received a $200 fine, and was stripped of his newly appointed title as captain of the Yankees. One month later, he battled another umpire. In a loss at Cleveland, the Yankees' eighth in a row, umpire Bill Dineen ejected Ruth for arguing a call. The Babe's "vile and vicious language" directed at the umpire drew a three-game suspension from the league president. Before the game the following day, Ruth and Dineen got into a heated argument. The Yankee star threatened the umpire and challenged him to a fight beneath the grandstand. When word of this incident reached Johnson, he added two days to Ruth's suspension. "Well, you can bet it's the last time I ever will be suspended for wrangling with an umpire," the Babe predicted.[74]

Ruth kept his promise for two months. At the end of August, the Babe objected to a called third strike and let the umpire know it. Johnson suspended him for the third time that season. In total, Ruth didn't play in 44 games in 1922. Clearly, something had the Babe agitated that summer. It may have had something to do with a new member of the Ruth family.

Helen Ruth made her first public appearance with daughter Dorothy in September. The young girl was said to be 16 months old, sparking confusion and plenty of rumors since no one could remember Helen being pregnant in the past two-and-a-half years. Reporters asked her if the daughter was adopted. "I should say not," she replied, "the baby's mine, mine, mine!" Helen claimed the girl was born June 7, 1921 at St. Vincent's Hospital in New York. Mr. Ruth told a different version to reporters, asserting the baby was born February 2 at Presbyterian Hospital. "The Babe's always been careless about dates," Helen explained.[75]

In fact, Ruth's daughter was the result of a tryst with a woman named Juanita Jennings. After Dorothy was born, Ruth claimed the girl and gave her to his wife to raise. Dorothy Ruth didn't learn the identity of her birth mother until 1980.[76]

Ruth was now a father and a former Yankee captain who had spent much of the season brawling with umpires and receiving punishments and tongue lashings from baseball's highest authorities. Not even the Babe's teammates were immune to his volatile ways. Ruth and first baseman Pipp got into a dugout fight in St. Louis in June. Manager Miller Huggins and third baseman Frank Baker managed to pull the two apart. The Yankees won the game 14-5. "You birds ought to fight every day," Browns coach Jimmy Austin told them the following afternoon at Sportsman's Park. As a team, they practically did.

"The Yankees of 1922 were a collection of ball players operating as a team, but much divided in spirit," pitcher Waite Hoyt wrote years later. "There were frequent fights and arguments."[77] Hoyt himself took a swing at his manager in the dugout that season. Hoyt's teammate and fellow pitcher Carl Mays despised Huggins. The feeling was mutual. While Huggins always had the backing of Jacob Ruppert, the man who hired him, co-owner Til Huston never liked the manager, would side with players in disputes, and constantly worked to oust him from the job. There was a reason one Yankees' biographer called 1922 "the turbulent year."[78]

Despite the constant and contentious battles, the fractious, foul-mouthed, hard-charging, hell-raising Yankees arrived in Missouri in mid-September in first place. To leave town in the same spot, they would need to take two of three from the Browns. St. Louis was ready. "All the hopes and ambitions of local fans and players are centered in these games," wrote *The New York Times*. "Everything else was second – war clouds, Armenian massacres, rail strikes, coal shortages."[79]

Time to play ball.

*****

Fans began arriving at 11:00 p.m. on Friday. They came from "the valley of the Mississippi, the Northwest and the Southwest, Missouri and Kansas." By midnight, the line for bleacher tickets – sold at .50 cents apiece – began to stretch. They had to wait another twelve hours for the gates to open. When they finally did, fans with unreserved tickets sprinted to claim a place. One woman was spotted rushing with a seat cushion in one hand, a hot dog in another, and a scorecard clenched between her teeth. With three hours until game time, the crowd sang songs, booed the appearance of the umpires and Babe Ruth, and cheered when their hero, George Sisler, emerged from the dugout.

The sight of Sisler in uniform brought joy and relief to Browns fans. The St. Louis first baseman's shoulder was aching. He suffered the injury after stretching for a throw on Monday. He hadn't played since. Team physician Dr. Robert Hyland diagnosed Sisler with a strain of the deltoid muscle in his right shoulder. "For one week it is certain that he ought not to attempt anything on the ball field," Hyland explained on Tuesday, "but I guess he will try to get into the Yankees series, despite all advice." [80]

Hyland's prediction proved correct. After missing four games, Sisler, hitting .424 at the time of the injury, returned to the lineup against New York. The Browns first baseman and his teammates took the field to an overflow crowd. In a park that held roughly 18,000 people, the Browns sold around 30,000 tickets to each of the games.[81] Owner Ball managed to squeeze in extra fans by constructing temporary seats in front of the grandstand and by setting up a rope line behind the outfielders. Anything hit beyond the rope and in the field of play meant an automatic ground-rule double for the hitter. It also put thousands of partisans in closer proximity to the players. Police mounted on horseback kept an eye on them. Bleacher fans armed with cowbells added to the atmosphere of the event and the agitation of the horses.

The Browns had their best pitcher, Shocker, on the mound, while the Yankees countered with righthander Bob Shawkey. New York delivered single runs in the second and third innings to take the lead. St. Louis got one back in the bottom of the sixth, but with runners at first and third and one out, a bare-handed grab of a ball off the bat of Sisler put an end to the threat. Yankee second baseman Aaron Ward snared the ball behind the bag, flipped it to shortstop Everett Scott who completed the double play by throwing on to first base. Sisler's injury may have prevented him from beating the throw. He ran to first base with his right arm "hung close to his side." The score remained 2-1 Yankees heading into the bottom of the ninth inning.

Third baseman Eddie Foster led off for the Browns. St. Louis had acquired him off waivers from the Boston Red Sox in August. The Browns needed a replacement for their regular third baseman, Frank Ellerbe, after he injured his knee in July. Ellerbe, the son of a former South Carolina governor, only played in a handful of games the rest of the season. Foster, the son of a Johns Hopkins-trained doctor, took his place.[82] Thus, the Browns, like the Yankees with Dugan, depended on a Harry Frazee castoff to man the hot corner down the stretch in 1922. The 35-year old Foster hit .306 in 37 games for St. Louis, 42 points above his career average.

Facing Shawkey in the bottom of the ninth, Foster swung and sent a fly ball to deep right-center field where Yankee center fielder Whitey Witt and right fielder Meusel converged. Meusel made the catch. Witt never saw the out. A soda bottle thrown from the right-field bleachers hit Witt on the forehead and knocked him out. Players and umpires rushed to check on his condition. Several Yankees emerged from the dugout with bats in hand. Mounted police stormed toward the downed player. Fans left the stands and swarmed the field. "It had the makings of a good riot," according to one account. [83]

The anger and tension subsided, though, as fans, players and umpires got a closer look at Witt, now bloody and unconscious. He had to be carried off the field. Order was restored, and the game continued. But the once raucous and electric crowd no longer had the energy to carry on the fight. Sisler followed Foster in the lineup. With their star player at the plate, Browns fans did the unthinkable. They began to root for Yankee pitcher Shawkey to strike him out. It was "a cry the like which was never heard before in St. Louis," noted the *Post-Dispatch*. Sisler, who admitted after the game his shoulder was "aching terribly now," didn't even swing the bat. Attempting to bunt for a hit, he was easily thrown out at first. When Ken Williams flew out to right field the game was over, and the Yankees had increased their lead over the Browns to 1.5 games with two games left in the series and two weeks left in the season.

The Witt incident drew an immediate response from baseball officials. League president Ban Johnson offered a $1,000 reward for the arrest of the person who injured the Yankee center fielder. Calling it a "deplorable event," Browns owner Ball added a $500 reward and banned the selling of bottled soda on the field. The Cardinals matched the Browns with a $500 bounty. Even the St. Louis Pennant Rooters' Club got involved, offering $50 for information leading to the arrest and conviction of the bottle thrower. The incident took place nearly 15 years to the day that umpire Evans had been struck by a bottle at Sportsman's Park. Evans was on the field and a witness to the attack on Witt. Reports surfaced that there may have been multiple bottles thrown at the Yankee outfielder. The umpire disagreed. "The bottle that struck Witt was the only one I saw thrown," he said after the game.[84]

While the search for the guilty party intensified, the baseball focus shifted to the matchup in the second game. "It's all over if we win tomorrow," Yankees manager Huggins told reporters after the one-run victory on Saturday. He handed the ball on Sunday to righthander Waite Hoyt. The Browns countered by throwing left-hander Pruett.

"Shucks" Pruett, the screwball-throwing lefthander, had been the nemesis of Ruth all season. The two men had last faced each other on July 12 in New York. With the bases loaded, Pruett struck him out. It marked the ninth time Ruth had fanned against Pruett in 12 plate appearances. The other three times, Ruth tapped out to the mound and walked twice, once intentionally.[85] Pruett hadn't started since that game at the Polo Grounds two months ago. Bothered by a sore arm, the lefthander had only appeared out of the bullpen. With the season on the line, manager Fohl turned to the rookie from Malden, Missouri. Pessimism prevailed. "When Lee Fohl announced Pruett's name as the man to face the Yankees in the second game, it was received with great misgiving," wrote *Post-Dispatch* sports editor John Wray.[86]

The first man Pruett faced on Sunday was Witt. Diagnosed by Doctor Hyland with a mild concussion, Witt returned to the lineup wearing a bandage to cover the lump on his forehead, described as "not much smaller than his fist."[87] He got a "handsome ovation" from the crowd and went 1-4 on the day. St. Louis fans were not as kind to his teammate Ruth who received "the razzing of his life" when he batted in the first inning.[88] The Babe, who always fed off the energy of the crowd, had two hits, including a home run in the sixth inning that put the Yankees up 1-0. The blast marked Ruth's first hit in fifteen plate appearances off Pruett and his 33rd homer of the year. But Sunday belonged to the Browns.

Sisler lined a single to center in the sixth inning, extending his hitting streak to an American League record 41 games, topping a mark previously set by Ty Cobb. Ken Williams hit his major league-leading 38th home run of the season in the eighth inning, one better than the Cardinals' Hornsby, sending the crowd of 31,000 "into apoplexy." The star of the game, though, was the rookie lefthander. Pruett went the distance, allowing five hits and one walk, while striking out eight Yankee hitters. The Browns won the game 5-1 and had once again closed to within a half game of the league-leading Yankees.

A win on Monday would mean the Browns would have both momentum and the schedule on their side. After the series against New York, St. Louis had nine games left, all at home: three-game sets against Washington, Philadelphia and Chicago, a trio of visiting teams that would finish the season sixth, seventh, and fifth, respectively, in the American League. The Yankees still had ten games remaining, all on the road, including three at Detroit against Ty Cobb's third-place Tigers.

Huggins had Joe Bush lined up to pitch in the series finale. Already the winner of 24 games in the season, Bush accounted for twenty-eight percent of all Yankees victories in 1922 and finished the season fourth in the MVP voting. Fohl sent veteran right-hander Dixie Davis to the mound. Davis had been with the Browns since 1920, winning a combined 34 games over his first two seasons in St. Louis. He started 25 games in 1922, including one a few weeks earlier now seared into the mind of his manager.

On August 31, the Browns found themselves in Cleveland, playing the final game of a series against the Indians. Davis had given up six hits through eight innings and had a comfortable 6-2 lead when he returned to the mound for the bottom of the ninth inning. He proceeded to walk the leadoff hitter, allowed four of the first five hitters to reach base and made an error on a throw to first base. Still up 6-3 with one out and runners at second and third, Fohl pulled Davis in favor of Elam Vangilder, appearing in his third straight game. A tired Vangilder couldn't stem the tide. The Indians rallied for five runs in the bottom of the ninth to beat the Browns 7-6.

Facing the Yankees at Sportsman's Park on September 18, Davis was even more effective than that day in Cleveland. Through seven innings, he had shutout the Yankees on only two hits, both infield singles by Witt. Even better, St. Louis had broken through against Bush to take a 2-0 lead.

Leading off the bottom of the fifth inning in a scoreless game, Jacobson sent a fly ball to center field. With a rope line in place, Witt didn't have to worry about an outfield wall. But the Yankee outfielder did have to battle partisan fans with the ability to manipulate the field of play. Pull the rope back when the home team is in the field and an outfielder needs extra space to make a catch. Hold firm when the visitor is present. With St. Louis at-bat, fans weren't budging. The ball fell beyond the rope for a ground-rule double. It was the Browns first hit of the game. Jacobson later scored to give St. Louis a 1-0 lead.

The rope line came into play again in the bottom of the seventh. Ken Williams led off with a ground-rule double to right field. With one out, Marty McManus hit a ball beyond the rope line for a ground-rule RBI double. The Browns had five hits on the day. Three of them were ground-rule doubles.

New York pushed a run across the plate in the top of the eighth to cut the lead to 2-1. Following a double by Dugan, Pipp singled off the glove of Davis. When the ball reached second baseman McManus, he threw wide of first, allowing Dugan to score and Pipp to advance a base. With the tying run on second and two out, Davis struck out Bob Meusel to end the inning. He returned to the mound in the top of the ninth still clinging to the one-run lead. The Browns were three outs from first place.

Catcher Schang led off for New York and like Pipp in the eighth, he hit a ball off the glove of Davis for a base hit. On Davis' next pitch, Schang advanced to second on a passed ball by catcher Severeid. Browns manager Fohl had seen enough. With memories of the meltdown in Cleveland from a few weeks earlier likely fresh in his mind, he pulled his starting pitcher.[89] With left-handed pinch-hitter Elmer Smith at the plate, Fohl went for the lefty-lefty matchup and brought in Hub Pruett, one day removed from his 103-pitch complete-game performance. Huggins countered by pulling Smith for right-handed hitting Mike McNally. When McNally bunted the ball, Schang broke for third. Catcher Severeid's throw to Eddie Foster was low and wide of the bag. Pruett then (unintentionally) walked shortstop Everett Scott on four pitches. The Yankees had loaded the bases with no outs and had barely hit a ball past the pitcher's mound.

Pruett's day was done. Fohl replaced him with Shocker to face Bush, a very good hitting pitcher (career batting average of .253). Bush grounded to second baseman McManus who fired the ball to Severeid to get a force out at the plate. Bases still loaded. One out. Witt, the bruised and bandaged center fielder of the Yankees, walked to the plate. He promptly lined a single to center field and scored two runs. New York now led 3-2. Shocker induced a double play off the bat of Dugan to end the inning but the damage was done. Under completely different circumstances, Witt had once again sucked the oxygen out of Sportsman's Park. One New York writer called it "poetic justice."[90]

Bush faced Sisler, Williams and Jacobson in the bottom of the ninth, the heart of the Browns order. The trio didn't hit a ball out of the infield. When Sisler grounded out, it meant he had failed to get a hit in a game for the first time since July 26, snapping his hitting streak at 41 games. When Jacobson grounded the ball to Yankee shortstop Everett Scott, he stopped running halfway down the line. When Scott threw the ball to Pipp at first base, the game and series were over. The Yankees had restored their lead to 1.5 games. "It would not have been so bad," one fan told the *Post-Dispatch* after it ended, "if the Yanks had walloped their way to a one-sided victory. But for the Browns to be virtually in first place and then kick it away that was a heartbreaker." The headline over the box score the next day in the paper read "If You Have Tears."

*****

St. Louis still had nine games left and a schedule in its favor, but for many Browns fans, it felt like the season was already over. Playing in front of a crowd estimated at 3,000 to 4,000 the next day at Sportsman's Park, the Browns lost to Washington and

Walter Johnson 4-3 while the Yankees won at Detroit. By the weekend, New York had stretched its lead to 4.5 games.

The Browns, however, refused to quit. On the final Saturday of the season, St. Louis trailed New York by two games. They needed to win their last two contests and have the Yankees lose at Boston on Saturday and then Washington on Sunday to force a tie. The Red Sox were scheduled to start lefthander Herb Pennock. Instead, Boston started Alex Ferguson. He left in the first inning without retiring a single batter. Pennock relieved him and only allowed two hits over seven innings, but the Yankees' first-inning outburst made the difference in a 3-1 pennant-clinching victory. The final was posted on the scoreboard at Sportsman's Park in the middle of the Browns' victory over the White Sox. New York lost a meaningless game on Sunday while the Browns won at home to close the final gap to one game.

Fans and biographers are quick to blame Red Sox owner Frazee's tactics and trades as the reason why the Browns lost in 1922. His questionable canceling of the doubleheader in July and his trade of Joe Dugan to the Yankees later that month certainly didn't help the Browns cause. But St. Louis also acquired a third baseman late in the season from Boston. Dugan played 60 games for the Yankees, hit three home runs with 26 RBI, batted .286 with an OPS (on-base plus slugging percentage) of .696. Foster played in 37 games for the Browns, had no home runs with 12 RBI, batted .306 with an OPS of .727.

Others point the finger in the direction of Mack's Philadelphia A's and the improbable winning start of Otto Rettig. There are other reasons to look at Philadelphia. Witt spent the first five years of his career with the A's. He clashed with Mack over salary demands early in 1922. His frustration boiled over in the ninth inning of a spring training game against the Cardinals. Standing in the outfield in the middle of a downpour, he threw a ball over the catcher's head into the grandstand instead of attempting to cut down the lead runner at third base.

"After the game we come back to the hotel and Connie Mack is talking to Branch Rickey and Hornsby and Mack says, 'Whitey, come here, I want to talk to you. I'm going to get rid of you.'" When the manager asked the player where he would like to go, Witt immediately thought of New York because of the season-opening suspensions given to Ruth and Meusel. Mack then sold Witt to the Yankees.

Catcher Cy Perkins played all but two seasons of his big-league career for Philadelphia. Yankee pitcher Bush was once a teammate. Bush noticed how Perkins gave signs to pitchers, always moving his legs upward when he flashed the sign for a curve, while keeping them steady when he called for a fastball.

"I passed that along to our hitters and we had little trouble beating them," said Bush. "Connie Mack knew I was reading Perkins for pitches but neither he nor Cy knew what was giving it to me." New York went 17-5 against Philadelphia in 1922, their best mark against any team in the league. "The New York Yankees had the Philadelphia Athletics to thank for their 1-game margin over the St. Louis Browns," wrote Mack biographer Norman Macht.[91]

Of course, the Browns also have themselves to blame. Despite dominating every other opponent in the American League (the Browns outscored their opponents by 244 runs), St. Louis struggled against New York.[92] In 22 head-to-head matchups with the Yankees that season, the Browns won only eight of them. St. Louis dropped 10 of its last 14 games against New York. Six of those ten losses were by one run, including the final game that raised so many questions about Fohl's ninth-inning pitching strategy. Those questions lingered for years. When Dixie Davis died more than two decades later, *The Sporting News* noted that his start on Monday, September 18, 1922 "has been the subject of more telephone inquiries than any sports event (in) Mound City history."[93]

*****

On October 1, the last day of the regular season, baseball officials announced the "pop bottle mystery" of St. Louis had been solved. Witt hadn't been struck by a soda bottle thrown from the stands after all, at least according to the version accepted by American League president Johnson. James P. Hon was an eyewitness to the events on that Saturday at Sportsman's Park. In a letter to Johnson, Hon claimed that Witt stepped on the neck of a bottle already on the field. The bottle then propelled upward and smacked the Yankee outfielder on the forehead. Identified as a "meat salesman," Hon claimed in his letter that he was probably the only one who saw it since everyone else was focused on Meusel catching the fly ball. Johnson was so pleased by the explanation he awarded Hon a check for $100, round trip transportation between St. Louis and New York and a complete set of tickets to the 1922 World Series.[94]

For the second consecutive year, the Yankees lost the World Series to the Giants. New York's American League team then left Manhattan and the Polo Grounds to a new park across the river in the Bronx. Yankee Stadium, "The House that Ruth Built," opened in 1923, the same year the Yankees won their first World Series title, with a bevy of former Red Sox pitchers and four former Boston players in their everyday lineup.

Fohl returned to manage the Browns in 1923 but general manager Quinn departed. He became part of the ownership group of the Red Sox. Quinn's group bought the team in August, long enough for Frazee to make one last trade with the Yankees. Boston sent lefthander Pennock to New York. Over the next 11 seasons with the Yankees, the Hall of Fame pitcher won 162 games. "With the Pennock trade in January 1923," wrote author Henry Fetter, "the Red Sox transfusions to the Yankee system came to an end, if for no other reason than the Red Sox had nothing left to give."[95] Stripped of talent, Quinn's group owned the Red Sox for ten seasons, finishing last in eight of them. Winners of four World Series titles from 1912 to 1918, Boston didn't return to the Fall Classic until 1946.

Sisler suffered from sinus troubles and double vision in 1923. He didn't play in a single game that season. Danforth, the pitcher suspended and ultimately waived the prior year, returned to St. Louis and had a banner campaign. He won a career-high 16 games, fulfilling the potential the Browns saw in him when they traded 11 players to get him. But without their star first baseman, the Browns struggled, finishing in fifth place with a record of 74-88.

After the 1924 season, the Browns traded Shocker back to the Yankees. In exchange, St. Louis received pitcher Joe Bush, the winning pitcher in that fateful Monday showdown with the Browns. At the end of the 1925 season, Browns owner Ball did something he'd wanted to do ever since 1922 – expand Sportsman's Park. When it opened in 1926, the park held some 34,000 fans, an increase of more than 15,000.[96] No more rope lines for marquee matchups.

Ball picked the perfect year to expand the park. But it wasn't the Browns who needed the extra seats.

---

[1] The Browns drew an all-time franchise record 712,918 fans in 1922 while 536,998 people came to watch the Cardinals. The combined attendance was the most for the St. Louis teams until 1946.

[2] The Powell and Schimmel families opened competing parking lots near the stadium in the 1920s. "We were the only two lots there for a long time," remembered Mrs. E.L. Schimmel. A streetcar ride to the park cost a nickel. The parking lots charged fifteen cents. *St. Louis Post-Dispatch*, May 22, 1966.

[3] The Cleveland Indians experimented with numbers on jersey sleeves in 1916. The Cardinals introduced numbers on the sleeve in 1923. Fans proceeded to mock the players and the idea was shelved. "The effect upon the team was bad and 'busted up' the team morale or spirit completely," Rickey said later. "They really didn't want to show themselves on the field. Because of the continuing embarrassment to the players, the numbers were removed." See exhibits.baseballhalloffame.org/dressed_to_the_nines/numbers.htm for more. The Cleveland Indians and New York Yankees introduced numbers on the backs of jerseys in 1929, a concept all teams eventually adopted.

[4] Bryson, *One Summer*.

[5] Ibid. The doubleheader in question was played on September 26, 1926, the final day of the regular season. Since the Yankees had already clinched the pennant, there was little to play for on the last day, likely contributing to the accelerated pace. The Yankees won the first game 6-1 and the Browns the second contest 6-2 with Sisler coming on in relief to get the save.

[6] Rushin, Steve. *The 34-Ton Bat: The Story of Baseball As Told Through Bobbleheads, Cracker Jacks, Jockstraps, Eye Black, and 375 Other Strange and Unforgettable Objects.* Brown & Company. 2013.

[7] Ibid.

[8] Quote from Gleick's blog. See around.com/time-for-earth-time/ for more.

[9] Rushin, *The 34-Ton Bat*.

[10] Ibid. Also see *Sacramento Daily Union*, July 11, 1897.

---

[11] Ibid. The original quote comes from a Pegler syndicated column. "The decanters and bottles sometimes shattered and left fragments of glass lying about the field, multiplying the problems of the grounds keepers and causing the ball to take bad hops. *Detroit Free Press,* April 2, 1933.
[12] *St. Louis Post-Dispatch*, August 1, 1917.
[13] Ibid, September 17, 1922.
[14] Godin, Roger A. *The 1922 St. Louis Browns: Best of the American League's Worst.* McFarland & Company, Inc. 1991.
[15] For his career, Sisler pitched 111 innings in the big leagues. Seventy of them occurred in 1915. "Sisler easily could have been one of the top pitchers – a thirty-game winner," believed teammate Lavan. *Baseball Digest*, May 1944.
[16] Sisler's single-season hit record was broken by Ichiro Suzuki. In 2004, the Seattle Mariners outfielder compiled 262 hits.
[17] *Yank, The Army Weekly*, March 23, 1945.
[18] *The Sporting News*, February 5, 1977.
[19] Ibid.
[20] Runyon, Damon. *Guys, Dolls, and Curveball: Damon Runyan on Baseball*. Jim Reisler, Editor. Carroll & Graf Publishers. 2005.
[21] Allen, Lee. *The Hot Stove League*. A.S. Barnes and Company. 1955.
[22] Scout Charley Barrett first saw Vangilder in a game against a team from Perryville, Missouri. "I went to Cape Girardeau, Missouri to look over a big country pitcher by the name of Elam Vangilder, who was knocking the rural boys cold with a fast ball," Barrett recalled. *The Standard Union,* March 27, 1929.
[23] McDonald, Anna. "Pruett Heir Remembers Ruthian Legacy." ESPN.com. March 2, 2014. www.espn.com/blog/sweetspot/post/_/id/44743/pruett-heir-remembers-ruthian-legacy.
[24] *St. Louis Post-Dispatch*, April 9, 1922.
[25] Ibid, April 23, 1922.
[26] *The Sporting News*, May 4, 1922.
[27] *St. Louis Post-Dispatch*, May 1, 1922.
[28] James, Bill. *The New Bill James Historical Abstract.* The Free Press. 2001.
[29] James, Bill. *The Bill James Guide to Baseball Managers: From 1870 to Today*. Simon & Schuster. 1997.
[30] Seymour, Harold. *Baseball: The Golden Age*. Oxford University Press. 1971.
[31] James, *The New Bill James Historical Baseball Abstract.*
[32] Bryson, *One Summer.*
[33] Wagenheim, *Babe Ruth*.
[34] Leavy, *The Big Fella.* He also endorsed automobiles, including the Reo in St. Louis.
[35] Ibid. "The courts did not recognize celebrity as an exclusive property right until 1953," Leavy wrote.

---

[36] Montville, *The Big Bam. The New York Times* reported a lower amount, saying the tour "was expected to net the Babe about $23,000 for a dozen or so appearances." See "Extent Of Penalty Is Surprise Here," *New York Times*, December 6, 1921.
[37] Montville, *The Big Bam.*
[38] *New York Times*, October 17, 1921.
[39] Ibid, October 22, 1921.
[40] Ibid, December 6, 1921.
[41] Ibid, October 28, 1921.
[42] Depending on the source, Ruth's salary for 1921 is either listed at $20,000, $26,000 or $30,000. The highest figure comes from a 1932 article in *The Sporting News*. See www.baseball-almanac.com/tsn/babe_ruth_salary.shtml
[43] Montville, *The Big Bam.*
[44] *The Sporting News*, March 30, 1922.
[45] Wagenheim, *Babe Ruth*.
[46] *New York Times*, May 24, 1922.
[47] Macht, Norman L. *Connie Mack: The Turbulent and Triumphant Years. 1915-1931.* University of Nebraska Press. 2012.
[48] *New York Times*, July 10, 1982.
[49] *St. Louis Post-Dispatch*, July 7, 1922.
[50] The Red Sox received infielders Chick Fewster and Johnny Mitchell and outfielder Elmer Miller. The player to be named later was Lefty O'Doul. O'Doul was a pitcher when the Red Sox acquired him. He played the 1923 season for Boston and didn't return to the big leagues until 1928. He resurfaced as an outfielder and won two batting titles – hitting .398 for the Phillies in 1929 and .368 for the Dodgers in 1932. In his one and only year in Boston, O'Doul went 1-1 with a 5.43 ERA in 53 innings.
[51] *St. Louis Post-Dispatch*, July 25, 1922.
[52] *New York Tribune,* July 26, 1922.
[53] *St. Louis Post-Dispatch*, July 25, 1922.
[54] The New York Giants also influenced the new June 15 deadline. *The New York Times* noted that the Giants had made several midseason deals in recent years, acquiring pitchers Art Nehf and Hugh McQuillan, shortstop Dave Bancroft and outfielder Irish Meusel (brother of Yankees outfielder Bob Meusel). "One of John McGraw's most potent weapons was thereby taken away from him." See *New York Times*, December 15, 1922.
[55] *New York Times,* October 5, 1916. The *Times* wrote that Rettig "will report to John McGraw on Thursday morning, when it is understood he will be taken into the National League." The Paterson Silk Sox were also known as the Doherty Silk Sox, reportedly for the factory in New Jersey that sponsored the team.
[56] See seamheads.com/blog/2014/07/31/the-improbable-career-of-adolph-otto-rettig/ for more.
[57] Macht, *Connie Mack*.
[58] *St. Louis Post-Dispatch*, July 21, 1922.

---

[59] Ibid, August 6, 1922. The Browns won the game 4-1.
[60] *The Sporting News*, November 2, 1922.
[61] Macht, *Connie Mack*.
[62] Steinberg, Steve. *Dave Danforth*. SABR.org biography project.
[63] *New York Times*, September 22, 1970.
[64] Steinberg, *Dave Danforth*.
[65] *Baseball Magazine*, July 1916.
[66] *St. Louis Post-Dispatch*, March 28, 1922.
[67] *The Sporting News*, December 21, 1921.
[68] *Bluefield Daily Telegraph*, March 24, 1944.
[69] *St. Louis Post-Dispatch*, June 14, 1922.
[70] Steinberg, *Dave Danforth.*
[71] *St. Louis Post-Dispatch*, July 28, 1922.
[72] Graham, Frank. *The New York Yankees: An Informal History.* G.P. Putnam's Sons. 1943.
[73] *New York Times*, May 27, 1922.
[74] Ibid, June 22, 1922.
[75] Wagenheim, *Babe Ruth.*
[76] *New York Times*, May 20, 1989.
[77] Hoyt, Waite. *Babe Ruth as I Knew Him.* Dell Pub. Co. 1948.
[78] Graham, *The New York Yankees.* Huston sold his interest in the team to Ruppert after the 1922 season for a reported $1,250,000.
[79] *New York Times*, September 17, 1922.
[80] *St. Louis Post-Dispatch*, September 13, 1922.
[81] Estimates on crowd size for the first game vary. The *New York Tribune* estimated 26,000, the *St. Louis Post-Dispatch* put the figure at 27,000 while *The New York Times* listed attendance at 30,000.
[82] Nowlin, Bill. *Eddie Foster*. SABR.org biography project.
[83] *New York Times*, September 17, 1922.
[84] *St. Louis Post-Dispatch*, September 17, 1922. While attention was focused on who threw the bottle, Red Smith later speculated on who *sold* the bottle. "Bill DeWitt [Sr.] was a hustler. It may be that he sold the very bottle which, during a game between the Yankees and Browns, dented the sconce of Whitey Witt, a New York outfielder." *Baseball Digest*, April 1949.
[85] Ibid.
[86] *St. Louis Post-Dispatch*, September 18, 1922.
[87] *New York Tribune*, September 18, 1922. Witt's injury may have been more serious than anyone knew. Years later, he didn't recall playing in the second game of the series. See Rich Westcott's biography of Witt at SABR.org.
[88] *New York Times*, September 18, 1922.

---

[89] In a story on Fohl signing his contract for the 1923 season, Roy Stockton cited the Cleveland game as motivation for the manager's move against New York. "Fohl was justified in that move." *St. Louis Post-Dispatch*, December 2, 1922.
[90] *New York Herald*, September 25, 1922.
[91] Macht, *Connie Mack.*
[92] Based on Pythagorean win-loss projections, a formula based on run differential, the Browns should have won five more games (98 instead of the actual 93). The Yankees outscored their opponents by 140 runs. According to the same Pythagorean calculation, the Yankees projected to win three fewer games (91 instead of 94). See *Baseball Reference.*
[93] *The Sporting News*, February 10, 1944.
[94] *New York Times*, October 2, 1922. Also see *St. Louis Star* on the same date.
[95] Fetter, *Taking On The Yankees.*
[96] Seating for expanded Sportsman's Park: 25,663 grandstand seats, 5,070 bleachers, 3,290 pavilion. Total seating: 34,023. *St. Louis Post-Dispatch*, April 10, 1926.

The Seeds of Success

They came from miles around. With nothing more than an announcement in a local paper, the word spread rapidly. The young men, many of them just teenagers, would show up the night before and sleep in their cars. They frequently didn't have the money to pay for a motel. Hundreds came for the opportunity. One dozen or maybe even two left with contracts. The amateur baseball players were chasing a dream. Branch Rickey was fulfilling a vision. "I offered them a better way of life," he later recalled. "They rose from sand lots to big city diamonds. In a month they earned more than they could have earned in a year."[1]

Beginning in 1919, tryout camps became a staple of the Rickey playbook.[2] Local affairs at first, the auditions eventually spread regionally and ultimately to a national footprint. Lasting up to a week, the camps gave the Cardinals a cheap and efficient way to evaluate players. It was one part grand strategy. If Rickey wanted to build a vertically integrated minor league system, he needed a pipeline of talent. It was another part desperation. The Cardinals were a bad team with no money.

Refined over time, Rickey and the Cardinals eventually turned the tryout camps into an assembly line process. Starting at nine a.m. the first day, the camps would conclude by five p.m. the following day. Over the two days, team officials would observe, appraise and complete the paperwork on every single player. The vote had to be unanimous to dismiss. If even one scout or club official voted to retain, the player was kept.[3] In his history of the Cardinals farm system, Donald Ray Anderson tells the story of how a young North Carolina outfielder was kept by such a vote. When it came time to evaluate Enos Slaughter, no one saw a future for him in the Cardinals organization except for a local minor league owner. Because of him, the Cardinals signed Slaughter in 1934. The rest is Hall of Fame history.[4]

Dizzy Dean, the pitcher who led the Gashouse Gang Cardinals to a World Series title in 1934, came out of a camp in Oklahoma. Teammate Pepper Martin is said to have arrived at a tryout camp in Greenville, Texas in 1925 on a freight train.[5] Marty Marion, who started at shortstop for three World Series and four pennant-winning teams in the 1940s, was signed after a tryout camp in Georgia.[6] An estimated three hundred players auditioned at a camp in Pine Bluff, Arkansas in 1938, a year in which the Cardinals had 14 summer tryout camps and 12 spring training camps. The camps "are more important than the farm system," contended Rickey, adding he believed the gatherings would eventually replace the role of scouts.[7] The vast numbers the camps produced allowed Rickey, the best talent evaluator in the business, to audition thousands of young players in a single year.[8] "The mass production gave us 50 percent of the men we signed in my last five years with the Cardinals," Rickey later recalled.[9] (In spring training of 1941, the Cardinals had 21 rookies in camp. All of them "eventually got to the big leagues for at least a cup of coffee," Bob Broeg later wrote.)[10]

It began under more modest circumstances. With Rickey still the field manager, the camps were confined to the St. Louis area. Fortunately for the Cardinals, the region was fertile ground. "St. Louis...will send somewhere around a hundred players to the majors and minors this year," *The Sporting News* noted in early 1920. Author Lee Allen later noted that although Missouri constituted roughly two-and-a-half percent of the country's population during the period, the state supplied nearly five percent of major league talent between 1929 and 1949.[11] First baseman Jim Bottomley and outfielders Ray Blades and Heinie Mueller all played instrumental roles in the rise of the Cardinals in the 1920s. All grew up in the area. All were under contract by 1920.[12]

The son of a coal miner, Bottomley was born in April of 1900 in the Illinois town of Oglesby. In Nokomis, Illinois, about eighty-five miles from St. Louis, he quit high school at the age of 16. Three years later, he wrote a letter to the Cardinals. "I am nineteen years old and I love to play ball." Scout Charley Barrett kept the handwritten note for the rest of his life.[13] Barrett and Rickey loved Bottomley's work ethic. "We had gone hungry to play. We had slept with the pungent leather glove under the pillow, awakened at dawn and walked the miles," remembered Rickey. "Bottomley was a symbol of the thing that has always made baseball great."[14]

Bottomley, who threw and hit lefthanded, was in the big leagues with the Cardinals by the end of the 1922 season. In his first full year in St. Louis, Bottomley hit .371, good enough for second-best in the National League, only behind teammate Rogers Hornsby. A new generation of Cardinal fans were introduced to Bottomley's talents after outfielder Mark Whiten produced 12 RBI in a game in 1993. Whiten's feat tied a record set by Bottomley in 1924, when he had six hits and 12 RBI in a game against the Brooklyn Dodgers.[15] A National League MVP in 1928, "Sunny Jim" was elected to the Hall of Fame in 1974.

Teammate Ray Blades followed a similar path. A native of Mount Vernon, Illinois, about eighty miles east of St. Louis, Blades caught the eye of Rickey in an exhibition game. "He was almost twenty-two, and not too much as a pitcher, but oh, how he could run, like a deer."[16] Signed and sent to play minor league ball in Memphis, Blades, like Bottomley, was in the big leagues in 1922 and became a regular soon thereafter. A second baseman converted to the outfield, he hit a career-high .342 in 1925. As we'll see later, a Blades injury in the summer of 1926 played a key role in the season.

When Rickey signed Clarence "Heinie" Mueller, he knew he was acquiring a confident young man. The St. Louis manager had plenty of questions for the Creve Coeur, Missouri native when he first met him.

"I understand, you're quite a ball player," he said to Mueller.

"Yes, Mr. Rickey."

"As good an outfielder as Tris Speaker?"

"Yes, Mr. Rickey."

"Can you run the bases like Ty Cobb?"

"Yes, Mr. Rickey."

"I suppose you can hit like Home Run Baker?"

"Yes, Mr. Rickey."

"Judas Priest!" an astonished Rickey exclaimed.

"I never heard of him, Mr. Rickey, but I'm just as good as he is."

"I don't think," Rickey said years later, "I would trade that meeting for the presidency of the United States."[17]

"I had two weaknesses," Mueller once said. "One was base-running, the other was keeping my mouth shut. I never knew which caused me more trouble." His most famous base-running story involved a hit-and-run play where he took off from first base and wound up on third, only to discover the batter had fouled out to the catcher. "That was the longest pop foul in history," Mueller said. "It sent me all the way from St. Louis to Houston (home of a Cardinals minor league team)."[18]

Bottomley, Blades and Mueller were just the start of a pipeline of talent that would eventually feature more than thirty minor league teams with more than 700 players under contract. "Starting the Cardinals farm system was no sudden stroke of genius," said Rickey. "It was a case of necessity being the mother of invention. We lived in a precarious existence. Other clubs would outbid us; they had the money and the superior scouting system. We had to take the leavings, or nothing at all."[19]

That "precarious existence," a part of the Cardinals DNA since the nineteenth century, began to stabilize in 1920. The fortunes of the franchise would dramatically improve over the coming decade. Rickey brought experience, a vision, and a grand plan to compete. What he needed was the financial backing to succeed. Enter Sam Breadon.

*****

Americans went mad for the automobile in the 1920s. Henry Ford's assembly line production dramatically cut costs, making vehicles affordable for the masses. The Model T debuted in 1908 at $950. By 1923, Ford had reduced the price to $269. "Nothing in the millennia of human history, at least until the 1950-55 spread of television sets into the American home, rivals the speed with which automobile ownership spread in a mere two decades between 1910 and 1930 to the majority of American households," wrote economist Robert J. Gordon.[20] More than 10 million Americans had cars by the late 1920s. It was a perfect time to be in the automobile business. Ford made his money from manufacturing vehicles. The president of the St. Louis Cardinals made his money from selling them.

Breadon was born in New York City in July of 1876. One of eight children born to parents of Irish and Scottish descent, he grew up on Manhattan's Lower East Side. "I was born in New York and grew up in the old Ninth Ward in old Greenwich Village," remembered Breadon. "Nothing fancy, a tough neighborhood. You had to be able to handle yourself, or you did not do so well."[21] By the age of 15, he had quit school. He spent time as a young man working as a bank clerk. Two of his friends, Gus and Oscar Halsey, had moved to St. Louis and by 1901 had established the Halsey Automobile Co. They sold Wintons and Packards.[22] Breadon wrote to Gus Halsey asking for a job. He arrived in St. Louis in January of 1902 and began work as a mechanic for $75 a month.[23] From those humble beginnings, Breadon would eventually control his own car dealership, become the majority owner of the St. Louis Cardinals and develop into a shrewd real estate investor, with business interests and properties worth millions of dollars.

Working for the Halsey brothers, he learned the art of the sale. "The automobile was a new contraption," Breadon later admitted. "However, the customers who came to the Halseys looked upon me as the expert from New York."[24] Ambitious and successful in his new role, Breadon began thinking about going into business for himself. When the Halseys heard about his plans, they fired him. Undeterred, he traveled to Detroit and bought two early (pre-Model T) Fords, had them shipped to St. Louis, and opened a temporary salesroom in the city.

One of those impressed by "the expert from New York" was Marion Lambert, whose family had a long and colorful history in St. Louis. Marion's father, Jordan W. Lambert, founded Lambert Pharmaceutical, best known today as the original manufacturer and marketer of Listerine. The patriarch passed away in 1889. Originally sold as a mild antiseptic, sales skyrocketed when son Gerald came up with the idea to market the product as a cure for bad breath. Near the peak of the roaring stock market of the 1920s, Gerald cashed out to pursue a career in international yacht racing.[25] Lambert Airport in St. Louis is named after another of Marion's brothers, Albert Bond Lambert, who learned to fly with the Wright Brothers. When Marion married in 1899, the *Post-Dispatch* reported that his annual income from his father's trust was $30,000.[26] He was 18 years old. So was his bride, the former Florence McRae Parker from Richmond, Virginia. She later swapped the pharmaceutical heir for a brewery heir, divorcing him in 1912 and marrying Adolphus Busch III in 1913.

In 1903, Marion Lambert had just become a vice president in the family firm and was an avid auto enthusiast. (When Lambert and three chauffeurs were all arrested for speeding a few years later, it made front-page news. The St. Louis County speed limit at the time was nine miles per hour.)[27] Lambert had the money. Breadon had entrepreneurial gumption. To make money after getting fired by the Halsey brothers, he got the idea to sell popcorn at the World's Fair dedication parade. The venture was a success. He turned a profit of $35. "That money fixed me up," he remembered years later.[28]

Breadon and Lambert started the Western Automobile Company. While the dealership sold a variety of cars over the years, including Fords and Buicks as well as brands now largely lost to history (i.e., Reo, Columbia), the Pierce-Arrow, a luxury car, became Breadon's staple. In the early days, "you sold autos only to 'sports,'" said Breadon, "the conservative people stuck to the horse and buggy."[29] He once sold 280 Pierce-Arrows in a single year, the cheapest of which cost $5,000.

At some point, Breadon bought out Lambert's interest in the dealership and by 1914 had established a permanent home for the Western Automobile Company at the intersection of Euclid Avenue and Washington Boulevard in St. Louis.[30] He had also started his second marriage. First married in October of 1906, Sam and Frances Josephine Breadon soon had a daughter, also named Frances. Five years later, his wife filed for divorce, charging that her husband "associated with women and persons of loose moral character." Frances Breadon claimed her husband had property worth $25,000 and an income of more than $8,000 a year (approximately $650,000 and $210,000 in 2020 dollars). A judge awarded her $2,000 annual alimony and custody of their daughter when the divorce became final in February of 1912.[31]

Four months later Breadon married again, this time to twenty-three-year-old Rachel Wilson. The couple married on June 25 in Stamford, Connecticut, although the announcement didn't make the local papers until September.[32] Breadon cited his divorce earlier in the year as the reason for the delay. His new bride was identified as living in St. Louis before the marriage but "formerly of New York." Three years later, the second Mrs. Breadon made the front page of the *St. Louis Star* for having won first prize at the San Francisco Exposition for the "most perfect profile." Described as having auburn hair with hazel eyes, she stood five feet seven inches tall and weighed 140 pounds. "Before she married Breadon," the paper noted, "she was Miss Rachel Wilson of Winfield, Kansas."[33] The union never produced any children, but the couple later adopted a daughter, Janet. The lack of a male heir would have an impact on both Breadon and the Cardinals late in his career.

Breadon's involvement with the local baseball team began in the spring of 1917, at a time when Cardinals attorney James C. Jones was actively soliciting stockholders for a community-backed, fan-owned franchise. He spent $200 on eight shares of stock. At a dinner for the team and stockholders at the beginning of the season, a friend opened his eyes to bigger possibilities. "He said I was foolish (for having such a small stake), that the club was going to make money and I should have more." Breadon took his friend's advice and bought more, upping his stake to $2,000. He still had no designs on a career in the business. "To tell the truth, I thought I was just throwing my money away in a good cause. I certainly never thought about going into baseball as a business."[34]

The financial instability of the Cardinals franchise fueled further involvement. The club had to meet note obligations to pay off former owner Helene Britton. When a

$25,000 payment came due and a stockholders meeting was called, only a handful of the more than 600 shareholders showed up. Breadon invested another $5,000. "It went on like that until the first thing I knew I had $18,000 in notes and $2,000 in stock."[35] To protect his investment, he took a seat on the board of directors and became president of the team in January of 1920. Just a few days before he officially took the position, Breadon was involved in an automobile accident in New York City. While he was only slightly injured, his traveling companion was killed when the car overturned.[36]

Breadon inherited a club $150,000 in debt and one that had lacked the funds to travel for spring training the prior year. The team he took charge of had never once finished higher than third place in the National League. He quickly moved to make one of the biggest swaps in the history of the franchise, one that didn't involve a single player.

Since 1893, the team had played in a park built by Chris Von der Ahe. Known by various names over the years – "New" Sportsman's Park, Robison Field, League Park, Cardinal Field – the wooden structure had burned frequently and had suffered from years of neglect. By the spring of 1920, the park's condition had reached a crisis state. "What a firetrap! When we had crowds at all we had twenty men with hoses under the stands putting out small fires," Breadon recalled. "The building inspector, who was a friend of mine, said he was afraid he couldn't let us go another season with those stands. I didn't blame him. I'd lie awake at nights worrying they'd collapse and kill somebody."[37]

Breadon's solution was to trade his old ballpark for an even older one, Sportsman's Park, the original home of the National League team – a park now occupied and owned by Phil Ball and the American League Browns (the park had been updated to a steel structure by former owner Robert Hedges). Ball wanted no part of Breadon's plans, rebuffing him on multiple occasions. The Cardinals president persisted and Ball eventually relented. For $20,000 a year, the Cardinals became tenants of the Browns. The team returned to the intersection of Grand and Dodier, just six blocks away, on July 1, 1920.[38]

Breadon now had an asset he could sell. His original idea was to demolish the old park and subdivide the land into residential lots. Plans soon changed when the St. Louis Board of Education came calling. For $200,000, or about $75,000 higher than the estimate of what the team thought it could get from the lots, the Cardinals sold the property to the city.[39] Beaumont High School soon replaced Von der Ahe's ballpark at Vandeventer and Natural Bridge. Before that sale, the team had received $30,000 when United Railways bought a parcel of the land for a terminal point in a streetcar line.[40] By 1922, the Cardinals had spun a depreciating wooden firetrap into a $230,000 pot of gold. It is difficult to overstate the impact of these transactions on the history of the franchise. Ball and the Browns may have acquired a renter, but Breadon and the Redbirds now had the financial flexibility to pursue Rickey's dream. The Cardinals needed minor league teams, or more specifically, *control* of minor league teams, to house all the talent Rickey was signing at tryout camps.

*****

Breadon and Rickey were baseball's odd couple. Breadon was urban, Scotch-Irish and a former choirboy in an Episcopal Church. The former high school dropout never lost his New York accent. Rickey was a Midwestern, Methodist farm boy and a Michigan law school graduate. Republican Rickey was an enthusiastic backer of Prohibition. Democrat Breadon liked his highballs.

"They were completely different," said Bill DeWitt Sr., who worked under both men. "Rickey never took a drink." Breadon, however, "belonged to a little club at the Hotel Jefferson. And he'd go down and have two or three drinks at lunch, and then he'd drink at night. And after he'd drink a while he wanted to sing."[41] Part of a barbershop quartet association in St. Louis, "Singing Sam" was active in the group until members asked him to help sponsor an event. The ads in the program cost $100 a page. Breadon turned them down and never showed up at another meeting.

Stories about Breadon's frugality (players just called him cheap) are legendary. When he was fired by the Halsey brothers, he claimed to live on a budget of .15 cents a day. In the 1930s, in the midst of the Great Depression, he walked into his office one day, pointed to an electric clock on the wall and asked an assistant how much electricity it used. Traveling secretary Clarence Lloyd didn't bother to answer. He just unplugged the clock.

"He is an optimist clear through, a hard worker, and a saver," is how one newspaper described Breadon before he got involved with baseball.[42] Working for the Browns and Cardinals, Rickey had also learned how to stretch a dollar. (Later with the Dodgers, a New York sportswriter dubbed him "El Cheapo.") United in common cause, battling teams with deeper pockets, the Cardinals executives got creative in a number of ways. Not all the ideas involved money.

Rickey, "The Great Rotarian," was forever speaking to groups in the community. In 1921, he traveled to the St. Louis suburb of Ferguson to address the First Presbyterian Church. The table decorations that day featured the image of a single bright red cardinal perched on a twig. The design caught Rickey's eye. The creation of Allie May Schmidt inspired a permanent change in the uniform of the team. The Cardinals debuted the iconic "Birds on the Bat" logo the following season.

Two years later, the National League began its Most Valuable Player award in controversial fashion (Hornsby finished second to Dodgers pitcher Dazzy Vance). Breadon was among those who pushed for the creation of the prize. Sunday doubleheaders in St. Louis became commonplace under Breadon, who also became an early backer of night baseball. "It makes every day Sunday," he would say.[43] Breadon and other National League owners backed the idea of a designated hitter in the 1920s.[44] It was American League owners who opposed the idea.

Under Breadon and Rickey, the Cardinals became the first team in baseball to hire a full-time publicist (Gene Karst), and the first team to include a position player who wore glasses. George "Specs" Toporcer played his entire big-league career for the Cardinals, spending parts of eight seasons in St. Louis. Before he debuted with the Cardinals in 1921, only a handful of baseball players wore glasses. All were pitchers. Their ranks included right-hander Lee Meadows, who debuted with St. Louis in 1915. (The team's success with Toporcer and Meadows led officials to advise Chick Hafey to begin wearing glasses when his eyesight faded in the late 1920s.)[45]

The single greatest innovation of the Breadon-Rickey era, however, came from their approach to the minor leagues. The Cardinals were not the first team to own a minor-league franchise. Brooklyn and Cleveland were among the teams that had minor league investments before World War I. Working for Browns owner Robert Hedges, Rickey had been considering the idea for years. What Breadon and Rickey accomplished was a complete transformation of the relationship between the major and minor leagues, establishing a vertically integrated chain of clubs, whereby a player could advance a level at a time, all within the continuity of a single franchise. Before this time, the minor leagues largely behaved as independent actors, typically owned by businessmen in the local community. They had no affiliation or loyalty to any major league team, opting to sell the contracts of their players to the highest bidder.

It was this economic stumbling block, the lack of dollars to sign talent, that motivated Rickey. He would dispatch scout Charley Barrett to some far-flung locale to evaluate a player. Once properly vetted, Barrett would make an offer only to see some other team, one with deeper pockets, trump his bid. It didn't take long for Rickey to abandon these efforts. His frustration boiled over when Barrett identified a minor-league prospect and offered the club $1,000 for him. The owner told Barrett he wanted time to think it over. A week later, the player was sold to John McGraw's New York Giants for $2,500.[46] "Pack up and come home," Rickey wired Barrett in Texas. "We'll develop our own."

It was Barrett who helped the Cardinals break into the business of minor league ownership. The Cardinals' scout knew Blake Harper, president of the franchise in Fort Smith, Arkansas. Barrett brought him to meet with Rickey in St. Louis where they worked out a deal for the Cardinals to acquire a half interest in the club.[47] In 1920, while playing spring training baseball in Texas, Rickey and the Cardinals developed a relationship with the owners of the Houston franchise. An equity investment in the Texas League team soon followed.[48] In early 1921, the Cardinals struck a deal to take a fifty-percent stake in the Syracuse club in the International League.

Club officials soon discovered that a half-interest in a minor league club wasn't much better than no interest. Their partner in the enterprise still wanted to sell players to the highest bidder. The Cardinals found that out when the club wanted to call up Jim Bottomley from Syracuse. Team president Ernie Landgraf had a different idea. He wanted to put the talented first baseman up for auction. Rickey had to convince him otherwise. The Cardinals got their player, but it took more money than the club had originally planned.

"Experience taught us that owning half of a minor league club, or even a majority of its stock, was unsatisfactory," said Rickey. "There naturally were many deals between the parent club and the minor league team. When we purchased the player from the minor league associate, we always had to be mindful of the minority holdings when determining a price. We had to make it high enough to avoid criticism. Then, when we sold a player from St. Louis to the minor league team, we had to be equally careful not to make the price too stiff. Or, again, someone would feel that he was getting hurt. *The solution, of course, was to own the minor league club outright.*"[49]

And that's exactly the strategy Breadon and Rickey pursued. The Cardinals eventually got control of Fort Smith, Houston and Syracuse (the New York franchise would later transfer to Rochester). By 1926, the franchise had added teams in Danville, Illinois and Austin, Texas. A decade later, the team had complete control of ten minor league teams. By 1940, near the end of the Rickey reign in St. Louis, the Cardinals had 32 minor league teams in their farm system, owning 15 franchises outright.[50] They included some of the most dominant minor league teams of the era. Every year, the champions of the International League and the American Association would meet in what was called the "Little World Series" or "Junior World Series." From 1928 to 1943, a sixteen-season stretch, a St. Louis Cardinals team played in the championship eleven times, winning seven titles.

When the Cardinals purchased the contract of pitcher Jesse Haines from a minor league team in Kansas City before the 1920 season, it marked the last time the team purchased a player from outside its system until the 1940s. St. Louis spent $10,000 to acquire Haines. By 1925, the club boasted a starting infield of first baseman Jim Bottomley, second baseman Rogers Hornsby, third baseman Les Bell and shortstop Specs Toporcer. The cost to sign the quartet totaled $3,000. Instead of spending their time on minor league talent potentially ready for major league baseball, Rickey and scout Charley Barrett focused on amateur talent and the lower minor leagues. "Anybody can follow a Class AA team [the highest minor league designation at the time] around the circuit and name the star players," said Barrett. "The trick is to get out in the 'peanut' leagues and recognize the future stars." In a more than six-month stretch in 1924, from April 15 to October 23, Barrett spent every day in the "peanut" leagues. He didn't see a single major league game the entire season.[51]

Like Barrett, Rickey was relentless and open-minded in his quest for talent. He took input and advice anywhere he could find it. Historian and baseball author Harold Seymour once wrote several major league clubs about a pitcher from the sandlots of Brooklyn. Only one team wrote back.[52] Rickey instructed the player to report to a Cardinals minor league team and present the letter to the manager. Pitcher Bill Lorhman spent nine seasons in the big leagues, winning 60 games. Another time, a history professor at the University of California wrote Rickey about a young player on campus.[53] Outfielder Taylor Douthit made his debut for the Cardinals later that year. "I had an increasing number of letters from many friends in baseball and in college coaching," recalled Rickey. "I was confident of getting promising young players in quantity."[54]

The manager and front office executive increasingly found his time consumed by the latter duties. More than any other baseball executive, Rickey was at the forefront of a major change in the game. "Between 1920 and 1935, with the development of farm systems, the responsibility for finding young players shifted away from the manager, and to the front office, the general manager, and the scouts who assisted him," wrote Bill James. "This transfer of responsibility is the most fundamental shift in the role of the manager in the history of baseball."

Lawyer Rickey pressed his advantage any way he could. Tryout camps could feature anywhere from 100 to 400 players. The Cardinals (according to a later investigation) would then sign 20 to 25 of them to "desk contracts" and not turn in the agreements to minor league officials. The franchise struck "gentlemen's agreements" with dozens of minor league teams it didn't own, paying them two to three thousand dollars to have first shot at their talent. At one point, Rickey and the Cardinals controlled every team in the Nebraska State and the Arkansas-Missouri Leagues.

The team also benefitted from the vacuum at the top of baseball in the period before Commissioner Landis took control of the game. When baseball struck a new agreement with the minor leagues in 1921, removed was any language forbidding major league ownership of minor league teams. It also permitted teams to transfer player contracts among minor league affiliates. After Landis took office, he became an opponent of big-league clubs controlling minor league teams, repeatedly clashing with Rickey over what he and other critics called "chain store baseball" or "Rickey's plantation." The Cardinals would eventually pay a price for Rickey's aggressive stance, and in the process, create a rift between the general manager and team president Breadon. Until then, the land grab for talent was on. The Cardinals needed more talent to assist the team's budding superstar.

*****

The record came with high drama. Facing Boston in his home park, he walked to the plate with two on and two out in the bottom of the ninth inning. His team trailed 6-4. When Boston pitcher Frank Miller delivered a high fastball, the batter connected and sent a drive to deep right-center field. The center fielder and right fielder converged at the outfield wall and waited for the ball to drop. It landed two feet beyond their reach in the bleachers. The home team had won the game 7-6, and the batter had set a new single-season home run record. The 18,000 fans at the park that day stormed the field and mobbed the hitter. He barely made it around the bases. As soon as he touched home plate, the enthusiastic crowd hoisted him on their shoulders and carried him to the clubhouse. The event occurred on July 19, 1922, at Sportsman's Park in St. Louis. The hitter was Rogers Hornsby.[55]

Lost in the shuffle amidst his many batting titles and overshadowed by Babe Ruth's exploits in the American League, Hornsby's 1922 home run assault is an impressive and historic achievement. He led the National League in home runs that season with 42. Before him, no hitter in the history of the league had even hit 30. His July 19th home run in St. Louis – his 25th of the season – set a modern (twentieth-century) National League record. A few weeks later in Philadelphia, he set the all-time NL record for single-season home runs when he eclipsed Ned Williamson of Chicago's mark of 27 set back in 1884. In Winters, Texas, where the Cardinals star was born (but left at the age of two), a drug store would post news of every Hornsby home run on its display window. "Even the Bohemian farmers in the territory surrounding Winters are pulling for him," noted one newspaper account.[56]

Twenty batters in baseball history hit .400 or better from 1876 to 1941. Only five of them did so more than once. Of those five, only three repeated the performance after 1900. Only three in the .400 club ever won a triple crown. Only Hornsby can claim all those achievements. No one, not even Ted Williams – the last player to hit .400 in 1941 – ever paired a .400 season with as many home runs as Hornsby did in 1922. Along with his 42 home runs, he batted .401 that year, the first of three seasons where he eclipsed the .400 mark.

Hornsby's progression as a hitter developed gradually, then suddenly. From 1918 to 1922, his batting average had steadily advanced, from .281 to .318, skyrocketing to .370 in 1920, then .397 before climbing above .400 in 1922. Hornsby led the league that season in runs, hits, doubles, home runs, RBI, batting average, on-base percentage and slugging percentage. His 450 total bases not only led the league but marked a high for his entire career.

By 1922, Hornsby was the best player and the highest-paid player in the National League. He signed a three-year deal at the beginning of the season that paid him $18,500 annually. His accomplishments were celebrated on the pages of the nation's newspapers nearly every day. He was well-known, highly paid and largely a mystery to his teammates.

"Hard to approach, difficult to understand," remembered Specs Toporcer, "he seemed to have nothing but contempt for the usual likes and dislikes of the average player." Ferdie Schupp played with Hornsby in 1919. "You never see him except on the ball field, and he never talks to anybody. After a game he comes into the club house, takes his shower, dresses, and walks out without a word, and nobody knows where he goes."[57]

Where Hornsby was going with increasing frequency was the dog and horse tracks around the St. Louis area. The Cardinals second baseman enjoyed placing a wager, especially on the ponies. It became a habit that developed into a life-long addiction. To his credit, Hornsby was always upfront and honest about where he enjoyed spending his time when not in uniform. To his discredit, he never saw the downside of his gambling debts, ignoring the impact on relationships and how it made him a potential target of criminal elements. In the aftermath of the Black Sox scandal, baseball tried to drive the bookmakers out of the ballparks. But the ballplayers still found the bookies. While no one ever accused Hornsby of betting on baseball or attempting to fix a contest, his habits found a way of leading him to men who didn't have the best interests of the game at heart.

Tony Foley grew up in the Kerry Patch section of St. Louis and was one of the founders of the Bottoms Gang. When his brother was shot dead after robbing a newsstand and the killer escaped justice, Foley blamed the police and sought revenge. Along with other gang members, he attacked and nearly killed a cop in early 1907. He was convicted of assault and served time in the penitentiary in Jefferson City, Missouri. He was released in November of 1912 with time off for good behavior.[58] By 1913, he had a saloon at Twenty-third and Olive streets in St. Louis that police called a "thieves' hangout." Neighborhood residents referred to it as "Tony Foley's dump."[59] He later ran several gambling joints in the St. Louis area including the one at Campbell's Forest Home backed by Kid Becker.[60]

There is evidence Hornsby knew Foley, or was at least familiar with his business, as early as 1918. Sometime during that season, manager Jack Hendricks fined Hornsby $50. Afterward, the Cardinals player invited sportswriter Sid Keener to dinner. The pair eventually wound up at one of Foley's establishments where Hornsby proceeded to trade $50 in bills for $50 in coins. "He just thought it would be funny to pay off Jack that way," said Keener.[61]

In 1922, Hornsby began an affair with a woman he knew as Jeannette Pennington. Both were married. Hornsby had been married since 1918 to the former Sarah Martin. Like Hornsby, she was a Texas native. The couple had one child, Rogers Hornsby Jr., born in November of 1920. Pennington's real name was Mary Jeannette Pennington Hine, the wife of a local automobile-supply salesman. According to Hornsby biographer Charles Alexander, she "had a reputation around St. Louis as a flapper who loved the nightlife and enjoyed friends of questionable propriety." She claimed to be twenty-three years old, but a local attorney told Rickey, "She is much older than she claims to be – older than Hornsby, even, and is a tout for Tony Foley's gambling place and has another married man on the string and is strictly a woman of the town and out for money."[62]

By the end of 1922, Hornsby and his wife were separated. She and the couple's son moved to California. By February of 1923, Jeannette Pennington and John Hine were officially divorced. But the ex-husband quickly changed his mind after shuffling through some of his ex-wife's paperwork. He found a letter addressed to "My Dear Little Sweetheart." It was signed by "Roge." Hornsby had mailed the letter from Florida, where the Cardinals were conducting spring training. Claiming his divorce was granted under false testimony, Hine filed in court to have the decree overturned.

"You ask in your letter whether my wife will come back to St. Louis," wrote Hornsby in a letter read aloud in court. "I am not sure, but it will be better for us two if she don't [sic] as you know the detectives were pretty hot on my trail." Those detectives had been hired by Hornsby's wife to confirm evidence of an extramarital affair, an allegation denied by Pennington. She did concede she had met Hornsby a few times in 1922, originally at a dog track in Illinois and a second time in a hotel lobby in New York City. On the trip to New York, Pennington was accompanied by her mother and Flavia Foley, Tony Foley's wife. Under oath, she also admitted he had called on her once at her home, stopping by after a hunting trip to give her a dozen quail.[63]

Hornsby never took the stand but was deposed in the case. He confirmed the meetings at the dog track and in the lobby of the New York City hotel and added that he had also seen Pennington in Florida earlier in the year. As for the letter, Hornsby denied using any terms of endearment in his correspondence with Pennington. He said she had written him a letter about baseball, one of many he received from both men and women. He answered her questions about the game and addressed the letter to "Dear Miss Pennington." When the attorney for Hine wanted to know if Pennington had ever telephoned Hornsby's wife, he became angry. "I don't want you to ask anything about my wife," he snapped. "Don't ask a lot of foolish questions," Hornsby added when the attorney insisted the question was proper. [64]

The deposition came in the same month Hornsby was officially divorced from his wife and in the middle of a baseball season where he battled not only attorneys but also injuries and his manager.[65] The Cardinals second baseman missed games for the first time since 1920, appearing in just 107 contests in 1923. In May, a spike to his left knee caused him to miss several games and ultimately put Hornsby in a plaster cast for nearly two weeks. He returned briefly in the middle of June but then left for nearly a week to visit his ailing mother in Texas. By the time he returned to the lineup on June 20, he had missed 27 of the team's first 57 games. He stayed healthy until early September when he was injured and later suspended, missing the final 17 games of the season.

The suspension arose over the severity of the injury. Sidelined by a skin rash, Hornsby missed two weeks of games. When physicians pronounced him healthy, the club expected him to return to the lineup. But Hornsby claimed his knee was still bothering him and refused to play. Breadon fined him $500 and suspended him for the remainder of the schedule. Hornsby finished his season batting .384, good enough for his fourth straight National League batting title, but his home run output fell to 17 and his RBI total of 83 was a little more than half of what he produced the previous year.

Before the suspension, the headstrong Hornsby had battled with manager Rickey, no shrinking violet himself. Tensions erupted following a game in New York in August. With Hornsby on third base and a 3-1 count on the batter in a tie game, manager Rickey gave the take sign. When the pitch was called a strike, an exasperated Hornsby threw up his hands in disgust. Hornsby didn't score. The Cardinals lost the game. In the locker room afterward, Hornsby let his manager know of his disapproval. Rickey later called his language "vile and unspeakable." He took a swing at Hornsby before players and coaches intervened.[66] "I'm no brawler," said Rickey. "There are, however, some things that even peace-loving persons will not put up with."

Whether it was the showdown in New York, the disputed injury in St. Louis, or a combination of the two incidents, stories began to circulate that Hornsby would be traded. "Rogers Hornsby May Be Traded By Rickey In Shakeup Of Team," read a headline in the *St. Louis Star* even before Hornsby was suspended. Both Ricky and Breadon downplayed the story and insisted Hornsby was going nowhere. "Hornsby is the one man on the entire club who is not for trade or sale," said Rickey. "The Cardinals club POSITIVELY will not trade him," said Breadon. "I can imagine no offer that any other club would make that we could consider for a moment. Hornsby is the keystone of our team and if we are ever to have a winner here he is the man about whom we must build."[67] Hornsby insisted he would no longer play for the Cardinals as long as Rickey was manager and cast himself as the victim. "I am convinced the club is taking this course for the avowed purpose of bringing the public mind to a point where it will regard me as a troublemaker and would view my departure from St. Louis as good riddance."

Rumors of a Hornsby trade had been around nearly as long as the Cardinals star had played in St. Louis. It was no secret that both the Chicago Cubs and New York Giants coveted Hornsby and made several offers over the years. Chewing gum magnate William Wrigley Jr. owned the Cubs. One legendary story involves Wrigley and Breadon meeting at the Chase Hotel in St. Louis. "Mr. Breadon, I won't mince words. I've come here to buy Rogers Hornsby." Breadon told him Hornsby wasn't for sale. "But you don't understand," Wrigley replied. "The price is no object. You name your price on Hornsby and we will meet it."

The New York Giants took much the same approach, seemingly offering an all-cash deal for Hornsby every year. In 1923, Giants manager John McGraw acknowledged his team had offered $300,000 for Hornsby in 1920 (after the Yankees had purchased Ruth for $100,000 prior to the season). "I offered the Cardinals $250,000 cash for Hornsby and $50,000 bonus payment if we won the pennant," recalled McGraw. Just as they did with Wrigley's overtures, Cardinals management rejected the offer.[68]

To the public, Breadon and Rickey presented a united front. Hornsby was untouchable. But there was a player that had long intrigued the Cardinals. He was New York Giants second baseman Frankie Frisch. The switch-hitting infielder debuted with the Giants in 1919 and led the league in hits in 1923 while batting .348. In his conversations with McGraw and Giants owner Charles Stoneham, Rickey turned the tables on them and said he would be interested in purchasing Frisch for $50,000. "You haven't got $50,000," Stoneham replied. "You haven't got a quarter." McGraw confirmed that over the years the Cardinals had expressed an interest in a cash *plus* Frisch deal for Hornsby. "The Cardinals have wanted me to throw in Frisch in addition to the purchase price, but I wouldn't make that trade even up, because Hornsby is 30 years old (actually 27 in 1923) and has a very bad leg."[69] McGraw would eventually change his mind.

In the interim, with the Cardinals unwilling or unable to deal Hornsby, the infielder wasn't going anywhere. In the days before free agency, Hornsby's options were to play for the Cardinals or not play at all. To a man who famously spent his winters staring out the window and waiting for spring, the choice was an easy one. Hornsby met with

Breadon and Rickey in St. Louis in February of 1924, shortly before the beginning of spring training. He issued a statement to the press the following day. "Mr. Rickey and I have talked things over," it read. "There is no longer a misunderstanding between us."

The *St. Louis Star* credited the manager for healing the wounds of the previous season. "Rickey, like some baseball managers we know, has never gone to the newspaper writers and asked them to print his angle of a grievance. Through thick and thin, in shadow and sunshine, he has never named Hornsby save to praise," the paper noted. "He is a distinct creation. He has a heart of gold and we have never been able to understand allegations that Hornsby, the stormy petrol of baseball, did not fancy him."[70]

Hornsby did fancy Jeannette Pennington. One week after the reconciliation between player and manager, the Cardinals second baseman was again a married man. A circuit court judge married Hornsby and Pennington in secret on February 28. "After the ceremony," remembered Judge Robert W. Hall, "there was an awkward pause, which was broken when the bride put her arms around Hornsby's neck and kissed him."[71]

It had been an eventful few months for Hornsby. He ended his 1923 season suspended and in a feud with management. One month later, a judge denied John Hine's motion to overturn his divorce decree, clearing the way for his ex-wife to wed again. Normally an insurance salesman in the offseason, Hornsby decided to go into the Christmas tree business. But he made the mistake of flooding the market. Prices collapsed and Hornsby lost his entire investment. If he was tempted to make up his losses with bets at one of Foley's gambling establishments, the events of that offseason surely gave him pause. In January, Foley was indicted by a federal grand jury for election fraud in St. Louis County. Foley acquaintances Hornsby and Pennington married five weeks later. After a one-night honeymoon, his bride stayed behind in St. Louis while Hornsby hit the road to Bradenton, Florida, where the Cardinals conducted spring training in 1924. (It was the Cardinals last year in Bradenton. Rickey discovered bootleggers trying to sell alcohol to his players.)

Healthy, newly married, and free of detectives on his heels, Hornsby proceeded to have one of the greatest seasons in the history of baseball. To go along with his .424 batting average, Hornsby also led the league in hits, walks, doubles and on-base percentage. When he lost the first National League MVP award to Dodgers pitcher Dazzy Vance that season (a Cincinnati voter omitted Hornsby from his ballot), Hornsby expressed no bitterness to the sportswriters who made the selection. "More power to Vance. He's a great pitcher. I certainly have no complaint to make."

For all of Hornsby's greatness, the Cardinals continued to wallow in mediocrity. The team finished the season 65-89, in sixth place in the National League. The team scored 740 runs. Only the league champion New York Giants scored more. But Rickey's pitchers allowed 750 runs, third-worst in the circuit.

Since becoming the manager of the Browns at the end of the 1913 season, Rickey had managed eight full seasons in organized baseball. He had nothing better than two third-place finishes to show for it. True, the Cardinals farm teams had begun to produce major league talent – Bottomley and Blades were already regulars – and other names that would generate dividends in the years to come had already appeared on the big league roster: outfielders Taylor Douthit, Chick Hafey, and Heine Mueller, as well as infielders Les Bell and Tommy Thevenow. But a full-scale minor league system needed a full-time overseer. Change was coming in St. Louis. Rickey didn't know it at the time, but 1924 marked his last full season as a major league manager.

*****

The Cardinals manager didn't have to worry about Florida bootleggers in March of 1925. The team found a new home for spring training in Stockdale, California. Despite the new location, Rickey was as busy as ever, working with his players during the day and giving speeches to area groups at night, as many as five a week. "If the native sons had their way," noted the *St. Louis Star*, "Branch would be giving all his time to speech-making instead of training." Writer James M. Gould also offered this assessment of the team. "Too bad victories in exhibitions cannot count. If they did, the Cards, one of the poorest starters in either of the major leagues, would be off in fast fashion. But the 1925 hunch is that things will be reversed this year and that the Rickeymen will get off on the right foot, even though they begin on the road."[72]

Poor starts had plagued the Cardinals nearly every year under Rickey. Since 1919, the club had a winning record by the end of May only once. The end of year trend was just as bleak. Under Rickey, the Cardinals won 87 games and finished in third place in 1921. The club repeated the third-place performance in 1922, winning 85 games. The win total dropped to 79 the following year and plunged to 65 in 1924. Attendance, which had spiked to 536,998 in 1922, fell by nearly fifty percent two years later. The 1924 attendance of 272,885 ranked seventh in the eight-team league. Team president Breadon, who now owned a majority stake in the team, wanted more from his investment.[73] Sensing the pressure, Rickey had reportedly offered to resign in the spring of 1925. The plan was to make the announcement in California but the manager changed his mind. "I can't Sam," he told Breadon. "I look at this team I have put together and I can visualize it winning the flag. I have the stuff here and I want another chance. I think I deserve it because I assembled all this talent."[74]

The talent Rickey had assembled finished April at 5-9. Near the end of May, with the club ten games under .500, Breadon decided to change managers. At a Pittsburgh hotel, Breadon informed Rickey of his decision and told Hornsby his plans. The entire conversation lasted five minutes.[75] The Cardinals had a new manager and Rickey had a new role. Freed of the day-to-day managing duties, Rickey retained his front office position and could now focus on scouting, evaluating talent and developing the farm system. "My fault as a manager, as I diagnose it, was due to my apparent zeal," Rickey said years later. The former football player and coach brought a gridiron mentality to the game of baseball. "I discussed the game every day, dealing with the game of the previous day in my discussion, as if the game coming up was the game of the year."

With coach Burt Shotton as acting manager on Saturday, the Cardinals lost a doubleheader to Pittsburgh, dropping their record to 13-25. The team headed back to St. Louis for a series at Sportsman's Park with Hornsby officially assuming the position as manager. "The Pupil...Succeeds the Master," read one headline, in part. With 12,000 fans on hand, the Cardinals beat the Reds 5-2 in Hornsby's managerial debut. "There was a dash that had been missing for some time," observed the *Post-Dispatch*. "It was hustle every minute."[76] By July, the club had reached .500 and finished the season one game over at 77-76, fourth place in the National League. With Hornsby leading the way, the rejuvenated Cardinals went 64-51. Attendance jumped by more than 130,000.

Under their new manager, the Cardinals abandoned the rah-rah approach to baseball. Rickey's Redbirds had endless chalkboard talks. "We had more signals than a freight yard," remembered one player. "Some of the boys thought they had to raise their hand to go to first base."[77] Hornsby canceled the daily meetings as well as daily morning workouts. "You can't drill for two hours and then get out in the afternoon with all your pep and play some more," said the new Cardinals manager. He also relaxed the rules when the club traveled, extending curfew by an hour.[78]

Hornsby focused his daily efforts on the pitcher and the catcher, spending ten minutes with them before every game reviewing the opponent's lineup. He also believed the manager should stick with the starting pitcher as long as possible. "You won't see me taking my pitcher out every time he walks a batter or there is a home run." In short order, the new manager put his stamp on the team. Gone were Rickey's theories. In its place was simple sandlot baseball. "The players play the game," said Hornsby. "Don't fill the minds of the players with too many signals, too many intricate plays."

While distinguishing between himself and his predecessor, Hornsby offered praise for Rickey and his ability to evaluate talent. "If this club gets up I want to say that Rickey is entitled to as much credit as anybody. Because it must not be forgotten that barring (backup outfielder) Jack Smith and myself every member of the team has been discovered by Rickey," Hornsby said shortly after taking the job.[79]

The new manager engineered a turnaround in his team without limiting his on-field contributions. Appearing in 138 games, he won his sixth consecutive batting title and his second triple crown, hitting .403 with 39 home runs and 143 RBI. Denied postseason honors the previous year, Hornsby could be denied no longer. His performance earned him the National League's Most Valuable Player Award, as well as the love and admiration of Cardinals fans. "I have seen many managers in action, but never saw a man work near as perfect as Rogers," wrote one fan after the season ended. "We have, in the Cardinals, I believe, the best team in the league."[80]

The belief in what Hornsby had accomplished and what it portended for the upcoming season extended well beyond hometown boosters. The manager of the perennially contending New York Giants identified the Cardinals as a team to watch in 1926. "If Rogers Hornsby gets some good pitching next season, or is able to land another experienced hurler, his club will be most formidable," said John McGraw.[81]

Having signed a three-year $100,000 contract before the 1925 season, Hornsby ranked as the best player in the National League and its highest-paid.[82] Only Babe Ruth made more. He had multiple batting titles and multiple job titles. Hornsby was a player, manager, and now a director of the franchise. When he took the job as manager, he also invested in the organization. Rickey, upset about being removed as manager by Breadon, made an emotional and short-sighted decision. "If I can't be manager of the club, I don't want to hold any stock," he told Breadon. Hornsby was the beneficiary of Rickey's decision, purchasing 1,167 shares at $43 a share, a total investment of $50,181.[83] Rickey sold stock in a club struggling near the bottom of the standings. Hornsby would later sell at the top.

Hornsby officially took on his newest role at a meeting of the Cardinals board of directors in February of 1926. Vice president Rickey retained his seat on the board while adding the title of business manager. The club also announced a new treasurer, Bill DeWitt Sr., who had begun his baseball career as a teenager working for Rickey and the Browns.

The day after the board meeting, Hornsby's ex-wife made news. The former Sarah Martin Hornsby was now Mrs. Roy M. Finley of Denison, Texas. She married the man who represented Rogers Hornsby in the couple's divorce proceeding. "I wish them the greatest happiness," said the Cardinals player/manager. Sarah had left St. Louis for California when she divorced Hornsby, taking the couple's son, Rogers Hornsby Jr., with her. With his new bride, Hornsby added a second son in the summer of 1925, William Pennington Hornsby.

In late February of 1926, it was time to leave the second wife and second child behind. Hornsby and his team headed for Texas for spring training. Before settling in San Antonio, the club spent time in the hot baths and sulphur resorts of Terrell Wells, Texas. "Hornsby is enthusiastic about its merits and thinks the revising of the system, will be highly advantageous, especially to the pitching corps," noted one newspaper account.

With former Rickey assistant and Sunday manager Burt Shotton now off to manage the Cardinals minor league team in Syracuse, Hornsby added two new coaches in 1926, Otto Williams and Bill Killefer. While Williams was hired to serve as a "Handy Andy" for the club, Killefer had a specific and unique role for a team of the 1920s. "Killefer will devote all his time to coaching the pitchers," the *Post-Dispatch* explained to its readers. "As the Cardinals chances hinge on the hurlers' ability this year, 'Paw' Bill's time will not be idly spent."[84] The team had added two pitchers, Vic Keen and Art Reinhart, in the offseason who made contributions in the new year (each won 10 games in 1926), but the club's biggest pitching acquisition was still to come. Killefer, who spent years as a catcher for both the Phillies and Cubs, as well as time managing in Chicago, was in a unique position to evaluate the man who would ultimately save the Cardinals season.

Just as he did in the regular season, Hornsby made changes to the Cardinals spring training routine. He abandoned Rickey's practice of having a morning and afternoon session in favor of a single extended mid-day workout.[85] In his first meeting with his club that spring, Hornsby told his players they were going to win the pennant. Anyone who doubted the manager's words was asked to leave. No one did. Winning spring training games became a priority. "No game is unimportant," he told his team, "the more of'em you win, the better, regardless of the conditions." The players bought in to the message, finishing the spring with a record of 22-1. "He is the squarest, bluntest, cussingest and most convincing man I ever met in baseball," admitted one New York writer, assigned to cover Hornsby for a story that season.[86]

Valued by management, respected by players, and adored by fans, the success of Hornsby projected permanence in St. Louis. From the perspective of the spring of 1926, it was easy to envision the star player spending his entire career in a Cardinals uniform. But Hornsby was always a double-edged sword. With promise came peril. Even those who respected him knew to be wary of his prickly personality. His leisure activities also brought scrutiny. The same maniacal focus he brought to hitting a baseball he also brought to his gambling habits. And he now had a new bookmaking friend who helped fuel the fire.

Any Hornsby association with Tony Foley had now faded into the background. Acquitted of election fraud charges, Foley became ensnared in another scheme. Before prohibition, whiskey manufacturer Jack Daniels operated a distillery in St. Louis. When the country went dry, nearly 1,000 barrels of whiskey simply sat and aged at a warehouse on Duncan Avenue. In 1923, bootleggers got the idea to siphon off the alcohol through a hose. Thirty-one thousand gallons of whiskey made their way to trucks positioned in an alley and were eventually sold for more than a million dollars. Legendary Cincinnati bootlegger George Remus, already in prison on another charge, spilled the beans on his co-conspirators.[87] In December of 1925, a federal jury convicted 24 people, including a Missouri state senator, a former federal circuit court clerk, and Foley, who received a fifteen-month prison sentence.

Earlier that same year, Hornsby made a new acquaintance. Frank L. Moore was a Kentucky bookmaker who specialized in horse racing. Hornsby had first met him in Cincinnati. The following year, Moore visited with the Cardinals star during spring training in San Antonio and over the summer in St. Louis. Each time, Hornsby picked up the hotel tab. Allegations would later surface that during the early months of 1926 the Cardinals player/manager had placed thousands of dollars of horse-racing bets with Moore. The explosive charges became public a year later in the middle of one of baseball's stormiest offseasons.

For now, those clouds were well off in the distance. Hornsby had his team primed for the season, ready to go in a newly refurbished and expanded Sportsman's Park. Over the previous six seasons, a hitter had crossed the magical batting average of .400 seven times. St. Louis hitters, Hornsby for the Cardinals and Sisler for the Browns, claimed five of those performances. Local fans had celebrated individual excellence but not team performance. The Cardinals and Browns were the only two clubs in all of baseball yet to win a pennant. Expectations ran high.

The anticipation of watching Hornsby play extended well beyond St. Louis. In the spring of 1926, The *Cleveland Press* had conducted a contest to find the most popular player in each league. Hornsby won the award for the National League while Ruth won in the American League.[88] Hornsby and Ruth, the Yin and Yang of baseball, had dominated the sport since the beginning of the decade. Just as the right-handed hitting infielder loomed over the NL, the left-handed-hitting outfielder reigned supreme in the AL. Ruth had set the home run record in the AL with 59 in 1921. Hornsby set the mark for the NL with 42 in 1922. Hornsby had won six straight batting titles. Ruth had already claimed the home run title six times. Hornsby had started his second marriage. Ruth's first marriage was all but over. Like Hornsby, Ruth had invested in money-losing schemes and lost plenty on longshots at the horse track. Throughout their careers, Commissioner Landis would rebuke both men for their off-field behavior.

The Rajah and The Sultan. The blunt and the bawdy. The king of the NL and the toast of the AL.

The new season would be a transitional and pivotal year in the careers of both men. Appropriately, the final play of 1926 featured the Cardinals star and the Yankees slugger. Literally and figuratively, Rogers Hornsby and Babe Ruth were on a collision course.

---

[1] *Baseball Digest*, February 1948.

[2] Mann, *Branch Rickey*. "We had our first Cardinals tryouts that summer [1919], though they were humble compared with later efforts. Still, they attracted boys," recalled Rickey.

[3] The unanimous vote didn't apply to a test that was administered at the beginning of camp. Dividing into groups of thirty, the players would run the 100-yard dash. Anyone who didn't run the distance in 11 seconds or less was "considered by Rickey as unworthy of further inspection, for he regards speed as the first and foremost asset of a young player." *Nashville Banner*, February 17, 1935. Basic arm strength was another weed-out factor. "After a good warm-up period we have them throw from the outfield and we can soon tell if the arms are good," said scout Charley Barrett. "If they fail in that test they quickly are eliminated." *St. Louis Post-Dispatch*, February 7, 1932.

[4] "He was awkward and clumsy, and he threw tennis lobs in from the outfield," said scout Frank Rickey, remembering the first time he saw Slaughter. "But he was a strong runner, faster than he looked at first glance. And you could sense the power in his frame." *Baseball Digest*, October 1947.

[5] Mann, *Branch Rickey*.

---

[6] There are conflicting stories about the signings of many Cardinals prospects. Part of it had to do with the way Rickey and the Cardinals went about it. Prospects would sometimes be discovered by a scout and then get invited to a camp. It was at the camp where the critical evaluation was performed. In 1935, the Cardinals had 1,200 players in spring training camps for 400 jobs at the major and minor league levels. *St. Louis Globe-Democrat*, December 20, 1934. The practice of signing players to contracts that were not turned in to league officials later became a focal point of the investigation into the Cardinals minor-league system.

[7] *St. Louis Star-Times*, February 9, 1937. While Rickey put a premium on scouting, he also predicted its demise, telling reporters "within the next decade the baseball scout will have gone the way of the Indian scout. There will not be any," he said. He envisioned a day where all teams would adopt summer tryout camps. "The outmoded scouting system cannot provide enough talent to care properly for the major and minor clubs. One scout can inspect only a dozen or so prospects in a year, and even then his deductions are hit or miss."

[8] "I believe in mass production of ball players," Rickey said in January of 1943. "Why, in the past I looked at as many as 3,500 young players in one year."

[9] *Brooklyn Eagle*, November 3, 1942.

[10] *The Sporting News*, April 4, 1975.

[11] Allen, *The Hot Stove League.*

[12] Multiple biographies and histories claim Bottomley, Blades and Mueller were all signed from the Cardinals initial tryout camps. Other evidence suggests they may have been discovered by other means (see footnote 6). *The Sporting News* once claimed a St. Louis cop tipped off Rickey to Bottomley's talents. Rickey dispatched Charley Barrett to evaluate. The scout signed Bottomley for $150 a month. *The Sporting News*, December 23, 1959. Barrett is also credited with discovering Mueller (and many others). *St. Louis Post-Dispatch*, July 5, 1939. A SABR.org biography of Ray Blades claims he was signed after the Cardinals played an exhibition game against his Mount Vernon, Illinois team. Enos Slaughter wrote in his autobiography that Rickey was familiar with Blades as early as 1913. Blades played high school baseball in St. Louis, and Rickey was an umpire for a championship game. A 1925 article referred to Blades as "the former McKinley High School star." *Post-Dispatch*, March 29, 1925.

[13] Lowenfish*, Branch Rickey.*

[14] Mann, Arthur. *Branch Rickey: American in Action.* The Riverside Press. 1957.

[15] Bottomley and Whiten are the only two players in major league history to have a 12 RBI game.

[16] Mann, *Branch Rickey.*

[17] Ibid.

[18] *New York Times*, January 25, 1975.

[19] Polner, *Branch Rickey.*

[20] Gordon, Robert J. *The Rise and Fall of American Growth: The U.S. Standard of Living Since the Civil War.* Princeton University Press. 2016.
[21] Daniel, Daniel M. *Baseball,* July 1949.
[22] *St. Louis Post-Dispatch*, April 3, 1904. The article describes the company as the "oldest auto house in St. Louis." A Winton touring car, the "Vermont" became the first to cross the United States coast-to-coast in 1903. Dr. Horatio Nelson Jackson completed the transcontinental journey in 63 days.
[23] Ibid, May 24, 1946.
[24] *St. Louis Globe-Democrat*, February 21, 1943.
[25] *St. Louis Post-Dispatch*, August 4, 1938. At the time, Gerald Lambert's "legal residence" was in Princeton, New Jersey where he owned a 52-room mansion set on 400 acres. At one point, he held 240,000 shares of company stock but sold out by the fall of 1928, one year before the market crashed.
[26] Ibid, December 14, 1899.
[27] Ibid, October 30, 1905. "Time records as accurate as those of horse races will be brought into court in Clayton Thursday as evidence against four alleged automobile scorchers arrested Sunday in St. Louis County by deputy sheriffs, who used revolvers and shotguns in halting offenders," the story begins.
[28] *St. Louis Globe-Democrat*, February 21, 1943.
[29] *St. Louis Post-Dispatch*, July 26, 1946.
[30] The company moved to the location in July of 1914. The dealership featured a "chauffeur's clubroom, to be equipped with a pool table, reading lounges and other attractions." *St. Louis Globe-Democrat*, July 10, 1914.
[31] *St. Louis Post-Dispatch*, November 17, 1911, and February 4, 1912.
[32] Ibid, September 8, 1912.
[33] *St. Louis Star*, August 27, 1915.
[34] *New York Times*, March 18, 1940.
[35] Ibid. *St. Louis Post-Dispatch,* May 24, 1946. Like many stories involving the early history of the Cardinals, there are multiple versions of how this unfolded. Breadon himself gave different versions of his early involvement with the team. In the 1946 *Post-Dispatch* story, the $5,000 investment is represented as a loan. In 1940, he told John Kieran the $5,000 gave him additional equity in the club. "That gave me 280 shares," Kieran quoted Breadon in the *Times.* "I was a big stockholder, comparatively."
[36] *St. Louis Post-Dispatch*, January 12, 1920.
[37] *New York Times*, March 18, 1940. Cardinal Field had the last wooden stands in the major leagues. In 1912, Browns owner Hedges offered Britton's Cardinals a half interest in Sportsman's Park for $12,000 a year and half the upkeep. She declined the offer. *St. Louis Globe-Democrat,* July 11, 1920.
[38] The Cardinals lost to the Pirates 6-2 in their return to Sportsman's Park. An estimated 20,000 fans marked the occasion which also featured the annual "Tuberculosis Day" at the

park (benefit for the Tuberculosis Society), an Army-Navy game beforehand, a marathon race for boys, and a car giveaway. *St. Louis Star*, July 1, 1920.

[39] Why the Board of Education paid $200,000 for land valued at $125,000 is not clear. "$200,000 is too much money to pay for that ground," wrote A.W.B. in a letter to the editor of the *Post-Dispatch* on February 4, 1922.

[40] "Cardinal Park Corner Sold To U.R. For $30,000." *St. Louis Post-Dispatch*, July 3, 1921. Several histories of the team claim the tract was sold for $75,000.

[41] Vecsey, *Stan Musial.*

[42] *St. Louis Star*, July 13, 1913. That same story claims Lambert sold his stock in the Western Automobile Company to Breadon by 1907. A later story mentions Lambert sold his stock to Breadon in 1906. "In the deal, Lambert offered me very liberal terms. He certainly was most generous." *St. Louis Globe-Democrat,* February 21, 1943.

[43] "If night baseball would bring twice as much revenue as afternoon baseball why isn't it sound business to go where there is larger income?" said Breadon. The Cardinals president created what were called "synthetic" doubleheaders by canceling a scheduled weekday game (typically Monday) and moving it to Sunday, a move that met with criticism that he was cheapening the game. "Whose game am I cheapening when we play to 177,461 fans for eight doubleheaders? If this franchise loses on a season's play then the salaries of the players must be reduced the following year." *St. Louis Star*, August 20, 1930.

[44] National League owners approved the idea of a designated hitter in December of 1928. *St. Louis Star*, December 12, 1928.

[45] *St. Louis Star-Times*, January 13, 1930. Hafey "reported his eyes weakening following the close of the 1928 season" and "was ready to give up his baseball career in disgust." Wearing glasses in 1929, Hafey hit .338. Team physician, Dr. Robert Hyland, suggested Hafey begin wearing glasses.

[46] *St. Louis Star-Times*, January 14, 1946.

[47] While working for the Cardinals, Harper served as president of minor league teams in Fort Smith, Topeka, Kansas, and Dayton, Ohio. He later became director of concessions at Sportsman's Park. Over a period of nineteen years, the number of concession stands at the park increased from two to 80. *St. Louis Post-Dispatch*, January 29, 1950.

[48] The Cardinals purchased a 25 interest in the Houston franchise in 1922. It took another three years to acquire the majority of stock. The Cardinals purchased the Fort Smith team in 1922. *St. Louis Star*, May 16, 1922 and April 30, 1927.

[49] Lieb, *The St. Louis Cardinals.* In August of 1924, the Cardinals purchased Chick Hafey from Houston. "Because of the lively bidding for Hafey, we have been forced to pay for him a greater sum in cash than we have ever paid for any player," said Sam Breadon. The amount was not disclosed. *St. Louis Post-Dispatch,* August 7, 1924.

[50] Lieb, *The St. Louis Cardinals*. *Baseball Reference* puts the total in 1940 at 31 teams. www.baseball-reference.com/register/affiliate.cgi?year=1940

---

[51] *St. Louis Post-Dispatch*, July 5, 1925.
[52] Seymour, *Baseball.*
[53] Latin American history professor Charles E. Chapman later became a scout for the Cincinnati Reds.
[54] Mann, *Branch Rickey.*
[55] *St. Louis Post-Dispatch,* July 20, 1922.
[56] Ibid, August 9, 1922.
[57] Alexander, *Rogers Hornsby.*
[58] *St. Louis Post-Dispatch,* April 16, 1919.
[59] Ibid, April 4, 1913.
[60] After Becker's death, authorities discovered $18,000 in his safe at Campbell's Forest Home. Foley opened the safe for investigators on the condition that they not look for gambling evidence. *St. Louis Post-Dispatch,* April 17, 1919.
[61] Alexander, *Rogers Hornsby.*
[62] Ibid.
[63] *St. Louis Post-Dispatch*, June 24, 1923.
[64] Ibid.
[65] Sarah Hornsby received a $25,000 lump-sum settlement and custody of the couple's son. *St. Louis Post-Dispatch*, June 27, 1923.
[66] In another version of the story, it's Hornsby who takes a swing at Rickey before the two men are separated. *St. Louis Star*, September 10, 1923.
[67] *St. Louis Post-Dispatch,* September 27 and 28, 1923.
[68] The bonus payment represented a conflict of interest and would have been illegal under baseball rules. Multiple histories of the Cardinals date the huge cash offer for Hornsby as coming in 1919 with the amount offered at $300,000 with a $50,000 bonus payment. The source of that date and amount is likely a J. Roy Stockton article from 1935. See *Saturday Evening Post*, March 9, 1935. The John McGraw account appears twelve years earlier. See *St. Louis Star*, December 22, 1923. Giving the McGraw version additional credence is the fact that Babe Ruth debuted with the Yankees in 1920 with the American League team outdrawing the Giants that season. The Giants wanted a drawing card to counteract Ruth and an impact bat at second base (Frisch played third and shortstop for the Giants in 1920). "After the 1920 season," wrote Westbrook Pegler, McGraw "did need Hornsby as Larry Doyle had gone to pot at second for the Giants."
[69] *St. Louis Star*, December 22, 1923.
[70] Ibid, February 22, 1924.
[71] Ibid, April 1, 1924.
[72] Ibid, March 18, 1925.
[73] Breadon gained controlling interest in the team when he bought out James C. Jones, the man who came up with the idea for a fan-owned franchise. *St. Louis Post-Dispatch,* May 8, 1922. Breadon acquired a majority of stock in the Cardinals for $90,000. Four years earlier,

---

Charles Stoneham paid $960,000 for a majority control of the New York Giants. Fetter, *Taking On The Yankees.*
[74] *St. Louis Post-Dispatch*, June 19, 1925.
[75] *St. Louis Star*, July 2, 1925. The *Star* account of the details of the meetings were first published in the *Boston Globe.* According to the *Globe*, the meeting with Rickey lasted three minutes. The meeting with Hornsby took two minutes. Hornsby said he asked Breadon for time to consider the offer before accepting. "I want a few hours to consider your proposition," he told the owner. *St. Louis Post-Dispatch*, May 31, 1925.
[76] *St. Louis Post-Dispatch*, June 1, 1925.
[77] Alexander, *Rogers Hornsby.*
[78] *St. Louis Star*, July 2, 1925.
[79] Ibid.
[80] Ibid, January 23, 1926.
[81] Ibid, December 30, 1925.
[82] The *St. Louis Star* placed the value at $100,000 over three years. Other sources estimated the value at $90,000 over three seasons, or $30,000 per season.
[83] *St. Louis Globe-Democrat*, Feb 2, 1927. Another newspaper account estimated the total price paid for the stock at between $60,000 and $70,000. *St. Louis Star*, June 11, 1925.
[84] *St. Louis Star*, January 30, 1926.
[85] *St. Louis Post-Dispatch*, February 21, 1926.
[86] Ibid, October 3, 1926. The story, written by J. Roy Stockton, doesn't give the identity of the New York writer.
[87] Ibid, September 14, 1925. Remus had purchased the distillery in St. Louis. He used medicinal alcohol, which was legal during Prohibition, as the cover for his operations. Some have claimed Remus was the inspiration behind F. Scott Fitzgerald's *The Great Gatsby.*
[88] Alexander, *Rogers Hornsby*. The author found a poll that listed Hornsby as the most popular player in the National League in 1926, but the winner in the American League was pitcher Walter Johnson, not Ruth. *Dayton Daily News,* April 12, 1926.

The Class of '26

For the New York Yankees, the 1926 season began the previous year in St. Louis, on the afternoon of August 29, 1925. On that date, manager Miller Huggins paced anxiously in the visitor's clubhouse at Sportsman's Park. With a game against the Browns about an hour away, Babe Ruth was nowhere to be found. The manager waited. And waited. And then waited some more. By the time Ruth arrived, Huggins had officially had it with his star outfielder. Tired of his off-field antics, Huggins fined the slugger $5,000 and suspended him indefinitely. The two men exchanged words. Ruth said he would fight the suspension and fine and take his case to the Yankees owner. Huggins told him he needn't bother. He was confident of Jacob Ruppert's support. Ruth departed for the Buckingham Hotel. Huggins returned to the dugout. A team executive would later call the showdown in St. Louis "a turning point in the history of the New York Yankees."

Without Ruth in the lineup that day, the Yankees beat the Browns 4-1 behind pitcher Urban Shocker. The righthander had returned to New York after spending seven seasons in St. Louis. The Yankees were so eager to acquire the spitball pitcher from the Browns, the club would have given their young first baseman to get him. "I would hate to think of the terrible mistake I would have made had I sent you to the Browns for Urban Shocker," manager Huggins later told Lou Gehrig. "If they had insisted, you would have gone." (Instead of Gehrig, the Browns received pitchers Joe Bush, Milt Gaston and Joe Giard.)[1] Shocker won 12 games that season for a Yankees team that won only 69, lost 85, and finished seventh place in the American League. It would be another 65 years before the franchise recorded fewer victories.

The Yankees' record mirrored Ruth's troubles. The Babe missed the first 40 games of the 1925 season. When he returned on June 1, the Yankees were ten games under .500 and 13.5 games back in the standings. Ruth played 98 games, hit 25 home runs, and had 67 RBI while batting .290. Compared to his 1924 campaign, the slugger appeared in 55 fewer games, hit 21 fewer home runs, and saw his RBI production fall by 57 and his batting average plummet by 88 points.

Ruth's woes began early in the year. Launching a relationship with the city that lasted decades, the Yankees conducted spring training for the first time in St. Petersburg. Ruth was hit with a lawsuit while in Florida. A bookmaker claimed Ruth owed him $7,700 for horse racing losses. This came after Commissioner Landis had issued an order forbidding players from betting on races, an edict that both Ruth and Hornsby had ignored. In the same month, the Babe also broke a finger. Then his troubles really began.

Departing St. Petersburg on March 25, the Yankees and the Brooklyn Robins, as the National League team was called at the time, embarked on an ambitious six-state exhibition swing through the South. On April 4, the teams met in Atlanta in a game cut short by rain. Scheduled to play in Chattanooga, Tennessee the following afternoon, Ruth was still in Atlanta the morning of the 5th. Suffering from chills and a fever, Ruth received treatment from a physician then made his way to the train station "heavily muffled in sweaters and looking a little pale." He slept all the way to Chattanooga and did not participate in any pre-game warmups. But when the curtain rose, the showman responded. The crowd of nearly 8,000 people jammed Andrews Field that day to see one man and one thing. "The fans came to see Babe Ruth hit home runs," noted an account in *The New York Times*. "He hit them." The Babe hit two that afternoon, including one thought to be the longest home run in the history of the park.

Another train ride. Another city. Another home run. Ruth went deep again the next day in Knoxville with a blast off Brooklyn pitcher Dazzy Vance. In the fifth inning, some 5,000 fans at Caswell Field watched as the Babe connected on a ball that cleared the park and knocked a limb off a dead tree. It was Ruth's seventh home run of the exhibition series. It would be his last.[2]

The traveling circus moved on to North Carolina. On the train ride through the Smoky Mountains, Ruth became ill again. Stepping off the train in Asheville, the Babe collapsed. Unconscious on the ride over to the Park Hotel, Ruth revived under a doctor's treatment. Media reports indicated he was suffering from the flu. But Yankees management, increasingly concerned about their star player, decided to send him home to New York to receive extended care. Accompanied by scout Paul Krichell, the Babe began to make the trek northward.

By the time the train arrived in Washington D.C., rumors were rampant that Ruth was dead. Missing a connection along the way, he arrived at Union Station later than expected. Panicked railroad officials immediately boarded the train to check on Ruth's condition. Informed he was in better shape than when he left North Carolina, relieved authorities departed the platform. Ruth continued onward to New York, but not before the rumors had made their way to England. British papers gave the reports of Ruth's death front-page coverage, referred to him as "The King of Baseball" in premature obituaries, and focused on his salary ($52,000 at the time), "a sum which has always caused amazement in conservative England."[3]

Waiting at Penn Station in New York were Ruth's wife, Helen, Yankees general manager Ed Barrow, and thousands of concerned baseball fans. What they didn't know at the time was that Ruth was again unconscious. To clean up before his arrival, he had gone to the bathroom where he fainted and cracked his head on the washbasin. Krichell found him crumpled on the floor. Ruth's condition created a logistical nightmare for emergency officials, tasked with getting the slugger off the train and into an ambulance. An hour elapsed before an unconscious Ruth emerged on a stretcher passed through a window. Taken to a baggage room on a freight elevator, Ruth's departure was delayed again. A steering gear on the St. Vincent's Hospital ambulance had broken. While waiting for a new ambulance to arrive, Ruth went into convulsions. As his arms and legs flailed wildly, six men had to hold him on the stretcher. "I feel rotten, Helen," Ruth told his wife when he briefly regained consciousness.

Lapsing back into a comatose state, Ruth's body shook violently on the trip to the hospital. On two separate occasions, a hypodermic injection was administered. When he arrived at St. Vincent's, he suffered another attack. It took seven attendants to keep him on the stretcher. Finally transported to a hospital room, Ruth regained consciousness and a doctor announced the crisis had passed. The Babe was in no danger from the flu or the fall on the train. "Ruth's condition is not serious," read a statement from Dr. Edward King. "He is run down and has low blood pressure and there is the indication of a slight attack of the flu. What he needs is rest. He should have been in bed a week ago."[4]

"Fried potatoes for breakfast yesterday morning are said to have contributed to his sudden relapse," read one newspaper account. The episode became known as "The Bellyache Heard 'Round The World.'" The lighthearted coverage masked more serious issues. A week later, Ruth was still in the hospital with a temperature fluctuating between 100 and 101 degrees. He underwent surgery to remove an intestinal abscess. While media reports focused on influenza and indigestion, the Yankees suspected additional problems were plaguing Ruth. General Manager Barrow thought the Babe was suffering from syphilis. Teammates were also convinced that Ruth had a sexually transmitted disease. "He wasn't allowed to shower with the other players or anything like that," pitcher Bob Shawkey later admitted. By early May, the Babe's weight was down to around 180 pounds.

By this time, wife Helen had joined him in the hospital, suffering a nervous breakdown shortly after her husband was admitted. The couple's relationship had deteriorated. In his annual trip to Hot Springs before spring training, Ruth arrived with Claire Hodgson, the woman he first met in 1923. The Babe and his wife owned a farmhouse in Massachusetts. They put it up for sale in the summer of 1925, around the time Helen was finally released from the hospital. She spent about a month longer at St. Vincent's than did her husband, who was released near the end of May.

When the Babe returned to action, he was soon joined by a new starter in the lineup. Lou Gehrig had barely played the first two months of the year, logging just 26 plate appearances in April and May. That all changed beginning on June 2, when Gehrig started in place of regular first baseman Wally Pipp. The swap was just one of many changes Huggins made to his starting lineup. "The most radical shakeup of the Yankee lineup in many years left only three regulars of last season in the batting order," wrote reporter James R. Harrison.[5] In addition to Ruth, the other regulars were fellow outfielder Bob Meusel and third baseman Joe Dugan. Gehrig hit sixth and went three-for-five with a run scored as the Yankees beat the Washington Senators 8-5. Pipp, the team's first baseman since 1915, never started again for New York. Gehrig's consecutive game streak had started. He didn't miss a contest for the next 13 years.[6]

Gehrig's spark and Ruth's return could only do so much. Even after beating Washington, the Yankees still lagged league-leading Philadelphia by 13.5 games and were ten games behind the Senators, the eventual pennant winners. Already in a struggling marriage, the Babe had returned to a struggling team. "1925 was a tough year for the Babe," remembered teammate and pitcher Waite Hoyt. "He had made involved business commitments. He was deep in debt. He was wrangling continuously with Miller Huggins. Besieged on all sides, Ruth met the situation the only way he knew; he fought with everyone, engaged in maudlin self-pity. And he blamed everyone but himself. It was the lowest point in Ruth's career."[7]

One of the legendary dustups between Ruth and Huggins likely occurred during this period. Standing on a train platform, Huggins was lecturing players for their late-night carousing when Ruth picked him up. He and teammate Bob Meusel dangled their diminutive manager over the side.[8]

In August, Huggins hired a private detective to shadow Ruth, first in Chicago and then in St. Louis. When the Browns beat the Yankees 1-0 in St. Louis on Friday, August 28, it marked New York's eighth loss in its last nine games. The Yankees were now 22 games under .500 and 27 games behind first-place Washington. When Ruth showed up late the next day, his manager was ready. "You don't have to dress today, Babe," Huggins said. The manager then told Ruth he was fined and suspended, and to take the next train back to New York.

"Why you little runt!" the Babe exploded. "I wish you weighed 200 pounds. I'd beat your ears off."

"I wish I did weigh 200 pounds," Huggins responded. "I might beat your ears off."[9]

The meeting ended. Huggins got up and walked to the dugout. The Babe headed back to the hotel where employees reported, "Ruth was smiling and seemingly not worried about the turn of events."[10] Defying his manager's order, Ruth made other plans. He canceled his reservations at Union Station and departed for a residence in the West End of St. Louis.

The initial report was that the Babe had deserted the team, but Huggins explained the fine and suspension after the game, telling reporters Ruth was penalized for "misconduct off the field." One reporter asked the manager if Ruth's misconduct included alcohol. "Of course, it means drinking," Huggins replied, "and it means a lot of other things besides. There are various kinds of misconduct. Patience has ceased to be a virtue."[11]

Ruth spent Saturday night in St. Louis and headed to the train station the following day. He arrived in Chicago where he planned to plead his case before Commissioner Landis. He also drew a line in the sand. "If Huggins is manager, I am through with the Yankees," Ruth declared. "I will not play for him. Either he quits or I quit, regardless of my contract, which expires next year."[12]

Ruth admitted to reporters breaking curfew three times during the season, including Friday night in St. Louis. "I had been out with some friends at the home of John Wollmershauser, 3715 Hartford Street, until midnight and then we took an automobile ride because it was so warm. I arrived at the Buckingham Hotel at 2:30 a.m. We were ordered to be in at 1 o'clock." He denied the drinking charge and considered the fine, the largest in baseball history at the time, excessive. "They don't fine bootleggers $5,000 and men get out of murder charges for less. I haven't killed anybody." The fine was a matter between Ruth and the Yankees. As for the suspension, league rules prevented the commissioner from hearing any appeals for ten days. Landis was also out of town, spending time at his summer home in Michigan.

Denied the opportunity to meet with the commissioner, Ruth then headed to New York to meet with Ruppert. If Ruth thought the Yankees owner would be more sympathetic than his manager, he was mistaken. Ruppert unequivocally backed his manager. "I don't know all the details, but I'm behind Huggins in everything he does." American League president Ban Johnson also threw his support behind Huggins. At the same time, rumors began to float that Helen Ruth planned to sue her husband for $100,000 and separate maintenance, a charge she denied. But it was clear that the Babe had no support, either from the baseball establishment or his wife.

Backed into a corner, the slugger quickly abandoned his hardline stance. "Babe Ruth, maker of home runs, may have played his last game as a Yankee," began a story in *The New York Times* on September 1. "The Dove of Peace hangs over Babe Ruth today," read a story in the same paper just one day later after a repentant Ruth met with Ruppert and Huggins to express regret over his behavior. "I made a fool of myself," he admitted. "I don't know what made me talk about Huggins the way I did." The manager was willing to take Ruth back, but on his terms. "I may reinstate him, but not until I believe that he has let this lesson seep into him," Huggins told reporters. "I don't know how long I will keep him on the suspended list. It all depends on him." A shift in the relationship had transpired. Backed by his owner and with the Yankees out of the pennant race, Huggins had the upper hand. If Ruth once dangled his manager over the side of a train, Huggins was now responding in kind, dangling playing time in front of his star player in exchange for a change in behavior.

Ruth returned to the lineup on September 7 in Boston. He finished with a flurry. Over the last 29 games, the Babe blasted ten home runs and hit .346. But at season's end, a humbler Ruth admitted his lifestyle needed a change. "I have been a Babe and a

Boob," he admitted. "And I am through – through with the pests and the good-time guys. Between them and a few crooks I have thrown away over a quarter-million dollars."[13]

In October, Ruth went on a hunting trip to Canada with a group of teammates. When he returned, the Yankee star made a career-altering decision. He skipped the fall barnstorming tour and his regular pre-spring-training visit to Hot Springs. The thirty-year-old Ruth decided to try something new.

*****

Artie McGovern was a former amateur boxing champion, a physical fitness guru to the stars and a personal trainer to the elites of New York. From his gym on the East Side of Manhattan, he would dispatch an army of recruits to wake up his wealthy clients. "I have about 20 boys out every morning," he once explained. "In winter you will see them going into houses and apartments along Park and Fifth Avenues almost before it's light. They have keys – they just walk right into the bedrooms and yank the covers off millionaires."[14]

His client list over the years included boxer Jack Dempsey, golfer Gene Sarazen, and dance instructor Arthur Murray. In November of 1925, Ruth darkened his door. The Babe showed up at McGovern's gym weighing 254 pounds. "His muscles were flabby," his trainer recalled. "He panted at the slightest physical exertion. He suffered from severe indigestion and insomnia."[15] Ruth's waistline measured just shy of 50 inches.

McGovern put Ruth on a two-meal-a-day schedule, recommending fruits, vegetables, salads, lean meats and milk. The Babe would spend two hours every afternoon in the gym, tossing around a medicine ball, lifting dumbbells and other weights, then spend time boxing or playing handball. McGovern also focused on core exercises and abdominal muscles, explaining that "most persons of sedentary habits get some sort of arm and leg motion during the day. The abdomen, however, gets no exercise at all."

The discipline McGovern imposed was unlike anything Ruth had experienced as an adult. "He eats often – probably on average of ten times a day," Arthur Robinson had written in *Collier's* magazine just two years earlier.[16] But his trainer thought the new regimen harkened back to an earlier part of Ruth's life. "The habits formed at St. Mary's Home in Baltimore, where he was placed at the age of seven, were invaluable aids to us many years later," McGovern remembered. "The first thing I did was to put Babe back on the old St. Mary's schedule, or something very similar – regular hours, no eating between meals, simple foods, exercises – abdominal and other – and strict compliance with discipline."

Babe would sometimes complain. "Diet and exercise, exercise and diet – that's all I ever get!" he once said to McGovern, but he quickly embraced the routine. "He had to get in condition," McGovern wrote years later, "and he COOPERATED." With his trainer's help, Ruth lost a lot of weight, up to 43 pounds over the winter by one account, and shaved nearly 12 inches off his waistline. On the first day of workouts in spring training of 1926, "a new, slimmer, brisker Babe," had owner Ruppert rubbing his eyes in amazement. "Ruth's remodeled figure is such as to give the illusion of greater height," wrote one reporter.[17]

For the rest of his career, Ruth would spend the offseason toiling under the watchful eye of McGovern. The Babe was reborn. With the svelte slugger leading the way, so too were the New York Yankees.

*****

The 1926 Yankees had an experienced outfield with Earle Combs roaming center field between corner outfielders Ruth and Meusel. Typically hitting in the lead-off spot in the lineup, Combs scored more than 100 runs for New York eight straight seasons.[18] Meusel led the American League in home runs and RBI in 1925 and had a reputation for the strongest throwing arm in the game.

It was the infield where the Yankees retooled for the new season. With Gehrig now established at first base, New York sold Wally Pipp to the Cincinnati Reds. At second base, the club purchased the contract of Tony Lazzeri from Salt Lake City in the Pacific Coast League. Lazzeri hit 60 home runs in PCL play in 1925, a record number tempered by the thin mountain air, and a minor league schedule that featured 200 games.[19] Still, the impressive totals attracted attention from many teams, including the Chicago Cubs and Cincinnati Reds. Both clubs took a pass. Lazzeri suffered from epilepsy, and neither team wanted to take a chance. The Yankees scouted him heavily, dispatching multiple observers out West, including Bob Connery, the former Cardinals scout who had signed Hornsby. The Yankees became convinced Lazzeri's talents outweighed his disorder. "As long as he doesn't take fits between three and six in the afternoon, that's good enough for me," said general manager Barrow, who sent three players and $50,000 to Salt Lake to acquire the twenty-two-year-old Lazzeri.

The Yankees turned to another rookie at shortstop. Mark Koenig had played briefly for New York in 1925 after being purchased from the St. Paul Saints. But when New York dispatched Pee-Wee Wanninger in the offseason, the twenty-one-year-old Koenig assumed the job. Joe Dugan, the player whose trade from Boston to New York in 1922 had caused such an uproar in St. Louis, still manned third base for the Yankees. Pat Collins and Hank Severeid, both former St. Louis Browns, caught games for Huggins' squad.

The pitching staff featured familiar names acquired over the years from other teams. Waite Hoyt, Sad Sam Jones and Herb Pennock had all pitched for the Boston Red Sox before coming to the Yankees, while Bob Shawkey had started his career with the Philadelphia Athletics. Former St. Louis Brown Shocker also returned for another season in New York.

A skeptical press expressed doubts about whether the Yankees had improved. "Correspondents with the club at St. Petersburg, almost scathing in their arraignment, say the 1926 Yankees are terrible," read one account in the middle of March. [20] Yet the young infield, mature outfield, and veteran pitching staff clicked almost immediately.

The Yankees won their final 18 exhibition games of the spring, including 12 straight over the Brooklyn Robins, as the teams again paraded their way around the South.

When the regular season opened in April, Huggins' team showed no signs of letting up. By the end of April, the Yankees first place record was 12-3. The club reeled off 16 straight wins in May, a stretch that included a four-game sweep of the Browns. As the calendar rolled over to June, New York was six games better than anyone else in the American League. On May 31, Pennock improved to 10-1 with a victory over second-place Philadelphia. A healthy Ruth had started every game and was hitting .374 with Meusel not far behind at .371. Two weeks later, with a Sunday afternoon victory over the Browns at Sportsman's Park, the Yankees first-place record stood at 40-15, a lead of 10 games in the standings.

It is easy in hindsight to see what the Yankees had assembled. The club featured two future Hall of Fame infielders in Gehrig and Lazzeri, two more in the outfield with Combs and Ruth, and a pair of pitchers bound for Cooperstown in Hoyt and Pennock. These six players would form the core of what is remembered today as the legendary 1927 Yankees, a club that won 110 regular-season games and swept a World Series. No one refers to the 1926 team in the same glowing terms, but the rosters were virtually identical. The 1926 lineup of Collins, Gehrig, Lazzeri, Dugan, Koenig, Ruth, Combs and Meusel scored 84 percent of the team's runs and hit 94 percent of the club's home runs. In 1927, the identical starting eight generated 81 percent of the club's offense and produced 96 percent of the team's home run output. In 1926, the three winningest pitchers on the staff – Hoyt, Pennock, and Shocker – won 58 games. In 1927, the three winningest pitchers on the staff – Hoyt, Pennock and Shocker – won 59 games. In other words, the 1926 Yankees were just a young, unproven version of the greatness still to come.

Over in the National League, the 1926 St. Louis Cardinals roster would also eventually feature six men honored by the Hall of Fame: two infielders, two outfielders, and two pitchers.[21] But at the beginning of June, Hornsby's team stood one game under .500 and seven games back in the standings. The momentum of the exhibition schedule had long since faded. The club needed help. It would soon arrive.

*****

A Babe Ruth biographer once noted that Grover Cleveland Alexander is "one of the few men in baseball known to not only drink more than Ruth but feel the effects less."[22] Alexander's reputation as an alcoholic has been frequently documented over the years to the point it often overshadows his many accomplishments in the game. But long before he succumbed to the bottle, the righthander had already established himself as one of the greatest pitchers in the history of the game. It took a world war to change his behavior.

Born just outside Elba, Nebraska in February of 1887, Alexander grew up on a farm. According to his family, it was farming and hunting that helped make him a successful pitcher. Alexander's father claimed that his son once husked thirteen hundred bushels of corn in thirteen days, "which is pretty near a record for these parts," he added. "Perhaps that exercise to his wrist was what gave him his strength to pitch." Strength in his legs developed from plowing fields, while bird hunting gave him accuracy. "He always had a good eye," remembered younger brother Ray. "But when he was little he used to go around with his pockets full of stones and throw at birds. He got so that he was almost a dead shot with a pebble." [23]

Alexander's farmer father was a Democrat. In 1887, the President of the United States was Grover Cleveland. That's how the sixth of the eight surviving children of William and Margaret Alexander got his name. His family called him "Dode." As a baseball player, he got the nickname Ol' Pete. Many just called him Alec or Alex.

In nearby St. Paul, Nebraska, where he would later live as an adult, Alexander played amateur baseball. He pitched and played second base. "We were short on second basemen," his manager once explained. His pitching talents needed no explanation. They attracted the attention of teammates and foes alike. In 1908, a semi-pro team in Central City, Nebraska offered Alexander the chance to join their team at $50 a month. He hesitated. He had a job digging postholes for the telephone company. It paid $1.50 a day. "It doesn't seem like the proper thing to throw up a good job to play ball for a few months. I might not be able to get my job back again," he told the Central City manager, who converted him with a sales pitch. "I told him to grab the chance at once. It ought to lead to something better and very likely to something so much better that his present job would be small in comparison."[24] Alexander's days of digging postholes were over.

Just as his manager predicted, the pitcher got the chance to do something better. Alexander soon left Central City for another semi-pro team that paid him $125 a month. The next year, 1909, he was playing professionally in Galesburg, in the Illinois-Missouri League. It was here that his career nearly ended.

While running the bases on a ground ball hit on the infield, a shortstop's throw hit Alexander in the head and knocked him unconscious. For the first few days, it was feared he might die. He spent 36 hours in a coma and three weeks in the hospital. The incident left him with blurry vision. Fearing Alexander might never pitch effectively again, the Galesburg team sold him to Indianapolis. He never played for the American Association team, but a doctor did confirm he had nerve damage behind his left eye. Indianapolis passed him on to Syracuse.

With his vision recovered in 1910, Alexander dominated the New York State League playing for the Syracuse Stars. He pitched 33 consecutive shutout innings and was one out away from reaching 34 when an infielder made a ninth-inning error and a base runner scored. Alexander lost the game 1-0. He then reeled off 53 scoreless innings. Alexander won 29 games for the Stars with an ERA of 1.53. The performance attracted the attention of major league scouts. In 1911, the former posthole digger was in the big leagues. The Philadelphia Phillies spent $500 to acquire Alexander. The club also paid $3,000 to acquire George Chalmers, another pitcher in the New York State League.

Over a seven-season major-league career, Chalmers won 29 games for the Phillies. Alexander won more than that in a single season – three separate times.

In 1911, in one of the greatest rookie years in baseball history, Alexander led the league with 28 wins, 31 complete games and seven shutouts. But it was the period from 1915 to 1917 that the righthander hit his stride. During these three years, Alexander won 30, 33, and 31 games, respectively. In addition to leading the National League in wins all three years, he paced the circuit each year in ERA, complete games, shutouts, strikeouts, and innings pitched. He accomplished those feats in a home ballpark – Baker Bowl – where the home run distance down the right-field line was 280 feet. His pinpoint control, honed by hurling rocks on the plains of Nebraska, never shone brighter than during this period where he never pitched less than 376 innings and never walked more than 64 batters. His WHIP (walks plus hits per innings pitched) in 1915 was a microscopic 0.842, meaning he averaged well under a baserunner per inning.

He pitched four one-hitters that year, including one in St. Louis where, with two outs in the ninth inning, shortstop Artie Butler "just managed to catch a wide curve on the end of the bat and pop a little Texas Leaguer over second." When the ball landed safely for a base hit, Phillies catcher Bill Killefer threw his mitt to the ground. Alexander tossed his glove in the air in disgust.[25] "I wouldn't have minded so much," the pitcher later said, "but the thing he struck at was so much of a ball that it was almost a wild pitch, and yet he hit at it and drove it safe." For all his accomplishments, Alexander never threw a no-hitter in the big leagues.[26]

He faced both Hornsby and Ruth for the first time in 1915. Hornsby's first double of his major-league career came off Alexander in a regular-season game in September. The righthander faced Ruth in a World Series game in October. He got him to ground out to first base. Alexander and the Phillies won the game. Ruth and the Red Sox won the World Series.

At six foot one and weighing 190 pounds, Alexander threw with a side-arm motion. He had a smoothness and ease to his delivery that *The Sporting News* once compared to that of Yankees lefthander Pennock. "For sheer artistry on the mound, rhythm and grace, Alex had no superior," the paper contended. His repertoire consisted of fastballs and curveballs. "Perhaps I use about six fastballs to three or four curves," he said after the 1915 season. In Philadelphia, he once showed a rookie teammate how to throw a curve. "Be sure to let the ball roll off the bottom knuckle of the first finger near your palm," he told Stan Baumgartner. "You don't have to snap it. Let it roll and it will curve itself."[27]

After his incredible three-year stretch, the Phillies decided to sell high. Since the United States had entered World War I in April 1917, club officials also feared the 30-year-old Alexander might soon get drafted. In December, Philadelphia traded Alexander and battery-mate Killefer to the Chicago Cubs for two players and $55,000. Just days before the 1918 season started, Alexander and the Cubs got the news from the U.S. military. "That certainly is a wallop – a serious shock to the Chicago club," Cubs owner Charles Weeghman said when informed that Alexander had been drafted and ordered to report on April 26.[28]

Alexander made just three starts for Chicago in 1918. He made his Cubs debut in St. Louis against the Cardinals on opening day. He lost 4-2 to St. Louis and their bespectacled righthander Lee Meadows one day before the draft board refused Alexander's request to enlist in the U.S. Navy.[29] He won his next two starts then reported to Army boot camp. During basic training at Camp Funston near Manhattan, Kansas and with departure for Europe imminent, he married Nebraska native Aimee (Amy) Arrant, a woman he would wed and divorce twice in his life.

By June, he had set sail for England. He soon found himself on the front lines of the battlefield in France as a member of the 342nd Field Artillery, 89th Division. Exposed to constant howitzer fire, the shell-shocked Alexander came home from the war deaf in one ear and an epileptic.[30] He began drinking to relieve the stress and disguise the symptoms of his disease. He would battle epilepsy and alcoholism for the rest of his life.

He returned to the Cubs on May 9, 1919. He lost the game 1-0 in a season where he frequently suffered from a lack of run support. Alexander finished the year 16-11, but his ERA of 1.72 remains the lowest of any Cubs pitcher at the park soon to be controlled by William Wrigley Jr.[31] His best season in Chicago came the following year when he won 27 games while leading the league in ERA, strikeouts, and innings pitched. Bill Killefer, who had been Alexander's teammate and catcher since 1911, became Cubs manager near the end of the 1921 season. But when he was fired halfway through the 1925 season and replaced with Joe McCarthy, Alexander's days in Chicago were numbered.

"Joe didn't like Alex," recalled Cubs shortstop Jimmy Cooney Jr., acquired from the Cardinals before the 1926 season. "He thought he was a bad influence on the younger players and certainly not a good example." Alexander would sip ammonia to prevent epileptic seizures and he always kept a bottle of booze in the locker room. "He knew McCarthy was on to him, so he would hide it in the locker of one of the rookie pitchers," said Cooney. "He'd slip down there during the game and take a few slugs. Things got so bad after a while and it was no surprise when the Cubs cut him loose."[32]

After the 1925 season, Alexander checked himself into the Keeley Institute in Dwight, Illinois, about 85 miles south of Chicago. Like all other efforts during his life to ween himself from the addiction to alcohol, this attempt failed. His drinking was so excessive near the end of spring training in 1926 that McCarthy sent him back to Chicago. He soon rejoined the team, and near the end of May, Alexander had a record of 3-3. In a start on May 16, he faced just eight batters and lasted just two-thirds of an inning in a game the Cubs rallied to win. His next time out, on May 22, he lost 7-1 to the Boston Braves on Grover Cleveland Alexander Day at Cubs Park. Before the game, he was feted with flowers, speeches and a brand-new Lincoln automobile. It would be his last appearance in a Cubs uniform. A few days later in Pittsburgh, Alexander collapsed in the dugout. In Philadelphia in mid-June, McCarthy suspended him and ordered him back to Chicago after the pitcher had gone missing for several days. "He has stayed away from the field, not appearing in uniform here or at Boston," McCarthy told reporters. "I am not going to stand for such stuff. I don't intend to let Alexander or any other player break up my ball club."[33]

Less than a week later, the Cubs put Alexander on waivers. Team owner William Wrigley Jr. sent his manager a note. "Congratulations," the telegram to McCarthy read. "For years I've been looking for a manager with the courage to do this." Any team could now claim the pitcher for the price of $4,000. A rival National League team did just that. And that is how thirty-nine-year-old Nebraska native Grover Cleveland Alexander, an epileptic, alcoholic, war veteran, and star pitcher, became a member of the St. Louis Cardinals.

*****

The pickup of Alexander off the waiver wire was the second of two acquisitions that influenced the Cardinals 1926 season. On June 14, the team acquired Billy Southworth from the New York Giants in exchange for Heinie Mueller. Both were left-handed-hitting outfielders, but Southworth was seven years older. He didn't have a lot of power but his career batting average of .297 made him an asset.

For the Cardinals, the thirty-three-year-old Southworth was spectacular. Of his 52 career home runs, he hit 11 of them for St. Louis in 1926. He also drove in 69 runs, stole 13 bases, while hitting .317 for the Cardinals. Combined with his numbers earlier in the year for the Giants, Southworth reached a career-high in runs scored (99), home runs (16), and RBI (99). Compared to Mueller's statistics on the season – seven home runs, 56 RBI and a .256 batting average – it became a deal that John McGraw would regret. In New York, Southworth frequently battled with his manager. In St. Louis, he had some of the biggest hits of the season.

Southworth joined a Cardinals outfield that now featured Taylor Douthit in center field and Ray Blades in left. On the infield, the team returned their veteran superstars in Hornsby and Jim Bottomley. Sunny Jim led the league in doubles with 40 and RBI with 120. He also led the team in home runs with 19 and batted .299. Bottomley just missed joining a list of five Cardinals to hit .300 on the season – Southworth, Douthit, and Blades in the outfield; Hornsby and third baseman Les Bell on the infield. Bell led the club in batting average at .325 while adding 17 home runs and 100 RBI.

With the trade of shortstop Cooney to the Cubs in the offseason, Tommy Thevenow became a regular for the first time in his career. He started every single game of 1926, and while he hit just .256 and committed 45 errors at short, he received praise for his wide-ranging and effective defense. Thevenow's range factor per game, a measurement of his assists and putouts, was the highest of any shortstop in baseball.[34]

Rounding out the starting eight was catcher Bob O'Farrell. The Cardinals acquired him the prior season when the catcher became expendable in Chicago with the emergence of Gabby Hartnett. For St. Louis, O'Farrell emerged as an offensive and defensive weapon. He hit seven home runs with 68 RBI while batting .293. Starting 142 games behind the plate, O'Farrell caught more pitches than any other backstop in the league. He logged 1,235 innings in 1926, a league-leading number 156 innings greater than his nearest rival. "There's no better catcher in baseball," Hornsby said that summer.[35] Sportswriters agreed. For his 1926 regular season performance, O'Farrell won the National League MVP award.

On the day the Cardinals acquired Southworth, a loss to Brooklyn snapped a six-game St. Louis winning streak. With Southworth in the lineup the following day, the club started another stretch of six consecutive victories. On June 21, the Cardinals saw that winning streak broken when the club lost at Forbes Field to the Pittsburgh Pirates. The two teams met the next day at Sportsman's Park where the Pirates beat the Cardinals 3-1 behind former St. Louis righthander Lee Meadows. These were the most important losses of the year. Cincinnati, Pittsburgh and St. Louis all claimed Alexander when Chicago put him on waivers.[36] The Reds were in first, Pirates in second, and the Cardinals – thanks to those back-to-back losses – stood in third place, two games behind Pittsburgh. The waiver wire worked in reverse order of the standings. The lowest-ranked team to make a claim was awarded the player. If the Cardinals had stretched their winning streak to eight games, Grover Cleveland Alexander would have belonged to the Pirates.

Exactly who in St. Louis gets the credit for picking up Alexander is not clear. One version is that owner Sam Breadon quickly made the claim. Another theory is that Hornsby, who had faced Alexander for more than a decade, pushed for the move. Still another version has Killefer, Alexander's former catcher and manager, and now a pitching coach with the Cardinals, strongly backing the action. Most versions agree that Rickey was out on a trip with the farm system and had no input into the decision.[37] "I'm tickled to be with the team and Hornsby and Killefer," said Alexander. "All Rog has to do is nod his head and I'll jump through a hoop for him."[38]

Alexander joined a rotation that included staff ace Flint Rhem, a 20-game winner in 1926, knuckleballer and future Hall-of-Famer Jesse "Pop" Haines, lefthander Bill "Wee Willie" Sherdel, and Vic Keen. Alexander and Keen had been teammates in Chicago. Keen went just 2-6 for the Cubs in 1925, but Killefer knew he had pitched with a sore arm that season and thought he could contribute. With Keen, Killefer, and catcher O'Farrell, Alexander had three familiar faces from his days in Chicago. Alexander and O'Farrell knew each other so well that the catcher flashed fake signs. The righthander threw whatever he wanted. "He don't pay no attention to me and I don't pay no attention to him. I just pitch whatever I want to pitch and I know Bob will get'em all."[39]

Adding new manager Hornsby to the list of Alexander boosters, the righthander had landed in a comfortable and supportive environment.[40] Gone were the days of McCarthy's lectures and suspicious glares. "Hornsby was a great manager as far as I'm concerned," O'Farrell said years later. "He never bothered any of us. Just let you play your game."

On Sunday afternoon, June 27, Alexander the Great made his St. Louis debut against McCarthy's Cubs. Lines began forming outside Sportsman's Park by 8:00 a.m. By noon, the main entrance to the park on Dodier Street had to be roped off. By 1:00 p.m., the police assigned to the stadium called for backup. By 2:00 p.m., more than 37,000 fans had jammed into the recently expanded park to watch the first game of a doubleheader. "It was the greatest throng that had ever paid to watch a baseball attraction in this city," wrote *The Sporting News.* Alexander held his old team to just four hits, and he went the distance in a 3-2 Cardinals victory that took ten innings. "Note to McCarthy: Have You Any More at Home Like Alex?" asked the *St. Louis Star.*

The Alexander victory pushed the Cardinals to 10 games over .500 at 38-28. But the impact of the two key acquisitions quickly faded. The club proceeded to drop eight of its next ten games.[41] An Alexander loss – his second since joining the Cardinals – knocked the team six games back in the standings on July 6. A big reason for the disappointing play was the absence of Hornsby. He was battling injuries, and soon he would be battling management. Again. But unlike 1923 when Hornsby feuded with Rickey, the second baseman now called the shots from the dugout, owned stock in the club, and served on the board of directors of the franchise. This battle would reach the highest levels of the organization. For Hornsby, the stakes and the consequences were never higher.

*****

On May 22, 1926, before a game that afternoon between the Philadelphia Phillies and the St. Louis Cardinals at Sportsman's Park, National League president Jon Heydler handed Hornsby a bag of gold. Valued at $1,000, it represented Hornsby's cash prize for winning the 1925 National League MVP award. Following the ceremony, Hornsby collected two hits and the Cardinals beat the Phillies. A month later at Sportsman's Park, on June 23 against the Pittsburgh Pirates, Hornsby again had two base hits in a Cardinals victory. The first one, a single, marked the 2,000th hit of his career. The second one, a grand slam off Pittsburgh pitcher Don Songer, proved to be the difference in a 6-2 St. Louis win. On that day, Hornsby's batting average stood at .346. It would never be higher that season. By the end of the year, it had dropped nearly 30 points.

Hornsby's injury-plagued 1926 season got an early start. He displaced two vertebrae and battled back problems all season. Late in the year, with the Cardinals in Pittsburgh, he paid a visit to Bonesetter Reese in Ohio, the legendary amateur physician many ballplayers considered an expert in treating aching arms and bothersome backs. Although sore the next day, Hornsby said he felt better and "that something snapped back into place."[42] While the back injury proved persistent, what caused Hornsby to miss the most time that season were boils on his body.

He missed the first of two ten-day stretches when he underwent an operation for the removal of a carbuncle on his thigh on June 29. Team physician Robert Hyland performed the operation. The issue with the infected pus-filled bumps sidelined Hornsby until July 9. He returned too soon and against the advice of Hyland. At a game in New York later that month, a throw from the outfield took a bad bounce and hit the second baseman in the eye. "It felt like Jack Dempsey had hit me," said Hornsby after the game with the eye swollen shut. He played the entire series against the Giants, going 1-13. The sole base hit was a single. "There is no punch in his swing," wrote Roy Stockton.

Hornsby took a second ten-day sabbatical starting on July 25. When he returned in early August, the team had dropped four straight and stood in third place, five games behind the league-leading Pirates. Despite his health issues and his struggles – his lowest batting average since 1918 – Hornsby still finished the year hitting .317 with 11 home runs and 93 RBI. With their manager in the lineup, the Cardinals were 30 games over .500. In his absence, the team went 8-14.

"The Cardinals need Hornsby and they need Hornsby badly," wrote Stockton on the eve of his August return. "Without Hornsby, the Cardinals are only a second-division ball club, and unless he returns to duty soon the team will not tarry in the first division long."

Swinging at the first pitch he saw when he returned to the lineup on August 4, Hornsby smashed a single off the outfield wall at Ebbets Field. He later scored on a Jim Bottomley double as the Cardinals beat the Robins 8-4 in the first of six straight victories and a stretch where the team won 18 of 21 games. The hot streak vaulted the club into first place. When Alexander beat the Boston Braves 4-3 in 11 innings at Sportsman's Park on August 25, the Cardinals boasted a record of 71-51 and had a one-game lead over the Pirates.

Hornsby's impact was more psychological than statistical. He batted just .265 in August with no home runs and 15 RBI. The key was the pitching staff that logged an ERA of 2.75 for the month. Alexander had his most productive month, appearing in 10 games, starting five of them, going 4-2 with one shutout. The team had its best month of the year, compiling a 22-8 record. Hornsby's squad capped off August with a doubleheader sweep of Pittsburgh, the defending World Series champs. The next day, September 1, the Cardinals finished the series with a 5-2 win and stood atop the standings with a one-game lead over Cincinnati and two over Pittsburgh.

The series also brought an end to regular-season home games at Sportsman's Park. St. Louis finished the schedule with twenty-four straight on the road, a stretch that would take them to every city in the National League. Not on the schedule were a series of exhibition games scheduled by owner Sam Breadon. In a span of five days starting on September 8, the Cardinals had three open dates. Breadon had scheduled games against two minor league squads in New York with a third game in New Haven, Connecticut. The owner wanted the money the games would provide. The manager wanted to focus on the games that mattered. He viewed the exhibitions as a distraction and a chance for a needless injury.

The disagreement between Breadon and Hornsby escalated into a war of words. Following a loss in Pittsburgh, Breadon told Hornsby the commitments had to be honored. The manager exploded, insisting he wouldn't play his starters and told the owner to get the hell out of his clubhouse. When his club departed for upstate New York, Hornsby left for Yankee Stadium with six of his pitchers and catcher O'Farrell to scout his potential World Series opponent.[43] Breadon returned to St. Louis, still stewing about the behavior of his manager. "He was flushed and angry when he left the clubhouse," Hornsby later said of the owner. "I believe he made up his mind then and there that, come pennant or last place, Hornsby wouldn't be with the Cardinals the next season."

On Sunday, September 12, the Cardinals played the third and final exhibition game in New Haven. The Connecticut minor-league team was owned by George Weiss, the future farm director and general manager of the New York Yankees. Breadon had tried to convince his counterpart to cancel but Weiss wouldn't hear of it. The Cardinals had played the game in years past when the team wasn't a draw, but now St. Louis had vaulted to the top of the National League standings. "Now that you are up, and you are the attraction, you'll have to keep your end," Weiss told him.[44] The game was played with Hornsby's worst fear realized. Chick Hafey was injured in the exhibition. The twenty-three-year-old outfielder had become a regular in August when Ray Blades suffered a season-ending knee injury when he crashed into the Sportsman's Park outfield wall. In New Haven, Hafey suffered an injury to a finger. Two years earlier in the same ballpark, he had fractured his ankle.[45] Fortunately for Hafey and the Cardinals, his injury in 1926 wasn't as serious. He missed just one game.

Hafey's return coincided with a five-game winning streak, a run that included a 23-3 win over the Phillies and a stretch where the Cardinals outscored their opponents 59-11. St. Louis entered the Polo Grounds on Friday afternoon, September 24, against McGraw's New York Giants, needing a victory and a Cincinnati Reds loss to clinch the pennant. The nation's sports fans were still abuzz over what had transpired the night before.

*****

More than 120,000 fans jammed into Philadelphia's Sesquicentennial Municipal Stadium on Thursday night to watch Jack Dempsey defend his heavyweight title against Gene Tunney. The paid crowd – a record number that stood for nearly 67 years – was joined by an estimated 15 million people who listened to the event on the radio. If there was a sport that matched, or maybe even eclipsed, the enthusiasm American sports fans had for baseball in the 1920s, it was boxing. Babe Ruth's salary, the subject of endless fascination in the media, peaked at $80,000. For his September 1926 defense of his title, Dempsey received more than $700,000.[46] Five years earlier, in a fight against French World War I hero Georges Carpentier, Dempsey was paid $300,000 and two years after that, his payday climbed to more than $500,000 when he squared off against Argentinian Luis Firpo. In three boxing matches, Dempsey earned nearly double the amount Ruth did for his entire baseball career. [47]

Boxing promoter Tex Rickard helped create the buzz surrounding the event originally planned for Yankee Stadium. When New York officials refused to grant Dempsey's permit request (state authorities demanded he oppose a different fighter), Rickard shifted the match to Philadelphia. The fevered pitch followed the title bout to Pennsylvania. Special trains from around the country coordinated trips to Philadelphia in the days before the event. Thousands flocked to the city's sold-out hotels. The roster of luminaries scheduled to attend included Calvin Coolidge's Vice President Charles Dawes, Treasury Secretary Andrew Mellon, actor Charlie Chaplin, and newspaper publisher William Randolph Hearst. Days before the match, two Philadelphia boys staged a schoolyard fight. When one youth pretending to be Dempsey struck a blow against another acting as Tunney, it didn't just knock him out. It killed twelve-year-old Manual Kin. "I didn't mean to hit him," said ten-year-old Carl Weinstein after police arrested him on the charge of homicide.[48]

The City of Brotherly Love also happened to be the home of crime boss Max "Boo-Boo" Hoff. Leading up to the heavyweight bout, Hoff had struck a deal with challenger Tunney and his manager Billy Gibson. Tunney, an ex-marine from New York City, needed money. Hoff loaned the boxer $20,000 with curious conditions. If Tunney lost the match to Dempsey, only the loan amount had to be repaid. But if the underdog could somehow defeat Dempsey, he owed Hoff 20 percent of all his future earnings. Why would Tunney, whose purse for the fight was $200,000, agree to such a deal? What did Hoff know that would move him to strike such an arrangement?

On the day of the fight, a Dempsey bodyguard gave the champion a small glass of olive oil, meant to aid in digestion. "Dempsey suffered something akin to food poisoning," wrote author David Pietrusza. "The Manassa Mauler" fought poorly that evening. The man who broke Carpentier's nose with his first punch and knocked out Firpo in four minutes lost all ten rounds. "From the time the bout started," Dempsey recalled, "I was aware that my body and my brain weren't communicating properly."[49] Gene Tunney was the new heavyweight champion of the world.

Suspicions and rumors about that evening dogged the new champion and his manager. Before their rematch in Chicago a year later, Dempsey published an open letter to Tunney in the *Herald and Examiner*. "You knew that if you won the title it would be worth at least $1,000,000 to you," Dempsey pointed out. "Why were you agreeable to paying Hoff approximately $200,000 bonus for a loan of $20,000? What could Hoff do to help you on to victory that would be worth $200,000?"

Dempsey charged that both Tunney and his manager conducted secret meetings with former boxer and longtime sports fixer Abe Attell and that Attell had met with Philadelphia gang lord Hoff. Attell was at Gibson's side before the fight and was in Tunney's dressing room after the fight.

Also in attendance that night in Philadelphia was Arnold Rothstein, Attell's former boss, and the financier of the Black Sox scandal in 1919. At 4-1 odds, Rothstein had placed a $125,000 bet on Tunney. He won $500,000 when the challenger upset

Dempsey.[50] After Rothstein's death two years later, his private papers revealed that one of the people hiding his assets was one "William Gibson of 505 Park Avenue" – Billy Gibson, Tunney's manager.[51] Seven years after the Black Sox, corruption in American sports was alive and well. Rothstein and crew had merely shifted their focus from baseball to boxing. So much easier to manipulate a single man in a ring than nine players on a diamond.

*****

Less than twenty-four hours after Tunney defeated Dempsey, New York Giants pitcher Hugh McQuillan took the mound at the Polo Grounds against a Cardinals lineup that featured Taylor Douthit leading off, followed by Billy Southworth, Rogers Hornsby, Jim Bottomley, Les Bell, Chick Hafey, Bob O'Farrell and Tommy Thevenow. It was a lineup that manager Hornsby had consistently employed since Blades' injury the previous month. Pitcher Flint Rhem, winner of his twentieth game of the season in his previous start at Philadelphia, got the start for St. Louis.

The Giants jumped out to a quick lead when outfielder Bill Terry connected for a three-run homer off Rhem in the bottom of the first. The Cardinals quickly countered. Cleanup hitter Bell led off the second with a double, advanced to third on a passed ball, then scored on an infield single by catcher O'Farrell. When shortstop Thevenow doubled to put runners at second and third, Hornsby decided to pull his starting pitcher. He tapped pinch-hitter Specs Toporcer, "a New York sandlotter who never got a chance in his hometown."[52] Toporcer lined a double to the outfield and the Cardinals tied the game. With two outs, another New York connection, former Giants outfielder Southworth, came to the plate with his manager and second baseman yelling encouragement from the on-deck circle.

"I can still hear his raspy voice," Southworth said years later. "Have your cut, Bill. Have your cut," Hornsby told him. "This could be the pennant." The outfielder proceeded to blast an upper-deck home run to right field, and the Cardinals had a lead they would never relinquish. "That was the timeliest home run I ever hit," Southworth remembered, "and to have it against the Giants, with McGraw snarling his defiance from the bench, made it doubly thrilling and satisfying."[53]

Sherdel came on in relief of Rhem and held New York to one run over eight innings. With a 6-4 win over the Giants and a Reds loss to the Phillies in the first game of a doubleheader, the Cardinals clinched their first pennant in franchise history and the first championship for St. Louis since the 1888 American Association Browns.

A raucous party erupted in the streets of the city. Thousands of fans had gathered on downtown sidewalks to listen to radio reports of the action from New York. With speakers set up at the Federal Building and the Railroad Exchange Building, an estimated 25,000 fans had gathered in downtown St. Louis. With victory came pandemonium. Residents made 128,000 telephone calls within an hour of the final out, the greatest deluge of calls in the history of the city. The downtown crowd quadrupled. "Impromptu parades by freakishly-costumed marchers infested the already choked streets and sidewalks," noted the *St. Louis Times*. "Placards appeared, urging the election of Rogers Hornsby for President."[54] The party peaked around 9:00 p.m. but continued until the early morning hours of Saturday.

Members of the throng made their way to the Buckingham Hotel where revelers began "beating drums and yowling defiance."[55] The choice of the Buckingham, located at the corner of Kingshighway and West Pine Boulevards, was no accident. Sleeping there that evening – or at least trying – were Ruth and his teammates. They were in no mood to party. The Yankees still had work to do.

*****

It rained in St. Louis on Friday, September 24. Not enough to stop any of the Cardinals' clinching victory celebrations, but just enough to cancel the scheduled afternoon game at Sportsman's Park between the Browns and the Yankees. The rainout meant the Yankees would finish the season with back-to-back doubleheaders in St. Louis on Saturday and Sunday.

With four games to go, New York clung to a two-game lead over second-place Cleveland. On August 6, the Yankees had an eleven-game lead and the race looked all but over. But New York was not healthy. Catcher Pat Collins suffered an elbow injury that sidelined him for much of the second half of the schedule. Catching 85 of the team's first 90 games, Collins played in just 17 games the rest of the year. Outfielder Meusel was hitting .365 when he broke a bone in his foot in late June. When he returned to the lineup in August, his performance lagged, much like the rest of his club. Meusel's batting average plunged fifty points over the last two months of the season. During that same timeframe, the Yankees lost four more games than they won. The surging Indians went 30-22 in August and September.

Cleveland had the opportunity to cut New York's lead to one-and-a-half games on September 19. The final game of a series at Dunn Field, the Indians home park, attracted a Cleveland record crowd of 31,000. Yankees manager Huggins gave the ball to veteran southpaw Walter "Dutch" Ruether. Acquired in a deal with the Washington Senators in August, the lefthander had won 18 games for the Washington Senators the previous year and had World Series experience. He started and won Game 1 for the Cincinnati Reds in the infamous Black Sox Series of 1919. Like St. Louis mid-season acquisition Grover Cleveland Alexander, Ruether had a reputation as a heavy drinker.

The lefthander won only two games for the Yankees in 1926, but one of them may have been the team's biggest win of the year. Ruether gave up three runs to Cleveland in the bottom of the first but then pitched six shutout innings. The Yankees got home runs from Ruth and Gehrig and two innings of relief from Shawkey to close out an 8-3 victory on a Sunday afternoon. With a week to go, the Yankees lead stood at three-and-a-half games. New York moved on to Chicago, where the White Sox took three of four games, while Cleveland took two of three from the Red Sox. Watching the rain fall in St. Louis and looking over their shoulder at Cleveland, the Yankees got some good news when the Athletics defeated the Indians Friday afternoon. New York needed two victories in St. Louis to celebrate an American League championship.

One day after the Cardinals clinched a pennant in New York, the Yankees clinched one in St. Louis. In sweeping the Saturday doubleheader, Huggins' crew got victories from their future Hall-of-Famers, Hoyt and Pennock, and outscored the Browns in the two games 20-6. Ruth dominated the day, going 5-8 with three home runs and eight RBI across the two contests. Considered a growing liability just one year earlier, the thirty-one-year-old Ruth responded in 1926 with 47 home runs and 153 RBI, his highest output since 1921. The Babe's workouts with Artie McGovern would pay dividends for years to come. In the six years following the initial workouts with his trainer, Ruth averaged 50 home runs, 147 runs and 156 RBI. The Babe's performance also reflected well on the hardline approach taken by Huggins in the clubhouse of Sportsman's Park that fateful day in August of 1925. "You can call it a turning point in the history of the New York Yankees," general manager Barrow said later. "Thereafter the so-called bad boys realized we meant business."[56]

While finishing in seventh place, the Browns nevertheless had an impact on the championship race. The American League St. Louis team went 6-16 against New York while splitting its 22 games against Cleveland.

Neither the Cardinals nor the Yankees won another regular-season game once the race was decided. The hungover Cardinals lost to the Giants on Saturday 12-2. To finish out the season, the team had to travel to Cincinnati for a game on Sunday. Hornsby and several of the veteran players didn't bother making the trip, preferring to spend their time in New York. The Browns swept the Yankees on the last day of the regular season in St. Louis, with George Sisler getting a three-inning save in the second game of the doubleheader.

The Cardinals and Yankees had arrived at their World Series destination through distinctly different routes. New York never spent a day under .500 during the season, claimed sole control of first place of the American League in the middle of May and never relinquished it. In compiling a record of 91-63, the Yankees scored 847 runs on the season while allowing 713. St. Louis struggled out of the gate, found themselves eight games back near the end of May, and didn't reach first place until mid-August. In compiling a record of 89-65, the Cardinals scored 817 runs while allowing 678. The two clubs featured slugging first basemen, young shortstops, speedy centerfielders, veteran pitching staffs, and the marquee players of their respective leagues. "Mr. Ruth and Rogers Hornsby undoubtedly represent the greatest amount of pounding power that baseball has ever known," wrote Damon Runyon on the eve of the World Series. "I mean to say they hit the ball harder than any batsmen that ever lived."

The Yankees scored 30 more runs on the season while the Cardinals had given up 35 less. New York's rookie combination of Lazzeri and Koenig had recorded 86 errors and turned 117 double plays. The middle infield duo of Hornsby and Thevenow for the

Cardinals had committed 72 errors with 141 double plays. Defense would be a difference in the Series.

"We'll beat them," Ruth told reporters after the team arrived back in New York on Monday night. "There'll be nothing to it." His manager agreed. "We're confident we're going to win," said Huggins. "We have a more experienced team and a more experienced pitching staff. We're about even in the strengths of our infield, but ours is steadier. Our outfield is better, stronger, and more experienced, and all the boys are cocky and ready to go. There's no doubt in their minds or in mine that the Yankees will win."

Contacted by *The New York Times* after the Yankees had clinched, Hornsby was equally confident in his team. "Most of our players are young," said the Cardinals second baseman and manager. "They have been on edge, with their nerves strained throughout the past six weeks, but they have played good ball. Now, with the strain of the National League pennant ended – and that, of course, had to be the first consideration – they are physically and mentally prepared to play better than ever. They are on their way to the world's championship."

Hornsby's squad had the entire week to get ready. The twenty-third World Series was scheduled to start Saturday afternoon at Yankee Stadium. After the first two games in New York, the teams would travel to St. Louis for Games 3, 4, and 5 in an already sold out Sportsman's Park. Box seats for the 1926 affair cost $6.60 each, with reserved tickets priced at $5.50, general admission at $3.30 while fans in the bleachers could watch for $1.10.

With ticket sales and last-minute preparations underway, Hornsby got news from Texas three days before the start of play. His mother had passed away. It was not unexpected. She died after a long illness. It was also her wish, newspaper accounts noted at the time, that Hornsby remain with his team in New York. Her son complied and asked that her funeral service be delayed until the Series was complete. Over the years, writers have criticized Hornsby for his actions, claiming he chose baseball over his mother's funeral.[57] In fact, he did no such thing. In the days before commercial airplane service, it simply wasn't practical to take a train trip to Texas. Suffering from back problems nearly the entire year, he would have endured a lengthy round trip while likely missing the first two games in New York. The Cardinals star player and manager had missed games in the past to visit his mother. He would pay one last visit after a week of baseball. The year 1926 was like that for Hornsby – moments of euphoria and celebration on the baseball field followed by the sobering reality of outside events.

His roller coaster ride had only just begun.

---

[1] After being fined and suspended by Huggins, Ruth criticized the trade. "He (Huggins) took Shocker from the Browns and gave away Bush, Gaston and Giard. He had never seen Giard, but he let him get away, and Giard is one of the best pitching prospects in the

league today. The only reason the Browns are in the first division is that Huggins gave them a pitching staff for practically nothing." *New York Times*, August 31, 1925. The Browns finished the year in third place with a record of 82-71. Pitcher Joe Giard went 10-5 with a 5.04 ERA. The Browns later traded him back to New York where he appeared in 16 games in 1927, his final year in baseball. He finished his career with 13 wins and 15 losses.

[2] A later spring training blast by Ruth in Knoxville was caught by fifteen-year-old Carden Gillenwater. The teenager became a major league baseball player, debuting with the Cardinals in 1940. *Tampa Bay Times*, May 14, 2000.

[3] *New York Times*, April 10, 1925.

[4] Ibid.

[5] Ibid, June 3, 1925.

[6] Gehrig officially began his streak of appearing in 2,130 straight games on June 1. He appeared in the game as a pinch-hitter. His streak ended on May 2, 1939. The record stood for 56 years when it was broken by Baltimore Orioles shortstop Cal Ripken Jr.

[7] Hoyt, Waite. *Babe Ruth As I Knew Him*. Dell Sports. 1948.

[8] Ruth's biographers are split on the question of whether the incident took place, but Huggins' biographers Steve Steinberg and Lyle Spatz believe it did. "The evidence suggests that the incident did indeed occur." See *The Colonel and Hug*.

[9] Hoyt, *Babe Ruth As I Knew Him.*

[10] *New York Times*, August 30, 1926.

[11] *St. Louis Post-Dispatch*, August 30, 1925

[12] *New York Times*, August 31, 1925.

[13] *Collier's*, October 31, 1925.

[14] Montville, *The Big Bam.*

[15] McGovern, Artie. *The Secret of Keeping Fit. An Easy and Sure Way to Better Health*. Simon & Schuster, Inc. 1935.

[16] *Collier's*, September 20, 1924.

[17] *New York Times*, March 2, 1926. There are conflicting reports about how much weight Ruth lost that offseason. The 43-pound figure comes from McGovern's book, published in 1935. Contemporaneous reports and some Ruth biographers put the total in the 20-to-25-pound range.

[18] The 1926 Yankees started the year with shortstop Mark Koenig hitting first with Combs batting second. By the end of the year, their positions in the lineup had switched.

[19] Lazzeri played in 197 games with 710 at-bats in 1925.

[20] *St. Louis Star*, March 15, 1926. Asked to handicap the 1926 pennant race in February, manager Miller Huggins said he expected his team to compete for a "first division berth." He was also intrigued by a longshot. "If there were a Winter book, as there is on some horse races, and if I were to bet on the Winter book, I would take the St. Louis Browns were the odds long enough." *New York Times,* February 27, 1926.

[21] The six St. Louis Cardinals on the 1926 roster in the Hall of Fame are first baseman Jim Bottomley, second baseman Rogers Hornsby, outfielders Chick Hafey and Billy Southworth,

and pitchers Grover Cleveland Alexander and Jesse Haines. Southworth is in Cooperstown as a manager, not as a player.
[22] Montville, *The Big Bam.*
[23] *Baseball Magazine*, January 1916.
[24] Ibid.
[25] *St. Louis Post-Dispatch*, June 6, 1915.
[26] Alexander did throw a no-hitter in the minor leagues while pitching for Galesburg in 1909.
[27] *The Sporting News*, November 15, 1950.
[28] *St. Louis Post-Dispatch*, April 12, 1918.
[29] *St. Louis Star*, April 17, 1918.
[30] Weeks of exposure to the sounds of war left Alexander deaf in his left ear. His right outer ear was damaged when it was hit by shrapnel. He later developed cancer in that same ear which resulted in its amputation. Skipper, John C. *Wicked Curve: The Life and Troubled Times of Grover Cleveland Alexander*. McFarland & Company, Inc. 2006.
[31] Former Cardinals pitcher Mordecai Browns holds the Cubs' single-season ERA record at 1.04, but the performance came before the team moved to what is now called Wrigley Field.
[32] Kavanaugh, Jack. *Ol' Pete: The Grover Cleveland Alexander Story.* Diamond Communications, Inc. 1996.
[33] *New York Times,* June 17, 1926.
[34] Range factor is calculated by adding putouts and assists divided by games played. Thevenow handled 1,013 chances at shortstop for the Cardinals in 1926. The next highest in all of baseball was 908. His range factor per game was 6.21. The league average was 4.98. Yankees shortstop Mark Koenig handled 755 chances that season with a range factor/game of 4.99. www.baseball-reference.com/leagues/MLB/1926-specialpos_ss-fielding.shtml
[35] *St. Louis Post-Dispatch,* August 27, 1926.
[36] Ibid, June 23, 1926. In his article on the pickup, Roy Stockton asserted that Cincinnati, Pittsburgh and St. Louis all claimed Alexander. Cubs manager Joe McCarthy told reporters only the Cardinals made a claim.
[37] Years later, Sid Keener claimed that Rickey did not want Alexander. "Rickey tried to block the negotiations. He didn't want Alex because of his off-duty habits." *St. Louis Star-Times*, February 22, 1950.
[38] *The Sporting News*, July 1, 1926.
[39] Alexander, *Rogers Hornsby*.
[40] The Cardinals had reportedly tried to acquire Alexander in the offseason prior to 1926. Hornsby "tried to arrange a swap with the Cubs during the winter, but his efforts to land Alex failed and instead the Cooney-for-Keen deal was consummated." *St. Louis Post-Dispatch*, June 23, 1926.
[41] Ibid, June 28, 1926. After Alexander's St. Louis debut, the Cardinals lost the second game of the doubleheader against the Cubs. The game was delayed 20 minutes in the top of the

ninth inning when fans threw soda bottles and seat cushions onto the field, in protest of an umpire's call. Amazingly, four years after Yankees outfielder Whitey Witt was knocked out cold, Sportsman's Park still sold soda in glass bottles. "In other cities it has been found dangerous to sell soda in bottles because excited fans will throw anything they can get their hands on. In many cities drinks are served in paper cups and it would be well to make a change here before players or umpires are killed by the morons."

[42] Ibid, September 8, 1926.

[43] On September 8, 1926, the Yankees hosted the Boston Red Sox. According to an account in *The New York Times,* Hornsby's six pitchers in the stands that day at Yankee Stadium were Grover Cleveland Alexander, Flint Rhem, Bill Sherdel, Alan Sothoron, Vic Keen and Jesse Haines. According to *Times* reporter James R. Harrison, Miller Huggins "instructed his athletes to keep their good stuff under cover." It must have worked. "Hornsby left the field gnashing his teeth bitterly." See *New York Times*, September 9, 1926. Some histories of the Cardinals have conflated the date of Hornsby's trip to New York with the team's exhibition game in New Haven. The game in Connecticut took place on Sunday, September 12. The Yankees were in Detroit that day where the game was canceled due to cold rain and light snow. *New York Times*, September 13, 1926.

[44] Lowenfish, *Branch Rickey.*

[45] *St. Louis Post-Dispatch*, September 13, 1926.

[46] The day after the fight, *The New York Times* put the Dempsey payday at $850,000 in one article and "as much as $800,000" in another story. Other estimates range between $700,000 and $800,000.

[47] Ruth likely earned somewhere between $850,000 and $900,000 from his major league career. Those totals don't reflect the considerable amount of money Ruth received from barnstorming tours and numerous endorsement deals he struck over the years.

[48] *New York Times,* September 16, 1926.

[49] Hauser, Thomas. "Jack Dempsey Revisited." www.secondsout.com/usa-boxing-news/usa-boxing-news/jack-dempsey-revisited

[50] "A flood of Tunney money…swept into Philadelphia at the last minute…" *New York Times*, September 24, 1926.

[51] Pietrusza, *Rothstein.*

[52] *New York Times*, September 25, 1926.

[53] Carmichael, John (editor). *My Greatest Day in Baseball: Forty-Seven Dramatic Stories by Forty-Seven Stars.* University of Nebraska Press. 1996.

[54] *St. Louis Times*, September 25, 1926.

[55] Graham, Frank. *The New York Yankees: An Informal History.* G.P. Putman's Sons. 1943.

[56] Steinberg and Spatz, *The Colonel and Hug*.

[57] For instance, in 2015 John Marsh wrote that "Hornsby skipped his own mother's funeral." See www.hardballtimes.com/trading-disgruntled-players/

A Fall Classic Begins

"I wonder if the Cards will ever win the pennant?"

"Not in our lifetime," Bill said.

"Gee, they'd go crazy," Nick said.

Ernest Hemingway's short story, *The Three-Day Blow*, featuring the dialogue between Bill and Nick, came out in 1925, just one year before the Cardinals achieved what Hemingway's characters could only dream about. The author may have had first-hand experience with the frustrations of Cardinals' fans. Of Hemingway's four wives, the first three grew up in St. Louis. The trio of women all came from well-to-do families and attended private schools in the area. Elizabeth Hadley Richardson (Mary Institute), Pauline Pfeiffer (Visitation Academy), and Martha Gellhorn (John Burroughs) would all go on to marry and eventually divorce the author.[1] "If one is perpetually doomed to marry people from St. Louis, it's best to marry them from the best families," Hemingway once wrote. "Anyone who's married three girls from St. Louis hasn't learned much," replied Gertrude Stein.

As part of the "Lost Generation" of American expatriates living in Paris after World War I, Hemingway traveled to Pamplona, Spain in the summer of 1925. The writer loved Spain, relished being ringside at bullfights, and soon became obsessed with one of his traveling partners, Lady Duff Twysden. Any attempt at a relationship was complicated by the fact that Twysden brought two of her lovers on the trip. The quartet drank heavily and fought repeatedly. Hemingway's six weeks in Spain became the basis of his first novel. It proved to be enormously influential. "I'm not sure that there was ever another moment when one novelist was so obviously the leader of a whole generation," said *Paris Review* editor Lorin Stein. "You read one sentence and it doesn't sound like anything that came before."[2] *The Sun Also Rises* was published in October of 1926.

October of 1926 brought the death of Harry Houdini in Detroit and the birth of Chuck Berry in St. Louis. The period also marked the end of one speculative boom while another marched on unabated. Land could be purchased in the backcountry of Fort Pierce, Florida for $150 an acre in 1922. Similar land fetched $1,000 an acre by 1925.[3] One year later, the real estate boom in the Sunshine State came crashing down when a massive hurricane smacked directly into Miami Beach. The Category 4 storm had winds of 128 MPH with storm surges of 12 to 15 feet. The "Great Miami" hurricane of September 18, 1926, killed more than 300 people and was described at the time as "probably the most destructive storm in the history of the United States."[4] Damage from the hurricane and the resulting publicity led to an immediate downturn in demand for land all over Florida. Among those impacted was Jacob Ruppert. The New York Yankees owner had significant real estate holdings on Florida's Gulf Coast and was planning a resort community near St. Petersburg when the hurricane hit. "Ruppert Beach" was never built.[5]

As the bottom fell out of the Florida real estate market, the boom in the 1920s stock market was just getting started. The Dow Jones Industrial Average stood at just over 150 in the fall of 1925, some 25 percent higher than where it ended the previous year. The index crossed 200 in December 1927 and hit 300 by the end of 1928. It reached a generational peak of 381 in September of 1929, a figure the index would not eclipse until 1954.

Among those caught up in the speculative fever was the star of the St. Louis Cardinals. Hornsby bought 1,000 shares of stock (largely on margin) in the Radio Corporation of America (RCA) in 1926, paying $52 a share. Formed in 1919, RCA quickly became the dominant communications company in the United States and the poster child for the infectious bubble of the decade. Three years after his purchase, RCA stock split 5-1. It would hit a post-split high of $114 a share, making Hornsby's stake worth hundreds of thousands of dollars.[6] He didn't sell, supposedly on the advice of his broker (and one-time Cardinals director) Mark Steinberg.[7] Hornsby's avarice was hardly unique. "When they pick up a newspaper now," Yankees manager Miller Huggins said of his players in 1927, "they turn to the financial page first and the sports page later."

The market crash of October 1929 triggered a grinding down of stock prices that lasted three years. By the summer of 1932, the market had lost 89 percent of its value. RCA stock bottomed at $2.50 a share.[8] Hornsby would miss an interest payment on his St. Louis County farm, triggering its foreclosure. Around the same time, Steinberg's firm went bankrupt and the New York Stock Exchange expelled the company for misrepresentations. But the misery of the stock market and the Great Depression belonged to the decade still to come.

These were The Roaring Twenties. Radio had entered a golden age.

*****

When Pittsburgh station KDKA broadcast the Harding-Cox presidential election returns in November of 1920, few people heard it. The overwhelming majority of Americans had no access to a radio. "Will anyone hearing this broadcast communicate with us," the station requested when it went on air just days before citizens went to the polls, "as we are anxious to know how far the broadcast is reaching and how it is being received." By the time President Warren Harding installed a radio in the White House in 1922, the nation had begun to rapidly embrace the transformational technology. Americans spent $60 million on radios and accessories in 1922. By 1926, that figure climbed to more than $500 million. In 1921, RCA earned a profit of $426,799. In 1923, the company reported net income of $4,737,774. The more than ten-fold increase was almost solely due to the increase in radio sales.[9]

Early radios were large, clunky, and difficult to operate. "They ran on batteries that weighed forty pounds," according to one historical account, "batteries that had to be recharged, batteries that sometimes leaked, that stained the carpet, that burnt holes in the floor." They were also expensive. A radio in 1921 could cost more than $100. That didn't include the headphones, antennae and battery. By 1930, the typical price had dropped to less than $20, speakers included.

The reduction in price coupled with user-friendly technologies and content the audience found compelling led to widespread adoption. "St. Louis is suffering from an acute attack of radiomania," one newspaper proclaimed in January of 1923 with radio sales in the city averaging $7,000 a week. "In street cars and elevators, across office desks and around lunch and bridge tables there is no other topic of conversation," touted the *St. Louis Star*. "Politics, sport, recipes for home brew and the fluctuating skirt level are dead issues by comparison."[10] What had once been considered a fad quickly mushroomed into a multi-million-dollar business. By the summer of 1927, one out of every three dollars Americans spent on furniture was spent on radios.

The sports world played a substantial role in the rise of commercial airwaves. The 1921 Dempsey-Carpentier fight was broadcast. So was a game of the 1921 World Series. A newspaper editor sitting at the Polo Grounds relayed the action between the Giants and Yankees to station WJZ in Newark, New Jersey where an announcer recreated the action for the listening audience. Radio broadcasts extended to the entire World Series in 1922, the same year the number of stations in America broadcasting zoomed to nearly 600. KDKA broadcast its first Pirates game in 1921. WLW in Cincinnati carried the Reds opener in 1924. Chicago radio stations began daily baseball broadcasts in 1925. The reaction was immediate and overwhelmingly positive. "Don't stop it," a farmer wrote to Cubs officials. "I have a radio in the field with me. I plow one turn, sit down for a cool drink out of the jug and listen to the score. It's grand."[11]

KMOX in St. Louis, which made its debut in December of 1925, experimented with live reports early in the 1926 season. "Baseball scores, inning by inning, direct from Sportsman's Park," read a published lineup of programming that also featured orchestra music and the "Housewives' Hour."[12] The live broadcast updates from the park ended after just a few weeks. Officials thought the cost was too expensive.[13] Another local station, WIL, carried recreations of Cardinals games during the team's September pennant drive, including the team's pennant-clinching win in New York. But what St. Louis fans had yet to hear was a live at-the-scene broadcast of a game, complete with the sounds of peanut vendors and passionate fans. Thanks to Graham McNamee, that all changed in the fall of 1926.

When McNamee wandered into station WEAF in New York City in 1923, he was unemployed and broke. But the concert baritone performer had a voice for radio. On lunch break from jury duty, he auditioned for a job. He was immediately hired as an announcer-singer. His big break came in the fall of that year when WEAF broadcast the World Series between the Yankees and the Giants. McNamee was assigned to the games along with sportswriter Grantland Rice. In the middle of the third game, Rice stepped aside.[14] McNamee did the rest of the Series solo.

A star was born. McNamee's enthusiastic style and vivid descriptions won fans over, despite the fact he knew little about baseball. "I don't know which game to write about," sportswriter Ring Lardner once admitted, "the one I saw or the one I heard Graham McNamee announce." McNamee would go on to broadcast every World Series through 1934 and become the voice of Universal Pictures newsreels. The concert singer viewed a baseball game as a theatrical performance. He paid close attention to the positioning of microphones around the stadium, giving his audience an earful of ballpark sounds. The effect was to transport the action from the field directly into a fan's living room. His style influenced a generation of future broadcasters. "The Series was sport and McNamee was the Series," remembered Jack Buck.[15] At the peak of his career, McNamee made more money than Babe Ruth.

Now, as Ruth and his teammates prepared to take on the Cardinals in the World Series, McNamee was again behind the microphone. St. Louis fans heard a familiar voice. McNamee was one of two broadcasters who called the Dempsey-Tunney fight carried by KSD less than two weeks earlier. The St. Louis station had joined a network of roughly two dozen stations that would carry the World Series broadcast to an audience across the United States and Canada. As a result, the 1926 Fall Classic was "the first true, easy-to-hear broadcast of the event."[16] The stations carrying the games formed the basis of the National Broadcasting Company (NBC) radio network, which made its debut one month later.[17]

Sixty-three thousand fans, including former heavyweight champion Dempsey, filed into Yankee Stadium on Saturday, October 2, for the first game of the Series, while an estimated 15 million listened on the radio.[18] "We are just about to go on," McNamee told his listeners. "The diamond and the ground and everything look beautiful. The dark brown chocolate color of the base line and the beautiful ground is wonderful."[19]

Some 10,000 fans gathered in downtown St. Louis to listen to the broadcast of the game with radios and loudspeakers set up in multiple locations. An enterprising twelve-year-old boy attracted a crowd by listening to the game with headphones then announcing the results with a megaphone. At the Odeon Theater on South Broadway, fans could watch every play diagrammed on an electric miniature playing field. Admission was $1. Most fans, though, were content to simply listen. "It is not necessary to have seen Babe Ruth, Rogers Hornsby and the rest in flesh," wrote *The New York*

Times, explaining the attraction of baseball on the radio. "All real fans have conceptions of these stars." But there was one concern on the minds of Cardinal fans listening on that fall Saturday afternoon. "McNamee's voice has a Yankee twang," warned the *Post-Dispatch*.

As the broadcaster described the scene at the ballpark, New York lefthander Herb Pennock stood on the mound and St. Louis center fielder Taylor Douthit walked to home plate. For the first time, a matchup between the Yankees and Cardinals mattered.

*****

On the sixth pitch of the game, Douthit rifled a ball into right field for a leadoff double. When Billy Southworth grounded out, Douthit advanced to third base. With one out, Hornsby came to the plate. "He is getting a hand from this New York crowd such as few men have gotten," McNamee told his radio audience. "His reception far outdid that of his rival Ruth," the *Times* noted the next day. The reception for Hornsby was as much sympathy as admiration. Fans knew his mother had died just days earlier. Hornsby grounded out to Pennock in what proved to be the start of a difficult day for the Cardinals second baseman and manager. He went 0-4 in the opener and only hit one ball out of the infield. "The edge was off his game," wrote Heywood Broun.

With Douthit still at third base, Jim Bottomley came to the plate with two outs. When the Cardinals first baseman hit a ball to deep short that Mark Koenig fielded on a bounce, Bottomley had an infield RBI single. Douthit scored to give St. Louis a 1-0 lead.

The advantage was short-lived. In the bottom of the first, Cardinals lefthander Bill Sherdel walked the bases loaded with one out. Lou Gehrig hit a ground ball to shortstop Tommy Thevenow who flipped to Hornsby for a force out at second base. But when Hornsby tried to complete the double play, his throw pulled Bottomley off the bag. Gehrig was safe at first while Yankees leadoff hitter Earle Combs raced across home plate to tie the game.

Both pitchers then settled in with each throwing four consecutive scoreless frames. The game was briefly interrupted in the bottom of the third inning when Ruth tore his pants as he slid into second base. "Babe Ruth, possibly having grown a bit in the past few days, has split a part of his accoutrements, which he needs very much in the game of baseball," McNamee explained. Out came the Yankees trainer with needle and thread to repair the uniform, much to the slugger's embarrassment. "Babe is the color of a nice red brick house," the broadcaster told his listeners.

In the top of the sixth, Pennock continued his mastery of St. Louis, retiring the Cardinals in order. Ruth led off the bottom of the inning with a base hit to left field. Playing for a single run, Yankees manager Miller Huggins had cleanup hitter Bob Meusel sacrifice Ruth to second base (although the Yankees led all of baseball with 121 home runs in the regular season and the Cardinals topped the National League with 90, both managers employed the sacrifice throughout the Series). When Gehrig knocked a single to right field, the Yankees had their first lead of the day.

In the top of the eighth inning and still down one run, the Cardinals had a chance when Pennock walked leadoff hitter Bob O'Farrell. St. Louis manager Hornsby employed the same small ball tactic that had previously paid off for Huggins. He had Thevenow bunt over Farrell. A big mistake, according to John McGraw. "Instead of stepping out boldly to win, they deliberately played for a tie, and got neither," said the New York Giants manager.[20] Farrell was out at third on an infield ground ball, and after the Yankees pitcher walked Douthit, pinch-hitter Wattie Holm ended the threat with a flyout to centerfield.

Still leading 2-1 in the top of the ninth inning, Pennock returned to the mound. With one out, Bottomley singled. It was the Cardinals first hit of the game since his RBI single in the first inning. But the lefthander proceeded to strike out Les Bell and induced a ground ball out off the bat of Chick Hafey. The Yankees had won the first game of the 1926 World Series. Their ace pitcher dominated the St. Louis lineup, allowing just three hits while going the distance for the victory. "The credit goes to Pennock. He deserves all the praise for pulling us through," said Huggins from a jubilant Yankees locker room where players were yelling and singing while Ruth was busy putting his signature on countless baseballs.[21]

From a decidedly quieter Cardinals locker room, manager Hornsby remained optimistic. "Our confidence is unshaken and the team came out of its first Series skirmish in great style. There may be a different tale to tell tomorrow." The tale of Game 2 would feature pitcher Grover Cleveland Alexander, the only member of the Cardinals alive when the city of St. Louis won its last championship. The storyline would once again be relayed to millions by McNamee. If Alexander gave St. Louis fans hope, so did the performance of the broadcaster in Game 1. "A Yankees fan, he nevertheless gave the Cards a square deal," the *Post-Dispatch* conceded.

*****

At five feet tall and weighing about 115 pounds, Morris "Butch" Yatkeman may have been one of the few men in baseball smaller than Miller Huggins. A St. Louis native, Yatkeman got his start in the game in 1923 working as the batboy for the visiting team at Sportsman's Park. The following year, he became the batboy for the Cardinals. "The batboy didn't have a uniform then," he recalled years later. "I did it in my street clothes." By 1938, Yatkeman had become the team's full-time equipment manager, a position he held until he retired after the 1982 season. The only member of the St. Louis Cardinals organization to have been a part of each of the franchise's first nine World Series titles, Yatkeman took his first road trip with the team in 1926. He was at Yankee Stadium that October.

Later dubbed the "indispensable man" by Bing Devine, the Cardinals general manager at the time, Yatkeman once explained the creativity he employed to became popular with players. One of them involved alcohol during Prohibition. The players wanted to drink on their long road trips but needed a way to smuggle the booze on the train. Yatkeman hired a carpenter to cutout a hiding space inside an equipment trunk.

Once accomplished, he could then stash bootleg whiskey inside the trunk, all the while avoiding spot checks from authorities at train stations.

Recalling the St. Louis players of that era, Yatkeman had especially fond memories of "Sunny Jim" Bottomley. "He really had that kind of disposition. I remember once he did me a favor and when I thanked him, he said, 'That's kind of you to say that, but if I've done something nice for you, pass it on,'" Yatkeman remembered. "He was a special man."[22]

Yatkeman never forgot an encounter with another member of the 1926 team, the starting pitcher for the second game of the World Series. "I was whistling a tune – 'Ain't Gonna Rain No More,' I think – and Alex, a quiet man, told me to knock it off. I don't know whether he was drunk or sober, but other players told me to forget it, that the old master just didn't like to hear whistling in the clubhouse."[23]

"The old master" was just four months shy of his fortieth birthday in the Fall of 1926. As Alexander warmed up on the infield on Sunday, October 3rd, a World Series record crowd of 63,600 jammed into Yankee Stadium on a warm and sunny day. Manager Hornsby mingled with New York City Mayor Jimmy Walker. Ruth had his picture taken that weekend with his family. It marked one of the last times Babe and wife Helen were seen together in public.

Yankees manager Huggins sent Urban Shocker to the mound, a veteran who had been in the game nearly as long as Alexander. The thirty-five-year-old spitballer and former St. Louis Brown, had gone 19-11 for the Yankees in the regular season. He quickly retired the first two Cardinals hitters when Hornsby walked to the plate. The Cardinals star once again received a "glowing reception" from the New York crowd. "He has a peculiar style," McNamee told his radio listeners, "he stands almost outside the box." When Hornsby lined the ball to right field for a double, he had his first hit of the Series. The threat quickly evaporated when Shocker got Bottomley to ground out to end the inning.

The Yankees struck first in the bottom of the second inning when Meusel scored on an RBI single by Tony Lazzeri. The New York second baseman added to the lead when Huggins ordered a double steal with runners at first and third and Shocker at the plate. The Cardinals had Lazzeri in a rundown between third and home, but he crossed the plate safely when Alexander made an errant throw. The unearned run put St. Louis in a 2-0 hole.

The Cardinals had an immediate answer. Both Douthit and Southworth reached on base hits and advanced to second and third on a bunt by Hornsby. Both scored on a single by Bottomley, who now had all three RBI for the Cardinals in the Series.

The two pitchers then settled down. Alexander and Shocker matched zeroes on the scoreboard until the top of the seventh inning. O'Farrell led off with a double and made it to third on a single by Thevenow. Just when it looked like St. Louis would fail to take advantage of the opportunity – Alexander and Douthit both popped out – Southworth came to the plate. On an inside pitch from Shocker, the Cardinals outfielder drove a fly ball to right field. As it drifted to the wall, Ruth backed up and ran out of room. The ball landed in the bleachers for a home run and the Cardinals had a three-run lead.

Many in the Yankee Stadium crowd roared their approval. Among those at the game was Colleen Moore, one of the biggest stars of the silent-screen. The actress who "personified the 'flapper' era" appeared in roughly 100 films and earned a million dollars a year at the peak of her popularity.[24] She rocketed to fame with the 1923 movie *Flaming Youth* in which she appeared with a Dutch bob haircut, spawning imitators across the country. The trend-setting performer married four times. She attended the game with her first husband, Hollywood producer John McCormick. As she watched Southworth's ball leave the yard, she joined the St. Louis rooters in celebration. "I hugged John so hard I almost wilted his collar."[25]

Just as he had done in the Cardinals pennant-clinching victory against the Giants just across the river at the Polo Grounds, Southworth had connected for what proved to be a game-winning blast. The Yankees manager wasn't impressed. "A foot shorter and it would have been a putout," said Miller Huggins after the game. His right fielder disagreed. "I couldn't have pulled in that drive with an eight-foot ladder," said Ruth.

New York had no answer. After a Combs leadoff single in the top of the third, Alexander set down 21 straight batters. He struck out the side in the fourth inning, becoming the first pitcher to perform that feat in a World Series game since Dutch Ruether, then with the Cincinnati Reds, in 1919 against the Chicago White Sox. Alexander went the distance, limiting the Yankees to just four hits and one earned run, while striking out ten. "His arm is no longer the arm of steel that pitched the Phillies to a pennant eleven years ago," observed Richard Vidmer. "His legs wobble when he walks. His eyes have grown dim in the service of baseball. But under the little gray cap, tipped sidewise and slanting, his brain has lost none of its cunning and still can outguess the younger generation of batters most of the time." [26] Of the 27 New York putouts, only one was recorded by a St. Louis outfielder.

In the top of the ninth, Thevenow hit a ball down the right-field line Ruth couldn't locate. "Not one of those birds in the bleachers would tell me where the ball was," the Yankees slugger said later. The Cardinals shortstop had an inside-the-park home run.[27] St. Louis had a 6-2 victory and tied the Series at one game apiece.

The newspapers the next day focused on Alexander's performance – "He held them. He toyed with them. They were thoroughly beaten," wrote James Gould in the *St. Louis Star* – and the behavior of the crowd. All those Cardinal fans in Yankee Stadium had the locals confused. "STADIUM CHEERS FOR CARDS," read part of a headline in the *Times*. "Sentiment is Strangely Against the Home Team."

"When Billy Southworth hit his home run, you would have thought Ruth hit it," Hornsby told reporters. "No home team today," McNamee told his radio audience.

After the win, the Cardinals quickly departed. Limousines waiting outside Yankee Stadium rushed the players to Penn Station. The team had a train to catch. The city of St. Louis had a party to throw.

*****

It had been thirty-three days since the Cardinals had last played a game at Sportsman's Park when the team arrived home on Monday, October 4th. The team left town at the beginning of September in the middle of a pennant chase. The Cardinals returned home as pennant winners. To commemorate the occasion, city officials had planned an elaborate celebration and parade for the team. Airplanes escorted the train the last 100 miles into the city. Crossing the Mississippi River, riverboats blew their whistles to signal the team's arrival. A dozen bombs on the levee were set to explode as the train crossed into Missouri. Not everything went according to plan.

Like the Cardinals, the Yankees had also left the stadium in a hurry following the Sunday game. The two teams and their respective railroad lines had engaged in a friendly competition to see who could make the westward trek from New York City to St. Louis the fastest. Taking the New York Central, the Yankees made it to St. Louis in 23 hours and 25 minutes, eclipsing the previous record by 15 minutes.[28] The "Flying Yankees Special" reached speeds of 72 MPH in parts of Indiana. Riding the Pennsylvania Railroad, the Cardinals had their train delayed nearly an hour by an accident. Eager St. Louis crews mistakenly took the train carrying the Yankees for the one carrying the home team. By the time the Yankees pulled into Union Station, many of the levee bombs had already been detonated.

The Cardinals arrived at the Washington Avenue station minutes later.[29] An estimated 100,000 fans had jammed into downtown to welcome the club. As players emerged from the train, bedlam ensued. St. Louis Mayor Victor Miller had to resort to his fists to battle his way to the front of the line. The mayor was attempting to escort Hornsby to his new Lincoln sedan, a gift from fans. When the crowd got their first look at the Cardinals star player and manager, they rushed toward him. Women ran their hands through his hair with some trying to kiss him. Men pounded him on his shoulders. "For a time, his predicament was precarious," the *Post-Dispatch* declared, "perilous from the threat of physical injury." Police had to form a flying wedge to subdue the crowd and give Hornsby space. His "disheveled and tearful" wife appeared a few minutes later. Their son, Billy, began to cry.[30]

Despite the chaos and deafening roar, the mayor briefly attempted to turn the event into a formal presentation. "Guess you didn't expect this?" the mayor asked. "Beyond expectations," Hornsby shouted in reply. "Nor this," Mayor Miller added, showing the Hornsbys their new automobile.

With three players to a car and the Hornsby family bringing up the rear (at the manager's request), the team paraded through thirty-four city blocks. It took four policemen on the running boards on each side of the Lincoln to escort Hornsby. Fans pressed forward all along the route to catch a glimpse of the man who had guided St. Louis to its first pennant in thirty-eight years. Young boys hung off the rear of the sedan. The Lincoln "was new when Hornsby arrived. Before he got home with it, it was scratched and marred by the pawing and frantic scratching of the mob, through which it had passed."[31]

In addition to the players, coaches, and front office personnel, the parade featured two bands, city authorities and baseball officials. Mounted police attempted, sometimes in vain, to clear the clogged route. Red was everywhere. Red ties, red flowers, red dresses, red hats. Horns blew. Cowbells rang. Confetti and torn paper rained down on the procession. The scene drew comparisons to celebrations last seen in the city at the end of World War I. "Never in the history of St. Louis has there been so much excitement over baseball," noted an account in the *Times.*

Lines formed Monday night for 7,500 unreserved pavilion and bleacher seats along with 3,500 standing room only tickets which were to go on sale Tuesday morning before Game 3. Scalpers offered tickets at $25 to $50 each, roughly five to ten times their face value. Anticipating a rowdy and sold-out crowd, the Cardinals announced a change in their soda bottle policy. To avoid a repeat of the 1922 "Little World Series" and the incident involving Yankees outfielder Whitey Witt, under no circumstances were the vendors to give the bottles to the fans. All attendants were instructed to open the bottles and pour the contents into a Lily cup

The city's hotels were full. The Hotel Statler, at the corner of Washington Avenue and 9th Street, accepted 750 reservations and refused another 375. Among the Coronado's 850 reservations were those of New York Giants manager John McGraw and owner Charles Stoneham. The Hotel Jefferson on Tucker Avenue acted as official baseball headquarters for the World Series. Its roster of guests included Commissioner Kenesaw Mountain Landis, National League president John Heydler, his American League counterpart, Ban Johnson, and dozens of East Coast baseball writers. Chicago Cubs owner Bill Veeck preferred to stay at the Chase while Chicago White Sox owner Charles Comiskey made reservations at the Mayfair. The former captain of the St. Louis Browns during their great run of the 1880s was "elated" by the Cardinals winning the pennant. "There is no city in the world that appreciates a winner better." From whatever downtown hotel the umpires resided, a limousine provided by St. Louis undertaker Arthur Donnelly would take them to and from games.[32]

The Yankees returned to the Buckingham Hotel. The New York contingent included owner Jacob Ruppert and Mayor Jimmy Walker. Only three Yankees received individual rooms: Manager Huggins, pitcher Bob Shawkey, and Ruth, although the Babe reportedly only received a room with a bath instead of his normal two-room suite.[33]

St. Louis players slept in their beds for the first time in over a month. Hornsby and his family returned to their apartment on Maple Avenue. The whirlwind of the past few weeks had taken its toll on the Cardinals star. It had only been ten days since the club clinched the pennant and just five since he got the news that his mother had died. In two World Series games, he had just one hit in seven at-bats. "Hornsby looked worn – unmistakably worn," when he arrived in St. Louis earlier that day. To a man consumed with baseball, the events in the city must have been a surreal experience. In the middle of a World Series, St. Louis residents responded with revelry normally associated with the end of the affair, the equivalent in football of fans storming the field and tearing down the goalposts at halftime. With the pandemonium of the parade behind him, the player/manager could now get back to the game he loved. October 5, 1926, marked the first modern World Series game ever to be played in the city of St. Louis. Hornsby had pitcher Jesse Haines ready to go.

*****

Growing up in Ohio, Jesse "Pop" Haines loved baseball so much, he'd hide his uniform in a corncrib. "My parents, good, honest, God-fearing people, objected to Sunday sports," he explained. On Sundays, Haines would take his uniform to a nearby cornfield to get dressed and then return it to the corncrib after the game was over to hide his participation from his deeply religious parents.

Born in Clayton, Ohio in July of 1893, the family moved to nearby Phillipsburg, just outside of Dayton, when Jesse was five years old. The son of an auctioneer, Haines began playing baseball at a young age. After high school, he started playing semi-pro ball and soon caught the attention of professional scouts. By 1913, he was playing in the minor leagues, where he'd spend parts or all of seven seasons. His only taste of the big leagues came when he threw batting practice for two months in 1915 for the Detroit Tigers and in one appearance for the Cincinnati Reds in 1918. With the Tigers, Haines received encouragement from Ty Cobb. "Say kid, you've got something on that fastball. It's hard to follow and some day, they're going to be talking about you."[34]

Despite the kind words from the legendary hitter and an effective appearance with the Reds (one run in five innings), Haines' career had stalled by the summer of 1919. Playing for Tulsa in the Western Leagues, he had a 5-9 record with an ERA over four. "I was just about ready to give up when I was traded on July 1, 1919, to Kansas City in the American Association." Motivated to give it one last try, Haines was spectacular for the Kansas City Blues, going 21-5 with an ERA of 2.11. The performance caught the eye of Rickey, who wanted to purchase Haines for the Cardinals. But the franchise didn't have the money to pull it off. "He (Rickey) got on his knees at every bank in St. Louis and they all turned him down," Haines recalled. Sam Breadon and some other stockholders kicked in the money to allow Rickey to make the move. For $10,000, Haines became a Cardinal in 1920.

Haines' former manager in Tulsa, Spencer Abbott, was so upset about the transaction he placed a wager with the manager in Kansas City. "Abbott, unhappy because he felt Haines had shown him up, bet Clarence Rowland a suit of clothes that Haines wouldn't last six weeks with St. Louis," said Commissioner Bowie Kuhn in 1970. "Jesse topped that by 930 weeks."[35] Kuhn told the story to a crowd assembled in Cooperstown, New York for Haines' induction into the Hall of Fame. Haines won 210 games for the Cardinals and wore the uniform of the National League team until he retired in 1937.[36]

The three-time 20-game winner threw a no-hitter in St. Louis in 1924 when he beat the Boston Braves 5-0. "Casey Stengel made the last out," Haines remembered. "He grounded out to Rogers Hornsby." It marked the first National League no-hitter in the city since George Washington Bradley had thrown the first one in league history for the original St. Louis Brown Stockings in 1876. After Haines performed the feat, there wouldn't be another NL no-hitter in St. Louis for fifty-four years.[37]

Despite the no-hit game in 1924, Haines struggled that season with a 13-14 record and an ERA of 4.57. He had experimented with a knuckleball for years and began throwing it regularly in 1926. He won 13 games again for the Cardinals that season but lost only four. He sliced more than a run off his ERA. "I worked on a knuckleball quite a while before I started using it consistently. Mine acted like a spitball. I had very good control of it and threw it from different positions." Unlike traditional knuckleball pitchers, who grip the baseball with their fingertips, Haines would rest the ball on the joints of his fingers. Given his grip and his ability to control the pitch, Haines possibly threw a knuckle-curve instead of a knuckleball. "He threw the knuckler harder than anyone you ever saw," remembered sportswriter Red Smith. Whatever it was called, the pitch probably extended his career by years. The man who didn't have a full-time big-league job until the age of 26 celebrated his 44th birthday his final year with the Cardinals.

Haines spent his winters repairing and selling cars with his brothers back in Ohio. Mild-mannered and pleasant off the field, he demanded perfection on the baseball diamond from himself and his teammates. When his batterymate, Pickles Dillhoefer, made a wild throw on a pickoff attempt in a game in 1920, allowing the only run of the game to score, Haines' teammates had to restrain the pitcher from jumping on his catcher in the clubhouse. A more mature Haines handled things differently as he got older. "He was noble of purpose," said Pepper Martin, who played with Haines in the 1930s. "After losing a tough low-score game, he'd flash vivid green eyes and kick a hole through a bucket filled with water."[38]

Nearly 38,000 paid fans flocked to Sportsman's Park for the third game of the World Series to witness Haines' fiery game-day demeanor. A career National Leaguer, the righthander had never faced the Yankees. New York pitcher Dutch Ruether, who spent the first eight years of his career in the NL, had faced St. Louis nearly three dozen times. His career record against the Cardinals was 12-11, but the lefthander struggled at Sportsman's Park, compiling a career ERA of more than six.

When the gates opened at 8:30 a.m., thousands dashed to fill the bleacher seats. Outside the stadium, thousands more, denied entrance to the sold-out game, milled around the streets where vendors charged as much as twenty-five cents for a sandwich. Neighborhood residents gathered on rooftops and chimney tops to catch a glimpse of the action. Downtown at the Boatman's Bank building, located at the corner of Broadway and Olive, hundreds of fans gathered on the roof to listen to the game on radio. St. Louis public schools closed early, as did just about every business in town.

Inside the park, Hornsby and Ruth signed autographs before the game for the St. Louis Chief of Police. Commissioner Landis and his son Reed, a World War I flying ace, had front row seats along the first-base line, close to the Yankees dugout. Giants manager McGraw was spotted in the upper deck. Red was again the color of the day. The iconic redbird logo was seemingly everywhere, except on St. Louis uniforms. Only the Cardinals road wear in 1926 featured the birds on the bat.

"Mardi Gras at Coney Island has nothing on St. Louis," Graham McNamee's broadcast partner, Philip Carlin, told the radio audience. Fans came armed with bells, horns, whistles, at least one bass drum, and whatever else they could find to make noise. "Mother is doing no cooking because Father has all the kitchen utensils fastened to his car," Carlin said.

The raucous crowd had some polite applause for the Yankees, but this was no bipartisan affair. Unlike Hornsby's warm reception in New York, Ruth was greeted with boos, hisses and groans when he came to the plate in the bottom of the first inning. "There was not a hypocrite in the St. Louis crowd," noted the *Times.*

The game remained scoreless until the fourth inning. In the top of the frame, Ruth singled and advanced to second on an infield groundout by Meusel. With Gehrig up, a heavy rain shower delayed the game for thirty-two minutes. As the grounds crew struggled to cover the infield with the tarpaulin, umbrellas popped up all over the park. As the crowd waited for the rain to end, McNamee stayed busy in the press box. "Everybody is writing me notes and bringing me telegrams," he said on the air. "Everybody having a good time but me."

When play resumed, Haines stranded Ruth at second by getting the next two hitters out. In the bottom of the inning, Bell led off with a single and advanced to second on a sacrifice by Hafey. When O'Farrell walked, the Cardinals had runners at first and second with one out. When Thevenow hit what looked to be an inning-ending double-play ground ball to second baseman Lazzeri, Ruether and the Yankees looked to escape the jam. But on a wet and muddy field, shortstop Koenig's throw to first sailed past Gehrig. Bell scored and the inning continued. Up to the plate came the Cardinals pitcher. In sixty-six plate appearances in the regular season, Haines hit .213. That was a big improvement over 1925 when he hit .176. He had one career home run. On the first pitch from Ruether, he added his second. When the ball landed in the right-field bleachers, the Cardinals had a 3-0 lead and St. Louis erupted. "There has never been a noise like it on a ball field," the *Times* pronounced.

The Cardinals added a run in the fifth inning but they didn't need it. Haines induced two double plays on the day, including one to end the game. In going the distance and pitching a shutout, the righthander allowed only five hits, all singles. Thanks to his arm and his bat, St. Louis won 4-0 and now had a 2-1 lead in the Series. "There was nothing to the game but Haines," Hornsby said from a celebratory Cardinals locker room. "I believe he could have shut out the Yankees for nine more innings the way he was going."

The Yankees and the New York media focused on the weather and Koenig's crucial error. "Mark Anthony Koenig tossed away the third game of the world's series with a double play and salvation in sight," asserted Richard Vidmer. Yes, he conceded, the muddy infield was not ideal, "but no one else, Cardinal or Yank, had any apparent difficulty in getting the ball where it was intended to go."

Koenig's defense had been a source of concern all year. At one point in the regular season, Huggins even experimented with Lazzeri at shortstop. But after three errors in six games, the manager returned the second baseman to his better position and reinstated Koenig into the lineup. The Yankee shortstop's performance stood in stark contrast to that of the young Cardinals middle infielder. Tommy Thevenow had handled all 17 chances cleanly in three World Series games. The shortstop the *Post-Dispatch* called the "fielding hero" was also hitting .333 against the Yankees.

Koenig (.083) was struggling at the plate along with the rest of the New York lineup. In three games, the Yankees had scored four runs and had 15 hits, all singles. "I can't see the Cardinals as a (better) ball club no matter if they did lick us," said a frustrated Ruth after the opener in St. Louis. "There are at least two better clubs in the National League – Pittsburgh and Cincinnati." The Yankees slugger thought the Cardinals caught a break when the game was delayed by rain in the top of the fourth inning. "Haines was clearly nervous at that moment," Ruth said.

The Yankees outfielder had just two hits in ten at-bats against the Cardinals. If New York had any chance of rebounding, their big slugger needed to get going. "When we start hitting," Ruth predicted, "it will be a different story."

*****

In the long and glorious career of George Herman Ruth, his most iconic and infamous baseball achievements occurred between 1926 and 1932. There was his magical 60-home-run season of 1927 and his called shot in the 1932 World Series. But perhaps no season and no Series featured as many moments as October of 1926. In that month, he achieved something no hitter had ever done before and did something no baserunner has done before or since. He also made a promise to a sick child that became the stuff of legend. The first of those moments came in the fourth game of the World Series.

St. Louis was riding high after Game 3. "CARDS CAN VIRTUALLY CLINCH SERIES TODAY," announced a headline from the *St. Louis Star.* "We are mighty confident today. And why not?" asked catcher Bob O'Farrell in the same newspaper. "I think we have an edge on the Yankees – a huge edge." A citywide party that started Monday afternoon with the arrival of the team rolled on Tuesday afternoon at Sportsman's Park. "If this city will go into ecstasy merely because the Cardinals came home...and leap to delirium on seeing them win a game," wondered *Times* reporter James Harrison, "what will it do if the Cardinals win the series?" The answer to that question would have to wait.

When Ruth would trot out to the outfield in Yankee Stadium, he would always head to right field. But at Sportsman's Park, Ruth played in left. He always drew the corner outfield post with the most shade. Meusel had to battle the sun. Standing in left field during batting practice before Game 4, showman Ruth began working the crowd. As bleacher fans called out for souvenir baseballs, the Babe tossed a few into the stands. Now in possession of a World Series baseball, the same fans wanted an autograph on their prized possession. Ruth obliged. Fans would hand their ball down to the slugger who scrawled his signature across it and then give it back. It was a good day to be in the bleachers. It was an even better day to be Babe Ruth.

The slugger hit his first home run of the day on the first pitch he saw from righthander Flint Rhem. The blast into the right-field bleachers gave the Yankees a short-lived 1-0 lead. A Hornsby RBI single off Yankees pitcher Waite Hoyt tied the game in the bottom of the first. That's where things stood when Rhem faced Ruth for a second and final time on the day.

Rhem and Ruth were teammates briefly on the Boston Braves near the end of both men's careers. If there was one man on the Cardinals who would have enjoyed the Babe at the peak of his late-night prowess, it was Charles Flint Rhem. The South Carolina native and former Clemson University engineering student is best known for drinking stories that might be described as Ruthian.

"I thought I was doing you a favor," he once explained to his manager in a hotel lobby after a late night out with fellow pitcher Grover Cleveland Alexander. "Me'n Alex were having a couple of drinks and I knew Alex was more important to the club than I was, so I drank twice as much and twice as fast so Alex wouldn't get too much to drink."[39]

His biggest drinking tale came in 1930 when the Cardinals were in Brooklyn for a key late-season series. Rhem went missing for 24 hours. When he finally surfaced, he told manager Gabby Street he'd been kidnapped by a group of gangsters who took him to a speakeasy and poured whiskey down his throat all night. They finally released him with a warning not to pitch against the Dodgers. It took thirty years, but the pitcher eventually told the truth about the incident. At an anniversary reunion of the pennant-winning team, Rhem admitted the story wasn't true. "I never left the hotel in New York," he confessed in 1960. "I had too much to drink, so I didn't make it to the ballpark."[40]

Although he pitched for four pennant-winning teams in St. Louis, Rhem never won a World Series game. His performance in 1926 was defined by 20 regular-season wins and the pitch to Ruth that came next. In the first inning, Rhem unsuccessfully tried to sneak a fastball past the Yankees outfielder. On his first delivery to Ruth in the third inning, he thought an off-speed delivery made more sense. It didn't. Ruth launched the ball over the pavilion in right-center field. It bounced on Grand Boulevard and smashed into a glass window of the Wells Motor Company. The five-feet by nine-feet pane was shattered. Only a portion of glass remained in place the next day when the company posted a sign: "This window broken by Babe Ruth." The car dealer awarded Ruth a Chevy sedan.[41]

Rhem lasted one more inning, giving up an RBI double to Joe Dugan in the top of the fourth inning to extend the Yankees lead to 3-1. But in a wild game that saw the two teams combine for a World Series record 28 hits, the Cardinals again had an answer. With one out in the bottom of the inning, Hafey singled. O'Farrell reached when Koenig committed an error, his second of the Series, on a ground ball. Thevenow, emerging as one of the stars of the Series, doubled down the right-field line, scoring Hafey. With runners at second and third and one out, Hornsby removed Rhem for pinch-hitter Specs Toporcer. His sacrifice fly tied the game. A Douthit double scored Thevenow and the Cardinals had their first and only lead of the day while the record crowd of 38,825 went wild. The booming applause lasted two to three minutes. With Hoyt and the Yankees reeling, Southworth came to the plate. He lined a single to left field. Douthit made the turn at third and headed for home. Ruth fielded the ball cleanly and the former pitcher fired a strike to the plate. The ball was waiting inside catcher Eric Severeid's glove as the runner arrived. Douthit was out and the Cardinal rally, three unearned runs, came to an end.

Although Douthit finished the game, he never appeared again in the 1926 World Series. He and Hafey collided in the outfield on Dugan's double in the top of the fourth. Third baseman Bell had to retrieve the ball. "They came together like two express trains," said McNamee. The collision knocked both men unconscious. Dr. Robert Hyland and the Cardinals trainer rushed onto the field. Smelling salts, cold water, and waving towels revived the players. Just minutes later, Douthit gunned down Dugan at home plate after a single by Severeid. The Cardinals center fielder ended the top of the fourth inning with a great throw and was the victim of a great throw by Ruth in the bottom of the frame. Backup outfielder Wattie Holm replaced him in the lineup for the final three games.

With the Cardinals leading 4-3, Hornsby went to reliever Art Reinhart in the top of the fifth. The lefthander hadn't pitched in fourteen days. The rust quickly showed. He walked four of the first five hitters he faced, including Ruth. The Yankees scored four runs on one base hit and led 7-4.

The Yankees struck again in the sixth. In hitting his second home run in the third inning, Ruth had tied a World Series record shared by three players, including himself. No one had ever hit three in a single postseason game. With one on and one out, Ruth came to the plate facing reliever Hi Bell. With the count at 3-2, McNamee described the scene to those listening on radio.

"The Babe is waving that wand of his over the plate. Bell is loosening up his arm. The Babe hits it clear into the center field bleachers for a home run! For a home run! Did you hear what I said? Where is that fellow who told me not to talk about Ruth anymore? Send him up here.

"Oh, what a shot! Directly over second. The boys are all over him over there. One of the boys is riding on Ruth's back. Oh, what a shot! Directly over second base far into the bleachers out in center field, and almost on a line and then that dumbbell, where is he, who told me not to talk about Ruth! Oh, boy! Not that I love Ruth, but, oh, how I love to see a shot like that! Wow!

"That was probably the longest hit ever made in Sportsman's Park. They tell me this is the first ball ever hit in the center field stand. That is a mile and a half from here. You know what I mean."

"If the bleachers hadn't been there," Cardinals third baseman Les Bell said later, "I think that ball would have torn down the YMCA across the street." Ruth's blast made the score 9-4 in favor of the Yankees. Each team would score one more run to make the final 10-5 in favor of New York. Hoyt went the distance for the Yankees to gain the victory and tie the Series at two games each.

Ruth came to bat one last time in the eighth inning, but the Cardinals wanted no part of him. He walked on four pitches, his second free pass of the afternoon. He finished the day three-for-three with three home runs, four RBI, and four runs scored.

After his third home run, Ruth returned to left field for the bottom of the inning. The crowd began to stir as soon as he emerged from the dugout. By the time he made it to the outfield grass, the bleacher fans in left field stood as one to acknowledge the Yankee star. As they "cheered, and cheered, and cheered," Ruth stopped, put his hands on his hips, and paused to acknowledge the reception. Clearly relishing the moment, the Babe then turned to the center field bleachers and tipped his cap in their direction. The gesture ignited another round of cheers and standing ovations. With one last acknowledgment in the direction of the left-field faithful, the long and thunderous applause finally came to an end.

It all happened at Sportsman's Park in St. Louis on the afternoon of October 6, 1926.

---

[1] Richardson and Gellhorn were born in St. Louis. Pfeiffer was born in Iowa, grew up in St. Louis, and graduated from the University of Missouri School of Journalism in 1918. She met Hemingway in Paris in 1926 while working for *Vogue*.

[2] Blume, Lesley M. *Everyone Behaves Badly: The True Story Behind Hemingway's Masterpiece The Sun Also Rises.* Houghton Mifflin Harcourt Publishing Company. 2016.

[3] *New York Times*, November 22, 1925. That same year, the *Miami Herald* sold so many ads, it needed 504 pages to print a single edition, setting a record at the time for American newspapers. Eig, *Get Capone.*

[4] Quote from Official-in-Charge Richard Gray of the Miami Weather Bureau Office. See www.weather.gov/images/mfl/events/1926hurricane/1926_hurricane_WBO1.jpg

[5] "Ruppert Beach On Pass-A-Grille-Key: Where Every Breath Brings Added Health And Every Moment Pleasure." *The Evening Independent*, March 10, 1926.

[6] RCA stock split five-for-one in February of 1929. www.gold-eagle.com/article/rca-1925-1929-and-microsoft-1994-1998-0

[7] Alexander, *Rogers Hornsby*. "Steinberg predicted the stock would continue to rise so Hornsby held on to his 1,000 shares."

---

[8] www.worststockmarketcrashes.com/crash-of-1929/rca-stock-price-after-the-1929-stock-crash/
[9] *New York Times*, September 21, 1924.
[10] *St. Louis Star*, January 6, 1923.
[11] Ehrgott, *Mr. Wrigley's Ball Club.*
[12] *St. Louis Post-Dispatch*, May 17, 1926.
[13] "St. Louis Cardinals' Radio History" at stlmediahistory.com. www.stlmediahistory.com/index.php/Radio/RadioArticles/st.-louis-cardinals-radio-history
[14] Barber, Red. *The Broadcasters*. The Dial Press. 1970.
[15] baseballhall.org/discover/awards/ford-c-frick/2016-candidates/mcnamee-graham
[16] Montville, *The Big Bam*. The 1927 Rose Bowl, which Graham McNamee also broadcast, is frequently credited with being the first coast-to-coast sports broadcast. But the 1926 World Series came three months earlier. "In a fraction of a second," *The New York Times* noted after Game 1, "the thrill of each exciting incident ran from coast to coast and probably from below the Mexican border to points around Hudson Bay."
[17] The World Series was also carried in St. Louis by radio station KMOX. It was a recreation based on wire reports. "Through the courtesy of the Associated Press and the *Globe-Democrat*, the story of the game will be a running description of each pitched ball." *St. Louis Globe-Democrat,* October 5, 1926. Porter Brown, who played in the KMOX radio orchestra, was the broadcaster. Since KSD was owned by the *Post-Dispatch* at the time, the *Globe-Democrat* ignored its competitor's coverage and touted its own.
[18] The paid crowd at Yankee Stadium was listed the next day at 61,658.
[19] *New York Times*, October 3, 1926. The *Times* published a transcript of the radio broadcast for every game of the series.
[20] *St. Louis Post-Dispatch*, October 3, 1926.
[21] Ibid.
[22] *New York Times*, October 25, 1982.
[23] *St. Louis Post-Dispatch*, October 13, 1977
[24] *New York Times*, January 26, 1988.
[25] *St. Louis Star*, October 4, 1926.
[26] *New York Times*, October 4, 1926.
[27] Thevenow never hit a home run over the wall. He hit two home runs in the 1926 regular season – both were inside-the-park. After the one in the 1926 World Series, he didn't hit another home run the rest of his career.
[28] *New York Times*, October 5, 1926. The *Times* recorded the Yankees arrival at 3:40 p.m. on Monday afternoon. The *Post-Dispatch* had the New York team arriving at 3:45 p.m. Both papers agreed the time beat the previous record by 15 minutes.
[29] The Cardinals would have normally stopped at Union Station, but "fearing that people might be trampled in the scramble to see the home-coming heroes," Union Station officials contacted the Cardinals to ask them to stop at Washington Avenue instead, according to

Stationmaster Ray O'Neill. "We breathed a sigh of relief when they agreed." *The Sporting News*, January 10, 1962.
[30] *St. Louis Post-Dispatch*, October 5, 1926.
[31] Ibid.
[32] The tradition to give umpires rides to and from games was started by Donnelly in 1909 after seeing an umpire attacked by fans at Sportsman's Park. At his funeral in 1930, eight umpires acted as pallbearers. One of them, Bill Klem, worked the 1926 World Series. Donnelly's son continued the tradition following his death. *St. Louis Globe-Democrat,* November 17, 1929 and July 15, 1951. *St. Louis Post-Dispatch,* December 31, 1930.
[33] *St. Louis Post-Dispatch*, September 30, 1926.
[34] Ibid, January 26, 1969.
[35] *The Sporting News*, August 8, 1970.
[36] The Veterans Committee selection of Haines was not without controversy. Bill James and others have criticized the pitcher as one of the worst players to make it to Cooperstown. The righthander finished his career with a 210-158 record and an ERA of 3.58. Haines' selection came at a time when his former manager Frankie Frisch and *St. Louis Post-Dispatch* sports editor J. Roy Stockton served on the Veterans Committee (the same body elected Chick Hafey in 1971 and Jim Bottomley in 1974). Haines' Hall of Fame class included Yankees outfielder Earle Combs, another Veterans Committee selection. In July of 1934, Combs crashed into the outfield wall at Sportsman's Park. Knocked unconscious, he suffered a broken collarbone and a fractured skull. Combs retired after the 1935 season.
[37] The next National League pitcher to throw a no-hitter in St. Louis after Haines in 1924 was Bob Forsch in April of 1978. He shutout the Phillies 5-0. Making his first start for the St. Louis Browns, Bobo Holloman threw the last American League no-hitter in the city in May of 1953. He shutout the Philadelphia Athletics 6-0. Holloman finished the year with a record of 3-7 and an ERA of 5.23, his one and only season in the major leagues.
[38] *St. Louis Post-Dispatch*, February 10, 1964.
[39] Ibid, October 20, 1976.
[40] Ibid, August 7, 1960.
[41] The company wasted little time in posting a larger and more formal sign that read: "WELLS MOTOR CO., WINDOW BROKEN when BABE RUTH Drove The Ball Over Right Field Pavilion Breaking All Records For Home Runs In One Series Game." Ruth had his picture taken with the sign that was turned into an ad for the company. Wells Motor Company then started selling cars with a "Babe Ruth Steering Wheel" that featured a likeness of the Babe in the center.

A Fall Classic Ends

The following day, October 7, began with a warning from the city's chief of police. "The gangsters and Italian gunmen must get out of St. Louis if we have to shoot them out," declared Chief Joseph Gerk. The night before, just hours after Ruth's epic performance, local cops auditioned a new riot pistol that fired shotgun shells loaded with buckshot that "worked so perfectly that more of the same type may be ordered." The recipient of one of the blasts was twenty-one-year-old Joseph Bommarito, identified as a former gangster with a criminal record that included 59 prior arrests. In a car chase through downtown St. Louis, Bommarito was driving with his left hand while holding a .45-caliber automatic with his right hand. Police fired buckshot from the rear that fatally struck Bommarito in the neck and head. He was still holding his weapon when police pulled his body from the car.[1]

"Detectives added another death to the growing toll in the deadly bootleg war between Cuckoo gangsters and the Italian gunmen last night," explained the *Post-Dispatch.* The Cuckoo Gang was one of five outlaw groups that dominated St. Louis in the 1920s.[2] Determined to win the war to control illegal booze, the gangs often resorted to violence. Their victims included Missouri State Senator and theater owner Joseph Mogler. Making the rounds of his establishments on a Monday morning, Mogler was killed instantly when a masked gunman shot him in the face. The murder "had all the makings of a professional hit" and remains unsolved.[3]

Mogler was known to sign bail bonds for various gangsters and underworld figures. A judge once asked him why he would get involved with such a crowd. "I know it, judge," Mogler replied, "but I can't help it."[4] His death came at a time when nine members of a Cuckoo Gang rival – Egan's Rats – were behind bars. One of the members of the Egan crew once took orders from Al Capone. Fred "Killer" Burke was among the suspected gunmen in the St. Valentine's Day massacre of 1929.

"I tell them I want peace," Capone said in the fall of 1926 regarding gang violence, "because I don't want to break the hearts of people that love me – and maybe I can make them think of their mothers and sisters. And if they think of them, they'll put up their guns and treat their business like any other man treats his, as something to work and forget when he goes home at night."[5] One day before the start of the World Series between the Cardinals and Yankees, Capone was indicted on charges of conspiracy to violate Prohibition laws. The charges were later dropped. The U.S. Attorney decided to wait. In May of 1927, the Supreme Court ruled that bootleggers must file income tax returns. Thanks to the high court and Eddie O'Hare, the notorious gangster's days were numbered. By one estimate, 33 people died as a result of Capone's decisions over the years.[6]

"Too many policemen are being killed, too many innocent bystanders are being wounded, too many bootlegger feudists are shooting it out on the streets, too many murders are being committed," editorialized the *St. Louis Star* in October of 1926. "The criminal no longer fears the consequence of his acts."

A more peaceful battle played out at the intersection of Grand and Dodier.

*****

He was known as a world champion and his fame spread from Australia to the United Kingdom. In the fall of 1926, he made his way to St. Louis. Lowell, Massachusetts' native James Leo "One-Eyed" Connolly started as a boxer, but his career ended when he lost his left eye in a fight.[7] No longer able to jump in the ring, he started crashing the gate of boxing matches. He became so accomplished at talking his way into arenas, he expanded his scope to baseball games, horse races, and political conventions. By the 1920s, his fame had reached a level to where newspapers tracked his every movement. "One-Eyed Connolly Invades New Orleans For Racing Season," read a headline from the *Post-Dispatch* in 1922.

His ventures were not always successful. "Last week I had a little trouble in Baltimore getting into a National Guard meeting," he admitted in 1924. "When I appeared in uniform they put handcuffs on me and threatened to ship me to Atlanta. I'm not going to play any more gates as close as that," confessed a chastened Connolly.[8] Attempting to get into a boxing match in England a few years later, British authorities sent him packing. Connolly called it his first defeat in thirty years of gate-crashing.[9]

Near the end of his life, he found an easier way to access sporting events. Connolly became a ticket-taker in Chicago. At the 1945 World Series between the Cubs and Detroit Tigers, he halted a man hurrying through a gate. "Where d'ya think you're going, buddy?" Connolly demanded. "To my office. I'm Phil Wrigley," came the reply from the Cubs owner. "Baloney," snapped Connolly. "They all give me that." The ticket-taker was soon "laid off temporarily."[10]

At the fifth game of the 1926 World Series, McNamee spotted him from the broadcast booth. "I see One-Eye Connolly up there. He crashed the gate again," McNamee told his listeners. "Did you pay your way in? He says he didn't."

Connolly joined a Thursday afternoon crowd to watch a rematch of Game 1 pitchers, Sherdel for the Cardinals and Pennock for the Yankees. Before the game, Ruth counted 813 telegrams and messages of congratulations for his performance the day before. The anticipation of what the Babe might do next and the last game of the year at

Sportsman's Park drew a record St. Louis crowd of nearly 40,000 paid customers and at least one gate-crasher.[11] "One-Eyed Connolly, the nationally known gate-crasher, is standing up with his hat in his characteristic manner," McNamee said in the fourth inning. "I don't know why he always wears the peak of his cap over on his right ear."

The Cardinals broke out on top in the bottom of the fourth on a Bottomley double and an RBI single from Bell. In the top of the sixth, Hafey slipped on a Pennock fly ball to left field and the pitcher had a leadoff double. With Combs up, Cardinals catcher O'Farrell fired the ball down to second on an attempted pickoff play. Thevenow had Pennock blocked from the bag, but the Cardinals shortstop dropped the ball. Thevenow was charged with an error. When Sherdel walked Combs, the Yankees had runners at first and second with no one out. After two bunt attempts by Koenig, the shortstop then singled to left field. Pennock scored and New York had tied the game at one.

Ruth came to the plate. A walk would have loaded the bases with no outs. After a visit to the mound by Hornsby and Bottomley, Sherdel began pitching to the Yankees slugger. With the count 2-2, Sherdel delivered a pitch over the heart of the plate. "If there was ever a ball that Ruth should have hit it was this one," declared *Times* reporter Harrison. Instead, the Babe swung and missed, much to the delight of the St. Louis crowd. "The tumult that greeted Mr. Ruth's three homers yesterday was a golden silence compared to the demonstration following his one strikeout today," Harrison wrote.

The anxious crowd soon had another worry. Sherdel injured a finger on his pitching hand on a return throw from the catcher. After running to the bench for treatment, the pitcher returned to the mound. Sherdel retired Meusel on a fly ball but then walked Gehrig. With two outs, the Yankees had loaded the bases with Lazzeri coming to the plate. On the fifth pitch, the New York second baseman drove the ball to deep right field. Southworth ran to the fence. With his back scraping the wall and the wind blowing in, the Cardinals outfielder caught the ball for the final out of the inning. Sherdel had escaped wlth Just one run allowed.

The game remained tied at one until the bottom of the seventh inning. Bell led off with a double to left field. When O'Farrell singled, Bell scored, and the Cardinals had regained their one-run lead. Sherdel, despite the injured finger, managed to hold the Yankees to just one run and five hits through the first eight innings. He returned to the mound in the top of the ninth with a chance to win the contest and give the Cardinals a crucial three-games-to-two-lead in the Series.

Sherdel's tough luck inning started immediately. Gehrig hit a wind-aided fly ball that landed for a double down the left-field line. The ball barely eluded the outstretched glove of shortstop Thevenow. Lazzeri's bunt turned into a base hit when he beat the throw from third baseman Bell. With runners at first and third, Huggins swapped out Dugan for pinch-hitter Ben Paschal. The Yankee third baseman had gone 0-3 on the day. "Dugan was so annoyed by this managerial move that he flung his bat to the ground, walked out through the St. Louis bench and turned his back on the inning," recorded the *Times.*

Huggins' move paid off. With the infield in and the outfield deep, Paschal hit a fly ball to short left-center field. It dropped for a single and the Yankees tied the game when Gehrig crossed the plate. With runners at first and second, Severeid attempted a bunt. When the ball bounced directly in front of the plate, O'Farrell grabbed it and threw to third base. Bell tagged out Lazzeri attempting to advance and the Cardinals had the first out of the inning. Although he pinch-hit for Dugan, Huggins elected to keep Pennock in the game. The lefthander grounded out as did Combs. Sherdel sidestepped any further damage.

Pennock made quick work of the Cardinals in the bottom of the ninth, retiring Bottomley, Bell, and Hafey in order. The starting pitchers and the game moved on to extra innings. Just as he had in the top of the ninth, Sherdel found himself in immediate hot water. Koenig singled to lead off the inning. After a wild pitch advanced him to second base, the Cardinals pitcher walked Ruth. Still playing small ball, Huggins had Meusel bunt the baserunners over. Gehrig was given an intentional pass and for the second time in the game, Lazzeri batted with the bases loaded. He drove the ball to deep left field where Hafey caught it for the second out of the inning. But Koenig easily trotted home with the go-ahead run, and for the first time all day, the Yankees had a lead. Sherdel then ended the inning by retiring Severeid on a pop fly to Hornsby on his 154th and final pitch of the day.

The Cardinals had no answer. When Pennock retired Holm with one on and two outs in the bottom of the tenth, the Yankees had a 3-2 win in the game and a 3-2 lead in the Series. In beating the Cardinals for the second time, the New York pitcher had now thrown 19 innings against St. Louis, walking just four batters and allowing only three runs. The game also marked a vindication of sorts for Yankees shortstop Koenig. Blamed for the loss in Game 3, he drove in the tying run in the sixth inning and scored the game-winning run in the tenth. "Mark Anthony Koenig has balanced the books," wrote Richard Vidmer. "He became indebted to the New York American League baseball club and the members thereof when he tossed away the third game of the current classic. Today he paid his debt in full."

In a series largely dominated by starting pitching and defense, Hornsby blamed his fielders for the loss. "Hafey misjudged that fly of Pennock's in the sixth inning," he said after the game. He also thought Gehrig's leadoff double in the ninth inning should have been an out. "Even with the sun and twice as much wind, the ball should have been caught," the manager claimed.

The Cardinals now faced the prospect of heading to New York and having to win both games in Yankee Stadium over the weekend to celebrate a championship. Just as he did in Game 2, Hornsby would again turn to his veteran righthander claimed on waivers from the Cubs back in June. "On the good right arm of Grover Cleveland Alexander rest all the hopes and ambitions of baseball mad St. Louis," Harrison wrote in the *Times*. The

Cardinals would indeed rely on the "good right arm" of Alexander in their attempt to win the Series. But not even the thirty-nine-year-old righthander realized how integral he would be. The Game 6 starting pitcher would be the last man standing on the mound Saturday. Sunday, too.

*****

Following the final game in St. Louis, all the players and officials of both teams quickly exited the ballpark and again dashed to the train station. All, that is, except for Ruth. The Babe had plans to spend another night in town. He left Sportsman's Park and went to the home of Louis Nolte, the longtime comptroller for the city of St. Louis.[12] Once there, he either remembered or was informed his team was heading out. Nolte then drove Ruth to Union Station. Too late. The train had already departed. Nolte then rushed Ruth to the North St. Louis station where the Babe climbed on board just in time. With the slugger in tow and with a lead in the Series, the Yankees had a happy ride home.

The Cardinals arrived first in Manhattan. Departing St. Louis at 5:00 p.m. on Thursday, the team pulled into Penn Station at 3:20 p.m. Eastern time on Friday. The 1,051 mile-long-trip on the Pennsylvania Railroad lasted just 21 hours and 20 minutes, the fastest trip ever from St. Louis to New York, forty minutes ahead of schedule. Traveling on the longer New York Central route (1,158 miles), the Yankees arrived that evening at Grand Central in 23 hours and 35 minutes.[13]

The Cardinals returned to a city that considered them heavy underdogs. "The feeling in New York is that the Yanks, despite the fact that Alex is to pitch, will win today and end it all," James Gould informed his St. Louis readers the following morning. "No provision has been made for an advance sale of Sunday tickets."[14]

Cardinals owner Breadon, who arrived on the train with his club, voiced confidence in his players. "We still have the best chances to win," he told reporters. "We have two better pitchers ready to go than the Yankees have. Pennock was the only man they had who could have beat us and he is through for the Series. We have Alex and Haines." Breadon's vice president did not make the trip to New York. Rickey stayed behind in St. Louis, where just like thousands of others in the city, he tuned in to KSD radio on Saturday afternoon to hang on every word from Graham McNamee. "The weather is just a little bit cooler than at any of the other games," McNamee told his radio listeners as the action got underway at Yankee Stadium. "Clear with a lovely speckled sky."

Heavyweight champion Gene Tunney was spotted in the crowd wearing a sombrero, but the cooler weather kept many others away. Just 48,615 paid to see a game thoroughly dominated by the visiting team. The Cardinals jumped on Yankees starter Bob Shawkey for three runs in the first inning and never looked back. St. Louis pounded out 13 hits, including four doubles, a triple, and a Les Bell home run that drew the largest applause of the day. After the game, a Cardinals fan complained to the *Times*, "The fans here do not even bring megaphones to help things along. The only place I can get plenty of noise here is in the subway."

The Yankees had their chances. Their leadoff man reached base six times against Alexander. The Cardinals made two errors. On two separate occasions, Ruth came to bat with two men on. In each instance, he failed to get the ball out of the infield. With runners in scoring position, New York had just one hit in 15 opportunities. St. Louis converted five of 12 such chances.

When the Cardinals knocked Shawkey out of the game with a five-run seventh inning, St. Louis had a commanding 9-1 lead. Hornsby kept Alexander in the game. Despite allowing eight hits and two walks and looking "older and (acting) more tired," the righthander still went the distance in a 10-2 Cardinals win. Alexander had his second victory against the Yankees and St. Louis had evened the Series with New York.[15] Bell was the star of the day. The Cardinals third baseman went three-for-four and tied a World Series record with four RBI. He joined a list of standout offensive performers on the St. Louis squad that included Southworth (.400 batting average in the Series with ten runs scored), Thevenow (.350 Series average), and Bottomley (.346 batting average with 12 total bases).

The marquee players of the matchup, though, had either struggled or largely been contained, and the papers on Sunday morning offered a review of their past performance and a clue to future actions. Hornsby had five hits in the Series, only one of them for extra bases. Ruth had been spectacular in Game 4, but outside of his three-home-run showing, the slugger had just two singles in the other five contests. He did have the Yankees first and only stolen base in the Series. It happened late in Game 6 and it came off Alexander and Cardinals catcher O'Farrell. Few people noticed. But Ruth remembered.

Sunday morning, October 10, 1926, arrived with cloudy skies and a steady drizzle of rain. The sun didn't peek out of the clouds until around 1:00 p.m., about an hour before game time. Poor weather, combined with the decision not to sell any Game 7 tickets in advance, suppressed attendance. A stadium that attracted more than sixty-thousand fans for each of the first two games of the Series drew only 38,000 paid customers for the finale. "It is very dark," McNamee told his radio audience as the game began. "It is a good day for fastball pitching."

The pitching matchup featured Haines, the Game 3 winner for the Cardinals, and Hoyt, the Game 4 winner for the Yankees. Ruth brightened the day for the hometown fans in the third inning with a solo home run, snapping a World Series scoreless streak by Haines that came up one out short of 12 innings. With four home runs in seven games against the Cardinals, Ruth set a World Series record. The Yankees had a 1-0 lead but it didn't last long.

With one on and one out in the top of the fourth inning, the Yankees defense fell apart. With Bottomley at first base, Bell hit a ground ball to Koenig that looked like a certain double play. But when the Yankees shortstop fumbled the ball, Bell reached on the error and the Cardinals had a threat brewing. When Hafey singled on a bloop fly ball to left field, St. Louis had loaded the bases. O'Farrell then lifted a fly ball to the outfield.

Playing in left field at Yankee Stadium, strong-armed Meusel waved off center fielder Combs and prepared to make a throw to home plate. Bottomley stood on third base and waited for Meusel to make the grab. In a hurry to make the throw, he forgot to make the catch. Meusel stunned the Yankee Stadium crowd by dropping the ball. Bottomley raced home and the Cardinals had tied the game on back-to-back errors.

With the bases still loaded, Hoyt had two strikes on Thevenow and looked to exit the inning with the game tied. But the St. Louis shortstop, in the middle of many World Series rallies, delivered one more time. His single to right-center field scored two runs and the Cardinals had a 3-1 lead. All the runs were unearned. St. Louis wouldn't score again.

The Yankees got one back in the bottom of the sixth inning. Dugan singled with two outs, and Severeid drove a ball to left field that Hafey charged aggressively. When it got past him, the catcher had a double instead of a single. Dugan scored to cut the lead to 3-2.

Huggins went to his bullpen in the seventh as Pennock replaced Hoyt. Haines remained in the game for the Cardinals. Combs led off the bottom of the inning with a single. Koenig sacrificed him to second and the Cardinals intentionally walked Ruth. With two on and one out, Meusel hit a ball to third base. Bell had the opportunity to step on the bag and fire the ball across the diamond to complete the double play. Instead, he elected to go around-the-horn and threw to second base. Hornsby stepped on the bag for the second out but his relay throw to first base was too late. When Gehrig walked, the Yankees had a runner on every base with two outs.

With Lazzeri coming to the plate, a base hit likely meant the lead for the Yankees. The Cardinals also had other issues. Haines, the knuckleball pitcher, had worn the skin off the index finger of his pitching hand. With his pitcher bleeding and the bases loaded, Hornsby elected to go to his bullpen. Since Alexander went the distance the day before and the teams had a travel day on Friday, Hornsby had a well-rested staff. With a full complement of options, the manager chose the oldest guy on the team and the pitcher with the least amount of time off. On a dull and cloudy Sunday afternoon, a ghostly figure emerged from the bullpen beyond the outfield wall at Yankee Stadium.

"Over the long green stretch of left field he lumbered, his shoulders bent, his crooked legs wobbling, his shoulders drooping," wrote Vidmer in the *Times*. "Not an imposing figure, nor a fearful one. He looked more like an old man, bent with age. But as he drew nearer it was seen that his little gray cap was tipped sidewise and slanting at a disdainful, cocky, devil-may-care angle. And the crowd roared one word as it recognized him:

"Alexander!"

Not even 24 hours after finishing off the Yankees on Saturday, Alexander was back on the mound with no margin for error. He likely didn't take a single warmup toss in the bullpen before walking in.[16] On the way to the mound, he assessed the situation as Lazzeri waited to hit. "Tony is up there all alone, with everyone in that Sunday crowd watching him," he recalled. "So I just said to myself, 'Take your time. Lazzeri isn't feeling too good up there and let him stew,'" Alexander said of the Yankee second baseman who led all American League hitters in strikeouts during the regular season.

The epileptic veteran pitcher now faced off against the epileptic rookie second baseman.[17] With the count 1-1, Lazzeri drove a deep fly ball down the left-field line. It was foul.[18] Back in St. Louis, Branch Rickey's radio had gone out. He was now listening to McNamee's broadcast from a neighbor's house. "Wait and see, Jane," Rickey told his wife. "Alexander will take it nice and easy and get impatient Lazzeri out."[19]

On the next pitch, O'Farrell signaled for a curveball. Alexander delivered a breaking ball, low and away from the right-handed hitter. "Everything I had was on that pitch," he said afterward. Lazzeri swung and missed. "I looked up and saw the crowd cheering madly," Alexander remembered. "It was a great moment for me; the greatest that I had ever experienced in the big leagues. But there were two more innings to be played and Ruth yet to be heard from."[20]

After a scoreless eighth inning and top of the ninth, Alexander faced the top of the Yankees lineup in the bottom of the inning. He quickly retired Combs and Koenig on ground balls to third base. The Babe came to the plate as the Yankees last chance but still a threat to tie the game. Hornsby went to the mound to talk strategy with his pitcher. "It seems that Hornsby wanted Alexander to pass Ruth and Alexander didn't want to do it," McNamee told his radio listeners. Alexander pitched him carefully. With the count 3-2, he just missed on a ball outside. Ruth walked for the fourth time on the afternoon.

Modern-day sabremetricians calculate that with a runner on first base and two outs, stealing second increases the odds of scoring a run by roughly ten percent. They've also determined that over the long run, a base runner needs to be successful about 75 percent of the time for the stolen base to make sense. In the regular season, Ruth had snared 11 bags. He had also been caught nine times making his success rate just 55 percent. But he had stolen second just the day before in an almost identical scenario – Alexander on the mound and O'Farrell behind the plate. On the righthander's first pitch to Meusel on Sunday, the Babe decided to try it one more time.

As Ruth steamed toward second, Alexander sent the ball toward the plate. The pitch was a strike. His catcher then fired the baseball over the mound to the second base bag. "I caught the blur of Ruth starting for second as I pitched and then came the whistle of the ball as O'Farrell rifled it to second," the pitcher recalled.

Waiting for the greatest American League player of the 1920s was the greatest National League player of the same decade. Hornsby grabbed the throw and tagged out Ruth. The game was over. For the first time in the history of the franchise, the St. Louis Cardinals were World Series champions. "My biggest thrill in all of baseball," Hornsby later wrote in his autobiography, "was making a simple tag on a runner trying to steal second base."

For the third time in less than a month, St. Louis erupted. Thousands poured into the streets of downtown for what the *Post-Dispatch* called a "9-Hour Rampage." The roar of the radio was quickly eclipsed by bells, horns, sirens, and shouts. South of town on the Meramec River, three shotgun blasts indicated a Cardinals victory. At least 30 people were injured, and one person was killed, amidst the celebration. Seventeen-year-old William G. Troll Jr. was clinging to the running board of a sedan when the car made a turn and came too close to an approaching streetcar. Troll was knocked off and suffered fractures to his skull, collarbone, left shoulder and left leg. He died two hours later.[21]

The seven-game affair set 19 World Series records and brought the highest attendance and most receipts ever for a Fall Classic. Despite bad weather the final weekend, 328,051 fans turned out for four games in New York and three in St. Louis, paying a total of $1,207,864 to witness the action. Ruth alone set 10 records and tied three others. In addition to the most home runs in a single game, Ruth's accomplishments included scoring the most runs in a single game with four and receiving the most walks in a Series with 11. The Yankee slugger participated in his seventh World Series, also a record. Ruth and his teammates each received a check for $3,723, while the winning St. Louis players celebrated a payment of $5,594.50.

The achievements of the 1926 Cardinals marked the capstone of a change in philosophy at the very top of the organization. Under owner Breadon and general manager Rickey, the Cardinals committed to developing homegrown talent. Bell, Bottomley, and Thevenow in the infield joined Blades, Douthit and Hafey in the outfield as players who came up through the St. Louis farm system. Through player development and shrewd acquisitions, the club developed a blueprint for how smaller market teams could compete. Twenty-one players on the Cardinals roster cost the franchise a grand total of $39,000 to acquire.[22] "In all the talk about the late World Series, I heard no mention of the name of Mr. Rickey nor of [scout] Mr. Barrett. Yet they are indubitably the master-minds of the outfit," wrote Damon Runyon.[23]

Back in New York, the papers focused on the Yankees sloppy defense and the three unearned runs in the finale. "Koenig and Meusel Hand Cardinals Title On Silver Platter," read a headline from *The Brooklyn Daily Eagle*. Ruth's caught stealing, the only time in the history of the World Series when the affair has ended on such a play, received far less coverage.[24] His manager defended Babe's decision. If Ruth had been successful, Huggins pointed out, the Yankees would have needed only one more hit instead of two to tie the game. Cardinals catcher O'Farrell went on a barnstorming tour with Ruth a year or two after the events of October 1926 and asked the slugger about it. "Ruth said he thought Alex had forgotten he was there," O'Farrell recalled.[25]

What Alexander hadn't forgotten was how to pitch. He won Games 2 and 6 and saved Game 7. The pitcher who struck out just 47 hitters in 200.1 regular-season innings, fanned 17 Yankees in just 20.1 innings in the postseason. Cut loose by the Cubs in June, he stood tall for the Cardinals in October. While shortstop Thevenow was the offensive star of the Series (ten hits in twenty-four at-bats for a team-best batting average of .417 with one home run, four RBI and five runs scored), it's the legend of Alexander that lives on.

O'Farrell claimed Alexander was drunk the night before the final game. "Alex didn't really intend to take a drink that night," he explained later. "But some of his 'friends' got hold of him and thought they were doing him a favor buying him a drink. Well, you weren't doing Alex any favor buying him a drink, because he just couldn't stop."[26]

Years later, the pitcher attempted to set the record straight in an interview that appeared in *Baseball Digest*. "I don't want to spoil anyone's story, but I was cold sober that night," Alexander told Gerry Hern. "There were plenty of other nights before and since that I have not been sober, although I have been cold, but the night before I struck Lazzeri out, I was as sober as a judge should be."[27] He and Hornsby had talked after Game 6, so he knew he might be called on the next day. Another part of the tale involves Alexander napping or having a pint of whiskey with him when summoned in the seventh inning of Game 7. According to teammate Sherdel, Alexander spent most of his time that Sunday afternoon talking to Pennock, the Yankee pitcher sitting in the nearby bullpen of the home team.[28] The denials, however, came long after the legend had taken hold. "Hornsby told me later," Alexander's wife once confessed to a reporter, "'The biggest mistake we made, Amy, was not in denying the story from the start. At the time it made for good reading, so we let it go.'"[29]

There is one final legacy of the 1926 World Series. It involves Alexander and his former club, the Cardinals rival to the North. Since 1916, Chicago's National League team played in a stadium called Cubs Park. After the 1926 season, the franchise announced plans to double-deck the venue. It reopened in 1927 with the name it has held ever since, Wrigley Field. "In most people's minds Cubs Park meant the place where Grover Alexander worked," wrote author Roberts Ehrgott, "and that would never happen again."

For all but a brief period in 1930 with the Phillies, Alexander would spend the rest of his career with the Cardinals. In his first half-season in St. Louis, the pitcher helped deliver to the Cardinals what would elude the Cubs for another nine decades. A World Series defined by Alexander's arm and the Babe's bat ended on a play involving Ruth's legs and Hornsby's glove. "I'll always remember putting the ball on him. He didn't say a word," Hornsby remembered. "He just picked himself off the ground and walked away to the dugout and I had lived through the greatest day any man could ask."[30]

---

[1] *St. Louis Star*, October 7, 1926.

[2] In addition to the Cuckoos, there were Egan's Rats, the Hogan Gang, the Pillow Gang and the Green Ones. themobmuseum.org/blog/double-crossing-mob-murders-green-ones-st-louis/

[3] Waugh, *The Gangs of St. Louis: Men of Respect.* The History Press. 2010.

---

[4] *St. Louis Star*, December 3, 1929.
[5] Eig, *Get Capone.*
[6] The list of Capone's victims can be found at Chicagology.com. See chicagology.com/notorious-chicago/capone/. The list includes Anthony Russo and Vincent Spicuzza, allegedly imported from St. Louis to assassinate Capone. The pair was gunned down in Chicago on August 11, 1927. The Mob Museum story disputes this account, pointing to the Green Ones as the likely culprits.
[7] Sometimes spelled as "Connelly" in press accounts.
[8] *New York Times*, October 4, 1924.
[9] *Ibid*, July 1, 1927.
[10] *St. Louis Post-Dispatch*, October 9, 1945.
[11] Paid attendance was 39,552. Total crowd was estimated at 41,000.
[12] "The Bambino, Hart Chandler of Pittsburgh, and George E. Thomas of St. Louis were the guests of Louis P. Nolte, City Comptroller, following the game at Sportsman's Park." *St. Louis Globe-Democrat*, October 8, 1926. First elected in 1917, Nolte served as the chief financial officer of the city for 32 years. Shortly after the death of his wife, the 78-year-old Nolte took his own life on New Year's Day, 1950. *St. Louis Post-Dispatch*, January 4, 1950.
[13] *New York Times*, October 9, 1926.
[14] *St. Louis Star*, October 8, 1926.
[15] "Resting" a pitcher wasn't a consideration during this era of baseball. "It is a fallacy that a pitcher can ruin his arm with too much work. I've never heard of it yet," Rickey once said. "Arms are hurt by slipping off the pitching rubber, by favoring a leg as for sciatica or trying new trick deliveries. But overwork? Never." *Baseball Digest*, August 1946.
[16] Accounts vary but most support the idea that Alexander didn't warmup in the bullpen. According to Sherdel, "he wasn't warmed up when he walked in from the bullpen. I know because I was in the bullpen with him," the pitcher recalled years later. "In those days, an incoming pitcher was allowed five pitches. After the five, the umpire dusted the plate and you were on your own." *The Sporting News*, March 5, 1966. Alexander told a similar story. He said his arm was "free and loose" and that he "threw four or five practice balls to O'Farrell." *St. Louis Post-Dispatch,* October 11, 1926. "So in I walked to that game without even taking off my sweater," he recalled years later. "I was cold, but if Hornsby needed me, I was ready to pitch." *Baseball Digest*, January 1951.
[17] Lazzeri died from a fall at the age of 42. Some people thought he may have suffered an epileptic seizure, but the coroner ruled it a heart attack. *New York Times*, March 4, 1991.
[18] Various accounts over the years have played up Lazzeri's foul ball. Taylor Spink of *The Sporting News* described it as a "ball which was foul by inches." Hornsby said it was foul by ten inches. Catcher O'Farrell, with as good a vantage point as anyone that day, said it was "foul by maybe ten feet." Alexander gave a similar account. The foul ball was barely noted in newspaper accounts the following day.
[19] Lowenfish, *Branch Rickey*.

---

[20] *St. Louis Post-Dispatch*, October 11, 1926. Alexander's Hall of Fame plaque reads in part: "Won 1926 World Championship for Cardinals by striking out Lazzeri with bases full in final crisis at Yankee Stadium." After Lazzeri died, Red Smith wrote that the Yankee second baseman never told how he felt about the moment. "Interviewing that guy," one reporter complained, "is like mining coal with a nail file." *Baseball Digest*, October 1946.
[21] Ibid. A fourth celebration was planned when the team returned to St. Louis. Nine players showed up at Sportsman's Park on Monday where an estimated 35,000 fans had gathered. "Horns shrieked, cowbells clanked and clattered, and the throng shouted itself hoarse," read one account the following day. "It finally became so unmanageable that the program had to be abandoned and the players, who were scheduled to address the fans, left the park without being heard." *St. Louis Star*, October 12, 1926.
[22] *St. Louis Post-Dispatch,* September 17, 1926.
[23] *Dayton Herald*, October 22, 1926. Like Barrett, Jack Ryan was a scout for the Cardinals in 1926. "Barrett and I were responsible for seven of the nine men that started on the '26 club, and we didn't even get a pack of cigarettes out of the Series." *Baseball Digest,* November 1945 (Winter Issue).
[24] Game 3 of the 1911 World Series also ended on a caught stealing. Ruth's out ended the game and the Series. *The Brooklyn Daily Eagle* defended Ruth's decision. "Ruth Was Justified In Attempt to Steal," read one sub-headline the following day. In 2011, author Bill Jenkinson wrote a detailed description of Ruth's stolen base attempt, the reasons behind it and the reactions to it. See newyork.cbslocal.com/2011/07/29/by-the-numbers-judging-babe-ruth%E2%80%99s-attempted-steal-of-second-base-in-the-1926-world-series/ for more. Sheldon Hirsch also defended Ruth's action in a 2013 article at Real Clear Sports. www.realclearsports.com/articles/2013/11/13/babe_ruths_miscue_was_no_blunder.html
[25] Yankees GM Barrow said he never asked Ruth about the play. But he admitted years later, it was the only time "that I felt like killing him." *St. Louis Star-Times*, February 6, 1950.
[26] Ritter, *The Glory of Their Times.*
[27] *Baseball Digest*, January 1951. The story had originally appeared in the *Boston Post*.
[28] "I answered the phone when Hornsby called. I thought he wanted me," Sherdel said in 1966. "'I don't want you, Bill. I want Pete,' Hornsby said. Pete had spent most of his time down there talking to Herb Pennock. The bullpens were close." *The Sporting News,* March 5, 1966. Sherdel's memory may not be entirely accurate. The earliest anyone has ever been able to place a phone in the bullpen at Yankee Stadium has been 1930. "Dugout Phones: Last Bastion of the Landline," *New York Times*, October 22, 2011. Hornsby later wrote that he just waived in Alexander from the bullpen.
[29] Kavanaugh, *Ol' Pete.*
[30] Carmichael, *My Greatest Day in Baseball.*

St. Louis Browns owner Chris Von der Ahe brought beer and championship baseball to Sportsman's Park in the 1880s. *(Library of Congress)*

The 1899 St. Louis "Perfectos." One year later, the team would adopt the name it has been called ever since, the Cardinals. *(Library of Congress)*

Shown here with fellow National League owners, Helene Britton became the first female owner of a major professional sports team when she took control of the Cardinals in 1911. *(Library of Congress)*

Britton's first manager was Roger Bresnahan (foreground). After the 1912 season, Britton fired Bresnahan and replaced him with Miller Huggins (background).
(Library of Congress)

Cardinals manager Huggins (left), shown here in 1913 with New York Giants manager John McGraw and umpire Bill Brennan, made quite an impression in St. Louis. "There is no smarter man in baseball today than Miller Huggins," said McGraw.
(Library of Congress)

Britton's divorce from husband Schuyler led to the sale of the Cardinals, and the hiring of Branch Rickey. *(Library of Congress)*

Before he joined the Cardinals, Rickey played for and later managed the St. Louis Browns. "Rickey is a practical baseball man in every sense of the word, having made good as a player, coach, and scout," said *Sporting Life* magazine, "he ought to become one of the really great leaders of the national game." *(Library of Congress)*

First at the University of Michigan and later with the Browns, George Sisler was Rickey's first big star. *(Library of Congress)*

Sisler (left), shown here with Babe Ruth and Ty Cobb, won the inaugural American League MVP Award in 1922. Ruth won it the following year. *(Library of Congress)*

Ruth, shown here in 1919 with the Boston Red Sox, was primarily a pitcher in his early days. His first start in the outfield came against the St. Louis Browns in 1918. He loved coming to the city. "I always had a lot of high-living friends [in St. Louis]," Ruth said. *(Library of Congress)*

Ruth battled Commissioner Kenesaw Mountain Landis (left) over his betting and drinking, and Yankees owner Jacob Ruppert (right) over contracts. Ruppert owned a brewery and his background and history are strikingly similar to that of Gussie Busch. *(Library of Congress)*

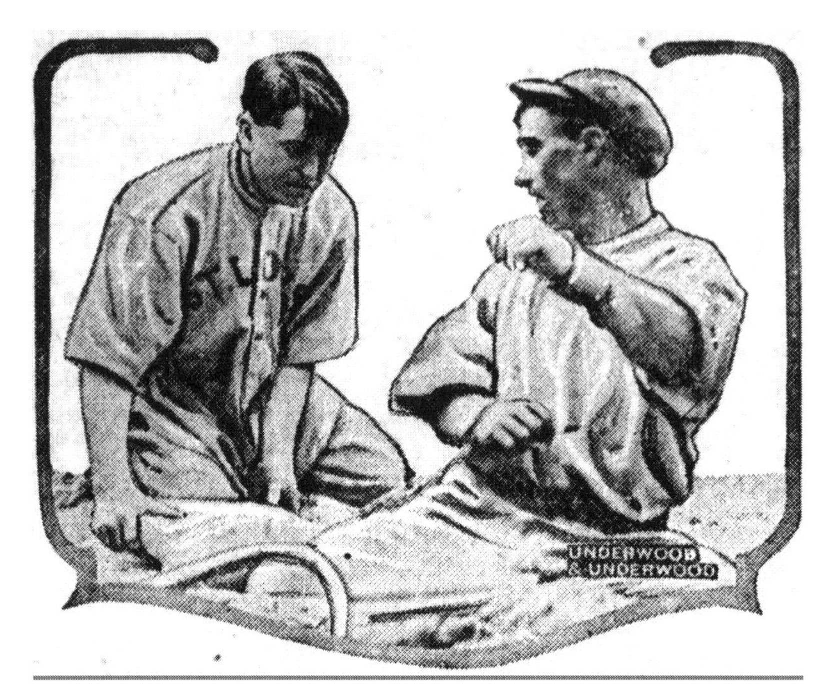

Rickey had a passion for coaching and teaching. Here, in spring training of 1921, Cardinals manager Rickey (left) is helping an unidentified rookie learn the proper way to slide into a base. *(Newspapers.com)*

Rogers Hornsby in 1921, at the beginning of one of the greatest five-year stretches in baseball history. From 1921 to 1925, Hornsby hit .402 and won two Triple Crowns. "He is the squarest, bluntest, cussingest and most convincing man I ever met in baseball," said one writer. (*Newspapers.com*)

By 1922, Rickey was not only managing the Cardinals, he was also building the game's first great farm system. His tryout camps would lure thousands of potential players over the years. "I offered them a better way of life," Rickey said. (*Newspapers.com*)

Hall of Fame pitchers Dizzy Dean (left) and Grover Cleveland Alexander (right) each won a World Series with the Cardinals. Dean won two games in 1934, while Alexander recorded two victories and a save in 1926. For both men, it was the only World Series win of their careers. (*St. Louis Globe-Democrat Photo/St. Louis Mercantile Library Collection)*

Lindy Gives Cards World Series Rings

LINDBERGH was presented with a handsome model of the Spirit of St. Louis in gold and then made distribution of the world championship rings to the Cardinals. This picture shows, left to right: Rogers Hornsby, Mayor Miller, Lindbergh, himself; Umpire Moran and Pitcher Reinhart of the Cards.

After making his historic trans-Atlantic flight on the *Spirit of St. Louis* in 1927, Charles Lindbergh returned to the city to raise the World Series flag and hand out World Series rings. *(St. Louis Globe-Democrat Photo/St. Louis Mercantile Library Collection)*

For many Cardinals fans, the 1926 World Series represented the first-ever live radio broadcast of a baseball game they had heard. The man behind the microphone was Graham McNamee (shown here in 1924). McNamee broadcast every World Series from 1923 to 1934, and Lindbergh's return to the United States in 1927.
(Library of Congress)

First in St. Louis and later in Brooklyn (shown here in 1946), Rickey kept track of every player in the organization. His blackboard in St. Louis became so popular with curious visitors, he had window shades installed. (*Look Magazine Photograph Collection, Prints and Photographs Division, Library of Congress)*

More than a decade after Rickey's Brooklyn Dodgers broke baseball's color barrier, Bill White and the Cardinals helped bring an end to spring training segregation in the 1960s. *(St. Louis Globe-Democrat Photo/St. Louis Mercantile Library Collection)*

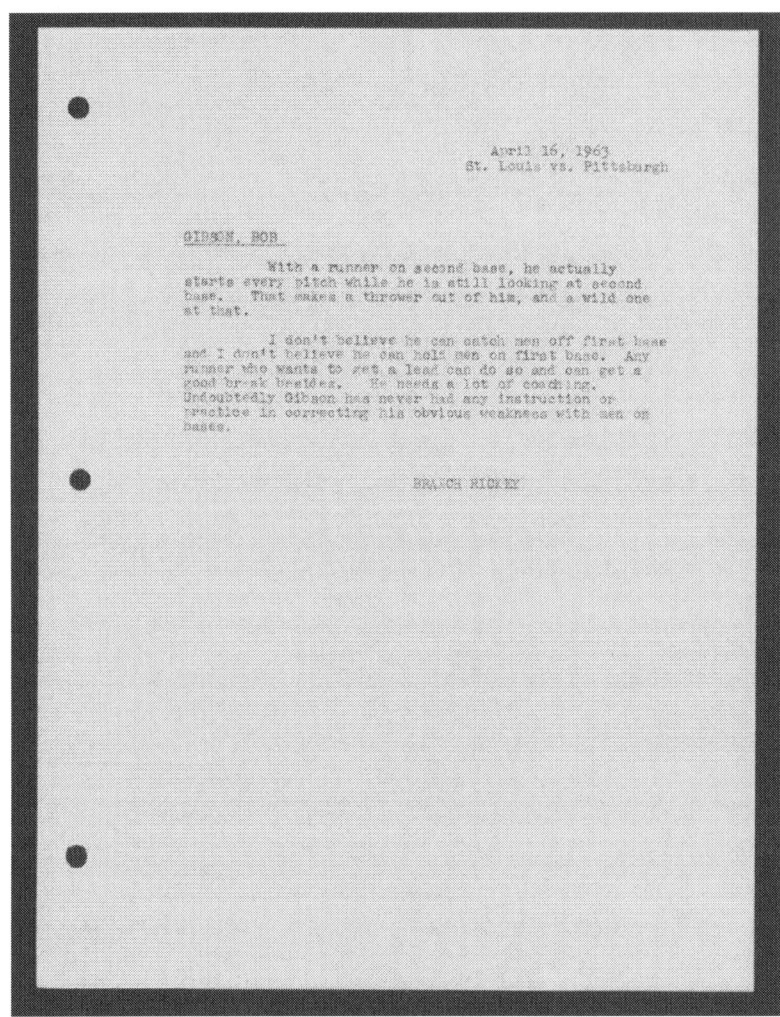

April 16, 1963
St. Louis vs. Pittsburgh

<u>GIBSON, BOB</u>

With a runner on second base, he actually starts every pitch while he is still looking at second base. That makes a thrower out of him, and a wild one at that.

I don't believe he can catch men off first base and I don't believe he can hold men on first base. Any runner who wants to get a lead can do so and can get a good break besides. He needs a lot of coaching. Undoubtedly Gibson has never had any instruction or practice in correcting his obvious weakness with men on bases.

BRANCH RICKEY

"He is considered the greatest judge of ballplayers in the world," is how columnist Roy Stockton once described Rickey. Here, in 1963, Rickey is not crazy about a young Bob Gibson's ability to hold runners on base. "He needs a lot of coaching," Rickey wrote. A talent evaluator nearly his entire adult life, Rickey filed his last scouting report for the Cardinals in October of 1964, just days before the team let him go. *(Library of Congress, Manuscript Division, Branch Rickey Papers)*

Legends, Lies, and Lindbergh

By the time his team boarded the train at Penn Station to head home after winning the first World Series in franchise history, the thoughts of majority owner and Cardinals president Sam Breadon had already turned to 1927. At odds with his manager over a series of exhibition games late in the season, Breadon was also increasingly worried about Hornsby's relationship with a bookmaker. The owner had seen him more than once sitting on the team bench before a game. He was also upset that several players were spotted looking over racing forms in the dugout.[1] Breadon had the racing forms banned, but the bookmaker, Frank L. Moore of Fort Thomas, Kentucky, continued to make appearances. With Hornsby's behavior weighing on his mind, he summoned coach Bill Killefer to his compartment. "Would you be interested in managing the Cardinals next season?" Breadon wanted to know.

When the Cardinals train pulled into Union Station Monday afternoon, Hornsby remained in his compartment for thirty minutes. He was both anxious to avoid the crowds and irritated that Breadon didn't come into the locker room at Yankee Stadium to congratulate the team. When he did venture out, he discovered he couldn't completely avoid the throngs that had shown up to greet the World Series champions. Besieged by fans in a celebratory mood, Hornsby had to run across tracks and through other trains. Accompanied by his wife and son, he then boarded a train headed to Texas. His mother's postponed funeral was now two days away.

Hornsby and his family arrived in Austin on Tuesday night. He had last seen his mother at her sixty-third birthday party in March when the Cardinals were in the middle of spring training. He first viewed her body three days after clinching the World Series. "Early in the day it was feared he would collapse," Louis La Coss informed readers of the *Globe-Democrat* the next morning, adding that Hornsby "was believed to be close to a nervous breakdown." He spent the funeral with his head buried in his hands.[2]

Later that day, the Hornsbys were traveling to the gravesite after the funeral. A cousin of Rogers was driving and had to slam the brakes to avoid hitting the vehicle in front of him. The close call threw Rogers' son Billy into the windshield. On the same day Mary Rogers Hornsby was buried, her grandson had to have three stitches sewn in his forehead. A difficult offseason for Mary's son and Billy's father had only just begun.

Rumblings of a split between Hornsby and Breadon soon reached the papers. "Rogers Hornsby May Go to Giants in Trade for Frisch," read a headline in the *Globe-Democrat* just 17 days after the World Series ended. "There has been gossip that there is not much harmony between Hornsby and Breadon and Rickey," wrote sports editor Glenn L. Wallar. Citing a report out of New York that Hornsby would be dealt for the Giants second baseman, Wallar explained that it would be "impossible to verify the matter at this time." But with just one year left on Hornsby's contract, conjecture about his future quickly consumed St. Louis. "It has been said in the street that Hornsby will not be with the Cardinals next year," Roy Stockton told his *Post-Dispatch* readers in November. "You can hear in any gathering place the 'inside story' of the trouble between Hornsby and Breadon."

As far as Hornsby was concerned, there were three sticking points. Two of them involved alcohol and gambling.

Earlier in the season, Branch Rickey had asked Prohibition enforcement officers to catch a bootlegger allegedly selling whiskey to the team. Hornsby wasn't consulted about the move and viewed the request by the Cardinals vice president as interfering on his turf.[3]

Hornsby and Breadon had argued in the past about the manager's bookmaker friend. Hornsby's connection with Moore so worried Breadon that he planned to insert a clause in the player/manager's new contract that banned him from gambling of any kind as well as any association with professional betting agents. Knowing Hornsby as he did, he likely knew his manager would vociferously object to any oversight of his off-field behavior. "The races have cost me a lot of money, it is true," Hornsby once admitted, "but it's my dough and as a free-born American citizen, I can do what I want with it."[4]

The final source of friction between Breadon and Hornsby involved that postgame conversation in Pittsburgh when the owner informed his manager that the team had to honor some previously scheduled exhibition games. Hornsby had unloaded on Breadon when told the decision. The owner didn't forget how he was treated. When the team celebrated the World Series title in New York, Breadon was noticeably absent from the locker room. This upset Hornsby and some of the players as well, many of whom already felt slighted by only receiving two tickets each to the World Series.

"However, there is no cause for worry," Stockton assured his readers. "The chances are good Hornsby and Breadon will come to an agreement." But when the two men met in early December, it was apparent they had considerable ground to close before any deal could be struck. The primary issue wasn't money but length of the deal. Breadon was only interested in offering Hornsby a one-year contract. Hornsby insisted on a three-year arrangement. "The length of the contract was the first thing we talked of and the last," Breadon said afterward. "We never got around to anything else."

With the two men still at odds, Breadon headed to New York the following week for baseball meetings. While there, he again approached Killefer about becoming the manager. For the second time, the Cardinals pitching coach of 1926 turned down the opportunity to manage the team in 1927. Steadfastly loyal to Hornsby, he soon took a job as a coach with the St. Louis Browns. "I do not think that Hornsby was treated fairly during the season and I do not think he is being treated fairly now," Killefer said.[5]

The acknowledgment, first reported in the *St. Louis Star* on December 16, that Breadon had offered Killefer the manager's job on two separate occasions spawned another round of rumors. The day after the story broke, speculation focused on former Cardinals player/manager Roger Bresnahan as a replacement for Hornsby in the dugout and a trade to acquire Frisch as his replacement in the lineup. Breadon denied both rumors while also explaining his version of the conversations with Killefer. He hadn't offered him the manager's job, Breadon somehow told reporters with a straight face, but rather wanted to know if Killefer would be in a receptive mood if the position just happened to be vacant. A follow-up meeting with Hornsby was set for Monday, December 20th.[6]

The final Breadon-Hornsby meeting ended with a slam of the door. While the men agreed on an annual salary of $50,000, an increase of $20,000, Breadon firmly held the length of his offer at one year while Hornsby still insisted on a three-year term. The manager also demanded absolute control of the team. Hornsby reportedly wanted Rickey fired, a charge he later denied.[7] Breadon's insertion of a no-gambling clause escalated the tension. The contract offer was contingent on Hornsby agreeing to never bet on a horse race, never give any of his teammates money to bet on a horse race, never associate with anyone connected to horse racing or bookmaking and never go to a race track.[8] Any violation would have made the contract null and void. "It is true that Mr. Breadon and I got pretty hot over the contract that I wanted," Hornsby later admitted. "I steamed up, told him where he could go, slammed the door as I left the office and the next thing I knew I was traded to the Giants for Frankie Frisch and Jimmy Ring."[9]

The long-rumored swap of Hornsby for Frisch, who came to St. Louis with pitcher Jimmy Ring, took place not long after Hornsby stormed out. Breadon picked up the phone, called Giants owner Charles Stoneham, and the two men quickly worked out an agreement. Breadon's next phone call was to Hornsby at his home.

"Hello, Rog?"

"Yea"

"This is Sam Breadon. I have traded you to New York."

Before Hornsby could reply, Breadon hung up the phone.[10]

The deal stunned St. Louis and sparked an immediate backlash. Breadon walked into the lobby of the Hotel Jefferson for lunch the day after the trade. "It was the worst moment of my life," the Cardinals owner remembered. "No one said a word to me. Friends I had known for years turned their back on me. I ate alone – and in silence."[11]

The St. Louis Chamber of Commerce protested the deal, called it "a terrible blow" and asked the Commissioner to block it. Judge Landis responded by saying it was a matter for the team to decide. Breadon responded by resigning from the Chamber. Mark Steinberg, who served as both Hornsby's broker and member of the board of directors for the team, was furious. "The trade of Hornsby is an insult to the fans of St. Louis and to the directors of the Cardinals club, in that Breadon did not consult the board members before making the trade." Steinberg soon left the board and was replaced by William Walsingham, Breadon's brother-in-law and partner in his automobile business.

Condemnation of the deal was widespread with one writer from Hornsby's home state of Texas blaming Rickey, calling him a "statistical crank" and "jealously inclined."[12] A few people with ties to St. Louis, however, took a contrarian viewpoint. "My experience with Mr. Breadon is that he is a clever trader," said Browns owner Phil Ball. "I do not think he would let sentiment interfere with a business deal that he thought was for the best." In New York, Giants outfielder, former Cardinal, and Creve Coeur, Missouri native Heinie Mueller welcomed the opportunity to reunite with Hornsby. "This is the greatest news I've heard since my mamma told me about Santa Claus."

Giants manager McGraw now had the player he had long coveted to compete with the star power of Babe Ruth. He also admitted he'd had conversations with Breadon about a deal involving Hornsby in New York on December 13, seven days before the trade was consummated. He walked into Stoneham's office that day and found the two owners deep in conversation over Hornsby. Breadon originally asked for Frisch and first baseman Bill Terry, but McGraw told him he couldn't trade both. Breadon then asked if he would trade Frisch and a pitcher and the blueprint of a deal was struck. "We came to an agreement then," McGraw said.[13] But Breadon still had a meeting with Hornsby on the calendar. "I was so determined to get rid of Hornsby that I was afraid he might accept my one-year offer," he later admitted.

The Cardinals president, in his zest to rid himself of the longtime second baseman, had traded Hornsby, the *player*. But he still had to deal with Hornsby, the *shareholder*. Outside of Breadon, no one owned more shares of Cardinals' stock than the man he had just dealt.

Baseball officials took notice. So did a Kentucky bookmaker.

*****

Frank Moore first met Hornsby in May of 1925 in Cincinnati. Once pleasantries were exchanged, Hornsby got right to the point. "His first question after he met me was to inquire if I had any good tips on the horses. I replied that I had and he authorized me to place bets of $10 each on ten horses," Moore recalled.

The two men developed a close friendship. The bookmaker claimed Hornsby started calling him from whatever city the Cardinals happened to be playing. Hornsby had a three-way telephone circuit installed in his St. Louis home, so his wife could help him place bets. The men would see each other every time the Cardinals played in Cincinnati.

Moore and his wife would frequently travel to St. Louis. Hornsby invited the couple to spring training in San Antonio in 1926. At trial, Moore's attorney showed jurors a picture of the bookmaker dressed in a Cardinals uniform standing next to a smiling Hornsby.

The ten-dollar bets quickly escalated. Over a two-month period, Moore alleged he bet $70,000 for Hornsby. The smallest bet was $400, the largest $4,300. Moore claimed he advanced Hornsby $14,930 to pay off a bookmaker in Jersey City, and he paid off another of Hornsby's bookmakers in New York to the tune of nearly $5,000. The financial relationship expanded over time. Moore maintained he loaned Hornsby $7,500 to purchase a new apartment home on Kingsbury Blvd. He said Hornsby came to him on more than one occasion needing money and asking for loans of $5,000 and $4,770 to pay off various debts. Hornsby's wife called him once to explain she had lost $7,950 betting in Rogers absence (he was in spring training at the time). Moore admitted to her he had lost $10,000 betting the same day. He sent her a check for $18,000.[14] Moore bought stock in a dog-racing operation in Jacksonville, Florida for $8,000. Hornsby was supposed to be his 50-50 partner but never paid his $4,000 share. Moore later admitted Hornsby had advised him against the purchase.

Why was Moore so willing to lend Hornsby and his wife so much money? "I guess it was hero worship," Moore admitted. "At any rate, it was expensive." (Hornsby's attorney used the same description. "My impression is that Moore is a hero-worshipper," said William Fahey.)[15]

In early January of 1927, Moore came to St. Louis to meet with Hornsby and his attorney. He brought copies of canceled checks. He also met with Breadon. The plan was to attach Hornsby's assets – including his ownership in the Cardinals and his new home – as part of any potential lawsuit claim.

One month after Hornsby was traded to the Giants, Moore made it official and filed suit in St. Louis County court for $70,075. The total included $26,800 Moore alleged he had advanced to Hornsby's wife and $500 for collect calls Moore said Hornsby had made to him. Hornsby responded by saying he "did not owe Moore a dime" and threatened to sue the Cardinals and team president Breadon. The team hadn't paid a dividend on its stock since the 1922 season. Hornsby wanted back dividends paid on his 1,167 shares. His attorney offered to sell those shares to Breadon at $105 each, more than $60 higher than Hornsby had paid. When Breadon refused the offer, Hornsby's attorney made a counteroffer. He told the Cardinals president he would buy his 5,904 shares at the same price, valuing Breadon's stake in the Cardinals at $619,920. Breadon also rejected that proposal.[16]

Hornsby claimed that while he never bet through Moore, he did receive horse racing tips from him. "The tips were bad of late," he told reporters. "I lost money and Moore lost money." Moore was seen in New York during the World Series. The bookmaker was asked directly if the two men bet on baseball games. "I frequently made bets on baseball," Moore admitted. "I bet heavily on the Cardinals every time I had the chance."

What about Hornsby? "I have never known him to make a bet on a baseball game or a baseball series, directly or indirectly," Moore stated. "He has bet heavily on the races, but never a cent on baseball as far as I know."[17] Reporters also confronted Hornsby. "I did not bet on the Cardinal games or the Cardinal chances to win a pennant or World Series," he said. "I do not believe in betting on ballgames and never expect to make a bet on baseball."

While Hornsby's relationship with Moore would remain a source of debate for the rest of 1927, it was clear the former Cardinals star had overextended himself. He had borrowed money to buy stock in the team. He had borrowed money for a new home. Whether or not he had borrowed money to bet with Moore, he admitted losing money from the bookmaker's tips. Threatening a lawsuit to receive back dividends on his stock in the team was another signal Hornsby needed cash. His one source of leverage was his ownership in the Cardinals. The National League wouldn't allow Hornsby to play for one team while holding stock in another. "Rule or no rule, it goes without saying that Hornsby could not play with the Giants and continue to hold stock in the St. Louis club," said NL president John Heydler. The matter had to be settled before the start of the new season.

If they couldn't agree on a contract, how could they agree on a stock price? Breadon originally offered his former player/manager $50 a share for his stock, giving Hornsby a profit of less than $10,000. Hornsby's $105 per share demand would mean a profit of roughly $70,000. Shares of Cardinals stock sold in a range between $60 and $75 in the days after the World Series ended but demand dried up after Hornsby was traded. Breadon had first option on the shares but there were other interested parties in the stake, including entertainer Al Jolson. The singer, dancer, and comedian was a minority shareholder in the St. Louis franchise. He sent a telegram to Hornsby asking for his price. Hornsby didn't reply.[18] The ex-Cardinal's stake represented about 12.5 percent of outstanding common shares. (The man who tried to buy Hornsby's shares attended the same school as Ruth. Jolson, like the Babe, spent time at St. Mary's Industrial School in Baltimore.)[19]

Thanks to his sizable ownership interest and support from fellow stockholders – notably friend and former director Steinberg – Hornsby was re-elected to the franchise's board in February. He also got a check for $2,917.50 as the directors approved a $2.50 per share dividend. But his days as a director and shareholder were numbered if he wanted to play for the Giants. "There are seventy business days in which to adjust this business arrangement and there is no cause for alarm or scandal," said Heydler.[20]

But it was apparent to many that neither Breadon nor Hornsby had any interest in compromise. Any reduction in playing time for Hornsby hurt the Giants and benefited the Cardinals and the rest of the National League. Any reduction in share price hurt Hornsby, already facing the lawsuit from Moore and needing money to satisfy other obligations. He did get a raise when he signed a two-year contract with New York at $40,000 annually. With so much invested in their new second baseman, the Giants had incentive to broker a deal and break the logjam. Reports began to surface that New York owner Stoneham was considering making up the difference between Breadon's offer and Hornsby's demand.[21]

The matter dragged on for weeks. Spring training came and went with no resolution (even with no agreement, the league allowed Hornsby to play in exhibition games). At one point, Hornsby suggested swapping his stock in the Cardinals for ownership of the franchise's minor league team in Houston. Since the club had previously drawn offers in excess of $200,000, the suggestion was not taken seriously.[22] Near the end of March, the Giants new second baseman reiterated his hardline stance and his rationale behind his asking price. "The stock is mine. It represents everything I have to show for 12 years of service with the Cardinals and also it stands for my reward for lifting the Cardinals from last place in 1925 to the world's championship in 1926, using the same players that Branch Rickey failed with," Hornsby told a reporter, conveniently ignoring the acquisitions of Alexander and Southworth during the 1926 season, the trade for 1926 MVP O'Farrell shortly before he became manager, and the emergence of Thevenow at shortstop.

Deal or no deal, Hornsby insisted he would play for the Giants. "There is no baseball law that says a player shall not own stock in one club and play for another. I realize it is not ethical, but I am the victim of a peculiar situation," he told a *Post-Dispatch* correspondent. "If the league thinks its principles are being jeopardized, it can come to the rescue and help make up the difference."[23]

The league took Hornsby's advice. Baseball authorities convened a special meeting of owners in Pittsburgh on April 8, just four days before the start of the season. After a follow-up meeting in New York the next day, a compromise agreement was struck. Hornsby would get $100 a share for his stock with Breadon paying the vast majority, the rest of the league's owners kicking in $14,000 or $2,000 each, and the Giants covering his legal fees.[24] Four months after the trade, Breadon and the Cardinals had finally cut all tles to thelr former player/manager/shareholder. "I am glad It Is over," Hornsby sald. "The settlement is absolutely satisfactory to me." At $100 a share, his profit exceeded $60,000.[25]

The *Times* called him an "Undisputed Giant Now." With a new baseball season starting, his first in New York, comparisons to Ruth were inevitable. "Babe Ruth vs. Rogers Hornsby," wrote John Kieran shortly after the season got underway. "That was the ticket to the World Series last fall and that will be the ticket all through the season which has just broken away to a rousing start."

Kieran closed the column with a prediction. "Hornsby is his closest rival, and playing in the same city, this battle of bludgeons should be well worth watching. Each one is out to outdo the other, but the general suspicion is that Ruth will prevail. For even the ball players agree there is only one Babe Ruth."[26]

*****

Johnny Sylvester turned eleven years old in 1926. Growing up in Essex Fells, New Jersey, about twenty miles outside New York City, he rooted for the Yankees in the World Series. In the middle of the seven-game affair, both the Yankees and the Cardinals sent autographed baseballs to his house. On the New York baseball, next to Ruth's signature, the Babe had written a note. "I'll knock a homer for you on Wednesday." Ruth was true to his word. Wednesday was Game 4, the day the Yankees slugger set a World Series record with three home runs. A legend was born.

The Sylvester saga has its origins in a horse-riding accident that summer on the New Jersey shore. "The horse stepped in a hole along the path," Sylvester explained later to writer Brian Sobel. "We both went down and the horse got up before I did and stepped on my head." Sylvester was later diagnosed with osteomyelitis, an inflammatory infection of the bones. Before antibiotics came along, it was life-threatening.

By early October, his condition had deteriorated. Johnny told his parents he would like a baseball, preferably one from a World Series game. His father, a vice president at National City Bank in New York, had a colleague with baseball connections. He arranged to have a telegram sent to St. Louis, explaining the situation. During a rain delay of Game 3 of the World Series, two St. Louis policemen went to the dugouts to secure player autographs. Hornsby and fourteen of his players autographed the one from the Cardinals. Ruth and five of his teammates signed the one from the Yankees.[27] A package that included the two autographed balls and the Ruth prediction soon arrived in New Jersey. Doctors had supposedly given the boy just thirty minutes to live, but upon seeing the baseballs and hearing about Ruth's performance (the airmail delivery arrived the day of Game 4), his physical condition dramatically improved. "His fever began to abate at once," noted an account in the *Times.*

The irresistible story sparked national attention and additional gifts. Sylvester received a football and a promise to score a touchdown from Red Grange, an autographed tennis racquet from Bill Tilden, and a letter from Rogers Hornsby.

"Dear Friend John," the letter began, "I was thinking of you all day and wondering if you were not feeling better. I am sure you are going to win out in your fight for your recovery and if Babe Ruth is going to hit a home run for you, I can only hope I can hit two for you. Cheer up and be a good boy and I hope to see you next summer when the Red Birds come to New York. Your friend. Rogers Hornsby."

The Hornsby letter was dated October 9, the day of Game 6. The Cardinals player/manager didn't hit two home runs, but his team did win two games that weekend. Less than twenty-four hours after getting tagged out by Hornsby to end the World Series, Ruth showed up at the Sylvester house. "Glad to meet you, Johnny," Ruth said as he entered his bedroom. "How are you feeling?"

"F-fine," is all a stunned Sylvester could say. "I'm sorry the Yanks lost the Series," the boy told Ruth. A silence fell over the room until a Sylvester sibling entered. "Nice looking brother you have there," Ruth remarked. "That's my sister but you should see my kid brother," Johnny told him, sparking a conversation about brother Peter. Ruth, on his way to an exhibition game in Bradley Beach, New Jersey, then got a phone call and soon departed.[28] The visit lasted about a half hour.[29]

Proving William Faulkner correct – "The past is never dead. It's not even past." – the Sylvester story entered the popular culture zeitgeist and never left. The incident was featured in the 1948 movie *The Babe Ruth Story*, but the film took liberty with the facts of the case. The movie has Ruth making the promise to a hit home run in person rather than on a note scrawled on a baseball and moves the date to the 1932 World Series against the Cubs. In the 1992 movie, *The Babe*, John Goodman's Ruth hits two home runs for Sylvester after visiting him in the hospital. "You're the best," an adult Johnny tells him at the end of the movie, "you're the best there's ever been." In 1996, the tale inspired an episode of the television show *Seinfeld* involving Kramer and Yankees outfielder Paul O'Neill. This plot also involved a sick child in a hospital, although there's no evidence that Sylvester ever spent time in one during his illness. Sylvester's family was wealthy. They had a maid and had hired a nurse to help care for him.

Sylvester's great-nephew made a documentary about the enduring baseball legend. Andrew Lilley unveiled *I'll Knock a Homer for You: The Timeless Story of Johnny Sylvester and Babe Ruth* in 2013. "The whole story behind the baseball is history. And I think it was a history that got distorted over the years through embellishments," he explained. "It seemed like in every movie they could never get it right. And I always felt the whole story never needed any embellishments. It was amazing enough as it was."

In the documentary, Sylvester's voice can be heard in audio recordings. "By the fall, they didn't really expect me to live," he said of his condition in 1926. "I was sinking very slowly, day after day. The doctor felt the only way that I could recover was I had to develop a will to survive." That will to survive arrived in the form of an autographed baseball with a promise from the Babe. A year after the documentary debuted, that baseball sold at an auction for $250,000. Two letters Babe had sent Sylvester each fetched more than $70,000 at the same 2014 event. Omitted from the coverage entirely or barely mentioned was Hornsby's correspondence with Sylvester. A letter from the winning manager of the 1926 World Series and the greatest right-handed hitter in the history of baseball brought $3,000.

More than nine decades later, John Kieran is still right. There is only one Babe Ruth.

*****

Ruth was at his peak financially and physically in the late 1920s. He took part in a twelve-week vaudeville tour following the 1926 season. Combined with barnstorming tours, ghost-written articles, commercial endorsements, a movie, and his baseball salary, Ruth pulled down nearly a quarter-million dollars in the two years starting in 1926. In 1927, Ruth made more money in endorsements than in salary, "making him undoubtedly the first professional athlete to earn as much or more off the field than on it," according to author Jane Leavy[30]

His agent and public relations man Christy Walsh had brought financial ballast to his life, getting Ruth to invest some of his growing cash pile. Ruth set aside $33,000 in early

1927 to invest in a trust and announced plans to increase the fund to $100,000. (He reached that goal in October of 1929 and added $50,000 to the account in both 1930 and 1931.) Walsh "controlled every aspect of Ruth's financial life: investments, annuities, insurance policies, endorsements, personal appearances, and taxes," wrote Leavy. "I did everything but sleep with him," Walsh would later say.[31]

Separated from wife Helen, he spent more time with Claire Hodgson. The two would later marry after Helen's death. She put him on a budget. A man who once bet thousands on a single horse race had to content himself with $50 checks.

His 1926 vaudeville tour started in Minnesota and ended on the West Coast. It was the perfect place to end the act. Signed to make a movie called *The Babe Comes Home*, Ruth spent much of the winter in Hollywood. The film featured a love story between Ruth's character, Babe Dugan, and the woman who did his laundry, played by Swedish actress Anna Q. Nilsson (perhaps best known for a cameo role in *Sunset Boulevard* in which she played herself). Shot in 22 days, no copy survives. Long forgotten (when Nilsson died, the *Times* didn't mention Ruth or the movie in her obituary) and poorly received, the film had its biggest fan in Ruth. "Every time I hit a town where it's playing, I go down and look at myself again!"

Trainer Artie McGovern followed the Babe to Hollywood to keep the slugger in shape and help him avoid the temptations of Southern California life. "Hollywood was at its peak then," remembered writer Marshall Hunt, "and, Jesus, the Babe would see all this luscious stuff on the streets, in the hotel lobbies, and out on the movie lots, but none of it was for him."[32] McGovern had Ruth up every morning at 6:00 a.m., running, working out, and staying on a strict diet. The trainer fed Ruth dry toast, thin soup, and lean meat, while making sure he drank plenty of warm water. In between workouts, Ruth spent ten hours a day in front of a camera. "You ain't got much time for hell-raising," he admitted. By the end of February, McGovern pronounced the Babe fit and ready for another season. "Ruth is in perfect physical condition," he said. "He has ten years of good baseball in his system if he takes care of himself."[33]

Like Hornsby, Ruth had a contract battle with his owner that offseason. Unlike Hornsby, he and Jacob Ruppert came to an amicable agreement. Shortly after the World Series, an annual figure of $150,000 was floated in the press (a number that originated with Walsh). Ruppert called the figure – nearly three times what Ruth received in 1926 – "preposterous" and stated emphatically, "he won't get it."[34]

A few months later, Ruth's demands had dropped to $100,000 annually, and he threatened to leave baseball entirely to open a string of gymnasiums with McGovern. Ruth spelled out his salary request in a letter to the Yankees owner. It also included a demand to return various fines over the years, including the one he paid after the showdown in St. Louis with manager Huggins in 1925. "The letter mailed by Ruth to Colonel Ruppert is a logical document, which is proof positive that the Babe didn't write it," proclaimed Kieran in the *Times.* "That demand for the return of $7,700 in fines, however, is something that only a ball player would think of inserting. It sprang from the heart. It's a personal touch."

In the end, Ruth and Ruppert settled on a three-year deal at $70,000 annually, an $18,000 increase over his 1926 salary. In a fifty-five-minute face-to-face meeting in Ruppert's office, the Yankees owner impressed on Ruth that his extracurricular income depended on his baseball career. "I pointed out to Ruth that his loss would be as great as ours if he ever quit baseball and that movie contracts wouldn't be so freely offered in such a contingency," he told reporters afterward. "Our talk was cordial, businesslike, and, as you can see, very much to the point and successful for both of us."[35]

Physically fit and financially sound, Ruth joined his teammates in a season for the ages. After reeling nine straight victories in the middle of June, the Yankees stood 27 games above .500 and had a ten-game lead in the standings. With a final record of 110-44, New York finished nineteen games ahead of second-place Philadelphia. The Yankees beat the Browns twenty-one straight times in 1927, losing only the finale to finish 21-1 against St. Louis. New York pounded Pittsburgh in the World Series, outscoring the Pirates 23 to 10 in a four-game sweep.

The lopsided victory by the Yankees was viewed as a positive by baseball officials, still haunted by gambling rumors and the specter of the Black Sox scandal. In addition to allegations involving Hornsby and a bookmaker, league authorities had to contend with charges of game-fixing involving two of the game's biggest stars, Ty Cobb and Tris Speaker. Like the Black Sox scandal, the charges stemmed from the 1919 season, specifically a late-season game between the Tigers and Indians. The news broke on the same day as the Hornsby trade to the Giants.

While the two players were later exonerated by Commissioner Landis, Cobb was released by the Tigers and never again played for Detroit, and Speaker left Cleveland for Washington. The two veterans never managed in the big leagues again.

That same winter, former White Sox player Swede Risberg claimed the 1917 Detroit Tigers "sloughed off" in two games against Chicago and hinted at even greater scandal. "I can give baseball's bosses information that will implicate twenty big leaguers who have never been mentioned in connection with crookedness," said Risberg, one of the eight Chicago players banned by Commissioner Landis in 1920.[36] First baseman and fellow Black Sox conspirator Chick Gandil backed up Risberg's claims but every other player on the two teams denied it. Landis investigated the charges, but like Cobb and Speaker, the commissioner exonerated the players.

"If there's scandal in baseball, let's admit it, pay the price in gate admissions and clean house," said Rickey in January of 1927. "The stark tragedy of these revelations which have jarred the baseball world lies not in the disgrace to the players involved, not in the shame forced upon their families, but in the shaking of the faith of the twenty-million boy hero worshippers," he told a gathering in Moline, Illinois.[37]

"The fans of 1927 will be watching, more or less with suspicion, games this coming season and woe betide the player whose 'boot' may cost the decision in a close game," wrote James Gould in the *St. Louis Star.*[38]

"Won't these goddamn things that happened before I came into baseball ever stop coming up?" remarked a frustrated Landis.

The Yankees sweep in the 1927 World Series gave Landis and baseball officials reason to breathe a sigh of relief. "Critics of the game are almost unanimous in accepting that result as clear proof that baseball, at least on the higher levels is now free from any suspicion of jockeying the public with 'fixt' games," contended an article in *Literary Digest*.[39]

"There can be no talk now of stringing a Series out," said Yankees owner Ruppert.

Ruth hit .400 in the World Series. This followed a .356 batting average in the regular season. That mark wasn't the highest of his career (he hit .393 in 1923). His slugging percentage of .772 was easily eclipsed by his .847 mark in 1920. Neither his RBI total nor his runs scored that season marked a career best. But in one category, home runs, the Babe hit one more than he did in 1921. Because of the nice round figure in the home run category and the dominating team performance, Ruth is more closely linked to his 1927 numbers than any other.

Ruth's quest for 60 home runs was a two-man race for much of the season. On July 1, both Ruth and teammate Lou Gehrig had 25 round-trippers. Entering September, Ruth had 43 with Gehrig just two behind. But the Yankee first baseman hit just six more the rest of the season while the Babe went on a tear. Ruth hit 17 home runs the final month of the season, including three in the last week against Washington. His record-setting sixtieth home run came off Senators pitcher Tom Zachary. "Sixty!" Ruth boasted after the game. "Let's see some son of a bitch try to top that one!"[40]

Ruth's reaction belied a more measured response from the baseball public. There were only 8,000 fans in Yankee Stadium that Friday. "There wasn't the excitement you'd imagine," remembered Yankees longtime equipment manager Pete Sheehy. "He'd already hit 59 another year and the feeling was that next year he would probably hit 62."[41]

A victim of high expectations, Ruth also had to contend with something else for much of the season. A new media star had taken over the front pages of newspapers across the country. Eclipsed by the St. Louis Cardinals in the fall of 1926, the Babe was overshadowed in the summer of 1927 by the *Spirit of St. Louis*.

*****

The airmail service that delivered the package to Johnny Sylvester had only been operating in St. Louis for six months when the autographed baseballs arrived in New Jersey. Brothers Frank and William Robertson, owners of the Robertson Aircraft Corporation, were awarded the contract for service between St. Louis and Chicago.[42] With that connection, it became possible to deliver mail to New York City in fifteen hours.

The Robertson route made its initial flight on the afternoon of April 15, 1926. In the cockpit was the company's chief pilot, a twenty-four-year-old Minnesota native. He made the journey from St. Louis to Chicago, with a stop in Springfield, Illinois, in about three hours. Charles Lindbergh would soon have a much longer and more difficult journey on his mind.

Lindbergh had an independent streak and a mechanical mind. He learned to drive by age 11 and was running the family farm by the time he was 16. The son of a U.S. congressman, Lindbergh dropped out of the University of Wisconsin. He was twenty years old when he enrolled in flight training in Lincoln, Nebraska. He bought his first plane a year later and made his way to St. Louis in the fall of 1923 for the International Air Races.

The young pilot became a stunt performer. Billed as "Daredevil Lindbergh," he barnstormed across the country. Along the way, he enlisted as an aviation cadet and entered U.S. Army flight training. He graduated at the top of his class. He later joined the Missouri National Guard and was commissioned as a First Lieutenant. His military training served him well. Lindbergh had four plane crashes before he became famous, escaping each time by parachute.

In May of 1925, near Lambert Field in St. Louis, he was roughly three hundred feet from the ground when he was forced to parachute out of his plane. While evacuating, he barely missed hitting the plane's propeller. When mechanics from the field reached him, blood was coming from his nose and mouth. "A little close," he said with a grin as the mechanics unwrapped his parachute. His demolished plane had crashed on a nearby road. Lindbergh escaped with minor injuries and a dislocated shoulder. With a different plane, he was back in the air in two hours.[43]

This was the second time Lindbergh had to employ his parachute. The first incident occurred just a few months earlier while he was still in military flying school. Conducting air maneuvers in Texas, Lindbergh and another cadet collided in midair; their planes locked together. Lindbergh climbed out of the right side of the cockpit and jumped backward. The other pilot did the same. They parachuted to safety while their planes burst into flames upon contact with the earth. Lindbergh returned to the sky in an hour.[44]

He had two close calls while delivering the mail. The St. Louis-Chicago route "was considered one of the most perilous runs in the country, because of the changing weather. Navigation was rudimentary at best, with pilots relying on visual contact with the ground," wrote Lindbergh biographer A. Scott Berg. "De Havilland planes had neither landing lights nor navigation lights." The pilot's lighting equipment "consisted of a pocket flashlight (pilot furnished) and a compass light attached to a button on the end of a stick," Lindbergh remembered.

In heavy fog sixty miles from Chicago and five-thousand feet from the ground, Lindbergh was forced to parachute to safety in September of 1926. He landed in a cornfield and walked to a farmhouse a mile away. The farmer soon got a call from a neighbor about a wrecked plane near his barn. With the help of a local sheriff, Lindbergh salvaged the mailbags from their compartment and put the letters and packages on a train.

Just two months later, blinded by snow and sleet, he ran out of fuel looking for a place to land. He parachuted headfirst off the side of his plane at 13,000 feet. "There wasn't a chance to see where I was falling up to the time I struck the ground," he later told a reporter. He landed on a barbed wire fence not far from Covell, Illinois, near Bloomington. The plane was located the next day and the mail was recovered. Despite the weather challenges, Lindbergh and the other Robertson pilots completed more than ninety-eight percent of their scheduled flights.

Restless and ambitious, Lindbergh began to set his sights on a more audacious goal. The De Havilland DH-4 plane he flew on the mail route had been around since World War I. Lindbergh knew more modern craft could fly at faster speeds and go for longer distances. The prize offered by New York hotelier Raymond Orteig, which promised $25,000 to anyone who could fly nonstop from New York to Paris, had gone unclaimed since 1919. Lindbergh now had more than four years of experience in the cockpit, and no one else in America could claim four-time membership in the "Caterpillar Club," the informal group of pilots who had saved their lives by jumping from airplanes.[45]

Approaching his twenty-fifth birthday, "Slim" Lindbergh stood six feet three inches tall, weighed 160 pounds, and had 20-15 vision. He had thrilled crowds as a stunt flyer, matured with military training, and had successfully navigated multiple life-threatening experiences. "Why shouldn't I fly from New York to Paris?" he thought to himself. Was there anyone else in America more qualified to take on the challenge? Lindbergh's time as a St. Louis mail pilot, "the only paycheck job in the normal sense of the word he ever had," was about to come to an end.[46]

Due to North Atlantic weather conditions, May was thought to be the earliest one could safely make the trip. Lindbergh had just months to raise the money, secure a plane, and get to New York. Thanks to a group of St. Louis businessmen, his dream became a reality.

The airmail service that employed Lindbergh originated from Lambert Field, which got its name from Major Alfred B. Lambert. An early flying enthusiast, Lambert built the field and later sold it to the city of St. Louis at cost. Lambert became president of the St. Louis Aero Club when it formed in 1907. Balloon races started the following year. The city quickly became a hub for flying activity. Former President Theodore Roosevelt took an airplane ride when he came to St. Louis in 1910, the same year Lambert took his first flying lesson from Orville Wright. Lambert became the fifth person in the country to hold both pilot and balloonist licenses.[47] He later commanded a school for balloon pilots in World War I.

The oldest son of the founder of Lambert Pharmaceutical and brother to Marion Lambert – the man who initially staked Cardinals president Breadon in the automobile business – Alfred served as president of the family company from 1896 until he retired in 1925. When Lindbergh went to see him, Lambert immediately agreed to back him and pledged $1,000 to the effort. The roster of backers also included Harry H. Knight, who ran a brokerage firm, and Harold Bixby, a bank vice president and the president of the St. Louis Chamber of Commerce (a busy time for Bixby, backing Lindbergh around the same time the Chamber was protesting the trade of Hornsby).[48] With $13,000 raised from St. Louis investors and $2,000 of his own money, Lindbergh quickly gained the capital needed. The Ryan Aeronautical Company in San Diego agreed to build the plane for $6,000. With the engine expense, the total came to less than $11,000.

Built in two months under Lindbergh's watchful and demanding eye, the plane had no brakes (like most aircraft of the era) and lacked a fuel gauge. The single-seat, single-engine plane had a fuel capacity of 450 gallons. Over the Atlantic, he switched to a different fuel tank every hour, noting the change with a pencil mark on his instrument panel.

Dubbed the *Spirit of St. Louis* at Bixby's suggestion, the plane made its first appearance in the city that inspired it in the spring of 1927. Lindbergh flew it from San Diego, arriving on the morning of May 11. At an average speed of 107 miles an hour, he made the 1,550-mile journey in 14 hours and 23 minutes. The voyage marked the longest solo non-stop flight in American history, and Lindbergh became the first pilot to navigate the Rocky Mountains at night.

On the day he arrived, the St. Louis Browns hosted the New York Yankees. In a foggy afternoon at Sportsman's Park, Ruth connected for one of his sixty home runs that season. The ball landed in the center field bleachers and brought back memories of his World Series shot from the previous fall. The Yankees won the game 4-2.

It was possible on that cool spring afternoon to see a Ruth blast and the Lindbergh plane on the same day. As Lindbergh enjoyed a meal at Louie's Café and caught up with his financial backers, the *Spirit of St. Louis* was on display at Lambert Field. Floodlights allowed visitors to get a look at the *Spirit* until 9:00 p.m. that evening. The next morning, Lindbergh flew to New York. Nine days later, he flew off to immortality.

When Lindbergh landed at Le Bourget Airport in Paris thirty-three hours and thirty minutes after takeoff from Roosevelt Field on Long Island, the moment reverberated around the world. The relatively obscure St. Louis mail pilot quickly became the most photographed person on the planet. ("Impossibly photogenic," wrote Berg, "there was not a bad picture to be taken of him.") Mobbed in Paris, feted in Brussels and London (the King of England wanted to know how many times he peed during the flight. Answer: Two), Lindbergh had given no thought to how he would return to the United States. Thanks to President Calvin Coolidge and the U.S. Navy, he didn't have to worry about it. Coolidge dispatched the *USS Memphis* to bring back the conquering hero. As the navy cruiser and a flotilla escort sailed up the Potomac River on the way to Washington D.C. on June 11, people around the country tuned in to their radios to get a live description. The ever-present Graham McNamee broadcast the event to a national audience estimated at 30 million people. A publicity-savvy Missouri company was also there. "Anheuser-Busch Inc., Welcomes Captain Lindbergh with the *Spirit of St. Louis*," read the advertisement on a truck parked in the navy yards of the nation's capital.[49]

Two days later, four million people turned out in New York City as Lindbergh paraded from the southern tip of Manhattan to Central Park. It nearly ended before it began. As the parade got underway, Lindbergh was standing in the back seat of an open car. As police pushed the crowd back to make way, the anxious driver hit the gas once he saw a clearing. As Lindbergh flew backward, the chairman of the welcoming committee managed to grab him by the leg and haul him back to safety. A four-hour march northward began.

The event practically paralyzed the city. Businesses and schools closed, courts recessed, and a blizzard of confetti and ticker tape rained down on the world's most eligible bachelor. "Girls were so busy looking at Lindbergh to think of weddings, so only thirty-nine marriage licenses were issued at the Bureau in the Municipal Building," noted the *Times*. "This was the lowest daily figure since the establishment of the institution." The paper devoted its first sixteen pages to Lindbergh the following day. "New York City is yours," Mayor Jimmy Walker told Lindbergh. "I don't give it to you. You won it."

As the breathless coverage amplified and endorsement offers poured in, the aviator suddenly glowed in a spotlight normally reserved for Hollywood headliners and baseball's biggest star. "Lindbergh was the Babe times two or three or four or maybe ten," wrote Ruth biographer Leigh Montville. "The offers that had come to the Babe – for books and movies and vaudeville tours, for endorsements and charity appearances – now came to Lindbergh with bigger numbers, more zeroes on the end." William Randolph Hearst offered him $500,000 plus ten percent of the gross receipts to star in a film about his life. Another movie offer, sort of a precursor to the television show, *The Bachelor*, came with a $1 million price tag if Lindbergh would marry the girl of his dreams with the cameras rolling. He rejected both deals.

Lindbergh arrived in New York on a Monday and spent the week in the city. He and his mother stayed at a Park Avenue apartment owned by Harry Frazee, the former owner of the Boston Red Sox and the man who sold Ruth to the Yankees. On Thursday, Lindbergh was scheduled to go to Yankee Stadium and be recognized in a pregame ceremony, the same day the borough of Brooklyn honored the aviator with a parade. The route stretched for twenty-two miles. The lengthy celebration delayed his departure to the Bronx where the umpires had delayed the start of the game between the Yankees and the Browns. The contest began twenty-five minutes late with Lindbergh still snarled in traffic. In the bottom of the first inning, Ruth hit his twenty-second home run of the year. "I had been saving that homer for Lindbergh, and then he doesn't show up," the Babe told reporters after the game. "I guess he thinks this is a twilight league." Ruth's blast came off Tom Zachary, the same pitcher who yielded the slugger's sixtieth home run at the end of the season. Two weeks after the June game in New York, St. Louis traded Zachary to the Washington Senators.[50]

Lindbergh didn't arrive at Yankee Stadium until after 5:00 p.m. with the game all but over. He and his entourage turned around and headed south to Manhattan. That evening, Lindbergh received the Orteig Prize and the $25,000 reward that came with it. The next day, he flew to St. Louis.

Lindbergh's adopted hometown enthusiastically embraced the record-setting aviator. A *Spirit of St. Louis* poetry contest generated four-thousand entries. No detail of his life now went unnoticed. At a banquet in his honor, a St. Louis society matron preserved his used corncobs, stashing them in her purse.[51]

On top of the customary banquets, speeches and lengthy parade, the former stunt-flying pilot thrilled a crowd of 100,000 spectators at Forest Park with his aerial acrobatics.[52] At Sportsman's Park, Breadon announced a special box had been built for Lindbergh near the team's dugout. City officials and baseball executives made sure he arrived in time to see it. Secretary of War and St. Louis native Dwight Davis was among those who greeted him, while National League president Heydler awarded him a lifetime pass to games. Among the speeches Lindbergh heard that Saturday afternoon was a brief one from Rogers Hornsby. "You're a great fellow," Hornsby told him. "And you did a great thing. I congratulate you." The weekend Lindbergh celebration coincided with a visit from Hornsby's new team, the New York Giants.

In his first week back in the United States, Lindbergh visited three cities and scheduled visits to a pair of sporting venues: Yankee Stadium and Sportsman's Park. The voice of McNamee welcomed him to Washington D.C., Ruth slugged a home run for him in New York, and with Hornsby at his side, Lindbergh hoisted the World Series flag in St. Louis. Marquee names that attracted crowds and a radio audience in the fall of 1926 all played ancillary roles in *the* story of 1927.

At Sportsman's Park, the capacity crowd roared its approval as Lindbergh raised the flag and later presented the champions their World Series rings. Hornsby was the first player to receive one. Sitting in his custom box, the guest of honor watched the first three innings before departing.[53] "Lindbergh was the quietest person in the park and still the most conspicuous," noted *Times* columnist Vidmer.

Despite his quiet and modest manner, the aviator dominated the headlines for months. He wrote a best-selling book called *We* and toured the nation in the plane that helped make him famous. With backing from the Guggenheim Fund, the aviator embarked on a blitz of all 48 states to raise awareness of America's fledgling aviation industry. It lasted three months and covered 22,350 miles.

He wasn't done. From December to February, he toured 16 Latin American countries. The relentless pace of his travels was only exceeded by the adulation from an adoring public. In the first month after his flight, Lindbergh received 3.5 million letters, a hundred thousand telegrams and fourteen thousand parcels. He donated much of his memorabilia to the Missouri Historical Society, continuing to send items until the early 1940s. Over the years, the St. Louis region honored the pilot and recognized his achievement in various ways, including the Spirit of St. Louis Airport, Lindbergh Boulevard and the Lindbergh School District. "Schools across the country bear Lindbergh's name," *St. Louis Magazine* stressed in 2007, "but this is the only Lindbergh *district*."

In April of 1928, the *Spirit of St. Louis* made its final flight. Lindbergh departed the city that inspired the name of the plane and headed to Washington, D.C. After landing in the nation's capital, the plane was disassembled, towed to the Smithsonian Institution, then reassembled for display. It has remained there to this day.

That same month, Hornsby began playing for his third team in three years.

*****

Playing in New York, the National League's highest-paid player got along fabulously with his new manager, John McGraw. "They were like two peas from one pod," recalled Giants outfielder Mueller. "They were together all the time, went to the races together, and we all thought Rog would be manager some day."[54] McGraw named his new second baseman team captain. When the longtime Giants manager was away from the club during spring training and later missed some games during the season, Hornsby filled in. The two men admired one another. In the team's first trip to St. Louis in June, McGraw told Roy Stockton he was planning to retire at the end of the season and Hornsby should be his replacement. "I am getting tired of traveling," the manager confessed. "I expect to step out as manager. Hornsby is the man to carry on."[55]

Healthy and happy with his manager, Hornsby didn't miss a game in 1927. He led the league in runs scored and hit .361. With 133 runs scored, 26 home runs and 125 RBI, the Giants second baseman finished third in MVP balloting at the end of the year. Hornsby was the same player he was in St. Louis. His game hadn't changed. Neither had his personality. While he enjoyed McGraw's company, Hornsby clashed with teammates, yelled at the traveling secretary, and offended the owner.

A sportswriter once asked Hornsby his opinion on the Giants outfield. Always blunt, always honest, the New York second baseman insisted he be quoted on the record. "Now, I'll tell you what I think of the outfield. I think it stinks." While having dinner one night with infielder Eddie "Doc" Farrell, a sportswriter spotted the pair and asked Hornsby if he thought the Giants could win the pennant. "Not with Farrell playing shortstop," he replied. A heated argument with Freddie Lindstrom that season ended with the Giants third baseman telling Hornsby, "When you drop your bat, you're just a handicap around a ball club."[56]

After a game in Chicago, Hornsby shared a cab with traveling secretary Jim Tierney. Giants shortstop Travis Jackson had made a costly error that day. When Tierney broached the subject, Hornsby lit into him. "You run your end of the ballclub and I'll run mine," Hornsby told him. "See that our players are taken care of properly at the hotels and don't be grabbing the best accommodations for yourself."

News of the clash made its way back to Giants owner Charles Stoneham, who had his own run-ins with Hornsby that season. The two men had heated words after a tough loss in Pittsburgh (just as Breadon and Hornsby did the previous year) with Stoneham questioning the manager's strategy. Hornsby unleashed a verbal tirade on his owner and then delivered an ultimatum. "If you don't like the way I'm running the club, get somebody else to do it," he told Stoneham.[57]

Hornsby spoke openly during the season about succeeding McGraw, but admitted there would be conditions before he accepted. "There would have to be a new ownership of the Giants before I would consent to being manager," Hornsby told a reporter for the *Times.* "There are too many men attempting to dictate the club's policy. I had a taste of that in St. Louis with Breadon and Rickey each having a finger in the pie. As manager I would want complete authority in the playing end."[58]

This was the final straw. Once the season ended, Stoneham began shopping the second baseman to several teams, including Cincinnati. Reds manager Jack Hendricks had clashed with Hornsby when he managed the Cardinals in 1918 and wanted no part of him. Stoneham eventually found a suitor. In January of 1928, with McGraw en route to his racetrack and casino in Cuba, the Giants owner dealt Hornsby to the Boston Braves for outfielder Jimmy Welsh and catcher James "Shanty" Hogan. Welsh played a year and a half for the Giants and was out of baseball after the 1930 season. Hogan played five seasons for New York and was a career .295 hitter, a solid player, but nowhere near Hornsby's status.

A headline the next day in the *Post-Dispatch* was typical of the reaction. "Baseball World Is Mystified By Hornsby Trade." Stoneham said he made the deal "in order to avoid any future conflict in the management of the club." The owner made it clear he took exception to discussions of Hornsby's possible role in the organization. "Statements have been made throughout the country that Mr. Hornsby would be the future manager of the club. I have never been consulted about this," he explained after the trade was announced.

Hornsby's gambling addiction always lurked in the background as a possible reason behind the deal. Stoneham and McGraw supposedly didn't object to his gambling but were offended about reports of him refusing to pay off his bookmaker. They weren't the only ones. Shortly after the trade to Boston, the story of a Hornsby murder plot hit the papers.[59] A reported $25,000 had been offered to gangsters to knock off the baseball player for "welching" on bets, and stories circulated that the Giants unloaded him before he was "killed or crippled." Hornsby dismissed the rumor as "hokum and propaganda," but it came on the heels of a decision in his case against bookmaker Moore.

Somewhere in this maelstrom of rumor and discontent, Breadon had to be smiling. Challenged by Hornsby's prickly personality and worried about his gambling habits, the Cardinals owner had offloaded his problem on the Giants while getting real talent in return. Frisch hit .337 for the Cardinals, with ten home runs and 78 RBI, while leading the league in stolen bases with 48. "In all the years I have had the Cardinals, no player ever played such ball for me as Frank Frisch did in 1927," Breadon said years later.

While the Cardinals failed to repeat as National League champions, the club won 92 games, three more than the previous season. Despite shortstop Tommy Thevenow's broken leg and ailments that caused new manager and 1926 MVP Bob O'Farrell to miss more than 90 games, the club won just two less than the NL champion Pittsburgh Pirates. In addition, while Hornsby spent just one year with the Giants (who also won 92 games that season), Frisch remained in St. Louis for the rest of his career. He also managed the team for six seasons, winning a World Series title as a player/manager in 1934. The trade for Frisch deeply influenced Breadon's approach toward marquee talent. "After the season of 1927, I never again was afraid to dispose of a player, regardless of his ability or popularity. I knew after that year that what fans want is a winner, and that a popular player is quickly forgotten by one who is equally popular."

*****

Former toast of the town Hornsby returned to St. Louis after the 1927 season. In December, he took the stand in the lawsuit against him. Either he or Frank Moore was lying about their gambling relationship and it was up to a St. Louis County jury to decide.

Questioned on the second day of testimony, one of Moore's attorneys wanted to know if he was a professional gambler. "No," Hornsby replied. "Are you an amateur gambler?" came the follow-up question. "That is for you to decide," Hornsby said with a laugh.[60]

A jury heard Hornsby and his attorney claim two defenses. While the baseball star insisted he owed Moore nothing, his attorney also claimed that all the transactions were gambling-related, and therefore inadmissible in a court of law. Moore and his attorneys claimed the bookmaker simply loaned Hornsby money. It was not Moore's fault, they contended, that the player bet and lost money on horse races.

The judge agreed and instructed jurors that gambling debts were inadmissible. He also reduced Moore's claim to $36,320.[61] The judge instructed the panel to return judgment for Hornsby if it decided he and Moore had gambled jointly, but to side with Moore if the Kentucky bookmaker had merely loaned Hornsby money without the intent to gamble.

While Hornsby was no longer a member of the Cardinals, he was still wildly popular. Just six months earlier, on his first trip to the city as a member of the Giants, he was honored with "Rogers Hornsby Day" and a pregame celebration in which Mayor Victor Miller presented him a watch engraved "From the Fans of St. Louis." Could an out-of-uniform ex-Cardinal still have sway over the locals? It took the jury less than two hours to decide the case. By a vote of 10-2, the panel sided with Hornsby. The jurors were "much impressed by the straightforward way in which Hornsby gave his testimony," the foreman admitted afterward.[62] "I'm through with this case and with St. Louis," said a frustrated Moore.

Hornsby maintained Moore never had a claim on his finances. But after the case was settled, he did confess to previously owing one bookmaker $7,000 and another $8,000. He paid off both from proceeds of his stock sale. Left unsaid was how he had planned to pay them off had he not liquidated his investment in the Cardinals. The chronic gambler's financial affairs were forever in a state of flux.

Hornsby had little time to celebrate the Moore verdict and enjoy the offseason as he was traded to the Braves just weeks later. Off for Boston in 1928, his last-place team was awful, but Hornsby was spectacular. Braves Field had a reputation as a pitcher's park with the wind constantly blowing from the mound toward home plate. "Nobody can hit up here," a player once complained to Casey Stengel. "All I know," Stengel replied, "is that Hornsby played here one whole season and batted .387."

Manager Jack Slattery was fired after 31 games with Hornsby named his successor. The player/manager's talents didn't translate to the roster as the team finished with a record of 50-103. Players on the 1928 Boston Braves included former Cardinals third baseman Les Bell, former Browns great George Sisler, and the man Hornsby disparaged at dinner in New York the previous year, Doc Farrell. The other distinguishing characteristic of the season was an investigation into horse-race betting. Illinois authorities suspected a jockey of "race tipping" by placing long-distance calls to several people, including Hornsby and McGraw. Both men denied any knowledge of the jockey.[63]

Hornsby found himself playing for his fourth team in four years when the Braves traded him to the Cubs for five players and $200,000. In Chicago, he found a home. Other than St. Louis, it was the only city where he spent more than one season. The 1929 Cubs won the pennant and Hornsby won his second MVP award. The slugging second baseman hit .380 with 39 home runs and 149 RBI as Chicago won 98 games but fell to the Philadelphia Athletics in the World Series.

By 1932, Hornsby was still in Chicago. Thirty-six years old and plagued by various injuries, he played sparingly, but he also managed the team, having replaced Joe McCarthy at the end of the 1930 season. The Cubs were on their way to another championship. Over in the American League, the Yankees claimed their last pennant of the Ruth era. But a second World Series matchup between Hornsby and Ruth never materialized. By the time October rolled around, Hornsby no longer had a job in Chicago.

His absence set the stage for the biggest Ruth legend of all.

---

[1] After the season, *Post-Dispatch* columnist John Wray told a story related to him by an unnamed official with the Cardinals. "In the seventh inning," the official said, "I heard one of the players remark: 'I wonder if that second race has been run yet – I'd like to know if our horse went over.' 'Let's send out and get a paper and find out,'" his companion suggested. "Imagine that, in the middle of a hot game and a hot flag race! And that's what

betting has done to a baseball club. The minds of those players were more on their money than on winning the game and earning their salaries." *St. Louis Post-Dispatch*, January 9, 1927.
[2] *St. Louis Globe-Democrat*, October 14, 1926.
[3] While the Breadon-Hornsby battle consumed the headlines in the fall and early winter of 1926, friction between Hornsby and Rickey had existed for years. "Salary increase is certain for Hornsby," wrote John Wray. "What will happen to Rickey, not what will happen to Hornsby, seems to be the question." *St. Louis Post-Dispatch*, November 10, 1926.
[4] *The Sporting News,* December 29, 1938. "If I had my last 20 years to live over, I'd do just as I have done," Hornsby told Dick Farrington. "It's the only real fun I get – betting on the horses."
[5] *St. Louis Post-Dispatch*, December 18, 1926.
[6] The fateful meeting happened to occur on Branch Rickey's birthday.
[7] "When I sought to sign Hornsby to a new contract, Rog stipulated that I should oust Rickey from the organization," said Breadon. *St. Louis Star-Times*, August 31, 1932. "Hornsby, insisting upon the removal of Rickey, preferred the one-man rule, with himself dictating the policy of the club," wrote Sid Keener. "Breadon refused to heed Rog's final demand to fire Rickey." *St. Louis Star-Times*, October 25, 1932. "Rickey never entered the picture on that debate as press comment had it at the time," Hornsby told Dick Farrington. "I never said anything about 'Rickey goes or I go' at that time." *The Sporting News*, December 29, 1938. Hornsby *did* try to oust Rickey in 1923. Did Breadon conflate that episode with the one in 1926 years later when talking with Keener?
[8] *St. Louis Post-Dispatch*, December 22, 1926.
[9] *The Sporting News*, December 29, 1938.
[10] *St. Louis Star*, December 21, 1926. "Sam Breadon said that listening to Rogers Hornsby was like having the contents of a rock crusher emptied over his head," former player Dick Bartell once wrote. Bartell, Dick with Norman L. Macht, *Rowdy Richard*. North Atlantic Books, 1987.
[11] *St. Louis Globe-Democrat*, May 11, 1949.
[12] "Branch Rickey is really to blame for [the trade]. Breadon, the president, is merely a figurehead in the move. He does what Rickey says [to] do. And Rickey is a statistical crank. Along with this, he is egotistical and jealously inclined." Duby Du Bose, Sports Editor, *The Austin American,* December 22, 1926.
[13] *St. Louis Post-Dispatch*, December 22, 1926. Article reprinted from *New York World.*
[14] Admitted under oath, the comments are among the more curious statements that Moore made. "What were your transactions with Mrs. Hornsby?" he was asked. "On March 5, 1926, Mrs. Hornsby phoned me at my home in Fort Thomas and said, 'Boy, I've had a bad day. What luck did you have?' I replied 'Terrible,' and added that I had lost over $10,000 that day. She told me that she had been trying to make some money for Rogers in his absence and had lost $7,950 and needed money. The next day I sent her a check for $18,000 to cover my losses and hers." *St. Louis Post-Dispatch,* December 20, 1927. Why

would Moore send her $10,000 to cover his losses if Hornsby was betting with borrowed money?
[15] *St. Louis Globe-Democrat,* January 14, 1927.
[16] *New York Times,* January 28, 1927.
[17] *St. Louis Post-Dispatch,* January 10, 1927.
[18] Ibid, December 28, 1926. When Jolson died in 1950, he left an estate valued at more than $3.2 million. Published accounts vary. At least one account put the value at $4 million. *New York Times*, October 27, 1950.
[19] Jolson was nine years older than Ruth. It's not clear how long he spent at St. Mary's. "That stuff about Al going to a Catholic school. Al was only there a few days," his brother Harry said after his death. In a 1950 Associated Press story about the school closing, Jolson was quoted as saying he was there "about the time of the Spanish-American War."
[20] *St. Louis Star*, February 3, 1927.
[21] *St. Louis Post-Dispatch*, February 5, 1927.
[22] *New York Times*, April 6, 1927.
[23] *St. Louis Post-Dispatch*, March 29, 1927.
[24] The details of what Hornsby received vary depending on the report. The *Post-Dispatch* reported he received $100 a share or a total of $116,700. The Times reported he received $100,000, with Breadon paying $86,000 and the rest of the league making up the difference. In January of 1928, Hornsby attorney William Fahey claimed Hornsby received $102.50 a share for his stock plus the $2.50 dividend, making the total $122,535. *St. Louis Post-Dispatch,* January 13, 1928.
[25] The *Times* mentioned the idea that the friction between Breadon and Hornsby went back to Hornsby's purchase of the stock in 1925. Having paid $43 a share, Hornsby allegedly discovered Breadon was buying additional stock from Rickey at $41 a share. *New York Times*, April 10, 1927.
[26] Ibid, April 27, 1927.
[27] Poekel, Charlie. *Babe & the Kid: The Legendary Story of Babe Ruth and Johnny Sylvester.* The History Press. 2007.
[28] *New York Times*, October 12, 1926.
[29] A few days later, Sylvester received a second baseball from the Yankees, this one from first baseman Lou Gehrig. "Without telling anyone, including the press, he simply took a baseball, one that was the last out in a World Series game, and sent it to me with a note saying he had saved it and thought I might like to have it," he recalled years later. "I guess everything you read about his quiet elegance is true." *Baseball Digest*, March 1986.
[30] Leavy, Jane. *The Big Fella: Babe Ruth And The World He Created*. Harper. 2018. In those two years, Ruth earned a salary of $52,000 and $70,000, respectively, while generating endorsement income of $50,243.50 in 1926 and $73,247.34 in 1927.
[31] Ibid. Walsh was born in St. Louis on December 2, 1891 but didn't grow up in Missouri. He attended St. Brigid's Grammar School in San Francisco. He graduated from St. Vincent's College in Los Angeles in 1911.

---

[32] Wagenheim, *Babe Ruth.*
[33] *New York Times*, February 27, 1927.
[34] Ibid, October 12, 1926.
[35] Ibid, March 3, 1927.
[36] Spink, *Judge Landis and Twenty-Five Years of Baseball.*
[37] *St. Louis Post-Dispatch*, January 11, 1927.
[38] *St. Louis Star*, January 11, 1927. The headline of the article was, "Baseball and Gambling."
[39] *Literary Digest,* October 22, 1927.
[40] Umpire Bill Dinneen was behind the plate that day, the same umpire who had called Ruth out at second base to end the 1926 World Series. A former pitcher, Dinneen played for the St. Louis Browns from 1907 to 1909.
[41] Smelser, *The Life That Ruth Built.*
[42] The Robertson Aircraft Corp. later became a part of Universal Aviation Corp., which eventually became part of American Airlines.
[43] Pisano, Dominick A. and van der Linden, F. Robert. *Charles Lindbergh and the Spirit of St. Louis*. Smithsonian Institution. 2002. *St. Louis Post-Dispatch*, May 22, 1927. The authors place the event in May of 1925. The newspaper account dates the event to the "fall and winter" of 1925.
[44] Berg, A. Scott. *Lindbergh.* G.P. Putnam's Sons. 1998.
[45] The name is a tribute to the silkworm. Silk threads made the original parachutes.
[46] *New York Times,* August 27, 1974.
[47] *St. Louis Star-Times*, October 8, 1939.
[48] Lindbergh's financial backers also included Knight's father, Harry F. Knight, the Robertson brothers, Earl C. Thompson, J.D. Wooster Lambert (Alfred's brother), and *St. Louis Globe-Democrat* publisher E. Lansing Ray. Many of the contemporaneous accounts refer to Harry H. Knight as Lindbergh's "chief backer."
[49] *New York Times*, June 12, 1927.
[50] In 1928, Zachary became Ruth's teammate when the Senators traded him to the Yankees. He defeated the Cardinals in Game 3 of the 1928 World Series.
[51] Primm, *Lion of the Valley.*
[52] Covering the St. Louis parade, reporter Louis La Coss wrote that it was "useless" to estimate crowd size, adding that "virtually the only persons in St. Louis who did not witness the spectacle were those confined to hospitals or too feeble to be out and around." *St. Louis Globe-Democrat,* June 19, 1927.
[53] Lindbergh spent just a little more than an hour at Sportsman's Park, arriving at 2:57 p.m. and departing at 4:03 p.m. *St. Louis Post-Dispatch*, June 19, 1927.
[54] Ibid, January 11, 1928.
[55] Ibid, June 15, 1927.
[56] *New York Times*, January 13, 1936. The quote has also been printed as, "When you put that bat down, you're no bargain."
[57] Durso, Joseph. *Casey & Mr. McGraw*. The Sporting News Publishing Co. 1989.

---

[58] *New York Times*, January 13, 1928.
[59] *St. Louis Post-Dispatch*, January 13, 1928.
[60] *New York Times*, December 21, 1927.
[61] *St. Louis Post-Dispatch*, December 22, 1927. That same day, The *Globe-Democrat* put the total at $35,275.
[62] *St. Louis Star*, December 22, 1927.
[63] *St. Louis Post-Dispatch*, September 14, 1928.

Last Call

Rogers Hornsby's tenure as manager of the Chicago Cubs ended on August 2, 1932. On that day, club president Bill Veeck Sr. fired him as a manager and released him as a player. "It was to the best interests of the club that Hornsby retire at this time," he said. Other details soon emerged regarding the possible reasons for Veeck's decision. To the surprise of no one familiar with Hornsby's past, the behavior involved betting.

Shortly after Hornsby was fired, Commissioner Landis launched an investigation into a rumor that Cubs players had run up a $38,000 debt to bookmakers in a horse-race betting pool. With the Cubs in St. Louis for a weekend series, Landis summoned Hornsby, three of his former players and a Cubs coach to the Chase Hotel. Under questioning from the commissioner, Hornsby admitted borrowing more than $4,000 from players to pay off various debts and then borrowing $7,000 more after convincing one player to sign his notes. But he refused to divulge any details of possible betting behavior. "I am not going to say," Hornsby responded when asked by Landis if he had placed a horse racing bet since 1930. "I refuse to answer that question." The Cubs players denied the betting pool allegations. Landis released a transcript of the meeting but did not take any further action. "The transcript speaks for itself," he told reporters. "There will be no ruling made by me."[1]

With their former manager out of the picture and the Landis investigation concluded, the Cubs caught fire. In second place with a record of 53-46 when Hornsby was terminated, Chicago went 37-18 the rest of the way, at one point reeling off 14 straight wins. Guided by their new manager and longtime first baseman, Charlie Grimm, Chicago finished with a record of 90-64, four games ahead of second-place Pittsburgh.

Known as "Jolly Cholly," the new manager's personality stood in stark contrast to the previous regime. Grimm, a St. Louis native, spent his teenage years reading meters in the summer for Laclede Gas every morning, then hustling over to Sportsman's Park where he would shag fly balls and take batting practice in the afternoon.[2] Spotted one day from the dugout by an impressed Philadelphia manager, Connie Mack, Grimm debuted for the Athletics in 1916. He was seventeen years old. He had been the Cubs everyday first baseman since 1925. (Grimm played one season in St. Louis. He and Hornsby were teammates in 1918.)

While Grimm now called the shots from the Cubs dugout, Mark Koenig took Hornsby's place on the roster. The former Yankee shortstop's four errors in seven games helped the Cardinals clinch their first World Series title.[3] Considered by some the "goat" of the 1926 Series, Koenig redeemed himself by hitting .500 the next year when the Yankees swept the Pirates. Remaining with the Yankees until early in the 1930 season, Koenig was playing minor league ball in the Pacific Coast League when he got the call from the Cubs.

In Chicago, Koenig helped lead the charge down the stretch. He hit .353 for the Cubs over the last two months of the season with three home runs and 11 RBI. Signed three days after Hornsby was fired, Koenig also served as insurance for regular shortstop Billy Jurges. Shot by a jilted lover at a Chicago hotel, Jurges missed more than two weeks of games in July as he recovered from gunshot wounds. (Some have claimed the Jurges story is the basis for the story of Roy Hobbs, the fictional ballplayer shot in the novel *The Natural*, later turned into a movie starring Robert Redford. Others point to a 1949 shooting incident involving Phillies first baseman Eddie Waitkus.)[4] After Koenig arrived, the former Yankee got the majority of starts at shortstop as Jurges struggled down the stretch (hit just .192 in August). When the World Series opened at Yankee Stadium on September 28, Koenig was the starter. He scored a run and knocked in another with a triple, but the Cubs lost the opener 12-6.

Koenig didn't start another game. He hurt his wrist on the triple and only made a single pinch-hitting appearance the rest of the way, but perhaps more than any other player, Koenig's spot on the Cubs roster set the tone for a raucous and contentious World Series atmosphere.

Before the start of postseason play, the Cubs decided how they would split their share of World Series money. The team voted to give twenty players full shares. Despite helping to ignite the team in the final months of the regular season, the Cubs allocated Koenig just a half-share of the money. Upon hearing the news of their former teammate's award, players on the Yankees feigned shock and outrage. Ruth called the Cubs "a bunch of cheapskates, nickel-nursers, and misers." The jawboning and bench-jockeying between the two clubs began almost immediately. "So they're going to give you a half-share, are they, Mark?" the Babe barked as Koenig took the field for Game 1. "Well, you had better collect that five bucks right now."[5]

Resenting how the Yankees portrayed their decision, the Cubs began firing verbal volleys of their own. With Ruth the ringleader on the New York side, it was only natural for Chicago to focus their catcalls and jeers in the direction of the Yankees slugger. The insults and taunts reached their peak in Game 3, the first game in Wrigley Field.

With the Yankees leading 2-0 in the Series and the game tied at four, Ruth came to the plate in the fifth inning against Cubs pitcher Charlie Root. Ruth had already homered off Root in the first inning and flew out to deep right field in his second plate appearance. With 51,000 fans on their feet and the Cubs players standing on the top step of their dugout jeering and screaming, John Drebinger described the scene in the *Times* as Ruth walked to the plate for the third time that day.

"A single lemon rolled out to the plate as Ruth came up in the fifth and in no mistaken motions the Babe notified the crowd that the nature of his retaliation would be a wallop right out of the confines of the park," Drebinger wrote. "Root pitched two balls and two strikes, while Ruth signaled with his fingers after each pitch to let the spectators know exactly how the situation stood." After the second strike, Ruth not only signaled with his fingers, he also pointed. Exactly *where* Ruth pointed is a source of debate to this day. Some claim he was gesturing toward the bleachers where a notorious Cubs heckler, Amos "Loudmouth" Latimer, was stationed. Many suspected he was pointing in the direction of the Cubs dugout, where pitcher Guy Bush was leading the verbal abuse against the Babe. Others thought he was communicating with the Cubs pitcher. "I am going to knock the next one down your goddamn throat," was the message Lou Gehrig thought Ruth was sending. (Readers can decide for themselves by looking at a pair of home movies discovered years later and available on YouTube.)

There is no mystery as to what happened next. For the first time in the at-bat, Ruth swung at a Root pitch. The ball rocketed off his Louisville Slugger and disappeared beyond the wall in right-center field. The Babe had crushed his second home run of the day to give the Yankees a lead they wouldn't relinquish and a story that would live forever. Wrigley Field fans, a group that included Democratic Presidential nominee Franklin Roosevelt and future Supreme Court Justice John Paul Stevens, gave a jubilant Ruth a standing ovation as he circled the bases.

While the legend of Ruth's "called shot" in the 1932 World Series has been frequently chronicled, there has been far less attention to the Babe's behavior four years earlier in an almost identical situation. Like the 1932 World Series against the Cubs, the Yankees swept the Cardinals in 1928. In both Series, Ruth stole the show. In his second World Series against St. Louis, Ruth repeated a feat he first accomplished in 1926 by hitting three home runs in a single game. Did Ruth also call his shot that day at Sportsman's Park?

The evidence comes from author and longtime *Sports Illustrated* editor Robert Creamer. In his 1974 biography of Ruth, Creamer wrote that after *SI* published an article skeptical of the Ruth called shot in Chicago, the publication received a letter about the slugger's performance against the Cardinals. K.E. Dougan claimed to be in St. Louis that October.

"Not having been there, I have no opinion [about 1932]," Dougan wrote. "However, I was a personal witness to either two or three home runs which Babe did call in one game. A friend and I skipped school and took a street car at 4 a.m. to get bleacher seats to the fourth game of the 1928 World Series. We sat in the left-field bleachers behind Ruth. He took a lot of good-natured booing. About the middle of the game, as he took his position in left field, he held up the number of fingers for the next inning and pointed to the right-field bleachers. And the next inning he hit a home run. As I recall, he did this twice during the game."[6]

Corroboration for Dougan's account came from the Babe himself. "I told those friends of mine in the bleachers I'd hit two home runs, and I hit three!" said Ruth after the game. The Babe's three home-run performance in Game 4 of 1928 capped off a World Series in which he hit .625 and made a nice running catch to end the final game. Before a contest against the Browns in 1929, a reporter asked Ruth, "What was the biggest thrill you ever got out of a ballgame?" Ruth, eating a hotdog at the time, paused to answer the question. "Biggest thrill? That's easy. It happened right here in St. Louis when I got three home runs in one World Series game and made that running catch off Frankie Frisch. Picked the ball right out of the stands."[7] In his two World Series against the Cardinals, Ruth hit seven home runs. His dramatic fifth-inning shot off Charlie Root was the fifteenth and final World Series home run of his career.

The Babe and his teammates each collected a winning check for $5,231.77 in 1932. Defeated Cubs players voted a full share received $4,244.60 apiece. Koenig, Hornsby's replacement on the Cubs roster and the inspiration behind much of the World Series banter, received half that amount, or $2,122.30. The man who guided the team for the first 99 games of the season received nothing. The Cubs didn't vote Hornsby a single dime. The former Chicago player/manager complained about the omission but an appeal to Commissioner Landis was denied.[8]

Hornsby didn't play or manage the rest of the season after getting released. "We suggest to baseball that it hire Hornsby as a baseball player, which he certainly is," editorialized the *Post-Dispatch*, "and quit trying to hire him as an exemplar for Boy Scouts, or the patron saint of Thrift Week, which he certainly is not."[9] Out of a baseball job, he returned to his farm in St. Louis County. When he bought it in 1928, he stocked it with horses, cattle, hogs, and chickens and had visions of selling his bluegrass sod to major league teams.[10] But four years later, the country was increasingly in the grips of the Great Depression, with one in four men soon to be out of work. Hornsby owed the federal government roughly $22,000 in back taxes.[11] In December, after he missed a $900 mortgage payment, his 80-acre foreclosed farm was sold at auction for $15,000.[12]

*****

Ruth played two more years for the Yankees and then ended his big-league career in the city where it began. Finishing out the string with the Boston Braves, the forty-year-old Ruth played in just 28 games. The highlight of his season came on May 25, 1935 in Pittsburgh, where he hit the final three home runs of his career. The last two home runs – career numbers 713 and 714 – came off Guy Bush, the former Chicago pitcher whose taunting from the Cubs dugout ingloriously backfired in the World Series three years earlier.[13] A week after his three-home-run game and struggling with a batting average of .181, the Babe decided to call it quits.

Ruth had often expressed a desire to manage in the big leagues, but he never got the opportunity. (Meanwhile, Hornsby got the chance everywhere he played. Both Ruth and his daughter Julia believed racial bias was a factor. "Judge Landis was absolutely against blacks," Julia told Jane Leavy. "He knew that if Daddy was a manager, Daddy would have had blacks on the team.")[14] Ruth did work as a first-base coach briefly for the Brooklyn Dodgers in 1938. That summer in St. Louis, he competed in a pre-game home run hitting contest. Challenged by Joe Medwick and Johnny Mize of the Cardinals and Dolph Camilli of the Dodgers, Ruth won the competition when he launched a 430-foot blast onto Grand Avenue.

He made his final visit to the city where he created so many memories a decade later. The Browns declared June 19, 1948 "Babe Ruth Day." The team honored the former Yankee great with a pre-game ceremony that featured an automobile ride around Sportsman's Park and a trophy presentation from *The Sporting News* that recognized the legend's contributions to American Legion baseball. The tribute occurred just one week after his final appearance in uniform at Yankee Stadium where Ruth's number 3 was retired.

The day in St. Louis began with Ruth conducting a baseball clinic at the park. Ten-thousand young boys showed up. A picture in the next day's *Post-Dispatch* shows Ruth surrounded by smiling youth. For his entire career, the Babe had a special bond with his young fans. "He was like the Pied Piper," a teenager once said of Ruth, "always surrounded by children and carrying one of them on his shoulder or in his arms."[15]

The *Globe-Democrat* pictured Ruth in a suit swinging a baseball bat with the batboy of the Browns by his side. The image captured the Yankees past – and the Cardinals future. Bill DeWitt Jr., the chairman of the Cardinals, was six years old when he met the Babe. Standing next to Ruth gave him instant credibility with the crowd, which sought his autograph as he circulated through the stands. "Being six, I signed 'Billy,'" DeWitt recalled. "My mother said, 'You might want to add your last name.'"[16]

With New York in town for a series, Ruth also posed with a St. Louis native and a man who would represent the next generation of Yankee greatness. "Found out later it was the last time Babe ever appeared in a ballpark," said Yogi Berra.[17]

On his final weekend in St. Louis, Ruth was also honored at a luncheon at the Chase Hotel. For likely the last time in his life, a reporter asked the Babe about his attempted steal of second base in Game 7 of the 1926 World Series. "All those writers were wonderful to me during my active days. They made me the hero when I hit home runs and never mentioned the biggest blunder I pulled as a player," Ruth replied. "I can see it all now. I was sore at Alex because he didn't put that last pitch close enough for me to swing at it. I felt sure I could belt a home run and tie up the score. When I got to first base, I said to myself that I'd get even with Alex and cross him by stealing second base. I didn't, of course, and I lost that Series for the Yanks."[18]

While Ruth's visit rekindled stories of his postseason clashes with the Cardinals, it also echoed with memories of his battles with the Browns and the "Little World Series" of 1922. Among the guests at the Chase that day was Ruth's old nemesis, Hub "Shucks" Pruett, the former Browns screwball pitcher. In his career, the Malden, Missouri native and University of Missouri product struck out Ruth fifteen times in 30 plate appearances. "Thanks for putting me through medical school," now Dr. Pruett told Ruth. "If it hadn't been for you, nobody ever would have heard of me."

"It's a good thing there weren't more like you," Ruth replied, "or nobody ever would have heard of me."

It was the first and last time the two men ever spoke. Ruth returned to New York and soon checked into a hospital. Battling cancer, he died two months after his final St. Louis visit. He was fifty-three years old. Over the next two days, an estimated 77,000 fans filed past his casket at Yankee Stadium while a similar number of onlookers gathered outside St. Patrick's Cathedral for his funeral. Pallbearers included former teammates Joe Dugan and Waite Hoyt.

"I'd give a hundred bucks for a cold beer," said Dugan on that August afternoon. "So would the Babe," Hoyt replied.

*****

Like Ruth, Hornsby returned to the town where he got his start. In October of 1932, Rickey convinced Breadon to give him another shot. He signed a one-year contract for $15,000. "I'm willing to admit I made the one big mistake of my career when I slammed the door in Mr. Breadon's face six years ago and refused to accept the contract that was offered," an unusually contrite Hornsby admitted.

Signed only to play and not manage, Hornsby began the season as the starting second baseman with Frisch playing shortstop. But when the Cardinals acquired shortstop Leo Durocher from Cincinnati in early May, Frisch returned to second base and Hornsby moved to the bench. With no room for him in the Cardinals lineup, a lifeline from the Browns soon emerged.

In the middle of a last-place season, Browns manager Bill Killefer resigned in July. The man Breadon wanted as Hornsby's replacement after the 1926 season found himself replaced by Hornsby in the middle of the 1933 season. Knowing that Phil Ball admired Hornsby, Cardinals vice president Rickey played matchmaker. He arranged for the Browns owner to meet with Hornsby and represented the player in the negotiations. On July 26, a deal was announced. Hornsby cleared waivers and joined the Browns as player/manager. (With the Cardinals, Hornsby hit .325 in 83 at-bats.) His final years with the American League team followed a familiar arc; he played sparingly, managed controversially, and was fired abruptly when his betting behavior became an issue too large to ignore.

The 1933 St. Louis Browns drew just 88,000 fans for the entire season. The team won 55 games while losing 99 (19-33 under Hornsby). "This is a fine ball club I'm turning over to you," Browns owner Ball told Hornsby when he hired him. "It's a lousy ball club," his new manager replied.[19] In October, Ball died and his heirs put the team up for sale. Rickey again played the role of intermediary. An executor of the estate turned to the Cardinals executive for possible ideas on new ownership of the Browns. Rickey thought of his former office assistant, Bill DeWitt Sr. Dewitt had risen to become the Cardinals treasurer in 1926 and a decade later had the title of assistant vice president and business manager of the St. Louis National League franchise.

Through his wife, DeWitt had a connection to Donald Barnes, president of a local investment company. The duo cobbled together a group of investors to buy the Browns for $325,000 in the fall of 1936. Barnes put up $50,000 and became president, and DeWitt invested $25,000 and became the general manager. For brokering the sale of his hometown rival, Rickey received a $25,000 commission. [20]

Barnes and DeWitt took over a struggling franchise that had finished in last place or next-to-last in three of the past four seasons. A sixth-place team in 1934 that finished twenty-two games under .500 was the high-water mark of the Hornsby era. That season was punctuated by the final appearance of Ruth in a Yankee uniform at Sportsman's Park in September. On Sunday, September 9, Ruth went 2-3 with one RBI and two runs scored. Hornsby appeared as a pinch-hitter and went 1-1 with one RBI in a 6-5 loss to the Yankees. It marked the last time both men appeared in the same game.

In between ownership groups and left to his own devices, Hornsby practiced an increasingly authoritarian style of management. The man who objected to constraints on his behavior banned the playing of cards in dressing rooms, hotels, and trains during the 1936 season. His unhappy players once stood outside his Pullman compartment and yelled for him to come out. He refused.

"Hornsby didn't coax or coddle anybody. He wasn't capable, and didn't believe a big-league player should need it. He had no feelings and didn't think anybody else did, either. He would criticize mediocre players unmercifully," wrote longtime National League player Dick Bartell. "He didn't care about his players as people. They all looked alike to him. He didn't care what effect his words might have on his target. He said what he thought, and he thought he was always right."[21]

Well aware of Hornsby's reputation and his chronic gambling habits, Barnes and DeWitt kept a close eye on their player/manager. They soon began noticing a pattern of behavior. Hornsby "would always go into one of the phone booths in the ballpark," DeWitt remembered. "Then during the game, the clubhouse boy would go out two or three times and spend ten or fifteen minutes away. We couldn't figure out what he was doing. So we finally checked around and found out that he was running bets for Hornsby to a saloon across the street, where they used to make book on the horses and the ball games and everything else. He'd come down and give Hornsby the results on the bench."[22]

The club had once enlisted the help of a St. Louis newspaper reporter to monitor Hornsby's activities. After a series in Detroit, the Browns had an off day in Chicago before playing the White Sox. "The *Globe-Democrat* had word that if Hornsby went to the race track in Chicago that day that baseball emissaries would swoop down on him and he would be summarily dismissed from baseball," Bob Burnes recalled years later. He was told he got the assignment instead of the regular Browns reporter because Hornsby didn't know him. Upon arrival in Chicago, Hornsby set up in one corner of the hotel lobby, Burnes in another, keeping an eye on the Browns player/manager all day long. The reporter turned spy watched Hornsby get up to make several telephone calls and venture over to the coffee shop a few times, but otherwise he never left the lobby of the Palmer House. At ten p.m., a yawning Hornsby finally departed for the elevators. Burnes' undercover mission was over.[23]

According to DeWitt, the owners decided in 1937 to take their surveillance to the next level. "Barnes got the idea of tapping the telephone, and we hired some Pinkerton's guys to get on the other end of the line to see what was going on. The guy gave us a report every day; we had all Hornsby's bets: what he lost, what he won, everything. Listen, he was a big bettor. He'd bet $50 across the board or $100 across the board. Sometimes, he'd bet $1,500 on a race. He'd bet eight or nine different races. And he was placing bets all over the country."

As an incentive to invest in something other than horse racing, Barnes had loaned Hornsby approximately $5,000 to buy stock in his firm, the American Investment Company. "And one day, Hornsby had a hell of a day at the tracks, won about $3,000 or $3,500," DeWitt recalled. "So he came in the office and he said, 'I want to pay off some of that money, about $2,000.' Barnes said, 'You must have had a windfall.' Hornsby said, 'Well, a guy owed me some money and paid me.' Of course, we knew where he got it, so he and Barnes got into an argument. Barnes wound up firing him, right then." Hornsby lasted 77 games under the Barnes/DeWitt regime. The owners replaced him with his former Cardinal teammate, Jim Bottomley.

That offseason, Hornsby attempted to strike deals with multiple teams. "Since last September, I have been approached a dozen times with good offers in baseball, but something always comes up," he said at the end of 1937. "A club representative will talk to me enthusiastically one day and then drop me like a hot rock. Why? Is it because I play the horses or what? Certainly, they should tell me," he demanded before adding, "No, I don't intend to stop playing the ponies."

Asked if Hornsby was now on baseball's blacklist, Commissioner Landis dodged the question. "Hornsby was a great ball player. A fine fellow. Too bad he likes the horses."[24] For the rest of the commissioner's reign, Hornsby didn't work for a major league team.

Elected to the Hall of Fame in 1942 (receiving 182 of 233 votes), Hornsby was otherwise rejected at the highest levels of baseball. He wandered the landscape of the minor leagues for years. He coached or managed in Minneapolis, Baltimore, Chattanooga, Oklahoma City, and Forth Worth. He had a baseball school in Hot Springs, Arkansas and even spent a year in the Mexican League. He did a radio show in St. Louis and then left for Chicago, where he broadcast games on television for the Cubs.[25]

After spending 1950 in Beaumont, Texas and the following year in Seattle, Hornsby finally returned to the big leagues. At the end of 1951, he reportedly entertained offers from both the Cardinals and Browns.[26] With Landis long gone (he died in 1944), baseball's unofficial blacklisting of Hornsby had lifted. He accepted an offer to manage the Browns from new owner Bill Veeck Jr. It was Veeck's father who had fired Hornsby in Chicago, prompting junior's mother to send him a note after the hire was announced: "What makes you think you're smarter than your daddy was?"

Veeck was a risk-taker who was not afraid to buck baseball's conventional wisdom. As owner of the Cleveland Indians, he signed Larry Doby, the first black player in American League history, who made his debut shortly after Jackie Robinson. In his first year with the Browns, Veeck signed legendary Negro League pitcher Satchel Paige and three-foot-seven-inch Eddie Gaedel. Making his debut in the uniform of Browns batboy DeWitt, Gaedel walked in his only major league plate appearance.

The hiring of Hornsby came after a season in which the Browns finished last in the American League in both victories and attendance. Less than 300,000 people watched the Browns in 1951 while more than a million fans came to Sportsman's Park to watch the Cardinals. Hornsby's return would pique the interest of Browns and Cardinals fans alike. At the same time, his recent performance as a manager – his Beaumont Roughnecks won the Texas League in 1950 while the Seattle Rainiers won the Pacific Coast League title in 1951 – demonstrated he could motivate players. Veeck paid him $36,000 a year, making Hornsby the highest salaried manager in franchise history.[27]

Fifteen years after getting fired the first time from the Browns, Hornsby lasted 51 games in his return to St. Louis. Just months after he called him the "best manager in baseball," Veeck let him go in June. His players hated him. "He doesn't have a friend in the world and he doesn't deserve one," said pitcher Gene Bearden. To show their approval of Hornsby's termination, Browns players presented Veeck with a three-foot-high trophy. "For the greatest play since the Emancipation Proclamation," it read.[28] "I just made a mistake," said Veeck. "I thought Hornsby had mellowed but he hadn't."[29]

Hornsby's humiliating treatment by the Browns didn't dampen interest in his services. He was soon hired to manage the Cincinnati Reds (Cincinnati general manager Gabe Paul got his start in baseball working for the Cardinals minor league team in Rochester). On Labor Day of 1953, the former Cardinal and Brown was in the visiting dugout at Sportsman's Park when he was handed a note. Estranged from his second wife, Hornsby had been living with another woman. The note informed him that the woman – Bernadette Ann Harris – was dead. The fifty-five-year-old Harris plunged to her death when she jumped out the window of a Chicago hotel. Authorities discovered a note in her purse. "In case of accident, notify Rogers Hornsby," it read. Believing she was going blind and deaf, a coroner's investigation ruled she committed suicide "while temporarily insane due to despondency." Hornsby, who testified at the inquest, described Harris as his personal secretary and friend. He was named the sole beneficiary of her estate. In the same safe deposit box where her will was discovered, authorities also found $25,000 in cash.[30] According to Hornsby biographer Alexander, Hornsby had been using Harris to hide money from his estranged wife Jeannette, who was seeking an increase in her separate maintenance allowance.

One week later, with the Reds in sixth place, general manager Paul dismissed Hornsby as manager of the team. "I wish the players and the club the best of luck,"

Hornsby told reporters. "I'm going back to Chicago and will make that my home while waiting for something else to show up."

He never managed in the major leagues again. He donned his 1926 uniform for an old-timers' game at Yankee Stadium in 1959 and more than once, regretted ever leaving St. Louis. "I loved St. Louis, had a house there and everything," he recalled.[31] "Planned to spend the rest of my life there." He coached for the Chicago Cubs, where he became an early booster of Billy Williams ("get this kid up here as fast as you can," he told club officials), and the New York Mets.[32] Hornsby was the hitting coach for the 1962 Metropolitans, Casey Stengel's infamous crew that went 40-120 in their inaugural season. Along the way, he divorced his second wife and married again. He remained married to Marjorie Bernice Frederick Porter for the rest of his life.

One of the last public feuds of Hornsby's career involved the man who broke Ruth's single-season home-run record. Roger Maris hit 61 homes runs for the Yankees in 1961. Before a spring training game in 1962, a photographer wanted Hornsby and Maris together for a photograph. The previous year, Hornsby had criticized Maris, saying the only thing he could do better than Ruth was run. Maris remembered. When Hornsby walked over to Maris for the photograph, the Yankee outfielder turned his back on him. Hornsby found a reporter and unloaded, calling Maris a "little punk ballplayer," a "swelled-up guy," and a "bush-leaguer." The Yankees responded the next day by defending Maris. "Let Hornsby take care of his ball club and I'll take care of mine," said manager Ralph Houk, but the Rajah wouldn't forget it. "The Maris snub has left a deep scar on Hornsby," Dick Young wrote weeks later.[33]

In the early 1960s, writer Bill Surface spent time with Hornsby for the Rajah's book, *My War with Baseball*, and a profile in the *Saturday Evening Post* that was published posthumously. In the magazine story, Surface told of how Hornsby would pretend to be on the phone in the mornings with his stockbroker. "Number Four in the first one at New York. Ten shares. You know. Five first and five second." When Surface told the Hall-of-Famer he was a former turf reporter and knew exactly what he was doing, Hornsby abandoned the subterfuge. From then on, the two spent their days talking at the racetrack. After watching Hornsby beg a trainer for a tip and lose $400 on the first seven races one day, Surface asked him if it was time to leave. "Leave?" he replied. "Hell, there's nine races today. Only one way to go out of this place." In seven hours at the track, Surface noticed that Hornsby had not eaten nor drunk a thing, nor had he spared a moment to go to the bathroom. The gambler was entirely consumed by the betting action. "He looked neither tired nor discouraged," Surface wrote.[34]

In December of 1962, Hornsby underwent cataract surgery. His legendary vision protected all those years, he insisted, by never going to movies or reading a book, was fading. A few days later, he suffered a stroke. On January 5, 1963, sixty-six-year-old Rogers Hornsby died of heart failure. Eight months after his death, the Academy of Sports Editors voted him the greatest National League player in history.

"He was a stranger, even to those who knew him best," wrote Red Smith. "He was a hard and lonely man who loved kids, hated phonies, and worshipped the truth."[35] After his death, when writers had something nice to say about Hornsby, it often revolved around his affection for youth. "Hardboiled Hornsby was a pushover for kids," wrote Bob Broeg in 1969.[36] When working at his various baseball camps, Hornsby "was characteristically patient, forbearing, and anxious to get them to love the game as he did," wrote his biographer, Charles Alexander.

He left his estate, "savings estimated at no more than $25,000," and various mementos, to his son Bill.[37] The final irony in the life of the man who didn't drink alcohol was that he left his money to a man who earned his living in the beer business. Bill Hornsby had a distributorship in Tennessee with Johnny Beazley, the hero of the 1942 World Series. Beazley won two games for the Cardinals against the Yankees, including the Game 5 clincher.

Hornsby outlived the pitcher who won two games against the Yankees in 1926 and the man he embraced in its most crucial moment. Grover Cleveland Alexander battled alcoholism to the end. He died in 1950 at the age of 63. He didn't outlast, however, the man with whom he had a sometimes fractious, sometimes friendly relationship. Just a few months before Hornsby died, Branch Rickey returned to the city where he got his start as a major league player, manager, and general manager. Not only was Rickey returning to St. Louis after a twenty-year hiatus, the one-time ardent prohibitionist went to work for a brewery.

Beer and baseball. It wasn't the first time Rickey did the unthinkable.

---

[1] *St. Louis Globe-Democrat,* August 14, 1932. The paper published the transcript.

[2] *St. Louis Star*, August 14, 1931.

[3] "I was a lousy shortstop," Koenig conceded decades later. "I had such small hands. We had little gloves, not the butterfly nets they've got now. I made quite a few errors, but not throwing errors because I had a good arm." *Los Angeles Times,* September 27, 1987.

[4] In fact, both incidents may have served to inspire the story. See sabr.org/research/eddie-waitkus-and-natural-what-assumption-what-fact

[5] Sherman, Ed. *Babe Ruth's Called Shot. The Myth and Mystery of Baseball's Greatest Home Run*. Lyons Press. 2014.

[6] Creamer, *Babe.*

[7] Ibid. Creamer says the "biggest thrill" quote occurred in 1930 but its origin is a 1929 profile of the Babe in St. Louis. *St. Louis Star*, May 23, 1929.

[8] In 1926, Hornsby's Cardinals voted to give every player on the roster a full share. That included pitcher Edgar Clough, who didn't pitch until after the team clinched the pennant. *St. Louis Globe-Democrat*, September 29, 1926.

[9] *St. Louis Post-Dispatch*, August 16, 1932.

---

[10] "The Cubs will have the finest infield and outfield in baseball – if they buy my grass." *Pittsburgh Press*, December 5, 1928. Hornsby lived on the property in a fourteen-room-house. "He is enthused over this thing of raising bluegrass and it is a distinct hobby with him. He even went so far as to have a couple of darkies come up from Texas when he first bought the place and set it out in the grass. They made a good job of it." *The Sporting News*, December 27, 1928.

[11] *St. Louis Star-Times*, December 17, 1932, and *St. Louis Post-Dispatch*, December 18, 1932. The Star mentions a figure of $22,283. The Post-Dispatch says the back taxes totaled $21,283.

[12] *St. Louis Post-Dispatch*, December 20, 1932. Depending on the account, the size of the farm is listed at 80, 85, 86 or 87-acres. It was located on Bridgeton Station road, near the airport. In August, Cubs pitcher Guy Bush told Landis that Hornsby had told him he needed money to pay back taxes. Under questioning, Hornsby admitted that none of the borrowed money went to pay the tax debt. *St. Louis Globe-Democrat*, August 14, 1932.

[13] Bush finished his career with the Cardinals in 1938. While in the minor leagues, Cardinals pitcher Mort Cooper credited Bush with giving him career-changing advice. "Get mad," Bush told him. "Not mad enough to lose control, but mad enough to swap punches with the batter." Cooper believed it was "the best advice I ever had." *Baseball Digest,* October 1944.

[14] Leavy, *The Big Fella.* The quote is part of a longer story in the book involving rumors of Ruth's ancestry. The granddaughter of Ruth's sister Mamie (his closest proven biological relative) had her DNA tested. According to a consultant, a saliva sample revealed no evidence of African "admixture" in her DNA, which would indicate Ruth had no "significant amount of African admixture" in his DNA, "if Ruth's biological parents were who they were believed to be."

[15] Macht, *Connie Mack.*

[16] Leavy, *The Big Fella.*

[17] Ibid.

[18] *St. Louis Star-Times,* June 22, 1948.

[19] *New York Times*, January 8, 1963.

[20] *The Sporting News*, November 19, 1936. The publication reported that Rickey's commission was "approximately ten percent, or $25,000 on the basis of a $325,000 sales price." The Barnes and DeWitt group purchased the franchise but not the ballpark. Phil Ball's heirs still owned the Dodier Realty Company, which agreed to lease the park to the Browns at $30,000 annually and to the Cardinals at $35,000 annually. The Browns purchased the park in 1946 under the ownership of Richard Muckerman.

[21] Bartell, *Rowdy Richard.*

[22] Golenbock, *The Spirit of St. Louis.*

[23] *St. Louis Globe-Democrat*, January 19, 1963. "While Hornsby spent much of his time lobby sitting, frequently that apparent idleness was also a matter of waiting out race results," wrote biographer Charles Alexander.

---

[24] *St. Louis Post-Dispatch*, December 10, 1937.
[25] Hornsby broadcast Chicago Cubs games on WENR-TV in 1949, a precursor to WLS.
[26] "(Fred) Saigh's interest in a more aggressive manager, a desire which first caused him to approach Rogers Hornsby…" wrote Bob Broeg. *The Sporting News*, December 5, 1951. The Cardinals hired Eddie Stanky to replace the recently fired Marty Marion.
[27] "I gave him exactly what he wanted, a 3-year contract at $36,000 a year." Veeck, *Veeck as in Wreck*. "Saigh had sent an emissary to sound out Rogers Hornsby about replacing Marty Marion as the Cardinals' manager. His emissary was thoughtful enough to pass the information on to me," Veeck recalled. "I couldn't allow that to happen."
[28] *Post-Dispatch* columnist and longtime Hornsby ghostwriter Roy Stockton strongly disapproved of the move, calling the trophy presentation a "public humiliation," and done in "woefully bad taste." *St. Louis Post-Dispatch*, June 12, 1952. Stockton claimed Hornsby "wanted them to win so badly that he was a sourpuss about it," a comment that drew a reaction from Veeck. "A man who would call Hornsby a sourpuss would wonder why everybody was complaining about Attila the Hun's table manners." Veeck, *Veeck as in Wreck.*
[29] Bill DeWitt Sr. had tried to warn Veeck before he hired Hornsby. "This guy will never change," DeWitt told him. WHAT DID I TELL YOU? Veeck's mother wired him after the firing. Veeck, *Veeck as in Wreck*.
[30] Ibid, September 9, 1953.
[31] He also regretted signing on as manager of the Browns and not the Cardinals in the fall of 1951. "That's where I booted one." Alexander, *Rogers Hornsby.*
[32] *The Sporting News*, July 4, 1964.
[33] *New York Daily News*, April 19, 1962.
[34] *Saturday Evening Post*, June 15, 1963.
[35] *St. Louis Post-Dispatch*, January 8, 1963.
[36] *The Sporting News*, February 22, 1969.
[37] Alexander, *Rogers Hornsby.*

The Seeds of Discontent

The 1934 season marked the culmination of an incredible turnaround in the fortunes of the St. Louis Cardinals. A franchise that consistently struggled and frequently finished in the bottom half of the standings from its inception through the 1925 campaign could point with pride to five pennants and three world championships in the previous nine seasons. Under Sam Breadon and Branch Rickey's leadership, the club had made a bold bet on developing talent through a vertically integrated farm system, an approach radically different than other dominant franchises of the era.

The 1934 Cardinals, a team that became known as the "Gashouse Gang," featured James Anthony "Ripper" Collins at first base (35 HR, 128 RBI, .333 batting average), Johnny Leonard Roosevelt "Pepper" Martin at third base (club-leading 23 stolen bases), and Joe "Ducky" Medwick (18 HR, 106 RBI, .319 batting average) in left field. All had risen through the ranks of the Cardinals organization. On player/manager Frankie Frisch's pitching staff were brothers Dizzy and Paul Dean. The former St. Louis farmhands claimed 49 of the team's regular-season 95 victories and all four of the club's wins in the World Series against Detroit. But what should have been a victory-lap moment for the franchise quickly devolved into a turbulent and contentious offseason in which the owner openly talked about selling or moving the franchise. It is in this window of time that some speculate the bonds began to fray between Breadon and Rickey, a professional relationship eventually terminated the following decade.

Breadon's winter of discontent began early. With two games to go in the season, the Cardinals and Giants were tied for first place. New York dropped its remaining contests on the schedule while St. Louis won its final two games against Cincinnati to clinch the pennant. National League president John Heydler had observers watch the games closely and reportedly even hired detectives to shadow players on that final regular-season weekend. Fifteen years after the Black Sox scandal, baseball officials were still haunted by the specter of tainted play. "I had ex-umpires and other trusted observers attend the games and report to me every night whether there had been any close plays which might have caused protests against the umpires," Heydler admitted, while denying any detectives were involved. While Heydler claimed the move was purely precautionary, Breadon was outraged. The St. Louis owner viewed the action as a smear against the character of his team and wrote an "unfortunately cruel letter" to Heydler. The National League president resigned in November.[1]

That same month, Breadon began negotiations to sell the team. The potential buyer was Lew Wentz, an Oklahoma businessman who made his millions in oil. Wentz arrived in St. Louis in November and checked in at the Hotel Jefferson under an assumed name. A week later, he was still there when negotiations came to a halt and word leaked to the press. "He has my price and I consider it a good one for a world championship ball club," Breadon told reporters. The president of the Cardinals was reportedly asking between $1,000,000 and $1,250,000 for his roughly 76 percent stake in the team.[2]

Why would Breadon even consider selling? A few days later, *Post-Dispatch* columnist John Wray speculated on why the owner wanted out. "Measured by the yardstick of success, Sam Breadon ought to be the most popular man in baseball, particularly in his hometown," Wray began. "Yet one of the reasons for his willingness to withdraw from the ownership of the Cardinals is a feeling that he is something of a pariah in his own baseball bailiwick."[3]

Breadon a pariah? Wray believed it all started with the trade of Hornsby following the 1926 season. Despite the performance of Frisch in a Cardinals uniform, local fans never quite got over the Rajah's departure and blamed Breadon for the breakup. (More than 36 years after the deal, *Globe-Democrat* columnist Bob Burnes wrote that he knew three people who were still fuming over the trade and hadn't been to a game since 1926.)[4] At a time when the franchise experienced unparalleled success, fans also watched an impatient owner cycle through multiple managers. During the same nine-year stretch of five pennants and three World Series titles, the Cardinals had six different men call the shots from the dugout. Hornsby gave way to O'Farrell in 1927, who was succeeded by Bill McKechnie in 1928, who was demoted in favor of Southworth, who lasted all of 88 games in 1929. The Cardinals won back-to-back pennants and a World Series title under Gabby Street in 1930 and 1931, but with the club struggling in 1933, he was cashiered in favor of Frisch. Finally, fans viewed Breadon as a cheapskate owner, less than generous with his players (a charge also leveled against Rickey). Breadon responded by pointing out his 1934 team was the fourth-highest paid team in all of baseball, a claim that fell on deaf ears. When Breadon clashed with the Dean brothers over salary demands that season, sportswriters joined the chorus of those critical of the owner. "Out-of-town writers pilloried Sam for his failure to do salary justice to the Dean brothers," Wray noted. "Many of the criticisms of Breadon and of his system were vitriolic and in some cases almost libelous."[5]

Beyond Breadon bashing, there were economic reasons why an owner would want to sell in 1934. The Great Depression had a huge impact on baseball attendance. Just six years earlier, the 1928 Cardinals drew 761,574 fans to games in St. Louis. By 1932, that number had plunged to 279,219 and dropped to 256,171 the following year, reflecting a trend across the game. Overall baseball attendance plummeted 40 percent from 1930 to 1933 and didn't fully recover until after World War II. Following the 1933 season, both the Cardinals and Browns banned the broadcasting of games at Sportsman's Park, believing that radio coverage dampened crowds. Attendance rebounded only slightly in the championship season of 1934 to 325,056. "Can you imagine drawing 300,000, no television rights, concessions were five cents a Coke and ten-cent hot dogs," recalled Marty Marion, who debuted for Breadon's Cardinals in 1940. "There wasn't much money around. What was admission, a dollar? Where did the money come from? Back in those days, they didn't have any money."[6] The radio ban was rescinded after the 1934 season.

The 1934 attendance figures reflected not only the desperate economic straits of the times but also how the season had played out. From the perspective of a St. Louis fan, the excitement of a pennant chase lasted only a few weeks. As late as September 7, the Gashouse Gang was seven games behind league-leading New York. After that date, the Cardinals won 18 of their final 23 games while the Giants dropped 13 of their final 21 contests. St. Louis spent just 13 days all season in first place.

With his club seemingly out of the pennant race in the summer, Breadon began to shop for potential buyers. Those efforts became public in September. "I'm surprised that this is not generally known," an unnamed baseball official told the *Post-Dispatch*. "I heard more than a month ago that Breadon had made it known that he would like to retire from baseball and that Branch Rickey had even gone so far as to make trips to New York and Indianapolis to confer with prospective purchasers."[7]

One of those prospective purchasers was Wentz. Born in Iowa and raised in Pennsylvania, Wentz made a name for himself in the oil business after moving to Ponca City, Oklahoma. The late billionaire J. Paul Getty once compared the oil boom of early twentieth-century Oklahoma to the California gold rush of the previous century. In the Sooner State, Wentz struck black gold. In one year in the 1920s, he paid taxes on earnings of $5,000,000, one of only seven men in the country to reach that income threshold. A life-long bachelor, Wentz lived in a suite at the Arcade Hotel in Ponca City, a hotel he owned.

Ponca City had a minor league baseball team that competed in the same league as the Cardinals' farm club in Springfield, Missouri. It was through this connection that Rickey became familiar with Wentz. He began actively courting the Oklahoma oilman in September. By November, Wentz had flown to St. Louis for face-to-face negotiations with Breadon.

By generation and bank account, Wentz and Breadon could identify with each other. The two men were born one year apart (the fifty-seven-year-old Wentz was a year younger than Breadon), and both were wealthy self-made entrepreneurs. But when it came to attitudes and beliefs, it was Wentz and Rickey who bonded. "They were both fervent Methodists, Sunday school teachers, teetotalers, and Rotarians," wrote Rickey biographer Lee Lowenfish, "and each was deeply involved in charitable activity and community service."[8]

Rickey hadn't worked with a teetotaling owner since his early days with Robert Hedges and the Browns. It is tempting to speculate how a Wentz-Rickey partnership would have influenced St. Louis and, indeed, baseball history, had the two men had the opportunity. Does Rickey remain in St. Louis for the rest of his career? How does the story of Jackie Robinson and baseball integration unfold without Rickey in Brooklyn? What would Sam Breadon do with the money?

It is this last question that *New York Times* reporter Roscoe McGowan attempted to answer when word leaked in mid-November that Breadon and Wentz were in negotiations. Claiming firsthand knowledge, "Breadon will not retire if he can purchase the club he frequently has spoken of to the writer." McGowan asserted that the Cardinals owner wanted to purchase the Brooklyn Dodgers. Citing a stipulation in the will of the late Charles Ebbets that his heirs should sell their holdings in 1935, the *Times* reporter identified Breadon as a likely candidate. "He would like to be established in New York, his hometown," McGowan wrote, "and although rated as a thorough business man, doubtless would make some sacrifice to acquire the Brooklyn franchise and retain the baseball associations he enjoys so greatly."[9] Friends of the Cardinals owner denied the report, but a parallel baseball universe where Breadon went to Brooklyn and Rickey stayed behind in St. Louis is one of the sport's more fascinating what-if scenarios.[10]

Regardless of his intentions in Brooklyn, Breadon was clearly ready to divest in St. Louis. Wentz "has my terms and the transfer of the Cardinals is up to his acceptance," he told reporters. Just a day later, he announced talks were off "indefinitely" as negotiations hit a snag. The on-again, off-again discussions remained fluid for the next few weeks. "I'm beginning to wonder myself what is causing this delay," Rickey said on November 24. At the end of the month, Sid Keener wrote that Breadon was holding out for $1,000,000, net of taxes, while Wenz wanted more time to dig into the finances of the Cardinals farm system.[11] "Putting two and two together," Keener told his readers, "the announcement of the Cardinals' sale will probably be made a few days after the National League magnates open their annual session in New York on Tuesday, December 11."

One week before the New York meeting, Breadon called it off. "I gave Mr. Wentz my price and I would have gone through with the deal, but now I'm glad he didn't accept my terms," he said after returning home from a ten-day trip to Florida.[12] (At one point, the two sides were reportedly only $35,000 apart.)[13] Several reports indicate negotiations broke down over the value of the Cardinals farm system. Other theories include Breadon raising the price of the team after the Cardinals won the World Series.[14] "The fact is," wrote *Post-Dispatch* columnist Wray, "Breadon himself was never solicitous about the deal, which was being engineered by others." The point man in the middle was Rickey, who turned out to be the biggest loser of all in the non-transaction. The front office executive would have reportedly made a $100,000 commission had the deal gone through.[15]

That detail, revealed years later, has suggested to some that a schism began to form in the relationship between Breadon and Rickey around this time and that the Cardinals vice president was eager – perhaps a little too eager – to see his boss dispose of his holdings. Columnist Roy Stockton later described the failed Wentz negotiations as "one of the disappointments of Branch's life with the Cardinals."

While the duo in charge of the St. Louis franchise had a professional partnership that lasted more than two decades, the two men were not afraid to cast each other in less than favorable light when discussing turning points in the success of the organization. "Sam Breadon never in his entire lifetime discussed with me anything along the lines of baseball having to do, for example, with the farm system. He wouldn't venture an opinion about it," Rickey once declared, saying "the idea of (Breadon) having an original idea about the so-called farm system is nonsense."[16] While Rickey wanted to make it clear who did have those original ideas, Breadon wasn't above poking holes in the reputation of the peerless talent evaluator. "I'll let you in on a secret," Breadon once told a sportswriter. "Few know it, but when Stan Musial began hitting at Springfield, the Giants offered us $40,000 for him. And a certain party wanted to sell him. I couldn't see the idea of selling Stan. I felt a hitter like that belonged on the Cardinals."[17]

Breadon's decision to keep Musial ranks as one of the greatest decisions of his ownership career. From a financial standpoint, so was his decision not to sell his team in the depths of a depression. In August of 1934, when the city of St. Louis was considering a tax on sporting events, Breadon testified before the Board of Alderman and pleaded poverty. "We've lost $100,000 a year for the past two years and expect to lose the same amount this year," Breadon said.[18] "Now this tax would be the last straw," the owner declared, telling the assembled crowd that the Cardinals would consider leaving town if such a measure passed.

Four months later, with the tax measure stalled and fresh off a World Series win, the Cardinals declared a dividend of $10 a share on common and preferred stock for a total distribution of $101,600. Omitted from the coverage was any mention of Breadon's statements in August, but the owner did explain how a projected loss suddenly turned into a profit. "The dividend this year was due to World Series money and undivided surplus," he told reporters.[19] Because he owned more than three-fourths of the common stock and held a large chunk of the preferred, Breadon's cash haul from the dividend approached or exceeded $80,000.[20] The 1934 dividend was the club's first since 1931 and began a string of four straight years of dividend payouts. From 1934 to 1937, the club paid out roughly $400,000 to shareholders with Breadon's payments totaling more than $300,000.[21]

While the owner was busy cashing checks, the vice president had again sold out. Rickey, who had liquidated his holdings in 1925, had started buying shares again in the interim. But on the day Breadon declared the dividend in 1934, he also announced that Rickey had sold his shares in the team. Reporters wanted to know if there was any significance to Rickey's action. "No," Breadon replied. "He didn't own very much stock, you know. I guess he was merely trying to clean up little business details before the first of the year." Breadon's response didn't tamp down speculation that Rickey may be on the move. "Rickey's relinquishment of his holdings appeared to some observers as basis for the assumption that the club's vice-president was about to sever his ties to the organization," wrote Dent McSkimming a day later in the *Post-Dispatch*.[22] Both Rickey and Breadon denied there were any ulterior motives behind the stock sale, but it is worth noting that the man in charge of the Cardinals farm system sold stock in the team twice in his life: once after Breadon fired him as manager, and a second time after Breadon's deal with Wentz fell through. (In 1934, Rickey sold 500 shares to Clarence Howard Jr., a longtime shareholder and son of a multimillionaire steel magnate, for a reported $100 a share.)[23]

While Breadon was quick to assure reporters of Rickey's status with the team, he was still wrestling with the fate of the franchise. While the sports tax issue faded away, he still entertained thoughts of moving the Cardinals. Back in 1932, Breadon had reportedly considered Montreal as a home for the Cardinals.[24] Near the end of spring training of 1935, Breadon talked openly about moving the team to Michigan. "Detroit is a large, prosperous city. It can stand continuous baseball (meaning an American or National League game every day during the season). St. Louis was a large city about twenty years ago, but it has failed to progress in the meantime. It cannot stand continuous baseball."[25] St. Louis was the fourth largest city in the country according to the 1910 census. Twenty years later, with a population of 821,960, its rank had slipped to seventh place. During the same two-decade span, Detroit's population had tripled to more than 1.5 million. By 1930, only New York, Chicago, and Philadelphia had more people. (The Tigers' attendance in 1934 – 919,161 – was the highest in all of baseball.)

Breadon and Detroit had both linked their fortunes to the booming automobile business. The Cardinals owner had a long history with the city, having visited Detroit in 1903 when he purchased two of the first automobiles to come out of the Ford Factory. In September of 1934, Breadon became an exclusive Ford dealer. Six months later, he renamed the company. The Western Automobile Company, in business for more than three decades, became Sam Breadon, Inc. (An odd move for a man who shunned the spotlight and was so private, he once refused to give a reporter his age. "I am not sensitive about my age," Breadon said. "But it's my own business.")[26] Less than three weeks later, Breadon floated the idea of moving his team to the hub of the automotive business.

"I have been informed by many executives of industries in Detroit that they would like to have continuous baseball. They have told me that hotels, merchants and other business interests would profit by having two clubs in their city," he said from Florida. "I agree with them."

Breadon knew any move required the approval of league owners. He also knew Frank Navin, owner of the Tigers, had no interest in seeing competition in his city. As quickly as he floated the idea, Breadon dismissed a possible move a few days later.

"How could I move away from St. Louis?" he asked. "I have real estate investments here and an automobile company in addition to the Cardinals."[27] (He reinforced his commitment to St. Louis and the Cardinals one year later when he sold his dealership and decided to retire from the automobile business.)

While the Detroit story promptly faded, Breadon's comments in the spring of 1935 reflected a growing concern among league officials that became known as "the St. Louis problem." Breadon and other baseball executives believed the city couldn't support two teams. Every few years, a story would surface that suggested either the Browns or Cardinals were leaving town. In July of 1939, National League owners reportedly held a special meeting to consider moving the Cardinals to Columbus, Ohio.[28] That same month, Keener wrote in the *Star-Times* that both the Cardinals and Browns were "alarmed at the drop of cash customers in St. Louis. Something's gone wrong with their business."[29] Two years later, the concern had escalated. "It is reported that several club officials are ready to force the St. Louis issue to a showdown decision," Keener wrote in June of 1941, "and that steps will be taken at next winter's conference to review plans for moving one local club."[30]

Six months later, the Browns had a deal to move to California. The team planned to play in Wrigley Field in Los Angeles (a ballpark owned by Phil Wrigley). Browns general manager Bill DeWitt Sr. had even met with the man who made out the baseball schedules. Each American League team would make two train trips to the West Coast over the course of a season. "They'd take the Super Chief out of Chicago. We had the schedules made out," DeWitt recalled. He and Browns owner Don Barnes planned to get approval for their plan at league meetings in Chicago on Monday, December 8, 1941. West Coast baseball may have arrived nearly two decades before the Dodgers and Giants made it a reality had it not been for the events on Sunday. Japan attacked Pearl Harbor. "I didn't know where the hell Pearl Harbor was. I never heard of Pearl Harbor," said DeWitt. "We had the meeting the next day and killed the whole thing."[31]

Four years after the Browns move failed to materialize, it was the Cardinals who faced the prospect of California baseball when stories linked Hollywood mogul Louis B. Mayer to an attempt to buy the club and move it to Los Angeles.[32] Shortly after those rumors went away, National League president Ford Frick dealt a double-blow to the ego of Cardinals fans. In the summer of 1947, a year after the team won its third World Series and fourth pennant in five seasons, Frick called for the club to leave town. He recommended Chicago as the destination. "There is no doubt that we are confronted with quite a problem in St. Louis, and I believe that a solution is available," he told Dan Daniel in *The Sporting News*. He recommended the Cardinals move to the West Side of Chicago. "A second National League team in Chicago would engender a rivalry similar to that which exists between the Dodgers and Giants in New York," Frick offered. "I can see 22 games between the Cubs and the West Siders becoming fully productive as 22 between the Giants and Dodgers."

Breadon denied any interest in moving. Frick quickly regretted the comments. "I can see now I spoke out of turn," he stated a few days later.[33] The issues were not unique to St. Louis. Both Boston and Philadelphia had teams in each league with both cities seemingly only having the appetite or resources to support one. A solution didn't arrive until the 1950s when the weaker franchise in each city moved on to greener pastures. The Boston Braves left for Milwaukee in 1953, the Browns became the Baltimore Orioles in 1954, and the Philadelphia Athletics departed for Kansas City in 1955.

Breadon ran the Cardinals from 1920 to 1947, a timeframe in which his team shared a ballpark with the Browns. He also had to contend with the Great Depression and a World War during much of his reign. Starting in the 1930s, Breadon and Rickey had another battle to fight. The pioneers of the modern minor-league system suddenly had deep-pocketed competition.

*****

By the standards of the 1926-1934 era – five pennants in nine seasons – the years from 1935 to 1941 proved incredibly frustrating to Breadon, Rickey, and the Cardinals faithful. The club didn't win a single pennant in the seven-season stretch despite some marvelously talented teams. The Cardinals came in second-place four of those seven years. Two of those teams had victory totals in the high nineties. The 1935 Cardinals, just like the 1927 edition, won more games than the World Series team of the previous year but didn't make it to the postseason. A record of 96-58 fell four games behind the Chicago Cubs, which won an incredible twenty-one straight in September to clinch the pennant.[34] The 1941 Cardinals won 97 games. The Brooklyn Dodgers won 100.

The Cardinals had to battle it out in a competitive National League at the same time the Yankees were crushing their opponents in the American League. The Yankees claimed first-place five of six seasons from 1936 to 1941, finishing an average 15 games ahead of the second-place team. Only once during that same stretch did the National League have a runaway winner. In 1940, the Cincinnati Reds finished 12.5 ahead of Brooklyn. In the other five seasons, the winner claimed the pennant by five, three, three, four-and-a-half, and two-and-a-half games, respectively.

Starting in the early 1930s, the financially formidable Yankees added a weapon to their arsenal. They began to copy the Rickey playbook and invest in their farm system. In late 1931, Yankees owner Jacob Ruppert purchased the Newark Bears of the International League. "I will spend millions to perfect a farm system that will be as big as the Cardinals," he predicted. By 1938, only the Cardinals had more farm teams. When Ruppert purchased the Newark team, he hired George Weiss as farm director. "I want to go in the chain store business and I want you to create a farm system similar to Rickey's Cardinals," Ruppert told him.[35] He did.

With Ruppert committed to the model and Weiss in charge of the farm system, the Yankees steadily encroached on territory the Cardinals had dominated. The Yankees pitch to prospects included calling the Cardinals a "cheap outfit" while backing up their offers with money for college tuition. Thanks to Rickey, the National League had passed a rule preventing teams from signing college players until after their classes had graduated. Thanks to the Yankees influence, the American League had no such rule.[36]

The post-Ruth Yankees were even more formidable than when the Babe batted third in the New York lineup. Ruth's Yankees never won more than two consecutive World Series titles. In winning twenty-two pennants in twenty-nine seasons from 1936 to 1964, the Yankees won four straight World Series from 1936 to 1939 and five straight from 1949 to 1953.

Weiss, the man who caused Rogers Hornsby such consternation back in 1926 when his New Haven minor league team refused to cancel an exhibition game against the Cardinals, spent the first sixteen years of his Yankee career as farm director. His competition for the job included the man who discovered Hornsby. Yankees general manager Ed Barrow wanted to hire Bob Connery, the former Cardinals and Yankees scout, but Ruppert preferred Weiss. His farm teams won the "Little World Series" four times during the time he oversaw the Yankees minor league squads from 1932 to 1947. Only the Cardinals, with five titles in that same timeframe, won more. In 1937, Weiss's Newark Bears faced off against Rickey's Columbus Redbirds. Columbus won the first three games in Newark but lost all four at home to give the Yankees' farm club the title.

With the Yankees committed to funding a minor league system, what had once been revolutionary was now baseball conventional wisdom. The game "has been completely Rickeyized," noted *The Sporting News.* With increased competition for young prospects, the innovative Cardinals executive sought to expand the talent pool in unconventional ways. A decade before he signed the game's first African-American player, Rickey began to aggressively target college football players. "After all," Rickey noted, "it shouldn't be so difficult for a famed athlete to sock a little baseball that is delivered by the pitcher." Easier said than done. While the Cardinals signed at least a dozen college football stars, only a few reached the big leagues. None had sustained success.[37] A few of them, however, achieved stardom in their preferred sport.

Sammy Baugh played college baseball and football at Texas Christian University. He debuted with the Washington Redskins in the fall of 1937. In his rookie season, "Slingin' Sammy" led the Redskins to the NFL Championship. In the spring of 1938, he was in the Cardinals' training camp in St. Petersburg, Florida. "Mr. Rickey gave me $2,500 to sign and a good salary," he remembered years later. A third baseman in college, Baugh played shortstop for two Cardinals minor league teams that year, appearing in 53 games for Columbus and Rochester. He hit .200 in 130 plate appearances. He returned to the Redskins that fall and never played professional baseball again. He played in the NFL until 1952 and was a member of the Pro Football Hall of Fame's charter class. Like Rickey, Baugh was groundbreaking in his role. "He was the first guy we ever saw on film who passed the ball on first down," NFL Films president Steve Sabol recalled in 2008.[38]

Two years before Baugh, Don Hutson played minor league baseball for the Cardinals in Pine Bluff, Arkansas, before committing to a career with the Green Bay Packers. Like

Baugh, he's considered a trailblazer at his position. The former Alabama All-American is regarded as the first modern receiver.[39] Hutson later joined Baugh as part of the Pro Football Hall of Fame's first class. Of the 17 members inducted in 1963, two played minor-league baseball for the Cardinals. Baseball or football, Rickey knew how to spot talent.

*****

Rickey's profile and popularity exploded in the mid-1930s. A search of "Branch Rickey" in the archives of the *Globe-Democrat* and *Post-Dispatch* reveals 114 stories containing his name in 1930. Five years later, the number was 338.[40] In March of 1935, the *Star-Times* featured a syndicated 12-part series on Rickey's life and career. But it was in the national press that the Rickey name skyrocketed in prominence. Mentioned just 19 times in the New York *Daily News* in 1930, the same paper included the Cardinals general manager in 166 stories five years later. (Rickey was aware of his growing and glowing press coverage. "Please don't refer to me as a master mind," he told Keener of the *Star-Times* in January of 1935.)[41]

A father of six children, one son and five daughters, Rickey and family lived on a twenty-three-acre St. Louis County property in a development known as Country Life Acres.[42] An active member of the Grace Methodist Church and statewide Republican politics, Rickey also found time to serve on the board of trustees of his alma mater, Ohio Wesleyan University, and the board of directors of John Burroughs School in St. Louis. Passionate about baseball and his Methodist faith, his calendar was populated with frequent public speaking events.[43] He enjoyed hunting ducks and other small game in the offseason.[44] Wherever he went, he typically had company. Rickey hated to drive.

His constant travels were compounded by his absent-mindedness. Once, on a trip through Ohio, he shouted to his driver, "Turn around. We should have stopped at Dayton!" The driver promptly turned the car around to make the thirty-mile journey. "I was supposed to stop and pick up Mrs. Rickey," he explained. "She's waiting for me at a drugstore there...I hope."[45] On another trip, he remembered he needed an extra pair of socks after he had locked his suitcase. In a hurry to leave, he quickly placed the socks in a coat pocket. Making a speech that evening in a warm building, beads of sweat began to furrow his brow. He reached into his coat pocket to grab a handkerchief. The audience erupted in laughter as he began to wipe his face, not with a handkerchief, but with those extra pair of socks.[46]

A decade into his full-time role running the Cardinals front office and farm system, a confident Rickey had also mastered the art of negotiation. When he wasn't traveling, he'd be in his office, receiving – and answering – 200 letters a day. Telegrams would pour in. The phone would ring constantly.[47] On his blackboard were the names of every single player in the Cardinals organization. (He had window shades installed to cover the list so curious visitors couldn't glean any plans.)[48] Every offseason, players would stroll into his office seeking a raise. They would lumber out grateful their salary hadn't been reduced. As discussions got underway, Rickey had a trick up his sleeve, or rather, a pedal under the desk. When pressed, the pedal produced a sound simulating a ringing telephone, claimed Bill Veeck Jr.[49]

Pause to consider the scene. On one side of the desk sat a player with visions of a $5,000 raise. On the other side sat Rickey, who had interrupted negotiations to take a call with one of his minor league general managers. The fake conversation would steer to a prospect who, by sheer coincidence, just happened to share the same position as the player sitting across from the man who made the decisions. Hearing the one, and only side of the call, the player would listen to Rickey concede that maybe, just maybe, the young hotshot was ready to make the jump to the big leagues after all. Rickey would then hang up the phone and begin discussing his worries of pay cuts coming down the line. But he also had good news for the man in his office. "I am determined," the general manager would assure him, "to find some way of paying you the same salary you received last year."

The same kind of magic Rickey worked with his roster also applied to executives on other teams, "because he was shrewd enough to study the front office personnel as carefully as he studied the playing personnel," Veeck contended. "Like any practicing hypnotist, he was always looking for the perfect subject; i.e., the man who fell under his spell so easily that it was almost posthypnotic suggestion." The Cubs had a man who fit that description. "In Chicago, he could absolutely mesmerize Clarence Rowland, the club vice president," Veeck believed.[50]

In the 1930s, Rickey's negotiation skills would be tested by a player who was in constant raise-seeking mode. And when Rickey and the Cardinals had their patience tested one too many times, the master wheeler-dealer and hypnotist only had to place a call to a man already under his spell to rid himself of the problem.

Jay Hanna "Dizzy" Dean showed up unannounced at Sportsman's Park after the 1930 season.[51] He met with Rickey in his office. The subject was money. Dean wanted more of it. After a two or three-hour meeting, Dean walked out a rear door. Rickey walked out to face the press. "If there was one more like him in baseball, just one, as God as my judge, I'd get out of the game!" he told the assembled. At the time, Dean was just twenty years old and his major-league experience consisted of one game. "He told me," Rickey said, "after one game this 'busher' told me, 'Mr. Rickey, I'll put more people in the park than anybody since Babe Ruth!'"[52]

In 1931, the Cardinals sent Dean back to the minor leagues "on the amusing theory it would teach him humility," wrote columnist Red Smith. He told a reporter he could win 30 games for the Cardinals, "but that would sound kind of braggy and windy so I'll put it at 25."[53] That winter, the club sent him to live in the Missouri bootheel town of Charleston, where Cardinals minor league business manager Oliver French had family. Dean practiced pitching by attempting to throw coal into an open furnace door. "A piece of chestnut coal into the furnace was a strike. Missing the opening was a single. Missing the furnace was a double. When the house got unbearably hot, we knew Dizzy had set another strikeout record," remembered French.[54]

He talked a local car dealer into loaning him a car and proceeded to take "his half of the road out of the middle." According to Rickey biographer Arthur Mann, Dean spent time airborne in a Piper Cub. He quit when the engine malfunctioned and the plane crashed through a fence and landed in a field. Dean survived, apparently no worse for wear. He fell in love with a teenage girl and sent her a pair of silk pajamas for Christmas. Her parents sent them back.

Dean and French left early for spring training. He earned a spot on the big-league roster, then spent the month of April on the bench before being shipped to the Cardinals farm team in Houston, much to the disappointment of fans. "Dizzy Dean is the youngest baseball 'gate attraction' we've ever seen," reporter Martin Haley wrote in the *Globe-Democrat* in April, when Dean had *still* only pitched one game in the big leagues.

He returned to the major leagues, for good this time, in 1932. By 1934, he was doing what he had promised Rickey four years earlier. A record-setting Polo Grounds crowd of 62,573 watched Dean start and win the first game of a doubleheader against the Giants in September. Brother Paul won the second game. On the final day of the season, an overflow Sportsman's Park crowd of 37,402 cheered Dizzy as he shut out the Reds to win his thirtieth game of the year, the last time in National League history a pitcher has won that many. "City's Baseball Fans Acclaim Dizzy Dean as King of St. Louis," read the headline the next day in the *Globe-Democrat*. Henry Ford said that fall that Dean had "done more to bring the world out of its doldrums than any other man alive."

The high-profile pitcher now attracted all kinds of attention, not all of it desired. During the World Series, Breadon was so worried about gangsters and kidnappers he assigned police guards to the Dean brothers. The spark for the security detail happened after a game in St. Louis when Dizzy was invited to take a ride back to his hotel in a car with New York plates. Breadon saw it unfolding, had Dean pulled from the automobile, and assigned coverage for the brothers. Policemen, taking two-hour shifts, even guarded the Deans at their suite at the Forest Park Hotel.[55] (Dizzy would introduce his protectors to reporters. "That guy," Dean would whisper, "he's guarding just me.")

That offseason, Dean returned to the topic of Ruth. He resented the aging slugger coming to play in the National League. "He made all his money in the American League, so why doesn't he stay there?" he told reporters. He caught flak for the comments and later backtracked, saying his criticism wasn't of Ruth, but of the American League. (The Babe had met the Dean brothers at the World Series in Detroit, calling them "the two friendliest, politest kids I saw in my life.")[56] Dizzy's first regular-season meeting with the Babe occurred in Boston in May. A crowd of 30,000 saw Ruth go 0-2 with a walk. Dean not only threw a shutout, but he also hit a home run. The Cardinals beat the Braves 7-0. With Ruth's career all but over, the charismatic, quotable and talented pitcher was a natural replacement as the face of the game. The Ruth comparisons now came with increasing frequency.

In spring training, a Ruth game against the Yankees in St. Petersburg attracted 4,726 fans on a Sunday. Three days later, Ruth and the Braves faced Dean and the Cardinals.

A Wednesday crowd of 6,467 set a Florida record. "When you draw close to 6,500 in this town of about 90,000 winter population, you have a crowd which ranks with 80,000 in Yankee Stadium," wrote Dan Daniel.[57]

A few weeks later, Dean appeared on the cover of *Time* magazine. (Jerome Herman Dean read the caption underneath the picture, a name Dizzy frequently gave to reporters.)[58] "Dizzy Gains Luster As The Babe Fades," proclaimed a *Sporting News* headline in May. "The sun apparently has not fully set on King Ruth," wrote Dick Farrington just days before the Babe called it quits, "but out of the mocking shadows emerges the figure of the heir apparent, if not the actual ruler, of all that is color and accomplishment in the two major leagues – Dizzy Dean, the new gate god, the successor to the throne of public appreciation and idolatry. Dizzy stands tip-toe on the mountain top. Babe is hardly within hailing distance on the other side."[59]

Like the Babe, Dizzy began making more money off the field than on it. By 1935, Dean was generating $30,000 a year or more from endorsements and other ventures. General Foods paid him $15,000 to advertise Grape-Nuts cereal. There were Dizzy Dean baseball caps, suits, gloves and shoes. He received royalties for having his name attached to shaving cream, toothbrushes and toothpaste, stationery, pencils, pens, belts, and men's jewelry.[60] He and Paul even did a one-week vaudeville act at the Roxy Theater in New York. For serving as manager for both Dean brothers, Bill DeWitt Sr. took a ten percent cut of the revenue.[61]

Like Ruth, Dean kept his name in the press in the offseason by performing in frequent barnstorming tours. A favorite opponent was Satchel Paige. The pitchers dueled often. "Ol Diz was the one boy I wanted to run up against," Paige once admitted.[62] The son of a sharecropper, Dean grew up picking cotton in the fields of Arkansas and "wore his prejudices lightly," wrote author Robert Kuhn McGregor. "He was respectful of the Negro Leaguers, and I guess that came from his relationship with Satch," remembered former player and Birmingham Black Barons manager Piper Davis. "You never heard black players call Diz 'a cracker.' If all the guys in white folks' ball had been like Diz, we'd all have been better off."[63] If Ruth had wanted an integrated game, as his daughter Julia believed, Dean was more vocal in his support. "It's too bad these colored boys don't play in the big leagues, because they sure got some great players," he once said.[64]

While Dean is remembered for his cooperation with black players, he's also identified with bitter and contentious negotiations with Breadon and Rickey. Every year, Breadon would announce he didn't expect any trouble signing Dean to a new contract. Every offseason, Dean would prove him wrong. After his 1934 MVP season, he announced he wouldn't sign for less than $25,000, saying in February, "I'm fed up with the way I've been treated. I'm seriously thinking of getting out of baseball anyhow." That same day he signed his contract for $19,500.[65] The next year, he threatened to hold out for $40,000, and if he didn't get it, "I'll retire and go into the furniture business."[66] Near the end of March, he signed for $22,300. "Like Babe Ruth,

Diz asked for the best hotel suite," wrote Tom Meany. "Like Ruth, he had plenty to say about his contract. Like Ruth, he talked about quitting."

In 1937, Dean initially demanded $100,000 before dropping it to $50,000. "Diz could get it in New York," said Ruth, while the Babe's former boss, Yankees owner Ruppert, called Dean "the Babe Ruth of pitchers." Dean's demands were echoed by his wife. "Fifty grand or we don't pitch," Pat Dean would tell reporters. Those comments got the attention of New York *Daily News* columnist Jack Miley, who wrote a series of articles criticizing the couple. He called Dean "flabby and hog fat," during his holdout, writing that "Dizzy is a big man now – especially between the ears," adding that "for a guy who was picking cotton at 50 cents a day a few years ago, Diz has an amusing idea of his own importance." As for Pat, "the only time the sports writers can get a word in edgewise with Diz is when the Missus isn't around – which isn't often."[67] Dean wound up signing for $25,500 (shortly after asking the Cardinals to authorize his retirement), but Dizzy and Pat hadn't forgotten the words of Miley.

In early April, near the end of spring training, Dean and his wife spotted Miley and *Chicago Times* sportswriter Irv Kupcinet in the lobby of a Tampa hotel after a game. The player and columnist exchanged words. As his teammates gathered around the sportswriters, Dean took a swing at Miley and then quickly backed away as a brawl erupted. ("Dizzy Dean Starts Argument In Lobby, Leaves As Fists Fly," read the headline of the *Star-Times* the following day.) Seven or eight players took swings at the writers. One of them landed a pair of spiked shoes on Miley's forehead, leaving cuts above his eye. Another landed a punch on Kupcinet's left cheekbone, leaving him with a swollen face. Cardinals coach Mike Gonzalez eventually broke up the brawl. Dean later apologized.[68]

The in-season acrimony was just as bad. A spat erupted in 1934 when Dizzy and Paul skipped an exhibition game in Detroit. Manager Frisch issued a fine. Breadon and Rickey announced a suspension. Dizzy tore up two uniforms – the second one for the benefit of photographers – and walked out. The matter went before Commissioner Landis who sided with management, but not before Dean and Breadon engaged in a shouting match. "Don't you call me a liar, Dizzy!" said Breadon. "Well then, don't you call me a liar," Dean responded.[69] His suspension was lifted but the ordeal cost Dean $486 – $100 in fines, $36 for the uniforms and $350 in lost wages for missing a week of games.

For an exhibition game the following July in St. Paul, he refused to acknowledge a Minnesota crowd of nearly 8,000. Neither Dizzy nor Paul would leave the dugout and the pair declined to pose for photographers. "Ten years ago, the Babe was here with the Yankees and stood in the rain for hours autographing baseballs," noted a St. Paul paper. "Yes, that's why Ruth was great," said Frisch. "He made a man of himself and millions of friends for the game by being considerate of the feelings of fans. Diz has yet to learn that." (Incidents like the one in St. Paul did enormous damage to Dean's endorsement deals.)[70]

In 1937, he reportedly called National League president Ford Frick and umpire George Barr "the two biggest crooks in baseball," a statement he denied. But Frick believed the report and, when Dean refused to apologize, issued a suspension. Dean responded by threatening to sue Frick and the National League for $250,000. Frick reinstated him after a face-to-face meeting. Biographers can, and have, filled chapters with Dean's various disputes with teammates, opponents, management and league officials.

At the All-Star game that summer, Dean was one out away from a third scoreless inning when he gave up a base hit, then a two-run homer by Lou Gehrig. The next batter, Earl Averill, smashed a line drive off Dean's foot. It broke the big toe on his left foot.

Fourteen days later in Boston, pitching in a spiked shoe with a toe plate cut out, he went the distance but lost the game 2-1. His toe had yet to heal. "I couldn't pivot for my follow-through," Dean recalled, "and I hurt my arm favoring the toe." His overhand delivery became more of a side-arm motion. He developed bursitis in his right shoulder.

His career was never the same. In April of 1938, Rickey did what he did best. He called Clarence Rowland and engineered a trade with the Cubs, dispatching Dean to Chicago for three players and $185,000 in cash. That summer, a bitter Dean wrote an article for *Liberty* magazine with the headline: "I Was No Pop-Off – They Made Me One." In the piece, Dean claimed he played the part of the "stooge" during his time in St. Louis at the behest of Breadon and Rickey.[71] St. Louis wasn't buying it. "Dizzy's statements, of course, are ridiculous," wrote Stockton. "Dizzy Dean was as irresponsible as he was brilliant, and he went merrily on his madcap way."[72]

While Stockton was critical of the pitcher, he also recognized his one-of-a-kind ability. "There never was a more brilliant worker, a more colorful baseball character. He's still the greatest one-man asset in the history of the game in our book, and we haven't forgotten about Babe Ruth."[73]

Like Hornsby, Dean drew frequent comparisons to Ruth throughout his career: Hornsby for his hitting prowess; Dean for his talent, and also for his magnetic charm that attracted media and fans alike. At their peaks, both were the best in the game at their position with the salaries to match.[74] Both Dean and Hornsby could also be their own worst enemy. For all their abilities, the two Hall-of-Famers have something else in common. Each won only a single World Series in their careers, and for both players, it happened in a Cardinals uniform.[75]

It's unfair to call the career of a Hall of Fame pitcher a letdown, but it is fair to ask "What-if?" Dean was only twenty-four years old when he won 30 games and only twenty-seven when he threw his last pitch for the Cardinals. What if a healthy and more mature Dizzy had been able to continue to pitch for St. Louis after 1937? Before Dean, the last two pitchers to win 30 games in the National League were Grover Cleveland Alexander and Christy Mathewson. Starting at the age of twenty-eight, Alexander won at least 30 games three straight years. At the age of twenty-eight, Mathewson won 25 games and proceeded to win more than 20 contests in each of the next five seasons. After leaving the Cardinals, Dean won 16 games the rest of his career.

In the post-Ruth vacuum of the mid-1930s, the Cardinals stood as good a chance as any team of becoming the game's dominant franchise. But population trends, playing in a two-team town, a highly competitive National League, and a Yankee farm system on the rise, all conspired against them. Internal misfortunes and adversity didn't help.[76] No one Cardinal better represented the promises and disappointments of this era more than Dizzy Dean.[77]

*****

In March of 1938, the same spring where Baugh donned a Cardinals uniform and a month before the Dean trade, Commissioner Landis dealt a blow to the fortunes of the St. Louis franchise. Never a fan of Rickey's vision for the minor leagues, Landis declared dozens of farmhands in the St. Louis system free agents. A ruling that became known as the "Cedar Rapids case," the commissioner's decision had an impact on future pennant races and the relationship between Rickey and Breadon.

The battles between Landis and the Cardinals went back to the 1920s. "You are both guilty of raping the minor leagues," Landis told Breadon and Rickey at a baseball meeting in Chattanooga late in 1929. Rickey fired back a year later at a meeting in Montreal, defending his vision of the farm system. "Baseball is bigger than one club. It is bigger than I am. It is bigger than any one man," he said with Landis sitting in the front row. Attorney Rickey vs. Judge Landis (who frequently doubled as his own jury). The raging dispute lasted for years.

The disagreement centered around control and ownership of minor league teams. The commissioner viewed the leagues as independent operators and deplored control by major league teams. The Cardinals viewed major league interest in the lower rungs of professional baseball as a necessity. It started as a way to compete against wealthier teams and the Cardinals had reaped the results. By 1938, the tentacles of the organization stretched from New York to California. The franchise had direct investments in fourteen teams and working agreements with at least sixteen others. Through his vast network, Rickey had also developed several informal arrangements. If a club in the minors wanted to sell a player, the Cardinals frequently got the first call. It was these non-contractual relationships that got the attention of Landis.

Harry S. Johnson was president of the Cedar Rapids Raiders in the Three-I-League (Illinois, Indiana, and Iowa). Rickey described him as "one of my closest friends in baseball." Cedar Rapids competed against a Cardinals' team in Danville, Illinois in the same league. Johnson's team also controlled clubs in four other leagues in which the Cardinals also had entrants.

League	Johnson/ Cedar Rapids Raiders	Rickey/ St. Louis Cardinals
Three-I	Cedar Rapids	Danville
Arkansas-Missouri	Fayetteville	Monett
Northeast Arkansas	Newport	Caruthersville
Northern	Crookston	Duluth
Nebraska State	Mitchell	Grand Island

Landis spent two years investigating the relationship between the Cardinals and Cedar Rapids and the various affiliates. In examining the paper trail between the two organizations, the commissioner accused the Cardinals of controlling both groups, a violation of baseball rules. Landis believed the Cardinals, through training camps in Springfield, Missouri in 1936 and 1937, had supplied nearly all the players to Cedar Rapids. In addition, Landis accused the Cardinals of signing these players to contracts with their Springfield club, then destroying the evidence and never sending the documentation to the National Association, the minor league's governing body. "They [the players] sincerely believed that they were under the domination of the Cardinals' Springfield club," Landis said.[78]

The commissioner leaked his intentions a week before the official decision to Harry Grayson, sports editor of the Newspaper Enterprise Association. Given the scoop directly from baseball's highest authority, Grayson exaggerated its importance. "The most important decision in the history of baseball is about to be made here," read his lead sentence. National Association president William Gibbons Branham added to the hyperbole by telling him the story would "out-headline the Chicago Black Sox Scandal of 1919-1920."[79]

While guilty of overhyping the story, Grayson honestly captured the commissioner's attitude toward the Cardinals and the club's approach to the minor leagues. "Landis has waited eighteen years for the spot he now occupies," he wrote. The investigation was sparked by the Yankees. "Sometime back Landis heard a complaint unofficially made by George Weiss," Grayson claimed. Cedar Rapids had drafted a player from a Yankees farm team. Weiss then contacted Rickey. "He asked why the Cardinals were fooling with future Yankees," Grayson wrote. The matter was eventually settled, but "Landis got wind of what was going on."

When Landis officially made his decision public a week after the story, dozens of St. Louis Cardinals prospects suddenly found themselves declared free agents. (Estimates vary on exactly how many players were impacted. Early reports put the number at approximately 100; a later report revised the number to 74.) A furious Rickey wanted to fight the charges, but Breadon accepted the commissioner's verdict. Publicly, the owner supported his second-in-command and claimed Rickey did nothing wrong.

"This farm-system idea has proved to be the salvation of the minor leagues," wrote Breadon, pointing out the number of leagues had risen from a little more than a dozen in 1930 to forty, less than a decade later. In a twelve-hundred-word statement, Breadon did concede financial coordination between Cardinals' farm teams in Springfield and Monett, Missouri, but left unaddressed larger issues raised by the commissioner. "I do not have access to the records of the evidence at hand to answer fully other points in the decision. The Cedar Rapids situation is incidental to us for it was not part of us," he claimed.

"I want to say in conclusion that Branch Rickey has done much constructive work for baseball and, in my opinion, baseball owes a great deal more to him than to any man or official connected to the game. I have been associated with him for 19 years, and I have yet to know him to do a dishonest or unworthy thing. He has my fullest confidence, and I will go along with him in anything he undertakes."[80]

While offering full support for Rickey in writing, the owner did have his doubts. "Breadon, a tough bargainer, but a stickler for the rules, sensed that something was wrong in the Cedar Rapids affiliation, and suggested it be cleaned up," Stockton wrote later in a story for the *Saturday Evening Post*. "Rickey looked at it from a lawyer's viewpoint, insisting that the setup was within the law."

Among the players released by Landis was St. Louis native Pete Reiser. As a teenager, Reiser played baseball at Beaumont High School on land once owned by the Cardinals before Breadon sold it to the city of St. Louis. Originally a shortstop, he caught the attention of Cardinals scout Charley Barrett, who hired him to be his "chauffeur."[81] Barrett didn't want the prospect to come to the attention of the Browns. Signed by the Cardinals in 1937 after he graduated from high school, Reiser played 70 games that season for Newport in the Northeast Arkansas League, one of the teams flagged in the Landis investigation.

Barrett recognized Reiser as a special talent. "That kid is going to be a star," he predicted. His boss agreed. Rickey struck a deal with Brooklyn general manager Larry MacPhail whereby Reiser would sign with the Dodgers and later be returned to the Cardinals in a trade, exactly the sort of "gentlemen's agreement" that Rickey had been accused of orchestrating in the Cedar Rapids decision. Reiser became Brooklyn property for $100.

The plan backfired in 1939 when Dodgers manager Leo Durocher saw Reiser play in spring training.[82] By the end of March, Reiser's Grapefruit League batting average stood at .611, and the *New York Times* was calling him "the wonder boy."[83] The gentleman's agreement was null and void. Durocher insisted Reiser remain in the Dodgers system.

After spending a little more than a year on Brooklyn farm teams, Reiser made his Dodgers debut in 1940. Converted to an outfielder, he became Brooklyn's starting centerfielder the following season. In 1941, Reiser led the National League with a batting average of .343, 117 runs scored, and 17 triples, while leading the Dodgers to the pennant. Modern sabermetrics compute Reiser's WAR (Wins Above Replacement) at 7.5 that season. The Dodgers edged the Cardinals in 1941 by two-and-a-half games.

*****

By the end of the 1930s, the life Rickey had built in St. Louis began to change. His son, Branch Jr., who had worked in the Cardinals farm system since 1935, left to become farm director for the Brooklyn Dodgers. His defection came around the same time others identified as "strong pro-Rickey men" left the organization, including the president of the farm team in Columbus. "Persons close to the Cardinals organization have suspected lately that relations between owner Breadon and business manager Rickey are not as friendly as they formerly were," Stockton told his readers in February of 1939.[84]

By this time, Rickey had expanded his role beyond the farm system to contract negotiations and player trades at the major league level. At the same time, Breadon, out of the automobile business, had more time to focus on baseball. The two men clashed over deals, employee compensation, and advertising sponsorships.

They also mourned the loss of Charley Barrett. The long-time Cardinals' scout and Rickey friend died in the summer of 1939. Barrett spent three decades scouting talent. He had been with the Cardinals since 1919. Since that time, he had traveled from California to Cuba for the team, signing dozens of players who eventually made their way to the big leagues.[85] He had also been instrumental in Rickey's influence over the minor leagues. It was Barrett who guaranteed financial support for all eight teams of the Nebraska State League in exchange for giving the Cardinals the option to buy any of their players. "I would have bought up many other leagues, but Judge Landis broke up my little play-house," he said.[86]

Barrett had just returned from a scouting trip in Arkansas. He stopped by Sportsman's Park where the Browns were hosting the Chicago White Sox in a doubleheader. Browns general manager Bill DeWitt Sr. was one of the last people to see him alive. July 4, 1939, is an iconic day in baseball history, the day Lou Gehrig, dying from ALS, told a Yankee Stadium crowd, "I consider myself the luckiest man on the face of this earth." On that same day, Charley Barrett left Sportsman's Park, went home, and died in his sleep. He was sixty-eight years old.

"The death of Charley Barrett is a blow to baseball. I doubt if I ever had a better friend than Charley," said DeWitt. "The passing of Charley Barrett has been a terrific blow to me," said Breadon. "He was as fine a gentleman as I have ever known." Rickey called him his "closest friend in baseball." Bachelor Barrett spent every Christmas with the Rickey family. The scout left a $500 bequest to Branch Rickey Jr., "son of my dear friend, Branch Rickey Sr.," he wrote in his will.

DeWitt, Breadon and Rickey Sr. were all pallbearers at Barrett's funeral. So was one of the scout's former signees and favorite players. Just days before he died, Barrett had participated in "Pepper Martin Day" at Sportsman's Park. Amidst a pregame ceremony where fans showered the player with gifts, Martin walked over to Barrett and shook his hand. "Gee Charley, don't you know if it wasn't for you, I wouldn't even be here."[87]

"There was only one Charley Barrett," noted *The Sporting News.* "The success of the farm system, as developed by the St. Louis Cardinals, is as much a credit to his foresight as to the acumen of Branch Rickey, and it is doubtful if the system would have dominated the game as it did for years, without a Barrett to dig up the incoming material."[88]

*****

In the wake of the Cedar Rapids decision and a challenging 1938 season – the team finished in sixth place and reported a loss, despite the Dean sale for $185,000 – the Cardinals downscaled their farm system in 1939 and changed managers at the big-league level. Ray Blades replaced Frankie Frisch, who had been let go near the end of the 1938 campaign. Despite front office turmoil and the death of Barrett, the club bounced back with a record of 92-61, good enough for second place. Attendance jumped by more than 100,000.

In August, Breadon went horseback riding near his farm in Fenton, Missouri. Riding past a farmhouse where the residents were operating a noisy, gasoline-powered washing machine, the horse became nervous and started to act up. Breadon dismounted and began walking with the animal. The residents also noticed the skittish horse and turned off the machinery. But with Breadon and his ride at what they considered a safe distance, they flipped the washer back on just as the Cardinals owner attempted to remount the animal. The sound caused the horse to jump and threw Breadon to the ground with a foot caught in the stirrup. It dragged him several feet before he could untangle himself. The horse ran away. Breadon was unconscious for nearly an hour. The farmhouse residents recognized him and contacted both his wife and doctor, who took him to the hospital.[89]

Breadon suffered a concussion, a broken right hand, and lacerations to his face that required plastic surgery. Doctors feared he fractured his skull, but x-rays turned up negative. He remained at St. John's Hospital for three weeks. His condition was serious enough for the Associated Press to prepare an obituary. "Sam had a narrow escape," wrote columnist Keener.

Breadon's brush with mortality didn't lead to any additional patience with managers. With the Cardinals struggling early in the 1940 season, Breadon fired Blades and replaced him with another outfielder from his first championship squad, Billy Southworth, who had briefly managed the team in 1929. The move upset Rickey, who considered Blades perhaps his favorite Cardinals manager. Two years earlier, the two men had clashed over Frisch. "Sam Breadon Fires Frisch to Keep Peace With Rickey," read a headline in *The Sporting News.*[90]

All of this occurred in a timeframe when Breadon instituted across the board salary cuts for non-contract employees. After pushing through a round of cuts in 1939, Breadon instituted a second round a year later. Rebuffed in his efforts to stop them,

Rickey told the owner, "Sam, I will dig ditches at a dollar a day rather than work for you one minute beyond the expiration of my contract."[91] The statement suggests that Rickey's eventual decision to leave the Cardinals was his alone. It wasn't.

Rickey's five-year contract, signed at the end of 1937, expired at the end of 1942. Word began to leak out in the summer of 1941 that he would likely not return. "On His Way Out?" read the caption in the *Post-Dispatch* above a picture of Rickey in June. At a board meeting in February, Breadon had indicated the Cardinals may not renew Rickey's contract, citing economic and "uncertain world conditions," a reference to World War II already raging in Europe. With his $50,000 salary, bonus, and his ten percent cut from the sale of players, Rickey made more than $80,000 in both 1941 and 1942. Whether the departure had an economic basis or was simply a clash of personalities, the two men barely spoke in Rickey's final days.[92]

One of their last disagreements concerned the Hyde Park Beer sponsorship of Cardinals' broadcasts. Rickey, still a Prohibitionist at heart, opposed the move. Breadon backed the beer company. The owner prevailed.[93] Rickey's days of running the Cardinals organization came to an end in October of 1942.

Despite disputes with Breadon, departure of key personnel, and the death of Barrett, Rickey left St. Louis triumphantly. A historic campaign helped wipe away the frustrations of the seven previous seasons. The 1942 Cardinals were truly Rickey's Redbirds. Every single regular in the lineup, including rookie outfielder Stan Musial, came up through the Cardinals farm system. All were signed between 1932 and 1938 and arrived primarily from small towns throughout the Midwest and South. Only one of them, second baseman Jimmy Brown, was over the age of 30. "A number of them are still so fresh from the bushes," wrote Red Smith, "they still make their beds in the morning after arising in their hotel."[94]

(See table on next page)

Position	Name	Born	Signed	MLB Debut	Age*
C	W. Cooper	1915 Atherton, MO	1935	1940	27
1B	J. Hopp	1916 Hastings, NE	1936	1939	26
2B	J. Brown	1910 Jamesville, NC	1933	1937	32
3B	W. Kurowski	1918 Reading, PA	1937	1941	24
SS	M. Marion	1917 Richburg, NC	1936	1940	25
OF	S. Musial	1920 Donora, PA	1938	1941	21
OF	T. Moore	1912 Vernon, AL	1932	1935	30
OF	E. Slaughter	1916 Roxboro, NC	1934	1938	26

*In 1942. Musial turned 22 in November, after the season was over.

The pitching staff was led by National League MVP Mort Cooper, two years older than his brother, Walker. The righthander went 22-7 with an ERA of 1.78 for a Cardinals team that won 106 games, a franchise record. In Rickey's first full year in the front office, St. Louis met New York in the World Series. He ended his final contract under Breadon with a rematch. After losing in 1926, the Yankees appeared in eight World Series, winning all of them. During that stretch, New York won 32 World Series games, their opponents only four. Against the Cardinals in 1942, the Yankees won the first game at Sportsman's Park and didn't win again. The Cardinals reeled off four straight victories, and just as in 1926, the team celebrated a title in Yankee Stadium. Since both teams called St. Petersburg their spring training home, New York was not an unfamiliar opponent. "We weren't awed by the Yankees because we had played them five times during spring training," said Musial after the Series was over.

Rickey's influence was felt for years. "Sam Breadon could do a Rip Van Winkle in the Catskills for five years and not have to worry a wink about his team," Rickey said in 1943. Over the next four seasons, the Cardinals won three more pennants and two more World Series titles, capped by a 1946 team that won baseball's first-ever playoff against the Brooklyn Dodgers. Both teams finished the regular season at 96-58. A best-of-three playoff decided the pennant. St. Louis won two straight from Brooklyn. A core chunk of the 1942 regulars – Kurowski, Marion, Musial, Moore, Slaughter – was still in the lineup along with newcomers like catcher Joe Garagiola and second baseman Red Schoendienst who Rickey had signed. From the winning locker room, Cardinals manager Eddie Dyer paid tribute to the team's former executive. "It was Branch Rickey who assembled this team. It was Branch Rickey who signed me as a pitcher back in 1922 and, when my arm went dead, persuaded me to continue as an executive and taught me every bit of baseball I know."[95] Dyer's team went on to record a seven-game World Series victory over the Boston Red Sox.

It was the end of an era. 1947 saw the breaking of baseball's color barrier with the debut of Jackie Robinson. In the twenty-one-season stretch before Robinson's arrival, St. Louis won nine pennants and claimed six World Series titles. Over the next twenty seasons – 1947-1966 – the league's dominant franchise won 10 pennants and four World Series. It wasn't the Cardinals.

The new Kings of the National League wore Dodger Blue.

---

[1] Allen, *The National League Story. The Sporting News*, November 15, 1934, and May 18, 1949. "Almost as soon as I dropped that letter in the box, I knew I shouldn't have written it," Breadon later told Fred Lieb. "I made statements for which I immediately was sorry." The 1934 account mentions a letter that Reds vice president Larry MacPhail had written to Heydler. There were rumors that Reds shortstop Gordon Slade had received half of a $500 bill before the series began. "If you do the right thing, you'll get the other half after the series," the letter reportedly said. "Slade never received such a letter," said Heydler. "You can quote me as saying that the whole story is absolutely untrue." Slade made three errors in the first inning of one of the games, but Heydler said two of them could have been recorded as hits.

[2] *New York Times*, November 15, 1934. Was Breadon's price a reasonable ask? Combining the sale of a major league franchise with minor league teams make direct comps difficult to estimate. That same year, the *Times* published a story regarding rumors of a sale of the New York Giants in the wake of the death of manager John McGraw. The *Times* wrote that "the sum frequently mentioned as the one [Giants owner Charles] Stoneham would consider irresistible is $1.8 million." Ibid, March 9, 1934. That price included only the major league franchise. Six years later, the executor of the Jacob Ruppert estate put the value of the Yankees and seven minor league teams at $4 million. Ibid, July 18, 1940. One million dollars for Breadon's 76 percent stake would mean a $1.3 million valuation for the Cardinals and their minor league teams, 33% of the price of baseball's most valuable franchise. In 2019, *Forbes* estimated the value of the Cardinals at $2.1 billion, or 45.7% of the value estimated for the Yankees ($4.6 billion). Given the direct competition from the Browns, Breadon's price and the larger discount to the Yankees seems reasonable for 1934. When the Browns considered relocating to Los Angeles in 1941, Breadon was ready to pay Browns owner Don Barnes $250,000 to leave town. *The Sporting News*, January 17, 1946.

[3] *St. Louis Post-Dispatch*, November 18, 1934.

[4] *St. Louis Globe-Democrat*, January 19, 1963.

[5] Referring to the Dean brothers, Dan Parker of the *New York Mirror* wrote, "Any other club would recognize the value of this colorful brother act and pay them at least twice as

much as the Cards. But the nickel-nursing Cardinal owners only look at it from the angle of how much they can save by underpaying the brothers." Golenbock, *The Spirit of St. Louis.*
[6] Ibid.
[7] *St. Louis Post-Dispatch*, September 8, 1934.
[8] Lowenfish, *Branch Rickey.* Wentz did have his vices. In an interview at the Hotel Jefferson, Sid Keener reported that Wentz "consumed almost a pack of cigarettes in an hour." *St. Louis Star-Times*, November 15, 1934.
[9] *New York Times*, November 14, 1934.
[10] Years later, the *Globe-Democrat* provided corroboration for the original report in the *Times*, writing "had Wentz bought the club, Breadon, instead of retiring from baseball would have bought the Brooklyn club, or at least tried to buy it." *St. Louis Globe-Democrat*, February 21, 1943.
[11] According to Keener, the investigation into the Cardinals' minor league holdings revealed that St. Louis farm teams lost $60,000 in 1934, exclusive of Columbus and Rochester. *St. Louis Star-Times,* November 30, 1934.
[12] *St. Louis Post-Dispatch*, December 5, 1934.
[13] *The Sporting News*, January 17, 1935.
[14] Roy Stockton, described by Rickey biographer Lee Lowenfish as "Sam Breadon's closest ally," wrote this one week after the sale was called off. "The price, and this comes from good authority, was exactly one-million, and included only Breadon's holdings." *St. Louis Post-Dispatch*, December 12, 1934.
[15] *Saturday Evening Post*, February 13, 1943.
[16] Polner, *Branch Rickey.*
[17] Vecsey, *Stan Musial.*
[18] *St. Louis Star-Times*, August 24, 1934.
[19] *St. Louis Post-Dispatch*, December 18, 1934. The Cardinals had also received a $50,000 payment from the Cincinnati Reds earlier in the year. From 1931 to early 1934, the Cardinals traded or sold 14 players, including Chick Hafey and Jim Bottomley, to the Reds. *St. Louis Star-Times*, February 14, 1934.
[20] Estimates of Breadon's ownership and dividend income varied. "Breadon's share of the total sum divided this year amounts to between $70,000 and $75,000. He is credited with holding about 72 percent of all the stock of the Cardinals." *St. Louis Post-Dispatch,* December 18, 1934. "Breadon's share of 75 ½ percent of the 7833 shares of common stock and 88 percent of the 2327 shares of preferred, upon which he collects a dividend of about $89,000," the same paper wrote the following day. "Breadon owns 76 percent of the stock, while the remaining 24 percent is divided among 140 other persons." *St. Louis Star-Times,* November 18, 1934. Breadon later clarified to reporters that he owned 85 percent of the common stock and 75.5 percent of the combined stock. *St. Louis Globe-Democrat*, December 20, 1934.
[21] The Cardinals declared a dividend of $10 in 1935, $12 in 1936, and $8 in 1937. No dividends were paid after the 1938 season, but $10 payments resumed in 1939, followed

by $7 in 1940 and $10 in 1941. In 1942, with the United States involved in World War II, the club paid $2 a share, followed by $3 a share in 1943, 1944, and 1945. With the war over and St. Louis celebrating another World Series title, a $10 per share payment was sent to shareholders in 1946. Breadon's total dividends received from 1934 through 1946 approached $700,000.

[22] *St. Louis Post-Dispatch*, December 19, 1934. *Slate* profiled McSkimming in a 2014 story about the Post-Dispatch's coverage of the 1950 World Cup.

[23] *The Sporting News*, December 27, 1934. Dick Farrington wrote, "The feeling...still prevails that Breadon and Rickey are diplomatically friendly, but secretly at 'outs.'" Charley Barrett sold an estimated 75 shares at the same time. Howard's father was the one-time president of Commonwealth Steel, which was sold to General Steel Castings Corporation in 1929 for $35 million in cash and $10 million in preferred stock. His father died in 1931. In 1937, the estate of his mother was valued at $5,733,436. *St. Louis Post-Dispatch*, June 16, 1937. Howard Jr. was elected to the board of directors of the Cardinals in February of 1935, just months after purchasing Rickey's stock.

[24] Armour, Mark L. and Levitt, Daniel R. *In Pursuit of Pennants: Baseball Operations from Deadball to Moneyball.* University of Nebraska Press. 2015. Armour and Levitt wrote that Breadon traveled to Montreal twice to investigate possible ballpark sites. Both Breadon and Browns owner Phil Ball reportedly turned down offers from Canadian businessmen Leo Dandurand and Joseph A. Cattarinich *St. Louis Post-Dispatch*, October 5, 1932. Dandurand and Cattarinich owned the Montreal Canadians. Some reports linked Giants manager John McGraw to the negotiations. Nine years earlier, Breadon looked at land in Montreal. He was reportedly considering relocating the team's Syracuse franchise. It later moved to Rochester. *St. Louis Star*, November 23, 1923.

[25] *St. Louis Star-Times*, March 28, 1935.

[26] Associated Press, November 27, 1934.

[27] *St. Louis Post-Dispatch*, April 1, 1935.

[28] Ibid, July 19, 1939.

[29] *St. Louis Star-Times*, July 29, 1939.

[30] Ibid, June 3, 1941.

[31] Golenbock, *The Spirit of St. Louis.*

[32] *St. Louis Post-Dispatch*, October 15, 1946. *The Sporting News* had published a piece claiming two syndicates were bidding for the Cardinals. One was headed by Mayer and another by local businessman Mark Steinberg, who had rejoined the board years after a dispute with Breadon over the trade of Rogers Hornsby. "It was not made plain how Mayer hoped to transfer the franchise to Los Angeles but it is a fact that he had a representative in St. Louis discussing possible purchase of the club." *Baseball Digest*, February 1948.

[33] *St. Louis Star-Times*, August 2, 1947.

[34] "We lost in 1936 because Paul Dean developed a sore arm. We lost in 1937 because Paul failed to come back, Dizzy Dean and Leo Durocher were injured," said Rickey, responding

---

to charges from fans who believed he devoted more time to the minor league teams than the major league squad. *St. Louis Star-Times,* December 8, 1937.
[35] Boxerman, Burton A. and Boxerman, Benita W. *George Weiss: Architect of the Golden Age Yankees*. McFarland & Company, Inc. Publishers. 2006.
[36] Lowenfish, *Branch Rickey*.
[37] In addition to Sammy Baugh and Don Hutson, college football players signed by the Cardinals included Ernie Vick, All-American center from Michigan; Bill Glasgow, All-Western conference halfback at the University of Iowa; Wesley Fesler, All-American end from Ohio State; Fred Thomsen, All Big-Ten halfback; Ted Saussele, Washington University; Lynn King, All-Valley halfback from Drake; Lou Bush, Massachusetts State College; Joel Hunt, All-Southwest back at Texas A&M; Jim Grilk, University of California; and Joe Grant, All-Southern halfback at Georgia. "The Cardinals' executive is positively a crank on the subject," wrote Sid Keener, regarding Rickey's desire to turn a college football player into a big-league baseball player. *St. Louis Star-Times*, November 11, 1937. Hunt, King, and Vick all had brief major league careers with the Cardinals.
[38] *Washington Post*, December 19, 2008.
[39] ESPN.com. Sports Century. www.espn.com/sportscentury/features/00014269.html
[40] Queries conducted through *newspapers.com.*
[41] *St. Louis Star-Times*, January 11, 1935.
[42] Daughters were common among Rickey and his brothers. Younger brother Frank had seven children, six daughters and one son. Older brother Orla had two daughters. Branch's five daughters referred to their brother, Branch Jr. as "boy." *Brooklyn Daily Eagle*, October 30 – Nov 3, 1942. Harold Parrott profiled Rickey and his family in a five-part series for the paper after he joined the Dodgers.
[43] Rickey was later instrumental in the founding of the Fellowship of Christian Athletes. He was inducted into the FCA's Hall of Champions in 1995.
[44] "In Springfield, Mo., Branch Rickey just isn't vice-president and general manager of the St. Louis Cardinals. He's also kingpin of the 'Rickey-ducks' club, an informal organization of leading business men which meets once a year at an even more informal banquet. Everyone wears his hunting clothes to the big dinner, held at the Colonial Hotel, and all must 'let their hair-down' under the rules of the club." The club was formed after Rickey stopped at the hotel after a duck hunt and asked the chef to put his ducks in the ice box until the following day. When Rickey went to retrieve them, another chef had put the ducks on the menu. *The Sporting News*, December 23, 1937.
[45] Mann, *Branch Rickey*.
[46] *Baseball Digest*, September 1949.
[47] At busy times, Rickey sometimes preferred to work from home. "He doesn't have a moment to himself when he gets here," said club secretary Clarence Lloyd. *St. Louis Star-Times*, February 19, 1932.
[48] *St. Louis Post-Dispatch*, January 14, 1935.

---

[49] Veeck, *The Hustler's Handbook*. Bob Burnes once wrote about Rickey's negotiation tactics with pitcher Jim Lindsey. During their discussions, the phone would ring constantly. "To this day Jim swears Branch had some sort of contraption under the desk and was ringing that telephone himself," wrote Burns, "but he couldn't take a chance on being wrong." *St. Louis Globe-Democrat*, November 21, 1942.
[50] Ibid.
[51] According to biographer Robert Gregory, he acquired the nickname while in the Army. A sergeant had yelled at him, "you dizzy son of a bitch." Gregory, Robert. *Diz: Dizzy Dean and Baseball During the Great Depression.* Viking Penguin. 1992.
[52] *St. Louis Post-Dispatch*, July 17, 1974. According to Dean biographer Gregory, Dean wanted a $300 raise. In the early 1930s, Dean had a propensity to write hot checks and charge purchases to the Cardinals. By early 1932, the total had reached $4,000. A big chunk of that came in a three-week spring training spree when he charged $2,700 of items to the team. Rickey demanded to know what he had spent the money on. "A fella's gotta eat," Dean replied.
[53] Ibid, January 21, 1931.
[54] Mann, Arthur. *Branch Rickey: American in Action.* The Riverside Press. 1957.
[55] *St. Louis Post-Dispatch*, October 6, 1934. The reasons behind Breadon's fears are not clear, but the incident came on the heels of NL president Heydler's close monitoring of the final regular-season series and two years after the kidnapping of the son of Charles Lindbergh.
[56] Gregory, *Diz.*
[57] *The Sporting News*, March 28, 1935.
[58] "He took the name Jerome Herman out of friendship for a battery mate in the San Antonio City League." *New York World-Telegram*, July 26, 1934. Dean would also give another version to reporters. As a child, he claimed to know a Jerome Herman who died at a young age. He reportedly told the boy's grieving father that he would call himself Jerome Herman. "My name's Jay Hanna and they're the same initials, anyway." In addition to his name, Dean would confuse reporters by giving multiple versions of his birthplace and birth date.
[59] *The Sporting News*, May 23, 1935.
[60] *St. Louis Star-Times,* June 6, 1935.
[61] Dean and DeWitt later went to court over their business dealings. DeWitt filed a claim seeking $6,989 in commissions. For releasing all claims against him, Dean paid DeWitt $1,125. *St. Louis Star-Times*, August 15, 1939.
[62] Gay, Timothy M. *Satch, Dizzy & Rapid Robert: The Wild Saga of Interracial Baseball Before Jackie Robinson*. Simon & Schuster. 2010.
[63] Ibid. Gay credits Allen Barra and an interview he did with Davis for *Birmingham Weekly.*
[64] Ibid.
[65] *The Sporting News*, February 14, 1935. *Baseball Reference* lists his salary for 1935 at $18,500.

---

[66] Dean had an endorsement deal with the Slack Furniture company in East St. Louis. It paid him $5,000 a year "to advertise furniture over the radio and in person at the store." *St. Louis Star-Times*, June 6, 1935.
[67] *Daily News*, March 19, 1937.
[68] Afterward, Miley said to Frisch: "What's the matter, Francis, can't you control those ball players of yours?" "No, I can't," Frisch replied. Kupcinet, a former University of Notre Dame quarterback, challenged Dean to a fight. "I'll fight you any place any time you want to. Just name it." Dean refused the challenge and later blamed the brawl on Medwick. Like Kupcinet, Medwick invited Dean to settle the matter with his fists. "All that Hungarian bastard wants to do is fight," said Dean. Gregory, *Diz.*
[69] *St. Louis Star-Times*, August 20, 1934.
[70] Gregory, *Diz*. "There was...an instant collapse in the products he'd endorsed. His temperament had wrecked the market. Nobody was buying. The fans were in revolt," wrote Gregory.
[71] St. Louis Star-Times, July 29, 1938.
[72] Stockton knew Dean well. He served as his ghostwriter in Christy Walsh's syndicate.
[73] *St. Louis Post-Dispatch*, July 28, 1938.
[74] At his peak, Hornsby was the highest-paid player in the National League. Dean was the highest-paid pitcher in the league. roadsidephotos.sabr.org/baseball/1930SSALS.htm
[75] Hornsby and Dean both lost World Series as members of the Cubs; Hornsby in 1929 and Dean in 1938. Dean started and lost Game 2 in a Series swept by the Yankees.
[76] Those internal misfortunes include the career of catcher Bill Delancey. At the age of 22, he hit .316 in 1934 and caught every inning of the World Series. After one more season, his career was all but over. Suffering from tuberculosis, he died on his thirty-fifth birthday. "There was one of the dead-gamest, hardest fighting ball players I ever knew and the best catcher I ever pitched to," said Dizzy Dean. *Baseball Digest*, February 1947.
[77] While he didn't mention Dean, Rickey said this in the fall of 1942 after leaving the Cardinals. "Players' bad habits off the field cost me two pennants in St. Louis; they will never cost me any more." *Brooklyn Daily Eagle*, November 3, 1942.
[78] *St. Louis Star-Times*, March 17, 1938. Another way Rickey would seek control over minor league teams was to structure an option to purchase one or two players, without naming them. "Given that a Minor League team would be unlikely to have more than one or two Major League-ready players anyway, this would effectively allow Rickey to control well beyond forty players. The legality of this interpretation was debatable." Armour and Levitt, *In Pursuit of Pennants*.
[79] Ibid. The story of the Cardinals minor-league system and control over other farm teams wasn't exactly a secret. Three years earlier, the same reporter, Harry Grayson had written this: "The Cardinals control two complete four-team class D leagues, the Arkansas State and Nebraska. They have the pick of at least seven other clubs." *St. Louis Star-Times*, February 21, 1935.
[80] *St. Louis Post-Dispatch*, March 29, 1938.

---

[81] Parrott, Harold. *The Lords of Baseball: A wry look at a side of the game the fan seldom sees – the front office.* Longstreet Press. 2001.
[82] Reiser was scheduled to report to a Dodgers minor league training camp in Macon, Georgia. But over the winter, since both he and Durocher lived in St. Louis at the time, Reiser paid his manager a visit and asked if he could work out with the Montreal Royals in Lake Wales, because he wanted to see Florida. Durocher granted the request. *Brooklyn Daily Eagle*, March 25, 1939.
[83] *New York Times*, March 31, 1939.
[84] *St. Louis Post-Dispatch*, February 10, 1939.
[85] Barrett's trip to Cuba in 1934 became the stuff of legend. He arrived on the island during a period of political unrest and was "forced to flee for his life, hopping from post to post to dodge bullets that whizzed by his head." At the first opportunity, he took a boat back to the United States. "If there any good ballplayers in Cuba, let them stay there. I'll find mine out in Oklahoma, Arkansas, and all points west." *St. Louis Star-Times*, July 5, 1939.
[86] Ibid, July 6, 1939.
[87] Ibid, July 5, 1939.
[88] *The Sporting News*, July 13, 1939.
[89] *St. Louis Star-Times*, August 21, 1939.
[90] Rickey and Frisch reportedly had strained relations. Press reports at the time linked Rickey to the Chicago Cubs. Media speculation was that Rickey was using the leverage of a job offer to get Breadon to fire Frisch. Clarence Rowland of the Cubs "came to St. Louis in an effort to interest Rickey with an offer that would have made him general manager, if not the president, of the Cubs." *The Sporting News,* September 15, 1938.
[91] Mann, *Branch Rickey.*
[92] *St. Louis Post-Dispatch*, October 5, 1942. Breadon admitted that he and Rickey had not discussed a contract in nearly two years. "I had not talked with Branch on this matter since I informed him in February of 1941 that I would not renew his contract on present terms."
[93] Cardinals games in the early 1940s were carried on KXOK radio (one of many stations to carry the broadcasts) and the Hyde Park network of stations. In 1940, the network included stations located in Cape Girardeau, Columbia, Poplar Bluff, and Springfield, Mo., and Decatur, Il. *St. Louis Star-Times*, April 17, 1940. One year later, announcer France Laux left KMOX to broadcast games on KXOK. Dizzy Dean retired in 1941 and began broadcasting for KWK. His partner on broadcasts was Johnny O'Hara. In 1944, the duo switched to WEW for day games and WTMV for night broadcasts. A year later, Laux and O'Hara did games together, with Dean reuniting with O'Hara on WIL in 1946. In 1947, Dean and O'Hara broadcast Browns games only.
[94] *Baseball Digest*, December 1942.
[95] Mann, *Branch Rickey.* While managing the Cardinals minor league team in Rochester one season, Dyer sent Rickey multiple telegrams, pleading for more pitchers. A confused Rickey wired back: "Please advise your position in the standings." "Temporarily in first place by six games. Need pitchers badly," Dyer replied. *New York Times*, April 24, 1964.

Rickey Expands the Recipe

Rickey had plenty of options when it became obvious his contract with the Cardinals wasn't getting renewed. He considered politics and private business and entertained offers from several major league teams. Recurring reports linked him to the Browns, but when Dodgers president and general manager Larry MacPhail resigned from Brooklyn in September of 1942 to join the Army, Rickey's name vaulted to the top of the Dodgers list.[1] When the victorious Cardinals boarded the train in New York after the World Series, Rickey was nowhere to be found. "I do not know anything about Rickey's affairs," said Breadon. "I'm on this train, you'll note, enjoying this great victory with the players."

The two men couldn't resist trading jabs. A few days later, Rickey told a New York sportswriter, "Under the present setup, Sam Breadon hasn't got, and couldn't raise enough money to keep me," a comment that surprised his boss.[2] Breadon told *The Sporting News* he had paid Rickey "more than a million dollars during the past 23 years and that's more salary than I've received."[3] Later in the month, Rickey said on KMOX radio that the Cardinals would show a profit of "close to $200,000" for the year, adding that "income could be further increased to about $300,000 without impairing the organization in any way."[4] If Breadon wanted to make his departure about economics, Rickey wanted the public to know the club had a healthy bottom line. (But maybe not as healthy as he wanted people to believe. In December, the club declared a $2 per share dividend, an $8 per share reduction from the previous year.)

While Rickey had started discussions with the Dodgers, he wasn't the only man considered for the job. Another executive prominently mentioned for the role was George Weiss of the Yankees. Weiss removed his name from consideration on October 22. "I have a contract with the Yankees which has a couple of years to run, and I am not making any changes at this time," he announced.[5]

Perhaps Weiss knew he wasn't getting the job. A day later, a columnist for the *New York World-Telegram* reported that while the Dodgers considered the Yankees executive, Rickey was their first choice. A deal had been struck. "He was offered the job after the first game of the World Series in St. Louis, at which time he took it under consideration," wrote Joe Williams. The announcement came the following week. Rickey notified Breadon in a two-sentence telegram. "Have just made five-year contract with Brooklyn. Will you please notify press relative to satisfactory termination of my St. Louis contract." The Rickey reign in St. Louis was officially over. So, too, was his longtime partnership with Breadon.

"Nobody ever bluffed him, physically or financially," Taylor Spink once wrote of Breadon in *The Sporting News*. In the same article, he described Rickey as "always two jumps and a half a dozen thoughts ahead of the other fellow in any business or trade discussions."[6] In October of 1942, the immovable object met the unstoppable force. "It was a strange partnership always," wrote Roy Stockton, "with each having always a great respect for the ability of the other, while their personalities, habits and views of extra-curricular things were so diametrically opposed that there was never any strong bond of friendship between the two partners."[7]

Another St. Louis columnist, Sid Keener, tried to get Rickey to elaborate on his split from Breadon. Was it a difference in politics between Democrat Breadon and Republican Rickey? Or maybe it was the hiring and firing of different managers? Perhaps he was upset about the departure over the years of many Rickey loyalists, a group that included long-time Rochester Red Wings president (and future National League president) Warren Giles? "They'll never get the inside story from me," Rickey said.[8]

"There was obviously more than one reason Breadon let Rickey go," remembered columnist Bob Broeg. "Breadon knew areas of Rickey's hypocrisy and double-talk," providing an Enos Slaughter contract as an example. Breadon once approached the Cardinals outfielder and asked him what it felt like to make five figures. A confused Slaughter didn't know what he was talking about. "Obviously Rickey and Breadon had agreed to pay Enos $10,000, and Rickey had chiseled it down to $9,000," Broeg said.[9]

Breadon also intimated that he, and he alone, could now run the Cardinals organization. "The hint develops that Breadon has reached the stage where he feels he can operate the Cardinals and the farm system himself," Dick Farrington wrote in *The Sporting News* in the fall of 1941.[10] Appreciation for what Rickey created in St. Louis would take years to realize. In the meantime, his players were not sorry to see him go. "I was kind of glad Mr. Rickey left," admitted Marty Marion. "The players always talked bad about him behind his back. He was a demon. He was the law. We respected him, don't forget that, but we didn't like him."[11]

The man Cardinal players respected but didn't like, now focused his efforts at beating them on the playing field instead of at the negotiating table. "Just as in the American League, club owners who seek to improve their team use the Yankees as their yardstick, we in the National League must measure our clubs by the Cardinals," Rickey said shortly after joining the Dodgers. "There is neither fame nor money in finishing second."[12]

*****

With both Breadon and Browns owner Phil Ball, Rickey had worked with opposites. The same could be said for Rickey's relationship with the man he replaced in Brooklyn. If the new Dodgers executive could be an absent-minded workaholic, MacPhail could be described as a quick-tempered alcoholic. He was also brilliant and original. "My grandfather was bombastic, flamboyant, a genius when sober, brilliant when he had one drink and a raving lunatic when he had too many," Andy MacPhail once said.[13]

His bold and daring behavior began as a young man. At the end of World War I, he and a group of Army colleagues tried to kidnap Kaiser Wilhelm from Holland. Dutch troops blocked the effort but MacPhail came away with the Kaiser's ashtray as a souvenir.

MacPhail got his start in baseball working for the Cardinals. When St. Louis bought the minor league Columbus Redbirds in the early 1930s, he became team president. Working as an attorney in the Ohio city, MacPhail had a purchase option on the team and brought it to the attention of the Cardinals. Instead of paying him a commission on the deal, Rickey and Breadon hired him. In Columbus, MacPhail was both an innovator – he brought night baseball to the team and its new ballpark in 1932 – and an instigator of turmoil. A union worker became so upset with MacPhail during stadium construction he threw an eight-pound wrench at his head. It missed by inches.[14]

By 1933, the Cardinals had enough of the volatile MacPhail and let him go.[15] But he had done enough to impress Rickey, who recommended him for a job with the Cincinnati Reds. "He's a wild man at times, but he'll do the job," Rickey told the Reds. Under the direction of their new front office executive, Cincinnati became the first team in major league baseball to host a night game in 1935. While his accomplishments were similar to those in Columbus, so was his behavior. In Cincinnati, he reportedly punched a detective and clashed with Powel Crosley, the owner of the Reds.[16] Cincinnati fired him after the 1936 season.

With another boost from Rickey, MacPhail got the job in Brooklyn. "I'm not going to take another drink for a year," MacPhail told his former boss. "Why not make that a lifetime, instead of a year?" Rickey replied.[17] At his new home, MacPhail dusted off a familiar playbook. He had lights installed at Ebbets Field in 1938. Three years after the Reds made history, MacPhail's Dodgers became baseball's second major league team to host a night game (Cincinnati pitcher Johnny Vander Meer tossed his second straight no-hitter that evening). A few months later, the Dodgers hosted the Cardinals in a game featuring yellow baseballs. Brooklyn won 6-2, but after a few more contests with a brightly colored ball, MacPhail abandoned the experiment.

That was the same season the Dodgers executive hired Babe Ruth as a coach (as well as former Cardinal great Jesse Haines). The Dodgers finished in seventh place with a record of 69-80 but attendance jumped by nearly 200,000. New York City had a radio ban on baseball broadcasts for several years in the 1930s. MacPhail broke the embargo in 1939 when he hired Red Barber (who had been with him in Cincinnati) to broadcast Dodgers games.[18] The team steadily improved. The 1941 National League champions had three former Cardinals in the lineup – Medwick, Reiser, and catcher Mickey Owen. The 1942 club won 104 games but came in second thanks to a St. Louis team that went 43-8 in its last 51 contests. When MacPhail resigned from the Dodgers to accept a commission in the United States Army, the cupboard was far from bare. But Rickey did inherit an aging club. First baseman Dolph Camilli, who led the team in both home runs and RBI, was thirty-five. Nineteen-game-winner Whit Wyatt was thirty-four.

Reiser, the former Cardinal farmhand and a rising star with the Dodgers, crashed into an outfield wall at Sportsman's Park in the summer of 1942. Weaving and groggy from the incident – "He was traveling like a bullet when he hit the fence," Medwick said afterward – Reiser was taken to St. John's Hospital.[19] Dr. Robert Hyland, the Cardinals team physician, diagnosed the St. Louis native with a concussion. According to Reiser, his skull was fractured, and the doctor recommended he not play anymore that season.[20] He missed four games. Hitting .350 at the time of the injury, he batted just .244 the rest of the season. Rickey blamed MacPhail for allowing Reiser to continue to play. "That character should never have been entrusted with anything so fine." While the story has assumed perhaps an exaggerated role in the career of Reiser (he missed the next three years due to military service, and over the course of his career, he was carried off the field 11 times due to his aggressive outfield play), it's true he never again posted numbers like his fabulous 1941 season.[21]

With no Reiser around, an aging Dodgers lineup got even older. Six of the eight regulars in 1943 were over the age of thirty. To Rickey, a man who put a premium on speed and youth, changes had to be made. As president of the Dodgers (he was a vice president in St. Louis, reporting to Breadon), Rickey had free rein to revamp the franchise (including canceling the whiskey ads on the Ebbets Field outfield wall). He brought his St. Louis recipe to Brooklyn; a transition made easier with his son running the Brooklyn farm system and his former shortstop in St. Louis, Leo Durocher, managing the club.[22]

Tryout camps began almost immediately (twenty-five camps were conducted in 1943). Pitcher Ralph Branca was signed after an audition at Ebbets Field and was soon pitching for the minor-league Olean Oilers. He was seventeen years old. Future Dodgers Gil Hodges and Carl Erskine signed after tryout camps in Indianapolis. Future Hall-of-Famer Duke Snider was spotted in a camp in Long Beach, California. In 1944, the team sent letters – some 20,000 of them – to every single high school baseball coach in America, asking for recommendations. Under Rickey's direction, the Dodgers expanded baseball's boundaries on what was possible. In the middle of World War II, Brooklyn even extended tryout camp invitations to Japanese-American players living in internment camps. "The fact that these boys are American boys is good enough for the Brooklyn club," wrote farm director Branch Rickey Jr.[23]

While other teams cut back their investment during the war, Rickey and the Dodgers expanded. "We are, in effect, betting that the war is over in two years," Rickey said while outlining his plans in January of 1943.[24] Just as it happened with the Cardinals, signing dozens of players from tryout camps created the need for additional minor-league teams. By 1948, the Dodgers had twenty-six of them, the most in baseball, and seven more than Rickey's former club. Other than the Yankees, teams were still hesitant to fully embrace the Rickey playbook. "[Red Sox owner] Yawkey and [Cubs owner] Wrigley and [Pirates owner] Galbreath could have signed the same kids who became the [Enos] Country Slaughters and [Marty] Slats Marions and brothers like the Deans and Coopers, but they didn't," wrote Harold Parrott, who worked for Rickey in Brooklyn. "All their scouts seemed to have patent leather shoes and silk shirts and wouldn't think of sloshing through the canebrakes where Frank Rickey, Branch's brother and great scout, worked in a frayed windbreaker, searching among the mill teams and around the semipros."

Frank Rickey later joined his brother Branch in Brooklyn, as did a host of others with connections from their days together in St. Louis. George Sisler, the former Browns great whose ties to Rickey stretched back to their days together at the University of Michigan, became a scout for Brooklyn. Former Michigan Athletic Director Phil Bartelme served as president of farm teams in Syracuse, Dayton, and Sacramento while working for the Cardinals for more than two decades. He became a scout for the Dodgers in 1944. Scouts Bob Finch and Wid Matthews left Breadon's Cardinals to work for Rickey's Dodgers.[25] Rex Bowen played minor-league ball for the Cardinals in the 1930s before running tryout camps for the team in his native New Jersey. Rickey got him to switch loyalties. Cardinals public relations director Melvin Jones and secretary Edward Staples also departed for Brooklyn, as did Columbus Redbirds secretary Jane Ann Jones and Rochester secretary Ann Driver.[26] Ray Blades and Burt Shotton spent years in St. Louis playing and coaching. Both eventually joined the Dodgers.[27] Pepper Martin and Andy High played for Rickey in St. Louis.[28] Both men later coached in the Dodgers organization.

When Rickey bolted for Brooklyn, the Cardinals lost more than just his incredible mind. They also lost an infrastructure and collective wisdom that took years to develop. Frank Rickey alone, according to estimates from his brother, discovered or signed 77 players during his time with the Cardinals. Branch and his extended brethren had successfully turned around the Cardinals from perennial losers to consistent winners. Now they suddenly found themselves on the other side of one of baseball's hottest rivalries.

*****

Joe Medwick broke in with the Cardinals in 1932, became a regular in 1933, and won the National League MVP award in 1937. That season he led the league with 31 home runs, 154 RBI, and a batting average of .374. No one in the National League has won a Triple Crown since. He received a raise to $20,000 for 1938. Medwick followed up his MVP campaign by leading the league with 122 RBI, while batting .322 with 21 home runs. The Cardinals cut his pay by $2,000. Medwick compared negotiating salary with

Rickey to shaving without any soap. "I thought I'd seen more blood than Count Dracula."[29]

Productive on the field, Medwick was not popular with his teammates. "He was just not a real likable guy," remembered infielder Don Gutteridge. Medwick and pitcher Tex Carleton once got into a fistfight during batting practice. "He was completely self-centered," is how broadcaster Barber once described him. On June 12, 1940, Rickey's Cardinals traded Medwick to MacPhail's Dodgers along with pitcher Curt Davis for four players and $125,000 cash.[30] The following week, Brooklyn welcomed Medwick's old team for the start of a three-game series. In the first inning of the second game, pandemonium erupted at Ebbets Field.

Freshly arrived in Brooklyn, Medwick was living in the New Yorker hotel. Dodgers manager and former Cardinal Durocher, who still lived in St. Louis in the offseason, also spent his summers there. The Cardinals were staying in the same hotel. Medwick and Durocher happened to encounter St. Louis starting pitcher Bob Bowman in an elevator. As teammates, Bowman and Medwick had exchanged words the previous season. The verbal volleys continued in the elevator. Versions vary as to what was said, but according to Slaughter, Durocher told Bowman his team would send the pitcher to an early shower. Staring at Medwick, Bowman replied that he was looking at the one automatic out in the Brooklyn lineup.

Out at Ebbets Field, Slaughter contended the Dodgers could see Bowman was tipping his pitches. Brooklyn third base coach Charlie Dressen would whistle every time Bowman would twist his glove, knowing that a curveball was coming. The first three batters in the Dodgers' lineup reached base. With Medwick coming to bat, the Cardinals figured out what the Brooklyn hitters already had. Catcher Don Padgett went to the mound and told Bowman to twist his glove again, but instead of throwing a curveball, deliver a fastball to the plate. Bowman complied. His fastball hit Medwick on the temple. Benches emptied. An angry MacPhail ran down to the field and had to be physically restrained. The Dodgers believed Bowman intentionally hit his former teammate. Medwick was carried off on a stretcher and taken to a local hospital. Nearly 100 uniformed officers took their place near the Cardinals dugout.[31] An investigation by National League president Ford Frick ruled the incident an accident.[32]

Medwick returned to the Brooklyn lineup four days later but his approach changed. "Medwick was never the tiger again at the plate," wrote Barber. "He didn't dig in again as he had. His power was gone." According to the Dodgers broadcaster, MacPhail always blamed Rickey (who was nowhere near Ebbets Field that day) for the beaning. "MacPhail, with his fantastic memory," Barber noted, "deep down inside, this beaning of Joe Medwick changed for all time his feelings about Branch Rickey. Rickey had won. MacPhail had lost and lost heavily."[33]

The 1940 brawl was followed by hard-fought pennant races the next two seasons where the teams swapped first and second place. Rickey and his entourage arrived after the 1942 season, and following a few seasons of rebuilding, the Dodgers and Cardinals battled to the bitter end in 1946. The Cardinals finished in second place three straight years from 1947 to 1949. The Dodgers won the pennant in two of those seasons.

Rickey's decision to invest heavily in the farm system in 1943 with World War II still raging was a gutsy and brilliant stroke, the equivalent of a stock analyst correctly calling the bottom of a bear market. His timing was perfect, and his team reaped the rewards of his investments for years to come. "The Dodgers farm system was so strong," wrote Bill James of Brooklyn in the Rickey era, "that if the Dodger team plane had crashed, the Dodgers could have put together a contending team from the players trapped at Triple-A." The Cardinal Way, right down to the Knothole Gang, became the Dodger Way.[34]

But the Dodger Way included an element that had never been possible in St. Louis, where the bleachers remained segregated until 1944. Rickey's switch from St. Louis to Brooklyn came in the middle of a world war that sparked new thoughts on race relations. "Remember Pearl Harbor and Sikeston Too!" read a headline from the *Chicago Defender* in 1942, a reference to the lynching of a black man in Sikeston, Missouri, and an argument that linked oppression abroad with injustice on the domestic front. Rickey's awareness was also raised by several African-American journalists, who had been arguing for an integrated game since the 1930s.

By the time Rickey signed Jackie Robinson in October of 1945, World War II had ended. The battle over integrated baseball had not. The following summer, baseball owners took up the issue of whether to allow black players in the majors. The vote was 15-1 against with only Rickey dissenting. A six-member steering committee designed to investigate the matter included Cardinals owner Breadon and MacPhail, out of the Army and now one of the owners of the New York Yankees. "Comparatively few good young Negro players are being developed," their secret report read, in part. "This is the reason there are not more players who meet major league standards in the Negro leagues." A furious Rickey then met with Commissioner Happy Chandler (who was not part of the vote nor on the committee) who reportedly assured the Dodgers president that Robinson would be given a shot. "Let's bring him in and treat him as just another player," Chandler told him.[35]

Robinson spent 1946 playing for the Montreal Royals, a Dodgers farm club. Born in Georgia and raised in California, Robinson was a four-sport athlete at UCLA, lettering in baseball, basketball, football, and track. As a lieutenant in the Army in 1944, he faced court-martial charges for refusing to go to the back of a segregated bus. Acquitted of the charge, he received an honorable discharge. He played for the Kansas City Monarchs in 1945, a Negro league team that played its home games in a stadium bought by Jacob Ruppert in the 1930s for a Yankees farm club. Rickey, who'd been searching for a candidate to break the color barrier ever since he arrived in Brooklyn, soon focused his efforts on the former UCLA star. Matthews, the former Cardinals scout, and Sisler, the former Browns great, were two of the men Rickey dispatched to make an evaluation. The reports came back positive with Matthews calling him one of the best two-strike hitters he had ever seen. Sisler predicted that Robinson's arm was better suited for second base than shortstop. (In his Dodgers' career, Robinson played 745 games at second and one game at shortstop.)

Robinson enjoyed a spectacular season in Montreal, hitting .349 with 40 stolen bases. The International League Champion Royals then went on to defeat Louisville of the American Association in the Little World Series. There was nothing left for Robinson to prove in the minor leagues. On April 10, 1947, Brooklyn purchased Robinson's contract from Montreal. He made his Dodgers' debut five days later. Two teams quickly followed Rickey's lead. Bill Veeck's Cleveland Indians signed Larry Doby in July, and the Browns, under the direction of former Rickey acolyte Bill DeWitt Sr., signed outfielder Willard Brown and infielder Hank Thompson.

But 1947 was the story of Robinson and the Dodgers. Playing first base, Robinson won the first Rookie of the Year award and Brooklyn won its first pennant of the Rickey era. Along the way, Robinson had to battle long-held racial beliefs of teammates, endure racial epithets from opposing managers and hear talk of a strike by opposing teams. One team featured prominently in the chatter surrounding the last maneuver – Rickey's old squad in St. Louis.

*****

The Cardinals and Dodgers met for a series in Brooklyn in May of 1947, the first time the two teams had faced each other since the historic playoff of the previous year. A great deal had changed in the interim, most of it centered on the behavior of a man who wore the uniforms of both teams during his career.

Speculation about manager Durocher began soon after Brooklyn lost the pennant. "The secret charges against Leo Durocher," Bill Veeck Jr., once told sportswriter and author Roger Kahn, "were that he dumped the 1946 pennant race to the St. Louis Cardinals. At least that's what Shondor Birns told me." Alex "Shondor" Birns was a noted Cleveland mobster, "the city's No. 1 racketeer," according to the *Plain-Dealer.* "He said he and some other gamblers paid off Leo to mishandle the Dodger pitching rotation. Shondor said that's what Leo did," Veeck recalled. "Shondor said he personally made a killing."[36]

The best-of-three series began in St. Louis on October 1. Durocher gave the ball to twenty-year-old Ralph Branca in the opener, who started only ten games the entire year for the Dodgers. Two days later in Brooklyn, Durocher went with 14-game winner Joe Hatten.[37] The Cardinals won both games and the Dodgers season was over. Ford Frick was National League president at the time and later the commissioner of baseball. After he retired, Kahn asked him about the Durocher gambling rumors. Despite repeated attempts, Frick would never give him an answer. "This remains one of the more interesting no-comments of my experience," Kahn wrote.[38] Durocher forcefully denied the charge. "Outrageous. Fucking outrageous," he said years later. (Kahn once said if there's a quote in his book from Durocher that doesn't have the F-word in it, "it's a misquote, because that's how Leo spoke.")[39]

Other stories about Durocher's behavior had floated around as long as he had been in baseball. As a rookie with the Yankees, he helped Babe Ruth to bed after a night on the town in St. Louis. The next day, Ruth discovered his wristwatch was missing and suspected Durocher was the culprit. The Yankees traded Durocher to the Cincinnati Reds in 1930. Rickey's Cardinals acquired the shortstop from the Reds three years later.

"Bear down, damn it. I'm $10,000 in the red. I need that six grand," the captain of the Gashouse Gang would yell from the shortstop position to whoever was on the mound for the Cardinals, a reference to the purse paid to players on the winning team of the World Series.[40] Durocher got a World Series ring and a wedding band in the same year. He married Grace Dozier, a St. Louis dress designer, during the 1934 season.

Durocher played in St. Louis until the end of the 1937 season when Rickey traded him to Brooklyn. His playing career ended and his managing career began with the Dodgers. By the time Rickey joined the organization, Durocher's clubhouse "reeked with gamblers, bookmakers, racing handicappers, fast 'friends,' and ticket scalpers," according to Rickey biographer Arthur Mann. "This is the gamblingest ball club I ever saw," said Dodgers pitcher Larry French after joining the team. When word reached Rickey that Durocher was gambling with players in the clubhouse before games, the Dodgers president attempted to put limits on the manager's behavior. "From now on," Rickey instructed, "there will be no poker with a higher limit than fifteen cents."[41] He also fired coach Charlie Dressen for betting on horses.[42]

Durocher divorced his St. Louis bride in 1943. He began spending his winters at the California home of George Raft. The Hollywood actor reportedly once won $100,000 betting on baseball. Durocher's connections included Connie Immerman, who ran a casino in pre-Castro Cuba, bookmaker Max "Memphis" Engelberg, Las Vegas mobster Bugsy Siegel, and New York mobster Joe Adonis. As part of an investigation in late 1946, the Brooklyn District Attorney tapped Durocher's telephone. The associations raised eyebrows in the media and concern in official baseball. Commissioner Landis had booted Philadelphia Phillies owner William D. Cox in 1943 for betting on baseball, and now it was Chandler's turn to deal with threats to the integrity of the game.

Durocher had magnified the target on his back by marrying actress Laraine Day. Their affair began when Day was still married to Ray Hendricks, a former Air Force flight instructor. Sometime after the 1946 season, Durocher was at Day's house screening one of her movies, when Hendricks, a heavy drinker, fell asleep. What happened next Durocher related to Kahn on a train trip years later. "Leo and Laraine embraced and proceeded to have at it full blast on a piano bench." The affair might have continued in secret had the movie not ended. The film reel snapping in the projector woke up Day's husband. Day addressed her legal partner as Durocher pulled up his pants. "I love Leo," she confessed. "He loves me. We want to be married."[43]

A California judge granted Day and Hendricks a divorce on January 20, 1947, with the stipulation that the actress couldn't remarry for a year. To escape the judge's decree, she traveled to Juarez, Mexico on January 21 to receive a second divorce and married Durocher later that day in El Paso, Texas. When the California judge deemed her Texas marriage illegal, the couple remarried a year later.

A scandalous affair between a Hollywood actress and a major league manager captured headlines and brought extra scrutiny to Rickey and his team. The Catholic Youth Organization (CYO) in Brooklyn threatened to withdraw from the Knothole Club (as it was called in Brooklyn) if Durocher wasn't fired. Rickey stood by his manager. The CYO, with its 125,000 boys, withdrew from the group at the end of February.[44] (Others took a different approach. When the movie *Mr. Lucky* debuted, the marquee on a Brooklyn theatre read, "Starring Cary Grant and Mrs. Leo Durocher.")

Against this backdrop – gambling rumors, tapped telephones, an affair and illegal marriage, and a boycott of the team – Durocher assembled his Dodgers for spring training in 1947 with the expectation that his club would break camp and make history with an integrated roster. He was promptly hit with a revolt from his players. Some of the Dodgers began circulating a petition stating they wouldn't play with Robinson. Durocher's reaction was immediate. He dragged his team out of bed in the middle of the night and reprimanded his players. He also appealed to their economic interests. "He's going to put money in our pockets and money in mine," Durocher told his team before ending the discussion. "Fuck the petition. The meeting is over. Go back to bed."

No sooner had one spring training crisis been averted than another one began. At a Dodgers-Yankees exhibition game in Havana, Engelberg and Immerman – two of Durocher's questionable gambling connections – were sitting in or near the box of Yankees owner MacPhail. Rickey was incredulous. "There they are as guests of the president of the Yankees, while my own manager can't even say hello to this actor, George What's-His-Name." Durocher was also furious. "Are there two sets of rules?" he asked. "One applying to managers and one to club owners?"[45]

MacPhail responded by calling for an investigation by the commissioner. "I'd much rather have Engelberg as my guest at a ballgame than Rickey," he said. At war with his former mentor ever since the Medwick beaning in 1940, MacPhail couldn't resist revisiting some sensitive Rickey history. "Judge Landis told me his one mistake as baseball commissioner was in not barring Rickey from the game as a result of the Cedar Rapids deal where he was covering up players. Landis told me he never encountered anything to equal this case for brazen contempt of baseball law."[46]

Commissioner Chandler called two hearings regarding the matter. He settled it by fining both the Yankees and Dodgers $2,000 and suspending Durocher for a year "as a result of the accumulation of unpleasant incidents in which he has been involved and which the commissioner construes as detrimental to baseball." The announcement came on April 9. Robinson's official promotion to the Dodgers came the following day. The season started on April 15.

Rickey now had to scramble to find a manager. Durocher, for all his faults, had always been open to the idea of integration. "Hell, I've seen a million good ones," he once said when asked if black players could compete in the major leagues. After considering several candidates (including Rogers Hornsby), Rickey settled on Shotton, the former Brown and Cardinal outfielder and Sunday manager for Rickey during his days in the dugout in St Louis. Shotton was sixty-two years old and living in Florida when he received a telegram. "Be in Brooklyn tomorrow morning," Rickey instructed. "See nobody. Say nothing."

The Dodgers season started after a near player revolt in spring training, a last-minute change of the manager, and increased scrutiny and vicious taunting from opposing benches with Robinson in the lineup. None of it seemed to bother the players on the field. The Dodgers were in first place with a 9-3 record when the club opened a series at home against the Cardinals on May 6. It was the defending world champions who were struggling. With the same manager and essentially the same lineup as the year before, the Cardinals had just snapped a nine-game losing streak when the team entered Ebbets Field for the first time in 1947. St. Louis dropped the opener but rallied to win the next two games and take the series. Then a bombshell hit the newspapers.

The day after the series ended, Stanley Woodward published a story in the *New York Herald Tribune* claiming a National League players' strike protesting the presence of Robinson and led by members of the Cardinals, had been averted. Woodward had indirectly received the tip from Dr. Hyland in St. Louis. A week before the Cardinals played in Brooklyn, the Yankees played the Browns at Sportsman's Park. Hyland, team physician for both St. Louis teams, had dinner with Rudd Rennie, another writer from the *Herald Tribune.* Hyland told him about rumors of a strike; information Rennie passed along to his boss Woodward, the sports editor for the paper.

The strike rumors had also reached Cardinals owner Breadon, who took the issue to Ford Frick. The National League president told Breadon that any striking player would be suspended. Breadon passed along the message to his team. "It was just a tempest in a teapot," Breadon later told Frick. "A few of the players were upset and popping off a bit. They didn't really mean it."

Coverage of the incident quickly faded but its impact and truthfulness have been debated ever since. Players on the Cardinals immediately denied it. Terry Moore called it "highly inaccurate" and pointed out "if the Cardinals refused to take the field, we'd lose 9-0 by a forfeit score." Manager Eddie Dyer dismissed any strike talk as absurd. "At no time to my knowledge did my players consider such a foolish action." Breadon called "the whole thing ridiculous," while also conceding he did discuss the rumors with his team. "I was happy to find that there was no dissatisfaction among the Cardinals."[47]

Over time, other players addressed the strike issue in more depth. "Why in the hell would I have wanted to strike rather than play them?" Enos Slaughter wrote in his autobiography. "Other than being in a World Series, there was nothing I wanted to do more than play against Brooklyn."

"We never had a meeting. We never talked about having an organized boycott," Stan Musial said in 1997. In a separate interview, he gave a more expanded and nuanced answer to sportswriter Kahn. "First of all, everybody has racial feelings. We don't admit it. We aren't proud of it. But it's there. And this is the big leagues, not an English tea, and ballplayers make noise. So I heard the words and I knew there was some feelings behind the words, but I didn't take it seriously. That was baseball," Musial said.

"For me at the time – I was twenty-six – saying all that would have been a speech and I didn't know how to make speeches. Saying it to older players, that was beyond me. Besides, I thought the racial talk was just hot air," believed Musial.

Other players confirm Musial's stance that *something* was going on early in the 1947 season. Cardinals pitcher Freddy Schmidt recalled a letter being circulated through the clubhouse, urging players not to take the field against Robinson and the Dodgers.[48] St. Louis native Dick Sisler, George's son, was in his second year with the Cardinals. "Very definitely there was something going on at the time whereby they said they weren't going to play." Sisler also told author Jules Tygiel the planning was done "by a lot of older players. I don't think the younger fellows had anything at all to say."[49] Dodgers third baseman Spider Jorgenson also heard rumors. "Early in the season, the Cardinals were late getting out on the field. Only later were we told that their players almost didn't play us because of Robinson."[50]

Probably the biggest defender of how the Cardinals responded to Robinson was *Post-Dispatch* columnist Broeg. "As for the Cardinals – and this is important to me – some of the world champions didn't like it, but *none* conspired to strike against Robinson," he wrote in his autobiography published in 1995. "The team, many of them still my friends, received an unfair rap. This injustice has never been corrected. It's time the wrong done to them was made right."[51]

Broeg claimed a panicked Breadon had flown to New York to discuss his struggling team and the fate of manager Dyer with his players, not to address the squad regarding a potential strike. But even Broeg conceded the strike talk had Breadon worried. "Breadon was concerned that his players might not play against the Dodgers with Robinson in the lineup." The Cardinals owner passed along those concerns to Frick when he was in New York, then called the commissioner a few days later to say everything was settled.

Part of the confusion over a possible strike, and the Cardinals role in it, came from Woodward's belief there had been two different protests under consideration. The first version, "formulated by certain St. Louis players, was instigated by a member of the Brooklyn Dodgers who has since recanted," he wrote. This plan was for the Cardinals to strike on May 6, the date of their first game at Ebbets Field. "Subsequently, the St. Louis players conceived the idea of a general strike within the National League on a certain date," Woodward contended. He believed the Cardinals were considering a protest when Brooklyn came to St. Louis on May 21. "That is what Frick and Breadon have been combating in the last few days."

Fifty years after Robinson's debut, ESPN's *Outside the Lines* program interviewed 93 of his 107 living opponents. Players from the Cubs, Pirates and Phillies said their teams had taken votes to strike on opening day. Outfielder Al Gionfriddo was traded from

Pittsburgh to Brooklyn shortly after the season began. He believed that "every team had voted on whether to play the Dodgers." ESPN didn't go that far. According to the network, it appeared the Cardinals had also taken a vote while the Cubs were ready to boycott. Cubs catcher Dewey Williams claimed the team was just waiting on a call from Dodgers outfielder Dixie Walker that Robinson had taken the field. The call never came.[52]

Dixie's brother was Harry Walker, who began the season in St. Louis. Both Walkers were traded in 1947. Rickey sent Dixie to Pittsburgh shortly after the season ended. The Cardinals traded Harry and pitcher Freddy Schmidt to the Phillies three days before the series in Brooklyn.

The strongest evidence the Cardinals at least considered a strike came from the captain of the 1947 Cardinals. In 1991, just four years before he passed away, Terry Moore was living in Collinsville, Illinois, across the Mississippi River from St. Louis, when Kahn paid him a visit. Unlike his denials in the immediate aftermath, Moore now admitted a protest against Robinson was very much on the mind of the team. But when Breadon read Frick's message that players would be suspended for striking, reality set in. "None of us was making a lot of money," Moore said. "A suspension without pay would mean some fellers would lose their homes or the family farm. That killed the strike movement right there."[53]

Before Kahn left, he added this. "When you write about the strike thing please point out that I was only acting on what I had been taught to believe as a boy," said Moore, born in Alabama forty-seven years after the end of the Civil War.

Did players on the Cardinals lead the effort to strike against Robinson in his rookie year? Any attempt to answer the question requires another question. Which strike? Evidence points to a Robinson teammate, Dixie Walker, as the leader behind efforts to hijack opening day in 1947. According to Woodward, a player on the Dodgers – also believed to be Walker – attempted to get the Cardinals to strike on May 6. Walker was also one of the Dodgers behind the spring training petition. "I had a wholesale business in Birmingham and people told me I'd lose my business if I played with a black man," he told Kahn. "It was the dumbest thing I ever did in all my life and if you ever get the chance sometime, write that I'm deeply sorry."[54] If the Cardinals were the ringleaders of a strike scheduled for later in the month, the effort died with Frick's threat of suspension.

If the team received an "unfair rap," in the words of Broeg, it is in how the Cardinals became the focus of the media regarding strike talks when other teams (and some of his teammates) were just as committed to taking a stand against Robinson. But statements from Musial, Schmidt, Sisler, and especially Moore, make it clear momentum was building among team members toward some type of action until the commissioner stymied their efforts.

With a strike off the table, the Cardinals-Dodgers series proved to be remarkably calm. "There wasn't even any riding of Robinson from the bench in our series with the

Cardinals," said Dodgers manager Shotton.[55] The Cardinals' approach differed dramatically from the one taken by Phillies manager Ben Chapman just two weeks earlier. "They're waiting for you in the jungles, black boy!" Chapman screamed at Robinson. "Hey snowflake, which one of those white boys' wives are you dating tonight?" he taunted from the visitors' dugout. "We don't want you here, nigger." While the Phillies manager later claimed he was just giving Robinson the same treatment he would any other rookie, his efforts backfired. "Chapman did more than anybody to unite the Dodgers," said Rickey.[56]

Brooklyn headed to Philadelphia immediately after the St. Louis series, prompting a phone call to Rickey from Phillies general manager Herb Pennock. "You just can't bring a nigger here with the rest of the team, Branch," Pennock told him. Rickey responded by saying the Dodgers would gladly claim a win by forfeit. Pennock relented and the game was played. Robinson, though, was barred from the team hotel.

He couldn't stay at the Chase Hotel either. The St. Louis landmark didn't lift the restriction until 1954, but even then, black players couldn't use the dining room, swimming pool, or loiter in the lobby.[57]

In August, the Cardinals returned to Ebbets Field for a series against the Dodgers. The final game was marred by what has become the second-most famous incident involving the Cardinals and the Brooklyn rookie. In the top of the 11th inning, Slaughter hit a ground ball toward the right side of the infield. Robinson gloved the ball and began running to first base as Slaughter sprinted down the line. Robinson won the race and shoved his foot against the bag just moments before Slaughter's spikes came down on Robinson's heel. The Brooklyn first baseman began hopping around in pain but stayed in the game.

His teammates viewed Slaughter's actions as intentional. "Slaughter deliberately spiked Robinson," said Dodgers second baseman Eddie Stanky. "I've lost all respect for him." The Cardinals outfielder called it an accident. "I've never deliberately spiked anyone in my life."[58]

Always an aggressive player, Slaughter later pointed out he once spiked Bill Rigney while sliding into second base in a game at the Polo Grounds. The Giants infielder needed twenty-two stitches in his hand. "That didn't make headlines," he wrote in his autobiography. He had another incident with the Dodgers where he collided with Stanky. "He was carried off on a stretcher, but they don't talk about these things the way they talk about the Robinson play."

Both Slaughter supporters and detractors can find support or satisfaction for their side of the argument based on events the following day. Playing in Philadelphia, the outfielder collided with rookie shortstop Bernie Creger on a pop fly to left field, evidence the hustling Slaughter was always running hard and that his focus could cause him to be unaware of others around him. Those who believe Slaughter acted with malice in Brooklyn can find a certain cosmic karma in what happened next. The collision between the outfielder and infielder knocked Slaughter unconscious. He had to be carried off the field and was diagnosed with a concussion at Temple University Hospital. He missed the next four games.

A final incident between Robinson and the Cardinals took place the following month at Sportsman's Park. In a play like the one in Brooklyn, the feet of Cardinals catcher Joe Garagiola and Robinson collided at first base in the bottom of the second inning. Robinson displayed a spike cut on his shoe after the game. "He cut my shoes all to pieces," he told reporters. While stating he didn't believe Garagiola acted intentionally, he was still clearly irritated by the incident the next time he came to the plate. "Robinson must have been pretty steamed up about the situation because when he came to bat in the third inning, he did more talking than any of us have ever seen Jackie do in the course of a game," observed Tommy Holmes in the *Brooklyn Daily Eagle.*[59] Robinson's comments sparked a rebuttal from Garagiola, and soon the two men were in a "teeth-to-teeth exchange."[60] The umpire had to break it up.

The Dodgers took two of three games from the Cardinals in the series and left St. Louis with a six-game lead in the standings with just fourteen games to go. Brooklyn won the pennant with a record of 94-60, five games ahead of their longtime rival. Robinson missed just three games all season, hit .297, with 12 home runs, 48 RBI, and 29 stolen bases. In the first televised World Series, the Dodgers lost to the Yankees in seven games.

At the end of the season, Rickey could breathe a sigh of relief. Robinson's performance on the field and composure in moments of crisis demonstrated the Dodgers executive had selected the right man to make history. As other teams began to follow suit, there would be no turning back. With Robinson as the marquee draw, the Dodgers set a National League attendance record as more than 1.8 million fans poured through the gates at Ebbets Field. For the season, fans filled nearly 79 percent of the stadium's capacity. The team was an even bigger draw on the road as more than 1.9 million fans turned out to see the Dodgers and their barrier-breaking infielder. In St. Louis, Robinson and his teammates drew the four highest crowds of the season at Sportsman's Park.[61]

As 1947 marked the beginning of Robinson's major league career and a watershed moment for baseball, it also brought an end to the careers of Rickey's two greatest rivals. Sam Breadon sold the Cardinals after the season. Larry MacPhail exited the scene in New York, selling his interest in the Yankees. On the heels of a legacy-defining season, Rickey had every right to think he would spend the rest of his career in Brooklyn. But as old rivals disappeared, a new one emerged.

This new rival would force Rickey out of Brooklyn, never to return.

---

[1] Taylor Spink wrote that the Browns matched the offer from the Dodgers. "Yes, we went the limit trying to keep Mr. Rickey in St. Louis," said Browns president Don Barnes. *The Sporting News*, November 5, 1942. Spink believed one of the motivations for Rickey taking

---

the Brooklyn job was to compete in the same market as the Yankees. Rickey's insistence that his contract be effective for five years, whether or not baseball carried on during the war, was another factor. The Browns did not offer that guarantee. Brooklyn did. A year earlier, Rickey and MacPhail sat next to each other at the World Series, an event that did not go unnoticed. "Rickey's presence in MacPhail's box at the World Series started tongues a-wagging," wrote Sid Keener. *St. Louis Star-Times*, October 4, 1941.

[2] *St. Louis Star-Times*, October 9, 1942. "It is known that Breadon was nearly knocked off his presidential chair in his Sportsman's Park office...after he read quotes by Rickey..." *The Sporting News*, November 5, 1942.

[3] Ibid.

[4] *St. Louis Post-Dispatch,* October 23, 1942.

[5] *New York Times*, October 23, 1942.

[6] *The Sporting News*, November 21, 1935.

[7] *St. Louis Post-Dispatch*, October 29, 1942.

[8] *St. Louis Star-Times*, October 10, 1942.

[9] Golenbock, *The Spirit of St. Louis*. After the exchange with Breadon, Slaughter soon got his $10,000.

[10] *The Sporting News*, November 20, 1941.

[11] Golenbock, *The Spirit of St. Louis*. Outfielder Terry Moore made this prediction. "The Cardinals, in a few years, will realize what a valuable man they've lost in Branch Rickey."

[12] *The Sporting News*, November 5, 1942. As president of the Dodgers, Rickey reported to a board of directors. He signed a five-year contract that paid him a $35,000 base salary plus bonuses. One newspaper called it "one of the most complex baseball contracts ever to draw ink." *Brooklyn Eagle*, October 29, 1942.

[13] *Baltimore Sun*, November 9, 2012.

[14] Mann*, Branch Rickey.*

[15] Rickey biographer Lee Lowenfish cited three reasons why the Cardinals ended their relationship with MacPhail. 1. "Operational extravagance." In a visit to Columbus, Rickey and Breadon noted that MacPhail had a luxuriously decorated office, far better than the spartan furnishings they had for themselves in St. Louis. 2. MacPhail's complaints that the Cardinals called up too many popular and productive players. 3. His alcoholism. MacPhail got into a shouting match with a bartender in a hotel where the Columbus Redbirds were staying. Lowenfish, *Branch Rickey.* There were other reasons. MacPhail and Breadon got into a heated argument over Bob O'Farrell. MacPhail insisted he be named manager in Columbus. Breadon said he was needed in St. Louis. "St Louis officials term him [MacPhail] a 'lone wolf' instead of an organization man." *Louisville Courier-Journal*, May 24, 1933.

[16] Parrott, *The Lords of Baseball.*

[17] Ibid.

[18] Once the Dodgers led the way, the Giants and Yankees also broke their radio broadcasting embargo in 1939. Both teams targeted KMOX announcer France Laux, who

---

had been doing games at Sportsman's Park since 1929. He declined the offers and remained in St. Louis. Shea, Stuart. Gary Gillette, Executive Editor. *Calling the Games: Baseball Broadcasting From 1920 to the Present.* Society for American Baseball Research, Inc. 2015.

[19] *Brooklyn Daily Eagle*, July 20, 1942.

[20] *New York Times*, August 10, 1975. While Reiser mentions the fractured skull in his story of that day for the *Times* – "Dr. Hyland...said I suffered a severe concussion and a fractured skull" – contemporaneous accounts disagree. "The x-ray showed a slight concussion but no fracture," wrote Roscoe McGowen the day after it happened. "Reiser will remain here overnight and leave for New York tomorrow." *New York Times*, July 20, 1942. In the *Brooklyn Daily Eagle*, Tommy Holmes wrote that "Dr. Robert F. Hyland, the Cards' club physician, revealed that Pete had suffered a slight brain concussion and will be lost to the team for several days." Four days later, Holmes ended an article with this sentence: "Although he was told to rest a few days, Pete worked out in practice Wednesday and L.S. [Larry] MacPhail raised hell about it."

[21] *New York Times*, November 2, 1981. Citing author Bill Heinz as his source (*Once They Heard the Cheers*), columnist Red Smith wrote that Reiser "was carried off the field 11 times. Nine times he regained consciousness in the clubhouse or a hospital."

[22] In the middle of World War II, many teams banned players' wives from spring training camps. Rickey, a longtime proponent of marriage, specifically requested the players bring along their spouses in 1943.

[23] Lowenfish, *Branch Rickey.*

[24] *St. Louis Post-Dispatch*, January 22, 1943. The war in Europe officially ended two years and four months later. The war in the Pacific officially ended two years and eight months later.

[25] In 1946, Rickey had Matthews and Sisler scouting the Boston Red Sox as a potential World Series opponent. When St. Louis eliminated Brooklyn, Rickey had them turn over their notes to the Cardinals. *Brooklyn Daily Eagle*, October 9, 1946.

[26] Rickey also claimed for Brooklyn two minor league training camps previously used by the Cardinals: West Palm Beach and Lake Worth, Florida. *St. Louis Star-Times*, November 30, 1942. Although she never worked for the Cardinals, Ebbets Field organist Gladys Gooding was a Missouri native. "I learned the game in St. Louis," she said after getting hired by the Dodgers in 1942. Edelman, Rob. "Gladys Gooding, Ebbets Field Organ Queen." *Baseball Research Journal*. Society for American Baseball Research. Fall 2017. Volume 46, Number 2. Gooding is credited with pioneering walk-up music for players.

[27] Trainer Harrison "Bucko" Weaver and secretary Mary Murphy declined invitations from Rickey to join him in Brooklyn. Dizzy Dean claimed he also turned down Rickey. "Branch Rickey came to see me. He wanted me to pitch Sundays. I wouldn't accept it." *Baseball Digest*, August 1943.

[28] High was born in Illinois but grew up in St. Louis. Discovered by scout Charley Barrett, he was playing minor league baseball in Memphis when Brooklyn claimed him in a draft. The

---

Boston Braves later claimed him off waivers. After spending more than two years with Boston, the Braves traded him to the Cardinals for Les Bell before the 1928 season. In his four years in St. Louis, the Cardinals won three pennants and one World Series. After his playing days, he became a scout for the Dodgers, retiring as chief scout in 1963. A baseball field in Webster Groves, "Andy High Field," was dedicated in 1984. Andy's brothers Charles and Hugh also played major league baseball.

[29] Lowenfish, *Branch Rickey.*

[30] Reports of the amount of cash involved in the Medwick transaction have ranged from $125,000 to $200,000. Most, however, put the number at or near the lower boundary.

[31] Russo, Frank. *The Cooperstown Chronicles*. Rowman & Littlefield. 2014.

[32] *St. Louis Globe-Democrat*, June 22, 1940.

[33] Barber, Red. *1947, When All Hell Broke Loose in Baseball*. De Capo Press, Inc. 1982.

[34] Brooklyn's version of the Knothole Gang started under MacPhail, but the idea came from the Cardinals. MacPhail's first knothole gang was in Columbus, when he worked under Breadon and Rickey.

[35] Polner, *Branch Rickey.* Researchers have voiced doubts about what support Chandler gave Rickey. "I found no evidence that such a meeting between Chandler and Rickey ever took place, except for Chandler saying it did," author Jules Tygiel told columnist Ira Berkow. *New York Times*, June 29, 1991. Others were more supportive. "Some of the things [Chandler] did for Jackie Robinson, Roy Campanella, and Don Newcombe when he was commissioner of baseball – those are the kind of things we never forget," said Newcombe. *New York Times*, June 16, 1991.

[36] Kahn, Roger. *Rickey & Robinson: The True, Untold Story of the Integration of Baseball*. Rodale, Inc. 2014. Birns, the Cleveland racketeer and Veeck's source, was blown up in a car-bombing attack in March of 1975 when he entered his parked car and attempted to start it. Police said they suspected sticks of dynamite had been wired to the ignition. Explosives had been placed underneath the front seat. Birns' head shot through the roof of the car. His upper torso was found beside the opened front passenger door. *The Plain Dealer*, March 30, 1975.

[37] Kirby Higbe led the Dodgers in wins in 1946 with 17, but of all Brooklyn starters with more than 12 starts, Hatten had the best ERA at 2.84. No matter who Brooklyn pitched that season, the club had little success against St. Louis. The Dodgers went 8-16 against the Cardinals. St. Louis was the only team to compile a winning record against Brooklyn.

[38] Ibid.

[39] *Chicago Tribune,* September 30, 1993.

[40] *St. Louis Post-Dispatch*, October 9, 1991.

[41] Polner, *Branch Rickey*.

[42] Rickey later rehired Dressen. After the 1946 season, Brooklyn coaches Dressen and John Corriden left the Dodgers for MacPhail's Yankees. There was also speculation the Yankees wanted to hire Durocher, adding more fuel to the rivalry between MacPhail and Rickey and the two teams.

---

[43] Kahn, *Rickey & Robinson.*
[44] New York *Daily News*, March 1, 1947.
[45] While MacPhail was silent regarding Immerman, he did comment on Engelberg. "I know Memphis and, to my knowledge, he never bets on baseball games. What he does at the race track is his own business. He wasn't my guest at the game in Havana, but I wouldn't bar him from Yankee Stadium. I go to the races and do not forbid my players to. Incidentally, Memphis often visits the Dodger clubhouse as a personal friend of Durocher's. If he is harmful, why hasn't Rickey barred him from Ebbets Field?" New York *Daily News*, March 16, 1947.
[46] Polner, *Branch Rickey.*
[47] *St. Louis Post-Dispatch,* May 9, 1947.
[48] Vecsey, *Stan Musial.* Also see *Hartford Courant*, June 29, 2008.
[49] Tygiel, *Baseball's Great Experiment.*
[50] "Spider Jorgenson," from *We Played the Game: 65 Players Remember Baseball's Greatest Era 1947-1965.* Hyperion. 1994.
[51] Broeg, Bob. *Memories of a Hall of Fame Sportswriter*. Sagamore Publishing. 1995.
[52] *Chicago Tribune*, February 28, 1997.
[53] Kahn, *Rickey & Robinson*.
[54] Ibid.
[55] *Brooklyn Daily Eagle*, May 9, 1947.
[56] Rampersad, Arnold. *Jackie Robinson: A Biography.* Ballantine Books. 1997.
[57] Tygiel, *Baseball's Great Experiment*.
[58] *St. Louis Star-Times*, August 21, 1947. Part of the Slaughter-Robinson legend, written about in multiple accounts, is the claim that Dodgers pitcher Ralph Branca had a no-hitter when the spiking occurred. Branca did start that night but was not pitching in the 11th inning and did not have a no-hitter. Branca was removed from the game after 8 2/3 innings. He gave up two runs on one hit. Hugh Casey went the rest of the way in a game the Dodgers lost 3-2 in 12 innings. Stanky, the Dodger player most critical of Slaughter, managed the Cardinals from 1952 to 1955. He was the manager when St. Louis traded Slaughter to the New York Yankees.
[59] *Brooklyn Daily Eagle*, September 12, 1947.
[60] Tygiel. *Baseball's Great Experiment.* Tygiel wrote that a Robinson remark drew a racially slurred response from Garagiola.
[61] Pastier, John. "Brooklyn Dodgers Attendance in 1947." *SABR.org*.

A Battle in Brooklyn, A Death in St. Louis

Branch Rickey was cheap. His players complained about it. The media wrote about it. New York *Daily News* writer Jimmy Powers dubbed Rickey "El Cheapo." Over one seven-month stretch, Powers wrote eighty columns blasting the Dodgers executive. For good measure, he bashed Rickey with passing insults in seventy-four other stories.[1] "Shall we send him over Niagara Falls in a barrel?" he wrote in July of 1946. "Shall we maroon him on a Bikini Atoll?"

Everyone knew Rickey was frugal with his ballclub. Everyone, that is, except for Walter O'Malley. And O'Malley's opinion mattered most of all. An Ivy League-educated New York native, O'Malley was both an engineer and an attorney. When he graduated from the University of Pennsylvania in 1928, his father gave him a boat that slept eight. He started law school at Columbia, but when his family lost money in the stock market crash of 1929, he switched to Fordham University. Later, O'Malley started his own engineering firm and law practice, and was making more than $100,000 a year by the late 1930s.[2]

He first got involved with the Dodgers as the team attorney. By 1945, O'Malley, Rickey, and pharmaceutical executive John L. Smith each had a twenty-five percent ownership interest in the team. (They first bought into the club in 1944, with Rickey borrowing against his life insurance policy to invest.)[3] As an owner, O'Malley had firsthand knowledge of the team's finances and how Rickey ran the operation. He didn't like what he saw. It wasn't frugality that caught O'Malley's eye, but rather what he regarded as lavish spending by the Dodgers president and general manager.

The 1946 playoff loss to the Cardinals spurred more bile from sportswriter Powers and outrage from O'Malley, but for entirely different reasons. At the end of the season, Rickey wanted to buy every member of the team a brand-new Studebaker as a bonus. O'Malley tried to block the move, contending the money should go to shareholders.[4]

When Durocher was suspended the following season, Rickey paid him his full salary for the year. A new stadium for a minor league team cost more than $200,000. Expanding the Brooklyn farm system cost money as did relocating spring training to Vero Beach, Florida. The team bought a plane and hired a pilot so Rickey could get a first-hand look at the expanding empire.

Rickey had also launched a football team that competed in the All-America Football Conference, a rival to the NFL. The team, also known as the Brooklyn Dodgers, played its games at Ebbets Field. Rickey tried to recruit Pepper Martin to be his placekicker. Martin told his former boss he didn't know how to kick. "Don't worry, John," Rickey replied, calling Martin by his actual name. "I'll teach you."[5] The team, sans Martin, played three seasons in Brooklyn and never had a winning record. It also hemorrhaged cash, losing its owners hundreds of thousands of dollars.

By 1948, Rickey's salary and bonus were approximately $200,000 annually. His compensation included ten to fifteen percent of player sales. His pay package was roughly half of what the Dodgers paid the entire team. According to O'Malley biographer Michael D'Antonio, Rickey made as much as the president of AT&T, the largest company in the world at the time.[6]

Rickey's outsized remuneration came at a time when the Dodgers thrived on the diamond and at the box office. A pennant in 1949 marked the second of the Rickey era in Brooklyn. From 1945 to 1949 – a timespan in which the club played in two World Series and won fifty-nine percent of its games – the team generated profits totaling $2,364,500. Those figures, later revealed by a congressional subcommittee investigating monopoly power in baseball, demonstrated Rickey's investments had paid off. But they also offered evidence for O'Malley's argument. The profits did not include salaries and bonuses paid to certain club officers, including $730,000 in bonuses that had been paid to Rickey.[7]

O'Malley didn't like Rickey's compensation scheme, nor what he considered his free-spending ways. Rickey didn't trust his business partner. "Walter O'Malley is the most devious man I have ever met," he confided to Red Barber.[8] While both men were highly educated, successful businessmen, O'Malley moved in different circles than the Ohio-born Rickey. The native New Yorker knew how to navigate the Manhattan social scene. He belonged to eighteen different clubs and associations, including the Metropolitan Club, founded by J.P. Morgan.[9]

The culture clash extended to a topic long associated with Rickey. Just as with Phil Ball and Sam Breadon in St. Louis, O'Malley had different views than Rickey regarding alcohol. The two men fought over a beer sponsorship. O'Malley prevailed. "I knew then that Dad was leaving Brooklyn," said Rickey's daughter Elizabeth.[10]

After years of profits, O'Malley claimed the team lost nearly $130,000 in 1950. Things came to a head that summer when Smith, a former president of Pfizer, died of cancer. His wife, who inherited her husband's twenty-five percent interest in the Dodgers, gave O'Malley proxy to vote her shares. With control over fifty percent of the stock, nothing could be done without O'Malley's approval. Rickey's contract was scheduled to expire at the end of the season. O'Malley had no interest in renewing it. Rickey's private box at Ebbets Field was adjacent to the radio booth. Broadcaster Barber recalled a screaming match that season between the two men that grew in such intensity he had to point his microphone away from them so listeners wouldn't hear the heated exchange.

Their final battle concerned Rickey's shares in the team. O'Malley thought he had leverage and offered to buy out Rickey for roughly $350,000, the same amount that Rickey had invested in the team. But the son of the Midwest responded with a strategic move that caught the urbane O'Malley off guard.

He originally thought of approaching Joseph Kennedy, the patriarch of America's most famous political family. Rickey contacted new Cardinals owner Fred Saigh to ask if he knew him. "I do indeed," Saigh replied, adding he didn't think Kennedy would be interested in the Dodgers but knew of others who might. "How much do you want?" Rickey told him he needed more time to come up with a figure. Saigh never heard back.[11]

Rickey found another buyer, one he knew O'Malley wouldn't like. Thanks to his connections to Pittsburgh owner John Galbreath, a fellow Ohio native and fraternity brother, Rickey approached William Zeckendorf. The New York real estate developer agreed to pay Rickey $1,000,000 for his interest. Since the other owners had first right of refusal on the shares, Zeckendorf would receive $50,000 if his deal didn't go through. O'Malley didn't want any part of Zeckendorf, fearing he would team up with Jim and Dearie Mulvey, who had the final twenty-five percent interest in the team, and push to rehire Rickey. O'Malley paid the breakup fee and got control of the team. Rickey got his million dollars, paid out over several years, and left Brooklyn.[12]

A week after he left, Rickey was announced as Galbreath's new general manager in Pittsburgh. Four months after Rickey left, the Dodgers announced a five-year, $3 million deal with Schaefer Brewing Company to sponsor television broadcasts.[13]

Rickey spent eight years in Brooklyn, a time in which he completely revamped the franchise. "In 1943 the club organization numbered only five clubs. We had twenty-five in 1950," he wrote in a final letter to the Dodgers board of directors. "In 1943 we had approximately 250 players, almost 100 of whom were on inactive [military] lists. Our reserve lists for 1950 show 637 active players. In 1943 the Brooklyn Club did not own real estate in any major league city. Ebbets Field was heavily mortgaged. Today Brooklyn owns valuable properties other than Ebbets Field in Fort Worth, Montreal, and elsewhere. There is no indebtedness on Ebbets Field...there is no indebtedness throughout the entire organization, except between our own clubs. The assets are estimated in high figures. The book value exceeds four million dollars."[14] The book value – the difference between assets and liabilities – meant that Rickey's twenty-five percent interest was purchased for less than their net worth, and suggests O'Malley got a good deal, even though he paid nearly three times more than what he originally intended.

With Rickey gone, O'Malley banished the very mention of his name and redecorated the office of the former club president.[15] Rickey had hung a portrait of Abraham Lincoln on his wall (before him, MacPhail had mounted a moose). O'Malley put up Audubon prints and baseball illustrations. While a few of the Rickey men – including son Branch Jr., Rex Bowen, and George Sisler – moved on to Pittsburgh with their mentor, other key aides remained behind.

Buzzie Bavasi, who had been in the Dodgers organization since 1940, became the general manager. Rickey had tapped Bavasi to investigate the character of Jackie Robinson after the club had signed him to a minor league contract. Bavasi spent a night in the stands in Montreal watching Robinson's wife interact with the wives of other players. He was impressed with what he saw. "If Jackie Roosevelt Robinson is good enough for Rachel Robinson, he is good enough for the Dodgers," he reported back to Rickey. Bavasi, who admitted Rickey had taught him "everything [he] knew about negotiating and trading," remained the Dodgers general manager until 1968.[16]

For nearly a half-century, the Dodgers organization had incredible continuity. The O'Malley family controlled the franchise for forty-seven years. The team had only two general managers in a twenty-six-season period starting in 1943, and only two field managers from 1954 to 1996 (former Cardinal farmhand Walter Alston and Tommy Lasorda).[17] That stability contrasted sharply with the Cardinals during the same timeframe. When Rickey left St. Louis, Breadon refused to appoint a successor and divided his responsibilities among multiple people. Breadon himself remained in control of the hiring and firing of managers and the trading of players. "I am not disturbed over the fact that Rickey has left us," he said in November of 1942, while announcing that working agreements with eight minor league teams had been canceled.[18]

Five years later, Breadon was the one who was leaving. At the end of a season where a black man led the Brooklyn Dodgers to a National League Pennant, Breadon announced he was selling his team. But it was another New York club, Breadon insisted, that helped inspire the timing of his decision.

*****

In June of 1947, Breadon was in the middle of his twenty-eighth season as president of the Cardinals. One month shy of his seventy-first birthday, the longtime baseball executive claimed it was time to "ease up a bit." He announced that his nephew, William Walsingham Jr., would take on more responsibilities. "I find I'm in need of an official who will take some of the work off my shoulders," Breadon told the press. "I arrive around 10 a.m. and it was 2 o'clock this morning when I left the park."[19]

What Breadon didn't tell the media was that earlier that same month, he had a deal to sell the Cardinals. But word of the transaction had leaked. Annoyed by rumors and constant pestering from reporters, Breadon changed his mind. He returned the earnest money to the potential buyers, Bob Hannegan, the Postmaster General and former chairman of the Democratic National Committee, and Fred Saigh, a St. Louis attorney and real estate investor.[20]

The iconoclastic Breadon had always done things his way and on his timeline. In spring training of 1941, the Cardinals created a buzz by unveiling a pitching machine to use in batting practice. A glowing United Press account referred to the machine as a "deadly-looking contrivance," "a giant slingshot," and "the greatest pitcher the world has ever seen." Everyone seemed impressed by the display. Breadon preferred to talk about another spring training newcomer. "It's a great thing all right," he conceded, "but there's a better story than that in this camp. Heard about our vitamins yet?"[21]

Over the winter, Breadon took some Vitamin B-1 tablets before playing a round of golf. The energy the vitamins provided sustained him for the entire round. Breadon was so impressed by the spark the pills provided, he decided to order 25,000 of them for his team. Players consumed the tablets all spring. "Bottles of the things were lying around the clubhouse in such profusion that baseball writers wondered whether they were in a spring training camp or had blundered into the biennial convention of the American Pharmaceutical Association," read one dispatch. "If this keeps up, the slogan of the Cardinals is going to be: Pills produce pennants."[22] The Cardinals didn't win a pennant that season. For the following spring, the team ordered three pitching machines. Coverage of the pills disappeared.

Free of his automobile business, Breadon found other interests to consume his time when not at Sportsman's Park. An active real estate investor, Breadon was an early backer of Hampton Village, a retail development on the southwest side of St. Louis. Broker Henry Weisels represented Breadon in many of his deals. Weisels claimed that at its peak, Breadon's real estate holdings generated gross revenue of more than a million dollars. "None of his property was mortgaged," Weisels said. "Sam never wanted to be in debt to anyone and quickly paid off his obligations whenever he acquired real estate."[23]

The experience of being poor as a young man stayed with Breadon his entire life. "He was always afraid he was going to lose his money," recalled Bill DeWitt Sr., who worked with Breadon for years in the front office of the Cardinals.

In 1946, Breadon received a scare involving the club, the crown jewel of his holdings. Mexican League baseball began to aggressively court major league players. Three players on the Cardinals – pitchers Max Lanier, Fred Martin, and second baseman Lou Klein – all defected that season.[24] Jorge Pasquel and his three brothers, the owners of the league, also targeted Stan Musial, offering him $125,000 for five years and a $50,000 bonus in the form of five $10,000 checks. Musial turned down the offer, but Breadon was so worried about the incursion he flew to Mexico to meet with the owners. "I wanted to find out what was going on down here, so I just hopped on a plane and came," he told reporters in Mexico City.[25] The raid on St. Louis players ended. Breadon gave Musial a raise. Gerardo Pasquel was Breadon's guest at the World Series that fall.[26]

Over five years, the president of the Cardinals survived a World War, the loss of Rickey, and a South of the Border invasion. He also had a World Series championship team. Beginning his eighth decade, it was time to sell. Hannegan and Saigh agreed to pay $310 a share for Breadon's stake and had put down $100,000 earnest money. Then Breadon got cold feet, backed out of the deal, and returned the check. Despite finishing second to the Dodgers in 1947, the Cardinals drew nearly 1.25 million fans that season, an increase of nearly 200,000 people.

With the post-war boom underway and his team more valuable than ever, Breadon revisited the idea of a sale. At the end of the season, he told Hannegan and Saigh he would make the deal, but for $400 per share, a $90 per share jump from their previous arrangement. The two men agreed to the new price. Hannegan resigned as Postmaster General and the Cardinals had new ownership. Breadon – "the most successful operator the business has ever known," in the words of *Dayton Herald* columnist Bob Husted – had sold out.[27]

Breadon made the announcement on November 25, explaining that "younger men...will be able to do more to keep the Cardinals in their high position." With two daughters, Breadon lacked a male heir. This was also a key factor in the sale. When bachelor Jacob Ruppert died in 1939, his New York Yankees languished in his estate until 1945 when a group of buyers, including Larry MacPhail, emerged to buy the team. The St. Louis owner didn't want his Cardinals to meet a similar fate. Breadon "didn't want the baseball empire to disintegrate in the event of his unexpected death, with the club falling into the hands of women, as the New York Yankees did upon the death of Col. Jake Ruppert," explained the *Post-Dispatch.*[28] A comment that would spark a firestorm of protest in the twenty-first century drew little scrutiny in 1947. It was also a comment rich in irony. Breadon's original involvement with the team was only possible because Helene Britton, the first female owner of a major league franchise, decided to cash out.

Breadon's delay in cashing out proved profitable. The $400 share price valued the Cardinals at $4,060,000. Breadon's take came to roughly $3.1 million, a $690,000 increase from what he would have received had he sold at $310 a share.[29] The sale included the Cardinals and 16 minor league clubs. Most of the limited partners followed Breadon's lead and sold out. Within a few weeks, Hannegan and Saigh controlled all but a handful of shares.[30]

Hannegan's involvement with the club was brief.[31] Saigh bought him out in January of 1949, the same year that both Hannegan and Breadon passed away. The forty-six-year-old Hannegan died of a heart attack in October. Breadon died in May. Remembered as a man who started with a $200 investment in the Cardinals that eventually ballooned into a multi-million-dollar fortune, Breadon was also eulogized as "the man nobody knew."[32]

After his death, a St. Louis realtor told the story of introducing Breadon to a friend. When Breadon referenced his parents' Irish heritage, the new acquaintance asked what part of Ireland they had come from. When Breadon told him, the man replied, "Those lefthanded counties from the north, eh?" Breadon jumped up out of his chair and shook his finger at him. "My people were damned good Irishmen, no matter what county they came from."[33]

"There was a lot of John McGraw in Breadon," remembered Ford Frick, president of the National League in 1949. "Fierce fighters both. Rough and tough on the exterior," he told Dan Daniel. "Funny thing about Sam. He was supposed to be so hard-boiled. But if a man got into trouble, nobody pleaded his cause more ardently."

Former Cardinal pitchers Grover Cleveland Alexander and Mort Cooper both battled alcoholism and faced financial difficulties. Breadon provided frequent assistance to Alexander and once posted a $2,000 bond to get Cooper released from jail on bad check charges. "It would be a disgrace for baseball to allow Mort to go to jail," Breadon said in 1948. "The public hasn't forgotten him as one of its great Cardinal heroes. So I just couldn't let him down."[34] As for the hero of 1926, "Many's the time that Sam got the veteran pitcher's World Series ring out of hock. Many's the check that has gone out from the Cardinal office to Old Pete Alexander," wrote columnist Roy Stockton.[35] After his playing days were over, Alexander received a $100 monthly pension check from the National League. While Breadon may not have been the source of the funds, the *idea* of sending Alexander money came from the one-time Cardinals owner.[36]

"Much has been written about the things he did for Grover Alexander and Morton Cooper," said Frick. "Well, those beneficiaries were just minor details in the overall picture of Sam's generosity."

The discreet and private Breadon remained so until the end. He disliked funerals and had it written in his will that any rites would be strictly a family affair. His body was cremated and his ashes were scattered over the Mississippi River from an airplane near Chester, Illinois.[37] Sam Breadon, the man whose reign over the Cardinals featured the franchise's first nine pennants and six World Series titles, died of cancer at the age of 72.

---

[1] Polner, *Branch Rickey*. The vitriol got to the point Rickey considered filing a lawsuit against Powers. In 1949, Rickey received a copy of a letter Powers had written. "I talked to the captain last night [publisher of the *Daily News*] and he told me not to worry over latrine gossip picked up by the FBI. That if [Walter] Winchell and the rest of the Jews had their way America would be a vast concentration camp from Maine to California. There wouldn't be enough barbed wire to hold back all the decent Christians maligned by the Jews and those who run with them," it read in part. When Powers discovered Rickey had the copy, the negative attacks stopped.

[2] D'Antonio, *Forever Blue.* Calling him "the Great Manipulator" and "something of a novelist," Roger Kahn was suspicious of O'Malley's background. "He enjoyed making up stories, inventing familial wealth, and creating for himself a distinguished career, say as an admiralty lawyer, which had in fact not existed." Kahn, *The Era 1947-1957.*

[3] O'Malley, Smith and Rickey purchased a 25 percent stake in the Dodgers in 1944 for $250,000. A year later, they paid $750,000 for a 50 percent stake. *New York Times*, November 2, 1944 and August 14, 1945.

[4] Authors Polner and Kahn wrote that O'Malley blocked the plan, but not everyone agrees. Author Rudy Marzano quotes Brooklyn first baseman Howie Shultz. "We got our cars," he

---

said. "I got mine and all the rest of the guys got theirs. We heard nothing of the deal being canceled." Marzano, Rudy. *The Last Years of the Brooklyn Dodgers: A History 1950-1957.* McFarland & Company, Inc. 2008. In late September of 1946, Rickey announced to the press that "perhaps a dozen models of Studebaker cars will be on the field Saturday for the players to make their choices of the car they want." Three days later, "Ten Studebaker cars...were driven on to the field and the players, one by one, were called to the field microphone to pick publicly the model wanted." *New York Times*, September 26 and 29, 1946.

[5] Polner, *Branch Rickey.*

[6] D'Antonio, *Forever Blue.* D'Antonio wrote that Rickey's cut of player sales was 15 percent in Brooklyn. Other authors have claimed it was the same 10 percent he received in St. Louis.

[7] *New York Times*, November 8, 1951.

[8] Polner, *Branch Rickey*. The quote is similar to the one Barber used in describing O'Malley in his autobiography. "He is a devious man, about the most devious man I ever met." Barber, Red with Robert Creamer. *Rhubarb in the Catbird Seat.* Doubleday & Company. 1968.

[9] D'Antonio, *Forever Blue.*

[10] Polner, *Branch Rickey*.

[11] Ibid. Rickey reportedly mentioned to O'Malley on the flight back home from John L. Smith's funeral that he had discussions with Kennedy about buying his shares. A price of $1.3 million had been mentioned. Kennedy had even talked about his son Jack becoming president of the Dodgers if Rickey remained as general manager. D'Antonio, *Forever Blue*.

[12] Rickey biographer Arthur Mann broke down the payout, claiming $300,000 retired Rickey's debt, allowing him to reclaim his pledged life insurance policy. The remainder came in 10 installment payments from O'Malley to Rickey, $72,500 a year for 10 years, for a grand total of $1,025,000. Mann wrote that Zeckendorf received $50,000, while others have asserted that this money was then given to Rickey as a gift.

[13] *New York Times*, February 28, 1951.

[14] Polner, *Branch Rickey.*

[15] At the news conference announcing his purchase of Rickey's shares, O'Malley said, "You may be sure, that for the next seven to eight years, Mr. Rickey will be credited with the victories of the Brooklyn ball club and that its losses will be charged to somebody else." *New York Times*, October 25, 1950.

[16] Helyar, John. *Lords of the Realm: The Real History of Baseball.* Ballantine Books. 1994.

[17] Alston signed with the Cardinals in 1935. He played in his one and only major league game for St. Louis in 1936. He began managing in the Cardinals farm system in 1940. Like many others, he left the Cardinals organization for the Dodgers during Rickey's reign in Brooklyn. He started his minor-league managing career with the Dodgers in 1944 and began managing at the major-league level a decade later.

---

[18] *St. Louis Star-Times*, November 30, 1942. According to one account, Eddie Dyer "was being groomed to replace Rickey, but because of uncertain conditions in the baseball world, it was decided to postpone major changes until after the war." *St. Louis Post-Dispatch*, January 23, 1946. Dyer became the Cardinals manager in 1946.
[19] Ibid, June 28, 1947. Breadon's will, written in 1938 and never adjusted for the sale of the franchise, revealed that he wanted Walsingham to run the team after his death. *St. Louis Star-Times*, May 13, 1949.
[20] Prior to the DNC, Hannegan served briefly as the Commissioner of Internal Revenue, the head of the IRS, the agency that would later investigate Saigh.
[21] Ibid, March 7, 1941.
[22] Ibid, April 17, 1941.
[23] *The Sporting News*, June 8, 1949. In 1931, Breadon purchased a garage on the corner of Sixteenth and Spruce Streets in St. Louis for $325,000. Weisels represented him in the negotiations. The headline of an adjacent article read, "Gloomy Real Estate Market is Parallel of 1907 Depression." *St. Louis Globe-Democrat*, July 5, 1931.
[24] Yankees president Larry MacPhail later offered Breadon $150,000 for Lanier, Martin and Klein. Breadon turned down the offer. *St. Louis Star-Times,* February 12, 1947.
[25] *St. Louis Star-Times*, June 20, 1946.
[26] *St. Louis Post-Dispatch*, October 6, 1946. Commissioner Chandler fined Breadon $5,000 for his visit to Mexico, a fine that was later rescinded. The Mexican League later folded. Lanier, Martin and Klein all returned to the Cardinals in 1949. Musial's salary jumped from $13,500 in 1946 to $31,000 in 1947, the most money Breadon ever paid a player. Ibid, January 19, 2013.
[27] *Dayton Herald,* November 26, 1947.
[28] *St. Louis Post-Dispatch*, November 25, 1947.
[29] Ibid, August 3, 1949.
[30] *The Sporting News*, December 17, 1947. Out of 10,150 shares, Hannegan and Saigh owned all but 21 of them
[31] A Washington D.C. colleague once said of Hannegan: "Bob is a swell guy, one of the very best, but the trouble with him is that he has never quite gotten the soot of Northwest St. Louis out of his hair." *Baseball Digest*, February 1948.
[32] Ibid, May 25, 1949.
[33] Ibid, June 8, 1949.
[34] Ibid, October 27, 1948.
[35] *St. Louis Post-Dispatch*, April 17, 1949.
[36] Grover Alexander's former wife, Aimee (Amy) Alexander, told reporters after his death the checks came from the National League but that Breadon secretly provided the funds. According to her, Alexander died without ever knowing the source. Her account of the pension comes from a wire service story following Alexander's death. See *Moberly Monitor-Index*, November 7, 1950. However, in the same story, Bill Walsingham of the Cardinals said the pension *idea* came from Breadon "but [the money] came from the

---

National League." *The Sporting News* agreed. The St. Louis publication said the checks were made out to Alexander, mailed to the Cardinals, who forwarded the pension to Alexander. "The fact that the checks were mailed from St. Louis for a number of years led some persons to believe they were Breadon's personal gift to Ol' Pete, but they were actually from the National League." *The Sporting News*, November 15, 1950. The Cardinals did pay for Alexander's funeral. The franchise was the only team represented among the 150 mourners.

[37] "Members of the family explained that Mr. Breadon's desire to have his ashes scattered in this manner without formal funeral services was due to the fact that he disliked funerals and had never attended them." *St. Louis Star-Times*, May 13, 1949.

Hot Water and Cold Beer

When Saigh (pronounced like "sigh") bought out Hannegan, he owned nearly every share of stock in the Cardinals. Only the Boston Red Sox, solely controlled by Tom Yawkey, had a more limited ownership among major league clubs. Forty-three years old and five feet five inches tall, Saigh wore glasses and once sported a lush mustache. In a span of three years starting in 1946, the previously obscure lawyer had engineered business deals totaling $15 million. "Everywhere, St. Louisans are asking the same question," wrote a reporter for the *Star-Times* in January of 1949, "Where does this latter-day Golden Boy get the dough?"[1]

Born in Springfield, Illinois in 1905, Saigh attended college at Bradley University (known as Bradley Polytechnic Institute at the time) in Peoria and took a few graduate courses at Northwestern University. He didn't have a law degree but later passed the bar examination. He arrived in St. Louis in 1927 and began working small criminal cases. His office was literally "in his hat." As an officer of the court, he could be sloppy about following certain regulations. In 1937, after suffering a fine in a court case, police quoted records showing Saigh had been arrested 32 times for traffic violations. The fine was for having an altercation with his arresting policeman. Driving also got him into hot water with a neighbor who accused Saigh of running over his flower bed. The incident sparked a brawl that saw Saigh end up with a broken nose. He sued the neighbor for $15,000 in damages.[2]

An early business venture proved to be a failure. Saigh invested $40,000 in a cigarette vending machine and convinced outside investors to pony up an additional forty-grand. He had an idea for a console-style vending machine "which delivered cigarettes upward by power," one of his investors explained, rather than dropping them from a slot. Other than five machines built by hand as samples, the company never went into production. The business went bankrupt. "Saigh is a lawyer. Why did you think he had sufficient engineering ability to tell you this machine was mechanically correct?" a bankruptcy referee asked one of Saigh's investors. "I didn't. I just relied on his word," admitted Lee Niedringhaus, who lost $15,500 in the deal.[3]

It was real estate that made Saigh a wealthy man. He led a group of investors who purchased a large office building in downtown St. Louis that housed the Scruggs, Vandervoort and Barney department store. His future business partner in the Cardinals helped him put the deal in place. As his attorney would later acknowledge, it was through his connection with Hannegan that Saigh "acquired the knowledge of men who put up big money." Although Saigh and Hannegan only owned a minority stake in the company, the deal was valued at $5 million.[4]

The successful real estate syndication inspired additional investments. Saigh and Hannegan, along with their partners, then acquired the Railway Exchange Building in St. Louis, described at the time as the largest office building west of the Mississippi River. The property had an estimated value of more than $8.5 million. It was this deal, along with the acquisition of the Cardinals, that vaulted Saigh into prominence. Suddenly, he was flooded with offers around the country to investigate. He took 46 business trips one year to evaluate various proposals. Saigh, whose father was born in Syria, once took a ten-day trip to the Middle East to investigate opportunities in the oil business. He and his wife, the former Elizabeth Lewis of Cuba, Missouri, lived in the Sheraton Hotel (formerly the Coronado Hotel). When his efforts to buy the building were rebuffed, he moved west down Lindell Boulevard near the Chase Hotel and Forest Park.

Once he had total control of the Cardinals, he moved his office to Sportsman's Park from his downtown location, where he had a preference for red leather furniture and oil paintings. He had a flair for interior decorating, selecting the colors for the Cardinals clubhouse. His new office was set up to flash scores of all major league games in progress. [5] One profile described him as a light drinker and a borderline hypochondriac. At the dinner table, "a bottle of pills is almost always in evidence."[6]

It was real estate that first attracted Saigh to the Cardinals. Breadon owned a lot at the corner of Choteau and Spring in St. Louis, where he had intentions of building a new ballpark. Before Breadon sold the team, he had plans drawn up and began setting money aside to fund a new stadium. At the time he sold the Cardinals, up to $2.5 million had been set aside for construction.[7] The ballpark was never built. Saigh and Hannegan used that money to pay off loans they needed to buy the team. In fact, Saigh later admitted, the new owners hadn't put a single penny in the deal. Even the $60,800 in cash they applied to the total came from a bank loan. Leverage that Saigh had employed in his real estate deals had now gone to purchase the Cardinals. It was a brilliant idea but perhaps too clever by half. At some point, the Internal Revenue Service began to investigate the transaction. Saigh didn't do himself any favors by clashing with the commissioner of baseball. Happy Chandler had investigators digging into the affairs of the owner of the Cardinals. Some believe the two investigations were even linked.

In January of 1949, just as Saigh was wrapping up the deal to buy out Hannegan for $1 million, the Cardinals sold pitcher Murry Dickson to the Pittsburgh Pirates.[8] A long-forgotten transaction is one St. Louis players of that era always remembered. "The Cardinals lost the 1949 pennant on January 29, when Saigh and Hannegan sold Murry

Dickson to the Pirates for $175,000," wrote Enos Slaughter in his autobiography.[9] Stan Musial agreed, claiming the Cardinals could have won an additional four to five pennants during his career had it not been for the sale of players like Dickson.[10]

The 1949 Cardinals were the twilight of Rickey's Redbirds, the last really good St. Louis team largely compiled by their former executive. The Cardinals went 96-58 that year, one game behind the National League champion Dodgers.[11] Dickson, the pitcher sold for cash to the Pirates, beat his old team five times that season. The transaction fueled suspicion that Saigh needed the money to pay off Hannegan, a charge denied by the Cardinals owner. "Saigh resents any suggestion that the sale of any ball player helped buy out Hannegan," wrote Bob Broeg.[12]

Regardless of the motivation, two sources later confirmed to a columnist for the *New York Mirror* that Chandler had a dossier on the Cardinals owner and that the commissioner had employed former FBI agents as investigators.[13] This revelation came just days after published reports alleged Saigh was leading the charge to oust the commissioner from office. The president of the Cardinals got his wish in December of 1950 when he and other owners voted against renewing Chandler's contract. "They tell me Saigh is taking credit for having put me out," Chandler told reporters. "Well, that's O.K. with me."[14]

The two men had battled since Saigh took control. Their conflicts reflected a changing status between the owners and the man who ran the game. Chandler was just the second man to serve as commissioner. His predecessor, Judge Landis, had come to baseball in the shadow of the Black Sox investigation. Desperate for new leadership, baseball owners acquiesced to demands from Landis that he have absolute control. But a new generation of owners no longer wanted an overlord and desired a freer hand to run their affairs. These were wealthy men used to getting their way. Friction was inevitable.

Shortly after Saigh took command of the team, the Browns and Cardinals got into a dispute over the lease at Sportsman's Park. Saigh voiced his concerns to Chandler and National League president Ford Frick, but baseball officials insisted the dispute was between landlord and tenant and pushed the two sides to reach an amicable agreement. The dispute wound up in court.[15] Chandler reduced the footprint of the Cardinals radio network when he ruled in April of 1949 that broadcasts of games could not be carried in southwest Missouri, and parts of Oklahoma and Kansas. Minor league teams in Carthage and Joplin, Missouri; Miami, Oklahoma; and Pittsburgh, Kansas, had affiliations with other major league teams. A year later, Saigh criticized how the commissioner handled baseball's television rights. Chandler negotiated a six-year, $6 million contract for World Series and All-Star games. Saigh believed multi-year deals didn't make sense with television still in its infancy. "Television rights worth $1 million today may be worth several million dollars a few years from now."[16]

The men disagreed in 1949 over how to handle the return of players from the Mexican League and clashed a year later over Sunday night baseball. In the summer of

1950, Saigh planned a first-ever Sunday night game in St. Louis against the Dodgers.[17] Chandler ordered him to cancel the game, saying it would conflict with church services. Saigh refused and asked for a hearing. When Frick told him the game had to be canceled based on a strict reading of league rules, Saigh complied.[18]

The owner of the Cardinals soon had bigger problems than Sunday night baseball and a feud with baseball officials. A grand jury indicted Saigh in April of 1952 on five counts of tax evasion. He was accused of avoiding nearly $50,000 in personal income taxes from 1946 through 1949. One of the counts alleged that he filed a fraudulent tax return for the Cardinals. The grand jury saw evidence that Saigh used team money to purchase items for personal use. Those items included a Cadillac, a tractor, and a film camera.

In a separate civil case, the government had issues with how Saigh handled his purchase of the Cardinals. He and Hannegan had obtained a series of loans to buy the team, including one for $350,000 from Breadon.[19] The money used to pay off that debt came from the coffers of the Cardinals. The government viewed the loan payoff as income to the two owners. Since Saigh owned forty-nine percent of the team at the time, he should have reported forty-nine percent of $350,000 on his tax return.[20]

On January 28, 1953, almost four years to the day that he purchased Hannegan's interest in the team, Saigh was sentenced to 15 months in jail and fined $15,000 after pleading no contest to two charges of tax evasion. Three of the original five counts had been dropped. He still faced civil claims he owed the government more than a half-million dollars in taxes and penalties.[21]

Revealed at sentencing was a charge from the government that Saigh had attempted to hire an agent investigating his tax records. After calling the agent into his office, Saigh reportedly told the man he liked his ability and appearance and needed a replacement for the team's current bookkeeper.

"The defendant (Saigh) wanted to know if the agent knew anyone with the agent's background and ability who would be interested in the position which would pay $15,000 a year," said government attorney Ted A. Bollinger Jr. "The agent told the defendant he was well-satisfied with his present position."[22]

Bollinger also accused Saigh of being uncooperative with government agents. "Many obstacles were put in their way in gaining access to what records they might acquire."

In avoiding a trial and pleading no contest, Saigh thought he might curry favor from the judge and receive a more lenient sentence. He was wrong. "I think you have been too tough on me," he told the court. Judge Roy W. Harper took a dim view of Saigh's argument. "You plead that you are guilty to these essential elements and if you were not guilty you should have stood upon a plea of not guilty. Don't come in and plead before me and then ask me to say that you are wrong."[23]

The downfall of Saigh, coming on the heels of Chandler's ouster, has fueled speculation over the years that the events were connected. Before becoming commissioner, Chandler served as governor of Kentucky and as a United States Senator from the Bluegrass State. He returned to politics after baseball. Did the politician tip off the government to the behavior of his one-time nemesis? "Chandler never boasted that he put the finger on Saigh," Robert L. Riggs wrote in a *Saturday Evening Post* story in 1955. "But whenever anyone suggested he had supplied the information which did Saigh in, Happy was pleased to give a knowing wink and to refrain from refusing credit."[24]

Just as Sam Breadon invoked the name of Jacob Ruppert when his time as owner came to an end, Saigh's reign in St. Louis is linked to another owner of the Yankees. Like Saigh, Del Webb bitterly opposed Chandler. As a wealthy construction company owner, Webb built schools, factories, Veterans Administration hospitals and an internment camp for Japanese Americans in World War II. He also built hotels, including the Flamingo and Sahara in Las Vegas. Reports linked Webb to an ownership stake in the casinos. Just as Chandler had investigators build a file on Saigh, he had his agents dig into Webb's Vegas connections. His time in charge of baseball ran out before he could make his move. "If I had remained commissioner," Chandler later wrote, "I would have banished both Del Webb and Fred Saigh...from organized baseball."[25]

Webb left baseball on his terms. He and Yankees co-owner Dan Topping would later sell out to CBS. It was a luxury Saigh didn't have. The prison sentence sealed his baseball fate. He had to sell the Cardinals and sell quickly. The judge had given him just a few months to get his financial affairs in order before he had to report to prison.

Saigh set his asking price at $4.25 million. The race to buy a baseball team evolved into a battle between beer makers. A Milwaukee group emerged as a serious bidder. The contingent included Fred Miller, president of the Miller Brewing Company.[26] Talks between Saigh and the Milwaukee delegation developed to the point that employees of the Cardinals were told in early February of 1953 that if they wished to move to Wisconsin with the team, their expenses would be paid. If they sold their homes, the club would compensate them for any losses. On Friday, February 20, Saigh was scheduled to fly to New York to get National League president Frick's approval for the sale. He never got on the plane.[27]

Anheuser-Busch asked the Cardinals owner to postpone the trip. The St. Louis-based brewery offered to pay $2.5 million in cash and assume $1.25 million in debt. The $3.75 million deal was thought to be about a quarter-million-dollars less than what the Milwaukee group was willing to pay. Saigh decided to take less money and keep the Cardinals in St. Louis. The local brewery, led by president Gussie Busch, now had a baseball team. The media portrayal of how Anheuser-Busch kept the Cardinals in St. Louis is one that forever bothered Saigh, who received parole after serving six months of his sentence. "I didn't want the Cardinals to leave St. Louis. Anheuser-Busch's publicity department turned it around that Mr. Busch was a savior." During the entire time the brewery owned the team, Saigh never attended a game. "I was bitter and I was hurt – still am," he said in the early 1990s.[28]

The new owners of the club did things Saigh could not or would not do. Anheuser-Busch helped drive the Browns out of St. Louis. "Saigh was wealthier than me, of course, but he did not have unlimited wealth. That meant he could be run out of town," said Browns owner Bill Veeck Jr.[29] "I wasn't going to run Gussie Busch out of town." Veeck sold the franchise. The Browns left for Baltimore following the 1953 season. Veeck also sold Sportsman's Park to the new owners of the Cardinals for $800,000. For the first time in more than three decades, the team didn't have to pay rent to a landlord.

Six seasons had passed since Jackie Robinson broke the color barrier in baseball. The Cardinals still didn't have a single black player. The absence had not gone unnoticed. The NAACP threatened to picket all Cardinals games in 1952 if things didn't change soon. Saigh had been reluctant to sign a black player. "We were thought of as a team from the South," he said years later. "In '51, we sold over $200,000 in tickets from Texas alone, largely because of the mail we got – 'we're glad you're not succumbing' [to the pressure]. I had nothing against the black man, but I had a big debt to pay off."[30]

Under Anheuser-Busch, the franchise took a different tact. "Where are our black players?" Gussie Busch wanted to know at his first spring training in charge of the club. "Hell, we sell beer to everyone." Tom Alston became the first black player for the Cardinals in 1954. But breaking the color barrier didn't change the general direction of the franchise. The deterioration of the post-Rickey Cardinals was much like Hemingway's description of bankruptcy, "Gradually and then suddenly." A team that finished first or second every year from 1941 to 1949 finished as high as second place only once in the 1950s. By the end of the 1962 season, Busch was frustrated and growing impatient. A decade of owning the Cardinals had yet to produce a single pennant.

Busch took a business trip to the West Coast in October of 1962 and happened to meet with an old friend. Bob Cobb owned the Brown Derby, a chain of restaurants in Los Angeles, and is known as the inventor of the "Cobb salad." He had also owned a baseball team in the Pacific Coast League, a franchise that had been affiliated with both the Brooklyn Dodgers and the Pittsburgh Pirates. It was baseball that brought him into contact with Rickey. The two men had been friends for years. Cobb knew that Rickey, now retired, wanted to move back to St. Louis.[31] The Brown Derby owner told Busch, "The best brain in baseball is sitting in Pittsburgh doing nothing." Following Cobb's advice, Busch picked up the phone and placed a call. Two months shy of his eighty-first birthday and nearly twenty years to the day he left the Cardinals, Rickey returned to the franchise he once ran.

Busch hired Rickey to be a consultant. The business marriage of a beer baron and a one-time Prohibitionist seemed destined to fail. It did. Rickey's last ride in St. Louis ended in resignation and controversy, but not before his team would claim baseball's biggest prize. 1926 was Rickey's first full season in a front office. 1964 would be his last. The rhyming of history also included a familiar World Series opponent, a seven-game drama, and a shocking postseason shakeup. But before the Yankees and Cardinals met for the fifth time in a World Series, the two teams were front and center in another battle: the fight to improve shameful housing conditions of black players during spring training.

---

[1] *St. Louis Star-Times*, January 28, 1949.
[2] *St. Louis Post-Dispatch,* January 29, 1953. Saigh claimed he frequently double-parked near the courthouse because no parking was available.
[3] Ibid, January 28, 1941.
[4] Ibid, January 29, 1953.
[5] "Western Union's enlarged ticker score tape...flashes across his Sportsman's Park offices." St. Louis Star-Times, March 15, 1950.
[6] *St. Louis Star-Times*, January 28, 1949.
[7] This figure varies depending on the report. At the time of the sale, Taylor Spink reported the Cardinals had a $1.1 million reserve fund and $1 million on deposit as a sinking fund set up for the construction of a new ballpark. *The Sporting News*, December 3, 1947. In 1952, Saigh told the Post-Dispatch there was a surplus of $2,550,000 cash in the baseball club when he and Hannegan made the purchase. With their newly formed entity, National Sports Inc., the owners declared a dividend. "We declared a dividend into National Sports and used the money to pay off the banks which lent us the money to buy the Cardinals," said Saigh. *St. Louis Post-Dispatch*, July 6, 1952.
[8] *St. Louis Post-Dispatch*, May 2, 1950. Saigh paid Hannegan $700,000 in cash and $300,000 in stocks. Bob Broeg later wrote that Saigh paid Hannegan $1.6 million, borrowing against the Cardinals minor league team in Rochester, New York for $1 million and $600,000 coming from stock in the Syndicate Trust Building. *St. Louis Post-Dispatch,* May 24, 1981. Saigh claimed that Kennedy patriarch Joe Kennedy offered to buy out Hannegan for $1.1 million. *St. Louis Post-Dispatch*, June 14, 1992.
[9] Slaughter, *Country Hardball*. Other reports put the price on the deal at $125,000.
[10] *St. Louis Post-Dispatch, April 7, 1964.* The article is a preview of Musial's autobiography. Musial singled out the sales of Johnny Mize in 1941, catcher Walker Cooper in 1945, and Dickson in 1949. "With those three players, I'm certain we could have won close pennant races which we lost." Author Rob Neyer blamed the failure of the 1949 Cardinals on the performance of first basemen Nippy Jones and Rocky Nelson. "Jones wasn't terrible," wrote Neyer, "Nelson, on the other hand, was truly awful." Nelson's slash line was .221/.258/.336 in 260 plate appearances. "By the way," Neyer added parenthetically, "all of this would be moot if, eight years earlier, Branch Rickey – then running the Cardinals – hadn't traded Johnny Mize to the Giants for three nobodies and $50,000." Neyer, Rob. *Rob Neyer's Big Book of Baseball Blunders: A Complete Guide to the Worst Decisions and Stupidest Moments in Baseball History*. Fireside. 2006.
[11] The performance of the 1949 Cardinals had columnist Roy Stockton comparing Saigh to Rickey and Breadon. "All of the idea production that made Rickey so valuable. All the business astuteness of Breadon." Less than a year later, Stockton wrote, "the Redbirds

have so many acute problems to solve that you can't attribute their recent steady decline to anything except squad inadequacy, a condition that takes a long time to remedy." *St. Louis Post-Dispatch*, October 2, 1949, and August 16, 1950.
[12] Broeg, *Memories of a Hall of Fame Sportswriter.*
[13] *St. Louis Post-Dispatch*, August 6, 1950. One year later, columnist Vincent X Flaherty of the *Los Angeles Examiner* wrote a series of articles raising questions about Saigh's past business deals, lawsuits, and traffic tickets. The articles also focused on Red Sox owner Lou Perini and Yankees owner Del Webb. All three opposed retaining Happy Chandler as the commissioner of baseball. *Globe-Democrat* columnist Bob Burnes and others suspected that Flaherty received his information on the owners directly from Chandler. *St. Louis Globe-Democrat*, March 8, 1951.
[14] *New York Times*, December 12, 1950. Baseball officials were meeting in St. Petersburg, Florida at the time of the vote. Afterward, when Cubs owner Phil Wrigley and Webb of the Yankees informed Chandler of the decision, they found him having dinner with Jimmy Conzelman, a St. Louis native. Conzelman played and coached football at Washington University, spent ten seasons in the NFL and later coached the Chicago Cardinals. He was inducted into the Pro Football Hall of Fame in 1964. He also worked in the front office of the St. Louis Browns from 1943 to 1945.
[15] The Browns contended the Sportsman's Park lease was forfeited upon the sale of the Cardinals from Breadon to Hannegan and Saigh. The lease contained a non-assignable clause. A judge ruled in favor of the Cardinals.
[16] *St. Louis Post-Dispatch*, December 27, 1950. Saigh believed television broadcasts of regular-season games hurt attendance. One of his ideas was to have games shown on movie screens on a delayed basis. *The Sporting News*, June 28, 1950.
[17] In 1949, the Cardinals became the first team in baseball to open the season under the lights.
[18] *New York Times*, June 13, 1950. "No night game shall be scheduled on a 'getaway' date without the consent of a visiting team, or on Sunday," read the league rule. Saigh interpreted it as saying a game could be scheduled on a Sunday night with the consent of the visiting team. When he asked the Dodgers for consent, Branch Rickey gave it. But Frick believed the rule prohibited all Sunday night games.
[19] Hannegan and Saigh borrowed $3 million from First National Bank, $550,000 and $350,000 from Breadon, and $150,000 from Mrs. Mark Steinberg, wife of the Cardinals' director. Details of the financing came to light during the Browns' eviction lawsuit against the Cardinals. *St. Louis Post-Dispatch,* December 19, 1949. In 1952, he admitted the cash in the deal, $60,800, had also been borrowed money. Manufacturers Bank & Trust Co. provided the loan. Ibid, July 6, 1952.
[20] *St. Louis Post-Dispatch*, February 11, 1953. The story specifically mentions Saigh's forty-nine percent ownership interest. Other stories have claimed Saigh owned seventy-percent of the team, even before he bought out Hannegan.

---

[21] The civil claims against Saigh stretched on for years. In 1955, he entered into an agreement with the government to settle for $276,328 a claim for taxes, penalties, and interest that had totaled $623,267. A year later, the IRS filed an income tax lien against Saigh for $1,097,478. The lien was for Saigh's individual income taxes for 1946, a year before he bought the Cardinals and was related to the purchase of the Railway Exchange Building. *St. Louis Post-Dispatch*, March 9, 1956. Five years later, with interest and penalties, the amount had ballooned to $2,198,302. It was then reduced to $60,966 plus interest. *St. Louis Post-Dispatch*, August 20, 1961.
[22] *New York Times*, January 29, 1953.
[23] The day after the verdict, Saigh went on the *Today* show and complained to broadcaster Dave Garroway about the sentence. He later apologized for the remarks. *St. Louis Post-Dispatch*, January 31, 1953.
[24] *Saturday Evening Post,* October 15, 1955.
[25] Shapiro, Michael. *Bottom of the Ninth: Branch Rickey, Casey Stengel, and the Daring Scheme to Save Baseball from Itself.* Times Book, Henry Holt and Company, LLC. 2009.
[26] *St. Louis Post-Dispatch*, May 24, 1981.
[27] Ibid, February 20, 1953. Other reports mention a group from Houston that also had serious interest in the team. "Saigh went down to Houston to talk to some Texas millionaires." Veeck, Bill with Ed Linn. *Veeck as in Wreck*: *The Autobiography of Bill Veeck.* The University of Chicago Press. 2001.
[28] Ibid, June 14, 1992.
[29] Veeck, *Veeck as in Wreck.* Veeck described the Cardinals under Saigh as "weak in the front office."
[30] Interview with Fred Saigh, May 16, 1978. Louis B. Nunn Center for Oral History, University of Kentucky Libraries.
[31] Rickey's son, Branch Jr, died in 1961. His daughter Sue lived in St. Louis County. When the Rickeys moved from Pittsburgh, they bought a home in Ladue near her.

The Times They Are a-Changin'

On January 25, 1959, an American Airlines flight left Los Angeles bound for Idlewild Airport in New York City. It arrived about five hours later, marking the first nonstop commercial transcontinental flight in U.S. history. A new era of jet travel had arrived in America. The next day, pitcher Jim Brosnan departed his home in Morton Grove, Illinois, bound for spring training in Florida. Accompanied by his wife, "two kids, a dozen toys, and enough clothes for a two months' trip," the Brosnans made stops along the way in Virginia and South Carolina before finally arriving in St. Petersburg on February 22. We know this because Brosnan kept a journal of his 1959 season, a campaign that began with the St. Louis Cardinals and ended with the Cincinnati Reds. The result would be *The Long Season*, a book published the following year. A new era of sports writing had arrived in America.[1]

Brosnan pulled back the curtain on life in the big leagues. He wrote about late-night drinking and extracurricular activities that included "a bit of carousing – perhaps a strenuous exercise or two." He wrote of his disdain for sportswriters. "Baseball writers as a rule are by no means abnormal. Some people even claim that they are human." He didn't like Cardinals broadcaster Harry Caray, calling him "Old Blabber-mouth" and "Tomato-Face." He also clashed with his manager, Solly Hemus. "Solly and I didn't see eye-to-eye on much of anything. I probably couldn't criticize him objectively if I could," he wrote. "Hemus tried hard, I'll say that for him. Maybe he tries too hard. He tends to overmanage and he gets panicky for no good reason at all."

Published a decade before Jim Bouton's *Ball Four*, Brosnan's book marked the genesis of the tell-all baseball chronicle. He had no ghostwriter, no public relations department to present the image of a squeaky-clean role model. This was no book for Boy Scouts. He described his enjoyment of chewing tobacco, always mixed with a piece of chewing gum. "The gum isn't supposed to add taste or flavor to the tobacco," he explained, "just hold it together for a longer, chewier cud." Bullpen competitions included filling a cup with tobacco spit and betting on what inning the cup would begin to overflow. A bullpen seat had advantages over being in the dugout. "A certain type of fan will sit daily in the first row behind the bullpen bench," Brosnan explained. "There she can be seen with a ballplayer without her reputation getting hurt." After games, he'd soak his arm while drinking a Budweiser. When his friend Don Studt proposed a small drink one evening, Brosnan wrote that "Don spells 'drink' with a 'u' not an 'i'."

Brosnan debuted with the Chicago Cubs in 1954. Acquired by the Cardinals in May of 1958, he won eight games for St. Louis that season. "I came from a poor organization to one that was overtly organized," he remembered. "Everyone was a Cardinal. If we weren't Cardinal-bred but had come from another organization, we quickly learned how to act like a Cardinal. There was definitely a Cardinals' tradition."

Brosnan wore thick glasses and was an avid reader. "I maintain a small library in the locker in the clubhouse," he admitted. Teammates called him "The Professor." He'd yell at opposing hitters in French: *Ils ne passeront pas* (they shall not pass). He was inquisitive and skeptical. "Since my wife is from Virginia, I have heard both versions of the Civil War, as taught in the public schools," he wrote. "Somebody is lying." He spoke candidly about the self-doubt a professional athlete faces. "Where can you find a comfortable place to relax, at the top?" he asked in a letter to his wife. "It's a definite problem of balance, for there's no hand hold above, and damn little support to lean on."

Brosnan's memoir also touched on religion – "Catholics predominate on the Cardinals" – and race. Here, the enlightened pitcher reflected attitudes more traditional among his generation. He once got into an argument with teammate Brooks Lawrence over jazz music. "Do you only listen to Negro musicians?" Brosnan asked the black pitcher.[2] "This is the first time I'd talked seriously to Lawrence," he wrote. "Best to find out if he was stuffy about being a Negro. Some of them are. Why they feel they have to be better than us I don't know."

The season where Brosnan and Lawrence debated the merits of Dave Brubeck and Thelonious Monk marked an important milestone in baseball. On July 21, 1959, Pumpsie Green made his debut for the Boston Red Sox, the last team in baseball to integrate. Twelve years after Jackie Robinson broke baseball's color barrier, the game was slowly evolving. But on many fronts, the sport Brosnan describes in his journal is one more closely aligned with the era of Hornsby and Ruth than baseball of the twenty-first century.

Other than franchise relocations, teams largely played in the same parks they did in decades past. Cincinnati played at Crosley Field, a park the Reds had called home since 1912 (when it was known as Redlands Field). Pittsburgh had called Forbes Field home since 1909. Across the state in Philadelphia, Shibe Park had been around since 1909 (although the Phillies didn't start playing there until 1938). Sportsman's Park in St. Louis was now called Busch Stadium, but it was still the same park located at the intersection of Grand and Dodier. A new generation of parks, including one in St. Louis, didn't emerge until the 1960s.

The 1959 Cardinals had a four-man pitching rotation. Brosnan was the long reliever, the first man out of the bullpen. Traded to Cincinnati in June, the Reds made him a starter. His first start came against his old team. After seven innings, he had thrown 150 pitches and had a finger bleeding from a punctured blister. He went back out for the eighth inning and faced one batter before exiting. Pitchers in both leagues still hit for themselves. The introduction of the designated hitter was more than a decade away. Florida's wettest spring training in decades led the Dodgers and Reds to play games in Cuba, where Prime Minister Fidel Castro had recently taken power. Major League Baseball wouldn't return for forty years. Brosnan, who considered himself "an average professional baseball player," made $15,000 in 1958. Cardinals general manager Bing Devine offered him $16,000 for the new season. In the offseason, Brosnan worked at an advertising agency. Because so many players had jobs in the winter months, spring training served as a time to get in shape. It was an uphill battle for many, who drank frequently and ate poorly. "Ballplayers eat nothing but junk!" St. Louis trainer Bob Bauman told Brosnan.[3]

While it was now possible to take a nonstop transcontinental flight from Los Angeles to New York, no major league team needed to do so. Only American League baseball was played in New York. The Yankees had the city to themselves. With the Dodgers and Giants now in California, fans watched only National League baseball on the West Coast. While the 1950s saw several teams change cities, baseball still featured just 16 teams, the same number it had in 1901, when the country had a hundred million fewer people.[4]

That would soon change. Branch Rickey had left his post as general manager of the Pirates after spending five largely unsuccessful seasons in Pittsburgh. The Pirates finished in last place four straight years starting in 1952, but players acquired during the Rickey era – Clemente, Groat, and Mazerowski – did lead the team to a world championship in 1960. Never idle for long, the man who pushed integration in the 1940s now advocated for expansion. Rickey was introduced as the first president of the Continental League in August of 1959. His idea was to have a third eight-team major league. Rickey's vision included having the World Series be a round-robin affair, with the winners of all three leagues participating. The proposal never came to fruition, but the idea spurred the established leagues to action. The American League added two teams in 1961. The National League followed suit in 1962. The AL now had a footprint in California with the Angels. The NL now had a presence in New York with the Mets.[5]

By the time Busch had hired Rickey to be a consultant with the Cardinals, the pace of change in baseball had accelerated. Both leagues had ten teams, the National League was back in the country's largest city, and the American League had a reason to travel to the West Coast. One in ten major league players was African American. But one aspect of the game had been stubbornly resistant to any modifications. Spring training in the Jim Crow South had always been a segregated affair. But in the early 1960s, that all changed. A new generation of Cardinals played a central role.

*****

By 1961, both the Cardinals and the Yankees had called St. Petersburg, Florida their spring training home for decades. New York arrived in town in the 1920s, St. Louis in the 1930s. Both teams played their games at Al Lang Field, named for the former mayor who passed away a year earlier. The Cardinals also trained at Al Lang, while the Yankees practiced at Miller Huggins Field, named in honor of the man who spent his entire managing career in St. Louis and New York. The Yankees headquartered at the Soreno, a seven-story, three-hundred-room hotel located on prime waterfront property. Cardinals players, coaches, and staff enjoyed staying at the nearby Vinoy Park Hotel, described in one dispatch as "aristocratic." Ballplayers had the option of walking to Al Lang Field if they so desired. "Exactly 1274 steps," remarked Cardinals trainer Bauman, who had counted the distance between the ballpark and the Vinoy.

The convenient and palatial offerings came with a catch. They were only available to white players. The black players couldn't even enter the hotels. They had to find housing every spring in the African American neighborhoods of St. Petersburg. Bob Gibson, Curt Flood, and Bill White lived in a boardinghouse in the Southside neighborhood of the city. White restaurants, drinking fountains, and bathrooms were all off-limits to them. By law, white taxicab drivers couldn't accept black passengers. After games, white players would take a short stroll back to the hotel. Gibson, Flood, and White would leave in an orange station wagon rented for them by the team.

In March, the St. Petersburg Chamber of Commerce sponsored a "Salute to Baseball" breakfast at the local yacht club. Dozens of Cardinal and Yankee players were invited. Not one was black. The news hit Cardinals first baseman White hard. The player had experienced the indignities of racism since his days in the minor leagues. An Ohio native, "the anger and hatred in the Deep South was a shock," he later admitted. Signed by the New York Giants in 1953, the club sent him to Danville, Virginia to play in the Carolina League. He was the only black player on the team. He frequently heard taunts of "nigger," "coon," and "darkie." One night in Graham, North Carolina, White flipped off some fans who had aimed racial epithets in his direction. After the game, he and his teammates had to march out of the clubhouse with bats held high to fend off a mob.[6] Flood and Gibson recalled similar racial tensions while playing in the minor leagues. Both men spent time on teams in Georgia, where it was against the law for black players to even dress in the same locker room with white players.[7]

White broke into the big leagues with the Giants in 1956 and was traded to the Cardinals three years later. He found St. Louis "difficult but not unbearable." While he found plenty of examples of covert racism in Missouri, it was "constant, inescapable, and all pervasive" in Florida. The snub by the Chamber of Commerce was the final straw. White decided to speak out. "When will we be made to feel like humans?" he asked. "How much longer must we accept this without saying a word? This thing keeps gnawing at my heart. I think about this every minute of the day."

White's comments struck a nerve. "It's my fault, not the city's," explained Cardinals public relations director Jim Toomey. "I only asked those players living at our spring training headquarters (the Vinoy Park) hotel, players who would have to walk right by the St. Petersburg Yacht Club, where the breakfast was scheduled, on their way to Al Lang Field," he explained. White players like Stan Musial, who preferred a private beachfront condo to hotel life, were also not invited. "I felt they would have to get up too early to be at the breakfast at 8:15," said Toomey.[8]

Officials scrambled to correct the oversight and quickly issued invitations to black players. Elston Howard of the Yankees attended but not a single black player of the Cardinals made an appearance. (White wrote in his autobiography that the Yankees ordered Howard to attend. As for himself, "I hadn't wanted to eat with those bigots anyway.") Toomey said he tried to reach White before the event. "I wish I could get in touch with Bill now," he said. "But I haven't been able to reach him. He is welcome if he wants to come."

Influential African American sportswriter Wendell Smith was incredulous at Toomey's response. "Here is an official of a major league club who unwittingly admits that he does not know how to contact a player on the club. He does not, or cannot, know what procedures to employ when the time comes to contact one of his Negro performers," he wrote. "Suppose a serious emergency did develop – suppose, for example, that a member of Bill White's family was stricken with an ailment suddenly? How would Toomey, or any other Cardinal official, contact White, who has been shunted over into the squalor of 'Colored Town?'" [9]

Toomey was not the only official with the Cardinals caught off guard by the backlash over the treatment of black players in spring training. Gussie Busch told Flood he wasn't aware of the segregated housing arrangements. "Do you mean to tell me that you're not staying at the hotel with the rest of the fellas?" the team president asked his center fielder. "Mr. Busch, don't you know we're staying about five miles outside of town in the Negro section?"[10]

Given this event happened at the beginning of Busch's ninth season in charge of the Cardinals, one can draw his or her own conclusions about what the beer baron knew or had simply chosen to ignore. But he could ignore it no longer. Black newspapers in St. Louis and beyond picked up on the issue. If this was the way Anheuser-Busch treated its black players, they suggested, maybe it was time to boycott the company's beer. Cardinals' director of player development Eddie Stanky asked White to back off the issue and focus on baseball. White said he wouldn't. He was encouraged by Al Fleishman, head of the Fleishman-Hilliard public relations agency, the same PR firm that represented Anheuser-Busch and the Busch family. "You need to keep the pressure on their ass," Fleishman told him. "Al was a good guy, and like a lot of Jewish Americans, he had no patience with racial and ethnic bigotry," wrote White. "It probably didn't help Al's mood that many hotels in St. Petersburg excluded not only blacks, but also Jews."[11]

The Yankees departed St. Petersburg after 1961 and set up their spring training headquarters the next year in Ft. Lauderdale. The Cardinals took a different tact. A local St. Petersburg businessman had purchased two motels – the Outrigger and the Skyline

– and made them available to all the team's players, black and white. Players like Musial and third baseman Ken Boyer, who had rented their own places in years past, moved in with the rest of the club. Counting players, coaches, team officials, wives, children, and sportswriters, 137 people lived in close quarters for the duration of spring training.

Feature films were brought in nightly and shown in the motel recreation room. Musial ran the popcorn stand. Lil Musial, Stan's wife, and Lela Keane, wife of manager Johnny Keane, arranged for inexpensive, family-style meals on the motel menu to help the budgets of younger and lower-salaried players with children (players received an $8 daily food allowance). The team had frequent cookouts. Boyer and pitcher Larry Jackson manned the grill. Gibson and White cooked food and pitching coach Howie Pollet fixed the salads. Family outings included a trip to Busch Gardens in Tampa Bay and a cruise on Busch's yacht.[12] White and black children all swam in the same motel pool. The behavior exhibited by the Cardinals and their families, so unusual in the Jim Crow South, became a bit of a tourist attraction. "All this integration was so unheard of in Florida that people would drive by the motel all day just to gawk and stare," White recalled. "For the first time, black players felt comfortable bringing their families to spring training."[13]

White's outburst in 1961, coupled with the stands taken by influential African American leaders like Wendell Smith, Alex Haley (who profiled the segregated conditions for *Sport* magazine) and St. Petersburg doctor Ralph Wimbish (who refused to continue helping black players find separate housing), had enormous consequences. By 1964, all the teams that trained in Florida had eliminated segregated housing arrangements for their players.[14]

After drawing attention to the issue, White received a letter in the mail. "Dear Bill," it began. "I just wanted you to know that I appreciate everything that you've done for black baseball players. Keep up the fight." It was signed by Jackie Robinson.

This was the team Branch Rickey joined in the fall of 1962.

---

[1] Brosnan, Jim. *The Long Season*. Ivan R. Dee. 2001. (First published by Harper and Row in 1960.)

[2] While both Brosnan and Lawrence played for the Cardinals and Reds, they were only teammates in Cincinnati. Lawrence became the second African-American pitcher in St. Louis Cardinals' history when he debuted in June of 1954, one month after Bill Greason.

[3] Prior to the Cardinals, Bauman served as the longtime trainer for the St. Louis Browns. He also worked for the St. Louis University basketball team in the offseason. His brother was also a baseball trainer. Frank Bowman (who chose to spell his name phonetically) worked for the Giants, first in New York and later in San Francisco, from 1948 to 1966.

[4] The 1900 census counted 76,212,168 Americans. By 1960, the population of the country had grown to 180.7 million.

---

[5] The other team to join the American League in 1961 was the "new" Washington Senators. The "old" Senators moved to Minneapolis and became the Minnesota Twins. One year later, the National League added the New York Mets and the Houston Colt .45's. In 1965, the Houston franchise moved into the Astrodome and were renamed the Astros.
[6] White, Bill with Gordon Dillow. *Uppity: My Untold Story About the Games People Play.* Grand Central Publishing. 2011.
[7] Flood spent 1957 playing for the Savannah (Ga.) Redlegs in the South Atlantic League. Gibson spent part of the same year in the same league playing for the Columbus (Ga.) Foxes.
[8] *St. Louis Post-Dispatch*, March 9, 1961.
[9] *New Pittsburgh Courier*, March 18, 1961.
[10] Snyder, Brad. *A Well-Paid Slave: Curt Flood's Fight for Free Agency in Professional Sports.* Penguin Group Inc. 2006.
[11] White, *Uppity.*
[12] *St. Louis Post-Dispatch*, March 15, 1962.
[13] White, *Uppity.*
[14] The segregated living arrangements were unique to Florida. Teams that trained in Arizona faced no such restrictions by the early 1960s.

Rickey's Last Ride

Hired as a consultant by the Cardinals, Branch Rickey spoke to the media as if he were still running the show. "This club cannot be traded into prosperity," he proclaimed at his first news conference back in St. Louis. He pointed to 1965 as "a rational objective for a pennant." He also soon called for the retirement of the team's biggest attraction and only player left from his first stint with the Cardinals. "If the Cardinals don't want me, I know some other clubs that do," Stan Musial said when he heard the news. "Since when do you ask a .330 hitter to retire unless you've got his equal to replace him?" said a stunned Gussie Busch, who felt it necessary to reiterate Rickey's role. "I had a definite understanding of Mr. Rickey that he is to serve in an advisory capacity, as senior consultant on trades and player development." All this happened in Rickey's first week back in St. Louis.[1] His promise and peril were succinctly captured in two *Globe-Democrat* headlines:

RICKEY BACK AT SCENE OF TRIUMPHS (October 30).

RICKEY HAS CARDS IN TURMOIL (November 6).

He compounded his problems with an interview he gave over the winter to the *Saturday Evening Post*, predicting the Cardinals would finish in fifth place in 1963. "Their infield rates with any," Rickey told Frank Graham Jr., "but they only have two good men in the outfield – Curt Flood and George Altman." He also questioned the depth and experience of the pitching staff. Published at the beginning of spring training, the comments caused a "mild sensation" in the Cardinals' camp.[2] He also didn't endear himself to Johnny Keane when he publicly upbraided the manager in the middle of a game. The two men exchanged words over a prospect (Jimmy Harris) Rickey wanted to keep with the big-league club, but Keane decided to ship him off to the minor-league camp.[3] Issues extended to the players. Addressing the team one day in St. Petersburg, Rickey lectured the team on the proper approach to take at the plate. "One foolish player – who will remain nameless – has been around long enough to know how to hold a bat," Rickey said while looking directly at Tim McCarver. "Nameless? The whole team knew Rickey was talking about me," remembered the Cardinals catcher. "Rickey's comment was humiliating and needless."[4] (McCarver was even more blunt in an email to Rickey biographer Lee Lowenfish: "I despised the guy.")

Rickey turned out to be right about the infield – first baseman Bill White, second baseman Julian Javier, third baseman Ken Boyer, and shortstop Dick Groat were all in the starting lineup at the All-Star Game that summer in Cleveland – but wrong about the team.[5] The 1963 Cardinals won 93 games to finish second in the National League. With two weeks to go in the season, the club was just a game behind the Dodgers but won only two of its final ten contests to finish six back of Los Angeles. As expectations soared for 1964, Rickey kept a lower profile. Behind the scenes, tension was bubbling to the surface.

Rickey always claimed he had no ambitions to return to his former role as general manager. "It's absurd to think I'm after anybody's job," he insisted. "I'm too old." But his public pronouncements and interactions with the team told a different story. "Everybody in baseball except Busch and a few other equally well-informed owners was perfectly aware that Papa Branch is constitutionally incapable of moving into any kind of organization without maneuvering to establish himself as the dominant force," Bill Veeck contended.[6] To a man used to the spotlight and leading the charge, a backseat role was not easy to accept. How could it be for any man with Rickey's track record? He had revolutionized baseball's minor leagues, successfully led the charge to integrate the sport, and pushed baseball to expand.

His trailblazing efforts included protective headgear we take for granted today. As general manager of the Pirates and owner of the American Baseball Cap Company, he made batting helmets mandatory in Pittsburgh long before the sport required them. In Brooklyn, he hired statistician Allan Roth to track every pitch and every lineup. Roth would generate statistics commonly accessed today – home/road splits, specific pitcher/hitter matchups, how the team's pitching staff fared against any specific batsman – but revolutionary at the time. "For instance," the *Brooklyn Daily Eagle* pointed out early in the 1950 season, "the Dodgers, involved in a series at St. Louis, are duly warned to beware of two characters named Enos Slaughter and Stan Musial." Slaughter hit .413 against Brooklyn in 1949 while Musial batted .411 against the Dodgers. Stan was at his best in the opponent's park, hitting .523 at Ebbets Field. "That means Brooklyn held Stan the Man to a mere .304 at Sportsman's Park," the paper proudly pointed out.[7] With Roth's help, Rickey devised a formula that assessed a team's overall strength by measuring the difference between a team's offense compared to its pitching and defense. "Wow!" said Yankees general manager Brian Cashman when shown the formula. "The guy was generations ahead of his time."[8]

Rickey's pedigree presented the most problems for the man presumably responsible for making trades and negotiating contracts in St. Louis. "I was still the general manager in title, but he was going to run the club. Nobody told me that, but I developed that feeling," Bing Devine later confessed. "To be honest, I rather resented that Rickey was back," he wrote in his autobiography.

"Are we going to have trouble if I'm here to run the club?" Rickey once asked him. "Mr. Rickey, we are not *going* to have trouble. We *have* trouble right now." Devine was giving Rickey a ride home at the time. The men rode in silence the rest of the way. "That kind of put a period on the conversation," Devine remembered, as his mind began to race with possibilities. "What's this going to lead to? Am I going to get fired?"

*****

Vaughan Pallmore "Bing" Devine was born in the St. Louis suburb of Overland in 1916. He attended high school in nearby University City and college at Washington University, where he played both basketball and baseball.[9] In his early days with the Cardinals, he pitched batting practice. Hired to work in the team's public relations department, Rickey was still running the show when Devine started with the club. "I learned this game at the foot of Branch Rickey," he said years later.[10] Rickey would have the freshly minted college graduate run errands for him. "Is he giving you money for coffee and newspapers?" secretary Mary Murphy once asked Devine, who told her Rickey was not. "Well, you're supposed to see me when he sends you out for something. I'll give you the money."[11]

One of Devine's duties was to get attendance figures from the ticket manager. He'd then take the number written on a scrap piece of paper to Sam Breadon, seated in his box next to the dugout. The owner had the final say. Depending on the crowd, Breadon would sometimes tweak the figures. An attendance of 7,000 would magically become 12,000. Devine would write down the new number on a fresh piece of scrap paper and take it to the press box where it would be recorded for posterity.[12]

Devine became the business manager of the Cardinals farm team in Johnson City in 1941 before serving in the U.S. Navy during World War II. When the war ended, he returned to the club, working for the Cardinals farm team in Columbus, Ohio, then to the Triple-A affiliate in Rochester, New York. The 1950 Red Wings won the pennant with Devine running the front office and Keane, another St. Louis native, managing the club. In 1953, Devine hired a young Jack Buck to broadcast the team's games. Buck beat Devine to St. Louis, arriving in 1954. Devine returned home after the 1955 season to serve as assistant general manager to Frank Lane.[13]

"Trader Frank" loved to make deals. Among his many transactions, he shipped off second baseman Red Schoendienst to the New York Giants and sent 1955 Rookie of the Year Bill Virdon to the Pittsburgh Pirates. He would have dealt Stan Musial to Philadelphia for pitcher Robin Roberts had Gussie Busch not blocked it. In 1957, Lane requested a new three-year contract from ownership. The reply from an increasingly exasperated Busch came in the form of a telegram: KISS MY ASS.[14] Lane left at the end of the season. Devine got promoted.

One of his first acts was to unwind a deal his predecessor had set up. Lane wanted to swap third baseman Ken Boyer for Philadelphia outfielder Richie Ashburn. Devine wanted no part of it. "Stan Musial is the only player not tradeable," Devine said, "but Boyer comes close to it."[15] Boyer remained in St. Louis eight more seasons. By 1963, his teammates were touting him as the league's most underrated player. The Alba, Missouri native hit 24 home runs and drove in 111 that season while batting .285. His numbers would be even better in 1964.

Devine managed to work for years under Busch despite an aversion to alcohol. Whenever the boss would order a round of Budweisers, he would make sure to add a Coke to the tab for Devine. Described as a soft-spoken man, Devine could also speak rapidly. "His machine-like chatter would talk the ears off a donkey," remembered Jim Brosnan.

Devine's first deal as general manager netted the team a nineteen-year-old third baseman. The Cardinals made Curt Flood their center fielder. Over the next decade, Flood would win six Gold Gloves and play in three All-Star games as a member of the Cardinals. Devine played a central role in shaping the infield that made All-Star Game history in 1963. He acquired first baseman White in 1959, second baseman Javier in 1960 and shortstop Groat in 1963. Only Boyer came up through the St. Louis farm system.

The Groat trade marked an early turning point in the relationship between Devine and Rickey. Devine wanted to acquire the shortstop from Pittsburgh in exchange for Julio Gotay. Groat turned thirty-two in 1963 and was nine years older than the Cardinals shortstop. Rickey opposed the move. He never wanted to give up youth for a veteran, and since he had Busch's ear, all moves had to pass by his desk. Knowing the battle he would face, Devine stacked the deck in his favor. He brought in manager Keane, coach Harry Walker and farm director Eddie Stanky – all of whom supported the deal – to meet with Rickey. "You seem to have this meeting loaded," the elder statesman told Devine. Rickey told him he wouldn't support the deal, but he wouldn't oppose it, either. Groat hit .319 with a league-leading 43 doubles in his first season for the Cardinals. He finished second in the National League MVP voting, "but the Groat trade...started cooling the relationship between Rickey and me," Devine remembered.

One season later, Rickey went even further to block a move by the Cardinals general manager. Devine wanted a backup to McCarver, the team's young left-handed hitting catcher. Bob Uecker, a right-handed hitting backstop with Milwaukee, was available. Rickey wouldn't budge in his opposition. With spring training almost over, Devine had Keane pay a late-night visit to Gussie Busch to get approval for the move that sent backups Gary Kolb and Jimmie Coker to the Braves. Arriving in St. Petersburg, Uecker met Rickey in the clubhouse. The newest Cardinal extended his hand and introduced himself. "Yes, I know, and I didn't want you," Rickey told him. "I wouldn't trade a hundred Bob Ueckers for one Gary Kolb."[16]

The Cardinals emerged from spring training 1964 largely the same team that finished in second place the prior season. Other than Uecker, the club had also acquired pitcher Roger Craig from the New York Mets in exchange for outfielder George Altman. Craig had come up with the Brooklyn Dodgers and had been signed by Rickey's brother, Frank. The most notable difference was the absence of Musial. The Hall of Fame hitter decided to retire after the 1963 season, one season after Rickey had wanted him to call it quits.

St. Louis native Charlie James began the season as the new Cardinals left fielder. James had starred as a halfback at Webster Groves High School and later at the University of Missouri where he played both football and baseball. His decision to leave the Mizzou program after his junior year and sign with the Cardinals created a firestorm of protest in Columbia, where both football coach Dan Devine (no relation to Bing) and baseball coach Johnny "Hi" Simmons criticized the move. Simmons called the move "greedy" and believed that James, who became a Cardinal for an estimated $15,000 signing bonus, "was signed for a song."[17]

Football coach Devine soon became doubly disappointed with the Cardinals when the team signed another of his players and another St. Louis native just months later. Mike Shannon, a product of CBC High School, had spent his freshman year at Mizzou on the football team. In the summer of 1958, he signed with the Cardinals for upwards of $65,000.[18] "I'm bitterly disappointed and disillusioned by the mechanics of the signing for reasons I don't wish to discuss publicly," the coach told reporters. Shannon made his Cardinals debut in 1962 and became a regular two seasons later. Center fielder Flood was flanked at times by two former Mizzou athletes in 1964; James in left field to begin the season and Shannon in right field in the back half of the campaign. Both appeared in exactly 88 games. Elsewhere the lineup remained intact with the All-Star infield returning and McCarver behind the plate. Bob Gibson, Ernie Broglio, Ray Sadecki, and Curt Simmons anchored the pitching staff.

A promising start to the season – 25-20 by the end of May – turned into doubt and skepticism as the club fell below .500 by mid-June after getting swept by the Dodgers in Los Angeles. On a flight to Houston, general manager Devine told his manager the club had a chance to acquire a young outfielder with the Chicago Cubs. "What are you waiting for?" Keane replied when told Lou Brock was available. On June 15, 1964, the Cardinals traded two pitchers and an outfielder; Broglio, Bobby Schantz and Doug Clemens, for two pitchers and an outfielder; Jack Spring, Paul Toth, and Brock. The principals in the deal were Brock and Broglio, a former twenty-game winner.

Informed of the trade, players on the Cardinals reacted with less than enthusiasm. "I suspected that the deal would cause more problems than it solved," Gibson recalled. "We all thought Bing was crazy," first baseman White remembered. Reaction to the deal was similar in Chicago. "Thank you, thank you, oh, you lovely St. Louis Cardinals. Nice doing business with you. Please call again any time," wrote *Chicago Daily News* sportswriter and Brock critic Bob Smith. (While there's no indication he had input into the deal, this was one Rickey would have presumably supported. Brock had youth and speed. Broglio was four years older and battling a sore arm.)

Doubts about the deal from the St. Louis perspective centered around the loss of Broglio – an eighteen-game winner with a 2.99 ERA in 1963 – and questions about Brock

– a twenty-five-year-old outfielder who had never hit above .263 in three seasons with the Cubs. In Chicago, Brock struggled in right field and the sun of Wrigley Field day games. The Cardinals moved him to left field, batted him second in the order behind Flood (the two would later swap places in the lineup), and turned him loose on the base paths. Keane had long been attracted to Brock's talents and the swift outfielder responded by rewarding his manager's faith. "I never thought I had anything to prove with the Cardinals," Brock remembered. "Whatever I had to prove, they told me to prove it to the opposition."[19] He made his first start for the Cardinals on June 16 and didn't come out of the lineup the rest of the season. Brock hit .348 with 12 home runs, 44 RBIs, and 33 stolen bases his first year in St. Louis. "The Cardinals were the perfect organization for him because he was allowed to run any time he wanted," said McCarver.[20] "With the Cardinals, I knew...that *you had a right to fail*," Brock declared. "Failure at one thing was permissible in the interest of letting you succeed at another."[21]

Three weeks after Brock's arrival, Mike Shannon was called up from the minor leagues and became the team's starting right fielder. The lineup Keane would use the rest of the season was now in place. Despite the spark provided by Brock and Shannon (nine home runs and 43 RBI), the club continued to limp along in the standings for weeks. After a loss to the Phillies on July 24, St. Louis found itself ten games back of Philadelphia and one game under .500. A few weeks before, Keane had held a closed-door team meeting. Convinced one of his players was undermining his authority, Keane decided to get the issue out in the open. The results would have far-ranging consequences. The question Devine asked himself when driving Rickey home one afternoon – "Am I going to get fired?" – was about to be answered.

*****

Dick Groat was a Branch Rickey man. As general manager of the Pirates, Rickey first courted Groat after his junior year at Duke, where he was an All-American in both baseball and basketball. In college on a basketball scholarship, Groat felt obligated to complete his four-year commitment but told Rickey he would sign with him the following year. True to his word, Groat debuted with Pittsburgh in June of 1952. He never played a game in the minor leagues. The National League MVP with the world-champion Pirates in 1960, Groat became a Cardinal three seasons later.

Sportswriter Bob Broeg and author David Halberstam used the same description of Groat – "clubhouse lawyer." His personality stood in contrast to his new teammates. "On a club that preferred to bring things out in the open, he was more of a hush-hush kind of guy," remembered Gibson. "If he had anything to say to you, whether it was confidential or not, he'd get up real close and whisper it, so that you had to lean forward to hear him."[22]

With the Cardinals, Keane had given his shortstop carte blanche to call his own hit-and-run plays. But after it backfired multiple times in a game in 1964, the manager removed the privileges. Groat began to grumble. The tension began to divide the clubhouse. Right after the All-Star break, with the team in New York, Keane called a closed-door meeting. "To this day, when I recall that meeting, I still can't talk about it," McCarver said twenty-five years later. Keane made it clear he was tired of the second-guessing behind his back. "You guys might get me fired, goddamnit," the manager told his players, "but if you do you can bet your asses that I'm taking some of you bastards with me!"[23] Knowing full-well Keane had aimed the barbs at him, Groat stepped up and apologized. The strain disappeared. The club turned the page.

Back in St. Louis, Gussie Busch didn't know about the solution, just the problem. He'd also heard about it long after Keane and Groat had buried the hatchet. There are conflicting versions of how he became aware of the controversy. Many claim he got the news from his daughter Elizabeth via Eddie Mathews. The Busch daughter and the Milwaukee Braves third baseman would later marry. Gibson would claim in his autobiography that Busch belatedly heard the news at a brewery convention from a Miller rep. Regardless, Busch sensed trouble on his team and thought his management was keeping the news from him. He met with Keane and Devine in August and wanted to know if there was any issue with the club he should know about it. With the Groat issue long since resolved, they said no. Busch didn't like the answer. He suspected disloyalty among the ranks. A few days later, Devine was out of a job.

"Seven years was enough for Bing Devine," Busch told reporters. Technically asked to resign, Devine was fired along with business manager Art Routzong. "Bing made a lot of good deals," Busch conceded in a statement he would soon regret, "but he made some bad ones, too." The general manager and business manager were gone. The manager survived, but Keane knew he likely wouldn't last long. Rumors began to circulate that Keane would be out of a job by the end of the year. The rumors were not unfounded.

The 1964 Cardinals were a unique group. The team featured eight future broadcasters (McCarver, Shannon, Uecker, and White most prominent), three electrical engineers, three men destined to be managers, a future general manager, and a first baseman in White who would eventually become president of the National League.[24] The front office featured Rickey, who along with Babe Ruth, did the most to shape the game during the first half of the twentieth century. The man Rickey answered to knew little about baseball but a lot about beer. Aggressively using the team as a marketing vehicle, Busch's flagship product became the best-selling beer in America in 1955, surpassing Schlitz.

These were outsized, dominant personalities; accomplished and opinionated leaders who called the shots from the front office, combined with intelligent, articulate men on the playing field. "Although the phrase had not been coined yet, we were, without a doubt, baseball's best and brightest," asserted Gibson. Yet in 1964, perhaps the single most popular and influential person associated with the club didn't appear in a lineup card, never made a trade, nor signed a check. He called the games on radio.

From his perch in the KMOX radio booth, Harry Caray's voice boomed at night from the Rocky Mountains to the East Coast. His legion of fans included a young Elvis Presley, listening from Memphis, and a youthful Bob Costas, tuning in from Long Island.[25] A St. Louis native, Harry Carabina was born in the city in 1914. He later legally changed his last name and had been broadcasting Cardinals games since 1945. His career got a boost in 1947 when then-owner Breadon decided to expand the broadcasts to include road games and tapped Caray and former manager Gabby Street to describe the action. He could be highly critical of players (Boyer was a favorite whipping boy), but his broadcasting style resonated with fans because of his genuine enthusiasm and passion for the game. He was raw, opinionated, and unfiltered. "Gussie Busch loved him," remembered Jack Buck. "They both were the same kind of earthy guys. Harry wouldn't take any gruff. Neither would Mr. Busch."[26]

In August of 1964, Mr. Busch wanted Caray to act as a middle man. Busch heard Caray interview Leo Durocher on the radio a few weeks after Devine was let go and quickly became enamored with the former Brooklyn Dodgers and New York Giants manager. Accomplished, talented, and controversial, Durocher had won a pennant with the Dodgers and two pennants and a World Series with the Giants. A longtime favorite of Rickey, Durocher drew headlines for his flamboyant lifestyle, controversial relationships and gambling habits. In many ways, he was the exact opposite of Johnny Keane, a man who had studied for the priesthood before entering baseball.

Durocher hadn't managed a team in nearly a decade but was clearly interested in the right opportunity. "If someone came to me and asked me to manage a team with some talent on it – a team like the Cardinals here – well, I'd jump at it in a minute," Durocher told Caray during the radio interview. A day later, Busch had Caray deliver Durocher to his Grant's Farm estate and offered him the manager's job for 1965.[27]

Keane's days in St. Louis were now numbered. They would soon end, but not in a way that anyone imagined. One of Devine's final acts as general manager was to call up a veteran pitcher from the minor leagues. Along with the Brock trade in June and the insertion of Shannon into the lineup in July, the arrival of Barney Schultz in August would propel the Cardinals to heights the franchise hadn't seen since 1946. The aging knuckleballer was the final piece to a championship puzzle.

*****

Schultz didn't make his major-league debut until he was twenty-eight years old. After going 1-2 with a 7.89 ERA for the Cardinals in 1955, he didn't appear in the big leagues again for another four years. His minor league career featured stops in Columbus, Ohio, and Omaha, Nebraska where he played for Keane. His 1959 campaign for the Detroit Tigers marked his only year in the American League. He continued to bounce around the minors before returning to the National League two years later with the Cubs. In his third year in Chicago, the Cubs traded him to the Cardinals. But after making 24 appearances for the big-league club in 1963, St. Louis sent him to their minor league team in Jacksonville to begin the 1964 season. "I didn't make the roster [out of spring training] because the team figured it wasn't going to do much, and they wanted to give the younger players a chance," Schultz remembered.[28]

Growing up in New Jersey, Schultz learned how to throw a knuckleball from a neighbor. "When I was a kid, I always had a ball and glove in my hand. There was an older fellow who lived next door, and he could throw it. He could make it dance. And that, I guess, was the biggest help I ever had, because nobody else ever worked with me on the knuckleball." Signed by the Phillies right out of high school in 1944, Schultz hurt his arm in his second year of professional baseball. It had long-term implications for his career. "I could pitch, but I lost some speed, so I had to change my style and perfect the knuckler. It wasn't that I didn't know how to throw the knuckleball before that. I just didn't have to use it."[29]

At the end of the 1963 season, Shultz took a job as a salesman in a New Jersey mall clothing store.[30] By this point in his baseball career, his journeys had taken him to three different major league clubs and fifteen different minor league teams. He considered retiring. He rejected the idea and soon developed an additional wrinkle to his knuckleball, a pitch he'd been throwing for twenty seasons. "I did have a tighter grip on the ball. I popped my wrists more, as in a fastball. That seemed to cut down on my strikeouts, but I got'em out."

After dominating minor league talent in Jacksonville (8-5 with a 1.05 ERA), Schultz made his 1964 debut for the Cardinals on August 1 in a 6-5 loss to the Cincinnati Reds. He didn't allow an earned run in his first twelve St. Louis appearances. A routine quickly developed. "It became a trend in the dugout – a superstition, really – that the fellows wouldn't let me go to the bullpen until after the sixth inning," the pitcher recalled.

"Barney Schultz is 38 years old, with sad eyes, an honest face and an arm apparently made out of some indestructible plastic," the *Post-Dispatch* glowed on August 19. The prior night, Schultz entered a game against Houston with two outs in the seventh inning and the Cardinals clinging to a 3-2 lead. He retired all seven batters he faced. Adding two runs on the top of the ninth inning, St. Louis won the game 5-2 with Schultz recording the save for Ray Sadecki's fifteenth win of the season.

The victory marked the Cardinals seventeenth win in twenty-four games. Yet the team was running to stand still. St. Louis began August eight games behind Philadelphia. Nearly three weeks later, the club was in fourth place – and eight games back of the Phillies. Following a 3-2 loss in San Francisco on August 23, St. Louis found itself 11 games behind the league-leaders. Philadelphia stood twenty-nine games over .500 and in firm control of the National League. That control would soon collapse. From that day forward, no team in the National League played better baseball than St. Louis. Other than the expansion franchises in Houston and New York, no club played worse than Philadelphia.

It all came together for the Cardinals down the stretch. Brock saved his best for last, hitting .364 the last month of the season. Curt Flood hit .358 over the same timeframe and finished the season with a league-high 211 hits. "I don't know where you'll find a better all-around 200-hit ball player," said Keane near the end of the season. Gibson went 7-2 in his last nine starts of the season with an ERA of 1.95. Battling a sore shoulder in the first half of the season, first baseman Bill White blossomed in the second half. Fourteen of his 21 home runs and 72 of his 102 RBIs came after the All-Star break. Ken Boyer's MVP campaign featured 24 home runs and a league-best 119 RBI. "I've been on several pennant winners," said relief pitcher Roger Craig in September, "but this club has more spirit than any of them."[31]

The team's final push for the pennant also received an inspirational boost from an unlikely source. In September, the club began receiving notes written in red ink. Signed by *Fifi LaTour, an old stripper*, the notes started out providing encouragement and predicting various victories. Claiming to be a psychic, Fifi's predictions got bolder as the month went on. "When she predicted that we would win the pennant," Gibson recalled, "some of us began to wonder."[32]

While the Cardinals were busy reeling off 28 wins in 39 games, the Phillies were busy falling apart. The club dropped 23 of its final 39 contests. Ten of those losses came consecutively in September. After a 3-2 win over the Dodgers on September 20, Philadelphia had a record of 90-60 and a 6.5 game lead. On September 30, the Phillies still had 90 wins but trailed the new leaders of the National League, the Cardinals, by 2.5 games. The final three losses of that ten-game stretch came in St. Louis. The Cardinals swept the Phillies behind pitchers Gibson, Sadecki, and Simmons. Schultz came on in relief to get the save in the first two games. "Eleven saves in two months," remarked Phillies manager Gene Mauch. "That's more than Schultz has had in his whole big-league career. He never saw the day he could get us out before." Schultz didn't allow a hit to the Phillies in his final two appearances of the season against them and capped off a stretch where he saved five consecutive victories. For Sadecki (a 20-game winner in 1964) and Simmons (18-9), the games marked their final victories of the season. Gibson had one last regular-season win to register and Schultz one final save to claim.

The Cardinals finished the regular season with three games at home against the New York Mets. The Phillies wrapped up the campaign with two games against the Reds. Sandwiched in-between St. Louis and Philadelphia, Cincinnati had surged in the standings to close within a half-game of the Cardinals. With almost no margin for error, St. Louis lost on Friday with Gibson on the mound 1-0 and followed it up with a 15-5 loss to the Mets on Saturday. On the last day of the season, the Cardinals and Reds were tied in the standings with the Phillies one game back. Losses by both St. Louis and Cincinnati would have meant a three-way tie for first place. McCarver showed up at the St. Louis Cathedral that Sunday. "It was just me and God that morning," he remembered. "I prayed as hard as I could. I was fervent because I wanted to win and knew I might never have the opportunity to be in another World Series."[33]

The 1964 pennant race paralleled an earlier period of St. Louis baseball. Former Cardinal Dick Sisler was managing the Reds (having replaced former Cardinal manager Fred Hutchinson).[34] Dick's father, George, had signed with the St. Louis Browns in 1915, marking one of the signature moments of Rickey's career. Reds owner Bill DeWitt Sr.

had gotten his start in baseball working for Rickey and had spent years working in Breadon's front office. DeWitt's first year as treasurer of the Cardinals was 1926, the year Schultz was born. The veteran pitcher, born two months before the Cardinals first championship, drew comparisons to Jesse Haines, the knuckleballing righthander and Game 7 winner of the 1926 World Series. The boost provided by Schultz also brought back memories of Grover Cleveland Alexander, another aging pitcher who helped spark a pennant drive. Both pitchers last performed for the Chicago Cubs before arriving in St. Louis.

Both the 1926 and 1964 Cardinals featured trades in June for outfielders – Southworth and Brock; performances that earned the National League MVP award – O'Farrell and Boyer; and a season that ended with a seven-game World Series against the New York Yankees. The 1964 Cardinals earned that right by winning on the last day of the season while the Phillies beat the Reds in Cincinnati. Coming into the game in relief of Curt Simmons just two days after starting on Friday night, Gibson went four innings to get the win. With one out in the ninth, Schultz replaced him to get the final two outs of the game. When McCarver caught a foul ball pop fly off the bat of Ed Kranepool, his prayers were answered. The Cardinals had won the game 11-5 and clinched the franchise's first pennant since 1946. "Right there, that was one of the most memorable feelings I've ever had," Schultz recalled. "I was lifted up off the ground and to me personally, it was like such a load had been taken off my shoulders. For the past two weeks, every pitch and every game had been so crucial. Every opportunity, Keane had me in the game."[35]

Fired general manager Devine joined a jubilant Cardinals clubhouse to congratulate the players. "I'm sorry you're not in this," Gibson told him. "You deserve it more than anyone else." Bob Howsam had replaced Devine as general manager (after both Harry Caray and Bill Veeck had reportedly been offered the position). A former owner of a minor league team in Denver, Howsam had gotten the job on the recommendation of Rickey. Howsam's Denver club had been affiliated with the Pirates when Rickey ran the Pittsburgh organization. The two men worked closely on the unsuccessful launch of the Continental League.

While respected by the club's senior consultant, Howsam was not popular among players still loyal to Devine. The new general manager didn't help his cause when, at a later victory celebration at Stan Musial & Biggie's restaurant, he gave a speech where he told the assembled, "I just want to point out this turnaround didn't happen until I took over the team." First baseman White was among those who took offense at the comments. "I did a slow burn," he remembered. "He must have known something about baseball," the first baseman later wrote of the team's new general manager, "but hardly any of us liked the guy." Bob Gibson was among those who didn't like the approach by Devine's replacement. "Howsam felt compelled to assert complete control over the ballclub. He imposed rules about such petty things as how high we were to pull up our baseball pants."

The months of June, July and August set the course for the Cardinals of 1964 and years beyond. The acquisition of Brock, the insertion of Shannon into the lineup, and the callup of Schultz played a significant role in the turnaround. All those decisions traced back to a general manager no longer there, as White was quick to remind everyone following Howsam's remarks. "Bing put all this together. And Bing is the reason we're all here." As a struggling team transformed into a championship club, a celebratory mood gave way to reflection and recrimination. The mood darkened one day after the World Series ended when Johnny Keane announced he wouldn't return as Cardinals manager. "It was an accumulation of a lot of little things," Keane said at the time, but it was widely suspected that the firing of Devine and the rumors regarding Durocher were two key factors in his decision. Because of his longtime connections to both Durocher and Howsam, Rickey bore the brunt of the blowback. A memo revealed after the season exposed how far he would have gone to remake the Cardinals.

The bombshell landed on the pages of the *Post-Dispatch* on October 18. Bob Broeg published details of a memo Rickey had written in August, three days before Devine was fired. "Rickey Buried Cards' Chances Aug. 10," read the headline. The team's senior consultant had speculated that "an early move with Bing" could lead to a roster shakeup and focus the club on building for the following season. Rickey wanted the Cardinals to bring up three pitchers from the minor leagues – Nelson Briles, Steve Carlton, and Dave Dowling – and "pitch them regularly until such time as there was unity of agreement that the player could not possibly remain with the club for 1965." He wanted to replace Javier at second base with Ed Pacheco, waive backup catcher Uecker (among others), and return Schultz to the minor leagues. He also voiced skepticism about the baseball career of right fielder Shannon. "As an afterthought I would let Shannon go back to Jacksonville for the balance of the season. I would even let Shannon go to the draft at Triple-A if major league waivers could be secured."

Since joining the Cardinals in the fall of 1962, Rickey had consistently focused on building toward 1965 and consistently misjudged the team and the talent right in front of his eyes. Devine had assembled a squad that won 93 regular-season games in both 1963 and 1964. During that same time, Rickey had opposed the acquisition of Groat, tried to block the trade for Uecker, and misjudged the impact of Shannon and Schultz. From the beginning, he had clashed with Devine over trades, angered Musial over a premature retirement call and sparred with Keane over the fate of a minor leaguer who never made it to the big leagues. The revealing of Rickey's August missive – what Broeg called a "Memo of Surrender" – was the final straw. One day later, Rickey left his role as a consultant with the team.

"I have received Mr. Rickey's resignation as consultant to the St. Louis Cardinals baseball club," Howsam announced. In fact, Howsam had to deliver the news to Rickey that he had been fired. Busch had ordered the move. "He forgot that he was just a 'senior consultant' and tried to run everything," Busch said later. "I was sorry, but he had to go."

Burned by the publishing of the memo in the pages of the *Post-Dispatch*, Rickey took his side of the story to the *Globe-Democrat.* He told Rich Koster he often wrote memos to himself to clarify his thinking. "It was not from Branch Rickey to August Busch. It was from Branch Rickey to Branch Rickey. To my knowledge, Mr. Busch never saw it." Koster's article primarily focused on Keane's exit from the club as Rickey sought to distance himself from the Durocher rumors. "I am a Keane man. I repeat. I am a Keane man," he explained in an article headlined RICKEY SEES HIMSELF AS SCAPEGOAT. "The reports that I had advised Mr. Busch to hire Durocher are ridiculous. Anyone who knows me can tell you that."[36] He had the evidence to back up this claim. Busch and the Cardinals had long been intrigued by Durocher. Reports had linked Durocher to several clubs in 1958, including the Cardinals, who replaced Fred Hutchinson with Solly Hemus at the end of the season.[37]

While the Koster story stressed Rickey's opposition to any move regarding the manager, the former team consultant had nothing to say in the piece about the firing of Devine. "Rickey, back at the scene of his greatest triumph, was treated deferentially by all, including Devine," Broeg recalled. "Rickey, in turn, treated Bing as what Devine had been when B.R. first knew him in 1939 – a glorified office boy. Memos flew off Rickey's facile tongue to Busch down at the brewery, hailing Devine as "a nice boy, but – ."[38] The day after Devine was terminated, Broeg called Rickey "Branch Richelieu," a reference to the seventeenth-century Catholic Cardinal and statesman who consolidated power and crushed factions under King Louis XIII in France.

Rather than criticize the firing of Devine, Harry Caray sought to highlight it as the reason behind the club's late-season success. "The evidence points strongly to the fact that Gussie Busch's dismissal of Devine was the psychological hot-foot that turned a sleeping Redbird into a fighting tiger," he contended.[39] Caray was not alone in believing a bad move had led to a good outcome. "Almost all of them [Cardinal players] were Bing's boys, and Bing was known to be a ballplayer's lamb. Branch Rickey was now in the saddle, they knew, and whatever else might be said for Branch, he has never shown any inordinate affection, respect or loyalty to his players," Bill Veeck maintained. "The Cards became a running, hitting, fielding, fighting, hustling ball club."[40]

The back and forth finger pointing and credit taking continued through the winter. In December, Rickey went public with the spat between Groat and Keane and took credit for ending it. Rickey "admitted he was the one to go to Groat and urge him to apologize," wrote UPI columnist Milton Richman.[41] Upset that the news became public, Groat denied that difficulties with his manager had anything to do with revoked hit-and-run privileges but instead stemmed from a comment he made to teammates about the smartest managers in baseball. "I picked Al Dark and Gene Mauch and never thought more about it, but somebody carried the story to Keane and from that day on, I could feel a coolness between the manager and me."[42]

Rickey's comments also led the Cardinals former manager to give his version of events. "I'm sorry, especially for Dick that Rickey saw fit to bring this out, and I'm disappointed in Dick's version. He knows there's more to the story," Keane told the *Post-Dispatch.* "I've seen ball clubs win even with dissension, and I'm sure Rickey has, too."

With the former manager weighing in, the team's former general manager also felt compelled to speak. Devine told the paper that he, not Rickey, was the one who brokered the peace between Groat and Keane. "I suggested that Johnny talk to Dick, and he did. The situation was not cleared up immediately, so at the All-Star break Johnny asked me to talk to Dick. I did."

By Devine's account, and most others, the situation was settled in July. Rickey told Richman the Groat apology didn't come until August and that the peace offering provided the catalyst for the team's performance down the stretch. "That was the difference in the club," he recalled months later. "From that point on, the Cardinals were an entirely different ball club – a unified ball club." Devine, the man responsible for the roster construction of the team, took exception to Rickey's version. "I have no comment about anything concerning Mr. Rickey," he explained before adding his two cents. "To say, though, that this situation represented the difference for the Cardinals would be patently unfair to Brock, Shannon, and Schultz, the three players who were added to the team's all-stars at mid-season and enabled the club to jell."

The performances of Brock, Shannon, Schultz, and the rest of the 1964 Cardinals led *The Sporting News* to name Devine its Executive of the Year for the second year in a row. "If you weren't a grown man, you'd cry," he said at a dinner to honor him after the season.

The man at least partially responsible for the firing of Devine had received the Executive of the Year award three times in his career, including the inaugural honor back in 1936. Now, just two months shy of his eighty-third birthday, Rickey's baseball career had come to an end. The last Cardinal team to employ the legendary baseball innovator had won despite him, not because of him. The great irony of Rickey's failure with the 1964 St. Louis Cardinals was that the club represented what he had in mind when he broke baseball's color barrier nearly two decades earlier; an integrated roster full of intelligent and talented men united in cause and spirit. "Of all the teams I was on," Gibson later recalled, "of all the teams I've ever *seen,* there was never a better band of men than the '64 Cardinals."

Many of those players had been acquired by Devine. Some of their arrivals had been opposed by Rickey. As a longtime manager in the Cardinals farm system, Keane had experience with players such as Gibson and Flood long before they became major league stars. All of them had their checks signed by Busch. Those four men are forever linked to the intrigue surrounding the 1964 squad. That same quartet was living in the St. Louis area when the team won its first World Series title in 1926. Back then, Busch was busy trying to keep the brewery afloat in the middle of Prohibition, Rickey was busy expanding baseball's first great farm system, Devine turned ten years old that spring in the suburbs of the city, and teenager Keane waited in line that fall at Sportsman's Park to get a World Series bleacher ticket the day Babe Ruth blasted three home runs. "I was always a Cardinal rooter," Keane recalled. "I belonged to the Knothole Gang." Now thirty-eight years later, Keane would spend his final games in a Cardinals uniform managing against the Bronx Bombers, an American League team long intertwined with pivotal moments in Cardinals history and the team's most celebrated executive.

The hiring of Rickey by the St. Louis Cardinals in 1917 helped lead Miller Huggins to the Yankees in 1918. Relieved of his managerial duties by Breadon in 1925, Rickey's first full year as a front office executive in 1926 coincided with a World Series victory over the Yankees. Rickey's last year under Breadon in 1942 came with an identical outcome, a World Series win over New York. Rickey's arrival in Brooklyn set off a decade-long battle between the Dodgers and Yankees. From 1947 to 1956, the two clubs met six times in the Fall Classic. Back in St. Louis to end his career, his final year in a baseball front office featured a familiar battle. For the fifth and final time of the twentieth century, the month of October featured the Cardinals and Yankees facing off in a battle for baseball supremacy.

Just as Rickey defined an era of team success from 1926 to 1946, his absence hindered the team during its lengthy postseason drought. At the end of the 1946 season, St. Louis celebrated its sixth World Series title and ninth pennant in twenty-one seasons. The team that had most successfully copied Rickey's farm system formula could point to ten World Series championships and fourteen pennants by 1946. The current gap in postseason totals can largely be explained by what occurred over the next 17 seasons. During a period when the Cardinals did not make a single World Series appearance, the Yankees made it to the Fall Classic fourteen times.

The 1947-1963 timeframe encapsulated nearly the entire career of one of New York's most celebrated players. The St. Louis native could have enjoyed a career in his hometown. Yogi Berra was the manager of the 1964 Yankees.

Branch Rickey was the reason he never wore a Cardinal uniform.

---

[1] *St. Louis Post-Dispatch*, October 29 and November 6, 1962. "I know I'm 42, but it seems strange to have Mr. Rickey recommend my retirement when he's almost twice my age," said Musial. *New York Times*, March 20, 1963.

[2] Making predictions about the Cardinals was nothing new for Rickey. Coming off a World Series title, Rickey predicted the 1935 Cardinals would finish second and "might easily finish fourth and that's where they will finish unless they start to think right." The Cardinals finished in second place. *St. Louis Post-Dispatch*, March 31, 1935. His comments to Graham in the *Saturday Evening Post* article were similar to what he said about the Cardinals at his introductory news conference in 1962. "I don't think they are quite ready to challenge..."

[3] *St. Louis Post-Dispatch,* March 17, 1963. Harris, a twenty-year-old shortstop prospect, never made it to the major leagues.

---

[4] Kahn, Roger. *Rickey & Robinson. The True, Untold Story of the Integration of Baseball*. Rodale. 2014.
[5] Javier joined the All-Star game starting lineup when Pittsburgh second baseman Bill Mazeroski pulled out with an injury. In 2016, fans selected an all-Cubs starting infield.
[6] Veeck, *The Hustler's Handbook.*
[7] *Brooklyn Daily Eagle*, May 2, 1950.
[8] *New York Times*, August 1, 2004.
[9] He got the nickname "Bing" from an aunt because "I made a lot of noise throwing things around as a kid, and my aunt said I sounded like a real binger." Basketball, not baseball, was his favorite sport. "I was better in basketball than in baseball." *The Sporting News*, November 20, 1957.
[10] *The Sporting News*, June 2, 1962. Devine also shared some Rickey traits. "Like First Boss Rickey, Bing Pro at Double Talk," read one headline in the June 2 issue of the St. Louis publication. He could also be absent-minded, losing several pairs of sunglasses over the years. He once had three pairs returned to him by three different general managers in the same week.
[11] Devine, Bing with Tom Wheatley. *The Memories of Bing Devine: Stealing Lou Brock and Other Winning Moves by a Master GM.* Sports Publishing L.L.C. 2004.
[12] Both the Browns and Cardinals played their first night game at Sportsman's Park in 1940. The Browns played the Cleveland Indians on May 24. The Cardinals played the Brooklyn Dodgers on June 4. According to Devine, the official tally for the Cardinals first night game was less than the Browns so Breadon had it adjusted upwards to exceed it. When Devine showed the figure to Roy Stockton, the *Post-Dispatch* columnist voiced skepticism. The Cardinals adjusted the figure again, less than the attendance for the Browns, but more than what came through the turnstiles. The Browns attendance is officially recorded at 24,827; the Cardinals at 23,500.
[13] Keane arrived as the third- base coach for the Cardinals four years after Devine. Prior to 1959, Keane had spent twenty-eight years in the Cardinals organization as a player or manager. He became the Cardinals manager in 1961, replacing Solly Hemus. Born in south St. Louis, Keane played shortstop and was signed by the Cardinals in 1930. His playing career ended after suffering a double skull-fracture. *St. Louis Post-Dispatch*, May 19, 1959.
[14] Halberstam, David. *October 1964.* Villard Books. 1994.
[15] *The Sporting News*, November 20, 1957.
[16] Halberstam, *October 1964.*
[17] *The Sporting News*, January 15, 1958.
[18] The Cardinals called it a "large" bonus with one club official telling the *Post-Dispatch* "it wouldn't be far wrong to put 'large' near the $50,000 class." *St. Louis Post-Dispatch*, June 12, 1958. Bob Broeg later wrote that it was a "whopping $65,000 bonus." Broeg, *Memories of a Hall of Fame Sportswriter.*
[19] Jacobson, Steve. *Carrying Jackie's Torch: The Players Who Integrated Baseball – And America.* Lawrence Hill Books. 2007.

---

[20] "Tim McCarver," from *We Played the Game: 65 Players Remember Baseball's Greatest Era 1947-1964.* Edited by Danny Peary. Hyperion. 1994.
[21] Brock, Lou & Schulze, Franz. *Stealing Is My Game.* Prentice-Hall, Inc. 1976.
[22] Gibson, Bob with Lonnie Wheeler. *Stranger to the Game: The Autobiography of Bob Gibson.* Penguin Group. 1994.
[23] Ibid.
[24] Ibid. The four additional players who did broadcasting work were Brock, Flood, Gibson, and Groat. Ken Boyer (Cardinals), Roger Craig (Giants) and Joe Morgan (Red Sox) became managers. Charlie James, Dal Maxvill and Ron Taylor were electrical engineers. Maxvill later became the Cardinals general manager.
[25] Caray told the story more than once of spending the night in a Memphis hotel and getting a phone call from Presley. When Elvis identified himself, Caray didn't believe him, so Presley soon arrived at the hotel in a Cadillac (Caray was in Memphis at the time for a St. Louis Hawks basketball game. The Hawks played multiple games in Memphis during the mid-1960s). The two men spent hours at Graceland, Presley's home, "eating ribs and drinking Budweiser and shooting the bull until the wee hours. I'll never forget that phone call," Caray said. *Chicago Tribune,* May 5, 2005. Also see *St. Louis Post-Dispatch*, February 28, 1998. Growing up, Costas would get his dad's keys and listen to Cardinals games on the car radio. "On a real clear night, even from 1,000 miles away in Long Island, I could get Harry and Jack [Buck]," Costas recalled. "These games were unbelievably exciting."
[26] *St. Louis Post-Dispatch*, February 19, 1998.
[27] Dickson, Paul. *Leo Durocher: Baseball's Prodigal Son.* Bloomsbury USA. 2017. "When a man says to me, 'Do we have a deal,' and I answer, 'We have a deal,' and we shake hands on it, what does that mean?" said Durocher. Columnist Bob Burnes wrote that both Dodgers G.M. Buzzie Bavasi and team president Walter O'Malley had confirmed during the World Series that Durocher had reached an agreement to manage the Cardinals in 1965. *St. Louis Globe-Democrat,* October 17, 1964. Busch was reportedly set to pull the trigger in August but wanted to get permission from Walter O'Malley The Dodgers owner was out of the country on an African safari. Zminda, Don. *The Legendary Harry Caray: Baseball's Greatest Salesman.* Rowman & Littlefield. 2019. Durocher claimed to have known Busch since his playing days with the Cardinals in the 1930s through his membership in the "Bastard Club, a very small and exclusive club with a membership consisting of perhaps twenty-five of the most distinguished businessmen and bankers in the city and...well, me." The sole function of the Bastard Club was to have a weekly rotating dinner where one member picked up the tab for the group. When Durocher returned to Caray's car after meeting with Busch, "Harry was simply overjoyed when I told him what had happened." Durocher, Leo with Ed Linn. *Nice Guys Finish Last.* Simon & Schuster. 1975.
[28] Fedo, Michael. *One Shining Season*. Pharos Books. 1991.
[29] Ibid.
[30] Camden, New Jersey *Courier-Post*, October 8, 1964.
[31] *St. Louis Post-Dispatch*, September 8, 1964.

---

[32] Many on the team suspected trainer Bob Bauman to be the source of the notes. Bauman later confessed that "Fifi" was actually a male physician from Venice, Florida. Gibson, *Stranger to the Game.*
[33] "Tim McCarver," from *We Played The Game*.
[34] Hutchinson was in poor health. A heavy smoker, he died from lung cancer at the age of forty-five in November of 1964.
[35] *St. Louis Post-Dispatch*, January 29, 1989.
[36] *St. Louis Globe-Democrat*, October 23, 1964.
[37] Dickson, *Leo Durocher.*
[38] *St. Louis Post-Dispatch*, August 29, 1975.
[39] St. Louis Globe-Democrat, October 21, 1964.
[40] Veeck, *The Hustler's Handbook.*
[41] Richman played minor league baseball for the St. Louis Browns.
[42] *St. Louis Post-Dispatch*, December 21, 1964. Later, Groat said of Keane that "he was the only manager – or coach – I had any problems with in my career. We just differed on how the game should be played." "Dick Groat," from *We Played The Game.*

The Ones Who Got Away

He was destined to wear the Birds on the Bat. The Cardinals celebrated their first World Series title the year he was born. He grew up on Elizabeth Avenue, in the Italian section of St. Louis known as the Hill. His father was a bricklayer who helped build the St. Louis Arena. As a teenager, he became friends with Butch Yatkeman, the Cardinals equipment manager. In exchange for bringing him homemade wine, Yatkeman would let the boy and a friend take batting practice at Sportsman's Park.

As a left-handed-hitting catcher, he caught the attention of major league scouts. Growing up in the city and taking regular swings in their home ballpark, the young prospect was well known to the local team. At the age of 16, he signed a contract with the club. That is how Joe Garagiola became a St. Louis Cardinal.

Garagiola's boyhood friend was Yogi Berra. Born nine months earlier than Garagiola (in May of 1925, just a few weeks before Branch Rickey was fired as Cardinals manager and replaced by Rogers Hornsby), Berra also grew up on the Hill. The address of the family home was 5447 Elizabeth Avenue. Directly across the street, at 5446 Elizabeth, were the Garagiolas. Like Joe's dad, Yogi's father was a bricklayer who helped build the St. Louis Arena. Joe and Yogi would take batting practice together at Sportsman's Park. The homemade wine – "Dago Red" – came from Yogi's father. Like Garagiola, Berra caught and hit from the left side of the plate.

The parallel tracks continued even after they became professionals. Both Joe and Yogi worked at Sears and Roebuck in St. Louis after their first seasons in the big leagues. Each was best man at the other's wedding. Residents of the Hill flocked to Sportsman's Park to pay tribute to both. Garagiola received his night of honor in 1946, Berra in 1947.[1] Garagiola and the Cardinals won the World Series in Joe's rookie season. Yogi celebrated his first title the following year.

The stories of their early lives are almost identical, except for one important detail. Garagiola's audition for the Cardinals impressed Branch Rickey. Berra's tryout did not. Garagiola signed for $500. Berra wanted the same. Rickey offered half that much and no more. The Cardinals front office executive became the first baseball man to discover just how tough a negotiator Berra could be. He wouldn't be the last. Yogi refused the offer from the Cardinals and eventually signed with the Yankees. Berra never forgot the slight. "I was never supposed to be more than a Triple-A player," he wrote in his 2003 book *Ten Rings*. "At least that's what Branch Rickey said." Over $250, the Cardinals lost their chance at one of the greatest catchers in major league history.

*****

There was a third player of note who auditioned for Rickey on that fateful day. Red Schoendienst grew up in Germantown, Illinois, just across the Mississippi River from St. Louis. Born in 1923, one of the key factors in Schoendienst's career can be traced to events in the fall of 1926.

Just a few weeks after Grover Cleveland Alexander preserved a Game 7 Cardinals victory at Yankee Stadium, "Foulproof" Taylor was making a name for himself in New York. Born James Philip Leo Taylor, the Englishman had emigrated to America in the early twentieth century. Standing five feet six inches tall and weighing 125 pounds, he first drew international headlines in 1918 when he set a world record in a sack race. Spalding was so impressed by the ninth of a mile sprint at the Calgary rodeo, the sporting goods manufacturer began to produce Taylor's official sack-racing sack.[2]

Eight years later, Taylor was a member of the Metropolitan Opera chorus. On the night of November 18, 1926, he appeared as a second tenor in the American debut of Puccini's *Turandot*. While walking offstage after the first act, a spear-carrier accidentally kneed him in the groin. "I went from second tenor to baritone to boy soprano with the yelp I let out when he gave me the knee," Taylor told *St. Louis Globe-Democrat* columnist Bob Burnes in 1961.[3] The accident sparked an idea. The next night, Taylor showed up at the Met with a protective cup fashioned out of aluminum and rubber cigars. He found the offending performer from the previous evening and uttered the phrase that soon became a trademark line. "Kick me," he instructed the spear-carrier. When the spear-carrier complied and Taylor survived the incident without injury, he became an evangelist for the device. "He knocked me on my ear," Foulproof recalled, "but he didn't hurt me." Although protective cups had been around in some form for a decade or more (Claude Berry is believed to be the first baseball player to wear one in 1915 for the Federal League Pittsburgh Rebels), Taylor soon found a wider audience for his contraption.

Boxing had long been plagued by below-the-belt fouls. While an injured boxer reeling from a punch to the groin was an issue for the sport, the bigger problem involved the reaction of its fans. A boxing match ended by a below-the-belt punch meant all bets were off. Gamblers hated it.

"The prohibition gangsters sat at ringside and had thousands of dollars going," Foulproof told Burnes. "If their boy was losing, they'd just yell to him to foul the other guy. He wouldn't even feint it, he'd just sock the other guy. Down he'd go, moaning, and the fight would be off. So would the bets. All bets were canceled in the event of a foul."

Spotting an opportunity, Taylor lobbied for change. He began to wear the cup wherever boxers or boxing officials gathered; local gyms, at prizefights, even the offices of boxing regulators. "Kick me here," the request came from Taylor, a man *The New York Times* would later describe as having a "Don King-like white thatched frightwig hairdo."[4]

His big break came in June of 1930 at the heavyweight title fight in Yankee Stadium between Max Schmeling and Jack Sharkey. In the fourth round, Schmeling collapsed from a low blow. The fight was over. Judges awarded Schmeling the title by foul. Three weeks later, the New York State Athletic Commission made cups mandatory. Five years later, when Joe Louis knocked out Primo Carnera at Yankee Stadium, both boxers wore what Taylor called his "Foulproof Cup."[5]

Baseball, always slow to change, didn't make cups mandatory but thanks to Taylor and the approach taken by boxing, attitudes about them gradually evolved. As a player for the Gashouse Gang teams of the 1930s, Pepper Martin never wore a cup. "Pepper would play with nothing under his uniform," remembered Enos Slaughter. "No jock strap, no sweat socks, nothing." A decade later, as a manager in the Cardinals minor league system, Martin had changed his mind.

In 1943, Schoendienst received the call to join Martin's Rochester Red Wings, the Cardinals Triple-A team in the International League. Not long after he joined the club, Martin spotted him dressing before a game and wanted to know if Schoendienst wore a cup. When Red told him he didn't, Martin insisted he wear one. "If you're going to play the infield you're going to need it or you're going to get hurt," Martin told him. Schoendienst complied with the request and wore one that night against Newark, the Yankees top farm club. When a Newark player hit a hard smash toward second base, the ball hit off the edge of the grass and careened directly into Schoendienst's groin. The impact of the baseball shattered his cup in half. Red's major league career was almost over before it began. "That was the first day I ever wore a cup, and it was a lifesaver," he recalled decades later.[6]

The Germantown native had signed with the Cardinals after answering the call for a tryout camp. Three hundred ninety-eight players showed up, including Schoendienst, who hitchhiked from Illinois on a Pevely Dairy truck. Later in the week, Rickey singled out three players for an additional audition. Joining Red in Rickey's black Lincoln on the way to Forest Park were the two celebrated players from the Hill. "I remember two things about that experience," said Schoendienst, "that he [Rickey] was a terrible driver and throwing batting practice to Garagiola and Berra."[7]

Red hitchhiked home with no contract but the Illinois teenager made an impression on a scout who had seen him earlier in the week. Summoned back to Sportsman's Park, Red and the Cardinals made a deal. Schoendienst received a bonus of "a ham sandwich and a glass of milk." He received $90 a month to play for the Union City, Tennessee farm team in the Class D Kitty League. Garagiola impressed Rickey the most. Lured by the $500 signing bonus, Garagiola agreed to terms with the Cardinals and reported to their minor league team in Springfield, Missouri. Berra held out for the same amount his childhood friend had received. Rickey's refusal set baseball history on a different path. "It was the most colossally shortsighted blunder ever made by a baseball executive, surpassing even Boston Red Sox owner Harry Frazee's dealing Babe Ruth to the Yankees in 1920," wrote biographer Allen Barra.

*****

Like George Herman Ruth, Lawrence Peter Berra was better known by his nickname. Like the Babe, Yogi helped define an era of Yankee dominance. Both players extended their popularity and fattened their wallets with numerous endorsement deals. Image makers and marketers took advantage of the popularity of both men with deals that neither approved. The *Baby Ruth* candy bar was widely seen as cashing in on the popularity of the Babe, despite the Curtiss Candy Company's insistence that the inspiration behind the product was the daughter of President Grover Cleveland. When Hanna-Barbera debuted the *Yogi Bear* television show, Berra reportedly considered suing the animator. "Television is big enough for both me and Yogi Bear," he said in 1963. "I was going to sue the Yogi Bear program for using my name until somebody reminded me Yogi isn't my real name – it's Lawrence."[8]

Ruth made his last appearance at Yankee Stadium on June 13, 1948 to have his jersey retired. Berra homered that Sunday afternoon off Cleveland Indian pitcher Bob Feller. The night Ruth died, the Yankees played an exhibition game. Before it began, players participated in a home-run hitting contest. Berra won it. Ruth patterned his batting stance after Brother Matthias at his Baltimore reform school. Berra mimicked Cardinals outfielder Joe "Ducky" Medwick.

Both Ducky and Yogi were considered great bad ball hitters. "Medwick used to hit pitches over his head or near his toes and hit to all fields," Berra recalled. "He didn't make hitting into some science. I kind of used the same theory: If I could see it good, I could hit it good."[9] The Yankees would later hire Medwick to help teach Berra how to play the outfield.

Growing up, Berra would sell newspapers at the corner of Southwest and Kingshighway in St. Louis. Medwick was a favorite client. The Cardinals outfielder would give Berra a nickel for a three-cent newspaper and tell him to keep the change. "Joe Medwick was my idol and my favorite player too," Berra remembered. "I used to worship the ballplayers," he said of the Cardinals of that era. Medwick teammates and fellow outfielders Terry Moore and Enos Slaughter would occasionally show up at Sherman Park to give tips to Berra and other St. Louis youth. As members of the Knothole Gang, Berra and best friend Garagiola would watch Cardinals game from the outfield seats at Sportsman's Park. "We were at our shrine. Our Vatican," Garagiola recalled. "If the Cardinals won, it was almost a perfect day."[10]

Berra's connection to the team extends to his nickname (according to one of *many* versions of the story). Gordon Maguire was a scout for the Cardinals. His son, Jack Maguire was a childhood friend of Berra's. In his early teens, Berra had a different nickname – "Lawdie" – because his Italian mother couldn't pronounce Lawrence. At a movie theater in St. Louis, Lawdie, Maguire, and some other friends watched a feature on a cross-legged Indian yogi. "You know, you look just like a yogi," Maguire told him afterward. "I'm going to call you Yogi." The nickname stuck.[11]

After eighth grade, Berra knew he loved playing baseball and hated going to school. "I was no scholar and never saw much sense in going to school. I was pretty disinterested, played a lot of hooky, and generally frustrated my teachers. When anybody asked me how I liked school, I'd say 'Closed.'"

After a meeting with a priest, the family decided Yogi would be better off working. His formal education ended and he began a series of jobs. By the time he was sixteen, Berra was working as a tack puller at a shoe factory and playing American Legion baseball. His teams made it to the semifinals of the National American Legion Tournament two straight years.

Sometime in this period, an audition with the Cardinals occurred. Decades after the Rickey tryout, the basic facts of that day are still in dispute. Berra told author Dave Kaplan the tryout occurred in 1942.[12] Allen Barra later wrote that both Yogi and Joe believed it took place in 1941.[13] Conspiracy theorists have had a field day with the fact that Rickey, considered the game's shrewdest talent evaluator of his era, didn't sign Berra when he was with the Cardinals, but later tried to get Yogi to report to a Dodgers training camp shortly after he joined the Brooklyn front office.

Adding to the confusion, Berra told conflicting stories over the years about Rickey's intent. He originally dismissed the idea but later changed his mind. "Looking back, I think Rickey knew he was a lame duck with the Cardinals," he recalled for *Ten Rings.* "He knew he was going to the Dodgers and maybe was trying to hide me." Berra claimed a telegram from Rickey arrived in November 1942 instructing him to report to a training camp outside New York City the following spring. By that time, Yogi had already signed with the Yankees.

Was hiding Berra really Rickey's goal? Regardless of whether the audition took place in the summer of 1941 or the spring of 1942, Rickey had no idea he would wind up in Brooklyn. The man he replaced, Larry MacPhail, didn't resign from the Dodgers until September of 1942. "I tend to disbelieve the story of Rickey trying to 'hide' Yogi for the Dodgers," said Rickey biographer Murray Polner. "Rickey was a notorious tightwad, but painfully honest." What then explains Rickey's telegram in the fall of that year? In 1961, Berra offered a more innocent explanation for the invitation to join the Dodgers organization in the middle of World War II. "I think it's just that it was getting harder to get players as the war went along, and he remembered me and figured out it would be worth a few hundred dollars to see if I could help him."

Neither the Cardinals nor the Dodgers ever found out if Yogi could help. Neither did the Browns. The other St. Louis team also passed on Berra after the Cardinals failed to sign him.[14]

In October of 1942, in Rickey's last month running the St. Louis front office, the Cardinals defeated the Yankees in the World Series in five games. The final game took place in the Bronx on October 5. With the series concluded, one of the coaches on the

Yankees staff returned to his St. Louis home. Johnny Schulte soon arrived at the Berra house on Elizabeth Avenue.

Schulte and the Yankees had gotten wind of Berra's exploits from his American Legion post manager. Leo Browne was an oil company executive and former minor league umpire. "His form is all wrong and his coaches can't make him wait at the plate," Browne once said of Berra, "but he's the best hitter I've ever seen." This was no idle chatter. Berra's American Legion teammates included childhood friends Jack Maguire (two years in the big leagues), Bobby Hofman (seven-year MLB career), and pitcher Jim Goodwin, who appeared briefly with the Chicago White Sox in 1948. Roy Sievers, the 1949 American League Rookie of the Year for the St. Louis Browns, played for Browne in 1943. In addition to the future big leaguers, Berra's teammates included Russ Steger, a 1947 All-American fullback at Illinois. (Another Berra childhood friend, Benny Pucci, played professional football.)

The St. Louis area was teeming with talent by the early 1940s with players born right around the time the Cardinals celebrated their first World Series title. Berra, Garagiola, Goodwin, Hofman, Maguire, and Sievers were all born from 1925 to 1927. So too were shortstop Bill Jennings (1925), who played 64 games for the Browns in 1951, and outfielder Don Mueller (1927), who enjoyed a twelve-year career with the Giants and White Sox. Jennings played at Southwest High School in St. Louis while Mueller starred at CBC. Goodwin, Hofman, Maguire, and Sievers all played at Beaumont High School. The roster of successful Beaumont alums also featured Bob Wiesler (1930), who pitched six years in the big leagues for the New York Yankees and Washington Senators, and a scrappy second baseman named Earl Weaver, born the same year. Signed by the Cardinals out of high school, Weaver never made it to the major leagues as a player (Schoendienst was blocking his path), but he did go on to a Hall of Fame career as a manager for the Baltimore Orioles.[15] Also sitting in the stands at Sportsman's Park in the heyday of Rickey's Redbirds were other future major league managers all born in the St. Louis area in the 1920s and early 1930s: Dave Garcia, Dick Sisler, Hank Bauer, Vern Rapp, Dick Williams, and Whitey Herzog. Berra and Schoendienst had successful managerial runs following their Hall of Fame playing careers. In addition to Weaver, Herzog and Williams are honored in Cooperstown for their performances from the dugout. "I haven't counted," Bill James once noted, "but I'm fairly sure that more major league managers were born in St. Louis than in any other city."

These were Berra's contemporaries – athletes who would go on to perform at baseball's highest level. But even at a young age, those around him had no doubt who stood head and shoulders above the rest. "I wasn't even the best player on my block," Garagiola would tell writers in later years. That honor belonged to the jock once described by Larry MacPhail as having "a homely face, no neck, and the build of a sawed-off shotgun." With the help of another Missouri native, a talented St. Louis teenager was about to become the property of the New York Yankees.

*****

Browne endorsed Berra in a letter sent to George Weiss, the man responsible for the Yankees farm system. Yogi was ready to sign, Browne told him, if he got his five hundred dollar signing bonus. Weiss dispatched Yankees coach Schulte, a Fredericktown, Missouri native and former left-handed hitting catcher who played for both the Browns and Cardinals in a brief major league career, to the Berra household.

As a player, Schulte's best year came in 1927 for the Cardinals. The journeyman catcher reached career highs in home runs, RBI and batting average for the defending World Series champions. He got the opportunity because the Cardinals catcher-manager, Bob O'Farrell, was injured much of the season. Two years later, he became Rogers Hornsby's teammate on a Chicago Cubs team that won a National League pennant. He made an impression on Cubs manager Joe McCarthy, who later hired Schulte as a coach when he moved east to direct the Yankees.

As the Yankees bullpen coach and part-time scout, Schulte's nickname was "Eagle Eye." He's one of the reasons why Phil Rizzuto and Whitey Ford signed with New York. Both the Dodgers and Giants had passed on Rizzuto and the Yankees were ready to do the same. Schulte liked him and asked scout Paul Krichell how much a train ticket would cost to ship Rizzuto to a minor league team in Virginia. "Twenty bucks," the scout told Schulte, "and he ain't worth it."

"Okay," Schulte replied. "Then I'll pay the twenty dollars myself."[16] Rizzuto was a Yankee. The Hall of Fame shortstop spent thirteen seasons in the major leagues, all with New York.

A decade later, a first baseman had auditioned for the Yankees with less than impressive results. But he told Schulte he also pitched. "Show me," the Missouri native responded.[17] Edward "Whitey" Ford would go on to win 236 games in his Hall of Fame career. Like Rizzuto, he was a lifelong Yankee.

Sandwiched in between those two signings, a decade apart, Schulte was in St. Louis in the summer of 1942 for a series at Sportsman's Park between the Browns and Yankees. After one of the games, he happened to catch an American Legion contest at Fairground Park and came away impressed with one of the players. "The kid was awkward, but, damn, he could hit," he recalled years later regarding the first time he ever saw Berra play.

A few months later, Schulte arrived at the Berra home on Elizabeth Avenue with a Yankees contract and the promise of a $500 signing bonus. Yogi signed a contract that paid him $90 a month in 1943. Buried in the fine print of the contract was a stipulation that the bonus would only be paid out if Berra played the entire season. Yogi eventually got his elusive $500 but he had to wait another year.

Berra's minor league career was brief. He played the 1943 season for the Yankees farm club in Norfolk, Virginia. At the end of the season, he joined the Navy. As a volunteer on a landing craft support vessel, Berra manned a machine gun and loaded a rocket launcher on D-Day. His vessel was lowered into the water early in the morning on June 6, 1944. At Omaha Beach, he remembered, "we were closer than the hitter is to the left-field screen at Fenway Park." Later in southern France, he received a Purple Heart after getting wounded by a German machine gun at Marseilles. He also spent time in Italy and northern Africa.

Returning stateside at the end of World War II, Berra played for a service team in New London, Connecticut. Playing an exhibition game against the New York Giants, he drew comparisons to another former St. Louis Cardinal. "That fluid swing reminded me of Johnny Mize," said Mel Ott, the Giants slugger, who also doubled as the team manager in the 1940s. Ott was so impressed he offered the Yankees $50,000 for Berra. The Yankees refused the overture.[18]

Discharged from the Navy in May of 1946, the club sent Berra to their minor league team in Newark. His manager was George Selkirk, the man who replaced Ruth in right field for the Yankees. Berra played outfield and catcher for Selkirk, but it was his hitting that impressed most observers. "Believe me," wrote former *Kansas City Journal* sports editor Parke Carroll in a letter to *Post-Dispatch* columnist John Wray, "he is the best hitter in the International League."[19] At the end of the regular season, Berra's Newark team faced off against Jackie Robinson's Montreal club in the minor league playoffs. When Newark lost, Berra received the call to join the major league club. He made his Yankees debut on September 22, 1946, in the first game of a doubleheader against the Philadelphia Athletics. After being retired his first time at the plate, Berra hit a home run in his next at-bat, a two-run shot that proved to be the difference in a 4-3 New York win. The 1946 Yankees finished the season in third place, seventeen games behind the American League champion Boston Red Sox. Back in St. Louis, Berra watched Game 7 of the World Series from the stands of Sportsman's Park. With longtime friend Garagiola starting behind the plate and batting sixth, the Cardinals defeated the Red Sox to win the game and the title.

Berra didn't get many opportunities to just be an observer during the World Series. Over the next seventeen seasons of his Yankees career, Yogi would be on the field for fourteen Fall Classics. Only in 1948, 1954, and 1959 did Berra and the Yankees fail to play October baseball. In winning fourteen pennants and ten World Series rings, Berra also claimed three American League MVP awards along the way: in 1951, 1954, and 1955. After Mickey Mantle won the MVP award following his 1956 Triple Crown campaign, the Yankees paid him $60,000 the next year. He wasn't the highest-paid player on the team. Berra received a salary of $65,000 for 1957, the highest of any player in the American League.

As his fame and fortune multiplied, so did his connections to his St. Louis roots. Playing the Browns in St. Louis, Berra would take his Yankees teammates to the family home on Elizabeth Avenue for Sunday dinner. After the Browns left town, some of Berra's teammates jokingly blamed their failure to win the 1954 pennant on the lack of homecooked St. Louis meals. In 1956, fresh off catching Don Larsen's perfect game in the World Series, residents of the Hill honored him as "one of the three best-known Italians in the world – Columbia, Marconi, and Yogi Berra."[20]

He met his wife in St. Louis. Carmen Short was a waitress at Biggie's Steak House (Stan Musial & Biggie's came later) when Berra met her one day in the offseason early in his career. He asked her out but she initially rebuffed him, confusing him with Cardinals outfielder Terry Moore, a married man. Berra couldn't convince her otherwise. Her boss, Biggie Garagnani, had to intervene. "Biggie said I wasn't that good," Berra recalled.

The courtship escalated quickly. The night before the 1948 All-Star Game in St. Louis, he proposed to her at a family dinner, dropping the ring on her plate without saying a word. They were married in January of 1949 at St. Ambrose Catholic Church on the Hill. Former Cardinals farmhand Pete Reiser and Berra childhood hero Medwick attended the ceremony. Cardinals catcher, best friend, and offseason bowling partner Garagiola served as his best man. The duo would switch roles the following offseason when Garagiola married.

Garagiola wasn't the only Cardinal Berra spent time with. The Yankee catcher was an occasional golf partner of Stan Musial at Sunset Country Club in St. Louis. Even after Berra left his hometown for New Jersey in the offseason and the Yankees no longer traveled to St. Louis, the two would see each other at spring training in St. Petersburg and occasionally in New York when games against the Giants or Dodgers happened to overlap with a Yankee homestand. The three-time American League MVP was even linked to the three-time National League MVP in a trade rumor near the end of their careers. "Musial to Yanks – Berra a Redbird," read a headline in *The Sporting News* in August of 1959. J.G. Taylor Spink incorrectly predicted the trade would be the first deal of the offseason. Both men retired after the 1963 season with the franchise they started with.

When he wasn't bowling with Garagiola or golfing with Musial, Berra would attend area hockey and college basketball games, following St. Louis University Billikens basketball closely. At the end of the 1949 season, the Yankees celebrated another World Series title, the second of the Berra era. At a victory dinner in the ballroom of a New York City hotel, Berra spotted a St. Louis friend and went over to ask him a question. He had read a story in the paper that day about a blowout loss suffered by his favorite college basketball team. "So," Berra wanted to know, "what in the world was the matter with them Billikens?"[21]

By the mid-1950s, Berra had leveraged his talents and broad appeal to become the highest-paid catcher in baseball and a popular Madison Avenue pitchman. He endorsed Rheingold beer, Camel cigarettes, and Mennen shaving cream. He owned bowling alleys (one with teammate Rizzuto) and became a vice-president for the Yoo-Hoo chocolate-flavored drink. He began making more money off the field than on it. According to biographer Carlo Devito, Berra would retire as the most successful and financially secure of any of the Yankees of his era. Instead of taking a salary at Yoo-Hoo, he took stock in the company and did endorsements for the product. "Is Yoo-Hoo hyphenated?" a woman once asked him. "No ma'am," Yogi replied, "it's not even carbonated."

Sayings like that helped Berra become one of the most widely quoted athletes in history. The memorable and unintentionally humorous phrases became known as "Yogi-isms." St. Louis served as the inspiration for a few of them. Early in his career, he worked in the offseason as head greeter at Ruggeri's. "Nobody goes there anymore, it's too crowded," he later said of the Italian restaurant on the Hill when discussing dining plans with Garagiola and Musial. At Yogi Berra Night at Sportsman's Park, the Yankees catcher had taken time to write out a speech that included the line, "I want to thank everyone for making this night possible." But that evening, it came out a bit differently. "I want to thank everyone for making this night *necessary*," Berra told the hometown crowd.

Even when Berra said what he meant, he still drew laughs. At a baseball banquet in St. Louis shortly after getting married, Cardinals broadcaster Harry Caray asked him the name of his new bride. "Carmen Short," Berra replied. "That's not an Italian name," Caray responded. "How come you didn't marry one of those nice Italian girls on the Hill?"

"They had their chance," said Berra, as laughter erupted from the audience. Back at his seat, he asked Garagiola if he had said something wrong. "No Yogi," he replied. "You said just the right thing."[22]

Coming off a season in which he tied his career-high in home runs and the Yankees won another World Series title, Berra arrived in St. Louis in the summer of 1957 to play in another All-Star Game. He was one of three native St. Louisans to take part in the affair. One of them was former Rookie of the Year Sievers, who had left the St. Louis Browns for the Washington Senators. The other was a current Berra teammate on the Yankees. Like Yogi, he played catcher and outfield. Also, like Berra, he could have, *should* have been a St. Louis Cardinal.

*****

When Rickey's Brooklyn Dodgers signed Jackie Robinson to a minor league contract in October of 1945, a St. Louis teenager was among those who reacted to the news. "I was sixteen and already dreaming of a baseball career, but not in organized ball," Elston Howard remembered. The Robinson signing opened his eyes to what was possible for young black players. "I felt like dancing all over the floor. The path was opening up. Maybe I could become a major league player."[23]

The signing had just as big an impact at Howard's high school, Vashon. It didn't have a baseball team in the spring of 1946, but it fielded a squad the following season, Howard's junior year. The spring of 1947 also marked Robinson's debut with the Dodgers, a seminal moment that carried influence far beyond the baseball field. "Breaking the color barrier was a big thing in St. Louis. He was a role model like no other in black America. Teachers at our school constantly talked about him in our classrooms. If you showed up late for class, the teacher would say, 'Jackie Robinson wouldn't be late.' If you misbehaved, the teacher would say, 'Jackie Robinson wouldn't act like that.'

And we believed every word," remembered former Vashon student and Howard's wife, Arlene.[24]

Arlene and Elston both grew up on Compton Hill, a black neighborhood on the south side of St. Louis, where residents of an earlier era were more likely to follow the exploits of Cool Papa Bell and the St. Louis Stars of the Negro National League than the Browns or Cardinals. Howard's mother arrived in the city in 1928, pregnant and unmarried. The father of the baby, Travis Howard, was an educator and a graduate of the Tuskegee Institute. He once lived next door to George Washington Carver. The couple had met in southeast Missouri, where Emmaline Webb taught at a school in Sikeston. According to Arlene Howard, Elston's father refused to accept responsibility when Emmaline became pregnant and refused to marry her. In another version of the story, Emmaline and Travis married but divorced when Elston was six years old.[25] In any event, Travis Howard had little to no relationship with his son until Elston became an adult.

By the time he was a teenager, Howard was known as "Foots." His speed was on display in track as he ran the quarter-mile. So was his strength. He set a Vashon High School record in the shot put. In basketball, he became one of the first high school players in the area to develop a jump shot. "Elston was the finest basketball player around at the time, and I still think basketball was his best sport," Howard's high school coach, Jodie Bailey, said in 1962. His football skills included an attribute that served him well as a major league catcher. "He had sure hands," remembered coach Don Salter. "On the football field, Elston, an end, did just about everything. He kicked off and punted and was the team's No. 1 target for passes as well as an outstanding defensive man."[26] With baseball added to the mix his junior year, Howard became a four-sport letterman at Vashon and had multiple offers to play college basketball and football.

He turned down those opportunities to focus on baseball. What he really wanted was to play for the St. Louis Cardinals when he graduated from high school in the spring of 1948. The franchise, which Sam Breadon had just recently sold to Robert Hannegan and Fred Saigh, elected not to pursue him.[27] "I would have liked to have played for the Cardinals, and I went to one of their four-day tryout camps," Howard recalled more than a decade later. "I did all right, and survived the cuts, and after the final day I was told the Cardinals would write to me. They never did."[28]

Rejected by the Cardinals, Howard signed with the Kansas City Monarchs, the same Negro League team where Jackie Robinson got his start in professional baseball. His roommate one season was another rising star dismissed by the Cardinals. "I don't think he is a major league prospect. He can't hit, he can't run, he has a pretty good arm but it's a scatter arm. I don't like him," read the Cardinals scouting report on future Hall of Fame player Ernie Banks.

Howard spent two years playing for legendary Monarchs player-manager Buck O'Neil. Signed by the Yankees in the summer of 1950, his minor league career, like Berra's, was cut short by war. Drafted into the army during the Korean War, Howard didn't play any professional baseball the next two years. He returned to Kansas City in

1953, this time playing for the Yankees top farm club. After a 1954 minor league season in Toronto in which he hit .331 and won the International League's most valuable player award, Howard could no longer be denied. He made his major-league debut with the Yankees on April 14, 1955. Eight years after Robinson broke the color barrier, Howard became the first black player in the history of the Yankees.

It wasn't easy. In spring training, he faced the same segregated living conditions in St. Petersburg endured by black Cardinal players of the era. Just as the team had done for decades, the Yankees finished their spring training by making a caravan of stops at southern minor league parks. That practice ended after 1955 as the Southern Association decided to end the tradition. The addition of Howard on the Yankees roster was the likely reason for it. Howard didn't have a roommate on road trips until 1957 when Harry Simpson became the Yankees' second black player. In Baltimore, Chicago, and Kansas City his rookie season, he was told to find a separate "negro hotel" to spend the night. The pressure of being the first black player for the Yankees was immense. "You always felt you were on view, on stage. You had to be this perfect person," remembered Howard's wife, Arlene.

Playing mainly in the outfield his first season, Howard batted .290 with ten home runs and 43 RBI. Paid the league minimum of $6,000 his first year, the Yankees offered him a thousand dollar raise for the following season. At a YMCA dinner in St. Louis, he ran into Musial who told him not to take it; a better offer would be coming. When a second contract for $10,000 arrived, Howard signed. On the way to spring training, he had plans to spend a night at the home of Dr. Martin Luther King Jr. in Birmingham, Alabama. When he called to confirm plans, Dr. King told him his home had just been fire-bombed. Howard made other arrangements.

Howard spent the first six years of his career playing for legendary Yankees manager Casey Stengel. (Stengel's first name was Charles. His nickname derived from his hometown of Kansas City, Missouri.) In spring training of 1955, Stengel wasn't sure exactly what to make of Howard's versatility. "Howard's a good boy," said Stengel. "But I can't make up my mind where he's best at."

With Berra entrenched behind the plate, it wasn't until 1960, Stengel's last year with the Yankees, that Howard caught the majority of games. By 1962, Howard was catching exclusively. A year later, he received the American League MVP award for a season in which he hit a career-high 28 home runs and was awarded the Gold Glove for his work behind the plate. "Elston was a very good hitter and the best defensive catcher I ever saw," said pitcher Pedro Ramos, who joined the Yankees near the end of the 1964 season.

Howard blossomed as a Yankee with the help of his teammates. Berra and Mantle were two of his biggest backers (both men were later pallbearers at his funeral). Mantle would stay on the bus with Howard when he was barred from entering Southern restaurants. As for the two St. Louis natives, "Elston liked and respected Yogi Berra so much," remembered Arlene Howard. "There was never any professional jealousy." The connection extended to the wives. "He and Carmen became very good friends of ours, and as the years went by, our families became close," Arlene later wrote. "Carmen and I would take turns picking up Yogi and Elston at the airport after road trips. Let me say this: Of all the Yankees wives, Carmen was the best dressed. I tried to keep up with her. We had a mutual admiration society."

The mutual admiration society extended to the husbands. Manager Berra, who caught his last game for the Yankees in 1963, leaned on Howard heavily in 1964. The Yankee catcher appeared in a career-high 150 games. He continued to consistently start behind the plate for New York through the 1966 season. Howard's trade to the Boston Red Sox in 1967 marked the end of a two-decade run where nearly every Yankees lineup featured a starting catcher from St. Louis.

As Cardinal players gathered in Busch Stadium for the first game of the 1964 World Series, they could look to the opposing dugout and see a manager and a catcher who could have been their longtime teammates. There was one other tantalizing possibility.

*****

When Mickey Mantle arrived in St. Louis in the summer of 1947, he was a sickly sixteen-year-old ballplayer. The previous fall, he had been kicked in the shin during football practice. The leg became swollen and an infection set in. Diagnosed with osteomyelitis – an infection of the bone – Mantle eventually recovered thanks to penicillin treatments. "When he got that penicillin in him, boy, his body shot out and the muscles in his arms jumped out," remembered childhood friend Bill Mosely.[29]

The Commerce, Oklahoma teenager had come to St. Louis to try out for the St. Louis Browns. He never saw the field. Since the audition took place before his physical transformation, the team took one look at him in uniform and sent him home. Over the next year, Mantle would put on forty pounds and shoot up four inches. "When he came back in 1948, he stood about 5'10" and weighed 180 pounds and could run like a deer," recalled teammate Bill Johnson.[30] The other St. Louis team – Mantle's favorite – took notice.

Mantle grew up idolizing Stan Musial. On an earlier trip to St. Louis with his father to see a Cardinals game, the duo happened to run into Musial in a hotel elevator. His father, Mutt, prevented his son from asking for an autograph. His mother, Lovell, loved to listen to Cardinals games on the radio. "During the day, when the kids were in school and her husband was workin' in the mines, she had the St. Louis Cardinals game on the radio, and when she was ironing or doing her housework, she was keepin' score of what every one of those guys did!" Mosely recalled.[31]

In 1948, the year before he graduated from high school, a physically stronger Mantle began to make an impression on area ball fields. He had joined a team in Baxter Springs, Kansas called the Whiz Kids and one night hit three home runs – two right-handed and one left-handed. Cardinals scout Runt Marr paid a visit to the family home. "Promise me this," Marr asked the Mantles. "Mickey won't sign with another club until you give me a chance to make an offer." For reasons never explained, the offer never came. "I'm still waiting to hear from Runt," Mantle said decades later.[32] (In 1951, Marr denied ever seeing Mantle play before he signed with the Yankees.)[33]

Enter Tom Greenwade. The Willard, Missouri native spent his entire life in his hometown. He had a promising minor-league career that was cut short by injuries. He then spent time in the private sector before returning to baseball. He worked for Bill DeWitt's St. Louis Browns as both a minor league manager and scout. His work for Branch Rickey's former protégé must have impressed the master himself. When Rickey left St. Louis for Brooklyn, he offered Greenwade a scouting position with the Dodgers. Rickey assigned Greenwade to shadow Jackie Robinson in the months before he signed with Brooklyn.[34] He later left the Dodgers to work for the Yankees and another Rickey protégé turned rival – Larry MacPhail. The Missouri native would spend the rest of his professional career working for the New York organization.

Like Marr, Greenwade had seen Mantle play in 1948. Unlike the Cardinals, though, Greenwade and the Yankees kept watching Mantle closely in the spring of 1949. The distance from his home in southwestern Missouri to the Mantle home in northeastern Oklahoma was less than 150 miles. He'd make the trip in a Cadillac he'd trade in every two years. On the day Mantle's high school class was to graduate, Greenwade asked the school if Mickey could skip the commencement exercises. The Whiz Kids had a game that night and Greenwade wanted to make the star attraction available. The school consented to Greenwade's request. The scout also had fears that another team was closing in. "He was worried about the Cardinals because he knew that Mickey and his dad were big Cardinals fans," recalled Bunch Greenwade, Tom's son.[35]

The Yankee scout watched Mantle hit two home runs that evening in a game in Coffeyville. Just as significant to Greenwade was who wasn't at the game that evening. "The Cardinals scout in the area, Runt Marr, had heard of the kid, and I was a little surprised when he didn't show up that [graduation] night." He made plans to see Mantle again. "I told Mickey's father, Mutt, that I'd be back and made him promise that no matter what anyone else offered not to sign until I got back and I could try to match it. I got back Sunday night and no one had come after Mickey, Runt Marr or anyone else."[36]

The game that Sunday evening was washed out by a thunderstorm. With rain falling, scout, player, and father hammered out an agreement inside Greenwade's Cadillac. Mantle signed with the Yankees for a bonus of $1,150. The apparent lack of interest by the Cardinals had seemingly sparked a crisis of confidence. "I didn't think anybody else wanted me," Mantle later confessed.

He made his Yankees debut in 1951 after spending just two seasons in the minor leagues, including one in Joplin, Missouri where he hit .383 and became known as the "Commerce Comet." An erratic-armed shortstop in the minor leagues, the Yankees converted him to the outfield. He won the first of three MVP awards in his triple-crown season of 1956, where he crushed 52 home runs with 130 RBI while batting .353. His 1964 campaign was the last great season of his career, driving in 111 runs while smashing 35 home runs. His on-base percentage of .423 topped the league.

"We would have seen a pretty fair St. Louis Cardinals outfield, come 1951 or 1952," wrote author Roger Kahn. "Stan Musial in left field, Enos Slaughter in right field, and Mickey Mantle in center. I suspect that outfield would have wrenched pennants from the Dodgers and the Giants."[37] Perhaps it would have. But the Cardinals could have been playing with both Mantle in the outfield *and* Berra behind the plate starting in 1951. What difference would that have made? The answer: Maybe not as much as you think.

The post-Rickey Dodgers were dominant over a longer period than the post-Rickey Cardinals. Rickey's former Brooklyn team won four pennants in six seasons from 1951 to 1956. In 1955, the Dodgers won their only World Series title in Brooklyn history. During that same six-year stretch, the Cardinals came within ten games of the NL pennant winner only once – in 1952.

Year	Brooklyn	Place	St. Louis	Place
1951	97-60	2nd	81-73	3rd
1952	96-57	1st	88-66	3rd
1953	105-49	1st	83-71	3rd*
1954	92-62	2nd	72-82	6th
1955	98-55	1st	68-86	7th
1956	93-61	1st	76-78	4th

*Cardinals and Phillies tied for third in 1953.

The 1952 Cardinals finished eight games back of the Dodgers. That year, St. Louis catcher Del Rice and outfielder Peanuts Lowrey combined for three wins above replacement (WAR). That same season, Berra and Mantle generated a WAR of 12.4. (A similar pattern played out in the seasons from 1957 to 1962 where the Cardinals finished double-digit games behind the pennant winner in all years but one. The 1957 Cardinals finished eight games back of the Milwaukee Braves, a season in which two St. Louis catchers and outfielder Del Ennis combined to net a WAR of zero. The trio of Berra, Howard, and Mantle combined to generate a WAR of 14.3.)

While it's conceivable to add one or two pennants to the Cardinals total, the real difference could have been in the American League. The 1954 Cleveland Indians won the pennant and finished second to the Yankees in every other season from 1951 to 1956. In the years where the Indians finished second, the difference in the standings was always less than the combined WAR of the Yankee trio.[38]

Year	Yankees	Indians	GB	Berra/Howard/Mantle WAR*
1951	98-56	93-61	5	6.8
1952	95-59	93-61	2	12.4
1953	99-52	92-62	8.5	10.8
1955	96-58	93-61	3	15.6
1956	97-57	88-66	9	17.1

*Only Berra and Mantle before 1955.

Even with two Hall-of-Fame players (later joined by a future MVP) in the lineup every day for St. Louis, the 1950s Cardinals would have likely barely made a dent in the legacy of the post-Rickey Dodgers (in fact, the moves had the potential to enhance it since Brooklyn won only one of four World Series against the Yankees during this time.) But over in the American League, we may recall the 1950s as the decade of the Cleveland Indians had Berra, Mantle, and Howard taken a different path.

Instead, the three players ended up in pinstripes because of two Missouri natives. One of them was Greenwade, the scout whose list of Yankee credits include Howard.[39] But Greenwade would forever be linked to Mantle, a player he first saw in action in a small Missouri town seventy miles west of Willard.

While Busch Stadium in St. Louis and Yankee Stadium in the Bronx would be the physical locations for the 1964 World Series, the beating heart of the battle could be traced to Alba, Missouri, population 336.[40]

---

[1] At Garagiola's night, he received "a 1946 coupe, two suits and six white shirts. His mother received a huge bouquet. His father was given a wristwatch." *Baseball Digest*, February 1947.

[2] Rushin, *The 34-Ton Bat.*

[3] *St. Louis Globe-Democrat*, August 29, 1961. Taylor had family in St. Louis. Diane Taylor wrote about "Uncle Foulproof" for *Living Las Vegas*. living-las-vegas.com/2010/11/the-man-who-saved-boxing/

[4] *New York Times*, March 1, 1987.

[5] Rushin, *The 34-Ton Bat*.

[6] Schoendienst, Red with Rob Rains. *Red: A Baseball Life.* Sports Publishing. 1998.

[7] Ibid.

[8] "Yogi Berra Suing Over Yogi Bear? Take It With a Grin of Salt." *The Hollywood Reporter*, September 23, 2015.

[9] Berra's lack of plate discipline was viewed as a handicap early in his career. "I like to pitch to hitters like that," an unnamed Cardinals pitcher told Roy Stockton during spring training

of 1947. "No doubt about his being a good hitter, but he'll swing at bad balls...And it's easier to pitch to a hitter like that." *St. Louis Post-Dispatch*, March 27, 1947.
[10] Garagiola, Joe. *Just Play Ball.* Northland Publishing. 2007.
[11] There are multiple versions of how Berra became known as Yogi. Berra biographer Carlo DeVito credits childhood friend Bobby Hofman with coming up with the nickname. Berra told both broadcaster Bod Costas and author Dave Kaplan he got the name after sitting cross-legged with his arms folded when he played American Legion baseball because the facilities lacked dugouts and benches. A 1949 *St. Louis Post-Dispatch* profile cites multiple potential sources. South Side Y.M.C.A. director Joe Causino claimed Berra got the nickname because nothing worried or upset him. American Legion manager Leo Browne remembers Berra wrestling with a teammate and spinning out of his grasp. "That boy spins like a yo-yo," Browne said. "You mean he spins like one of them yogis," someone replied. Cardinals scout Maguire gave him the nickname "because of his walk. Garagiola says he gave it to him because he looked like a yogi they both saw in a movie one day," wrote Dickson Terry. "As for Berra, he doesn't recall where the name came from, and cares less." *St. Louis Post-Dispatch*, July 3, 1949. Less than a year later, Berra credited childhood friend Jack Maguire. "Some of us went to a movie with a yogi in it and afterwards Jack began calling me Yogi. Now everybody uses it except my own family." *St. Louis Post-Dispatch,* April 26, 1950.
[12] "When the Cardinals held a local tryout in 1942, Joe and I were eager, real excited." Berra, Yogi with Dave Kaplan. *Ten Rings: My Championship Seasons*. HarperCollins. 2003.
[13] Author Jon Pessah wrote that the audition occurred in July of 1941. Pessah, Jon. *Yogi: A Life Behind the Mask*. Little, Brown & Company. 2020. In a September 24, 2015, article about Schoendienst, *Post-Dispatch* writer Rick Hummel mentions spring of 1942 as the date. An earlier profile mentions 1941. *St. Louis Post-Dispatch*, March 4, 1945. There was a "Red" Schoendienst who signed with the Cardinals in August of 1941, but Schoendienst's brother, Julius, also played minor league baseball for the Cardinals and was also called Red. The article mentions no other first name, but says Schoendienst signed after a tryout. *Breese, (Il) Journal*, August 7, 1941. While *Baseball Reference* doesn't list any 1941 statistics for Red Schoendienst, there is this newspaper account; "Red played in thirty-four games here in 1941 and showed promise of developing into a classy infielder. He hit but .234 in those 34 games and accounted for 20 runs." Johnson City (TN) *Press-Chronicle*, March 29, 1942. The article describes Schoendienst as the "holdover shortstop from 1941." Those numbers correspond to figures produced by Julius Schoendienst as a member of the Johnson City Cardinals in 1941. Julius signed with the Browns in 1940 but was in the Cardinals organization a year later. *Breese Journal*, August 15, 1940. Also see www.baseball-reference.com/register/player.fcgi?id=schoen001jul
[14] Some reports claim the Browns did not offer Berra a signing bonus. Others maintain the Browns, like the Cardinals, offered Yogi $250 but no more. Scout Lou Maguolo "talked himself hoarse" trying to convince Bill DeWitt Sr. of the Browns to offer Berra $500, according to one account. McDonald, James. *Lou Maguolo*. SABR.org biography project.

---

[15] Weaver's dad had a laundry service that did the work for the Cardinals and Browns. "From the time I was five until I entered high school, I used to ride into Sportsman's Park in one of our trucks," Weaver remembered. "My particular heroes, I guess were Medwick, Terry Moore, and – from the Browns – Harold Clift." As a member of the Knothole Gang, Weaver was in Sportsman's Park the day in 1942 when Dodgers outfielder Pete Reiser crashed into the wall. *Boston Globe,* July 30, 1968.
[16] *St. Louis Post-Dispatch*, July 2, 1978.
[17] Ibid.
[18] *Baseball Digest,* June 1949. "If the truth must be told," said MacPhail, "I'd never even heard of Berra, but I figured if he was worth fifty grand to Ottie he must be worth fifty grand to me."
[19] *St. Louis Post-Dispatch*, August 4, 1946.
[20] Larsen made his major-league debut for the St. Louis Browns in 1953. Before he died on January 1, 2020, he was the Browns last living pitcher.
[21] Ibid, April 26, 1950.
[22] *Saturday Evening Post*, April 29, 1950.
[23] Tygiel, *Baseball's Great Experiment.*
[24] Howard, Arlene with Ralph Wimbish. *Elston and Me: The Story of the First Black Yankee*. University of Missouri Press. 2001.
[25] *The Sporting News*, February 4, 1967.
[26] *St. Louis Post-Dispatch*, January 31, 1962.
[27] Ibid, November 4. 1970. "The Cardinals were among the clubs not signing blacks at the time," wrote sportswriter Neal Russo in 1970. According to St. Louis native and Yankee scout Lou Maguolo, "Joe Mathes (Cardinals chief scout) turned Howard over to me. Howard had a commitment to the Kansas City Monarchs, and three of us scouted him after that until he signed."
[28] Ibid.
[29] Leavy, Jane. *The Last Boy: Mickey Mantle and the end of America's Childhood*. HarperCollins. 2010.
[30] *Newark (Ohio) Advocate*, November 5, 2001.
[31] Ibid.
[32] Kahn, *The Era*.
[33] *Des Moines Tribune*, April 23, 1951. "I drove 500 miles to his home at Commerce, Oklahoma, to see Mantle pitch, but I discovered he was already trying out with the Yanks at Granby, Missouri at the time," Marr told Tony Cordero. "I never saw Mantle in action until he was playing with Joplin and I wonder why he said that I had." Marr was responding to a story in which Mantle told Joe Trimble of the *New York Daily News*, "Another scout, Runt Marr of the Cardinals, also looked me over, but didn't think I was good enough." Both Mantle and Yankee scout Tom Greenwade mentioned Marr on multiple occasions. As a scout for the Cardinals, Marr made his home in Grove, Oklahoma, a thirty-one-mile drive from Commerce.

[34] "I followed Robinson for 22 days at one stretch on a 'secret mission,'" Greenwade said in 1947. *The Daily Oklahoma*, June 4, 1947.
[35] Leavy, *The Last Boy.*
[36] Castro, Tom. *Mickey Mantle. America's Prodigal Son*. Potomac Books, Inc. 2002.
[37] Kahn, *The Era*.
[38] What we don't know in this analysis is the WAR of the Yankee players who would have taken the places of Berra, Howard, and Mantle.
[39] Greenwade is often credited with signing Howard. Lou Maguolo also claimed him. "Lou Maguolo and Tom Greenwade have kept us in front with their ability to uncover great talent," Casey Stengel once said.
[40] Population number from the 1960 census.

Alba, the Architects, and the Series of '64

"Alba has one filling station in the entire town, one barber, only one chair in his shop, and there's no movie house, if you want to see a movie you gotta go 20 miles to Joplin," Clete Boyer once told a reporter. "There's no swimming pool either, so when we were kids we swam in the river. Spring River it's called. No bathing suits, either. We swam with nothing on. We played baseball in the summer, basketball in the winter and swam the rest of the time."[1]

Clete was one of seven Boyer boys who filled their days with baseball, basketball, and swimming. All of them would go on to play professional baseball, three of them at the highest level. If Runt Marr lost the battle for Mantle, he decisively won the Boyer War. Marr and the Cardinals signed all but two of the brothers. Clete was the fifth brother to sign a baseball contract and the first one to elude St. Louis. According to one account, the club would have signed him but passed "partly because they had just signed Dick Schofield and spent quite a bit for Lindy McDaniel." Instead, Clete signed with the Kansas City A's for $35,000 (McDaniel received a $40,000 bonus that same year from the Cardinals).

Under owner Arnold Johnson, the Kansas City franchise had an incestuous relationship with the Yankees in the 1950s. Johnson's general manager and PR director were former Yankee employees. He hired the construction company of Yankee owner Del Webb to update his Kansas City stadium.[2] Above all, Johnson proved to be a consistent and reliable trading partner. From 1955 to 1960, the year Johnson died, Kansas City and New York made 15 trades involving 59 players.[3] In those six seasons, the Yankees won five pennants and finished third once. In the same timeframe, the A's never finished above sixth place in an eight-team league. The crown jewels of all that trading activity were still in the Yankee starting lineup in 1964: third baseman Boyer acquired in 1957 and outfielder Roger Maris acquired in 1959.

The long-time speculation involving Boyer was that New York had put up the money to sign him and that he was really Yankee property the entire time. Clete was considered a "bonus baby" when he signed with Kansas City. The rules at the time required large bonus players to spend their first two years in the big leagues. Boyer made his debut with the A's on June 5, 1955. He became official Yankees property when he was traded to New York on June 4, 1957. The club promptly sent him to the minor leagues where he spent the entire 1958 season. He made his Yankee debut the following year and became a regular in the lineup in 1960. At the urging of Mantle, who understood the significance, Boyer wore number 6, the same number worn by Musial of the Cardinals. The 1964 World Series marked Clete's fifth straight appearance in the Fall Classic. He was not a good hitter (career .242 average) but was considered one of the best defensive third basemen in the game. "Clete Boyer was a pretty likable guy and a helluva third baseman, the best I saw other than Brooks Robinson," recalled Pedro Ramos. "Clete Boyer is the finest fielding third baseman I've ever seen," Robinson once remarked.[4]

While World Series play had become routine for Clete, it was brand new territory for older brother Ken. The third Boyer brother to sign a professional contract and the second to make it to the big leagues (pitcher Cloyd Boyer signed in 1947 and made his Cardinals debut two years later), his early life bore strong parallels to Mantle. Both were born in 1931, Depression-era babies who grew up in modest circumstances. "I didn't have a new shirt until I went to high school," Boyer once recalled. Alba was once considered lead and zinc mine territory, similar to Commerce, Oklahoma, just forty miles away. Mantle's father worked in the mines. Boyer's father was a marble cutter. He also had a farm, managed a grocery store, and served as mayor of the town. Wife Mabel was city clerk. The couple had 14 children, seven boys and seven girls (one of the girls died in infancy). Vernon Boyer also found the time to convert the open field across from the family home into a baseball field. "I got some of the other fathers together, we rented the land for a few dollars, we built the entire ball field by ourselves, lights included."[5]

With those seven sons, Papa Boyer supplied plenty of talent to the local baseball team. The Alba Aces played in the Cardinal Junior League that included, for a time, a squad from Baxter Springs, Kansas that featured Mantle. Just like Mickey, the competition for Ken came down to two teams – the Cardinals and Yankees. "The Yankees wanted me badly," Boyer recalled, "but from the time I was a kid we always listened to the Cardinals games on the radio and we didn't know there was any other team but the Cardinals." He signed his baseball contract in 1949, the same year Mantle became a Yankee. Mickey was a shortstop who became an outfielder. Ken was a pitcher who became a third baseman. Like his Oklahoma counterpart and his younger brother, Boyer grew up idolizing Musial. "Stan probably had as much influence on my career as anyone," he remembered. "He said so many things to me that you knew were right."

Both players seemed destined for great things in the big leagues. In 1951, the Yankees assigned Mantle number 6, since 3 (Ruth), 4 (Gehrig), and 5 (DiMaggio) were already taken. After being sent down to the minor leagues briefly during his rookie season, Mantle returned to the Yankees and wore number 7 for the rest of his career. Boyer wore number 14 for the Cardinals and long considered it his lucky number. In 1964, he won the National League MVP award, having received 14 first-place votes.

"Boyer could become the greatest third baseman in Cardinals history," the team's chief scout, Joe Mathes, predicted in 1955. Boyer made every all-star team from 1959 to 1964 and was a leader on the team. "He was the boss of our field," said Tim McCarver. "He was the guy everyone looked up to."

Ken Boyer and the Cardinals clinched their pennant on the last day of the season against Casey Stengel's New York Mets. Clete Boyer and his teammates clinched their pennant one day earlier for rookie Yankees manager Yogi Berra. With Mantle hitting a bases-clearing double in the eighth inning to break the game open, the Yankees defeated the Indians 8-3. The New York outfielder would finish second in the American League MVP voting in 1964 behind another player who grew up longing to play for the Cardinals, Baltimore third baseman and Little Rock, Arkansas native Brooks Robinson. The man who finished third in the MVP voting, Yankees catcher Elston Howard, had two hits and two RBI in the final regular-season win for New York while third baseman Boyer also contributed two hits with one RBI and a run scored. Early Monday morning, Clete called Ken to congratulate him and confide in his brother. "Clete told me he was glad his team had sewed up the pennant on Saturday," Ken told reporters. "Clete told me the Yankees were a little tight and nervous and might not have done it on Sunday."

For his part, Ken warned his brother about the wicked bounces that could occur on the Busch Stadium surface. "Kenny wrote me a note saying, 'Watch that infield of ours, it has a lot of bad hops in it,'" his brother recalled years later. "The next day, he missed a little pop fly and I wrote him a note saying, 'Watch the air out here, too. It's got a lot of bad pockets in it.'" Beyond the jokes, the love and respect the two had for each other was obvious to others. "I never saw any brothers closer than the Boyers," remembered Mantle.[6]

The Boyer brothers and their connections with the Cardinals and Yankees went well beyond Ken and Clete. After making his first appearance for the team in 1949, Cloyd spent three more seasons pitching for the Cardinals. In 1964, he was working for the Yankees as a roving minor-league pitching instructor. Brother Wayne signed with the Cardinals one year after Cloyd, spent three years in the minor leagues, and then quit baseball to become a dentist. Ken's contract with the Cardinals came a year after Wayne's, and he made his St. Louis debut the same year Clete signed with Kansas City. In between those two, first baseman Lynn spent two years in the Cardinals minor league system before a broken shoulder ended his career. Ronnie signed with the Yankees in 1962, and baby brother Lennie became the seventh Boyer to play professional baseball when he signed with the Cardinals in the summer of 1964, just months before his two older brothers faced off in a World Series.

By this time, the Boyer family had become the perfect metaphor for the symmetry that existed between the Cardinals and Yankees. Both teams had a brother on the major league club and each franchise had one in their minor league system. Back in Alba, the even split had created a dilemma. "The Cardinals were always the favorites there, but the Yankees have picked up a lot of followers since Clete and Ron joined them," Ken conceded. Their parents pledged neutrality for the World Series. "Oh gosh, we couldn't favor one team over the other," Vernon told reporters. "This is something we have wished would happen," said Mabel.[7]

If anyone understood how the Boyers felt, it was Joe Garagiola. When the St. Louis native retired from the game after the 1954 season, he spent years broadcasting games for his hometown team. By the early 1960s, NBC hired him to do national broadcasts, and in 1964 he was part of the team calling the World Series. With Berra managing the Yankees, the former Cardinal was asked for a prediction. "I hope it goes seven games, the score is tied in the ninth inning and it rains until November," Garagiola said the day the Series began.

"I was managing the Yankees, and my pal Joe was upstairs broadcasting. It was hard to believe. It was almost spooky," Berra remembered. "Could this be the same two kids from the Hill who used to sit by the lamppost in front of [Benny] Pucci's house holding a handful of dirt one of them had scooped up from the Sportsman's Park infield after watching their favorite team, the Cardinals, play?"[8]

Up in the broadcast booth, Garagiola joined a squad of announcers who all had either Cardinal or Yankee roots. Garagiola shared duties with former Yankee player Phil Rizzuto. In August of 1956, Rizzuto was a struggling thirty-eight-year-old shortstop hitting .231 in a part-time role. The Yankees released him to make room on their roster for former Cardinal outfielder Enos Slaughter (this marked the second time the Yankees had acquired Slaughter). Rizzuto spent the next forty years broadcasting Yankee baseball. The team of Garagiola and Rizzuto rotated World Series radio and television duties with the duo of Harry Caray and Curt Gowdy. St. Louis native Caray had been calling Cardinals games since 1945. (When Caray was later fired by the Cardinals after the 1969 season, his replacement was Jim Woods. Rizzuto had replaced Woods in the Yankee broadcast booth in 1957. After two years with the Cardinals, Woods would again be replaced by a former player who spent his entire career with one team – Mike Shannon). By 1964, Caray partner Gowdy had spent years as the voice of the Boston Red Sox, but he began his career in 1949 working for the Yankees with Mel Allen.[9]

Down on the field before the first game, former Yankee Bob Wiesler threw batting practice to Cardinal hitters. During the Series, Wiesler would be joined in that role by former Yankee farmhands Lloyd Merritt and Jim O'Reilly.[10] All three grew up in St. Louis and had been signed by Yankee scout Lou Maguolo, who once coached baseball at McKinley High School in the city and taught industrial arts at both McKinley and Beaumont High School.[11] Beaumont alum Wiesler had once been a teammate of Berra, Howard, and Mantle. After his baseball career ended, Wiesler returned to his hometown and went to work for Anheuser-Busch. Working for the brewery, a role for the lefthander with the brewery-owned baseball team soon followed. "I started throwing batting practice for the Cardinals in 1964 and here I am pitching for them and they're playing the Yankees in the World Series!" he recalled years later.[12]

Beer and baseball always had a way of intersecting in St. Louis. The 1964 World Series had ended years of frustration for Anheuser-Busch. In twelve years of ownership, the team had five different managers.[13] Gussie Busch could finally point with pride to a championship baseball team to go along with his dominant brands of beer. More than thirty years earlier, it was a different brewery and a different team struggling to find its identity in a new era of baseball. Back then, Jacob Ruppert and the Yankees found inspiration in the Cardinal Way. A three-decade run of dominance ensued. The man who launched the Yankees farm system played a central role. George Weiss, believed *New York Times* columnist Arthur Daley, "was a perfect cog in a perfect machine."[14]

*****

"George doesn't know a ballplayer from a billy goat but he's a great team balancer," Rickey said in 1963. By that time, Weiss and Rickey, the architects of baseball's most successful farm systems, had been drawing comparisons for more than three decades. "George Weiss has left here to become the Branch Rickey of the New York Yankees," noted a *Baltimore Sun* report shortly after the Yankees hired him.

Despite a lineup that included both Babe Ruth and Lou Gehrig, Ruppert's Yankees sat out the postseason for the third straight year in 1931. The Philadelphia Athletics had emerged as the dominant team in the American League, winners of three straight pennants. The A's averaged 104 wins over that stretch, a timeframe in which the Yankees best output was 94 victories. But it wasn't Philadelphia that had Ruppert's attention. Rather, it was the team that had just defeated Connie Mack's club in the World Series.

"It was the St. Louis Cardinals success in 1931 that convinced Col. Jacob Ruppert that Branch Rickey had the right idea," wrote Harry Grayson. That season, the Cardinals won their fourth pennant and second World Series title in six years. It was not only their success on the field that led Ruppert to St. Louis; it was the system established by Rickey he wanted to replicate. "It was becoming increasingly difficult to obtain stars, yet the Cardinals seemed able to come up with an outstanding youngster whenever they required one," Grayson explained. "They had no sour experiences with costly purchases because they had none."

Rickey's investment in a vertically integrated farm system was met with controversy and skepticism at the time. Rival teams loved to say the only thing Rickey would get out of it would be a headache and an aspirin tablet.[15] Instead, it had blossomed into the envy of baseball. In his quest to replicate Rickey's success, Ruppert went in search of a man who could run the Yankees farm system. He found Weiss, a New Haven, Connecticut native and Yale dropout. Weiss had purchased the minor league team in his hometown at the age of twenty-four. His investors included Ty Cobb and Walter Johnson. With the biggest stadium in the Eastern League, exhibition games against major-league teams became a staple of the Weiss playbook, an act that created headaches for the owners of both the Cardinals and Yankees, as both Hornsby and Ruth attracted headlines as conspicuous no-shows for the event at different times in the 1920s.[16]

Weiss left New Haven for a job in Baltimore, as general manager of the International League Orioles. Baltimore had an opening because Jack Dunn, the man who signed Ruth to his first professional contract, had passed away. After three years with the Orioles, Ruppert hired him. Weiss would spend the next twenty-nine years working for the Yankees, the first sixteen as farm director. Working with Yankees general manager Ed Barrow, Weiss went to work expanding the Yankees farm system. By 1938, the Yankees were spending $100,000 annually on scouting and only the Cardinals had more minor league teams. Like their National League counterparts, the Yankees became skilled at promoting talent instead of paying for it. "It isn't often that the world champion Yankees go out of their way to obtain material in the open market," Louis Effrat wrote in *The New York Times* before the 1942 season. "The vast system which Ed Barrow and George Weiss have developed generally produces whatever the New Yorkers require."[17]

The Yankees also had an advantage the Cardinals didn't have. Under Breadon, St. Louis consistently declared dividends and took money out of the franchise. Ruppert and the Yankees had a different philosophy. "Unfortunately, most of us by necessity are profit-minded," Rickey said in 1937. "Not so with the Yankee company. It puts every cent back in the business."

Rickey later attributed much of the Yankees' success to general manager Barrow. "The Yankee dynasty of superiority was not an accident of ownership or sagacity of managers or the luck of scouts or the prestige of the city name or the reputation of 'Yankee.' It was the wise production of players and fixing of team identity by Ed Barrow," Rickey wrote in *The American Diamond.* "In a grandstand visit during a game with him, he would quietly tell me the changes that confronted the Yankees as much as two years into the future." After Barrow retired and Larry MacPhail sold his ownership stake, Weiss became the GM. Weiss left the Yankees after the 1960 season, and just like Rickey leaving the Cardinals in 1942, his teams had four good years left before a long post-season drought began.

The two men's shared history included high profile executives who worked for both. When the St. Louis Browns left town, Bill DeWitt Sr. joined the Yankees as an assistant general manager under Weiss. After the Cardinals fired him, Bing Devine went to work for Weiss, who joined the New York Mets following his long run with the Yankees. Devine's successor, Bob Howsam, had exposure to both as a minor league owner in Denver. In 1952, Howsam's team became affiliated with Rickey's Pittsburgh Pirates. "I was like a puppy dog," Howsam recalled. "He allowed me to be right at his elbow." Three years later, Howsam's team became a part of the Yankee system and marveled at how Weiss could read his scouts. "When one scout said a player was 'fair' he knew that meant poor. When another scout called a man 'fair' he knew that meant to check him out right away."[18]

Like Rickey, Weiss had a reputation for being cheap and for being a brutally tough negotiator. Tony Kubek once responded to a contract offer with a letter stating he could make more money shoveling snow in his native Wisconsin. "Received your answer," Weiss replied. "Suggest you get a big shovel."[19]

While the similarities were many, the two men also had their differences, none more dramatic than the issue of race. When Rickey left St. Louis for Brooklyn, he went to work on integrating the game. Weiss and the Yankees dragged their feet. "The truth is that our box seat customers from Westchester County don't want to sit with a lot of colored fans from Harlem," said Weiss. "I had Branch Rickey behind me, the whole club behind me. You didn't have your club behind you. They didn't want black players there," Jackie Robinson told Elston Howard.

The decision by Rickey and Brooklyn rippled throughout the National League. The reluctance by Weiss and the Yankees had a similar impact on the American League. The results of the decisions made by these two men years before could be seen on the field in the 1964 World Series. Of the top five players most responsible for the success of the Cardinals that season, only one – Ken Boyer – was white. As for the Yankees top five most productive players, only one – Howard – was black.[20]

As the two teams took the field on Wednesday, October 7, 1964, for the first game of the World Series, all but one of those ten players were in the lineup; Cardinals ace Gibson was backed by a lineup that included Boyer, Brock, Flood, and White while Yankees ace Ford counted on teammates Howard, Mantle, and Maris. The last of the Yankee five – Jim Bouton – would start Game 3.

For the last time in the twentieth century, the Cardinals and Yankees played games that mattered.

*****

The first time these two teams met in a World Series, they combined for eight home runs in seven games. Each team blasted four of them in 1926, with Ruth accounting for all of New York's output. Outside of Game 4, when the slugger connected three times, the Series was largely dominated by pitching and defense. Thirty-eight years later, the squads combined to hit 15 home runs, 10 of them by the Yankees. Nearly every game featured a memorable or defining long ball.

In Game 1 in St. Louis, the Cardinals trailed 4-2 entering the bottom of the sixth inning. A long two-run home run by Mike Shannon off Whitey Ford tied the game, and St. Louis would later add two runs in the frame to take a lead they would never relinquish. On a cool, clear day that featured winds of 16 miles an hour blowing from the southeast, Barney Schultz came on in relief of Ray Sadecki to close out the Yankees in a 9-5 victory.

New York tied the Series a day later at Busch Stadium. The Yankees led 4-2 when shortstop Phil Linz, filling in for an injured Tony Kubek, knocked a lead-off home run in the ninth inning of Schultz. His teammates added three more runs in the frame to finish off the Cardinals. Rookie Mel Stottlemyre went the distance for New York, outdueling

Gibson in an 8-3 win that snapped a five-game World Series losing streak for the Yankees (Los Angeles had swept New York in the 1963 Series).

When the series moved to the Bronx, home runs made the difference in all three games played at Yankee Stadium. Tied at one in the bottom of the ninth inning, Mantle led off for New York. Coming on in relief of Curt Simmons, Schultz made his third straight appearance. He made one pitch. "Mickey Mantle turned Barney Schultz into a pumpkin today," wrote Bob Broeg in the *Post-Dispatch*. The outfielder connected for a home run that landed in the third deck of Yankee Stadium. The blast marked the sixteenth World Series home run in Mantle's career, breaking a record established by Ruth. "The ball got a good piece of the plate," said catcher Tim McCarver after the game. "And Mantle got a good piece of the ball," added manager Johnny Keane.

The Cardinals got their revenge the following day. Yankees rookie Al Downing, filling in for an injured Whitey Ford, had allowed only one hit through the first five frames. But in the sixth inning, back-to-back singles by pinch-hitter Carl Warwick and Curt Flood followed by a one-out error by Yankee second baseman Bobby Richardson on a ball hit by Dick Groat loaded the bases. Up to the plate came Cardinals third baseman Boyer. The National League MVP was hitting .067 in the Series, with just one hit in 15 tries. Downing's second pitch was a high change-up. "He got the ball up in my eyes, and that's where any hitter likes to swing," Boyer said afterward. "If Downing had gotten the ball down, I probably would have hit into a double play." A double play would have ended the inning and preserved New York's 3-0 lead. Instead, Boyer blasted the ball over the left-field wall for a grand slam, only the ninth bases-loaded home run in World Series history. Neither team scored another run. The 4-3 win by the Cardinals tied the Series at two games each.

With great pitching, controversial calls, and dramatic home runs, the Cardinals and Yankees served up a World Series classic in Game 5. One home run sent the game to extra innings and another long ball in the tenth inning accounted for the game's final score. In a rematch of the second game, Gibson once again faced off against Stottlemyre. An RBI single by Brock put the Cardinals up 1-0 in the fifth inning. With runners now at first and third and one out, White hit a ground ball to second baseman Richardson that looked like it could be an inning-ending double play, but umpire Al Smith ruled that the relay throw from the shortstop arrived too late. White was safe at first and the Cardinals had a two-run lead.

With the Yankees still down 2-0 in the bottom of the ninth inning, Mantle led off against Gibson and reached on an error by Groat. With two outs, Yankees outfielder Tom Tresh connected on a 400-foot home run that tied the game. It could have been a game-winner. After Mantle reached, Gibson struck out Howard before facing Joe Pepitone. The Yankees first baseman lined the ball off Gibson's hip. The ball bounced toward the third base foul line with Gibson in pursuit. The former Harlem Globetrotter grabbed the ball bare-handed and fired the ball to first baseman White. This time, umpire Al Smith called the runner out, sparking a furious argument from Berra and the

Yankees, while the Cardinals contended replays showed the umpire was correct.[21] With one man on base instead of two, Tresh followed with the home run that tied the contest. When Gibson retired the next hitter, Pedro Gonzalez, the game went to extra innings.

White led off the Cardinals tenth inning with a walk. Boyer singled on a sacrifice bunt attempt and with Groat at the plate, White stole third base. Groat then hit a ball to third baseman Gonzalez, only in the game because the Yankees had earlier pinch-hit for Clete Boyer. Holding White at third, Gonzales threw the ball to second base for a force out, much to the regret of his manager. "I just wish Pedro had thrown to first...not second. If first base is open, then that gives me an excuse to walk McCarver. And, the way he's been hitting this Series, I would have walked him," Berra said later. Instead, with runners at the corners, the Yankee manager elected to pitch to McCarver, who already had two hits on the day and was hitting .438 for the Series.

Like others in uniform that day, McCarver's decision out of high school came down to two teams: the Cardinals and Yankees. Hall of Famer Bill Dickey had swapped his catcher's mitt for a scout's notebook and first spotted McCarver on the ball fields of Memphis when he was just fifteen years old. The former Yankee great later offered the teenager a new catcher's mitt and a two-week fishing trip to sign with the Bronx Bombers. "I could have signed with the Yankees," McCarver recalled years later. "Me and (Dickey) were close friends. I could have been a member of the Yankees. They were my No. 2 (choice), and a very close No. 2 to the Cardinals. But I think I was swayed by the fact the Cardinals were only 290 miles away (from Memphis). That influenced me somewhat."[22] Perhaps also influencing his decision in 1959 was the fact that the Yankees already had two talented catchers on their roster, St. Louis natives Berra and Howard.[23]

Now, a little more than five years later, the spotlight fell on the Memphis native in a game tied at two, in a World Series tied at two, with Berra signaling signs from the dugout, Howard signaling the pitches behind the plate, facing the team he could have played for, in Yankee Stadium. "He's a Yankees-type player," Dickey had said more than once of the young catcher who chose proximity over pinstripes. Tasked with getting out the Cardinals' hottest hitter was righthander Pete Mikkelsen, a sinkerball pitcher. The count ran to 3-2 before Mikkelsen delivered a sinker that didn't sink.

"I didn't think it was going all the way," McCarver said afterward. "On the three-two pitch, I was just looking to get a ball to hit. I wanted to get that runner home from third." He did more than that. The "Yankees-type player" delivered a Ruthian-type moment in the house the Babe built, a three-run home run to give the Cardinals a 5-2 lead. With his parents looking on from the stands, McCarver joyously trotted around the bases. "By the time I got to third, I was laughing out loud," he told reporters. "This has got to be the biggest thrill of my life."

The Yankees had no answer. With one on and two outs in the bottom of the tenth, Boyer caught a foul-ball pop fly off the bat of Maris to secure the win. Gibson went the distance, finishing with thirteen strikeouts on the day. In World Series history, only two pitchers had ever struck out more. "It was probably the greatest game of my life to that point," he later wrote.

The intense competition on the field reflected a battle going on inside the broadcast booth. Pairing former Cardinal Garagiola with former Yankee Rizzuto didn't sit well with some observers. Broadcaster Red Barber had left the Dodgers for the Yankees following the 1953 season. "Garagiola kept interrupting Rizzuto on the air, cutting in on him, taking the mike away from him. It was as though Rizzuto wasn't good enough to detail a routine play – Garagiola had to explain it or make a wisecrack," Barber remembered. "Then we got doubly mad because Rizzuto sat there and took it like a sweet, little lamb. Rizzuto just let Garagiola cut in on him – and when Garagiola had the play-by-play, Our Little Phil let Old Joe run with it as he pleased."[24]

A pleased Cardinals team took a happy flight home. Just as they did in 1926, the club won the final two games of the Series played in Yankee Stadium. Only this time, there was still unfinished business. This World Series would be settled in St. Louis.

Ten thousand fans greeted the team when they landed at Lambert-St. Louis Field. "McCarver for President," read the sign of one teenage girl. The Cardinals catcher, now hitting .471 for the Series, would be back in the lineup hitting sixth. The pitching matchup would be a rematch of Game 3 with Simmons on the mound for St. Louis and Bouton back on the hill for New York. Home runs again told the story. Tied at one in the top of the sixth, Maris and Mantle struck back-to-back blows to give the Yankees a two-run lead. Schultz relieved Simmons in the eighth inning, faced five batters, and retired only one. He left trailing 4-1 and when Gordie Richardson gave up a grand slam to Pepitone, the Yankees could bask in a blow-out win. Bouton defeated the Cardinals for a second straight time. Game 7 would decide all.

Pitching just three days after his complete-game, ten-inning performance at Yankee Stadium, Gibson drew the starting assignment for the Cardinals. For the third straight game, he would be pitted against Yankee rookie Stottlemyre, also pitching on just two days of rest. Neither pitcher had his best stuff. The Cardinals were first to take advantage.

St. Louis reached Stottlemyre for three runs in the fourth inning, highlighted by a steal of home by McCarver as part of a double steal in which Shannon took second base. Brock led off the next inning with a home run and the Cardinals added two more runs in the frame to give Gibson a 6-0 lead heading into the sixth inning.

The Yankees got one back when Mantle homered off Gibson, his third long ball of the Series. It would be the eighteenth and final World Series home run of Mantle's career. New York added two more runs in the inning to cut the lead in half. A Ken Boyer home run in the bottom of the seventh inning gave the Cardinals a 7-3 lead heading into the ninth inning. With one out, Clete Boyer homered for New York, giving everyone in Alba something to cheer about. The blasts by the Boyers marked the first time in World Series history that brothers had homered in the same game. With two outs, Linz hit his second home run of the Series to cut the lead to 7-5. One more baserunner and New

York would have the tying run at the plate. Before the inning began, Keane told Gibson to throw nothing but fastballs, figuring the Yankees couldn't hit four home runs in the inning. They were halfway there. "I looked over to the dugout to Keane, wondering if he had overestimated my speed and underestimated the Yankees' power," Gibson recalled. "But Keane didn't waver."

Gibson would have to face his biggest nemesis in the Series, Bobby Richardson. The Yankee second baseman had 13 hits in seven games, a World Series record he would later share with Lou Brock.[25] Seven of Richardson's hits had come off the ace of the Cardinals staff. On the first pitch, Gibson got him to pop up on the infield. Second baseman Dal Maxvill, filling in for an injured Julian Javier, caught it for the final out. For the first time since 1946, St. Louis could revel in a World Series winner. For the man calling the shots from the dugout, the wait was even longer. "I've waited 35 years for this," a champagne-soaked Keane told reporters from the clubhouse. Signed by scout Charley Barrett as a teenager, the St. Louis native had spent three-and-a-half decades in the Cardinals organization, most of them in the minor leagues. "They're the greatest bunch I've ever managed," he said of his club. "They're a treat to watch. I'd pay to see them any day."

For many of his players, though, the celebration was brief. "I had a horseshit winter," Gibson remembered, despite two victories, 31 strikeouts, and Series MVP recognition. The winter of Gibson's discontent had its origins in the fate of Keane. For only the second time in history, the winning manager in the Fall Classic was leaving for another club. And just like Hornsby in 1926, Keane was headed to New York.[26]

*****

On Friday, October 16, 1964, one day after the conclusion of the World Series, the fate of two managers, both St. Louis natives, was revealed. In New York, the Yankees announced that Berra would not be returning. Just a few hours later in St. Louis, a stunned Gussie Busch announced the resignation of Keane. Although the news may have blindsided the Cardinals president, the timing was as coordinated as a perfectly executed double play.

Yankee management had become disenchanted with Berra's leadership over the summer. Citing a source "second to none in the Yankees hierarchy," Bob Hunter of the *Herald Examiner* later wrote that the club realized by July that Berra didn't have control of the team. One name quickly bubbled up to the top of the potential target list, but club officials didn't think they could get him. All that changed in August. When Devine was fired as general manager of the Cardinals, "we had a pretty good idea Keane would be available," the source told Hunter.[27] (Bill Veeck believed the offer to Keane came in early September and was delivered by Bill Bergesch, the Yankees traveling secretary. Bergesch, a St. Louis native, was the general manager of the Cardinals minor league team in Omaha when Keane was the manager.)[28]

In St. Louis, Busch read Keane's resignation letter on that Friday morning in October. It was dated September 28. Distraught over the departure of Devine and upset over the Durocher rumors, Keane had made up his mind to leave the Cardinals during the final week of the regular season. After the World Series, Yankee general manager Ralph Houk congratulated Keane in the Cardinals clubhouse, whispering in his ear, "Attaway podnah."[29]

Three days later, at the Savoy Plaza Hotel in New York, Houk and the Yankees introduced Keane as their new manager. Bombarded by questions from reporters as to when the decision had been made, both men insisted they hadn't talked about the job until Sunday, the day before. "When I knew Keane was out of the Cardinals, he went to the top of my list," Houk conceded but never stating exactly *when* he knew Keane's status. Houk also had to assure Commissioner Ford Frick, who had called him Sunday, worried about possible tampering by the Yankees. "Has anyone ever questioned your credibility?" one reporter asked. "Only my bank!" Houk replied.[30]

Just two hours later in St. Louis, the Cardinals introduced their new manager, Red Schoendienst. Stung by the loss of Keane, Busch and the Cardinals moved quickly to replace him with the popular former All-Star second baseman. Sensing a public relations backlash, Busch knew he couldn't follow through on his promise made to Durocher in August. So did Leo. "I knew Gussie couldn't afford to hire me. The popular view in St. Louis was that Gussie had done something underhanded in hiring me, which also seemed to mean that I had done something underhanded in being hired," Durocher wrote in his autobiography. "I understand the fix you're in," Durocher told Busch when Gussie called to tell him the news.[31]

The hiring of Schoendienst came on the same day Rickey was asked to submit his letter of resignation. Never again would he have a job in a baseball front office. But with Schoendienst in St. Louis and Keane in New York, the Rickey legacy would only grow. Both the Cardinals and Yankees were now managed by former Rickey farmhands. In another echo of an earlier era, Keane joined Miller Huggins as the second Cardinals manager to leave the team for the Yankees.[32]

So much had transpired in less than a week. Just four days earlier, Rickey had reflected on his career from a noisy and jubilant Cardinals clubhouse. "I'm a fortunate man to be associated with this team," the eighty-two-year-old executive told an Associated Press reporter. "Five times I've been with the Cardinals in some capacity when the team met the Yankees in the World Series. We've won three of them. That's a pretty good average." Neither before nor after Rickey's time with the team have the Cardinals and Yankees met in postseason play. Of all the National League clubs that have faced New York more than once in World Series play, only St. Louis has a winning record.[33]

All three victories over the Yankees came at transitional moments in Rickey's career. The 1926 celebration occurred just a season after he was fired as the team's manager, the 1942 victory took place amidst his negotiations with the Brooklyn Dodgers, and his moment in the winning locker room in 1964 came just days before his boss decided he had to go.

The action that had consequences for both the Cardinals and Yankees and started the tumbling of the dominoes in Rickey's last go-round was the firing of Devine. That development sparked Keane's unhappiness, which gave Yankees management confidence their preferred choice to replace Berra would be available at the end of the year. With Keane gone, Busch fingered Rickey as the fall guy and tapped Schoendienst to fill the managerial void in St. Louis. With a new manager in place in New York, the new owners of the Yankees (CBS) also wanted a new voice in the broadcast booth. They hired him in December. The transition was complete. The only thing lacking in the Cardinals-Yankees drama, *Philadelphia Daily News* columnist Larry Merchant later noted, was a love interest.

In the early 1940s, Schoendienst, Berra, and Garagiola took a ride in Rickey's Lincoln out to Forest Park for a tryout. By Christmas of 1964, every member of the trio had a new job. Schoendienst started his managing career with the Cardinals in 1965. Berra became a coach with the Mets in 1965. Garagiola replaced Mel Allen in the Yankees' broadcast booth in 1965.

As for the man who started it all, Branch Rickey wouldn't survive 1965.

---

[1] *Springfield Leader and Press*, March 8, 1966.

[2] Webb and fellow owner Dan Topping sold Yankee Stadium and the land underneath it to Johnson for $6.5 million in 1953. The price included the ballpark in Kansas City. Johnson then sold the land underneath the New York park to the Knights of Columbus for $2.5 million and leased the stadium back to the Yankees. A year later, in November 1954, Johnson bought the Philadelphia A's and moved the franchise to Kansas City.

[3] From 1955 to 1961, the A's and Yankees made a total of 16 trades involving 62 players, but the last deal, in June of 1961, occurred under new Kansas City A's owner Charlie Finley. After that trade, fans protested to the point that Finley promised to stop trading with the Yankees. See www.baseball-almanac.com/corner/c042001b.shtml for details.

[4] *Baltimore Evening Sun*, April 9, 1968.

[5] *St. Louis Post-Dispatch*, May 24, 1978.

[6] *Tampa Bay Times*, September 8, 1982.

[7] *St. Louis Post-Dispatch*, October 5 and December 13, 1964.

[8] Garagiola, *Just Play Ball*.

[9] Caray and Gowdy worked the television broadcasts on NBC for Games 1,2,6,7 and radio for Games 3,4, and 5, alternating television and radio assignments with Garagiola and Rizzuto.

[10] While Merritt signed with the Yankees in 1951, his only major-league appearances came for the Cardinals in 1957. One of Merritt's teammates on the 1951 Joplin Miners was another Maguolo signee – Whitey Herzog. As a scout for the Browns and the Yankees, Maguolo claimed to have signed 40 players who made it to the big leagues. Those players

---

included American League Rookie of the Year Roy Sievers for the Browns and Tony Kubek for the Yankees.

[11] *St. Louis Post-Dispatch*, October 14 and November 4, 1970. Both Wiesler and Merritt attended Beaumont High School. O'Reilly went to St. Mary's High School.

[12] "Bob Wiesler, climbed the Yankees ranks with Mantle, passes away at 83." Baseballhappenings.net. August 16, 2014. www.baseballhappenings.net/2014/08/bob-wiesler-climbed-yankee-ranks-with.html

[13] The five managers were Eddie Stanky, Harry Walker, Fred Hutchinson, Solly Hemus, and Johnny Keane. A sixth, Stan Hack, managed the club for 10 games at the end of the 1958 season after Hutchinson was fired.

[14] *New York Times*, March 9, 1952.

[15] *The Sporting News*, May 21, 1936.

[16] Ruth was a no-show for an exhibition game in New Haven in 1923. Weiss had guaranteed the Yankees $3,000. Weiss backed off the guarantee when Ruth failed to attend. Yankees owner Ruppert protested and the matter went before Judge Landis. The commissioner ruled that Weiss only had to refund the difference in cost between the exhibition ticket and a regular-season game. The amount came to $1,000. Boxerman and Boxerman, *George Weiss.*

[17] *New York Times*, February 6, 1942.

[18] Rhodes, Greg & Erardi, John. *Big Red Dynasty How Bob Howsam & Sparky Anderson Built the Big Red Machine.* Road West Publishing. 1997. Howsam's manager in Denver in 1955 was Ralph Houk. Nine years later, the two men would be opposing general managers in the World Series.

[19] Garagiola, *Just Play Ball.*

[20] Based on WAR (Wins Above Replacement). In order, the top five for St. Louis were Boyer, Gibson, Brock, White, Flood. For New York, the order was Ford, Howard, Mantle, Maris, Bouton.

[21] Gibson, *Stranger to the Game*. "It was a controversial call by the umpire, Al Smith, but replays showed that he was right."

[22] *Memphis Commercial Appeal,* March 13, 2017.

[23] Reports of McCarver's signing bonus with the Cardinals ranged from $75,000 to $80,000. "My mother is a good businesswoman, and she not only suggested I put most of the money in certain investments, she demanded it. As a result, I'm now financially independent," he told a reporter in June of 1963, four months shy of his twenty-second birthday. *St. Louis Post-Dispatch*, June 30, 1963.

[24] Barber, Red. *The Broadcasters*. The Dial Press. 1970.

[25] Three players share the record of 13 hits in a single World Series: Bobby Richardson in 1964, Lou Brock in 1968, and Marty Barrett of the Red Sox in 1986.

[26] Keane became the third manager to leave his team after winning a World Series, but the first, Bill Carrigan of the Boston Red Sox, retired as a player-manager after the 1916 season. Carrigan was Ruth's manager the first three seasons of the Babe's career.

---

[27] *St. Louis Globe-Democrat*, October 28, 1964. Hunter's reporting was corroborated by others, including Joe Trimble in the *Daily News.* "Bobby Richardson and Tony Kubek stated flatly that they would not return under Berra next season. Elston Howard, another veteran, had this opinion. 'The man can't control these guys,' Howard said honestly." *New York Daily News*, October 21, 1964.
[28] Veeck, *The Hustler's Handbook*.
[29] *St. Louis Globe-Democrat*, October 19, 1964.
[30] *New York Daily News*, October 21, 1964.
[31] Durocher, *Nice Guys Finish Last*. "Thank you very much, Leo. I knew you'd understand the predicament I was in," Busch told Durocher and then hung up. Durocher said he wasn't offered, nor did he take any money from the Cardinals to call off the deal.
[32] In a poll of 250 sportswriters, the moves surrounding Keane and Berra were named as the "Oddity of the Year" for 1964.
[33] Both the Diamondbacks and Marlins are 1-0 in World Series play against the Yankees. Two clubs have faced New York more often than St. Louis in the World Series. The Yankees are 8-3 in 11 World Series against the Dodgers (Brooklyn and Los Angeles) and 5-2 against the Giants (New York and San Francisco).

Is That Cool or What?

At the end of 1964, *Los Angeles Times* columnist Jim Murray sarcastically named the year's biggest comeback: "Branch Rickey who proved you're never too old to make mistakes." Out of a front-office job, Rickey kept a lower profile in the new year but managed to stay as busy as ever. He served on the Veterans' Committee for the Hall of Fame, narrated a documentary on the sport's history called "The Old Ball Game," and continued to push for baseball expansion. Calling the 10-team setup in each of the two leagues "terrible, shocking and illogical," Rickey argued baseball "should have three eight-team leagues and then four leagues to truly nationalize the sport," but conceded "first we'll probably have two 12-team leagues with sectional divisions of six teams each." He also offered his thoughts on the future of big-screen television sets – "the TV screen should be 2 ½ times as wide as it is high," and took on the role as national chairman for a fundraising campaign at Ohio Wesleyan, his alma mater.

In March, Pepper Martin's death at the age of 61 brought a flood of stories about Rickey's Redbirds at their peak in the early 1930s. "He's one of the few men I've known in my lifetime, who, if a game goes long enough, he'll win it," Rickey said at a banquet just a month before the death of the player also known as the "WIld Horse of the Osage." Later in the year, writers rekindled their memories of Rickey's time with Brooklyn. Nearly two decades after Jackie Robinson debuted with the Dodgers, baseball officials selected Emmett Ashford to become the first black umpire in the big leagues. He made his debut the following year.[1]

In April, a columnist noted that while Rickey hadn't been the general manager of the Pittsburgh Pirates in a decade, his influence was still present. "Sign up all available hands and there's a chance that a few of the diamonds in the rough will turn out to be real gems," wrote Tom Keys, noting the Pirates had 180 minor league players in camp verses 155 the year before. Rickey had invented the "out of quantity comes quality" formula decades before in St. Louis, a philosophy he continued to employ in Brooklyn and Pittsburgh. And while baseball had tinkered with the rules to make it more challenging, the basic structure Rickey had conceived worked more or less the same as it had for more than four decades; scour the country for talent, conduct tryout camps, and get as many players as possible under contract. That all changed in 1965.

Upset over escalating bonuses paid to high profile amateurs, baseball owners decided to act (Rick Reichardt had signed with the California Angels the previous year for a reported $205,000). The sport's first amateur draft took place in June. When the Kansas City A's selected Arizona State outfielder Rick Monday with the first overall pick, a new era of shepherding talent was underway. No longer could enterprising scouts like Charley Barrett or Tom Greenwade have first dibs on promising players. (The draft achieved the owners' financial goal. Monday's bonus was $104,000. Reichardt's bonus wasn't eclipsed until Andy Benes signed for $235,000 in 1988.)[2] In total, the twenty teams selected 826 prospects. With the final pick of the first round, the World Series champion Cardinals took Joe DiFabio, a pitcher from Delta State University. DiFabio spent seven years in the minor leagues but never appeared in the big leagues. The team should have looked closer to home. Pitcher Ken Holtzman, from the St. Louis County suburb of University City and a fourth-round pick of the Chicago Cubs, was the first of the drafted players to appear in a major league game. Other notable players taken in the inaugural draft included Johnny Bench, Craig Nettles, Sal Bando, Hal McRae, Nolan Ryan, Tom Seaver, and Carlton Fisk.[3] One distinguishing characteristic of these future major league stars was that none of them was drafted by St. Louis, a reminder that a once peerless talent evaluation system developed under Rickey had long since been surpassed.

One of those scouts in Rickey's vast army of baseball informants passed away in October. Born in Raleigh, Illinois, Wid Matthews grew up fifty-five miles south in Metropolis. After a brief major league career with the Washington Senators and Philadelphia A's, Matthews was coaching high school basketball and football in the Missouri bootheel town of Caruthersville when Rickey and the Cardinals arrived to hold a tryout camp. The Cardinals had a minor league team there that played in the Northeast Arkansas League. When Matthews offered his services to Rickey, the Cardinals executive accepted, making him the club's business manager.[4] A year later, Matthews began scouting for the Cardinals and when Rickey moved to Brooklyn, he followed. "He was regarded as Rickey's righthand man in building up the Dodgers dynasty," *The Sporting News* noted following Matthews' death. After the Dodgers, he became director of player personnel for the Chicago Cubs, where he was credited with signing Ernie Banks. He also spent time in the Milwaukee Braves organization and with the New York Mets, where he served as an administrative assistant to George Weiss. In 1965, he worked as a scout for the California Angels. Gathering with other officials for a postseason team meeting, Matthews suffered a fatal heart attack in a Los Angeles hotel. He was sixty-nine years old.

That same month, Rickey joined Cardinal icon Stan Musial (class of 1963) and Yankee legend Casey Stengel (class of 1952) as a member of the Missouri Sports Hall of Fame. Rickey's induction ceremony was scheduled for the following month. He was not in good health. He had suffered a heart attack in 1958 and another one in 1961, the same year son Branch Rickey Jr. died after a lengthy battle with diabetes. To make it to the event in Columbia, Rickey had to leave his bed at St. Luke's Hospital in St. Louis. Running a fever that at one point reached 105 degrees, he had been in the hospital for more than two weeks and promised his doctor he would return after the event. The great orator was not about to miss the chance to make a speech. ("The Demosthenes of the diamond," *Boston Globe* columnist Harold Kaese later wrote. "Baseball has never had a more eloquent speaker than Branch Rickey.")[5]

On the day of the ceremony, Saturday, November 13, Rickey, wife Jane, and other family members headed down Interstate 70 to the campus of the University of Missouri, where the hometown Tigers were hosting the Oklahoma Sooners in Big Eight Conference action. On a brisk fall afternoon, the former college football player and coach sat under a blanket and enjoyed the last game he would ever see. After Dan Devine's Tigers dominated the Sooners 30-0 to clinch a Sugar Bowl invitation, Rickey departed for the Daniel Boone Hotel in downtown Columbia where he would give his induction speech.

The night embodied much of Rickey's baseball career in the state, from his early days with the Browns to his most recent time with the Cardinals. Broadcaster Harry Caray emceed the event that honored not only Rickey but also fellow inductees George Sisler and (posthumously) *Sporting News* publisher Taylor Spink. Rickey's connection to Sisler at the University of Michigan helped bring the baseball star to the Browns, an event that widened the wedge between the feuding American and National Leagues. It was Spink who helped lead Miller Huggins to the Yankees after the Cardinals manager tried and failed to buy the St. Louis team, events that occurred during Rickey's first year with the franchise. And it was Caray's interview with Leo Durocher that began Gussie Busch's infatuation with the former manager, a rumored hiring that helped lead to the end of Rickey's second stint with the Cardinals.

Rickey had included both Sisler and Spink in *The American Diamond*, his book released for publication that same November weekend. In it, he named Sisler, along with Lou Gehrig, as the greatest first baseman he had ever seen. As for Spink, "Taylor edited all articles for all his publications, changed the substance rather than the style, and frequently substituted his name for the author's," Rickey wrote of the publisher of the St. Louis-based weekly.

That night at the Daniel Boone Hotel, however, Rickey was full of praise for both men. "I wanted to come because of George and Taylor," he told the crowd. "To be with them is to be with the immortals." In a speech on courage, he also mentioned the other Hall of Fame first baseman who called Sportsman's Park home in the 1920s. "There was a fellow on my team in years gone [by], Jim Bottomley," Rickey told his audience. "He had courage, he had that sort of thing that when you come to the testing point, it never occurred to him whether he had it or didn't have it," he explained, before telling the crowd about Bottomley sliding into second base on a bad hip, a play that set up the game's winning run. Bottomley, one of the first of Rickey's Redbirds, would be the subject of the last baseball story Rickey would ever tell.

He transitioned from physical courage to moral courage. "I will use an illustration from the Bible," he said, speaking a few more sentences before a long pause. "I don't believe I'm going to be able to speak any longer," he said shortly before collapsing into a chair beside the podium.[6] He had suffered yet another heart attack. Rushed to Boone County Hospital, he never regained consciousness. He died at 10:00 p.m. on December 9, still in the same hospital intensive care unit where he'd been for the past twenty-six days. Wesley Branch Rickey was eleven days shy of his eighty-fourth birthday.

Bob Broeg was among those in attendance the Saturday night Rickey collapsed. While conceding the baseball legend would have preferred sparing his wife and family a nearly four-week hospital vigil, he saw purpose beyond the poignancy about the end of a life lived in full. "But to have experienced his last lucid moment on his feet, his voice vibrant and a capacity crowd of some 150 persons open-mouthed, hanging on his every word, ah, that's the way Mr. Rickey would have wanted it – and that's the way it happened," wrote the *Post-Dispatch* columnist.[7] Several of Broeg's media brethren also took the occasion of Rickey's death to reflect on a one-of-a-kind career.

"When Mr. Rickey spoke, the angels listened. At the age of 82, he could come to Chicago, agree to speak for a few seconds, and then spellbind us for more than an hour," remembered Dave Condon in the pages of the *Chicago Tribune*.

"Very probably he was the greatest man ever to devote his life to a game, any game," wrote Larry Merchant in the *Philadelphia Daily News*. "We don't get this kind anymore."

"People either liked him immensely and looked upon him with awe and reverence or simply couldn't stand him," contended Lester Biederman in the *Pittsburgh Press*. "There was no middle ground."

"Branch Rickey was the greatest man in baseball. There was a lot of hustler in him and plenty of actor. But he came on strongest as an evangelist," believed *New York Journal-American's* Jimmy Cannon. "There has never been one like him connected with sports. I doubt if there will ever be another."[8]

As tributes poured in, nearly five-hundred people arrived at Grace United Methodist Church in St. Louis to attend Rickey's funeral four days after his death. Bill DeWitt Sr. had known Rickey since he was a teenager working as a vendor at Sportsman's Park. "I just can't say enough good things about Mr. Rickey," said the president of the Cincinnati Reds. "I guess he was my closest friend for many years and I saw his entire family raised." Warren Giles got his start in baseball working for Rickey's Redbirds in the 1920s as a business manager in the minor leagues. "No one in the game made a greater contribution to baseball than Mr. Rickey," said the National League president. Former Cardinals in attendance included Ray Blades and Stan Musial. "He helped me tremendously as a young player," Musial recalled. Former Browns great Sisler arrived with sons George Jr. and Dave. Cool Papa Bell, who dazzled crowds for the St. Louis

Stars when Rickey was first building his minor league system, also came to pay his respects.

The Dodgers contingent included Buzzie Bavasi, the man who replaced Rickey as the Dodgers general manager, and the player most connected to the Rickey legacy. "The passing of Mr. Rickey is like losing a father," said Jackie Robinson. Frank Duncan, Robinson's first manager for the Kansas City Monarchs, joined his former player in attendance.[9] Dr. Ralph Sockman, who had known Rickey since he was a student at Ohio Wesleyan, delivered the eulogy, calling him a "master mind" and the "master heart of baseball." The retired pastor of Christ Church Methodist in New York said Rickey had asked him several years ago to conduct his funeral. "It is quite a feat that he was able to extend his life so that it should become entwined in the heartstrings of millions of fellow citizens," he told the assembled. "By opening the game to all colors and creeds, he made baseball worthy of being called a national sport."

The Grace United Methodist pastor, Rev. Wesley H. Hager, delivered the eulogy the following day at the Rickey family plot in Scioto County, Ohio. The mourners that day included Jesse Haines, the pitcher who threw a shutout and hit a home run in the third game of the 1926 World Series against the Yankees, and Billy Southworth, the Cardinals manager who guided the team to a World Series title against the Yankees in 1942 just weeks before Rickey departed for Brooklyn. Joining the former Cardinals in honoring Rickey's memory were members of the Harlem Globetrotters and Satchel Paige, the great Negro League pitcher who finally got his chance to pitch in the major leagues at the age of 41, one year after Robinson broke baseball's color barrier.

More tributes arrived in 1967 when Rickey was voted into the Baseball Hall of Fame. One story regarding the announcement mentioned that "Rickey developed his infamous farm club chain gang, which was finally broken up by Commissioner Kenesaw Mountain Landis." Columnist Red Smith, who began his career in sports journalism for the *St. Louis Star* in the 1920s, took issue with the description. "If it was infamous, it was a brand of infamy eagerly embraced by the Yankees, the Dodgers, and, indeed, every other team in the major leagues. It was a farm system built by George Weiss on the pattern established by Rickey that kept the Yankees at the top from the 1930s into the 1960s," Smith wrote, while also pointing out that Landis never came close to breaking up the Rickey model. "The farm system not only survived," he noted, "it was copied everywhere."

Others wondered why it took so long for the tribute to come. "When you think about Mr. Rickey for a while you have to come to the conclusion that nobody has ever had anything remotely close resembling the effect he had on this game," wrote *Newark Star-Ledger* columnist Jerry Izenberg, noting that baseball had waived the rules for an early admission to the Hall of Fame for Stengel but not for Rickey. At Cooperstown, Izenberg predicted, "they will say a lot of things about him...things that should have been said there much sooner."[10] Whatever was said of Rickey that day was said in private. His wife Jane and his five daughters were among 24 members of his immediate family to witness the formal induction. While Jane accepted the replica of his Hall of Fame plaque, no one spoke on Rickey's behalf during the ceremony.

In death, stories of Rickey's antics and behavior proliferated, many of them focused on his legendary frugality. He appreciated and expected brevity from his scouts in Western Union wire reports. One day, Rickey wired a scout to ask if a particular player was ready for a promotion. "Yes," came the one-word reply. "Yes, what?" Rickey demanded to know in a follow-up telegram. "Yes, sir," the scout replied.

There was the one printed in 1968 about his time with the Cardinals negotiating with a star player down to the eve of opening day. The player finally managed to wrangle an extra $1,000 out of Rickey. "I beg you to make no public announcement of this deal," Rickey told him. "Let's keep this our little secret."

"Don't worry, Mr. Rickey," the player assured him. "I'm just as ashamed of this contract as you are."

The early 1970s brought more serious reflection. Rickey's wife Jane passed away in October of 1971 at the age of 89. That same month, the Pittsburgh Pirates won the World Series. Pittsburgh manager Danny Murtaugh got his start in professional baseball for Rickey's Redbirds, signed by the Cardinals in 1937. The infielder never made it to the big leagues with St. Louis, but after Rickey sold his contract to Philadelphia, Murtaugh debuted with the Phillies in 1941. He played his last game a decade later. That fall, he attended a Pittsburgh Pirates tryout camp in preparation to begin his managerial career with a minor league team in the organization. Pirates general manager Rickey conducted the camp. "I learned more about baseball fundamentals than I ever had before," Murtaugh recalled years later. "It was a good prep course taught by one of the masters of the game."[11]

Besides defeating the Baltimore Orioles (managed by another Cardinal farmhand, Earl Weaver) in the World Series, Murtaugh's 1971 Pirates have another distinguishing characteristic.[12] The Pittsburgh starting nine on September 1 of that year was the first in major-league history to feature an all-black and Latino lineup. "When it comes to making out the lineup," Murtaugh said, "I'm colorblind and my athletes know it."[13]

The athlete who made the trend toward a colorblind lineup possible died the following year. Jackie Robinson passed away in October of 1972 at the age of 53. "I considered Mr. Rickey the greatest human being I had ever known," Robinson wrote in his autobiography, published one month after his death. "Mr. Rickey received hundreds of hate letters," remembered former Cardinal Ray Blades, who was on the coaching staff of the 1947 Dodgers. "But he always believed in Jackie Robinson and he always believed he would be a great ballplayer."[14]

In 1987, the fortieth anniversary of Robinson breaking baseball's color barrier, Baltimore *Evening Sun* columnist Bill Tanton told the story of how Rickey hired black scout Ralph Jones for the Cardinals in 1964. Jones, a former college baseball player at Indiana, was working in the athletic department at Morgan State University in Baltimore when Rickey called. "Mr. Rickey's chauffeur picked me up at the airport in St. Louis,"

Jones remembered. "He told me, 'There won't be anything on the menu but baseball. That's all he talks, 24 hours a day.'"[15]

Rickey hired Jones to scout a thirteen-state region in the South. "I want you to comb that area and help me find some black youngsters who can someday help our ballclub," Rickey told him. The two men soon took off for a ten-day scouting trip, meeting every morning at 6:30 a.m. to discuss players. Meeting over breakfast one morning at a restaurant in the South, a white waitress spilled coffee on Jones' lap – twice.

"Mr. Rickey saw what the woman did and he told her, 'Young lady, the St. Louis Cardinals frequent this establishment. I can see to it they don't. Mr. Jones' trousers are too damaged for dry cleaning. I expect the restaurant to buy him a suit,'" Rickey demanded. "I got a new suit out of it, too," said Jones.

When the Cardinals won it all in 1964, the team gave Jones a World Series ring. He passed away in 1989. At some point, the family lost the ring. On April 15, 2015, Jackie Robinson Day in baseball, the Cardinals presented Jones' son, Earnest, with a replica of the 1964 World Series ring in a ceremony before the game. He made plans to put the ring on display at the Eddie Robinson Museum at Grambling State University in Louisiana where Ralph Jones' father, Ralph Sr., served as president for 41 years and coached its baseball team to more than 800 victories.[16]

One measure of Rickey's impact on the game could be seen in 1999 at the unveiling of baseball's all-century team. He had a direct connection with 12 of the players: teammate of Wee Willie Keeler on the 1907 New York Highlanders (Yankees); signed Sisler for the Browns; manager and/or general manager of the Cardinals during the era of pitchers Alexander and Dean, infielders Hornsby and Frisch, and outfielders Medwick and Musial; responsible for Campanella, Snider, and Robinson while running Brooklyn; acquired Clemente when he served as general manager in Pittsburgh.

Three players – Brock, Carlton, and Gibson – were a part of the Cardinals organization when he served as a front office consultant. There were also two celebrated misses; the previously chronicled case of Berra, and a young lefthander who spent two days at Forbes Field in Pittsburgh in 1954. "Mr. Rickey told me afterward that he was interested," Dodgers lefthander Sandy Koufax recalled in 1962. There was just one problem. "No money was mentioned at all. Had Mr. Rickey said, 'Here, we'll give you $20,000 or $25,000,' or maybe even less, we might have accepted."[17]

That is 17 of the 100 players on the all-century team the great man knew well. Considering that more than 70 of them were in the big leagues by 1964, Rickey's last year in the game, he likely played against, scouted, attempted to acquire, or just enjoyed watching play the vast majority of the twentieth century's best baseball talent. "To be Branch Rickey's guest at a game was a rare experience," Dr. Norman Vincent Peale recalled the year of his Hall of Fame induction. "His knowledge of every player was encyclopedic. He knew their characters, their families, their histories, indeed, everything about them."[18]

Rickey's influence on the game extended well beyond the players. In the 1980s, nearly two decades after Rickey's death, Dodgers general manager Al Campanis told author Roger Kahn he still listened to lectures on tape by his former boss.[19]

In 1981, Rickey was portrayed by actor David Huddleston in "The First," a Broadway musical about Robinson breaking baseball's color barrier (David Alan Grier played Robinson).[20] It wasn't the first time an actor portrayed Rickey (Minor Watson played him in the 1950 movie, "The Jackie Robinson Story"), and it wouldn't be the last. More recent movie-goers may recall Harrison Ford's depiction of Rickey for the 2013 film "42."

In 2000, Mets manager Bobby Valentine read aloud to the press from a magazine article he had recently come across. "The dominant factor in driving managers gray before their time and leaving them prey to hypertension is the unintentional base on balls," the passage began. "Pitchers' control has been steadily deteriorating because they know that almost any batter can hit a home run or one off the wall." The article in question had been written by Rickey for the October 7, 1950 edition of *Collier's* magazine. "Is that cool or what?" said Valentine.[21]

In 2007, infielder Joe McEwing was at the end of his career, trying to catch on with the Boston Red Sox in spring training. Luis Alicea worked on the Boston coaching staff, and like McEwing, the former second baseman had come up in the Cardinals organization. "I listen to Luis describing double-play depth with [rookie Dustin] Pedroia," he told author Howard Megdal for the book, *The Cardinals Way.* "And I go, 'I don't want to interrupt, but do you want me to finish this?' He goes, 'What do you mean?' I go, 'Do you want me to finish this speech?' He's like, 'You grew up under George [Kissell]. You know exactly what I'm gonna say.' I said, 'You're right.'"

George Kissell spent nearly 70 years in the Cardinals organization, most of them as a roving instructor in the minor leagues. He got his start in professional baseball after attending a tryout camp with the Cardinals in his home state of New York in 1940. He drove 125 miles to the camp, a trip that cost him $19.80. Rickey signed him and gave him twenty bucks. "Keep the change," Rickey told him, "that's your bonus."[22] Kissell never made it to the major leagues as a player but did for a time as a coach on Red Schoendienst's staff. He became best known for schooling young talent on the basics of the game, tirelessly teaching fundamentals to generations of up-and-coming players. On spring training mornings, he'd direct rookies on the field. "We're going to play Albert baseball," he would tell them. Met with a quizzical look, Kissell would respond by pointing to his head. "*Einstein.* We're going to play smart baseball." The man players would call "the professor" was never at a loss for words. "George Kissell is the only man I know who can talk for 15 minutes about a ground ball," Whitey Herzog once said.[23]

In 2005, the Cardinals named their spring training clubhouse in Jupiter, Florida for him. Kissell died in a car accident in October of 2008, about a year-and-a-half after former Cardinals Alicea and McEwing teamed up to school future American League MVP Pedroia on the basics of double-play depth. Kissell was eighty-eight years old when he passed away. To put his time with the Cardinals in perspective, a Rickey signee who got his start with the franchise in a pre-Pearl Harbor America was still teaching the organization's athletes seven years after 9/11.

In 2016, broadcaster Vin Scully called his last game for the Los Angeles Dodgers. Back in 1950, a position had become available in the Brooklyn Dodgers broadcast booth when Ernie Harwell left for a job with the Giants. The Fordham University graduate caught the eye and ear of Red Barber. "Red recommended me for the job but not before I was interviewed and approved by Branch Rickey," Scully remembered years later.[24] He went on to call Dodgers baseball for 67 seasons, a span that featured more than 9,000 games, 21 no-hitters and three perfect games.

In southern California, he became so popular, fans would bring their radios to games so they could hear Scully describe what they were seeing. "My life is just full of breaks," he told the *Los Angeles Times*, "but the greatest single break was the transistor radio."[25] He was at the mic for two of baseball's most iconic home runs. "A black man is getting a standing ovation in the deep South for breaking the record of an all-time baseball idol," Scully said when Hank Aaron broke Babe Ruth's career home-run record. "In the year that has been so improbable, the impossible has happened," a stunned television audience heard Scully say as a hobbled Kirk Gibson limped around the bases after hitting a game-winning home run off Dennis Eckersley in the first game of the 1988 World Series.

He was eighty-eight years old when he signed off for the last time. To put his time with the Dodgers in perspective, a Rickey personnel decision made nearly two decades before man landed on the moon still redounded to the benefit of baseball fans nearly two decades after the start of the twenty-first century.

Is that cool or what?

---

[1] It would be another decade before baseball had its first black manager. The Cleveland Indians hired player manager Frank Robinson in 1975.

[2] *New York Daily News*, May 26, 1999.

[3] Seaver and Fisk did not sign.

[4] *The Sporting News*, October 16, 1965.

[5] *Boston Globe*, November 15, 1965. Rickey comparisons to Demosthenes, the Greek statesman and orator, were common. In 1914, the *Post-Dispatch* praised his public speaking skills, contrasting Rickey to other speakers in the community who weren't as talented. "There wasn't a Demosthenes or even a Burke in the bunch," the paper said in an editorial. Four years later, the paper referred to him as "Demosthenes Branch Rickey." *St. Louis Post-Dispatch*, June 11, 1914, and June 10, 1918.

[6] *The Sporting News*, December 25, 1965. KMOX radio had a recording of Rickey's last speech.

[7] *St. Louis Post-Dispatch*, December 13, 1965.

[8] *The Sporting News*, January 1, 1966.

---

[9] Robinson mentioned Duncan and Bell when writing about his disappointment in the attendance at Rickey's funeral in St. Louis. "In my mind, it was a disgraceful and almost unbelievable thing that, when Mr. Rickey came to the end of the long road of life on this earth, not one of the present-day Negro greats of baseball was there to say a silent, grateful farewell." *Pittsburgh Courier*, December 25, 1965.
[10] Part of the delay was because while baseball honored former players, managers, and umpires, the eligibility rules had no provisions for former executives at the time Rickey died. "If Branch Rickey doesn't belong in the Hall of Fame, they had better padlock the place and throw away the key," proclaimed *The Sporting News* in an editorial shortly after his death (January 8, 1966). Baseball later modified its rules, allowing Rickey to be elected under a special provision governing executives 65 years or older.
[11] Wilmington, Delaware *Evening Journal*, December 1, 1971.
[12] Except for Eddie Sawyer (1950 Phillies), every single pennant-winning National League manager from 1939 to 1978 played or managed in the Cardinals organization, played or managed under Rickey, or was a St. Louis native. The list includes Bill McKechnie, Leo Durocher, Billy Southworth, Charlie Grimm, Eddie Dyer, Burt Shotton, Charlie Dressen, Walter Alston, Fred Haney, Danny Murtaugh, Fred Hutchinson, Alvin Dark, Johnny Keane, Red Schoendienst, Gil Hodges, Sparky Anderson, Yogi Berra, and Tommy Lasorda. McKechnie, Durocher, Southworth, Grimm, Dyer, Shotton, Alston, Haney, Murtaugh, Hutchinson, Dark, Keane, Schoendienst, and Anderson all played for or managed the Cardinals (or both), or one of its minor-league teams. Durocher, Shotton, Dressen, Alston, Hodges, and Lasorda managed, coached, or played for the Brooklyn Dodgers organization under Rickey. Berra, along with Grimm and Keane, was a St. Louis native. (Grimm began the 1938 season as the manager of the pennant-winning Cubs but was later replaced by Gabby Hartnett.)
[13] theundefeated.com/features/on-this-day-in-1971-the-pittsburgh-pirates-fielded-the-first-all-black-lineup/
[14] *Mt. Vernon (Il.) Register-News,* October 26, 1972.
[15] *The Evening Sun*, November 24, 1987. Tanton refers to Jones as the first black man in a major-league-front-office position. The 2015 stories on Jones don't go that far, only calling him one of the first African-American scouts for the Cardinals. In the late 1940s, Cleveland Indians owner Bill Veeck "integrated every level of his ballpark operation – special police, ushers, food vendors, scorecard sellers, grounds crew, and front-office personnel," according to biographer Paul Dickson.
[16] According to an Associated Press obituary, Jones's record as Grambling's baseball coach was 814-216 after World War II. Prewar records were lost in a fire.
[17] *Pittsburgh Post-Gazette*, June 6, 1962.
[18] *Philadelphia Inquirer,* October 24, 1967.
[19] Nearly two years later, Campanis was forced to resign as Dodgers general manager. To commemorate the 40th anniversary of Robinson's debut, he had appeared on the ABC

---

news show *Nightline* where he told anchor Ted Koppel that blacks may not have the "necessities" for management jobs.

[20] "I saw Branch Rickey come alive on that stage," Dick Young wrote after opening night. "David Huddleston was remarkable. The voice, the mannerisms, the walk, the articulation. He WAS Branch Rickey." New York *Daily News*, November 19, 1981. Huddleston appeared in dozens of films. He played the title role in "The Big Lebowski."

[21] *New York Daily News*, August 15, 2000.

[22] In another version of the story, it's a scout, not Rickey, who gives the $20 to Kissell. *Tampa Bay Times,* March 16, 1997.

[23] *Tampa Tribune*, June 12, 2005.

[24] *New York Daily News*, October 24, 1986.

[25] *Los Angeles Times*, September 25, 2016.

Birds, Bombers, and Beer: '65 and Beyond

In the days and weeks following the 1964 World Series, the man who brought Rickey back to St. Louis relished a World Series winner but also bore the brunt of criticism for his actions. In just a few months, Gussie Busch fired his general manager and front office consultant, and watched his manager jump ship to the Yankees. "What should have been unadulterated triumph ended as a public relations disaster," noted *New York Times* columnist Leonard Koppett.[1] Still, on the balance sheet of 1964, Busch's moments of pride far exceeded his embarrassing actions. St. Louis was a city on the move in the early 1960s. The iconic Arch on the St. Louis riverfront and a new downtown stadium were under construction. The brewery had contributed a quarter of the $20 million in equity to get Busch Stadium II built. A groundbreaking ceremony had taken place in May of 1964, the same year the city celebrated its bicentennial. Busch served on the steering committee that oversaw the year-long festivities.

In December, Anheuser-Busch celebrated a record-setting ten million barrels of production. In typical Gussie Busch fashion, the moment was commemorated with a brass band, a team of Clydesdales, and a speech to the public atop a beer wagon. A reporter asked the sixty-five-year-old executive about his future hopes. "Another world championship baseball team and another world beer production record, I hope, I hope."

"He would get what he hoped for, and then some," wrote *Bitter Brew* author William Knoedelseder. "But he would pay a terrible price for it all in the years to come. In some ways, on this day, standing on a beer wagon in the sun congratulating his employees for a job well done, he had reached his peak."

A fall from the apex took place for Busch's team and his city the following year. The 1965 Cardinals finished in seventh place in the ten-team National League. Manager Red Schoendienst's first team was eight games under .500 on June 29 and never became a factor in the pennant race, ending with a record of 80-81. Schoendienst did get some good news in August when his contract was extended through the 1966 season. The move, wrote Neil Russo in the *Post-Dispatch*, "ended speculation that either Leo Durocher or [former Cubs manager] Charlie Metro would be brought in to replace the Redbird manager."[2] The Durocher rumor, still alive in the summer of 1965, offered further proof that it was the owner, and not the team's former senior consultant, who seriously considered replacing Keane as manager in 1964.

In the spring, the team made news when it hired the man best known for replacing Lou Gehrig as the Yankees first baseman. No longer playing, fifty-two-year-old Babe Dahlgren became the Cardinals' film director. "I do believe that if use of films of our players – and of the opposition – will help us win three or four games a season, the expenditure of $20,000 or so will be worthwhile," said Bob Howsam.[3] The signing represented the first acquisition of a former Yankee by the Cardinals general manager. It wouldn't be his last.

In the fall, the club made a trade that demonstrated the Rickey influence on the man running the Cardinals front office. The team traded third baseman Ken Boyer to the New York Mets for third baseman Charley Smith and pitcher Al Jackson. Howsam, wrote columnist Broeg, "burns incense at the baseball shrine of Branch Rickey," citing the Rickey mantra of "better to trade a player a year too early than a year too late." Thirty-four-year-old Ken joined brother Clete in playing for a New York team.

As the Cardinals prepared to move into a new stadium the following year, Missouri native Walt Disney had a vision for an amusement park that would have added to the downtown renovation and complemented the team's new facilities. Designed for the area between the stadium and the Arch, plans for "Walt Disney's Riverfront Square" included "a Circarama film on St. Louis, an Audio-Animatronic exhibition, a New Orleans French district, a haunted house, an Audubon bird room, a Davey Crockett cave, and a pirate ship walk-through," wrote Disney biographer Neal Gabler[4]. At one point, *The New York Times* even reported Disney had committed to St. Louis, stating the 2.5 acre, five-story indoor park "is not expected to be completed until 1966 or 1967."[5] In July, however, Disney and officers with the St. Louis Civic Center Development Corporation confirmed their talks had ended. In a joint press release, the groups stated that plans "proved to be unfeasible." One of the whispers surrounding the scrapping of the proposal was that Busch wanted beer to be sold in the park. Disney opposed it. Gabler called the allegation untrue. Regardless of the reason, St. Louis's loss was Orlando's gain.[6]

*****

If the mid-1960s marked the peak for Gussie Busch and his empire, it also marked the end of the line for another brewery once associated with an iconic baseball franchise. Fourteen breweries were operating on Manhattan Island when Prohibition was lifted. Three decades later, only one remained. The Jacob Ruppert Brewery had operated on the Upper East Side for a century when it announced plans to close its doors. In the years since Jacob Ruppert's death, other beer makers, most notably Anheuser-Busch, had aggressively moved onto its turf. In 1953, the St. Louis brewery opened a plant in Newark, New Jersey. In 1965, the Ruppert Brewery, the financial engine that once allowed its owner to reinvest every cent of Yankee profit back into the team during the heyday of Ruth and Gehrig, ceased production.

*****

The CBS ownership of the Yankees was the least successful for the franchise since the days before the Ruppert era. The Yankees of 1964 were like the Cardinals of 1946, a dynasty at the end of a great run. Both franchises had been deeply influenced by general managers who had departed four years earlier. Rickey's reign as general manager of the Cardinals ended after the 1942 World Series against a Yankees lineup heavily infused by talent from Weiss's farm system. Weiss's run as GM of the Yankees ended after the 1960 World Series against a Pittsburgh Pirates team influenced by Rickey's management. Following Rickey's departure, the Cardinals dominated the National League for the next four years, winning three pennants and two World Series titles. After Weiss left the Yankees, New York played October baseball the next four seasons. It took St. Louis eighteen years and two ownership changes to return to the Fall Classic. New York was about to embark on a similar path.

From 1965 through 1972, the Yankees finished higher than fourth place only once. Key players on the team Johnny Keane inherited were old, injured, or both. "They want Mickey to play. But he can't do it," the manager said during his first spring training in pinstripes. "The way his legs are now, he couldn't play in anybody's outfield without hurting you."[7] Issues extended well beyond Mantle. Tony Kubek retired in 1965. Bobby Richardson played his last game in 1966. Whitey Ford called it quits in 1967. Mantle and Elston Howard (traded to Boston in 1967) hung up their spikes in 1968. A UPI sportswriter noted in the spring of 1969 that Clete Boyer was the last regular of the Yankees dynasty still playing, but he had long since left New York.[8] Traded to the Atlanta Braves after the 1966 season, Clete finished his career in 1971, two years after brother Ken retired.

Keane's first club finished in sixth place, eight games under .500. When the team dropped 16 of their first 20 games the following season, he found himself out of a job. The Yankees replaced him with the man who hired him, Ralph Houk. Eight months later, Keane was dead. He died of a heart attack at his home in Houston. He was fifty-five years old. Those who knew him best had great admiration for the man who gave up the priesthood for a baseball career. "He was, in fact, the closest thing to a saint that I came across in baseball," Bob Gibson later wrote. "A man could be pretty good," said Bing Devine the night Keane died, "if he only tried to be half as good a man as Johnny Keane."[9]

Just a few months before Keane died, Devine had succeeded Weiss as president of the Mets, an organization increasingly populated by men with ties to the Cardinals and Yankees. Stengel managed the Mets their first four seasons. Like the former Yankee skipper, Mel Allen had been ousted by the Yankees and found a home in Queens. He joined the Mets broadcast booth in 1965. One year later, a former Yankee farmhand and future Cardinal manager joined the team as its third-base coach.

Whitey Herzog grew up in New Athens, Illinois, just across the Mississippi River from St. Louis. Signed by the Yankees, he never made it to the big leagues with New York.

Traded to the Washington Senators, Herzog spent eight years in the big leagues with four different teams. When his playing career ended, he immediately went into coaching and scouting, working for the Kansas City A's for two seasons before joining the Mets coaching staff.

Herzog's first year with the Mets coincided with a decision that changed the direction of the franchise. University of Southern California pitcher Tom Seaver had signed a contract with the Atlanta Braves. Commissioner William Eckert invalidated the deal, ruling the Braves had improperly signed the pitcher after the start of the college season. Any team could enter a drawing to assume the contract that included a $50,000 signing bonus. The Mets entered the drawing and were awarded the deal. It was Devine who convinced Weiss that Seaver was worth the investment.

Meanwhile, Herzog left his third-base coaching duties to become the Mets director of player development in 1967. Over the next six years, Herzog led a farm system that developed future major league players such as Jon Matlack, Ken Singleton, Gary Gentry, Amos Otis, John Milner, and Wayne Garrett.[10] The 1969 "Miracle Mets" won a World Series and the 1973 club won the National League pennant. The latter club was managed by Berra. The Mets hired him following the death of Gil Hodges in 1972. Herzog wanted the job but didn't get along with Mets chairman Donald Grant. "Grant's people even ordered me to stay away from Gil's funeral just so there wouldn't be speculation that I'd be hired as the new manager," Herzog recalled. "I've never forgiven them for that." Rejected by the Mets, Herzog would leave the organization, a decision that had long-term ramifications in St. Louis.

*****

In December of 1965, Cincinnati Reds president Bill DeWitt Sr. made one of the worst trades in baseball history. He sent outfielder Frank Robinson to the Baltimore Orioles for outfielder Dick Simpson and pitchers Milt Pappas and Jack Baldschun. All were gone from the Reds by 1968, while Robinson would lead the Orioles to a World Series sweep of the Los Angeles Dodgers in the 1966 World Series, winning the Triple Crown and the American League's MVP award that same season. DeWitt compounded his woes the following season when he battled with Cincinnati city officials over the location of a new ballpark. The Reds owner wanted it close to the Kings Island amusement park or out in the suburbs. The city wanted it on the riverfront. When the two sides couldn't come to terms over the proposed stadium's lease terms, DeWitt decided to sell.

He sold the team in January of 1967 to Frank Dale, the publisher of *The Cincinnati Enquirer,* who quickly reached an agreement with city officials on the location of Riverfront Stadium. Having purchased the team from one former Rickey protégé, Dale went looking for a man to run the organization and focused on two others with extensive Rickey roots, Dodgers GM Bavasi and Cardinals GM Howsam. "We did make a feeler in Bavasi's direction. At the same time we made our initial feeler in Howsam's direction," said Dale. "Howsam was the only man we actually offered the job."[11] Howsam joined the Reds the same month Dale took over. He brought with him two associates from St. Louis, assistant Dick Wagner and Sheldon "Chief" Bender, director of player personnel. Howsam would later hire manager Sparky Anderson, who had previously spent time managing in the Cardinals minor league system. It was under this ownership and management group that the "Big Red Machine" blossomed. Cincinnati won the National League pennant in 1970 and 1972 and back-to-back World Series in 1975 and 1976.

While not popular with the players in St. Louis, Howsam left his mark on the franchise. "He found the front office in disarray," wrote *In Pursuit of Pennants* authors Mark L. Armour and Daniel R. Levitt. "There was no mechanism for selling season tickets or for promotions (beyond the close tie-in with Busch's brewery), and some of the ticket takers were stealing tickets from the club." Howsam fired farm director Eddie Stanky after Stanky walked into his office and told him how things would be run (Bender replaced him) and fired two women he believed responsible for leaking the infamous Rickey memo to Broeg in 1964.

He also made two key trades before departing. On May 8, 1966, he swapped pitcher Ray Sadecki for San Francisco Giants first baseman Orlando Cepeda. On December 8, 1966, just a month before he left, Howsam dealt infielder Charley Smith to the Yankees for outfielder Roger Maris. Howsam's last trade with the Cardinals mirrored that of another early career mentor. As part of his last deal with the Yankees, George Weiss had acquired Maris from Kansas City on December 11, 1959.

Cepeda was spectacular for the Cardinals in 1967, winning the National League MVP award. Maris played right field in St. Louis as Mike Shannon shifted to third base. During the two years Cepeda and Maris were in the lineup, the Cardinals played in two World Series, defeating the Red Sox before losing to the Tigers. Against Boston, Maris hit .385 with a home run and seven RBI. Batting third in the lineup, he drove in at least one run in each of the four Cardinal victories. Six seasons after a successful assault on Ruth's single-season home run record caused him so much stress he began losing his hair, Maris found peace in St. Louis. "I almost forgot how good it was to be in baseball," he said at the team victory party at Stan Musial & Biggie's restaurant. St. Louis traded Cepeda to Atlanta before the start of the 1969 season for Joe Torre. Maris decided to retire. To show his appreciation for his time in St. Louis, Busch awarded Maris a beer distributorship in Gainesville, Florida.

Baseball expanded by four teams and decided to split each league into two divisions for the new season (just as Rickey had predicted). The back-to-back NL champions arrived in spring training in St. Petersburg in an optimistic mood. It quickly soured. On March 22, Busch addressed the team, attacking the "high salaries" of baseball. "The speech demoralized the 1969 Cardinals," wrote Curt Flood. The club finished fourth in the newly formed National League East.

One of the issues that made Busch's blood boil was Flood's demand for a $100,000 salary. When challenged by players, the owner had a consistent and predictable response. He got rid of the challenger. The Cardinals traded Flood to Philadelphia in

October as part of a seven-player deal. Busch is "the most baronial of major-league club owners," Flood recalled. "He also has the shortest fuse." Flood refused to report to the Phillies and sent a letter to Bowie Kuhn. "After twelve years in the major leagues, I do not feel I am a piece of property to be bought and sold irrespective of my wishes," he explained to the commissioner. Flood filed a lawsuit against baseball's reserve clause. While Jackie Robinson, former Browns owner Bill Veeck, and former Cardinals pitcher Jim Brosnan testified on Flood's behalf, not a single active player was willing to take that risk. The baseball establishment took a dim view of Flood's efforts. Rickey had once claimed that anyone who opposed the reserve clause had "avowed communist tendencies." The case made it all the way to the Supreme Court, where the justices – by a vote of 5-3 – upheld baseball's antitrust exemption.

The same year the Supreme Court ruled against Flood, the Cardinals made likely the worst decision in franchise history, and the biggest mistake since Rickey let Berra get away. Once again, Busch's temper played a role. Upset over a salary increase request by Steve Carlton, Busch demanded the pitcher be dealt. General manager Devine, back with the club for a second stint, reluctantly complied, sending him to Philadelphia in exchange for pitcher Rick Wise. Over $5,000, the Cardinals lost the services of one of the greatest pitchers in baseball history.[12] Carlton, who had won twenty games for St. Louis in 1971, went 27-10 in 1972 for a Phillies team that won only 59 games. The lefthander, who made his Cardinal debut in 1965, pitched 17 seasons after leaving St. Louis, winning four Cy Young awards and 252 games. He was particularly effective against his old team, going 38-14, a winning percentage of .731, the highest mark against any team Carlton faced more than twice in his career.

The pitcher acquired for Carlton, Rick Wise, pitched two years in St. Louis and won 32 games before being dealt to Boston for Reggie Smith. The outfielder was an All-Star for the Cardinals in 1974 and 1975 before the team traded him to Los Angeles for Joe Ferguson. The catcher played one year in St. Louis, then was traded to Houston for pitcher Larry Dierker and infielder Jerry DaVanon, both of whom played one year with the Cardinals and never appeared in the big leagues again.

Busch compounded the Carlton mistake with another short-sighted move that haunted the franchise for years to come. The Cardinals had another promising young lefthander in the rotation, and like Carlton, he also wanted a raise in 1972. Jerry Reuss, from Ritenour High School in suburban St. Louis County, had won 14 games the previous season. He was just twenty-two years old. Reuss wanted a raise from $17,000 to $25,000. Busch would only go as high as $20,000. Five-thousand dollars cost the Cardinals another lefthander. St. Louis traded him to Houston for Scipio Spinks. Reuss won 220 games in his career, 198 after he left the Cardinals. Spinks won six games in two seasons with St. Louis as injuries took their toll on the righthander. After the Cardinals, he never pitched in the big leagues again. "Trading Carlton and Reuss probably cost the Cardinals three division titles," estimated author Rob Neyer.[13]

By 1978, a year where Carlton won 16 games while leading the NL East champion Phillies, the Cardinals had nothing to show for either trade. The club fired manager Vern Rapp seventeen games into the season while compiling a record of 69-93, the team's worst showing in more than four decades.

While the Cardinals would wander in baseball's wilderness throughout the 1970s, the Yankees returned to their winning ways. Just as it took St. Louis more than a decade and two ownership changes to right the ship in the 1960s, a similar pattern played out in New York. Eight seasons after Dan Topping and Del Webb sold the team to CBS, the broadcast network sold the franchise to a group led by George Steinbrenner for $10 million.[14] In 1976, the Yankees won their first pennant since the 1964 season.

The president of Steinbrenner's first pennant-winning team was Gabe Paul, a man who broke into baseball with Rickey's Redbirds, first as a batboy and later as a ticket salesman for the Rochester Red Wings. He followed Rochester president Warren Giles to the Cincinnati Reds, and when Giles became president of the National League, Paul became the Reds general manager. He frequently consulted with two colleagues. "I turned for help and advice to Mr. Rickey," Paul remembered. "We got to be very close. He would go out of his way to help you," he told Red Barber in 1969. "Also, I used to talk to Ed Barrow of the Yankees whenever I was in New York."[15]

Paul had been in baseball for more than forty years when he went to work for Steinbrenner. "Gabe Paul was a dear friend and the most knowledgeable baseball man I have ever met in my 25 years in the game," Steinbrenner said after Paul's death in 1998. "He was responsible for our group being able to purchase the Yankees from CBS."

Steinbrenner and Paul had even more reasons to celebrate in 1977. The Yankees brought home the franchise's first World Series title in fifteen years. Paul then left New York to rejoin his previous employer, the Cleveland Indians. In an article titled "The Yanks' Big Loss," columnist Dave Anderson called Paul "the Yankees' voice of reason," adding that "he was also their voice of experience, a 67-year old disciple of Branch Rickey..."[16] Absent Paul, New York won its second straight World Series by defeating the Los Angeles Dodgers for a second straight year in 1978. The Cardinals and Flood played a role in creating this dynasty.

Busch's decision to trade Flood and the outfielder's subsequent lawsuit set off a chain of events that eventually led to the end of the reserve clause and the beginning of free agency. "After the Flood case, it wasn't a question if the reserve clause would be restructured or annihilated, but when," John Gaherin, chief labor negotiator for the owners, later told *The New York Times*.[17]

An arbiter granted Jim "Catfish" Hunter free agency after a dispute with the Oakland A's following the 1974 season. The Yankees signed him. A year later, Dodgers pitcher Andy Messersmith directly challenged the reserve clause by playing an entire season without a contract. Messersmith, later joined in his case by pitcher Dave McNally, believed the reserve clause gave owners a one-year option on his talent, not a lifetime of service. When arbitrator Peter Seitz sided with the players, free agency became an official part of the game. "There is a direct line – one might even say an umbilical cord – connecting Flood to Messersmith," wrote Bill Veeck.

No one in baseball was more aggressive in the pursuit of free agents than Steinbrenner, who quickly signed outfielder Reggie Jackson and pitcher Don Gullett. The 1977 Yankees, with Jackson in right field and Gullett and Hunter in the starting rotation, won 100 games. The 1978 team added free agent Goose Gossage to anchor the bullpen in a carbon-copy campaign – a 100-win regular season followed by a six-game World Series victory.

Busch liked to talk about signing free agents but had little to show for his efforts. Near the end of the 1976 season, Busch spoke openly of his desire to bid on the free-agent market, specifically targeting a power hitter and a top relief pitcher. A reporter asked him about outfielder Joe Rudi of the Oakland A's. "You're coming awfully close," Busch replied. The reporter then asked him about Rudi's teammate, reliever Rollie Fingers. "You're coming awfully close again," Busch answered.[18] Oakland owner Charlie Finley saw the story, accused Busch of tampering, and protested to Bowie Kuhn. The commissioner fined Busch $5,000. That offseason, Rudi signed with the California Angels and Fingers went to the San Diego Padres. A few years later, Busch tried to lure Pete Rose to St. Louis with the promise of a $750,000 salary, possibly more if Rose agreed to do a few beer commercials. There was only one problem. Rose didn't drink. Rejecting the Cardinals offer, he joined Carlton in Philadelphia when he signed a free-agent contract with the Phillies. With Rose leading off and playing first base and Carlton winning his third Cy Young award with a record of 24-9, the 1980 Phillies won their first World Series in franchise history.

The Yankees returned to October baseball in 1981 against the Dodgers in a World Series remembered as much for Steinbrenner's antics than the results of any contest. After a loss in Game 5, the Yankees owner returned to the team's hotel in Los Angeles before flying back to New York the following morning. In an elevator, he claimed that two drunk and abusive Dodgers fans began talking about Yankee "chokers" and the "animals" who lived in New York. When Steinbrenner responded with an obscenity, one of the men hit him on the side of the head with a beer bottle. With three punches, the Bronx Boss would allege, he took down both men. "I clocked them," he told reporters that night. "There are two guys in this town looking for their teeth and two guys who will probably sue me." The men never sued, never came forward or were never even identified. "It just ended," Steinbrenner publicist Howard Rubinstein said years later.[19]

The entire incident was widely suspected as a fabrication, an attempt by Steinbrenner to motivate his team. It backfired. Down 3-2 in the Series, the Yankees lost the sixth and final game three nights later in Yankee Stadium. In dropping the final game 9-2, Yankee righthander (and former Cardinal) George Frazier became the first pitcher in baseball history to lose three games in a best-of-seven World Series.

Steinbrenner combined the worst traits of three Cardinal owners. He had the volatile temper of Busch, changed managers more often than Breadon (from 1978 to 1991, a span of 14 seasons, the Yankees had 18 managers), and drew comparisons to a third Cardinal owner for suspicious financial activity. Steinbrenner was indicted for tax evasion in the spring of 1974. His company – American Shipbuilding – was targeted for illegal campaign contributions to the committee to re-elect President Richard Nixon. Steinbrenner was thought to be the mastermind of the scheme. Commissioner Kuhn grasped the significance and drew the historical parallels in his autobiography. "This was not exactly a promising situation. People get put in jail for obstruction of justice. The last owner to be sentenced to jail was told by Commissioner Ford Frick to sell his baseball interest. That was Fred Saigh, owner of the St. Louis Cardinals, who in 1953 was sentenced to fifteen months in jail for tax evasion," he wrote in *Hardball: The Education of a Baseball Commissioner*. "I found it hard to avoid the conclusion that Steinbrenner was headed for the same fate as Saigh if indicted and similarly sentenced."

In August of 1974, Steinbrenner pleaded guilty to one count of the felony indictment. Although Federal Judge Leroy Contie Jr. could have imposed a jail sentence, he elected to fine Steinbrenner $15,000 and his company $20,000. Three months later, Kuhn announced a two-year suspension. Spared a prison term, Steinbrenner, unlike Saigh, would not be required to sell out. Kuhn later lifted Steinbrenner's suspension after 15 months. (Saigh's jail sentence had effectively blackballed him from ever returning to the game. When he tried to buy the Chicago White Sox, the commissioner vetoed the move. "He wrote an angry letter that I ignored," Kuhn remembered.)[20]

Busch, even more so than Steinbrenner, would forever be linked to Saigh due to their shared history. After selling out to Anheuser-Busch, Saigh would remain a thorn in the side of the brewery for years to come. In August of 1964, on the same day the Cardinals fired Devine, Saigh made an offer to buy the team for $4.5 million, stating in his letter to Busch that "St. Louis fans deserve a front office management that will make an educated effort to provide them with a winning ball club." The brewery quickly rejected the offer. Earlier that year, Saigh lost a lawsuit against the company in which he had asked the brewery to grant him the same stock option privileges given the company's president. As the company's largest outside shareholder other than the Busch family, Saigh publicly opposed a corporate reorganization plan in 1979. "It gives the chairman and president a blank check to do whatever he pleases, for the board of Anheuser-Busch is constituted in such a way that is merely a rubber stamp board," he argued unsuccessfully.[21]

Saigh was not the only one worried about an increasingly powerful Anheuser-Busch. "Their potential for mischief was enormous," Dodgers owner Walter O'Malley had once warned Kuhn about the St. Louis brewery. By 1981, Anheuser-Busch had radio or television affiliations with nearly every team in baseball. It wanted more. Playing catch up to Miller, its Milwaukee competitor that had been the first to focus on endorsements from ex-jocks and had introduced its wildly popular Miller Lite in 1975, the St. Louis brewer pushed for more national platforms to market its products. Specifically, A-B executives had their eye on baseball's network broadcasting contracts that Miller had with ABC and NBC. Brewery officials took their demands to Kuhn. When the commissioner pointed out those decisions were up to the networks, "they countered by arguing that in professional football, Commissioner Pete Rozelle had successfully interceded on Budweiser's behalf," Kuhn recalled, promising to review the situation when new network contracts were up for negotiation a few years later.

Later that year, Kuhn blocked a proposed Anheuser-Busch sponsored package of 52 telecasts of Cardinal and Yankee games to be carried on ESPN. "The deal would have violated our contracts with NBC, ABC, and USA Cable," he explained. "I could hear again Walter O'Malley's words of warning about the power of Anheuser-Busch."[22]

The 1981 baseball season featured a nearly two-month-long strike by the players, wiping out every scheduled game from early June through early August. As part of the deal to resume play, baseball authorities decided to split the season in half. Despite the best overall record in the National League East, the Cardinals missed out on the playoffs, finishing 1.5 games behind the Phillies in the first half and a half-game behind Montreal in the second half. One of the supporters and beneficiaries of the split season plan was O'Malley's Dodgers, winners of the first half in the NL West. Whitey Herzog derisively called the split-season schedule the "Bowie Kuhn Sweepstakes," pointing out the Cardinals played 30 games in the second half on the road and just 22 at home. Years later, he still wondered if the commissioner's issues with the brewery played a role in the decision. "I think that's why in 1981, (Kuhn) went with his buddies, like O'Malley," he said in 2007. "He had his friends, and he knew who his enemies were."[23]

Kuhn insisted his beef was never with Gussie. "I liked Busch, for all his impervious and curmudgeonly ways," he recalled. "I do not know any owner who loved the game more." The commissioner had a different take, however, on Busch attorney Lou Susman. Recalling a time when Susman asked to meet him for dinner, Kuhn suggested drinks instead. "I could not stand the prospect of having dinner with him." When nine owners, including Busch and Steinbrenner, called for the commissioner's resignation in December of 1981, Kuhn had a clear idea on the origins of opposition. "Susman had been secretly campaigning against me since December 1980," he contended. His suspicions were validated by Steinbrenner, who called the meeting "National League inspired. Susman was the organizer. The principal speaker. He did everything."[24]

One year later, the commissioner lost his job, thanks in part to the campaign by Susman and the Cardinals. Kuhn needed the support of 20 owners to extend his term. He fell two votes short. When the results were announced, the eighty-three-year-old Busch pounded his cane on the table. "He should clean out his desk tomorrow!" shouted the Cardinals president. Busch, like Saigh before him, helped lead an effort that ended a commissioner's reign.

The ouster of Kuhn was a small victory for a man who had experienced years of personal and professional losses. The 1970s were a wasteland of Cardinal baseball, in large part because of ill-tempered Busch decisions. In 1975, a boardroom coup at Anheuser-Busch saw him lose the role of president to his son, August Busch III. "The Third" was no baseball fan and no fan of Gussie. He did allow his father to continue in his role as president of the Cardinals but stripped him of his corporate perks. Gussie no longer had access to the company yacht or its fleet of planes. He had to fly commercial.

The biggest blow of all came the year before he lost his job. Busch had 11 children in all, delivered by three of his four different wives. By 1974, he had been married to his third wife, Gertrude Buholzer, known as Trudy, for more than two decades. In December, a family chauffeur was carrying eight-year-old Christina and her eleven-year-old brother Andrew on their way home from school when a tire blew on a tractor-trailer truck. The big rig then crossed the median on Interstate 44 and struck the Busch vehicle nearly head-on. The chauffeur, Nathan Mays, was killed immediately. Andrew was injured but survived. Christina suffered severe brain damage and was transported to St. John's Mercy Hospital. She died eleven days later. The death of his youngest and last child crushed Gussie. "When his daughter was killed that's what broke his heart," said longtime Busch publicist Al Fleishman. "He was never the same after that."[25]

Another of Gussie's eleven children, son Peter, had grown up with a fondness for guns and had once accidentally shot himself. In February 1976, Peter, twenty years old at the time, had a friend spend the night at the Busch family estate. David Leeker was three years older and didn't live far from Grant's Farm. The sleepover occurred one day after the pair had done some target practice with Peter's new .357-magnum revolver. Getting ready for bed, Peter had the pistol in one hand when he tossed a pillow with the other to his friend. What happened next had deadly consequences. "I was going to throw the .357 onto my bed," Peter later explained. "And as I was coming up to throw it, the gun somehow discharged." The bullet struck Leeker just above the lip before settling in his skull. He was killed instantly. Three weeks later, Peter Busch was indicted on manslaughter charges. According to a St. Louis homicide detective, powder burns around Leeker's face suggested the shot had been fired from a distance less than 14 inches.[26] After pleading guilty to the charge, a judge gave Busch a suspended sentence and five years' probation for the fatal shooting. Not accepting the Busch version of events, the Leeker family filed a $3 million wrongful death lawsuit against Peter and his parents. The two sides would later reach an out of court settlement for an undisclosed amount, confirmed by Leeker's father to be more than $150,000 but thought to be considerably less than $3 million.[27]

In February 1978, two years after a deadly shooting involving one of their children and a little more than three years after the death of their daughter, Gussie and Trudy divorced. That same year, the Cardinals turned to their third manager in three seasons. Ken Boyer was hired to reclaim the magic of the 1960s. His 1979 team showed promise, winning 86 games, finishing third in the NL East, with first baseman Keith Hernandez sharing MVP honors with Pirates first baseman Wille Stargell. But when the club began the next season by losing 33 of its first 51 games, Boyer was let go. At a meeting in June at his Grant's Farm estate, Busch turned the keys of the franchise over to a man raised on Yankee baseball. "I fell under the spell of Charles Dillon Stengel," Dorrel Norman Elvert "Whitey" Herzog confessed in his autobiography. "Of all the managers I've ever played for, Casey had the most influence on me, even though I never really got to play a regular season for him."[28]

*****

Whitey Herzog was born in 1931 and signed his first baseball contract in 1949; the same years as the man he replaced in St. Louis – Boyer – and the identical timeline as the man who blocked his way to the big leagues in New York – Mantle. Like Mickey, Whitey was an outfielder. He met the man who shaped his career at a Yankee rookie camp. "I'll bet Casey Stengel walked me down the third-base line 75 times a day teaching me that good base running boils down to anticipation and knowledge of the defense," Herzog once told the *New York Times.*

He spent five years in the Yankee minor league system. His stops included the Joplin Miners a year after Mantle starred there, and the Denver Bears, a team owned by future Cardinals general manager Howsam. Two decades after his last year in the Yankees organization, the Kansas City Royals hired him to manage. By the beginning of the 1980 season, Herzog was an unemployed former manager, in large part due to his inability to beat the Yankees. His Kansas City teams met New York in the playoffs three straight years. Each time, a Royals' loss sent the Yankees to the World Series. When Kansas City finished second in the American League West in 1979, Whitey was out of a job.

Herzog was summoned to the June meeting by Busch attorney Susman. Herzog received the call while playing in a golf tournament at Tan-Tar-A Resort at the Lake of the Ozarks. After a dinner that night to honor former Cardinals player and announcer, St. Louis native Buddy Blattner, Herzog headed to the city and checked into a hotel under an assumed name (Boyer had yet to be fired). He drove out to Grant's Farm the next morning to meet Busch, his fourth wife and former secretary, Margaret Snyder, and Susman.

When the conversation turned into a job offer, Herzog originally turned it down. The salary was fine, $100,000, but the deal was for only one season. "If you want to give me a one-year contract, then you'd better get someone else to manage. I just went through that in Kansas City," Herzog said.

"You're right," Busch conceded. "I'll give you a three-year contract." And just like that, the deal was done. Boyer was fired (in between games of a doubleheader in Montreal) and Herzog became the manager. A new hurdle soon developed.

To get things done with the Cardinals, Whitey knew he needed to communicate with Gussie. Easier said than done. "I was the manager, all right, but between the manager and the owner there were layers of club executives, PR men, and lawyers. It wasn't easy to get Gussie then, and later, it became almost impossible," he recalled.

A lunch meeting with Bing Devine sparked an idea. The on-again, off-again general manager of the Cardinals had been fired a second time by Busch during the malaise of the 1970s. Devine believed that one of the reasons he never bonded with the man in charge is because he didn't drink alcohol. "You've got a hell of an advantage," Devine told Herzog. "Just call him up and say you're coming out for a couple of beers." Herzog took the advice and began paying regular visits to Grant's Farm. "We'd sit and eat sandwiches, play gin, and drink beer," he remembered. More importantly, "It was the first time in my career as a manager, I'd had good solid access to the owner of the club, the man who could give me authority to make the decisions I needed to make."[29]

Herzog, two generations removed from the Hamburg area of northern Germany, and Busch, whose grandfather Adolphus was born in the Rhine River country of western Germany, bonded over beer and baseball. In the 1880s, important St. Louis Browns' discussions took place at Chris Von der Ahe's saloon. In the 1980s, consequential St. Louis Cardinals' conversations were held at the family estate of the world's largest brewery, whose founder was Von der Ahe's contemporary. Those discussions helped spark a complete revamping of the team.

Two months after the Cardinals installed Herzog as manager, Busch fired general manager John Claiborne. He'd only been on the job 22 months. The Cardinals, noted columnist Tom Barnidge, "change employees more than they change pitchers." Less than two weeks later, Busch named Herzog as Claiborne's replacement. Whitey then left his on-field duties for the rest of the season, replaced by Red Schoendienst on an interim basis. In October, Gussie made it official: Whitey would be both manager and general manager of the team. "I realize this is unique in baseball," he explained, "but we sincerely believe Whitey is capable of handling both jobs." For the first time since the 1920s under Rickey, the Cardinals now had one man giving signals from the dugout and making deals from the front office.

Herzog now had carte blanche to remake the team. He took full advantage. At the winter meetings in Dallas, he began changing the faces and the direction of the franchise. On Sunday, December 7, the club announced the signing of free-agent catcher Darrell Porter, who Herzog knew well from his days in Kansas City. One day later, the team made an 11-player swap with the San Diego Padres, receiving pitchers Rollie Fingers and Bob Shirley, along with catcher-first baseman Gene Tenace and catcher Bob Geren, while shipping seven prospects to the Padres, including highly regarded catcher Terry Kennedy. The next day, Herzog dealt first base prospect Leon Durham, third baseman Ken Reitz and minor-league infielder Ty Waller to the Chicago Cubs for relief pitcher Bruce Sutter. He wrapped up the week on Friday by sending the newly acquired Fingers, along with catcher Ted Simmons and pitcher Pete Vuckovich to Milwaukee for four players: outfielders David Green and Sixto Lezcano, and pitchers Dave LaPoint and Larry Sorensen. In six days, Herzog made transactions involving 23 players. It was the last deal that caught the most attention and flak from sportswriters and fans alike. "All Herzog really added was Sutter," wrote Steve Wulf in *Sports Illustrated*, "while losing the switch-hitting Simmons, one of the game's half-dozen toughest outs, in the process." Local reaction was also muted. Rick Hummel believed "the early vote was negative. Fans seemed to resent the [Simmons] deal."

Herzog remained resolute. "Teddy is a switch-hitter with a lifetime batting average near .300," he later wrote, "but he gave up a lot of passed balls and he couldn't throw worth a damn." Sutter cemented the back end of the bullpen and the roster shakeup enhanced team speed, a priority for a club that played its home games on the artificial turf of Busch Stadium. "Most of the guys [on the 1980 team] were so slow it took them two trips to haul ass," Herzog remembered.[30]

Herzog made three more key trades the following offseason to get the team even faster: acquiring outfielder Lonnie Smith in a three-team deal, swapping shortstop Garry Templeton for San Diego shortstop Ozzie Smith, and one involving a young outfielder. Herzog now had the elements in place to make a championship run. The last piece of the puzzle came courtesy of the Yankees.

*****

In the middle of their 1981 World Series loss to the Dodgers, Steinbrenner and the Yankees were already making plans for the following year. On the day of the second game of the Series, the team traded minor league outfielder Willie McGee to the Cardinals for pitcher Bob Sykes. It marked the second trade in less than a year between the Cardinals and Yankees. "We just felt he [Sykes] was worth taking a chance on, just like George Frazier last year," Yankees vice president Bill Bergesch said later that offseason (the same Bill Bergesch who, according to Veeck, made the team's offer to Keane in 1964.) Frazier, despite his World Series woes, had pitched well for New York, appearing in 16 regular-season contests, saving three games, and recording an ERA of 1.61. Sykes was expected to fill the role of a middle reliever. "We were especially impressed with his record (2-0, 1.88 ERA in 14 games) over the second half of last season," Bergesch told *New York Daily News* columnist Bill Madden.[31]

In most newspapers, the trade received only a few paragraphs of coverage. Most of the focus was on Sykes, a pitcher with five years of big-league experience. "I was a Mets fan," he said when contacted by a reporter after the deal was announced. "My dad was a Yankee fan. I hated the Yankees."[32] Little attention was paid to McGee, except to note the switch-hitting outfielder hit .322 for the Nashville Sounds in the Southern League. Free-agent Dave Winfield had joined a crowded Yankee outfield before the season. Knowing they would leave McGee off their protected 40-man roster (the team kept Ted Wilborn instead), the Yankees decided to trade him. *Post-Dispatch* reporter Hummel formally introduced the prospect to Cardinal fans the following spring.

"He speaks only when spoken to and goes largely unnoticed in the clubhouse," Hummel observed. "But he has skills that have marked him as a soon-to-be major leaguer, in Whitey Herzog's estimation. 'Got a quick bat,' said Herzog. 'It's unusual to see a young hitter with a quick bat from both sides of the plate.'"

An unnamed veteran pitcher on the team also liked what he saw from the young outfielder. "He's my long-shot choice to make this ballclub. Every spring, there's one guy who isn't supposed to make it that does, and I like Willie McGee. If he goes down, it won't be for long."[33]

The unnamed pitcher's prediction proved correct. McGee was sent down to the minor leagues to start the season. He didn't stay long. McGee made his major-league debut on May 10 and was in the starting lineup the following day. He rarely came out of the lineup the rest of the year. Appearing in 123 games, he hit .296, socked four home runs with 56 RBI, and stole 24 bases on a team that won the National League East. The third-place finisher in the race for Rookie of the Year in the National League (the Dodgers' Steve Sax won the award), the twenty-three-year-old outfielder saved his best for last. After sweeping the National League playoffs against the Atlanta Braves, the Cardinals had won a pennant for the first time since 1968. The 1982 World Series pitted St. Louis vs. Milwaukee, as Herzog's deal greatly boosted the Brewers. Vuckovich won 18 games, Fingers had 29 saves, and Simmons hit 23 home runs with 97 RBI. The three players in the deal still on the St. Louis roster contributed (Lezcano was a part of the Templeton/Smith trade), but none of them to the extent of the Milwaukee trio. In addition to featuring two Midwestern teams, the Series served as a proxy for two monster beer products: Budweiser and Miller Lite. The media dubbed it the "Suds Series."

The latter battle was a reminder of what caused so much agita for the St. Louis brewer and so much agony for Commissioner Kuhn. "Miller World Series 'Winner' Over Busch," read a headline in the *Post-Dispatch* in the middle of the Series, pointing out the Milwaukee brewer was the only beer company permitted to advertise on television broadcasts. Anheuser-Busch had to settle for radio ads.

Of course, A-B had other ways to remind a television audience of its products. Playing the opener in Busch Stadium and trotting out the Budweiser Clydesdales before the contest helped. What didn't help was what a few excited Clydesdales did to the first-base coaching box. On their way to deposit Gussie in his box seat, the horses left a deposit of their own on the stadium turf. It took a half-dozen grounds members to clean up the mess. For the Cardinals, it was an omen of things to come that evening. Milwaukee blasted St. Louis 10-0 in the most lopsided World Series opener since 1959. The Cardinals rallied to beat the Brewers 5-4 the following night to even things out.

For Game 3, the Cardinals returned to Milwaukee's County Stadium for the first time since the Braves left for Atlanta. After the first two games, "we began to wonder where the real heroes were," wrote Mike Lupica. "We wondered who would step forth and do something great, who would reach out from the television set, grab America by the front of the shirt and say: 'Watch *me.*'"[34]

The wait ended that night. "We wondered about all that until a 23-year-old Yankee reject named Wille McGee showed up at County Stadium in Milwaukee and for one glorious night turned into Wille Mays," Lupica told readers of his *Daily News* column. McGee began the evening by making a catch against the wall to rob Brewers leadoff hitter Paul Molitor. He smashed a three-run home run in the fifth inning and a solo shot in the seventh. Both home runs were off former Cardinal Vuckovich. In the bottom of the ninth inning, with one runner on base, and the Cardinals up 6-2, he robbed Gorman Thomas of a home run with a leaping grab at the wall that would have cut the lead in half. "I don't know if anybody ever played a World Series game better than Willie McGee did tonight," raved manager Herzog. McGee was asked if he had ever hit two home runs in a game before. "Little League," he said with a smile.

The impact of McGee's performance was magnified by what happened over the next two days. The Game 3 win would be the only victory for St. Louis in Milwaukee. Down 3-2 in the Series when the team returned to St. Louis, the Cardinals blasted the Brewers 13-1 in Game 6 and rallied to win 6-3 in the final game. When Bruce Sutter struck out Gorman Thomas in the ninth inning, St. Louis toasted a World Series winner for the first time in fifteen years. Despite one win and two saves in the Series, Sutter was not its MVP. That honor went to catcher Darrell Porter, who hit .286 with one home run and five RBI. McGee had two home runs and five RBI in the Series, but most of his damage was done in a single game.

All three had been acquired since Busch decided to change managers in 1980. Since that time, the roster had been reshaped by former Yankee farmhand Herzog, while the trajectory of the Series was reshaped by former Yankee farmhand McGee.

The Cardinals made two more World Series appearances in the 1980s under Herzog, and McGee played a key role on both teams. In 1985, he led the league in hits and triples, winning both the MVP award and a batting title with an average of .353 for a Cardinal team that won 100 games but lost the World Series in seven games to Kansas City.

Two years later, the team lost another seven-game Series, this time to the Minnesota Twins.[35] That season, McGee drove in 105 runs, the only time in his career his RBI total topped the century mark. He won his second and last batting title for St. Louis in 1990, hitting .335 for the Cardinals before being traded to the Oakland A's. He later returned to St. Louis and finished his career in a Cardinal uniform.

The year McGee came back to St. Louis, 1996, represented a dramatic change in the direction of both the Cardinals and Yankees. Busch had died in 1989. Herzog quit managing in the middle of the 1990 season. His replacement was Joe Torre. But with Gussie gone, Torrie lost the club's biggest advocate. Anheuser-Busch looked at the franchise as just another business line and an unprofitable one at that. In 1995, Torre's last year in St. Louis, the brewery said the club lost $12 million and put the franchise up for sale. In Herzog's last full season, the club led the league in attendance, averaging more than 38,000 fans a game. Six years later, and one year after a strike that wiped out the World Series, average attendance had plunged by 14,000 per contest.

The new ownership group of the Cardinals was introduced over the winter. Seven decades after his father became treasurer of the Cardinals, Bill DeWitt Jr., along with his partners, met with the media. DeWitt, Drew Baur, and Fred Hanser, all of them graduates of Country Day School in St. Louis, led a group of investors that paid $150 million for the team, the stadium, and parking garages. DeWitt got an early endorsement from the team's broadcaster. "If the kid is as nice as his father was, we're in good shape," said Jack Buck. "He [Bill Sr.] and his brother Charlie were like a pair of old slippers. They were wonderful to everyone," Buck said of the brothers who once owned the St. Louis Browns. While Bill DeWitt Sr. had once worked directly for Rickey, the other partners also had connections to Rickey's Redbirds. Hanser's great-grandfather was Adolph Diez, a minority owner of the Cardinals from 1917 to 1947. "He told my mother that he's the one who got automobile dealer Sam Breadon to buy the Cardinals. I don't know how much, if any, of this is true, but that's what he told her," Hanser recalled. Baur's connection was more personal. "Mr. Rickey was my mother's godfather, and his daughter, Sue, was my mother's best friend growing up," he said. "I remember my interest in the game began listening to Mr. Rickey and my grandfather talk about baseball on a Sunday afternoon on our porch."[36]

The new owners and general manager Walt Jocketty already had their manager in place for the next season. And it was a good thing they did. Steinbrenner and the Yankees were also interested in Tony La Russa before the Cardinals hired him. The Yankees had cycled through nearly two dozen managers in the past two decades and were looking for another one. In addition to La Russa, New York considered a couple of other candidates, but ultimately settled on one with plenty of experience, all of it in the National League and not a single postseason victory on his resume. "I got to admit," Torre said later, "I was their last choice."

*****

By the time Torre arrived for his first spring training with the Cardinals in 1969, he had already been in the major leagues for nearly a decade. He made his debut with the Milwaukee Braves in 1960. He was twenty years old. Primarily a catcher, Torre had also played first base and the outfield. He originally played first base and catcher for the Cardinals, but when Mike Shannon came down with a career-ending illness (nephritis, a kidney disease), Torre became the team's third baseman. George Kissell taught him how to play the position.

During spring training at Al Lang Field in St. Petersburg, coach and player would walk to the outfield. Kissell had him face the outfield wall, just eight feet away. Standing behind him, the coach would fire baseballs at the wall, leaving Torre to field the ricochet, similar to how a third baseman must react to a hot shot down the line. While it was Torre's offense that made him the National League MVP in 1971 (led the league with 230 hits, 137 RBI, and a .363 batting average), he never forgot the lessons he learned from the longtime Cardinal instructor. "A lot of people can play the game, but not as many people can teach the game," Torre said after his first season as Yankee manager. "And George, to me, was the ultimate. *Is* the ultimate."

Kissell's former student enjoyed an eighteen-year career in the big leagues. After his playing days were done, he managed the New York Mets, the Atlanta Braves and the Cardinals. In fourteen seasons, his only team to make it to postseason play, the 1982

Atlanta squad, didn't win a game in the NLCS against St. Louis. Fired as manager of the Cardinals in June of 1995, the Yankees came calling that fall. "CLUELESS JOE," read the headline of a skeptical *Daily News* when Torre was hired to lead a team that hadn't won a World Series game since before Steinbrenner was allegedly attacked in a Los Angeles hotel elevator.

The Yankees owner spent the 1980s making bad trades, firing managers and feuding with a star player. A year after the Yankees traded McGee to the Cardinals, New York dealt prospect Fred McGriff to the Toronto Blue Jays. Just like the McGee deal (Sykes never pitched in the big leagues again after leaving St. Louis), the McGriff trade proved to be one the Yankees would long regret. The first baseman went on to have a nineteen-year career, hitting 493 home runs. As for the players received in exchange, infielder Tom Dodd never played for the Yankees and pitcher Dale Murray won three games in two seasons for the club. Later in the decade, the team traded twenty-three-year-old outfielder Jay Buhner to the Seattle Mariners for thirty-three-year-old Ken Phelps, a trade so bad it was famously mocked in a *Seinfeld* episode. Buhner hit 310 home runs in a fifteen-year big-league career, while Phelps, a first baseman and designated hitter, hit 17 home runs in parts of two seasons in New York.

The owner compounded his problems with more off-field drama. Steinbrenner's feud with Dave Winfield resulted in a ban from management of the team by Commissioner Fay Vincent (he paid gambler Howard Spira $40,000 to dig up dirt on the outfielder). Reinstated in 1993, Steinbrenner watched his club improve under Buck Showalter, but when the Yankees lost a Division Series to Seattle in 1995, he fired the manager. By this time, fourteen years after the Yankees last World Series appearance, consensus opinion was that no manager could stand up to Steinbrenner and his impulsive, ranting ways.

Torre would prove the critics wrong. The "last choice" to manage the Yankees proved to be a perfect fit. In their first year together, the Yankees and Torre won the World Series, defeating the Atlanta Braves in six games. He almost faced La Russa's Cardinals. Up 3-1 in the National League Championship Series, the Cardinals dropped the next three games to the Braves. One story, often repeated in Atlanta, but lesser-known in St. Louis, is that when Cardinal relief pitcher Dennis Eckersley struck out Marquis Grissom to close out the victory in Game 4, he gave a fist pump into the air that offended the visiting team. Over the next three contests, Atlanta outscored St. Louis 32-1.

The Braves' momentum continued in the World Series, winning the first game in Yankee Stadium 12-1. Before Game 2, a nervous Steinbrenner paid Torre a visit in the clubhouse. "This is a must game," Steinbrenner said. "You should be prepared for us to lose again tonight," Torre told him. "But then we're going to Atlanta. Atlanta's my town. We'll take three games there and win it back here on Saturday."[37]

The manager proved to be a prophet. The Yankees would lose Game 2 before winning four straight to give the franchise their first World Series title in nearly two decades. Although the victory didn't come against the Cardinals, Torre had the team and its manager in mind that offseason. He reminded Steinbrenner that his contract called for a $550,000 salary for 1997, about a third of what the Cardinals were paying La Russa, a manager who also had one World Series victory on his resume. Steinbrenner bumped his pay by a quarter-million dollars to $800,000.

One of the keys to Torre's success could be seen in the exchange with his owner before Game 2 of the World Series. Just as Herzog figured out a casual conversation over beer was the best way to communicate with Busch, Torre had to navigate the terrain of an owner whose first instinct was to bully those below him. And the best way to beat a bully, Torre learned, was to engage in pre-emptive strikes. When the team was struggling, Torre wouldn't wait for a call from Steinbrenner. He'd dial up the owner and begin complaining about the team. "George always wanted to make me feel uncomfortable because he wanted that control over you," he remembered.[38]

Early in Torre's reign, he brought in relief pitcher Ramiro Mendoza in a game with the Yankees up 8-2. Mendoza gave up three runs in three innings, but the Yankees won the game 9-6. Afterward, Steinbrenner told general manager Bob Watson he wanted Mendoza shipped to the minor leagues. When Watson called Torre with the news, the manager had a plan. "Just make sure that George knows that when we do it and if the writers ask me why, I will tell them that George wanted to do it – that he wanted to send him out. I didn't." When Watson relayed the information to Steinbrenner, the Boss changed his mind. "That was a good lesson I learned early on. It was really my first confrontation with George. He backed off. Because he didn't want that responsibility of people knowing it was his call."

And that's how it went for 12 seasons; the anxious, overbearing owner and the cool, confident manager. "The lion would roar menacingly and Torre calmly would stick his head into the animal's mouth and come out smiling and unscathed," wrote author Tom Verducci. The career of Torre, the last Yankee manager to win a title in the twentieth century, bore a strong resemblance to the man who guided the team to its first championship decades earlier. Like Torre, Miller Huggins had arrived in New York after leaving St. Louis. Huggins managed the Cardinals for five seasons, never finished higher than third place, compiling a winning percentage of .455. Torre spent six years in St. Louis, never finished higher than second, and compiled a winning percentage of .498.[39] In New York, Huggins led the Yankees for 12 seasons, winning six pennants and three World Series. In his dozen years in the Bronx, Torre's teams won six pennants and four World Series.

Just as in 1996, the Cardinals and Yankees came within a single game of meeting in the World Series in 2004. This time, it was the Yankees' turn to blow a big lead. Up 3-0 in the American League Championship Series, New York saw Boston win four straight. The winning streak stretched to eight games when the Red Sox swept the Cardinals in the World Series. The 2004 Yankee team was the last under Torre to make it to the ALCS. He left the Yankees after the 2007 season. He collaborated with Verducci on the book *The Yankee Years* which was published in 2009. In the acknowledgments section, he singled out the people most influential in his career. One of those he mentioned was Kissell "for teaching me more about baseball than anyone."

The last Cardinal manager to work with Kissell was La Russa. In 2006, Tony's team delivered another World Series title to St. Louis, the team's first since Herzog's win over the Brewers in 1982. The game-clinching celebration took place in Busch Stadium III, which had just opened that spring. Three years later, the Yankees opened a new Yankee Stadium in the Bronx. The original had opened in 1923, the year of the first Yankee World Series title. History repeated itself nearly nine decades later. The 2009 Yankees, under manager Joe Girardi (whose last season as a player was 2003 as a Cardinal), enjoyed a World Series win in their new home, defeating the Philadelphia Phillies four games to two. Two years later, Albert Pujols accomplished something in World Series play previously only done by two Yankees. In the third game of the World Series against the Texas Rangers, Pujols hit three home runs to join an exclusive list previously featuring only Babe Ruth and Reggie Jackson. "It was fun to watch you," Jackson told Pujols in a telephone conversation after the game. "Albert elevated me by doing what he did," Reggie told columnist Bob Klapisch. "It was a reminder of what I did and what Ruth did."[40]

Ruth and Pujols could do what few others could. In the spring of 2006, researchers at Washington University in St. Louis put Pujols through a battery of tests similar to what psychologists at Columbia University in New York had conducted with Ruth eighty-five years earlier. The tests covered things like bat speed, visual response, and finger tapping. Pujols, like Ruth, was twenty-six years old at the time of the testing. The Cardinal first baseman produced a bat speed of 86.99 miles per hour with a 31.5-ounce bat. The Yankee outfielder generated a speed of 75 miles per hour with a 54-ounce bat. Pujols' visual response was 20 milliseconds faster than average. Ruth's eye stimulus tests showed he was 16 to 18 milliseconds faster than average. Researchers asked Pujols to depress a tapper with his index finger as many times as possible in 10 seconds. He scored in the 99th percentile, "a score almost identical to one earned by Ruth on a similar test of movement speed and endurance," noted an article published by Washington University.[41] In 1921, *The New York Times* called Ruth "supernormal." In 2006, one columnist called Pujols a "physiological freak."[42]

Pujols' performance in the 2011 World Series wasn't the first time a Cardinal had joined a home-run list previously dominated by Yankee players. In September of 1998, Mark McGwire launched his sixty-second home run of the season, breaking the single-season record set by Maris, a mark that had stood for thirty-seven years. Before Maris, Ruth's sixty-home-run-season set the standard for thirty-four seasons. Maris had passed away in 1985, but on the night McGwire hit number 62 off Chicago Cubs pitcher Steve Trachsel, his four sons and two daughters were in attendance at Busch Stadium. After crossing home plate, McGwire walked over to where the Maris family was sitting to embrace them and honor the memory of a man whose most famous moment occurred as a Yankee but who ended his career as a Cardinal.

In June of 2015, on the twentieth anniversary of Torre's termination in St. Louis, writer Will Leitch marveled at so many Cardinal-Yankee moments that had transpired in the previous two decades. "There were two franchises at their lowest point in decades when Joe Torre was fired, and since then, for 20 years, these have been the two most successful franchises in the sport. (And, perhaps not unrelatedly, the most despised by opposing team's fans.) And they both have changed the game of baseball in almost unfathomable ways. The planet is different because of one move, 20 years ago Tuesday. Sometimes a firing is just a firing. But sometimes it is so much more."[43]

---

[1] *New York Times,* April 11, 1965.
[2] *St. Louis Post-Dispatch,* August 2, 1965.
[3] The Cardinals let Dahlgren go after one season. Howsam said the team did not get as much use out of the films as they had hoped. Ibid, February 6, 1966.
[4] Gabler, Neal. *Walt Disney. The Triumph of the American Imagination.* Alfred E. Knopf. 2006.
[5] *New York Times,* July 3, 1964.
[6] According to Gabler, Disney had already purchased 27,400 acres of land in Florida by June of 1965.
[7] *Rochester Democrat and Chronicle*, January 8, 1967.
[8] Tom Tresh and Joe Pepitone were still active in 1969 but Boyer started his Yankee career earlier than either one.
[9] *Rochester Democrat and Chronicle*, January 8, 1967.
[10] *New York Times*, July 23, 2010.
[11] *The Cincinnati Enquirer*, January 23, 1967.
[12] "If I had to do it over again," Busch said in 1982, "I probably would have given Carlton the extra $5,000 he was asking for." *St. Louis Post-Dispatch,* September 21, 1982. "I sat with the bullheaded buzzard for seven hours, and Dick (Meyer), a great negotiator, tried for four hours," Busch recalled in 1978. "We couldn't budge him." Ibid, March 14, 1978.
[13] Neyer, *Rob Neyer's Big Book of Baseball Blunders.* Neyer believes those years were 1973, 1974, and 1981. Before Carlton and Reuss, the Cardinals traded pitchers Fred Norman and Mike Torrez in June of 1971. The two would go on to win 266 games for other teams. "So, in the span of eleven months – June 1971 through April 1972 – the Cardinals traded four pitchers who would, afterward, win 716 games. In return, the Cardinals essentially wound up with Rick Wise and not much of anything else. It might be among the worst eleven months any GM ever had."
[14] *New York Times*, January 4, 1973. The price was $3.2 million less than CBS had paid in 1964. Other published reports on the sale put the price tag on the Steinbrenner-led purchase at $8.7 million.
[15] *Miami Herald*, April 27, 1969.

---

[16] *New York Times*, December 4, 1977.
[17] Ibid, December 22, 1985.
[18] *St. Louis Post-Dispatch,* September 24, 1976.
[19] *New York Times*, June 17, 2004.
[20] Kuhn, Bowie. *Hardball: The Education of a Baseball Commissioner.* Times Books. 1978.
[21] *St. Louis Post-Dispatch*, April 18, 1979.
[22] Kuhn, *Hardball.*
[23] *St. Louis Post-Dispatch*, March 16, 2007.
[24] Kuhn, *Hardball.*
[25] Hernon and Ganey, *Under the Influence.*
[26] *St. Louis Post-Dispatch*, March 31, 1976.
[27] Ibid, September 16, 1981. According to authors Peter Hernon and Terry Ganey, one of the reasons the Leekers settled was a fear of David's sexuality being an issue at trial. David's parents regarded the allegation as a smear. "Afraid that their son would be slandered in death, they were also worn out by the long ordeal." Hernon and Ganey. *Under the Influence.*
[28] Herzog, Whitey and Horrigan, Kevin. *White Rat: A Life in Baseball.* Harper & Row. 1987,
[29] Ibid.
[30] Ibid.
[31] *New York Daily News*, November 27, 1981.
[32] *Ashbury (New Jersey) Park Press*, October 22, 1981.
[33] *St. Louis Post-Dispatch*, March 18, 1982.
[34] New York *Daily News*, October 16, 1982.
[35] The general manager of the 1985 and 1987 pennant-winning Cardinals teams was Dal Maxvill, the man who had caught the last out of the 1964 World Series against the Yankees.
[36] *St. Louis Post-Dispatch*, January 7, 1996.
[37] Torre, Joe and Verducci, Tom. *The Yankee Years.* Doubleday. 2009.
[38] Ibid.
[39] In St. Louis, Torre managed four full seasons – 1991 to 1994 – and parts of 1990 and 1995. He was fired 47 games into the 1995 season.
[40] *The Record (*Hackensack, New Jersey), October 24, 2011.
[41] source.wustl.edu/2006/08/st-louis-cardinals-slugger-pujols-gets-babe-ruth-test-at-washington-university/
[42] *The Baltimore Sun,* October 27, 2006.
[43] "The Move That Changed Baseball," *Sports On Earth*, June 16, 2015. www.sportsonearth.com/article/130956592/joe-torre-fired-st-louis-cardinals-20-years-ago-new-york-yankees. Ten years earlier, Dave Anderson had written a column titled "Cardinals Are Ghosts That Haunt The Yankees." *New York Times*, June 8, 2005. In 2017, Ed Gruver wrote about the Cardinal and Yankee teams of the mid-1930s. "The Greatest World Series Never Played." seamheads.com/blog/2014/10/17/the-greatest-world-series-never-played/

The Ghosts of Branch Rickey

Bill DeWitt Jr. grew up in an environment not bound by baseball conventions. In 1945, his father and uncle signed one-armed outfielder Pete Gray to play for the Browns. Two years later, the team became the third in all of baseball to sign and play African-American players, only behind Rickey's Dodgers and Bill Veeck's Indians. Desperate for attendance, the team touted its cutting edge in-game experience for fans. "We were the first to flash hits and errors on our big scoreboard," said Charley DeWitt in 1948. "We're the only city in the country where the up-to-the-minute batting averages and pitching records of the players are carried on the scorecards."[1] Under Charley and Bill DeWitt Sr.'s ownership, the Browns hired a psychologist.[2] Dr. David Tracy believed in hypnosis, a practice the team's rookies claimed helped them get adjusted to big-league crowds and competition. "I know Bill DeWitt has gone out on a limb to hire me, and I've gone out on a bigger limb," he said in February of 1950, shortly after going to work for the team.[3]

Bill DeWitt Jr. turned nine years old that summer. It later dawned on him where his father's baseball philosophy came from. "I got the sense, as I got to be a little older, how he operated, and Rickey's was the model he used."

As a teenager, the son got exposure to another baseball organization. After the Browns moved to Baltimore, Bill DeWitt Sr. joined the Yankees as assistant general manager to George Weiss. "I used to travel with my father when he was with the Yankees," DeWitt Jr. recalled. "As the assistant GM, he used to go scouting all over the place. I would go with him. He used to give me the stopwatch, to clock runners from home to first. I got to meet a lot of scouts, and high school and college coaches."[4]

DeWitt Sr. left the Yankees for a brief stint helping major league baseball administer a fund to aid the minor leagues. He then spent two years as president and general manager of the Detroit Tigers, where he once traded managers with the Cleveland Indians. The deal that swapped Cleveland's Joe Gordon for Detroit's Jimmy Dykes brought back memories of Rickey's deal with the New York Giants in the middle of the 1948 season that saw manager Leo Durocher change teams.

In the fall of 1960, DeWitt Sr. replaced Gabe Paul as the Cincinnati Reds general manager (Paul and DeWitt were part of a five-decade run of Reds general managers with Rickey roots and ties to the Cardinals).[5] The 1961 Reds won the National League pennant, and since DeWitt already had the 1944 American League champion St. Louis Browns on his resume, he became the first executive to win pennants in both leagues. A year later, he bought the Reds for $4,625,000. *Cincinnati Enquirer* sports editor Allan Haim called him "the modern Branch Rickey," a viewpoint shared by others. "After Rickey, he's the shrewdest trader and executive in baseball," said Veeck.[6] (With the Browns, DeWitt once traded two players to the Boston Red Sox for seven players and $310,000 in cash.) "I learned a long time ago from Mr. Rickey that you can't stand still. If you do, it won't be long before the other teams overtake you," said DeWitt.[7] It was a lesson from Rickey that his son would carry with him to St. Louis.

After college at Yale and getting his MBA at Harvard (where he wrote a paper on baseball business practices), DeWitt Jr. got his first baseball job from anyone other than his family when the Reds hired him in January of 1967. His father had just sold the team (for $7 million) and new owner Frank Dale welcomed him the same month Bob Howsam left St. Louis to become the Cincinnati general manager. The younger DeWitt became the team's treasurer, the same role his father had for the Cardinals decades earlier. Over the next three decades, DeWitt Jr. went on to hold minority ownership positions at various times with the Reds, the Texas Rangers (as a partner of future President George W. Bush), and the Baltimore Orioles. In 1993, he was poised to take control of the Orioles when the deal fell through. Two years later, he got the chance to buy the Cardinals. "I'm lucky that the Baltimore deal didn't work out. Because the Cardinals turned out to be a much better fit."[8]

By the end of 2002, DeWitt had been in charge of the Cardinals for seven seasons, a timeframe in which the team had won the National League Central three times and made the playoffs four times. The 2002 team won 97 games and made it to the NLCS before losing to the San Francisco Giants. While it featured a few homegrown stars drafted and developed by the organization – Albert Pujols, J.D. Drew, Matt Morris – the vast majority of key contributors had been acquired through trades or signed via free agency. DeWitt thought the balance needed to change; the entire talent evaluation process needed an overhaul.

"I'm totally committed to drafting and signing the best players," the owner told a gathering of scouts early in his tenure, calling the process "the lifeblood of the business." Searching for a better way, he found it in the summer of 2003. Michael Lewis's book *Moneyball* told the story of the small-market Oakland A's and how general manager Billy Beane managed to keep his team competitive through cutting edge data analysis. More than a half-century before, Rickey and Brooklyn statistician Allan Roth had developed a formula (based on run differential) they were convinced baseball would embrace. "If the baseball world is to accept this new system of analyzing games – and eventually it will – it must first give up preconceived notions," Rickey wrote of the formula that emphasized things like on-base percentage and isolated power, a modification of slugging percentage. Baseball yawned. "Ah, the famous equation," remembered *New York Times* columnist Leonard Koppett, "There was no response. No one followed it."[9]

By the early twenty-first century, a new group of number crunchers, aided by ubiquitous information and exponentially increasing computing power, saw a powerful advantage in taking a fresh look at the data. Lewis's book had an enormous impact on professional baseball. DeWitt read it, recognized it as a gamechanger and wasted no time taking action. "I wanted somebody fresh, to give an outsider's perspective," he recalled. "And to do more research and analysis."[10] In the fall, DeWitt hired Jeff Luhnow, a former McKinsey consultant and Internet entrepreneur, calling him a "high-level McKinsey talent at a below-market price." Hired as vice president of player development, Luhnow quickly rose through the organization. In 2004, he took charge of the organization's baseball academy in the Dominican Republic. A year later, he became director of amateur scouting and a year after that, became the club's director of player development.

Armed with engineering and economic degrees from Penn, an MBA from Northwestern, entrepreneurial experience and a consulting background, Luhnow brought process discipline, an analytical framework, and a fresh viewpoint. Early in his time with the Cardinals, he set up an advisory board that included fantasy baseball writer Ron Shandler. He also began hiring Ivy League-pedigreed former athletes, outsiders, and those versed in the language of standard deviation and regression analysis. Dan Kantrovitz played shortstop at Brown. Mike Elias pitched at Yale, illustrator and cartoonist Mike Witte had some interesting theories on pitching mechanics, Sig Mejdal had worked as a biomathematician for NASA's Fatigue Countermeasure Group. Luhnow hired all of them.[11] Baseball had all sorts of numbers and ratios. Mining the right ones could produce a competitive advantage.

Mejdal (pronounced "my-dell") recalled an early presentation for an audience that included the owner and his son, team president Bill DeWitt III. "I remember the look on Billy's face very well," said Mejdal. "He and his father both appreciated that the inefficiency was there, and I remember feeling a great relief. It was just a question of how much of it we could grab and how long would the inefficiency remain."[12]

Starting in 2005, when Luhnow took charge of scouting, the Cardinals began grabbing players in the draft who would later play key roles on the big-league squad. His first draft featured eight players who eventually made it to the major leagues (including outfielder Colby Rasmus and pitcher Jaime Garcia), twice as many as the year before. It could have been even better. Mejdal wanted to take Stanford infielder Jed Lowrie, still active in the big leagues in 2019. Instead, the team chose Tyler Greene from Georgia Tech, who played his last game in 2013. The 2006 draft included outfielders Jon Jay, Allen Craig, and Tommy Pham; pitcher Lance Lynn was taken in 2008.[13]

The fifth year of the new regime, 2009, featured what author Howard Megdal referred to as "peak Luhnow." In that draft, the Cardinals took five players who would soon be in St. Louis: pitchers Shelby Miller, Joe Kelly, and Trevor Rosenthal; third baseman Matt Carpenter and first baseman Matt Adams.

Under Luhnow's direction, the Cardinals gradually integrated analytics into their talent evaluation and development process. "From the very beginning in St. Louis, Jeff framed it as an *and* question," recalled Mejdal. "It's the scouting information *and* the performance information." Mejdal called it STOUT – half stats, half scouts.[14] Despite the take-it-slow approach, Luhnow and his band of outsiders rubbed the old-school front-office staff the wrong way. General manager Walt Jocketty saw Luhnow, with his vice president title and direct access to DeWitt, as more of a threat than a revelation. "I don't think Walt trusted him, and I don't think Walt liked him," remembered John Mozeliak, the assistant general manager at the time. Some members of the front office went so far as to refuse to talk to Luhnow. Factions developed. Morale plummeted. "I actually thought at one point of just leaving here," said Mozeliak. "It was getting so tense and it was very stressful."[15]

The stress level continued to rise as Luhnow brought on additional outsiders who challenged mainstream methods. Impressed with Witte, the cartoonist who would fax diagrams of pitching mechanics to the owners in St. Louis, Luhnow asked him if he knew a coach who had a similar philosophy around pitching practices. Witte recommended Brent Strom, the second player in major-league history to have Tommy John surgery. Strom had spent time in five different organizations after his playing days ended but was out of baseball and working with his wife on her dog-grooming business when Luhnow hired him to tutor minor league pitchers. Strom believed in throwing fastballs up in the strike zone, a direct challenge to the approach taken by St. Louis pitching coach Dave Duncan, who wanted his staff to keep the ball down. "Strommy would say stuff about throwing your high fastball, and that wouldn't go over too well," Luhnow remembered.[16] If it hadn't been for Luhnow's support, "I think I'd have been gone after the first year," Strom recalled. ("You know what? You're a pretty good guy," coach Mark DeJohn once told Strom in spring training. "You're not the asshole everyone tells me you are.")[17]

Luhnow did his best to steer Strom toward the lower minor leagues and away from the upper tiers of the organization, but the argument revealed deep fissures in the franchise. Luhnow and Jocketty ran distinct fiefdoms with little communication between the two groups. This feud was no longer just about abstract data. The Luhnow team had waded into the basic tenets of the game. The philosophical and practical civil war resulted in real casualties.

Even before the hiring of Strom, owner DeWitt decided a Cardinals house divided against itself could not stand. Coming off a 2007 season in which the team finished six games below .500, he fired general manager Jocketty. "There was basically a difference in philosophy," said Jocketty, "no different than if you have a difference of opinion with your wife, your parents or whatever."[18] Speaking about his relationship with Luhnow, Jocketty told *Post-Dispatch* reporter Joe Strauss, "There were probably things I could have and should have done to try and make it work better, but I wasn't comfortable. I didn't do it." A day after Jocketty was fired, the Cardinals dismissed former minor league director Bruce Manno. Minor-league hitting coordinator Gene Tenace soon left his job after clashing with Luhnow. "They bring in a guy that has no background in baseball and he wants to get involved in (player) development, and I don't think it works that way." Tenace told Kary Booher of the *Springfield News-Leader*. "I hope it all works out for them. But I don't see where it's going to work."[19]

Fueling the skeptic's doubt was the performance of Jocketty, who joined the Cincinnati Reds and soon became the team's general manager. In 2010, *The Sporting News* named him Executive of the Year after the Reds won 91 games and claimed the National League Central division title. The Cardinals finished second in the division and sat out the postseason for the third time in four seasons. The local media took notice. "There have been successes, but also failures," wrote *Post-Dispatch* columnist Bernie Miklasz. "Overall, I'd have to say Luhnow has improved the young talent pipeline, and we praise him for that. But the results haven't come close to matching the claims made by Luhnow's boosters."

Luhnow's boosters could point to a minor-league system winning percentage of .569 in 2010, the best in baseball. Validation at the major-league level came a year later when the Cardinals won the World Series. Seven players on the World Series roster, including pitchers Mitchell Boggs, Jaime Garcia, Lance Lynn, and Fernando Salas, had been signed under Luhnow's leadership. "If I'd known you were going to send me so many guys who can throw ninety-five plus, I wouldn't have been so hard on you for so long!" La Russa told him afterward. The Luhnow pipeline was just beginning. The 2013 National League champion Cardinals featured a World Series roster with 17 of 25 players signed when Luhnow oversaw scouting.

While the franchise would continue to benefit from the work of their vice president – the 2014 team lost in the NLCS and the 2015 team won a major-league best 100 regular-season games – the man who started the St. Louis revolution had moved on. The Houston Astros hired Luhnow to become the team's general manager in December of 2011.

In Houston, Luhnow climbed an even bigger mountain. He inherited a team that had lost 106 games in the previous season. He immediately hired Mejdal, the former NASA engineer he had brought to St. Louis and gave him a distinct title: Director of Decision Sciences. "Don't think this new breed is not impressed with itself," wrote *Sporting News* columnist Stan McNeal, just the beginning of withering criticism Luhnow would face early in his Houston tenure. In 2013, Miklasz described the Astros general manager – a man who had held high-level positions in baseball for a decade – as "business-school graduate Jeff Luhnow." The following summer, Miklasz colleague Joe Strauss posted on

Twitter that the "BFIB (best fans in baseball) longing for days of Luhnow blissfully unaware of worsening meltdown in Houston. Amazing."

The "meltdown" in Houston featured a 2012 team that lost 107 games. It didn't get any better the following year. The 2013 club lost 111 games. "They are definitely the outcast of Major League Baseball right now, and it's kind of frustrating for everyone else to watch it," former Astros pitcher Bud Norris said early in the 2014 season. On the day Strauss took to Twitter, Houston had the second-worst record in the American League and were twenty games under .500. It also came one month after Ben Reiter's *Sports Illustrated* cover story about the Astros appeared with the bold headline: YOUR 2017 WORLD SERIES CHAMPS.

Reiter had arrived in Houston one day before the 2014 amateur draft. For the third straight season, Houston had the first pick. The *SI* writer was granted access to draft room deliberations and given insight into Luhnow's approach to building a team. "They would not make cosmetic decisions, such as wasting money on a free agent or hanging on to a veteran who might be converted into future assets, in an effort to keep up appearances," Reiter wrote for the June 30 cover story. "When you're in 2017," Luhnow told him, "you don't really care that much about whether you lost 98 or 107 in 2012. You care about how close we are to winning a championship in 2017."

Through a combination of drafts, trades, and free-agent signings, Luhnow built a 2017 team that won 99 games and finished first in the American League West. After defeating Boston and New York in the playoffs, Houston faced Los Angeles for the sport's ultimate prize. Seventy years to the month after Rickey's Dodgers played in their first World Series since he left St. Louis, Luhnow's Astros won the first World Series title in Houston history. In his book, *Astroball*, Reiter credited a visionary owner and an author for laying the groundwork for Houston's success. "(I)f not for the intuition of a single person, Cardinals' owner Bill DeWitt Jr., and timely publication of a book called *Moneyball*, the men who made those calls would have likely remained in Silicon Valley and at NASA."[20]

Just as Rickey did when he left for Ebbets Field, Luhnow had several people follow him to Texas. In addition to Mejdal, Luhnow brought over others who played a role for the 2017 World Series winners. Mike Elias became the team's director of scouting. Oz Ocampo had once served as coordinator of Latin American scouting for the Cardinals. Luhnow hired him to oversee all aspects of international baseball operations for Houston. Scout Charlie Gonzalez left the Cardinals for the Astros while the pitching coach for the World Series winners was the man who had ruffled feathers in St. Louis for challenging the pitch-to-contact approach preached by Dave Duncan and Tony La Russa. "There are very few coaches like him," Luhnow said of Brent Strom in the summer of 2018, describing him in a way reminiscent of Rickey a century before. "He's always reading a book, always researching a new theory."

Even before Luhnow's success in Houston became abundantly apparent, his actions received scrutiny in St. Louis. For one member of the Cardinals' front office, the exploits of their former executive became an obsession.

Chris Correa was a doctoral student at the University of Michigan when he responded to an Internet posting by the Cardinals looking for a freelancer to tackle a data project. Correa got the job and so impressed club officials with the results (the project involved scraping data from the websites of college baseball teams), they later offered him a full-time position.[21] When Luhnow and Mejdal left for Houston, Correa remained in St. Louis and at the end of 2014 was named the club's director of scouting, Luhnow's old job (the position became available when Luhnow's replacement, Dan Kantrovitz, left for an assistant GM position with the Oakland A's).[22]

The following summer, Correa ran his first and only amateur draft for the Cardinals. The team's selections that June included pitcher Jordan Hicks, shortstop Paul DeJong, and outfielder Harrison Bader, players who quickly made it to the major leagues. It was an impressive draft with some possible illegal inputs.

In March of 2014, the *Houston Chronicle* featured a story on a database developed by the Astros, nicknamed "Ground Control." As reporter Evan Drellich noted, "Contract information, scouting reports, statistics common and proprietary – the Astros have centralized most every piece of useful baseball information at one password-protected web address." Luhnow had first presented the idea for the "complex, built-from-scratch database" when he interviewed with Houston owner Jim Crane. "Built from scratch" was an important phrase. "The similarities between 'Ground Control,' as described in the *Chronicle* story, and the Cardinals' in-house database was not lost on the Cardinals, team officials said at the time," explained Cardinals beat writer Derrick Goold. As for the system developed in Houston, "It's one of the coolest toys the public will never play with," wrote Drellich.[23] The public didn't. Chris Correa did.

Three months after the story appeared, *Deadspin* broke the news that ten months of the Astros internal trade talks had been leaked and posted online. Someone had hacked the Houston database. A year later, *The New York Times* claimed the FBI had traced the hack to a single house in Jupiter, Florida, the spring training home of the Cardinals.[24] When Mejdal left the Cardinals in December of 2011, he turned over his laptop – and his password – to Correa. When he started his new job in Houston, Mejdal used a similar password. Correa figured it out. Documents would later establish that Correa intruded into the Houston database 48 times and accessed the accounts of Mejdal and four other Astros' employees, including Luhnow. For two-and-a-half years, Correa had "unfettered access" to Mejdal's e-mail account.[25] As he explained to a judge, Correa suspected Luhnow and his team had taken proprietary data with them to Houston. As one source told the *Post-Dispatch*, "Correa's suspicions were aroused in part by a résumé in which a job seeker claimed expertise that Correa believed could have come only from working with Cardinals data."[26] The Astros consistently maintained no proprietary information of the Cardinals was in their database.

The skullduggery by Correa harkened back to another era when a high-profile executive left the Cardinals and sparked chicanery in St. Louis. Rickey's departure for Brooklyn after the 1942 season ignited an exodus of personnel and scouts who wound up working for the Dodgers. The rest of the decade saw plenty of heated battles and brawls between St. Louis and Brooklyn. Most of them were confined to the field of play, but one skirmish involving Cardinals owner Sam Breadon had Brooklyn blood boiling.

It happened in September of 1945 with the Cardinals in pursuit of a fourth straight pennant. The Dodgers had a series in Cincinnati before heading to St. Louis for three games. The team's last day in Ohio featured a doubleheader against the Reds. In between games, the Dodgers got the news that Breadon had scheduled a doubleheader in St. Louis for the following evening. Brooklyn players and manager Leo Durocher howled in protest. ANGRY DODGERS SET TO TEAR CARDINALS LIMB FROM LIMB IN TWO TILTS TONIGHT read a headline in the *Brooklyn Eagle.* On the morning after the Cincinnati finale, the team caught a 6:00 a.m. train, didn't arrive in St. Louis until 4:30 that afternoon, and headed directly to Sportsman's Park to play a Cardinals team just two games behind the first-place Chicago Cubs. A confident Breadon was making World Series plans. "We're gaining speed and it looks like the Cubs are faltering," he told columnist Roy Stockton. "Anyhow, I've made [World Series] reservations for the Cardinals in both Detroit and Washington."[27]

The Cardinals won the first game that evening, but the Dodgers caught a break when the second game was rained out. The next day, Thursday, featured more rain and no games were played. With time running out on the regular season and the Dodgers due in Chicago for a series starting Saturday, the teams played a doubleheader on Friday. Brooklyn swept the twin-bill. "Sam Breadon proposes, but Leo Durocher disposes," wrote Harold Burr in the *Brooklyn Eagle*.

A weary Dodgers team then caught a midnight train to Chicago. With no berths available, the club had to sit in coach for the overnight ride. Forty miles outside Chicago, the train crashed into an oil truck, killing the engineer and a crew member and severely burning the truck driver. None of the Dodgers was seriously hurt (outfielder Luis Olmo was cut on the right arm by flying glass), and the team somehow made its way to Wrigley Field to play that day. Brooklyn proceeded to drop three straight games to Chicago. When the Cardinals split a doubleheader against the Phillies on Sunday, St. Louis fell four games back. In the final standings two weeks later, the Cubs ended up winning the pennant over the Cardinals by a three-game margin.

Breadon's plan had backfired but it wasn't forgotten in Brooklyn. More than three decades later, Harold Parrott, the Dodgers traveling secretary in 1945, wrote about the incident for his book *The Lords of Baseball.* He named a chapter "Breadon's Dirty Trick and Lippy's Revenge" and claimed that "Rickey carried an open grudge" against the Cardinals owner.

An open grudge likely played a role in Correa's troubles. Both he and Mejdal admitted to the FBI "having heated disputes with each other." Documents unsealed in the U.S. Southern District Court in January of 2017 described Mejdal as "one of Correa's rivals." When his rival got glowing press from the *Sports Illustrated* piece, Correa decided to act. The article was released online on June 26, 2014. One night later, "after months of not intruding into Ground Control, Correa began trying to log back in." He was unsuccessful (the Astros had reset all passwords earlier in the year) but the next day found the usernames and passwords of three minor league players while searching Mejdal's e-mail account. Using the accounts of two of the players, Correa used an anonymous e-mail service to send months' worth of trade discussion talks to *Deadspin,* which quickly published the material. The disclosure of those discussions led the Astros to privately apologize to every team in the league. Investigators believed Correa's motivation was clear. "It was a humiliating episode for the Astros," noted authorities.

By the time the documents were released, Correa had long since departed St. Louis. The Cardinals fired him in the summer of 2015 shortly after the *Times* story broke. In January of 2016, he pled guilty to five counts of unauthorized access to a computer, was sentenced to 46 months in federal prison (later reduced), and ordered to pay the Astros $279,039 in restitution. The prosecution also struck back at Correa's main line of defense. "Ultimately, Correa was not intruding to see if the Astros took any information," according to the unsealed documents, "rather, he was keenly focused on information that coincided with the work he was doing for the Cardinals."

Correa's crimes also cost the Cardinals. While no one else in the organization was implicated in the scandal, Commissioner Rob Manfred stripped St. Louis of its first two picks of the 2017 draft, awarded them to Houston, and ordered the Cardinals to pay $2 million in compensation to the Astros. He also banned Correa for life from having a job in baseball. The announcement by the commissioner closed the books on one of the most sordid scandals in St. Louis baseball history and tarnished the reputation of the franchise. "Sadly for the Cardinals, few in baseball believe Correa acted alone," concluded *Post-Dispatch* columnist Jose de Jesus Ortiz.[28]

While general manager Mozeliak strongly denied that anyone with the Cardinals had anything to do with the actions of Correa, he did concede the loss of draft picks was a blow to the franchise. "When you think about the success of this organization, we've been, candidly, defined by how well we drafted," said the man hired to replace Jocketty as general manager, in large part because he could bridge the gap between the front office traditionalists and Luhnow's band of quants. Promoted to president in charge of baseball operations in the summer of 2017, Mozeliak pays tribute to Cardinals history (wears bow ties to honor Rickey), while his time as general manager drew comparisons to the Yankees (from 2008 to the time of his promotion, New York and St. Louis had the two best records in baseball).

With the hacking scandal, Mozeliak and the Cardinals ensured further comparisons to Luhnow and the Astros. The summer of 2019 brought additional scrutiny. At the trade deadline, the Astros shocked the baseball world by completing a last-minute deal to secure the services of Arizona Diamondbacks righthander Zack Greinke. In exchange for

Greinke, a former Cy Young Award winner, the Astros dealt four minor league players, including three of the top-eight ranked prospects in the organization. One of the players included, and one of the elite eight, was Corbin Martin, a pitcher the Astros selected in the 2017 draft. Houston took Martin with the 56th pick, a slot the Cardinals had to give to the Astros. The ability of Houston to pull the trigger on the Greinke trade reflected a deep pool of talent in the minor leagues. The only trade the Cardinals made at the deadline involved swapping infielder Jedd Gyorko to the Dodgers for a minor league pitcher and injured lefthander Tony Cingrani, who never pitched for St. Louis. The Cardinals had two prospects desired by other organizations – third baseman Nolan Gorman and outfielder Dylan Carlson – but otherwise lacked the reservoir of talent needed to pull off a Greinke-level deal. As *FanGraphs* columnist Craig Edwards noted at the trade deadline, "If you remove MLB roster, Gorman, and Carlson, the only player the Cards have among top 300 prospects in the game is their first-round draft pick this year."[29]

Whether it was a lack of trading chips or simply wise decision-making, the patience displayed by the Cardinals at the trade deadline paid off. ("Sometimes, the best deals are the ones you don't make," Rickey often said.) The team caught fire in the second half of the season, won the division, and made it to the NLCS before being dominated by the eventual World Series champion Washington Nationals. But concerns over talent in the minor leagues lingered.

Here, too, we can draw analogies to an earlier time. Breadon and the Cardinals prospered in the first four years after Rickey left St. Louis, winning three pennants and two World Series titles. In the first four years after Luhnow left the Cardinals, St. Louis made four consecutive postseason appearances. Although not a perfect corollary, the four seasons after that also produce some similarities. The Cardinals' long postseason drought that didn't end until 1964 began in 1947. Starting in 2016, St. Louis failed to make the postseason for three straight years, the team's longest stretch since the 1990s.

First Four Years in St. Louis

After Rickey					**After Luhnow**
Year	**Record**	**Result**	**Year**	**Record**	**Result**
1943	105-49	NL Champ	2012	88-74	NLCS Loss
1944	105-49	WS Winner	2013	97-65	NL Champ
1945	95-59	2nd Place	2014	90-72	NLCS Loss
1946	98-58	WS Winner	2015	100-62	NLDS Loss

Next Four Years in St. Louis

After Rickey			After Luhnow		
Year	**Record**	**Result**	**Year**	**Record**	**Result**
1947	89-65	2nd Place	2016	86-76	2nd NL Cent.
1948	85-69	2nd Place	2017	83-79	3rd NL Cent.
1949	96-58	2nd Place	2018	88-74	3rd NL Cent.
1950	78-75	5th Place	2019	91-71	NLCS Loss

Both Rickey and Luhnow brought championships to organizations where success had largely eluded them. It took Rickey five years after departing St. Louis to deliver a pennant winner in Brooklyn, just the club's second championship since 1920. Luhnow needed six years to bring a title to Houston, the first World Series winner in franchise history.

First Four Years in Brooklyn/Houston

Rickey			Luhnow		
Year	**Record**	**Result**	**Year**	**Record**	**Result**
1943	81-72	3rd Place	2012	55-107	6th NL Cent.
1944	63-91	7th Place	2013	51-111	5th AL West
1945	87-67	3rd Place	2014	70-92	4th AL West
1946	96-60	2nd Place	2015	86-76	2nd AL West

Next Four Years in Brooklyn/Houston

Rickey			Luhnow		
Year	**Record**	**Result**	**Year**	**Record**	**Result**
1947	94-60	NL Champ	2016	84-78	3rd AL West
1948	84-70	3rd Place	2017	101-61	WS Winner
1949	97-57	NL Champ	2018	103-59	ALCS Loss
1950	89-65	2nd Place	2019	107-55	AL Champ

Despite the loss in the World Series, the 2019 season capped an incredible three-year run by the Astros. The team became just the sixth in MLB history to win 100-plus games three straight years (a fraternity of teams that includes Rickey's Redbirds of the 1940s and Joe Torre's Yankees in the early 2000s).[30]

Rickey had led the push to expand the farm system. Luhnow was now leading the game in the opposite direction. After 2017, Houston reduced their minor league teams from nine to seven in the belief that fewer clubs could produce better talent. "In baseball," wrote Travis Sawchik at *FiveThirtyEight*, "top prospects spend years against lesser competition. How do you improve against *inferior* competition?"[31]

Luhnow gave Mejdal a new title and new responsibilities. He was no longer Director of Decision Sciences. Mejdal became Special Assistant to the GM, Process Improvement. Instead of sitting in an office evaluating numbers, Mejdal put on a baseball uniform for the first time since Little League and began traveling with the Houston farm teams. He was there to observe, make recommendations, and ensure the team's data-driven approach permeated even the lowest rungs of the organization.[32]

As the Cardinals found out earlier in the decade, success spawned imitators. Luhnow's top assistant, David Stearns, left to become the general manager of the Milwaukee Brewers (amateur scouting director Elias became the new assistant general manager). Jeff Albert had worked for six years in the Houston organization as a hitting instructor. St. Louis hired him to become their hitting coach at the major-league level. It was a roundtrip for Albert who started his professional coaching career for a Cardinals farm team.

Besides losing personnel, Houston's cutting-edge approach came with other costs. In 2018, the team stirred concerns, especially among female employees, when it traded for Roberto Osuna, a relief pitcher nearing the end of a 75-game suspension for domestic abuse charges (charges that were later dropped when the woman returned to Mexico and refused to testify.) The culture of the organization, several former Houston employees insisted, was toxic. "Cutthroat. Secretive. Not fun. But, winning, being first, innovative," one former and unnamed employee told *The Athletic*.[33] Strike One.

A year after the Osuna deal, on the night the Astros clinched the American League Championship Series, assistant general manager Brandon Taubman turned to *Sports Illustrated's* Stephanie Apstein and two other female reporters amidst the post-game celebration and repeatedly began yelling. "Thank God we got Osuna! I'm so fucking glad we got Osuna!"[34] The women had not been talking to, or about Osuna, who had allowed a two-run home run that tied the game in the top of the ninth inning. Instead of focusing their attention on the needless taunting of the women, one of whom was wearing a domestic violence bracelet, the Astros accused Apstein, the reporter who broke the story, of attempting "to fabricate a story where one does not exist." The team quickly backtracked. In the face of intense media scrutiny and criticism, Luhnow apologized, announced the firing of Taubman, but wouldn't say who wrote or approved the team's initial statement. "The Astros have a character flaw," wrote Peter Abraham in the *Boston Globe.* Strike Two.

In his column critiquing the Astros, Abraham brought additional evidence to bear regarding the team's win-at-all-costs attitude. "Under Luhnow, the Astros are generally considered to be at least bending the rules when it comes to video surveillance of other teams during games, especially at home," Abraham contended. "It was so blatant last season (2018) that the Indians tipped off the Red Sox to the falsely credentialed Astros staffer who was peering into their dugout during the ALCS." That evidence was first reported by *Yahoo's* Jeff Passan and included this note. "Two major league players said they have witnessed the Astros hitting a trash can in the dugout in recent years and believe it is a way to relay signals to hitters," Passan wrote.[35]

On November 12, thirteen days after the end of the World Series and less than a month after Passan's column appeared, former Houston pitcher Mike Fiers confirmed what many in baseball had long suspected. The Astros were stealing signs in 2017, thanks to a center-field camera, a monitor near the dugout, and players and team employees banging a trash can to relay information about the oncoming pitch to the hitter. "That's not playing the game the right way," Fiers told Ken Rosenthal and Evan Drellich of *The Athletic*. "They were willing to go above and beyond to win." (Three other sources inside the organization confirmed the existence of the scheme to the reporters on the condition of anonymity.)

Major league baseball officials quickly launched an investigation and confirmed the charges. Justice was swift. Commissioner Rob Manfred announced punishment in January. The Astros received a $5 million fine and forfeited their first and second-round draft picks in both 2020 and 2021. While the commissioner chose not to discipline any Astros players, he suspended Luhnow, manager A.J. Hinch, and former executive Taubman for the 2020 season. While Luhnow denied any knowledge of the banging scheme, investigators did find evidence he was aware of what was going on in the video replay room, "but he didn't give it much attention," according to the report. Just hours after Manfred's announcement, Houston owner Jim Crane fired both Luhnow and Hinch.[36] Strike Three.

Information revealed later cast doubts on Luhnow's claims. In February, *The Wall Street Journal*, citing a letter Manfred had written to Luhnow, placed the origins of the sign-stealing scheme inside the front office. An intern with the club had developed an algorithm that could decode the signs an opposing catcher was giving. *WSJ* reporter Jared Diamond claimed the system, called "Codebreaker," was used in 2017 and parts of 2018, at home and on the road. Codebreaker was explained in a PowerPoint presentation shown to Luhnow. The Astros GM also opened two emails that discussed the system, enhanced by players who banged on trash cans to communicate pitch information. Luhnow claimed he thought the algorithm would be used to study a previous game's footage, not live in games. The emails, written by Tom Koch, the team's director of advance information, had referenced "our dark arts, sign-stealing department." Luhnow admitted he saw the emails but claimed he didn't read either one to the end. "MLB couldn't decipher whose account was truthful," wrote Diamond.[37]

In just a few short years, the Astros had gone from victims in one scandal to the perpetrators in another. In less than a decade, Luhnow's team had risen from laughingstock to dynasty before plunging into disgrace. His now former team became front and center in a debate over tactics nearly as old as the game itself.

*****

At the Baker Bowl in Philadelphia, Phillies backup catcher Morgan Murphy would position himself in the center-field clubhouse armed with a pair of binoculars. He'd use a Morse-code buzzer linked to a receiver buried underneath the third-base coaching box. There, the Philadelphia coach could feel the vibration in his shoe – one buzz meant a fastball, two for a curve, and three meant a change-up was coming. The scheme was exposed when a visiting coach somehow got his spikes tangled up with the connecting wire. When he pulled on it, the cable led to center field. The year of this high-tech hijinks? Depending on the account, either 1898 or 1900.[38] (*The Sporting News* once traced the origins of sign-stealing to the 1876 Hartford Dark Blues.)[39]

In 1948, Veeck's Cleveland Indians employed a military-grade gun sight sixty times stronger than the naked eye (Bob Feller had brought it back with him from World War II) to aid their center-field spying. The Indians won 20 of their final 25 games (20 played at home) on their way to a World Series win over the Boston Braves.[40]

Twelve years later, Veeck had changed teams but not tactics. The Chicago White Sox had pitching coach Dizzy Trout positioned inside the Comiskey Park scoreboard where he would signal White Sox hitters the type of pitch they were about to see. If one particular light was blinking, a breaking ball was coming. If it stayed solid, the hitter could expect a fastball. The defending American League champions went 51-26 at home that season and just 36-41 on the road.

Near the end of the season, the White Sox had acquired pitcher Al Worthington. Pitching for the San Francisco Giants in 1959, Worthington complained to manager Bill Rigney when he heard the team had been stationing staff around Seals Stadium with binoculars to pick up the signs opposing catchers were giving pitchers and relaying the information to the dugout. Following Worthington's complaints, the Giants had the binocular patrol call it quits. In first place at the time, San Francisco dropped seven of their last eight games to finish in third place. [41]

A year later in Chicago, Worthington went to manager Al Lopez when he heard about the scheme and told him he didn't think it was right. Lopez told Worthington he didn't think it was wrong. The pitcher voiced his concerns to Hank Greenberg, then a front office executive with the team. "Baseball Is a game where you try to get away with anything you can," Greenberg told him. "Everybody tries to cheat a little."[42]

Getting nowhere with White Sox officials, Worthington packed his bags and went home to Birmingham, Alabama. "How can I be a follower of Christ and go along with something that's dishonest?" He spent the next two years pitching in the minor leagues as the White Sox tried to get rid of him. "We tried to sell him," said Greenberg, "but the word was out he was some sort of cuckoo."[43] Worthington didn't make it back to the big leagues until 1963.

By the early 1960s, scoreboard sign-stealing was baseball's biggest open secret. "Every team with a scoreboard in centerfield," Rogers Hornsby wrote in *My War with Baseball*, "has a spy hidden inside at one time or another. There's always a hole for the spy to peep out." The practice was so pervasive, American League president Joe Cronin put out a "cease and desist" letter to teams in 1962. That same year in the National League, Milwaukee Braves manager Birdie Tebbetts openly complained about sign-stealing, even sending a letter to Commissioner Ford Frick, who responded by calling the charge "a lot of bunk."[44]

Decades later, Associated Press columnist Hal Bock agreed with Hornsby and Tebbetts. "Teams routinely would post spies in manually-operated scoreboards to peek out and swipe signals," he wrote in 1988. More than a quarter-century later, only the technology had changed. "Electronic scoreboards eliminated those convenient peep-hole perches and satellite dishes made them unnecessary," Bock wrote. "Now teams tape other clubs' games and television's center field camera, peering in at the crouching catcher, provides the best sign-stealing arrangement imaginable."

In 2017, baseball officials discovered Boston players had used video cameras and an Apple Watch to signal "sign sequences." The evidence came to light after the Yankees filed a complaint following a game with the Red Sox. Boston responded by accusing New York of using a Yankee Stadium camera to steal signs from catchers.

The Yankees of the 1950s and early 1960s didn't need a spy in center field. They had pitcher Bob Turley, who had become so accomplished at reading opposing hurlers, manager Casey Stengel would have him coach first base on his off days to get a better look. Turley would signal pitches to Mickey Mantle by whistling.[45] "Two of the longest home runs I ever saw was one opening day in Washington when Mickey hit two over the trees in the old park on stolen pitches," Turley remembered. "I bet he [Turley] helped Mantle hit 50 homers over the years," contended Tony Kubek.[46]

Veeck once described gamesmanship as "the art of winning without really cheating," and contended "sign-stealing, even when done from the scoreboard is part of the real byplay of baseball, part of the battle of wits." His former player, Worthington, believed there was nothing wrong with a coach trying to steal signals. "But to spy with binoculars, I say that's cheating." The dividing line between what constitutes gamesmanship and what defines cheating extends well beyond the debate over stealing signs. In the book, *The Baseball Codes*, authors Jason Turbow and Michael Duca detail various ways players can skirt the rules or violate the spirit of the game. While the authors spend an entire chapter on stadium sign-stealing, they dedicate four more chapters to the methods players and managers can seek to gain an edge, much of it either illegal or in an ethically gray area.

A *New York Times* reader once posed this dilemma to a columnist. "I am puzzled how Gaylord Perry, who cheated on the field, gets into the Baseball Hall of Fame while Pete Rose, who cheated off but not on the field, is banned."

"This puzzles a lot of people," wrote columnist Ira Berkow. Perry had thrown a spitball for years (he titled his autobiography *Me and the Spitter*), a pitch outlawed in 1920, while Rose was banned for betting on games. Berkow asked Baseball Hall of Fame president Ed Stack about the difference. "That's a tough one," Stack said. "That's a tough one."[47]

Rickey managed cheaters, Hornsby being the most prominent. "You've got to cheat to win in baseball," Hornsby declared in the pages of *True* magazine in 1961. "I've been in pro baseball since 1914 and I've cheated, or watched someone on my team cheat, in practically every game." Hornsby claimed ninety-five percent of big-league pitchers cheat. The other five percent just hadn't learned how. Rickey was Hornsby's manager from 1919 until he was replaced in 1925. Did he endorse what Hornsby did or just look the other way? While Rickey was silent on Hornsby's charges, we do know he supported the legalization of the spitball. "A legal spitball could add years to the life of a pitcher's arm," he insisted in 1957. (After the 1947 season, Rickey acquired Preacher Roe from the Pirates. Roe later admitted he threw a spitball his entire seven years with the Dodgers).[48]

The most famous sign-stealing scheme of all featured the 1951 New York Giants. With ten weeks to go, the manager ordered a setup whereby a spotter in the center-field clubhouse at the Polo Grounds was linked to the Giants bullpen. A wire would trigger a buzzer on a telephone. When the kinks were finally worked out, New York went on a sixteen-game winning streak (after being down by thirteen-and-a-half games on August 11). Thirteen of those games were at home. Tied at the end of the regular season with the Dodgers, the Giants won the pennant on Bobby Thomson's "shot heard 'round the world" home run.[49]

Durocher, who played for Rickey in St. Louis and managed for him in Brooklyn, was the manager of the Giants in 1951. Herman Franks was one of his coaches and the man Durocher installed in the center-field clubhouse. Franks later coached in San Francisco and when he left after the 1958 season, the club asked him to return the following year to set up the system that caused Worthington so much angst. (As a player, Franks spent years in the Cardinals farm system and made his major-league debut for St. Louis in 1939).

Rickey and the Cardinals were slapped by Commissioner Landis in the Cedar Rapids case for misrepresenting contracts signed by dozens of players. How differently would we view Rickey's career today if he had ever been suspended from the game? That question was not just theoretical in 1938. On the eve of the Landis decision, Judge William Gibbons Branham, Landis' equivalent for the minor leagues, was asked if Rickey would be barred from baseball. "Landis once sentenced a minor league owner to five years on evidence that he schemed to take his old manager from a club he had sold to one he had purchased," Branham told a reporter. "I can't see how Judge Landis can penalize minor league owners without doing something about the director of the Octopus."

Other than losing dozens of minor league players, "the director of the Octopus" escaped unscathed.

Landis and other critics saw hypocrisy in Rickey's design of the minor leagues. "He could build championship clubs, and no one could fault him for that," wrote David Condon in the *Chicago Tribune* after Rickey's death. "The fact that he used slave labor – the farm teams – to ensure the success of those clubs, was something not many of us could appreciate."[50]

Negro league owners vilified Rickey for his refusal to offer compensation for players he signed. "Branch Rickey was just a businessman after money," believed former Negro league player Verdell Mathis. "He didn't care what Jackie was."[51] Rickey irritated members of the media for what they viewed as condescending, and sometimes, less than truthful answers. "Rickey was not as honorable a man as Breadon was," believed longtime columnist Bob Broeg.[52]

There are also the personal inconsistencies and stories rarely repeated that don't square with the image we have of Rickey today. "Rickey was an interesting guy, a man of many paradoxes," remembered Gene Karst, who worked with him in St. Louis. "I had been to Mexico, and one of his questions was about sex in Mexico. He wanted to know about it. I had been there several months, and I was young and inexperienced, so I didn't know much about sex in Mexico, and I wasn't able to give him very much information."[53]

Brooklyn traveling secretary Parrott recalled having dinner one night with Rickey and his wife. "Harold, will you order me a Manhattan cocktail, please. I know *he* never will," said Jane Rickey. "Would you believe that every year he used to take me to the Kentucky Derby? We had such fun," she remembered. "But that was before all this silly talk started about Branch being cheap, and a religious fanatic. Now he's afraid to be seen at the track for fear somebody will make a big story of it."[54]

Durocher, who worked for Rickey for years, once had this observation about his former boss. "You had to know him to understand that he was a shy, and in certain ways, an indecisive man."[55] Rickey shy and indecisive? A man of many paradoxes, indeed.

But these one-off stories are just a ripple in a pond compared to an ocean of accomplishments and a consistent behavior that many recall. "Whatever he did," remembered grandson Branch B. Rickey, "he did with zeal – and it was contagious."[56] Rickey biographers focus their attention, and rightly so, on his eight seasons with Brooklyn and his successful efforts to integrate baseball. It is one of the great accomplishments in twentieth-century American history. But Rickey spent more than thirty years in St. Louis between the Browns and the Cardinals, and his time there reshaped the sport and the trajectory of the Cardinals' franchise. Even without the Jackie Robinson story, Rickey's achievements in St. Louis would still merit a place in the Hall of Fame.

His successes in St. Louis and Brooklyn soared in hindsight. Over time, the criticisms and inconsistencies simply paled in comparison or just faded away. "He was not universally popular," remembered *Boston Globe* columnist Harold Kaese, "but he was universally respected."

In the wake of the latest sign-stealing scandal, Luhnow is more reviled than respected. (The Astros "are the universally most loathed organization in baseball," wrote *Daily News* columnist Bill Madden.)[57] Banned for a season and fired from a job, how will history judge him? Will the immediate and universal condemnation cool over time? Will he ever be given a second chance, or will he find himself like Rose, forever on the outside looking in?[58] Those whose livelihood depends on the game have differing views on just how far the Astros crossed the line.

"There's a gray area. But I think cameras are past the line. It's cheating, basically," said a scout not affiliated with the Astros. "I don't know if it's 'cheating-cheating.' But it's over the line."

The man who gave Luhnow his first job in baseball was surprised that opponents didn't figure out what the Astros were doing. "It was surprising to see it come out the way it did and how sophisticated the technology was," said DeWitt. "(But) banging the garbage cans doesn't sound sophisticated. I'm surprised the opposition didn't pick up on it."[59]

As spring training opened, the Astros faced a storm of boos from fans and a torrent of condemnation from other teams. Players from the Yankees and Dodgers, the last two clubs to lose to the Astros on their march to a title in 2017, were particularly strident in their criticism. "I just don't think it holds any value," said Yankee outfielder Aaron Judge of the Astros' World Series win. "It wasn't earned." Judge said he deleted his tweet congratulating Houston second baseman Jose Altuve for winning the 2017 American League MVP Award. The Yankee outfielder finished second. "I was just sick to my stomach," he admitted, when he heard the story of the sign-stealing scandal.

Cody Bellinger of the Dodgers said Altuve "stole" the MVP award from Judge and the World Series from his team. "Everybody knows they stole the ring from us," he said. Bellinger also gave voice to a popular, but unproven theory, that Altuve was using a buzzer connected to his uniform to know what pitch was coming when he hit a walk-off home run off Aroldis Chapman in Game 6 of the ALCS. "I don't know what human hits a walk-off home run against Aroldis Chapman to send your team to the World Series and, one, has the thought to say, 'Don't rip my jersey off,'" Bellinger said. "But to go in the tunnel, change your shirt, and then come out and do your interview – that makes no sense to me. Makes zero sense to me."[60]

The collateral damage from the disclosures rippled throughout baseball. Las Vegas linemakers expected retaliation to last all season. Oddsmakers set an over/under on the number of times Astros batters would get hit by pitches. Every day, it seemed, someone was coming forward to confess, explain, or defend their actions. Cardinals, past and present, got drawn into the scandal.

According to former pitcher Jack McDowell, the White Sox teams of the 1980s, under manager Tony La Russa, employed a sign-stealing scheme. "Gatorade sign out in right-center had a light, there was a toggle switch in the manager's office and a camera zoomed in on the catcher," McDowell told a Charlotte radio station in January of 2020. "Everybody knows, everybody that's been around the game knows all this stuff. Why all of a sudden it became a big thing, I have no idea. But it's frustrating being on the outside and watching what's going on with the game I played for so long." (McDowell didn't join the White Sox until after La Russa was fired. "Tony La Russa is the one who put it in," he claimed in the radio interview.)

Outfielder and former Cardinal Carlos Beltran retired as a player after spending the 2017 season in Houston. The New York Mets had named him their manager for the 2020 season, but after being the only player mentioned in the commissioner's inquiry, the club decided to part ways with him. Beltran became the third manager to lose his job as part of the investigation into the scandal. Alex Cora, the Boston Red Sox manager and former bench coach for Houston, also lost his job after being named in Manfred's report.

Cardinals hitting coach Jeff Albert spent 2017 working in the minor leagues for Houston but was the Astros assistant hitting coach the next season. "I don't feel like I was participating, or doing, or even asked to do something like unethical or that had issues with integrity of the game," he told reporters. "That was just my experience as far as what I was personally doing and the conversations and people that I was around."

According to the commissioner's report, the 2018 Astros team that Albert was a part of did engage in sign-stealing for part of the season but stopped "because the players no longer believed it was effective." As Ben Lindbergh and Travis Sawchik point out in their book, *The MVP Machine*, the 2018 Houston club was one of the great all-time statistical teams, posting the third-greatest run differential since 1954.[61] In 2019, a season in which no evidence of sign stealing has emerged, the Astros won more regular-season games than either of the two previous seasons.

How much of a difference did the trash can banging make in 2017? Writers Jayson Stark and Eno Sarris dug through the data, wrote more than 3,000 words on some interesting anomalies (the 2017 Astros struck out 365 fewer times than the previous season, the biggest drop in the live-ball era – 1920 to the present), but didn't reach any sweeping conclusions.

"How much of the Astros' championship season was about greatness, and how much was about sign-stealing?" asked Stark and Sarris. "We would love to tell you. But repeat after us: We. Have. No. Idea."[62]

We do know this. The lens of history has a different aperture than the increasingly condensed news cycle now measured in hours or even minutes thanks to the proliferation of social media. Rickey's career provides a great example of the difference between retrospective analysis versus contemporaneous opinion.[63]

*****

Rickey left his mark on the game with integration, the farm system, and a thirst for knowledge, never content with the status quo. In 1950, he asked General Electric engineers to design a machine with three mirrors and electric eyes. A pitch in the right zone would light up a lamp, indicating a strike.[64] Rickey's vision for technology featured a benefit to the game, not just for one team at the expense of the other. Seven decades after Rickey's idea, Commissioner Manfred announced an automated strike zone would be used (in some capacity) in minor league baseball in 2020.[65]

Rickey's fascination with statistics at the major league level started with the St. Louis Browns in 1914. That season, he had Travis Hoke, a young reporter, track bases, not hits. "A hit isn't a hit," Hoke explained to *Esquire* readers in 1935, "it is a one, two, three, four *base* hit. The unit of achievement in baseball isn't a hit, it is a base."[66] Rickey would have Hoke sit in the grandstand behind home plate, record the location of every pitch a batter swung at, and chart the destination of every ball hit into the field of play.

A century later, Luhnow disciples Mike Elias and Sig Mejdal are among those pushing the game in analytical directions Rickey could only dream of. In November of 2018, the Baltimore Orioles hired Elias to be their general manager. Mejdal was his first hire. They landed in a franchise that Bill DeWitt Jr. nearly purchased; a franchise his father once owned when it played in St. Louis and was known as the Browns; where Rickey got his start – as a player, manager and general manager. Rickey gave DeWitt Sr. his start in baseball, his son brought Luhnow into the game and gave him the freedom to hire and expand. "What began...as a small advisory group of Luhnow's analysts with salaries and hardware that cost less than $1 million has expanded into an arm of the Cardinals' front office that informs decisions everywhere from the boardroom to the dugout, the training room to trade talks," noted the *Post-Dispatch* in 2015.[67] Elias, the former Yale pitcher, and Mejdal, the NASA scientist, were an early part of that burgeoning empire, having been brought into the fold by Luhnow.

They now face a similar uphill climb as the man they once worked for. In Luhnow's first year in Houston, the club lost 107 games. In Elias' and Mejdal's first year with Baltimore, the team lost 108. In their last season in St. Louis, DeWitt Sr.'s Browns recorded 54 victories. The 2019 Orioles won 54 games. The Cardinals had never won a World Series before Rickey got involved with the franchise. The Astros had never won the title before Luhnow took control. The Orioles last World Series win came just one year after manager and St. Louis native Earl Weaver retired.

Perhaps it was only appropriate that the Cardinals were scheduled to open their 2020 home schedule with the Orioles.[68] The flywheel Rickey set in motion more than a hundred years ago just keeps on spinning.

---

[1] *Baseball Digest,* September 1948. Attendance at home games for the Browns that season was 335,564, the lowest in all of baseball.

[2] Bill and Charley DeWitt bought a controlling interest in the Browns in February of 1949. They sold to Bill Veeck in the summer of 1951. The brothers owned or controlled 156,225 shares of stock in the team. After paying off debt and capital gains taxes, Roy Stockton once estimated each brother walked away with between $200,000 and $250,000. *St. Louis Post-Dispatch,* July 1, 1951. Bill DeWitt was an executive with the team before and after his ownership. After selling out, Charley DeWitt returned to an insurance business he had founded years before. The DeWitt brothers' limited partners included a Metropolitan Opera star. Helen Traubel was a St. Louis native. In October of 1950, she invested "at

least $25,000 and perhaps more" in the team, according to reports. "My father was a great Browns' fan," she explained. "The first loves of my life were George Sisler, Baby Doll Jacobson and Urban Shocker." Her opera specialty was Wagner. *St. Louis Globe-Democrat* and *St. Louis Post-Dispatch*, October 19, 1950. The *Post-Dispatch* disputed the amount of her investment. "A report that her investment was $25,000 was said authoritatively to be somewhat excessive."

[3] *St. Louis Star-Times*, February 22, 1950. The experiment was short-lived. Tracy left the team at the end of May, a victim of the team's budget constraints. [The DeWitt brothers] "explained that a main factor in his release was meager crowds at Brownie home games. That meant, they said, that expenses must be cut." *South Bend Tribune*, May 30, 1950.

[4] Megdal, *The Cardinals Way.*

[5] From the 1930s to the late 1980s, every single Reds GM had started his baseball career with the Cardinals and/or Rickey. Larry MacPhail, Warren Giles, Gabe Paul, Bill DeWitt, Bob Howsam, Dick Wagner and Bill Bergesch ran the Reds organization during this time. All but Wagner, who joined the Cardinals under Howsam, and Bergesch (who started with the Cardinals in 1947) had worked for Rickey. Howsam had two stints with the Reds, replacing Wagner before retiring. The list of Reds general managers over the years also includes Bob Quinn, grandson of the former general manager of the Browns and Walt Jocketty, former Cardinals GM. The current Cincinnati owner, Bob Castellini, had been a limited partner with the Cardinals before buying the Reds.

[6] By the early 1960s, there were more than 100 executives in baseball with Rickey roots. In addition to DeWitt and Paul, the list included George Trautman, president of the National Association of Baseball Leagues, Fresco Thompson, vice president of the Los Angeles Dodgers, and several names previously mentioned: Buzzie Bavasi, Warren Giles, Larry MacPhail, and Wid Matthews among them. Salisbury, Maryland *Daily Times*, April 5, 1963.

[7] *Cincinnati Enquirer*, May 20, 1962

[8] Megdal, *The Cardinals Way.*

[9] *New York Times*, August 1, 2004.

[10] While he embraced the concepts, he didn't like the terminology. "I don't know what 'Moneyball' means," DeWitt said in 2007. "If it means using all the information at your disposal to make the best possible decision, then, yeah, that's what we're trying to accomplish." *St. Louis Post-Dispatch*, November 1, 2007.

[11] While the others were hired as full-time employees, Witte was brought on as a consultant. He once gave a presentation on the pitching mechanics of Bob Gibson, whose audience included the Hall of Fame pitcher. "If this guy is full of shit, I'm walking out," Gibson said the night before the presentation. He stayed. A St. Louis area native, Witte had attended St. Louis Country Day, the same high school as DeWitt, Baur and Hanser. After the new ownership group took control of the team, he began going to spring training games with Baur. *The New Yorker*, October 16, 2005. See also, "How a Baseball Revolution Happens," by Sean Cunningham at *Inside Hook*.
www.insidehook.com/article/sports/baseball-revolution-happens

---

[12] Megdal, *The Cardinals Way.*
[13] Luhnow's drafts from 2005 to 2007 produced 24 major league players, the highest total in MLB during those years. *Baseball Prospectus 2013*. John Wiley & Sons, Inc. 2013. Luhnow wrote the forward to the 2013 edition. He had previously hired Mike Fast and Kevin Goldstein from *Baseball Prospectus*, a website that focuses on sabermetric analysis.
[14] Reiter, Ben. *Astroball: The New Way to Win it All.* Crown Archetype. 2018.
[15] Megdal, *The Cardinals Way.*
[16] *New York Times*, June 1, 2018. Joe Strauss once described Strom as "a Luhnow hire who has no contact with Duncan." *St. Louis Post-Dispatch*, October 14, 2009.
[17] Megdal, *The Cardinals Way.*
[18] *St. Louis Post-Dispatch*, October 6, 2007.
[19] *Springfield News-Leader*, April 20, 2008.
[20] Reiter, *Astroball.*
[21] In June of 2014, an official with the Cardinals said the organization believed it "has a competitive advantage when it comes to looking for college players." *St. Louis Post-Dispatch*, June 5, 2014. That process had begun years before. In 2006, Mejdal "collected 22 months of statistics from every plate appearance for every player in four different levels of college baseball." Ibid, June 21, 2015.
[22] Kantrovitz ran the draft for the Cardinals for three years – 2012 to 2014. His selections included pitchers Michael Wacha and Jack Flaherty. The Chicago Cubs named him their director of scouting in November of 2019.
[23] *Houston Chronicle*, March 8, 2014. "Luhnow and Mejdal both had clear ideas of what they wanted after using the system the St. Louis Cardinals used, named 'Red Dog,'" Drellich wrote.
[24] *New York Times*, June 23, 2015.
[25] Ibid, January 28, 2017.
[26] *St. Louis Post-Dispatch*, July 3, 2015.
[27] Ibid, September 13, 1945.
[28] Ibid, January 31, 2017.
[29] twitter.com/craigjedwards/status/1156685728987922432. In February of 2020, Keith Law ranked the Cardinals as having the ninth-best farm system in baseball. In May of 2020, Mark Saxon of *The Athletic* gave the Cardinals 2017 draft a D+ grade.
[30] The six teams are the Philadelphia Athletics (1929-1931), St. Louis Cardinals (1942-1944), Baltimore Orioles (1969-1971), Atlanta Braves (1997-1999), New York Yankees (2002-2004), Houston Astros (2017-2019).
[31] fivethirtyeight.com/features/do-we-even-need-minor-league-baseball/
[32] Reiter, *Astroball.*
[33] theathletic.com/1317907/2019/10/25/taubman-saga-exposes-longstanding-questions-about-the-astros-culture-under-jim-crane-and-jeff-luhnow/
[34] www.si.com/mlb/2019/10/22/houston-astros-roberto-osuna-suspension

[35] sports.yahoo.com/sources-red-sox-warned-indians-astros-attempting-steal-signs-information-032027336.html
[36] Crane grew up in suburban St. Louis. As a teenager, he worked at Norwood Hills Country Club. At the age of 13, he caddied for Stan Musial, Ken Boyer, and Dick Groat. At 16, he worked at a parking lot outside Busch Stadium. He graduated from Lutheran North High School and Central Missouri State University. *St. Louis Post-Dispatch,* November 3, 2017.
[37] *The Wall Street Journal Weekend*, February 8-9, 2020.
[38] Turbow, Jason with Michael Duca. *The Baseball Codes: Beanballs, Sign Stealing, and Bench-Clearing Brawls: The Unwritten Rules of America's Pastime.* Pantheon Books. 2010. Nash, Bruce and Zullo, Allan. *The Baseball Hall of Shame 2*. Pocket Books. 1996. Turbow and Duca put the date at 1900. Nash and Zullo have it listed as 1898.
[39] "There was a shack outside the park (in Hartford), hung off a telegraph pole. A lot of dope came out of that little 'office,'" wrote Dan Daniel. *The Sporting News*, April 4, 1962. A similar setup occurred in St. Louis. "The club house at the old ballpark in St. Louis was in center field. There was a little coop atop of it, and in that coop during every home game was a very smart and alert youth. He would signal the pitch to the batter with a newspaper." *Baseball Digest*, August 1948.
[40] Turbow, *The Baseball Codes.*
[41] "I always thought," an unnamed player said later, "we would have won the pennant if we had kept the spy system." *The Sporting News*, April 4, 1962.
[42] *Saturday Evening Post*, May 2, 1964.
[43] Ibid.
[44] *The Sporting News,* July 14, 1962.
[45] *The Charlotte Observer*, April 4, 1965. In *The Baseball Codes*, authors Turbow and Duca discuss Turley's tactics as a first-base coach. Other press accounts reference Turley reading pitchers from the bench. Turley estimated he was accurate 60 percent of the time from the bench. "If I could call them from first base, I'd be right 80 to 90 percent of the time," he said in 1965. In 1958, he offered this caveat. "Reading a no-windup hurler is virtually impossible."
[46] Turley's sign-stealing talent started in St. Louis. "It started when I came to the St. Louis Browns. We lost so many games. I found it difficult at times to maintain keen interest unless I was working." Turley made his major-league debut for the Browns in 1951. Bill DeWitt Sr. had signed him. "Nobody else wanted Turley. He had pitched in high school in East St. Louis and hadn't been first-string even there. But the kid threw so hard, we felt he had a chance." Turley's talent had piqued interest from the Yankees, who accidentally signed one of his relatives. The Yankee scout found only one Turley in the phone book, Bob's grandfather, who assumed the team was interested in his son and Bob's uncle, Ralph Turley. *The Sporting News*, May 14, 1958.
[47] *New York Times*, July 28, 1991.
[48] Ibid, July 10, 1955.

---

[49] Thomson denied being tipped off to the pitch. "I used the signs off and on but not when I hit the home run," he said in 2001. "He knew it was coming. Absolutely," said Dodgers pitcher Ralph Branca. *New York Times*, October 1, 2001, and August 18, 2010. Branca's opinion changed over the years. "I always figured he just outguessed me," he said decades earlier. *The Sporting News*, April 4, 1962.
[50] *Chicago Tribune*, December 11, 1965.
[51] *The Sporting News*, April 14, 1997.
[52] Golenbock, *The Spirit of St. Louis*. "Breadon was smart and honest, and if Rickey wasn't so honest, he was smarter," remembered pitcher Flint Rhem. *Boston Globe,* November 15, 1965.
[53] Golenbock, *The Spirit of St. Louis*.
[54] Parrott, *The Lords of Baseball*.
[55] Durocher, *Nice Guys Finish Last*.
[56] *New York Times*, August 3, 1997.
[57] New York *Daily News*, December 1, 2019.
[58] In February of 2020, Rose asked Commissioner Manfred to remove his name from baseball's ineligible list, citing the Astros sign-stealing scandal in his petition. "There cannot be one set of rules for Mr. Rose and another for everyone else," Rose's lawyers stated in their petition for reinstatement.
[59] *St. Louis Post-Dispatch*, January 21, 2020. At least one opponent did. Danny Farquhar was pitching for the White Sox when he faced the Astros in Houston in 2017. "There was a banging from the dugout, almost like a bat rack every time a changeup signal got put down," he recalled. "After the third bang, I stepped off." He and his catcher switched signs. "The banging stopped."
[60] *Los Angeles Times*, February 14, 2020. Houston shortstop Carlos Correa told Ken Rosenthal there were two reasons Altuve didn't want his jersey ripped off. Altuve's wife had voiced disapproval after Correa had ripped off her husband's jersey following a walk-off home run in the regular season. "I ripped off his shirt, and his wife told my wife, 'Why is Carlos ripping Altuve's shirt? I don't like that.'" The second reason was a tattoo. "He's got an unfinished tattoo on his collarbone that honestly looked terrible. It was a bad tattoo, and he didn't want anybody to see it. He didn't want to show it at all." theathletic.com/1610301/2020/02/15/rosenthal-carlos-correa-rips-bellinger-passionately-defends-altuve-and-says-the-astros-deserve-their-2017-title/ Altuve showed reporters the tattoo in spring training. "Yes, there was a tattoo on his left collarbone," Jeff Passan wrote on Twitter. "I'm not sure if it was bad or not."
[61] Lindbergh, Ben and Sawchik, Travis. *The MVP Machine: How Baseball's New Nonconformists Are Using Data To Build Better Players.* Basic Books. 2019.
[62] theathletic.com/1573075/2020/01/31/does-electronic-sign-stealing-work-the-astros-numbers-are-eye-popping/ An Astros fan logged more than 8,200 pitches from Houston home games. He detected banging on more than 1,100 pitches. *Signstealingscandal.com*. The Astros also used other methods – including "clapping, whistling or yelling."

---

[63] Another example of the difference between contemporaneous opinion and retrospective analysis can be seen in Hall of Fame voting. Widely suspected of using performance-enhancing drugs, pitcher Roger Clemens and outfielder Barry Bonds received 37.6 percent and 36.2 percent of the vote, respectively, in their first year eligible for the Hall of Fame (2013). By 2020, sportswriters had pushed Clemens to 61 percent and Bonds to 60.7 percent. No statistic had changed in seven years. Only perceptions.
[64] *The Sporting News*, August 17, 1998.
[65] Plans announced before the disruption caused by the coronavirus pandemic.
[66] *Esquire*, October 1935. In St. Louis, Hoke had worked for a weekly publication called *Sport and Stage*.
[67] *St. Louis Post-Dispatch*, June 21, 2015.
[68] Postponed by the coronavirus, the Cardinals were scheduled to open their 2020 home schedule on April 2 against the Orioles.

Made in United States
Orlando, FL
17 May 2022

17951023R00278